THE CHRIST AND THE SPIRIT

Collected Essays of

JAMES D. G. DUNN

Volume 1

CHRISTOLOGY

THE CHRIST AND THE SPIRIT

Collected Essays of

JAMES D. G. DUNN

Lightfoot Professor of Divinity
University of Durham

Volume 1

CHRISTOLOGY

WILLIAM B. EERDMANS PUBLISHING COMPANY
GRAND RAPIDS, MICHIGAN / CAMBRIDGE, U.K.

Printed in the United States of America

03 02 01 00 99 98   7 6 5 4 3 2 1

Library of Congress Cataloging-in-Publication Data

Dunn, James D. G., 1939-

The Christ and the Spirit / James D. G. Dunn.

p.   cm.

Includes bibliographical references.

Contents: v. 1. Christology.

ISBN 0-8028-4175-9 (v. 1.: pbk.: alk. paper)

1. Jesus Christ — Person and offices — Biblical teaching.

2. Holy Spirit — Biblical teaching.

3. Bible. N.T. — Theology.

4. Jesus Christ — History of doctrines — Early church, ca. 30-600.

5. Holy Spirit — History of doctrines — Early church, ca. 30-600.

I. Title.

BT202.D79   1998

232 — dc21   97-26651

                                                CIP

CONTENTS

Preface   vii

Abbreviations   xv

GENERAL ESSAYS   1

1. New Testament Christology (1992)   3
2. Incarnation (1990)   30
3. Interpreting New Testament Christology (1990)   48

JESUS AND CHRISTOLOGY   55

4. The Messianic Secret in Mark (1970)   57
5. Messianic Ideas and Their Influence on the Jesus of History (1992)   78
6. Jesus, Table-Fellowship, and Qumran (1992)   96

SPIRIT AND CHRISTOLOGY IN PAUL   113

7. 2 Corinthians 3:17 — "The Lord Is the Spirit" (1970)   115
8. Jesus — Flesh and Spirit: An Exposition of Romans 1:3-4 (1973)   126
9. 1 Corinthians 15:45 — Last Adam, Life-Giving Spirit (1973)   154

PAULINE CHRISTOLOGY   167

10. Jesus Tradition in Paul (1994)   169

11. Paul's Understanding of the Death of Jesus as Sacrifice (1991)   190

12. How Controversial Was Paul's Christology? (1993)   212

13. Pauline Christology: Shaping the Fundamental Structures (1993)   229

CHRISTOLOGY IN ACTS   239

14. ΚΥΡΙΟΣ in Acts (1997)   241

CHRISTOLOGY IN THE MAKING   255

15. Maurice Wiles on *Christology in the Making* and Responses by
the Author (1982)   257

16. In Defense of a Methodology (1984)   270

17. Some Clarifications on Issues of Method: A Reply to Holladay
and Segal (1985)   279

18. Foreword to the Second Edition of *Christology in the Making*
(1989)   287

19. Was Christianity a Monotheistic Faith from the Beginning?
(1982)   315

20. Let John Be John: A Gospel for Its Time (1982)   345

21. Christology as an Aspect of Theology (1993)   377

22. The Making of Christology: Evolution or Unfolding? (1994)   388

23. Why "Incarnation"? A Review of Recent New Testament
Scholarship (1994)   405

24. He Will Come Again (1997)   424

Index of Modern Authors   440

Index of Scripture and Other Ancient Writings   443

PREFACE

Why Christology?

Here is a group of essays — 24 in number. The first was initially published in 1970, the last in 1997 — a span of nearly 28 years. And all of them on different aspects of New Testament christology, that is, the earliest Christian reflection on Jesus and his significance. Why this fascination with christology? Why such a focus on Jesus, known from the beginnings of Christianity as "the Christ," or simply "Christ"?

The question is a double one. It asks, first, why should anyone be curious about a figure now distant from us by nearly two millennia. The answer is so obvious that it hardly needs restating. As the founder of Christianity, or at least the primary inspiration for Christianity, he set loose in the world a movement of undoubted if incalculable influence, a movement which has shaped whole civilizations and national (as well as individual) destinies more profoundly than empires or democracies or warring hordes. Who would not be curious about such a figure? As the one whose birth came to mark the juncture between world epochs (BC and AD), for Christian culture and all cultures affected in due course, he somehow stands above time as well as within time. Who is he who could be accorded such significance?

Behind that broad-brush response there are equally profound answers, which become the very warp and woof of christological reflection. One is the power of the symbolic figure. These words are written in the week after the amazing and unforgettable scenes of national and international mourning over the sudden and tragic death of Diana, Princess of Wales, followed a few days later by the death of Mother Teresa of Calcutta. Here were figures who, despite any questions or controversy which surrounded them, were widely seen to embody and enact an ideal of practical care and profound

vii

concern for the poor, the disadvantaged, the afflicted. In so doing they touched literally millions to the heart, in their challenge to seemingly less caring authority and tradition, in their refusal to be numbed into stoic or pious (or despairing) inactivity by the overwhelming magnitude of the need confronting them. In the deeply felt and not easily understood reaction which their lives and deaths have aroused they demonstrate the power of the symbolic figure, the figure who embodies an ideal which evokes almost universal admiration, an ideal which both challenges and inspires millions to some degree of imitation.

Jesus was evidently a symbolic figure something like this. The extent of his personal influence is obscured as well as indicated by the records of his life (the Gospels). But he too must have embodied and enacted a symbolic ideal, particularly of insight, honesty, and compassion, which reached deeply into the hearts of individuals and moved them to follow, which is still power-fully reflected in the stories about him in the Gospels, and which centuries later through these same stories still illuminates and challenges millions. Within the sum total of human inquiry it would be astonishing if such a figure did not command considerable attention. Christology as in part the attempt to understand and appreciate the power of that symbolic figure is the affirmation by each generation of the power of what Jesus symbolized.

Beyond that we move on to particular aspects of the symbol and to the claims regarding his significance which he inspired. What was his status within his native Judaism, and does it matter subsequently? How can it be that his death makes a difference to the standing of countless millions before God, as Christians have claimed more or less from the first? Above all, the Christian claims that he was raised from the dead; the why and the what here become increasingly difficult to handle as they move beyond the more graspable human analogies; but the power of the claim that death was conquered in Jesus has been immeasurable. Equally difficult are the claims of Jesus' pres-ence still with those who meet in his name; and yet they have been such a potent factor in the subsequent centuries, at the heart of many a dispute among Christians, and still today. And most profound of all, the claim that in and through this Jesus God has somehow manifested himself in a definitive and final way. If there is any substance in any of this, then the answer to the question "Why christology?" is still more obvious. Christology, but of course: to make some sense of all this, to grasp better its grounding in the historic figure of Jesus and the first reactions to him, to attain a fuller appreciation of why it all exerts such power; *of course* this is a necessary exercise, with potentially vital and crucial conseqences for millions. Even if Christianity fell into total decay, the figure of Jesus the Christ would still exercise an endless fascination.

The question "Why christology?" is also a personal question: Why my own fascination with the subject? The answer comes partly in terms of my own faith as a Christian. Who is this in whom I believe? What and why do I believe it? In terms of Anselm's famous tag *(Credo ut intelligam)* it has been a case of faith in search of understanding. Not in the sense that faith has simply sought for clarification and confirmation. For faith itself is expressed in words and images which embody some kind of understanding. Consequently, the process has been much more one of dialogue — of inquiry into these words and images, their scope, their origin — the response clarifying and sharpening the inquiry — the freshly posed inquiry eliciting a more nuanced response — and so on, back and forth. A faith which sought understanding and ended up unable to express itself in different words and images would not have understood very much.

At one and the same time, as an academic — publication of the first essay coincided with my appointment to a lectureship in Nottingham, so the 28 years also span my career as a university teacher — I naturally had an intense intellectual curiosity in the subject. Why has Christianity made so much of this Jesus? How did Christian faith in and belief about this Christ Jesus first take shape and come to the expressions which have been so central in its confession and worship ever since? Why christology? Here the motivation moves beyond personal faith to one of legitimate intellectual inquiry, appropriate and necessary within even a "secular" university. As one of the great makers and movers of history, as one of the most inspiring and influential symbolic figures in world history, Jesus invites, demands even, the scrutiny that any significant individual or event calls for. Given the unique role of university theology within British universities — that is, as an academic discipline within the Arts and Humanities, and not at all in the business of confessional apologia, far less indoctrination — such an inquiry is bound to be at the heart of the academic enterprise.

These two aspects, the personal and the academic, the inquiry of faith and the inquiry into faith, I do not regard as contradictory or incompatible. On the contrary, the one feeds into the other. Some would say that it is not possible to critique a tradition except from outside that tradition. I refute that view. There are many examples in many disciplines of paradigms of interpretation and traditional perspectives being questioned and transformed from within — and theology has a record second to none in this respect. For myself, I have always been open to the possibility that my intellectual inquiry might persuade me of the impossibility of faith on individual points or even in the whole. Such openness I have deemed to be crucial not simply to the integrity of the academic inquiry, but also to the integrity of faith. Love of truth, commitment to truth is the great bond. I believe, not least because I believe what I believe to be true. If it were not true, I would not want to continue believing it. And if I were persuaded of the untruth of some statement of faith

I would cease to assent to it. Such a dialogue between starting point of presupposition and subject matter of inquiry I regard as the very heart of the search for truth and of the academic enterprise at its most profound.

What follow, then, are the fruits (or fumblings) of nearly thirty years of academic (but also personal) inquiry into the beginnings of christology. The subjects are the particular aspects of the whole which caught my attention at different times through these years. (I note with some curiosity that most essays seem to have been produced in three bursts, at the beginning of the '70s, '80s, and '90s respectively, though in some cases there was a gap of some years between the writing and the publication). For any who might be interested in tracing the developments in my thinking (and, hopefully, the deepening of my insights) I have indicated on the Contents pages the dates when the essays first appeared. But in arranging the structure of the volume it seemed more sensible and more user-friendly to group them by theme rather than to order them by date.

I am more ambivalent about whether I should have updated the essays to indicate where I have modified my views and particularly to take account of more recent studies. In the event, however, I decided against it. Part of the value of a collection like this is ease of reference: it brings together, between a single pair of covers, contributions to earlier stages of various discussions, several of which are referred to by other contributors to these discussions. It is not unimportant for a proper understanding of these discussions that the content and detail of the contributions be retained in their original form. Of course, some additional notes could well have been incorporated at the end of the earlier essays in particular. But in some cases the modification of perspective or of presentation (I think particularly of chapters 4 and 7–9) would have required too extensive an alteration to the text or a too lengthy additional footnote — and I am well enough content that the essays in question represent my developing views at the time they were written. In other cases (the Pauline material) I can most simply refer to my *Theology of Paul the Apostle* (Grand Rapids: Eerdmans/Edinburgh: Clark, 1997), where both discussions and bibliography have been fully updated.

There have been some minor alterations, including Americanization of spelling and punctuation and regularization of footnotes. Where practicable and necessary the language has been made more inclusive. That policy, however, became impracticable where Adam christology is involved (chapters 11 and 19). Where the theological point depends on a sometimes almost imperceptible shift along the continuum Adam-man-Christ, we are more or less locked into a historic cultural perspective. The point being made would be lost if we substituted "human beings" for "man"; the NRSV translation of Heb 2:6-9 demonstrates the problem and cost of such "modernization" of an ancient text. In such cases I can simply hope that the jolt of being confronted by a perspective different from our own will help focus (rather than distract) attention and help bring home the point being made.

The first three chapters (1–3) are survey articles for dictionaries. Coming from my "more mature period," they may provide a useful overview of where my understanding and appreciation of the christological debate had reached after twenty years.

The next three chapters (4–6) attest my enduring interest in what can be said about Jesus himself, his own ideas and teaching. This area has not been the primary focus of my research over the years, though I hope to remedy that as the first stage of my next large project on *Christianity in the Making*. But I remain convinced that the symbolic figure (to hark back to my earlier point) must embody and enact the symbol if the symbol itself is to have real and lasting power. So the challenge of having to check the symbol (alternatively expressed, the christology) against what may be known of the historical actuality will never disappear and has to be addressed again and again. A comparison of chapters 4 and 5, separated by about twenty years, will, I hope, indicate the sharpening of perception which the years have brought.

Chapters 7–9 indicate the earliest phase of my interest in christology and the angle from which I entered the larger dialogue on christology. My earliest research and writing was on the Holy Spirit and the experience of the Spirit. I will refer to this at greater length in the Preface to the second volume of these essays, which will be on pneumatology. These three chapters could have been included equally well in that volume, and in fact chapter 7 is not really on christology. But the cumulative thrust of the three essays is toward a clarification of the rather vital relation (for Paul's theology, but also for Christian theology generally) between the Christ and the Spirit, so it seemed to make better sense, or as good sense, to include the essays in this volume. The angle of this approach into christology is reflected in a distinct tendency toward what can properly be called a Spirit-christology. And my subsequent immersion in other aspects of christology have certainly qualified that view and, I hope, given me a more rounded and more nuanced grasp of Paul's christology in particular. But I remain convinced that an adequate apprehension of the role of experience in the shaping of earliest christology and pneumatology, as well as of the interaction of christology and pneumatology in earliest Christian theology, remains fundamental to an adequate apprehension of both.

The chapters on Pauline christology (10–13) reflect the fact that in the second half of the '80s and early '90s my research was intensively focused on Paul, in preparation, particularly, for my commentaries on Romans (WBC 38; Dallas: Word, 1988) and Galatians (BNTC; London: Black/Peabody: Hendrickson, 1993), though chapter 11 was a revision of an earlier 1974 essay. Between them they seem to cover a large portion of Paul's christology, from

Jesus tradition to God in Christ. I remain somewhat puzzled by several aspects, particularly the question of the controversial character of Paul's christology. The question which forms the title of chapter 12 remains a genuine question; the essay is simply giving the question substance, rather than presenting any kind of definitive answer. Here is one of the areas where I would hope that dialogue can continue and prosper (but denunciation or dismissal is not dialogue!).

I welcomed the opportunity to slip in a late contribution on Acts (chapter 14), which emerged from work for a semipopular commentary on The Acts of the Apostles (London: Epworth/Valley Forge: TPI, 1996) and which helps provide a little more balance for a volume which might otherwise be too dominated by Paul.

The largest group of essays revolve around my *Christology in the Making* (London: SCM/Philadelphia: Westminster, 1980), the debate it partly contributed to and partly engendered, and the several spinoffs which resulted. I hope the sequence indicates something of the character of debate which I see to be fundamental to effective theologizing. The exchange with Maurice Wiles was particularly fruitful for me (chapter 15); I have included his opening review but only my side of the resulting correspondence, which seemed sufficiently self-explanatory. Several of the reviews and critiques of *Christology* seemed to me to be so inadequate that a fairly robust response was called for (chapters 16 and 17). But an author cannot wholly excuse himself for the misunderstandings of his readers, so I hope the responses provided useful clarification and met at least some of the criticisms. The opportunity for a second edition of *Christology* gave me opportunity to summarize and extend these responses and to indicate where modification was called for as a result (chapter 18). Further debate has not been as extensive as I had hoped, but that may have been partly due to the lack of a North American version of the second edition, a defect now happily resolved by Eerdmans (1996).

One feature of my attitude to theologizing is that I see what I write as contributing to an ongoing dialogue. Which is also to admit that I do not find it necessary to have reached a completely rounded conclusion or stasis before I commit my research to paper. In writing I both clarify my own perception (I write in order to understand!) and invite those responses which will help to further clarify, modify, sharpen, etc. that perception or its articulation. In this case the lectures which make up chapters 19 and 20 gave me the opportunity to take further and already to modify the first edition of *Christology* (this is why I have placed them after the essays on *Christology* itself). The growing appreciation of how crucial was the issue of monotheism in late first-century Christianity as it emerged from second Temple Judaism and of how crucial was the role of John's Gospel in bringing this issue to focus and in promoting a full-blown christology-within-monotheism has been for me one of the most important insights to emerge from 28 years of research in christology.

I remain of the strong conviction that getting it right at this point is vital for several important aspects of Christianity and Christian theology. (1) It is vital for our understanding of Christianity as a monotheistic religion. The point is elaborated in chapter 21. The danger of a focus on christology is that it obscures the primary context of theology. And too many branches of contemporary Christianity lean dangerously close to a form of christolatry for the danger to be lightly dismissed. In the intensity of their focus on Jesus they forget that even the confession of Jesus Christ as Lord is/should be "to the glory of God the Father" (Phil 2:11). A christology which forgets its monotheistic matrix is more polytheistic than monotheistic in inspiration.

(2) It is equally vital for our understanding of Christianity's continued relation with the Judaism within which it emerged. Hence the reaction in chapter 22. The greatest stumbling block between Christianity and Judaism today is still the question whether Christianity has in fact abandoned belief that God is one. There is more to it, of course, given not least that Judaism and Christianity have gone their independent ways for so many centuries; I may refer simply to my *The Partings of the Ways between Christianity and Judaism* (London: SCM/Philadelphia: TPI, 1991). But so long as Christian theology remains ambivalent on its monotheism, and so long as any tendency to christolatry remains strong in Christian worship, for so long will Jew and Christian be unable to comprehend the other in regard to the most fundamental root of their common religion. And for a Christianity three-quarters of whose scriptures are the scriptures of Israel, that is a most serious crack in its own foundations.

(3) Not least is an adequate appreciation of Christianity's monotheism vital for Christian understanding of the continuities between Jesus himself and what was claimed for him subsequently. Without such continuity there is another flaw at the heart of a Christianity which claims that the self-revelation of God has been focused in a historical individual and particularly in his three-year ministry in Galilee and Jerusalem. And without such continuity, demonstrable or at least plausible, Christian apologetics on this crucial point have an almost impossible task. Hence the importance of the concept of incarnation (chapter 2) and of attempting to grasp why the concept and credo was formulated (chapter 23). As one who has always seen the heart of the Christian gospel in the proclamation of cross and resurrection, I confess to being somewhat bemused to find that my own dialogue and research have pushed me so far toward a strong affirmation of incarnation. And as one who started with some difficulties over classic formulations of God as Trinity I am amused that my work has progressed so consistently from Spirit, to Christ, to God.

Finally it seemed appropriate to include a lecture first delivered at the Presbyterian Church (USA) Theology Convocation "We Believe in One Lord Jesus Christ" (Pittsburgh, April, 1995), on the second coming (chapter 24). Oddly enough, this was a topic I had never addressed in depth until this time. But it gave me an insight into the character of Christian hope and of theological imagery which closely correlated with the results of earlier study. I hope it also gives a flavor of the dialogue which is faith in search of understanding and understanding in scrutiny of faith. It is a subject which is bound to come more and more to the fore at the turn of the millennium and which, one would have thought, those engaged in the dialogue of christology ought to be addressing with some energy. But, most important here, it is part of a full answer to the question "Why christology?" which in the end, as from the beginning, confronts us with God.

James D. G. Dunn,
Durham
September, 1997

ABBREVIATIONS

The standard abbreviations for the Qumran documents are used.

AB   Anchor Bible

ANRW   *Aufstieg und Niedergang der römischen Welt*

Apoc. Abr.   *Apocalypse of Abraham*

Ass. Mos.   *Assumption of Moses*

b.   Babylonian Talmud

BAGD   W. Bauer, *A Greek-English Lexicon of the New Testament and Other Early Christian Literature,* tr. and ed. W. F. Arndt, F. W. Gingrich, and F. W. Danker (Chicago: University of Chicago, 1979)

Barn.   *Epistle of Barnabas*

BBE   Beiträge zur biblischen Exegese

BDF   F. Blass and A. Debrunner, *A Greek Grammar of the New Testament and Other Early Christian Literature,* tr. and rev. R. W. Funk (Chicago: University of Chicago, 1961)

Ber.   *Berakoth*

BETL   Bibliotheca ephemeridum theologicarum lovaniensium

BNTC   Black's New Testament Commentaries

BJRL   *Bulletin of the John Rylands Library*

BZAW   Beihefte zum Zeitschrift für die Alttestamentliche Wissenschaft

CBQ   *Catholic Biblical Quarterly*

Cyprian

  Idol.   *Quod Idola Dii Non Sint*

Did.   *Didache*

DJD   *Discoveries in the Judaean Desert*

ÉBib	Études Bibliques
EKK	Evangelisch-katholisches Kommentar
1 En.	*1 Enoch*
2 En.	*2 Enoch*
esp.	especially
EQ	*Evangelical Quarterly*
ETL	*Ephemerides theologicae lovanienses*
ExpT	*Expository Times*
FS	Festschrift
Gregory of Nazianzus	
Ep.	*Epistles*
Ḥag.	*Ḥagigah*
HBT	*Horizons in Biblical Theology*
Hermas	
Mand.	*Mandates*
Sim.	*Similitudes*
HJ	*Heythrop Journal*
HNT	Handbuch zum Neuen Testament
HTR	*Harvard Theological Review*
ICC	International Critical Commentary
Ignatius	
Eph.	*Ephesians*
Rom.	*Romans*
Int	*Interpretation*
JB	Jerusalem Bible
JBL	*Journal of Biblical Literature*
JJS	*Journal of Jewish Studies*
Josephus	
Ant.	*Antiquities*
War	*Jewish War*
JSJ	*Journal for the Study of Judaism*
JSNT	*Journal for the Study of the New Testament*
JSNTSS	*Journal for the Study of the New Testament* Supplement Series
JSOTSS	*Journal for the Study of the Old Testament* Supplement Series
JSPSup	*Journal for the Study of the Pseudepigrapha* Supplement Series
JTC	*Journal for Theology and Church*
JTS	*Journal of Theological Studies*
Jub.	*Jubilees*
KEK	Kritisch-exegetisch Kommentar
KuD	*Kerygma und Dogma*

LCL	Loeb Classical Library
m.	Mishnah
MNTC	Moffatt New Testament Commentary
NCBC	New Century Bible Commentary
NEB	New English Bible
Ned.	*Nedarim*
NICNT	New International Commentary on the New Testament
NIGTC	New International Greek Testament Commentary
NJB	New Jerusalem Bible
NovT	*Novum Testamentum*
NovTSup	Supplements to *Novum Testamentum*
n. s.	new series
NT	New Testament
NTD	Das Neue Testament Deutsch
NTS	*New Testament Studies*
Od. Sol.	*Odes of Solomon*
OT	Old Testament
ÖTKNT	Ökumenischer Taschenbuchkommentar zum Neuen Testament
par(s).	and parallel(s)
Pes.	*Pesaḥim*
Philo	
Abr.	*De Abrahamo*
Agr.	*De Agricultura*
Cher.	*De Cherubim*
Decal.	*De Decalogo*
Det.	*Quod Deterius Potiori Insidiari Soleat*
Ebr.	*De Ebrietate*
Fuga	*De Fuga et Inventione*
Leg. All.	*Legum Allegoriae*
Migr.	*De Migratione Abrahami*
Mos.	*De Vita Mosis*
Mut.	*De Mutatione Nominum*
Opif.	*De Opificio Mundi*
Plant.	*De Plantatione*
Post.	*De Posteritate Caini*
Quaes. Gen.	*Quaestiones et Solutiones in Genesin*
Sacr.	*De Sacrificiis Abelis et Caini*
Somn.	*De Somnis*
Virt.	*De Virtutibus*
Pliny	
Ep.	*Epistles*

Pss. Sol.	*Psalms of Solomon*
RB	*Revue Biblique*
RHPR	*Revue d'histoire et de philosophie religieuses*
RSV⁻	Revised Standard Version
Sanh.	*Sanhedrin*
SB	H. Strack and P. Billerbeck, *Kommentar zum Neuen Testament aus Talmud und Midrasch* I-VI (Munich: Beck, 1922-28)
SBLDS	Society of Biblical Literature Dissertation Series
SBLMS	Society of Biblical Literature Monograph Series
SBLSP	*Society of Biblical Literature Seminar Papers*
SBS	Stuttgarter Bibelstudien
SBT	Studies in Biblical Theology
Sib. Or.	*Sibylline Oracles*
SJT	*Scottish Journal of Theology*
SNTSMS	Society for New Testament Studies Monograph Series
Ta'an.	*Ta'anith*
TBei	*Theologische Beiträge*
T. 12 P.	*Testaments of the Twelve Patriarchs*
T. Abr.	*Testament of Abraham*
T. Benj.	*Testament of Benjamin*
T. Dan	*Testament of Dan*
T. Job	*Testament of Job*
T. Jud.	*Testament of Judah*
T. Levi	*Testament of Levi*
T. Mos.	*Testament of Moses*
T. Reu.	*Testament of Reuben*
TDNT	*Theological Dictionary of the New Testament*
TDOT	*Theological Dictionary of the Old Testament*
Tertullian	
Prax.	*Adversus Praxean*
THKNT	Theologisches Handkommentar zum Neuen Testament
TLG	*Thesaurus Linguae Graecae*
TR	*Theologische Rundschau*
TRE	*Theologische Realenzyklopädie*
TS	*Theological Studies*
TU	Texte und Untersuchungen
TZ	*Theologische Zeitschrift*
Virgil	
Ecl.	*Eclogues*
WBC	Word Biblical Commentary

WMANT	Wissenschaftliche Monographien zum Alten und Neuen Testament
WUNT	Wissenschaftliche Untersuchungen zum Neuen Testament
ZNW	*Zeitschrift für die Neutestamentliche Wissenschaft*
ZTK	*Zeitschrift für Theologie und Kirche*

GENERAL ESSAYS

1

New Testament Christology

The main object of New Testament christology is to trace the emergence of Christianity's distinctive claims regarding Christ as documented in the writings of the New Testament.

A. Introduction

1. Aim

Prior to Jesus' ministry, we can speak only of a diverse Jewish hope of a new age often involving one or more intermediary or redeemer figures — messiah, prophet, exalted hero, archangel, even God himself. A century later all these categories and more were either superseded or focused in one man, Jesus Christ. Ignatius spoke of Jesus in straightforward terms as "our God, Jesus (the) Christ" (*Eph.* 18:2; *Rom.* 3:3) and showed how christology was well on the way toward the classical credal statements of the ecumenical councils. "There is one physician, who is both flesh and spirit, born and yet not born, who is God in man, true life in death, both of Mary and of God, first passible and then impassible, Jesus Christ our Lord" (*Eph.* 7:2). In the course of that hundred years, the claims of Christianity appeared and began to take definitive shape. The New Testament contains that first flowering and enables us to appreciate a good deal of how and why it came about and took the forms it did.

Originally published as "Christology (NT)," *Anchor Bible Dictionary* I, 979-91. Copyright © 1992 by Doubleday, a division of Bantam Doubleday Dell Publishing Group, Inc., and used by permission.

2. Method

Since a transition is involved, at the very least, from Jewish expectations to Christian faith, a developmental approach has been chosen. This assumes that a tradition-history analysis is able to uncover the main outlines of Jesus' own convictions and teaching and similarly that sufficiently reliable information can be had about the beliefs of the earliest Christian congregations. Thereafter we can trace the teaching and emphasis of the individual New Testament writers themselves, following consensus dating and location where necessary. This approach, of course, will not reveal all that Christians said about Christ during that period, but the New Testament writings were obviously regarded as of more than passing significance from the first and therefore can be said to have preserved the most influential material from the foundational epoch.

New Testament christology could properly confine itself to a description of the christology of each individual document, seeking to demonstrate such correlation and coherence as seems appropriate. Several standard treatments have focused on titles; and though titles cannot tell the whole story, the emergence and use of certain titles can tell us a good deal. Dissatisfaction with an excessive emphasis on titles has more recently resulted in calls for different approaches — motif-centered, transformation of categories, conceptual trajectories, and the like. The following analysis will use all these methods, as seems appropriate.

Most attempts to write a New Testament christology also use the benefit of hindsight and global perspective to trace the larger patterns and developments of which individuals were a part. They describe the process by which the earliest christological formulations came to expression, as it were, from "outside." The danger of such an approach is that it reads back later developments into the earlier material; it fails to respect the inevitably more limited horizons of the writers themselves. We will attempt the more difficult task of describing the process from "inside." That should not prevent us from recognizing any new or previously unexpressed formulation. On the contrary, we should be better able to distinguish the genuinely new from mere variation or transfer categories.

3. Chief Impulses

The principal stimulus in the formulating of New Testament christology was threefold: (1) the impact of Jesus, including the impact of his ministry in style and content as well as of his teaching in particular; (2) the impact of his death and resurrection; (3) the experience of (many of) the first Christians in which they recognized further evidence of Jesus' power and status.

The material with which New Testament christology worked was again primarily the first Christians' memories of Jesus and their own experience. But a principal tributary was the various main features of Jewish hope seen to cohere in Jesus. Also of increasing importance over the hundred-year period under review were various categories of wider currency in the Greco-Roman world.

B. Christological Claims Attributed to Jesus

Did Jesus have a christology? That is, did he make significant claims regarding himself? The Synoptics and John's Gospel are most markedly different at this point. Whereas in the latter Jesus' claims for himself are a prominent feature chapter after chapter, in the former he seems on the contrary to want to avoid drawing attention to himself. Since John's christology is so distinctive in comparison with the others, it is best to confine attention here to the Synoptics and treat John separately below.

1. Jesus and Jewish Expectation

At the time of Jesus, Jewish hope embraced a variety of messianic and/or prophetic categories.

a. Royal Messiah

A royal son of David (as in Isa. 11:1-5; *Pss. Sol.* 17:23; 4QFlor 1.10-13) was probably the figure of popular Jewish hope — a new king to restore Israel's independence and greatness. It is likely that anyone who roused the sort of popular interest and excitement which John the Baptist and Jesus provoked would have been regarded as a candidate for such a messianic role (cf. John 1:20; 6:15). And a basic fact is that Jesus was executed as a messianic pretender — King of the Jews (Mark 15:26 pars.). In the hearing before Caiaphas the question was also probably raised, "Are you the Messiah, son of the Blessed?" — on the basis of the accusation about destroying and rebuilding the temple seen in the light of 2 Sam. 7:13-14, interpreted messianically (as in 4QFlor). The distinctive features of Jesus' entry into Jerusalem and of his symbolic action in the temple ("the cleansing of the temple") would almost certainly have raised the same issue in broad (eschatological) or specific (royal messiah) terms. It would hardly be surprising then if his closest followers had themselves raised the question at an earlier stage of his ministry, particularly in the light of the success and popularity it clearly enjoyed (so Mark 8:27-30 pars.).

The key question, however, is how Jesus reacted when this option was put to him. And the answer of the earliest traditions seems to be not very positively. He never once laid claim to the title on his own behalf or unequivocally welcomed its application to him by others. Mark 6:45 strongly suggests that he rejected the messianic role of popular anticipation (cf. John 6:15), and Mark 8:30-33 and the entry into Jerusalem portray a rather different model. So far as we can tell, he did not reject the title "Messiah" outright when put to him (Mark 8:30; 14:62; 15:2), but as currently understood it was evidently unsuited to describe the role he saw for himself. It needed the events of the cross and resurrection to reshape and fill the title with new content for the first Christians.

b. Priestly Messiah

In one or more strands of pre-Christian Judaism a priestly messiah was accorded greater significance than the royal messiah (e.g., *T. 12 P.*; 1QSa 2.11-22). But apparently this was never seen as an option for Jesus, presumably because he was known to be of a tribe other than the tribe of Levi.

c. The Prophet

Jewish expectation took various forms here — the return of Elijah (Mal. 4:5; Sir. 48:9-10), the prophet like Moses (Deut. 18:15, 18), and an unnamed or eschatological prophet (Isa. 61:1-2; 1QS 9.11; 11QMelch). Whether these were different expectations or variants of a single expecation is not clear, and probably was not clear then either. What is clear, however, is that there was a readiness to recognize Jesus as a prophet or the prophet (Mark 6:15 par.; 8:28 pars.; John 6:14; 7:40, 52), though it should not be forgotten that others were accorded the same title in this period (Mark 11:32; John 1:21; Josephus, *Ant.* 18.85-87; 20.97f., 167, 169-72, 188).

Jesus himself seems to have accepted the designation in some degree (Mark 6:4 pars.; Luke 13:33) and in particular to have used Isa. 61:1-2 as a program for his mission (Matt. 5:3-4 = Luke 6:20-21; Matt. 11:5 = Luke 7:22; Luke 4:18-19). He also seems deliberately to have engaged in prophetic or symbolic actions (particularly the action in the temple and the Last Supper). But at times there are hints that he saw his role as transcending that of the normal prophetic figure: Mark 12:1-9; the claim, "I came," rather than, "I was sent" (as in Mark 2:17 pars.); and the use of the formula, "But I say," rather than the more typically prophetic, "Thus says the Lord."

d. Healer

Although miraculous restoration of physical faculties was expected to be a mark of the new age (Isa. 17–19; 35:5-7), it was not particularly associated with any of the above figures. Healings and exorcisms were widely practiced in the ancient world, by pagans and Jews (Mark 9:38-39; Acts 19:13-19; Josephus, *Ant.* 8.45-49). So although it is beyond dispute that Jesus was known as a successful healer and exorcist, it is not clear whether much significance would have been read into this activity by his contemporaries.

Jesus himself, however, seems to have seen in his own ministry clear evidence that God's final rule was already beginning to operate through his exorcisms (Mark 3:23, 27; Matt. 12:28 = Luke 11:20; Luke 10:18) and healing (Matt. 11:5-6 = Luke 7:22-23). This self-estimate included a claim to a plenary anointing by God's spirit, which marked out his ministry as distinctive and which should have been sufficiently clear to his critical onlookers (hence also Mark 3:28-29 pars.). Also distinctive was his exorcistic technique, since he seems neither to have used physical aids nor to have invoked some higher authority in a formula of adjuration. We may properly infer a consciousness on his part of his own authority or of an immediacy and directness of empowering from God (Mark 11:28-33 pars.).

e. Teacher

Jesus is regularly called teacher in the tradition (Mark 5:35; 9:17, 38; 10:17, 20, 35, etc.) and his characteristic style as a "parabolist," one who spoke in parables and pithy sayings, is clearly enshrined in the Synoptics. This would be relatively unremarkable in itself except that the authority with which Jesus taught seems to have provoked surprise and question (Mark 1:27 par.; 6:2 par.; 11:28 pars.). In a large part this must have been because of the same immediacy and directness which his teaching style embodied — the lack of appeal to previous authorities, the typical "Amen" with which he often began a saying, and not least his readiness to dispute established rulings even if given by Moses himself (as in Matt. 5:31-42).

As Jesus evidently saw himself as God's ambassador and spokesman (Mark 9:37 pars.) and as the climax of the prophetic tradition, so he may have seen himself not simply as a teacher of wisdom but as the eschatological emissary of divine Wisdom (Luke 7:31-35 pars.; 10:21-22 par.; 11:49-51 par.).

Such self-understanding must lie behind his pronouncement of sins forgiven without reference to the sacrificial cult (as in Mark 2:10) and the exclusiveness of the claim he made for his teaching and call (Matt. 7:24-27; 10:32 pars.; 10:37 par.).

In short, none of these various categories available or applied to Jesus seem to have proved entirely suitable to describe the role Jesus saw for himself. Four of the five caught aspects of his work, but only aspects.

2. Jesus' View of His Own Role

The evidence reviewed above indicates that Jesus saw his ministry as having a final significance for his hearers. He saw himself as the eschatological agent of God. This self-understanding seems to have been encapsulated in two modes of self-reference.

a. Son of God

This title, which eventually became *the* title for Christ in the classic creeds (God the Son), at the time of Jesus had a much broader reference and simply denoted someone highly favored by God. Hence it could be used of Israel (as in Exod. 4:22), of angels (as in Job 1:6-12), of the king (as in 2 Sam. 7:14), of the righteous man (as in Wis. 2:13-18), or of (other) charismatic rabbis (*m. Ta'an.* 3:8). The process by which the first Christians commandeered this title and gave it exclusive reference to Jesus is reflected in its increasing significance in the Gospel traditions during the second half of the first century — as indicated by the number of times Jesus speaks of God as his father (Mark 3 times, Q 4, Luke's special material 4, Matthew's special material 31, John over 100).

There is sufficient indication that the process that permitted Christians to call Jesus Son of God had already begun with Jesus himself. The basic data is Jesus' habit, as it appears to have been, of addressing God as "Father" in his prayers (as in Matt. 11:25-26 = Luke 10:1-22; the only exception being Mark 15:34). The word used was almost certainly the Aramaic *'abbā* (so Mark 14:36), since it was evidently remembered and treasured in the Greek-speaking churches as characterizing the sonship of Jesus (Rom. 8:15-16; Gal. 4:6). The point is that "abba" is a family word, expressive of intimate family relationship. So the deduction lies close to hand that Jesus used it because he understood (we may even say experienced) his relationship to God in prayer in such intimate terms. And though he evidently taught his disciples so to pray (Luke 11:2), the same Pauline passages clearly indicate that this mode of prayer was seen as something distinctive of the Christians in their dependence on the Spirit of the Son. To that extent at least we can say that the process of narrowing the concept of divine sonship by reference to Jesus did indeed begin with Jesus. Whether Jesus made this a subject of explicit teaching, however, may be doubted, since Matt. 11:27 and Mark 13:32 in particular may already evidence some of the christological intensification which comes to full expression in the Fourth Gospel. But at least we can say that the directness and immediacy of his relationship with God noted above seems to have cohered for Jesus in his "abba" prayer.

b. Son of Man

As our records stand, this seems to be the most obvious example of a self-chosen self-designation (e.g., Mark 2:10; 8:31; 14:62). But the significance of the phrase has been disputed in New Testament scholarship throughout this century.

Certainly the phrase must go back to Jesus in some form. It belongs almost exclusively to the Gospels (82 out of 86 times), and in the Gospels it appears in effect *only* on the lips of Jesus. Apart from Acts 7:56 we cannot speak of a "Son of man christology" outside the Jesus tradition. The most consistent explanation is that the usage originated in the Jesus tradition, and that means, in this case, with Jesus himself. That is not to exclude the likelihood that a number of particular examples within the Jesus tradition reflect some editorial reworking of the tradition (as in Matt. 16:28). But even that reworking follows what was probably the established and therefore original pattern of a speech usage confined to Jesus' own words. It must have been a firm and clear characteristic of Jesus' speech.

In some instances at least he seems to have used the phrase in the normal Aramaic idiom — "son of man" = man (cf. Ps. 8:4), though with something of a self-reference (the polite English style of referring to oneself by the general "one" is a useful parallel). This usage is probably reflected in such passages as Mark 2:10 (the use of the phrase occasions no surprise or offense in the story) and 2:28, and the variant traditions of Mark 3:28-29 pars. are best explained by an ambiguous son of man/man formulation in the original Aramaic. It would also explain why "I" appears in place of "the Son of Man" in other parallel traditions (as in Luke 6:22 = Matt. 5:11; Luke 12:8 = Matt. 10:32). In such cases, of course, the phrase would not have had a titular significance to start with.

The alternative suggestion that the phrase was already firmly established in Jewish thought as a title for a heavenly redeemer figure is not securely grounded. In Dan. 7:13 it is not a title: the manlike figure represents Israel over against the beastlike figures which represent Israel's enemies in a creative reuse of the familiar creation mythology — the saints of the most high fulfilling Adam's role of dominion over the rest of creation. Jewish apocalyptic writers certainly interpret the Dan. 7:13 vision with reference to a heavenly redeemer, but in each case (*Similitudes of Enoch* and 4 Ezra) the implication is that this is a fresh interpretation of the Daniel passage. The date of the *Similitudes* is disputed, but a date prior to Jesus cannot be assumed, and 4 Ezra is certainly later than A.D. 70. Nor is there any indication whatsoever that Jesus was thought to have identified himself with an already known redeemer figure of Jewish expectation or that such an identification needed to be confessed or defended. The likelihood that it was Jesus himself who first drew upon Dan. 7:13 to interpret his own role is part of the larger question which follows.

3. Jesus' View of His Death

It is highly probable that Jesus foresaw the likelihood of a violent or ignominious death. This was the typical fate of prophet and righteous man in Jewish tradition (Wis. 5:1-5; Matt. 23:29-37 par.), as his immediate predecessor (John the Baptist) showed all too well. The hostility which resulted in his eventual crucifixion must have been evident some time before that (cf. Mark 3:22 pars.; 14:8 pars.; Matt. 23:37 = Luke 13:34), and the prophetic action in the temple certainly invited the retaliation which soon followed. The sayings tradition which can be traced back to Jesus with some confidence suggests that Jesus saw a fuller significance in his death. The "cup" sayings (Mark 10:38 par.; 14:36 pars.) evoke the OT image of the cup of God's wrath (as in Isa. 51:17-23), and the "baptism" and "fire" sayings (Mark 10:38; Luke 12:49-50) probably take up the Baptist's metaphor of a fiery baptism to represent the final tribulations which would introduce the end. In applying such images to himself, Jesus presumably implied that his death was to have some sort of representative or vicarious meaning.

If, in addition, the Son of man passion predictions (Mark 8:31; 9:31; 10:34) already contained, in their original form, an allusion to the manlike figure of Daniel's vision, an even more explicit representative significance would be hard to exclude (= "the saints of the most high"). Similar implications are involved in Mark 10:45 and 14:24, though a more direct allusion to the suffering servant of Isaiah 53 is harder to sustain at the earliest level of the tradition.

It is also highly likely that Jesus expected to be vindicated after his death. The pattern was already well established in Jewish reflection on the suffering of the righteous (Isa. 53:10-11; Dan. 7; Wis. 5:1-5; 2 Macc. 7:23), and hope of vindication after enduring the eschatological tribulation would be an obvious way to correlate his expected suffering with his confidence in God's coming reign (as Mark 14:25 confirms). If he did express this hope in terms of resurrection (Mark 8:31; 9:31; 10:34), it would presumably be the final resurrection he had in mind, since the concept of the eschatological resurrection of an individual seems to have emerged as a Christian perception of what had happened to Jesus.

In short, while we cannot say that Jesus placed himself at the center of his own message or called for faith in himself as such, neither can we say that Jesus simply saw himself as the eschatological proclaimer of the kingdom of God. The claim to be the medium of God's rule, the sense of an immediacy and directness in his relation with God and the expectation of representative death and vindication, is well enough rooted in the Jesus tradition. It is also the sort of base we both need and anyway expect if we are to explain the subsequent development of christology.

C. The Beginnings of Christology Proper

Despite what has just been said, it is highly doubtful whether the movement begun by Jesus during his lifetime would have amounted to anything without the resurrection and the experience of the Spirit.

1. The Resurrection of Christ

The belief that God had raised Jesus from the dead was clearly foundational in shaping christology. It is the most prominent feature in the sermons in Acts, reflecting the emphasis both of Luke and of the material he uses (Acts 2:24-32; 4:1-2, 33; 10:40-41; 13:30-37; 17:18, 30-31). The pre-Pauline formula, "God raised him from the dead," may justly be described as the earliest Christian creed (Rom. 10:9; 1 Thess. 1:10; Rom. 8:11 [twice]; Gal. 1:1; Col. 2:12; Eph. 1:20; 2 Tim. 2:8). The centrality of Christ's resurrection for Paul himself is underlined in 1 Cor. 15:12-20, particularly 15:17, and Phil. 2:9-11. In all the Gospels the resurrection forms the climax to the whole presentation of Jesus. Its watershed character in determining christology is indicated variously: in Mark it resolves "the messianic secret" (Mark 9:9); similarly it is the hermeneutic key in John (John 2:22); Luke carefully monitors his use of the title "Lord" in reference to Jesus in acknowledgment of the fact that the title only became his by reason of the resurrection; and in Matthew it is only with the resurrection that the commission of Jesus becomes universal (Matt. 28:18-20; cf. 10:5-6).

Even where the concept "resurrection" is not prominent, the significance of what happened to Jesus after his death is central in assessments of Christ and his significance, as in Hebrews (e.g., 9:11-12) and Revelation (e.g., 5:5). And elsewhere there seems to be no attempt to distinguish resurrection from exaltation (e.g., Acts 2:32-33; Phil. 2:9; 1 Pet. 3:21-22; John 12:32). Nevertheless, it remains a striking fact that the concept of "resurrection" became established from the first, rather than what might otherwise have been the more obvious and recognized category of vindication in heaven of the dead hero. Indeed the earliest formulations seem to have assumed that Jesus' resurrection was the beginning of "the resurrection from the dead" in general (1 Cor. 15:20; cf. Matt. 27:51-53).

2. The Experience of the Spirit

That the outpouring of the Spirit expected for the last days was already a factor of their experience seems likewise to have been a basic and unifying claim of the earliest Christians. What is most relevant here is that the perceived influence of the Spirit seems also to have been a determinative factor in shaping christology. The Baptist's prediction that the coming one's ministry would be characterized by baptizing in Spirit is retained by all forms of the gospel tradition (Mark 1:8 pars.). The Pentecost outpouring is attributed explicitly to the exalted Jesus (Acts 2:33). The identification of the Spirit as "the Spirit of Christ" evidently became soon established (Acts 16:7; 1 Pet. 1:12; 1 John 5:7; Rev. 19:11; on John see below). In Revelation the seven spirits of God (= the Holy Spirit) are depicted as the eyes of the Lamb (Rev. 5:6).

3. Other Features of Early Christology

The search for scriptural explanations of what had happened must inevitably have been a primary objective for the first Christians. To show that Jesus was Messiah despite his shameful death would have been an urgent necessity, reflected in such passages as Luke 24:26, 46 and Acts 3:18, in the early formula "Christ died" (Rom. 8:34; 14:9; 1 Thess. 4:14), and in the established Pauline emphasis on "Christ crucified" (1 Cor. 1:23; 2:2; Gal. 3:1). Isaiah 53 undoubtedly came early into play (as in Rom. 4:25; 1 Cor. 15:3; 1 Pet. 2:24-25), though allusions in Acts 3–4 highlight the suffering-vindication theme rather than that of vicarious suffering.

On the theme of Jesus' exaltation, Ps. 110:1 quickly became a basic proof text (as, e.g., in Acts 2:34; Rom. 8:34; 1 Cor. 15:25; Heb. 1:3, 13; 1 Pet. 3:22). Also, to a lesser extent, Ps. 2:7 (as in Acts 13:33; Heb. 5:5). The consequence of such usage was to give what could be later regarded as an "adoptionist" ring to some early formulations (Acts 2:36; 13:33; Rom. 1:4). More important, however, was the fact that these texts gave added impulse to the two titles for Jesus which were most capable of providing a bridge of communication for the gospel from Judaism to the wider Hellenistic world — Jesus as Lord (1 Cor. 16:22; Jas. 5:7-8; and Acts 11:20; Rom. 10:9 = pre-Pauline baptismal confession; Phil. 2:9-11) and Jesus as Son of God (Acts 9:20; 1 Thess. 1:9-10; Heb. 4:14).

The early Christian use of these same texts left its mark on the Jesus tradition itself (as in Mark 1:11; 12:35-37; 14:24, 62; Luke 22:37), obscuring the issue of whether Jesus himself referred to them. The transformation of various "Son of man" sayings within the Jesus tradition into full titular self-references with consistent if often implicit reference to Dan. 7:13 must also have happened early on.

At the same time the use and reuse of the Jesus tradition throughout this whole period is sufficient indication of a lively desire to recall the words and character of Jesus' ministry because of their continuing relevance. This remains a compelling deduction despite the relative lack of interest shown in the content of the Jesus tradition outside the Gospels. The Q collection, for example, reflects a strong concern to present Jesus as (eschatological) teacher of wisdom (particularly Luke 7:35; 10:21-22; 11:31, 49; 13:34). Besides this, it is inconceivable that substantial elements of the Jesus tradition were not passed on to newly established congregations (cf. Acts 2:42; 1 Cor. 11:2; Col. 2:6; 2 Thess. 2:15). Such traditions must have provided a common ground between writer and readers to which allusion need only be made (e.g., Rom. 13:8-10; 2 Cor. 10:1; 1 Thess. 5:2; Jas. 5:12).

A strong feature of the earliest period was also the expectation of the imminent return of Christ. It was the corollary of the belief that Christ's resurrection was the beginning of the final resurrection (see above) and is reflected in such early formulations as Acts 3:19-21; 1 Cor. 16:22; and 1 Thess. 1:9-10. The Son of Man material used by Q also reflects a keen interest in his coming in glory and judgment (Matt. 19:28 par.; 24:27, 37, 44 par.). Such imminent expectation was slow to disappear, as the early letters of Paul demonstrate (1 Thess. 4:13-18; 1 Cor. 7:29-31), and retained a particular vitality in Jewish-Christian circles (Jas. 5:7-8; Rev. 22:20).

The short time lag anticipated between Jesus' exaltation and return may be sufficient to explain why no interim function in heaven seems to be attributed to Jesus in the Acts material. On the other hand, the understanding of Jesus as heavenly intercessor must have emerged early, prior to its development in Hebrews (Rom. 8:34), since the idea of heavenly intercession was already well established in Judaism (e.g., Tob. 12:15; *T. Levi* 3:5; 5:6-7).

While it is impossible then to gain a detailed picture of this earliest stage of christology, a sufficiently clear and coherent outline can be reconstructed.

D. The Christology of Paul

The background of Paul's christology has already in effect been given above. The impact of the Damascus road experience should not be underestimated (in view of 2 Cor. 4:6 and Gal. 1:16), though it can as easily be exaggerated. Likewise his continuing experience of being "engraced" or "enChristed" was fundamental (see below). The most important other influences came through Hellenistic Judaism (see below). The 20th-century entrancement with the hypothesis that Paul adopted an already widely spread Gnostic redeemer myth is neither justified by the pre-Pauline sources nor necessitated by the Pauline material itself.

The distinctive Pauline contribution can be summarized under three heads.

1. Adam Christology — Christ as Man

It is a fundamental conviction of Paul that in his life and death Jesus was one with humanity in his fallenness and that his resurrection inaugurated a new humanity. The latter is explicit in the passages in which he sums up the whole sweep of human history in the two epochs of Adam and Christ (Rom. 5:12-21; 1 Cor. 15:20-22, 45-49). The former is implicit in his use of Ps. 8:4-6 (1 Cor. 15:27; Eph. 1:22; Phil. 3:21), as its fuller exposition in Heb. 2:6-9 indicates. But it also comes to expression in Rom. 8:3 ("the actual likeness of sinful flesh"); Gal. 4:4 ("born of woman, born under the law"); 2 Cor. 8:9 ("his poverty"); and Phil. 2:7 ("form of a slave . . . as man"), though the majority of scholars would question whether these last verses are properly to be seen as expressions of Adam christology.

As many of the above references also indicate, this representative function of Christ's life achieves its point particularly in his death; if this one man dies, then all die (2 Cor. 5:14). This dovetails with Paul's readiness to interpret Christ's death under the category of "sacrifice" or "sin-offering" (Rom. 3:25; 1 Cor. 5:7). As several passages clearly imply, Paul saw the "mechanism" of sacrifice in terms of representative "interchange" (2 Cor. 5:21; Rom. 8:3; Gal. 3:13; 4:4-5). That is, the sinless one suffers the full effects of human sin (death) in order, not that death might be escaped (= substitution), but that the finality of death might be broken through a sharing in his death leading to resurrection (Rom. 6:5-8; 8:17; Phil. 3:10-11).

Since the obedience of his death was primarily an undoing of Adam's disobedience (Rom. 5:19; Phil. 2:8), a voluntary embracing of the human lot which was the consequence of Adam's folly, it is more accurate to speak of Christ's role as inaugurator of a new humanity as stemming from the resurrection (1 Cor. 15:21-22; Rom. 8:29; Col. 1:18). It is as resurrected, as "spiritual body," that Christ is "last Adam" and pattern of the humanity which at last fulfills the divine purpose in creating humankind (1 Cor. 15:45-49).

Somewhat surprisingly, some of Paul's other distinctive emphases can be included under this head. In particular, his intensive use of "Christ" (already established as a proper name) in corporate imagery — the characteristic "in Christ" (about 80 times), "into Christ" (as in Gal. 3:27), "with Christ" (as in Gal. 3:20), and "through Christ" (more than twenty times), not to mention the "body of Christ" (as in Romans 12 and 1 Corinthians 12). The language refers to the identification with Christ made possible by Christ's identification with fallen humanity — the process of salvation understood as a growing participation in Christ's death with a view to a complete participation in his resurrection as the final goal (Rom. 6:3-6; hence also the creation motif of "old nature/new nature" in Col. 3:9-11; Eph. 4:22-24). The Adam christology corresponds with the understanding of the process of salvation as corporate, more than individual (cf. Eph. 2:15; 4:13).

Other facets of Paul's christology also cohere effectively under Adam christology. For obvious reasons this applies to the relatively less important theme of Jesus as God's Son, as the prominence of this title in some of the material reviewed above makes clear (Rom. 8:3, 15-17, 29; Gal. 4:4-7; Col. 1:13) — the risen Christ as the eldest brother in the eschatological family of God. But it applies even more to an important aspect of Paul's most prominent designation for Jesus, that is "Lord," since it is only as risen Lord that Christ fulfills God's original intention in creating the first human — "to put all things under his feet" (1 Cor. 15:25-27 referring to Ps. 8:6). This may include the "Christus victor" theme of Col. 2:15.

2. Wisdom Christology — Christ as Divine

Perhaps the most enduring development was the application of Wisdom categories to Jesus. Divine wisdom had long served as one of the most important bridge concepts for a Judaism seeking to present itself intelligibly and appealingly within the context of the wider religiophilosophic thought of the time. Within Judaism itself, Wisdom (along with Spirit and Word) was one important way of speaking of God in his creative, revelatory, and redemptive imminence (Proverbs, Sirach, Wisdom, Philo). Judaism's distinctive claim was that this wisdom was now embodied in the Torah (Sir. 24:23; Bar. 4:1).

Already with Paul the equivalent association is being made between Wisdom and Christ (1 Cor. 1:30) — that is, Christ as the embodiment of divine Wisdom and thus as the definitive self-expression of God (Col. 1:19; 2:9). Paul uses Wisdom terminology boldly of Christ, particularly speaking of his

role in creation (1 Cor. 8:6; Col. 1:15-17). Whether Paul means by this that
Christ himself was preexistent, as most conclude, or, more precisely, that
Christ had assumed the role of preexistent Wisdom without remainder, is less
clear. At all events, he has no doubt that it is Christ crucified who is the
definition of divine Wisdom (1 Cor. 1:24), the determinative revelation and
redemptive act of God (2 Cor. 5:19).

The element of ambiguity here is not resolved by other references. The
concept of Jesus' divine sonship provides an important bridge between Adam
and Wisdom christologies, but the usage in Rom. 8:3 and Gal. 4:4 seems as
close to the imagery of Mark 12:6 as to that of the Fourth Evangelist. Potentially more revealing is the title "Lord," since it was such an important
indicator of Christ's status for Paul (note particuarly Rom. 10:9 and 1 Cor.
12:3; well over 200 times in reference to Christ). Its use in Hellenistic religion
for the cult god made it an important evangelistic and apologetic tool. Over
against Hellenistic tolerant syncretism Paul claimed exclusivity for Christ's
Lordship (1 Cor. 8:5-6; Phil. 2:9-11; 1 Cor. 15:25). In so doing he did not
hesitate to apply OT texts referring to Yahweh to the Lord Christ (Rom. 10:13;
1 Cor. 2:16; Phil. 2:10-11 — using the strongly monotheistic Isa. 45:22-23).
Yet, at the same time, Paul evidently did not see such usage as an infringement
on traditional Jewish monotheism (1 Cor. 8:6; also 3:23; 11:3; 15:24, 28). To
call Jesus Lord was as much a way of distinguishing Christ from the one God
as of attributing to him God's agency. Hence the frequent reference to "the
God and Father of our Lord Jesus Christ" (Rom. 15:6; 2 Cor. 1:3; 11:31; Eph.
1:3, 17; Col. 1:3).

The question whether Paul called Jesus "God" does not provide much
help on this point. For one thing, "God," like "Son of God" did not have
such an exclusive reference at this stage, even in Jewish circles (cf. Pss. 45:6;
82:6; Philo *Sacr.* 9; *Quaes. Gen.* 2.62). And for another, the only clear occurrence comes in the later or deutero-Pauline literature (Tit. 2:13). In the strongly
Jewish context of the earlier Rom. 9:5 it is unlikely that any Jew would have
read the benediction as describing "the messiah" as "God over all." The fact
that Paul evidently offered his prayers to God "through Christ" (Rom. 1:8;
7:25; 2 Cor. 1:20; Col. 3:17) confirms that for Paul Christ's role is characteristically as mediator. In other words, neither Adam christology nor Wisdom
christology should be emphasized at the expense of the other.

3. Spirit Christology — Christ as Spirit

Although "Spirit" was virtually synonymous with "Wisdom" in pre-Christian
Judaism (as in Wis. 9:17), Paul did not take what might have appeared to be
the logical step of identifying Christ with the divine spirit in the same way

as he had identified Christ and Wisdom. The identification with Wisdom took in Wisdom's role in creation; but the identification with Spirit is dated only from Christ's resurrection (Rom. 1:4; 1 Cor. 15:45; but not 2 Cor. 3:17, where "the Lord" is the Lord of Exod. 34:34). Hence the strong degree of synonymity between Christ and Spirit in passages dealing with Christian experience (particularly Rom. 8:9-11 and 1 Cor. 12:4-6); it is in Christian experience of the divine that Christ and Spirit are one; Christ experienced not independently of the Spirit but through and as the Spirit.

This also means that for Paul christology becomes a controlling factor in pneumatology. Paul takes it for granted that the Spirit of God is known now only by reference to Christ — "the Spirit of sonship" voicing Jesus' prayer, "Abba, Father" (Rom. 8:15), the Spirit known by the confession "Jesus is Lord" (1 Cor. 12:3), the Spirit who transforms us into the image of Christ (2 Cor. 3:18). The Spirit can now be defined as "the Spirit of Christ" (Rom. 8:9; Gal. 4:6; Phil. 1:19), and spirituality must be measured against the pattern of Christ crucified (2 Cor. 4:7–5:5; 13:4; Phil. 3:10-11). The Spirit is thus redefined as the medium of Christ's relationship with his people (1 Cor. 6:17). Beyond that it is much less clear that we can properly speak of an identification between Christ and Spirit. The Spirit is still preeminently the Spirit of God (Rom. 8:9, 11, 14; 1 Cor. 1:11, 14, etc.) and given by God (1 Cor. 2:12; 2 Cor. 1:21-22; 5:5, etc.). To speak of Christ as Spirit was evidently not the same as speaking of him as Wisdom and Lord. Judging by the convoluted syntax of Rom. 8:11, Paul did not perceive the relation between Christ and Spirit in such clear-cut terms as that between Christ and Wisdom. In other words, even at this early stage, the redefinition of God in his immanent self-revelation, which developing christology was already occasioning, was throwing up factors which were not going to find easy resolution either in simple polytheism or in some more sophisticated "binitarianism" (God as two in one).

E. Varied Emphases in Second-Generation Writings

1. Deutero-Pauline Letters

In Ephesians a distinctive note is struck immediately in the long opening benediction focusing on the theme of Christ as the predetermined redeemer and focus of cosmic unity in "the fullness of time" (Eph. 1:3-14). The idea of Christ as the revelation of God's hitherto mysterious purpose, already developed in Colossians (1:26-27; 2:2), is taken further and spelled out in still more emphatic terms (Eph. 2:11–3:13). All this is a variation of Paul's Wisdom

christology (Col. 2:3; Eph. 3:10), integrating it more fully with Paul's central
concern as apostle to the Gentiles. Note also the fuller confessional material
in Eph. 4:4-6 and the more elaborate images of the body of Christ (4:15-16)
and of Christ as husband of the church (5:23-27).

The Pastorals do not mark much further development in ways of speaking about Christ. The talk is still of Christ's predetermined appearing to fulfill
God's purpose of salvation (2 Tim. 1:9-10; Tit. 1:2-3), and in Tit. 2:13 the
reference is not to Jesus as a second God but rather to "the appearance of the
glory of our great God and Savior" — Jesus' coming as the manifestation of
the glory of the one God. The title "Savior" is much more prominent than in
the earlier Paulines and is used equally of Christ as of God (especially Tit.
1:3-4; 2:10, 13; 3:4, 6). But otherwise the christology is characteristically
contained in what are already well-established credal and hymnic formulae
(1 Tim. 1:15; 2:5-6; 3:16; 6:13; 2 Tim. 2:8; Tit. 3:5-7), "the teaching which
accords with godliness" (1 Tim. 6:3). So, too, the talk of the second appearing
has already assumed the more measured tones of a hope which no longer
expects imminent fulfillment (1 Tim. 6:14; 2 Tim. 4:1, 8; Tit. 2:13).

2. The Wider Circle of Pauline Influence

In 1 Peter we find the same conviction that Christ had been "predestined
before the foundation of the world" and "manifested at the end of the times"
(1:20) — clearly a widespread christological emphasis at this period. But
distinctive of 1 Peter is the continual focus on suffering, and this determines
the main christological concern. The Spirit is designated "the Spirit of Christ"
as having predicted the prophecies of Christ's sufferings (1:11). Christ was
the spotless sacrificial lamb (1:19). In the fullest use of Isaiah 53 in the New
Testament, Christ's patience in suffering is held up as an example (2:21-25;
similarly 3:17-18). In echo of the characteristic Pauline emphasis, experience
of "the Spirit of glory" is linked with sharing in Christ's sufferings (4:13-14).
The vicarious effect of Christ's suffering and death, however, is evidently
linked in the author's mind with Christ's resurrection, which he also regards
as a medium of salvation (1:3; 3:18-21). At the same time he gives evidence
of the earliest speculation about Christ's ministry between death and resurrection — preaching to "the spirits in prison" (3:18-20; 4:6). 1 Peter also
contains one of the best examples of a collection of OT texts used for evangelistic or apologetic purposes — the "stone testimonia" (1:6-8).

Next to the Fourth Gospel, Hebrews has the most carefully worked out
and sustained christology in the New Testament. It includes two of the most
developed expressions of Wisdom and Adam christologies (1:2-3; 2:6-17).
But its main objective is to present Christ as superior to all other potential

mediator figures — superior as Son to the prophets (1:1-2), to the angels (1:4-16), and to Moses (3:1-6). The principal thrust, however, comes in the presentation of Christ as High Priest — not of Aaron's line, though sharing the very human characteristics required of a good high priest (5:1-10), but of the order of Melchizedek (Ps. 110:4) "by the power of an indestructible life" (7:16). As such he is superior to the Levitical priesthood as a whole.

This central thesis is worked out in 8–10 by means of a magnificent blend of Platonic idealism and Hebraic eschatology. As also in Philo, the earthly world of everyday perception is only a shadow and imperfect copy of the real heavenly world. So the tabernacle with its priesthood and sacrifice is only a shadow of the real heavenly sanctuary, and Christ is the real High Priest and his sacrifice (of himself) *the* sacrifice which alone suffices to purify the conscience and make the worshiper perfect. In the blend with Hebraic eschatology, the shadowy "here below" is identified with the preparatory "then" of the old covenant, and the heavenly real with the eschatological "now" of the new covenant. Thus priesthood and cult are shown to belong to the outmoded age of imperfect and preparatory shadow. Christ has opened the way once for all into the real inner sanctum of God's presence. By such sophisticated means the writer clearly hopes to discourage his readers from harking back to the tangibility of the Jewish cult and to persuade them of the virtues of a Christianity whose only priest and atoning sacrifice is Christ, even if it means social ostracism (13:8-16).

Of the Gospels, Mark most closely shares Pauline concerns. His aim is to present Jesus as Christ, Son of God (1:1, 11). But if this claim is understood in terms simply of mighty works (as in 3:11 and 5:7), it is misunderstood (so also 13:22). Hence the secrecy motif (as in 3:12 and 5:43) and the theme of the disciples' dullness (as in 4:13 and 8:14-21). Hence, too, at what is obviously the center and turning point of the Gospel, Jesus responds to Peter's confession, "You are the Christ," by repeating the call for secrecy, and immediately goes on to teach that the Son of man must suffer and be killed (8:30-31). The second half begins with the heavenly voice once again hailing Jesus as God's Son (9:7), giving the stamp of divine approval to the christology and its consequences for discipleship just expressed (8:31–9:1). Thereafter the movement of the narrative is all toward Jerusalem, with repeated predictions of the imminent passion (9:12, 31; 10:33-34, 38-39, 45; 12:8, etc.). In the climax to the whole, the high priest poses the question of Jesus' messiahship and divine sonship only to reject him (14:61-64), whereas, with supreme dramatic effect, it is the Roman centurion who at last makes the right confession, "Truly this man was God's Son" — speaking of the crucified Jesus who has just died (15:39). In the light of this, several have concluded that Mark wrote his Gospel with an object similar to that of Paul in 2 Corinthians 10–13 — to correct a christology of glory (a so-called "divine man" christology), which emphasized too much the mighty works of Jesus, by means of a christology of the cross.

3. Luke-Acts

Any study of the theology of Luke must take account of the fact that he wrote two volumes. The significance of this fact is not reducible to the tracing of structural parallels (e.g., the two prologues and inaugural Spirit anointings — Luke 1–2 = Acts 1 and Luke 3:21-22 = Acts 2:1-4; the journey framework for narrative). Rather it implies that there is a continuity and interconnectedness between the two parts of Luke's twofold composition which should prohibit us from drawing conclusions regarding Luke's christology from only one part, or from one part independently of the other. So, e.g., Luke evidently did not think it necessary to include much reference to the ministry of Jesus in the sermons in Acts (only 2:22 and 10:36-39), since he could presume that his readers already knew the Gospel.

In particular, the two-volume scope of Luke's theology enables us to recognize the governing claim of his christology: that Jesus Christ is both the climax of God's purpose through Israel and the center of history. Hence the counterpoint themes of continuity and discontinuity by which Jesus both links and separates the epochs which precede and succeed him. On the one hand, the climactic note of fulfillment which marks not least the periods of transition from one epoch to the other (from Israel to Jesus — Luke 1:67-79; 3:4-6; 4:16-22; from Jesus to church — 24:26-27, 44-48; Acts 1:16-20; 2:16-21, 25-36). Likewise the subtle evocation of the Exodus theme in Luke 9:31 and 11:20, and the maintenance of a Moses/Prophet christology across the divide of his two volumes (Luke 24:19; Acts 3:22; 7:37). With similar effect, and even more marked, his emphasis on the Spirit, as heralding the coming of the Christ (Luke 1:15, 41, 67; 2:25), as distinguishing his ministry in special measure (3:22; 4:1, 14, 18; 10:21; Acts 1:2; 10:38), and as poured out in eschatological fullness on the first believers (Acts 1:5; 8; 2:4, 17-18, 33, etc.).

On the other hand, the period of Israel becomes increasingly superseded. The Jerusalem temple, which provides an important focus of continuity (Luke 1:8-23; 2:22-51; 24:52-53; Acts 2:46; 3:1-10; 5:20-21, 42), is attacked by Stephen as "made with hands" (7:48; cf. v. 41) and becomes the occasion for Paul's final rejection and arrest (21:7-36; 26:21), a development complemented by Paul's own repeated turning away from "the Jews" and to the Gentiles (9:15; 13:45-50; 22:21-22; 28:25-28). The discontinuity between epochs is also marked christologically, in the depiction of the successive modes of relationship between Jesus and the Spirit — first, as the one whose human life is created by the Spirit (Luke 1:35), second, as the one who is uniquely anointed by the Spirit (3:22; 4:18; Acts 10:38), and third, as the exalted one who in his exaltation has received divine power to bestow the Spirit (Acts 2:33), so that, as with Paul, the Spirit can be designated "the Spirit of Jesus" (Acts 16:7). The attempt to mark off the epoch of Jesus from the epoch of the Spirit by limiting the resurrection appearances to forty days so that there is a ten-day gap between ascension and Pentecost (Acts 1) is particularly noticeable.

An important factor in this reshaping of the christological focus of salvation history is the delay of the parousia. The extent of the delay envisaged by Luke should not be exaggerated: he still uses the language of imminent expectation in Luke 10:9, 11; 18:7-8; and 21:32. Nevertheless he does inject clear warnings of delay into the earlier tradition at Luke 19:11; 20:9; and 21:8, and in Acts a longer time scale does seem to be envisaged for the mission (Acts 1:6-8), with the talk of Christ's parousia reading more like a doctrine of the last things than a threat pressingly close (Acts 10:42; 17:31; 24:25). This stretching out of the period between exaltation and parousia reinforces the impression that Acts has an "absentee christology," with no further activity predicated of Christ other than through his name (Acts 3:6, 16; 4:10-12, 30; 10:43) or in visions (Acts 9:10; 18:9; 22:17-21; 26:13-19), in some contrast to the more intimate "in Christ" and mutual indwelling emphases of Paul and John.

Other distinctive features of Luke's christology include his focus on "salvation." Of the Synoptic Evangelists, only Luke calls Jesus "Savior" (Luke 2:11; in John only at 4:42) and attributes "salvation" to him (Luke 1:69; 2:30; 3:6; 19:9). The same emphasis is continued in Acts, in the use of both nouns (Acts 4:12; 5:31; 13:23, 26; 28:28) and of the verb (particularly 2:21; 4:12; 15:11; 16:31). Equally striking is the surprising lack of any clear atonement theology in Luke-Acts. As already noted, the references to the death of Christ in the Acts speeches, including the allusions to Jesus as "Servant," emphasize the suffering-vindication theme rather than the motif of vicarious suffering (Acts 3:13, 26; 4:27, 30; 5:30; 10:39-40; 13:29-30). The impression that this feature may be indicative of Luke's own theology of the cross is strengthened by the absence of the clearest Markan expression of atonement theology (Luke 22:27; cf. Mark 10:45) and by the textual confusion at the other two most sensitive points in the narrative (Luke 22:19b-20; Acts 20:28). Finally we may note that Luke's depiction of the substantial and objective nature of Christ's resurrection appearances (Luke 24:39-43; Acts 1:3), which in part at least may be simply the result of his own perception of the tangible character of spiritual phenomena (e.g., Luke 3:22; Acts 4:31; 8:18-19; 12:9), enables him to emphasize still further the contrast between the epoch of Christ and that of the Spirit and marks off the ascension from the resurrection in a way that is unparalleled elsewhere in the New Testament.

4. Outside the Circle of Pauline Influence

James almost seems to lack any christology worth speaking of, though the ambiguous "Lord" of 5:7-8 probably also refers to Jesus. But he does draw directly on the Jesus tradition (e.g., 1:5, 22-23; 4:12; 5:12) and may refer to Jesus as the "righteous one" (5:6) in a fine blend of Jewish wisdom teaching and prophetic fervor against social injustice. This can quite properly be called an implicit christology, since it shows how these emphases of Jesus' ministry were maintained, without necessarily having to be held all the time within a Markan passion framework (as in all the Gospels).

The twofold emphasis of the birth narratives also provides Matthew with his principal christological themes — Jesus as Son of David and Messiah (1:1, 17, 20; 2:4), but also Son of God (1:18, 20; 2:15). Evidently within a more Jewish context the assertion of Jesus' messiahship was still a matter of apologetic importance (hence the redactional insertions at 11:2; 16:20; 23:10; 24:5). Matthew also makes more use of the "Son of David" title than any other New Testament writer (9:27; 12:23; 15:22; 20:30-31 pars.; 21:9, 15). But "Son of God" is clearly the more important designation. For Matthew not only retains the high points of Mark's presentation (3:17; 8:29; 17:5; 26:63; 27:54) but takes pains to extend the motif (14:33; 16:16; 27:40, 43; 28:19).

On the one hand, this means that Christ recapitulates Israel's history to complete God's purpose for Israel (2:15; 4:3-6 = midrash on Deuteronomy 6–8) — an Israel christology rather like Paul's Adam christology. Hence also the implicit Moses typology (Jesus gives the first of five blocks of teaching on a mountain) and the sustained fulfillment of prophecy theme (1:22-23; 2:15, 17-18, 23; 4:14-16; 8:17; 12:17-21; 21:4; 27:9-10). But even more, this means that Jesus, Son of God, is the divine presence among his people (1:23; 18:20; 28:20). The process whereby "Son of God" gains in christological significance is already well advanced — as reflected also in the marked increase in Jesus' reference to God as "Father" (as in 7:21; 10:32-33; 12:50; 16:17; 18:10, 19). Hence, too, the evidently deliberate Matthean redaction whereby Jesus is presented not merely as the eschatological emissary of Wisdom but as Wisdom herself (11:19, 25-30; 23:34-36, 37-39).

The most striking feature of the christology of the Revelation of John is the relation envisaged between God and the exalted Christ — although the full force of the christology involved remains unclear since the apocalyptic imagery is open to diverse interpretations. The description of the initial vision of Christ is a fascinating mixture of elements drawn from previous apocalyptic visions (particularly Ezek. 1:24; 8:2; Dan. 7:13; 10:5-6) and is of a piece with the tradition of Jewish apocalyptic (or merkabah mysticism) in which a glorious angel seems to have the appearance of God (as in *Apoc. Abr.* 10). The difference is that elsewhere in the tradition the angel forbids the offer of worship, whereas in Revelation, Christ is as much the object of worship as God is (5:13; 7:10).

Christ, initially introduced as the Lion of Judah and Root of David, conqueror of death and lord of history (5:5), is referred to thereafter as the Lamb once slain (5:6, 8, 12-13; 6:1, etc.), whose blood enables his followers to conquer and who is the executor of divine wrath (6:16; 7:14; 12:11). More significant is the fact that the Lamb is also said to be "in the middle of the throne" (5:6; 7:17), whereas elsewhere it is God who is described as "he who is seated on the throne" (4:9-10; 5:1, 7, 13; 6:16; 7:10, 15; 19:4; 21:5). The one throne is evidently shared by both God and the Lamb (22:1). So, too, each can equally be called "the Alpha and the Omega" (1:8; 21:6; 22:13). In other words, Christ has not simply been exalted alongside God as a second divine power in heaven, but in the visionary imagery of the seer is somehow merged with God. This makes the promise of salvation as being given to sit on the same throne and as being given in marriage to the Lamb all the more profound (3:21; 19:7-8; 21:2, 9-14).

F. The Christology of John

The Fourth Gospel has the most fully developed christology in the New Testament. The contrast with the Synoptics is at once apparent in the public roll call of titles which climaxes ch. 1 ("Lamb of God," "Messiah," "Son of God," "King of Israel," "Son of Man"). The style and content of Jesus' teaching is strikingly different: in the Synoptics, Jesus speaks in epigrams and parables, principally about the kingdom of God/heaven and very little about himself; in John, Jesus speaks in long, often involved discourses, principally about himself and very little about the kingdom. Jesus' consciousness of having preexisted, as Son with the Father, as Son of man descended from heaven, as the eternal "I am," confronts the reader throughout. There is sufficient evidence that John's presentation is rooted in good tradition (cf., e.g., John 6:20 with Mark 6:50; John 6:51-58 with Mark 14:22-24 = Luke 22:19-20; John 10 with Luke 15:4-6), but the above emphases are so consistent in John and so lacking in the earlier Jesus tradition that they have to be attributed to a developed reflection on that earlier tradition.

The chief objectives of the Fourth Evangelist are clearly marked in the Prologue, which must have a programmatic function since it matches the subsequent emphases so closely, and in 20:31.

1. The Word Incarnate

In the Prologue the line of earlier Wisdom christology is extended. The concept "Word" is given preference over "Wisdom," perhaps simply because the masculine concept seemed more appropriate, but probably mainly because "Word" was the more serviceable concept to provide a bridge of communication between Jewish monotheism and Greek religious philosophy (as with Philo). In the line of Jewish Wisdom theology, the Word is not thought of as being other than God, but as God in his self-revelation, God insofar as he may be known by humankind. The Word was not a redemptive "afterthought" but was "in the beginning" (1:1-2), God's own power put forth in creation and revelation (1:3-5, 9-10). Jesus Christ is this Word become man, embodying the divine glory (1:14). He alone reveals God (1:18).

Although the concept "Word" disappears after the Prologue, what follows is in effect a massive elaboration of Word/Wisdom christology. In varied ways the message is constantly repeated — Jesus is the one who has finally and definitively revealed God. Nathanael is a "true Israelite" (= "one who sees God") because he will see the Son of man as the ladder between heaven and earth (1:47-51). No one has ascended to heaven; only the Son of man who descended from heaven can bear witness to heavenly things (3:11-13). He who comes from above is above all whose witness is from God (3:31-33). Only he who is from the Father has seen the Father (6:46). The "I am" statements unique to John pick up Wisdom language (shepherd, light, etc.) and in echoing the "I am" of Yahweh (Exod. 3:14; Isa. 43:10, etc.) make the claim even more emphatically — Jesus is the self-revelation of the covenant God (John 6:35; 8:12, 24, 28, 58, etc.), the definitive manifestation of that divine reality (1:14, 17; 14:6). Isaiah saw Christ because he saw God in his glory, God as manifested to humankind (Isaiah 6; John 12:41). Hence the charge leveled against the Johannine Jesus by "the Jews": he made himself equal with God, made himself God (5:18; 10:33). John does not dispute the charge; rather he makes it an article of faith on his own account (1:18; 20:28); only, Jesus as God must not be understood as another, a second God, but as God himself incarnate, God making himself present and known to humankind so far as that was possible within the confines of human experience.

This also is the function of the dominant category of John's christology — Son of God. Although the designation "Messiah" is still important (note 1:41 and 4:25), it is clear that he wants the Christ title to be understood in the light of the Son of God title (11:27; 20:31). The reason is also clear from the characteristic Johannine elaboration of the Son language: "Son" expresses well the intimate relation between Jesus and God and the authority of Jesus' revelation of God. As "Son of God," Jesus is unique: he is the *monogenēs*, "one of a kind" (like no other son, 1:14, 18; 3:16, 18); his sonship cannot be shared (he alone is "son"; believers are "children"; contrast Paul). As "the Son," he is not a different divine being from the Father, but God making himself visible to people: he and the Father are one (10:30); to have seen him is to have seen the Father (14:9). Hence also the repeated note usually taken subsequently as emphasizing the Son's subordination to the Father, but better understood as highlighting the continuity between Father and Son and the authority of the Son's witness on the Father's behalf (e.g., 5:19-23, 26-27; 6:35-40, 57; 10:25, 37-38; 14:25-31; 15:26).

With this as the chief emphasis of John's christology, the Christian redefinition of Jewish monotheism can be said to be already well under way. Clearly evident, too, are the strains which caused rabbinic Judaism to reject such redefinition as in effect an abandoning of the unity of God. The danger of an overemphasis on Jesus as God on earth is also evident, but John was aware of it and took steps to guard against it.

2. The Son Glorified

Although the Fourth Evangelist has nothing like the Adam christology with which Paul balanced his Wisdom christology, a somewhat different balance is nevertheless provided by important other strands of the Gospel. In particular, John takes pains to exclude the impression that Jesus was simply God in human appearance, not really part of the human species. The Word became "flesh" (1:14), that which constitutes the human born (1:13; 3:6). To have eternal life one must believe in Jesus, that is, accept his fleshliness in all its earthliness (6:53-56). He really died on the cross, as eyewitness testimony confirms (19:34-35). The emphasis is not prominent, but it does come at critical points in the Gospel, and John presumably thought the line was clearly enough drawn.

The subject of Jesus' rejection and death is, in fact, more intensively elaborated, in its own way, than in any other Gospel. The theme of the light opposed by the darkness, of the Word rejected by his own, first announced in the Prologue (1:5, 11), becomes a leitmotif of the whole Gospel. The light inevitably has a critical or divisive role, since some accept it but many hate it (3:19-21). "Judgment" as a sifting process separating into "for" and "against" is a thread which holds together the central section of the Gospel (6–12), with only the inner circle left before Judas, too, goes off into the night (13:30). The mention of "the hour" sounds a steady drumbeat throughout, heralding the coming passion (2:4; 7:30; 8:20; 12:23, 27; 13:1; 17:1). The soteriological significance of Jesus' death is still prominent (1:29; 6:51; 12:32; 13:10; 19:34), but more prominent is the christological point that his death forms a theological unity with his resurrection and ascension — a single act of being "lifted up" (3:14; 8:28; 12:32), of ascension (3:13; 6:62; 20:17), and particularly of glorification (7:39; 12:16, 23; 13:31; 17:1). As with Paul, the glory of Christ does not come into focus apart from the cross.

As with Paul, the concept of the Spirit is drawn into close correlation with christology. Despite the powerful Word/Wisdom christology, the Spirit is still depicted as given to Jesus at Jordan, but given to "remain on him" and "without measure" (1:32; 4:34). More to the point, the Spirit is now clearly a gift to be given by Christ (1:33; 4:10, 14; 4:34f.[?]; 7:39; 15:26; 16:7; 19:34); and here, too, the unity of the salvation climax of Jesus' ministry is underlined, since Jesus "hands over" the Spirit on the cross (19:30) and the (Pentecostal) bestowal of the Spirit for mission is effected on the day of resurrection (20:21-23). Most distinctive of all, the Spirit is described as the "Paraclete" or Counselor, or more precisely, as "the other Paraclete" (14:16). That is to say, the Spirit is Jesus' successor and takes Jesus' place, so that the promise of Jesus' return to dwell in his disciples can be immediately linked to the coming and indwelling of the Paraclete (14:15-26) — one of the most striking features of John's "realized eschatology." Significantly, the Paraclete's primary role is to maintain and complete the revelation of Christ (14:26; 15:26; 16:7, 10), to glorify Christ by taking what is Christ's and reproclaiming it to his disciples (16:12-15). Yet once again, as with Paul, this does not mean that John's christology has absorbed the concept of Spirit without remainder, as it has the concepts of Wisdom and Word. For distinct functions are still attributed to both — to the Spirit in worship and to Christ apart from the Spirit: despite his realized eschatology, John retains the promise of a future parousia (14:3); and despite having already given the Spirit and ascended, Christ reappears to Thomas a week later (20:26-29).

3. 1 and 2 John — Crisis over Christology

1 John was probably written after the Gospel and reflects a situation of some crisis in the Johannine congregations which the Gospel and its presentation of Christ may have helped bring about. A number of erstwhile members had evidently left (1 John 2:19), and the breaking point seems to have been a matter of christology, since they are described as "antichrists" and accused of failing to confess or acknowledge Christ (2:18, 22; 4:3; 2 John 7). In particular, they claimed that Jesus Christ had not come in the flesh (1 John 4:2-3; 2 John 7), a form of docetism which, conceivably, they may have derived from or defended by means of a lopsided reading of the Gospel. Consequently this second member of the Johannine school draws back somewhat from the bolder synthesis attempted in the Gospel. The opening verses clearly recall the Prologue to the Gospel, but they also recall the older idea

of Christ as the content of the word of preaching (cf. 1 John 1:1-3 particularly with Luke 1:2 and Acts 10:36). And 1 John 5:20 probably refers to Jesus as "the true God" (cf. particularly John 1:18). But the balancing emphasis is more clearly and sharply drawn: the word of life had a tangible historicity (1 John 1:1); the confession that "Jesus Christ has come in the flesh" is the key criterion for testing the spirits (4:1-2); any suggestion that the Christ did not really die is emphatically ruled out (5:6-8).

In short, 1 and 2 John provide vivid indications of the hazardous frontiers of reproclamation which christology at the end of the first century was beginning to explore.

G. Conclusions

1. Continuity with Judaism

Throughout the various New Testament writings there is never any slackening of a central claim: Jesus was a Jew and must be understood within the terms provided by Judaism and its sacred scriptures. Most striking is the way in which a range of diverse categories is focused on Jesus — Messiah and son of man, Lord and son of God, Wisdom and Word, atoning sacrifice and priest, Adam and Spirit, Servant and Lamb, Savior and God. Of course, most of the categories are redefined in one degree or other — son of man becomes Son of Man, son of God becomes only-begotten Son of God, Spirit becomes Spirit of Christ, and so on. But the categories remain essentially Jewish, even when they had wider currency in the Greco-Roman world, and it was evidently understood to be important, even if not stated explicitly, that Jesus should continue to be comprehended in Jewish terms — important that Jesus should be seen in continuity with the purposes of God from creation and in the calling of Israel. Clearly then the first Christians felt that Jesus was so much the decisive and definitive fulfillment of Israel's hopes that his significance could not be adequately expressed without pulling in all available categories provided by Jesus' own Jewish religion.

2. Continuity with Jesus' Own Self-Understanding

This second aspect is not so easy to recognize. The important reason is that so much of New Testament christology turns on the event of the cross and resurrection. That event so decisively reshaped the categories applicable to Jesus that their occurrences on either side of that event are not strictly comparable. For example, it is only as Christ crucified that the Messiah claim can be incorporated into christology. It is only as priest "in the order of Melchizedek," "by the power of an indestructible life," that the category of priest can be taken over. It is only as the man whose obedience in death reverses the disobedience of the first man that the title "Adam" can be given to the exalted Christ. Nevertheless, there are sufficiently clear antecedents within the historical Jesus tradition itself that a continuity can properly be claimed — particularly in Jesus' consciousness of intimate sonship, his premonition of suffering in a representative capacity, and his hope of vindication following death. Consequently the claim can justly be made that the cross and resurrection were not a distortion of Jesus' own claims for himself but an appropriate outworking of them. So also the subsequent claims of New Testament christology can fairly be seen not as a wholly new departure without foundation in Christ's own ministry, but a fuller insight into the reality of that mission in the light of the cross and resurrection.

3. Unity and Diversity in New Testament Christology

At the heart of New Testament christology is the claim that the man Jesus was raised from the dead to a status of supreme exaltation. This is the most constant element throughout all the New Testament documents. In its more expanded form, it takes on a double aspect — Christ as the culmination of God's purpose for humankind (and Israel) in creation and salvation, and Christ as the definitive revelation of God to humankind. The latter comes to increasing prominence in the later writings, explicitly as a doctrine of incarnation in John's Gospel, but not at the cost of removing the earlier emphasis on Jesus' death and resurrection as a decisive moment not only for Christ's work but also for his person. Neither aspect can be neglected and neither emphasized at the expense of the other in any christology which claims to be rooted in the New Testament, but consistently in the New Testament writings it is the fact and character of Christ's death and resurrection which provided the criterion and control for christology.

Particular emphases of the individual writers by no means reflect a uniform expression and weighting of this central core. Even the core itself is something of an abstraction, since no two writers express it in precisely the same terms. The differences of the writers themselves and the differences of the situations they address inevitably made for a rich diversity of expression of what nevertheless can be called a common faith in Christ. But beyond that core the range of presentations includes a wide-ranging diversity of motif, form, and image — wide enough to include the differences of Mark and Matthew, the absence of significant christological features in James and Acts, and the idiosyncratic elements in Hebrews and Revelation. Evidently the individual writers felt free to reexpress ("reproclaim" is John's word) the gospel that is Jesus in different ways and with different emphases to speak more pertinently to their own diverse situations. In all cases that included a concern to be true to the insights which had already become established. In some cases that concern dominated largely to the exclusion of all else (particularly the Pastorals). For the most part, however, christology was seen as no mere transfer of set traditions from one church to another, but as a creative response to the exalted Christ and his Spirit, which could sometimes have unpredictable results. But that, too, is part of New Testament christology.

4. The Foundation for Subsequent Christology

The context-specific and at the same time developing character of so much of New Testament christology made it inevitable that not all elements within New Testament christology would be carried forward — particularly the "adoptionist"-like notes in some of the earliest formulations and idea of Wisdom as created which came in as part of the pre-Christian Jewish Wisdom tradition. Some elements were caught up spasmodically — Paul's Adam christology is taken up in Irenaeus's doctrine of "recapitulation," Luke's schematization of the epoch of Christ followed by the epoch of the Spirit reappears in corrupt form in Montanism and modern dispensationalism, and the visionary magnificence of the Revelation of John retains its impact in the Byzantine Pantocrator. But the main highway into the future was provided by the Wisdom/Word christologies of Paul and John. That way was by no means smooth. The concept of Christ as God's self-revelation not only had to skirt around docetism (already in 1-2 John), but also resulted in an outright breach with Judaism over the question mark it seemed to pose to the unity of God (already foreshadowed in John), and it also gave scope to a modalist interpretation later in the second century. In the event, as it happened, the New Testament writings contained sufficient safeguards to prevent Christianity from abandoning monotheism (Christ as God incarnate), but also sufficient dynamic in the relationships implied between God, the exalted Christ, and the Spirit of Christ to require redefinition of that monotheism in a trinitarian direction. Whether subsequent formulations managed to take sufficient account of all the balancing elements in New Testament christology, however, remains an open question.

2

Incarnation

"Incarnation" means literally "enfleshment" or, slightly more fully, "embodiment in flesh." The question of where the concept of incarnation is to be found in the biblical texts is to a large extent dependent on whether that definition is interpreted in a broader or a narrower sense.

A. Definition

Encyclopedia Britannica defines "incarnation" as "a central Christian doctrine that the eternal Word of God (Logos), the Son of God, the second Person of the Trinity, became man in Jesus Christ, who was then truly God and truly man." This certainly reflects what has been the dominant meaning of the term itself within Christian thought. But it is doubtful whether the concept in such a developed sense can be found anywhere within the Bible, since clearly presupposed therein is the full-blown trinitarian doctrine as that came to expression in the fourth and fifth centures of the Christian era.

The question then becomes whether the Christian concept is present in a less developed or undeveloped sense in the New Testament. Alternatively expressed, it becomes a question of defining the beginnings or foundations within the biblical writings of the doctrine as later formulated. To what extent can these early adumbrations or embryonic formulations be described as expressing a belief in "incarnation"?

In turn, this raises the question of how distinctive was that less clearly

Originally published in *Anchor Bible Dictionary* III, 397-404. Copyright © 1992 by Bantam Doubleday Dell Publishing Group, Inc., and used by permission.

defined Christian teaching. Is "incarnation" a specifically "Christian doctrine" as such? Or in its earliest form, was the Christian doctrine of incarnation of a piece with a larger and vaguer understanding of incarnation or of incarnational possibilities? Can "incarnation" not be used quite properly for other forms of "embodiment in flesh"? And if so, what were the distinctive features of the early Christian use of this broader category which caused the Christian conception to stand out from that broader usage and in due course to become the dominant technical sense for the word itself?

B. Preliminary Clarifications

"Incarnation" could quite properly be used for any embodiment in any flesh. But we can limit the inquiry to *human* flesh most of the time, since that is the predominant range of reference. The incarnation of *what* is another question. Clearly implied is the assumption that the "what" is something other than flesh and something "higher" than flesh. It would be unwise, however, to limit the discussion to the idea of God or a god incarnate, even though that would give the most promise of finding an antecedent to the Christian doctrine; for the concept can apply quite properly to the incarnation of any spiritual entity or quality. More modern phrases, such as "an incarnate fiend" or "Liberty incarnate," should provide sufficient warning against narrowing the discussion prematurely. And it will soon become apparent that ancient usage was as broad.

It would of course be possible to define all humanity in incarnational terms — as offspring of the gods (cf. Acts 17:28), as sons of God by virtue of sharing the one divine reason, or as possessing a divine spark. But in such cases, the concept of incarnation has become so diluted as to require a quite different inquiry: What is the "divine" in humankind? What is "human"? A similar problem would arise where the embodiment was thought of in corporate terms — a nation or a large group embodying some ideal. Important as it is to bear in mind the continuity of conception among all these usages, this study will have to be limited to the sense of incarnation as denoting one individual or a number of individuals unusual in the degree or kind of their embodiment of the divine.

Can we bring our question to sharper focus by delimiting the concept of incarnation still further? The problems of conceptuality and definition can be highlighted by noting the overlap and difference between "incarnation/embodiment" on the one hand and "indwelling" and "inspiration" on the other. In both cases it is a question of how the gap or difference between the higher form of existence (spiritual, divine) and the lower (flesh) is perceived as capable of being overcome, so that the higher becomes embodied "in" the lower in some sense.

1. Incarnation and Indwelling

In a dualistic system, where spirit and flesh are seen as sharply and irreconcilably distinct and even antithetical, the resulting embodiment is probably more accurately described as indwelling than as incarnation. The point is that Hellenistic religion and philosophy, which determined the dominant worldview in the Mediterranean world during the period before and after the emergence of Christianity, was characteristically dualistic. The consequence was that in Hellenistic conceptuality the divine could manifest itself *in* the flesh but not *as* flesh. The axiomatic structures of thought made it literally unthinkable that the divine should *become* flesh, that the (by definition) eternal and unchanging should *become* flesh, that the (by definition) eternal and unchanging should *become* that which (by definition) changed, decayed, and perished. Gods might appear *in the guise* of human beings, but they were still gods and not flesh. The divine reason was *part* of the human species, but as "the inner person," quite distinct from the material body.

The extent of the problem here for Hellenistic thought is clearly reflected subsequently in the Christian difficulty in correlating its own emerging doctrine of incarnation with the "given" of divine impassibility. Nor is it surprising that the option of docetism (the divine Christ only seemed to be a man) proved so attractive to many Christians in the second century. And the Gnostic systems of the second and third centuries simply serve to underline the fact that Hellenistic dualism could only cope with the concept of divine indwelling (the splinter of light imprisoned within the mud of matter) and not with incarnation as distinct from indwelling.

2. Incarnation and Inspiration

Here, the problem is more difficult than has usually been realized. What is the difference between these two categories? — incarnation and inspiration — the latter not dependent on Hellenistic dualism and very highly regarded in Jewish thought. After all, the phenomenon of inspiration could be described as "god-possession" (Gk *entheos, enthousiasmos*) or, in Jewish terms, as a being filled or possessed by the Spirit of God (as in Judg. 6:34). An inviting distinction might be developed in terms of inspiration as essentially a temporary phenomenon; a prophet would not be described as an incarnation of the Spirit, a demoniac not as an incarnation of Satan. The difficulty arises, however, if one wants to speak of inspiration as continuous or unique — as indeed some Christians did (e.g., Acts 6:3, 5; Eph. 5:18). John the Baptist was described as "filled with the Holy Spirit from his mother's womb" (Luke 1:15). And Jesus was accused of being possessed by Beelzebul (Mark 3:22 pars.).

The problem here is that incarnation and permanent inspiration would be indistinguishable phenomenologically. This is illustrated by the fact that the early Fathers of the Church did sometimes speak of incarnation in terms of the *Spirit* rather than of the Son (e.g., Hermas *Sim.* 5.6.5; Tertullian *Prax.* 26; Cyprian *Idol.* 11). Consequently, there is a question as to whether the distinction between the two can be maintained beyond the conceptual level — rather like the distinction between "the eternal generation of the Son" and "the procession of the Holy Spirit," that is, a confession that there is and must be an important difference, but we are not at all sure what it amounts to.

Such reflection serves to emphasize the fact that "incarnation" was neither a clearly conceived category ready to be used in reference to Jesus nor an empty concept ready to be filled with specifically Christian meaning. "Incarnation" evidently emerged within a world of meaning where other concepts lay close to hand but which were not seen as adequate to express the Christian perception regarding Jesus. In other words, if we may already draw a preliminary conclusion, it looks as though it is not the overlap of meaning between "incarnation" and other categories such as "indwelling" and "inspiration" which was important so much as the distinction between them: incarnation being developed as a distinctive category in order to express the distinctive way in which the divine and human were seen to have come together in Jesus — incarnation as a particular way of conceiving the embodiment, as the divine *becoming* human, rather than simply indwelling or inspiring the human. This becomes clearer when we look for antecedents to what became the later orthodox Christian concept.

C. Antecedents

A representative range of ideas and idiom, all of which could warrant the description "incarnation" in some sense at least, would include those shown below (fuller details in *TDNT* VIII, 335-62; Boslooper, *Virgin Birth,* 170-78; Hengel, *Son of God,* 21-56; Dunn, *Christology in the Making,* 13-22). The categories are in no sense mutually exclusive and indicate overlapping usage along a more or less continuous spectrum of conceptuality:

(a) The gods themselves appearing in the form or guise of men, as recounted classically in Ovid's *Metamorphoses*.

(b) Descent from the gods, particularly legendary heroes like Dionysus and Heracles, sons of Zeus by mortal mothers.

(c) Pharaohs, kings, and then emperors as representatives of God/the gods, whether by descent or by adoption, and thus embodying divine presence/authority.

(d) The broad category often embraced by the phrase "divine men," as indicating individuals specially favored or empowered by God or the gods, who thus warranted the epithet "divine," Apollonius of Tyana being a much cited case in point.

(e) Poetic hyperbole, sometimes used in incarnational categories, as classically in the case of Augustus, represented by Virgil as Apollo come to earth (*Ecl.* 4.6-10) and by Horace as Mercury descended in the guise of man (*Odes* 1.2.41-52).

(f) Individuals understood as the embodiment of divine wisdom (Sophia), particularly as in Philo's portrayal of Abraham and Moses as archetypes of the wise man (*Leg. All.* 3.217, 244; *Cher.* 10, 18, 31, etc.; *Leg. All.* 2.87; 3.45, 140-47; *Cher.* 41; *Sacr.* 9, etc.) and of Sarah as the embodiment of Wisdom herself (*Leg. All.* 2.82; *Cher.* 9-10, 49; *Det.* 124, etc.).

In the light of our discussion above, however, we can put a question mark against most of these categories, if it is indeed antecedents to the concept of "incarnation" for which we are looking. Within Hellenistic conceptuality, the dualism which allowed the thought of gods appearing in the guise of men (*a* above) militates against the possibility of translating that into the idea of a god become man. And the questionable category of the "divine man" (*d* above) is anyway better set under the heading of "inspiration" (divine empowering).

It is equally doubtful whether the more intellectual circles of the time within the Hellenistic world would have recognized a category of "incarnation" as equivalent to other of the usages just listed. Whatever the popular view of such matters, about which we have only a few hints anyway, those who determined the intellectual climate of the day saw the myths about gods and demigods (*a* and *b*) as just that — myths and not factual truth. Likewise, talk of king or emperor as divine or as son of God (*c*) was largely a matter of political convention, and as such expressive of the symbolical power of the head of state and of an underlying desire for divine legitimation for the social and political structure; and as such regularly manipulated in bloody power struggles. And the poetic hyperbole of a Virgil lauding Augustus's success (*e*) was presumably seen as such — the exaggerated description quite proper in the eulogy of a remarkable man. Certainly, important attitudes and claims were embodied in all this language, but to use the word "incarnation" to describe them is at best of doubtful value and probably serves more to confuse than to help forward the discussion.

All this seems to indicate that while the "in"-put of the divine to the human was variously conceived within the wider Greco-Roman world, the idea of incarnation in the sense of the divine actually becoming human was nowhere formulated prior to Christianity. Whatever language might be proper within myth and poetic eulogy, the inherent dualism of the Hellenistic world-view was probably a decisive barrier which prevented such a narrower concept of incarnation from emerging.

Within the more specifically Jewish milieu, there is a similar range of usage:

(1) The anthropomorphism of early Hebrew thought facilitated the idea that God could appear in human form (cf. the appearance of "the angel of the Lord" in human form, as in Genesis 18; 32:24-30; Josh. 5:13-15).

(2) Equivalent to Heracles (descent from the gods) are the "giants" of Gen. 6:4.

(3) The king of Israel was occasionally called "son of God" or "god," particularly in the Psalms (Pss. 2:7; 45:6; 82:6; 89:26-27).

(4) Fully equivalent to any "divine men" in wider Hellenistic thought were the charismatic leaders in the period of the judges and the later prophets (e.g., Judg. 14:19; 1 Kgs. 18:46; Jer. 20:9; Ezek. 2:2), not to mention the righteous individual and charismatic rabbi (Wis. 2:13-18; *m. Ta'an.* 3:8).

(5) As classic an example as Virgil's eulogy of Augustus would be the Wisdom of Solomon's description of the plagues of Egypt (Wis. 18:15-16).

If parallels to or precursors of the subsequent Christian doctrine of incarnation are sought, similar qualifications would have to be made. Although later Christian thought took some of the anthropomorphisms as manifestations of the Son of God (already in the second century in Justin Martyr's *Dialogue with Trypho*), there is nothing of this in the New Testament itself; there is some christological use of angelomorphic language, particularly in the vision of Rev. 1:13-16, but not as a description of Jesus on earth or of incarnation. In Jewish circles, the episode of Gen. 6:1-4 was taken as one of the major sources to account for human sin (*Jub.* 5:1-10; *1 En.* 6:10; *T. Reu.* 5). Use of the language of deity to speak of the king was the idiom of representation and legitimation as much within Israel as beyond. Charismatic leadership or prophecy likewise belongs more to the category of inspiration than to that of incarnation. And the imagery of Hebrew poetry was as vivid and as vigorous as any of its Greek equivalents. There is nothing in all this which leads us to conclude that by a process of natural evolution any of these usages would have given rise to the more specifically Christian idea of incarnation.

The one exception, or nearest thing to an exception, would seem to be the talk of Wisdom noted previously under (f). Here, we cannot go into the question of whether Wisdom was understood as a divine being other than God, or as a hypostasis, or as a way of speaking (personification) of divine action and immanence within creation; in the framework of Jewish monotheism, the last of these seems most likely, with the concept of "hypostasis" a category which only emerged later in Christian theology, in large part at least as a *consequence* rather than as a *precursor* of the idea of "incarnation" (see Dunn, *Christology in the Making,* 168-76). The point here, however, is that Wisdom certainly denotes the divine as over against the human, so that a concept of divine "in"-put or of incarnation in at least a broader sense is involved. Even so, Philo's portrayal of such a figure as Moses or Sarah as an embodiment of divine wisdom does not actually bring us much further forward, for it is an example of Philo's characteristic use of allegorizing in his handling of scriptural texts and so remains within the broader range of poetic symbolism and hyperbole. Philo, himself, was too much influenced by Hellenistic philosophy for the antithesis between divine and human, rational and material, to be overcome so easily. Juxtaposed they were in the human mind and identified in allegory they might be, but for the one to become the other or be identified with the other in actual fact was probably a step beyond what was yet thinkable.

If anything, the closer antecedent to the concept of "incarnation" is to be found in the idea of divine wisdom as given to Israel, embodied in the Torah, for in this case the language of actual identification seems to be used. The clearest examples are Sir. 24:23 and Bar. 4:1. In the former, the hymn where Wisdom praises herself in the first person is immediately followed by the comment: "All this is the book of the covenant of the Most High God, the law which Moses commanded us." And in the latter, a description of Wisdom is followed in just the same way by a similar comment: "She is the book of the commandments of God and the law that endures for ever." Of course, we are still some way from a concept of incarnation, especially since we have restricted the definition of the term to embodiment in *human flesh.* Nonetheless, such usage of a word which so clearly betokens the divine, a usage which includes both the description of the unique inspiration of Moses and its identification with something as tangible as the book of the law, is clearly not far from the idea of incarnation in the more specifically Christian sense. All it needed was for the two to come together, unique inspiration and identification, in reference to a single individual for the distinctive concept of "incarnation" to be born.

And this is what seems to have happened with regard to Jesus. But in what way, and why, and how soon? Despite the well-known difficulties of stratifying and dating the material, and although other ways of structuring the examination are of course quite possible, we shall seek to maintain a chronological approach as the one most appropriate to an attempt to trace a conceptuality in process of evolution.

D. Jesus

Is the word "incarnation" appropriate to describe Jesus' self-consciousness or claims he made regarding himself? Did Jesus think or speak of himself in terms of the divine embodied in human flesh, whether as a divine being or as God himself become man? The question, of course, is complicated by the usual problem of distinguishing what in the Jesus tradition goes back to Jesus himself and what expresses the later perspective of the earliest Christians or of the Evangelists themselves. The Johannine portrayal of Jesus is the most supportive of an affirmative answer, inviting the evangelistic-apologetic challenge: "He who so speaks of himself is either mad, bad, or God." But it is precisely at this point, Jesus' explicit claims to have preexisted with the Father, at which the Fourth Gospel differs consistently and strikingly from the other Gospels, so that it is precisely the overt incarnationalism of that Gospel which is most likely to indicate a later perspective. As we shall also see later, there are some features of Matthew's portrayal which likewise seem to indicate a developed christology, but for the most part the words of Jesus in the Synoptic Gospels probably bring us closer to Jesus' own self-assertions.

Almost all of that material, however, fits most naturally under the heading of "possession" (whether indwelling or inspiration) rather than of "incarnation." This is certainly the case with the relatively strong use of prophet categories, as in Mark 6:4 and Luke 4:18-19; and the implication is that Jesus saw himself as spokesman for God and emissary of divine Wisdom, as in Mark 9:37 and Luke 7:31-35. Even if Jesus occasionally spoke of himself as "the son (of God)" or God's "beloved son" (Matt. 11:27; Mark 13:32), though the point is disputed, there would have been no implication in the category itself of any claim to preexistence, since divine and intimate sonship was already attributed to a messianic king and the righteous person within Israel (Ps. 2:7; Isa. 42:1; Wis. 2:16-18). And Jesus' talk of himself as "the son of man," even where an allusion to Dan. 7:13 is given, would not be understood as a claim to preexistence, since Dan. 7:13 was evidently not yet interpreted as speaking of a divine individual (see pp. 9-10 above).

Does the authority expressed by Jesus not carry with it an implicit claim to incarnation? The "But I say to you" of Matthew 5 seems to go beyond the prophets' "Thus says the Lord" and to set Jesus over against or above Moses. Even so, however, it is some way from the absolute claim of the Johannine "I am" formula, and it does not seem to have moved beyond the category of inspiration. The most striking expression of divine authority on the part of Jesus would seem to be his claim to forgive sins in Mark 2:5, 10, especially since in the narrative itself it prompts the response, "Who can forgive sins but God alone?" The issue here, however, seems to be that of authorization. After all, the priest was entitled to pronounce sins forgiven in the context of the cult on the authority of Leviticus 5. The provocative feature of Jesus' pronouncement was that he spoke neither as priest nor in the context of the cult. To pronounce sins forgiven or even to forgive sins is not of itself an indication of incarnation, since according to John 20:22 Jesus' disciples can do the same (Matt. 16:19; 18:18). Here again, we do not seem to have moved beyond the category of inspiration or authorization.

It has been suggested that in Jesus' parables he applied to himself OT imagery which depicted God, indicating that Jesus thought of himself as in some sense God. The flaw in this reasoning is the twofold non sequitur that Jesus consistently intended his parables to be understood allegorically and that he consistently intended to portray himself in them. For example, is the sower of Mark 4:3-8 a specific person or anyone who preaches the good news? And the farmer of Mark 4:26-29, who sleeps and rises night and day, is hardly to be understood as a portrayal of God. If any identification is intended by the figure of the father (as in Luke 15:11-32) or of the king (as in Luke 19:12-27), it is obviously God. The imagery of the shepherd (as in Luke 15:4-7) is certainly that of God, but in the same passages it is also that of those set over Israel by God (Jer. 23:1-6; Ezek. 34:10-16, 20-24). Most striking here is the use of wedding imagery (Mark 2:19; Matt. 25:1-13), but even here it is by no means clear if Jesus intended to refer to himself as the bridegroom, as distinct from simply using the symbolism of the wedding to denote the new age of the kingdom (Isa. 49:18; 62:5); and the parable of the king giving a marriage feast for his son (Matt. 22:1-10) hardly suggests an identification between the bridegroom and God.

In short, within the earlier strata of the Jesus tradition there is substantive evidence that Jesus laid claim to speak with divine inspiration and authorization as in some sense the representative of God. But there is nothing of consequence to support the thesis that Jesus saw himself in some sense as God, as the incarnation of deity.

E. Earliest Christianity

Here, the issue resolves itself down to the significance implied or understood in the claim that Jesus had been raised from the dead and exalted to heaven. The claim was clearly fundamental from the beginning of Christianity proper. What were the incarnational corollaries of this claim?

It is quite often assumed that any affirmation of Jesus as exalted to heavenly status would inevitably have carried with it the implication that he had thereby been restored to or had resumed a status already previously enjoyed (e.g., Knox, *Death of Christ,* 11; Moule, *Origin of Christology,* 138-40). Thus, it is argued that the assertion of Jesus' postexistence, after his life on earth, would have been seen to include as a corollary the assertion of his preexistence, before his life on earth. The more exalted the claims made regarding the risen Christ, or the more divine the functions attributed to the exalted Christ, the more unavoidable that corollary would have been. Consequently, even though the concept of incarnation as such was not yet formulated, its conceptualization must have been simply the outworking of that earliest belief in Jesus as raised from the dead. In which case, incarnation could be said to have been an integral part of Christian belief from the very first. So the argument runs.

The argument has power, and since the belief in Jesus as incarnate deity did emerge sooner or later within early Chrstianity, it can hardly be disputed that the doctrine of incarnation was in some sense a consequence of the Easter faith. But if our concern is to trace the emergence of the Christian idea of incarnation, the question to be asked is how soon that consequence was perceived and affirmed. The argument just stated sees it as an almost immediate consequence. But stated like that, it takes too little account of the range of belief and conceptuality at the time. In particular, first-century Judaism knew a good deal of speculation about hero figures who had been exalted to heaven and given some participation in God's judgment, e.g., Enoch, Abel, and the mysterious Melchizedek (*Jub.* 4:22-23; *T. Abr.* 13:1-6; 11QMelch 10). According to Matt. 19:28 and 1 Cor. 6:2-3, Christians themselves were to take part in the final judgment. None of this would have been understood to imply the deity or preexistence of the individuals named. The bestowal of the Spirit (as in Acts 2:33) may seem to take a step beyond anything affirmed of a human figure in pre-Christian Judaism, but John the Baptist attributed some sort of bestowal of the Spirit to the "coming one" (Mark 1:8). Even the confession of Jesus as "Lord," which is certainly very early, did not carry with it a necessary implication that the one so confessed was thereby identified with God, since there were many "lords" (1 Cor. 8:5) and since in Paul at least the confession of Jesus as Lord was bound up with the confession of God as one (1 Cor. 8:6; Phil. 2:9-11; see p. 16 above).

It is unlikely, therefore, that the thought of incarnation was part of earliest Christian faith, or that the conviction regarding Jesus' exaltation to God's right hand would have been seen more or less from the first to carry that corollary within it.

F. Paul

The issue of whether Paul's christology included the thought of incarnation has been obscured for most of the twentieth century by the debate regarding a pre-Christian Gnostic redeemer myth. Bultmann especially argued that there was already in existence before the emergence of Christianity the myth of a heavenly redeemer figure sent from on high to awaken to their true nature the sparks of light imprisoned within matter. According to Bultmann, early christology, including that of Paul, was indebted to this concept of a cosmic figure, a preexistent Son of the Father, who came down from heaven and assumed human form.

The fatal flaw in this whole thesis was that it read the fully developed form of the myth, first clearly attested in the second century A.D., back into the period before Christ. Elements of pre-Christian and early Christian thought, which are better seen as the building blocks from which the Gnostic redeemer myth was later constructed, were assumed to be the broken fragments of an already existing myth whose fuller expressions have been lost to us — a highly questionable argument from silence. In particular, the Christian belief about Jesus probably provided one of the most important of these building blocks, since the actual redeemer figures of the second and third-century Gnostic systems seem to be modeled on this Christian belief rather than vice versa. The thesis is also basically unsatisfactory since the postulated myth is fundamentally dualistic in character; that is to say, it would have led if anything to a docetic rather than an incarnational christology; whereas, in the event, Docetism seems to have emerged as an attempt to translate a newly evolved concept of incarnation into the more characteristically dualistic categories of Hellenistic thought.

The passages in Paul on which the debate mostly focused are the Christ-hymns of Phil. 2:6-11 and Col. 1:15-20. And even when the pre-Christian redeemer myth has been dismissed from the debate, these passages seem to offer the clearest examples of a preexistence and so incarnational christology in Paul.

1. Philippians 2:6-11

Here, the issue is largely reduced to the question of the christological imagery being used and its significance. More specifically, to what extent is the imagery that of Adam christology? The talk of being in God's form (or image) and of a grasping at equality with God (Phil. 2:6) certainly seems to be intended as a portrayal of Jesus in Adamic terms (Gen. 1:26-27 and 3:5 are clearly alluded to). But if that is the case, is it the preexistent Jesus who is in view (the heavenly Christ chose to humble himself to become a man), or is it the epochal significance of Jesus' ministry expressed in Adamic terms (Jesus refused the path of individual self-advancement and chose rather to identify himself completely with humankind in its enslavement to sin and to the death which is the consequence of that enslavement)?

Most commentators find the former more convincing. In which case, the talk of "taking the form of a slave, being/becoming in the likeness of men, and being found/having proved himself to be like man" (Phil. 2:7) is probably to be reckoned the earliest expression of incarnation christology. On the other hand, Adam christology elsewhere in Paul focuses on Christ's death and resurrection, not on his birth, as the decisive moments of epochal significance (Rom. 5:15-19; 1 Cor. 15:20-22, 45-50). And the distinctiveness of Adam christology from the Gnostic redeemer myth lies precisely in the fact that the life, and death, of a historic individual (Jesus) is perceived as imbued with suprahistorical significance for humankind as a whole, rather than that a preexistent divine being entered the alien territory of a human form. (Adam, properly speaking, was prehistoric rather than preexistent.) Moreover, the regular link between Ps. 110:1 and Ps. 8:6 elsewhere in earliest christology (1 Cor. 15:25-27; Eph. 1:20-22; Heb. 1:13–2:8; 1 Pet. 3:22; cf. Phil. 3:21) suggests that Christ's exaltation to lordship following his Adamic death was also seen in Adamic terms; that is, not as a restoration to a heavenly status previously enjoyed but as the fulfillment of God's purpose in creating humankind in the first place ("to put all things under his feet"), "to the glory of God the Father" (Phil. 2:11). So perhaps the issue is not so clearcut as is usually assumed to be the case.

The debate is the same in other expressions of Adam christology. In 1 Cor. 15:47, "the second man, from heaven" is almost certainly the exalted Christ. Although some have argued along the lines of the Gnostic redeemer myth that "the man from heaven" is the spiritual, preexistent prototype of Adam (the Primal Man), Paul explicitly denies this: the spiritual comes *after* the natural; it is the risen Christ who is the prototype of resurrected humankind (15:46-49). In 2 Cor. 8:9, on the other hand, there is an ambivalence similar to that in Philippians 2. Is Christ's richness his preexistent state, and is Christ's becoming poor his incarnation? Or is the richness that of unbroken fellowship with God (such as Adam had enjoyed before the fall) and the poverty the state of separation from God, particularly in his death (cf. Mark 15:34)? The parallel with 2 Cor. 5:21, if anything, suggests the latter.

In Gal. 4:4 and Rom. 8:3 the issue is again more open and depends on how the talk of God sending his Son is to be correlated with Paul's description of the Son as "born of woman, born under the law" and as being sent "in the likeness of sinful flesh." Again, the emphasis seems to be on describing Christ's complete oneness with the human condition ("under the law," "sinful flesh"), which made redemption necessary so that the redemption achieved (on the cross) might be effective for that condition ("to redeem those under the law," "condemned sin in the flesh"). The language of "sending" may have been drawn from the idea of commissioning a prophet (e.g., Jer. 1:7; Ezek. 2:3; Mark 12:2-6), as in the case of Isaiah, conscious of his solidarity with the sinfulness of his people (Isa. 6:5-8), or indeed of the Servant to bear the iniquity of his people (Isa. 49:1-7; 53:4-6). Had Paul intended to evoke the thought of a sending from heaven, it is questionable whether he would have used the word "likeness" in Rom. 8:3, since within Hellenistic thought the word could lend itself too readily to a docetic-type interpretation — not a genuine solidarity with human sinfulness, and so not an actual redemption.

2. Colossians 1:15-20

Here, the matter seems to be more straightforward. Christ is described as "the image of God, the firstborn of all creation," as the one in, through, and for whom all things were created, the one who is "before all things" and in whom all things hold together (1:15-17). There is no reference to incarnation (a descent from heaven, or becoming man), but the language is clearly that of preexistence, and since the preexistence is predicated of Christ himself, the idea of incarnation, rather than that of indwelling or inspiration, must be implicit. Much the same could be said of 1 Cor. 8:6: "one Lord, Jesus Christ, through whom all things. . . ."

There are some difficulties even in this case, however: (1) The language is generally recognized to be that used of Wisdom in the Jewish wisdom literature (Prov. 3:19; 8:22, 25; Sir. 24:9; Wis. 7:26). In the same passages, Wisdom is spoken of as God's first creation, which, if the language of personal preexistence is pressed, leaves us with a rather Arian understanding of "first-born of creation." (2) Equally awkward for subsequent classic credal christology would be the assertion of the personal preexistence of Christ, since in subsequent orthodoxy it is clear that Jesus Christ is the man whom preexistent Wisdom became. The preexistence is attributed to Wisdom; Jesus is the incarnation of preexistent Wisdom. (3) Within the Colossian hymn itself, there is the problem of the second half, often ignored in such discussions. There Christ's exalted preeminence is described as the result of his resurrection (1:18) and as the consequence of God having been pleased to dwell in him in all his fullness (1:19; cf. 2:9) — language more appropriate to the concept of indwelling, or of adoption, than to that of incarnation.

Once again, therefore, the thought does not appear to be so clearcut as it first appeared. The hymn writer does not seem to have been attempting to achieve a consistent christological statement. If by reading the text as straightforward factual affirmation, we find ourselves with unlooked-for corollaries and contradictory assertions, that may be sign enough that we are reading the text with a different meaning than that the author intended, that the author was simply drawing on diverse theological imagery and language to describe the significance of Christ rather than to make a dogmatically coherent claim of incarnation. Even so, the use of Wisdom imagery and language for Christ in both 1 Corinthians 8 and Colossians 1 is striking. Never before, so far as we can tell, had such affirmations been made of a man who had lived and died within living memory. More is being said here of Jesus than Philo said of Moses or the wisdom writers said of the law; more than Virgil said of Augustus. At the very least, we have to say that Jesus' life, death, and resurrection were being seen to possess a divine significance, a revelation of the divine wisdom, a self-disclosure of God himself, so that it was taken as wholly proper to speak of him as that Wisdom, as the manifestation of the one God, with the death of Jesus in particular serving as a definitive expression of that Wisdom (1 Cor. 1:22-25). The explicit concept of incarnation lies very close at hand in such language; and in the way that language is used here we may indeed even be able to observe the concept of "incarnation" on the point of emerging into conscious thought.

G. Between Paul and John

In the period following Paul, the conceptuality is more varied, but the same question as that posed by Paul's Wisdom christology remains of uncertain answer. Has the Christian understanding of Jesus begun to break through the older categories, images, and hyperboles? The focus of such language on Jesus certainly indicates that he was seen as the focus of divine revelation for the first Christians. But has the conceptuality of indwelling and inspiration been stretched to express a new category, that of incarnation? Here again, the answer is more open than many have assumed to be the case.

For example, if the Pauline talk of the sending of the Son (Rom. 8:3; Gal. 4:4) is read as an expression of Wisdom christology on the parallel of

Wis. 9:10, then it should also be read in parallel with Philo's description of Moses, sent by God "as a loan to the earthly sphere and suffered to dwell therein" (*Sacr.* 9). If the latter is an expression of Philo's allegorical hyperbole (Moses as the archetype of the wise man; cf. above), what does that say of the former? Similarly, the talk of the appearing of the one predestined from the beginning of time, in passages such as 2 Tim. 1:9-10, Heb. 9:26, and 1 Pet. 1:20, seems to be a fairly clear expression of preexistence and incarnation, until we remember that similar language is used of Moses in *T. Mos.* (14: "chosen and appointed, and prepared from the foundation of the world, to be the mediator of the covenant"). The christology of Heb. 1:1-3 is also dependent on Jewish wisdom language (e.g., Wis. 7:26; Philo, *Plant.* 8-9, 18) and shares the same difficulty with Col. 1:15-20 as to how its reference to Christ should be interpreted, particularly as later on (Heb. 2:6-9; 5:7-10) we find one of the most fully developed expressions of Adam christology in the New Testament. The language of Heb. 7:3 seems to envisage Melchizedek as an ideal type of the Platonic model, while 10:5 assumes that the Jewish idiom, "those who come into the world," is a circumlocution for human beings.

Even the idea of virginal conception (and birth?), which may be thought to have broken new ground, does not seem to have gone beyond Philo's talk of Zipporah as "pregnant through no mortal agency," and of Sarah as "ranked as a pure virgin" even after giving birth (*Cher.* 47, 50). Of course, the birth narratives of Matthew 1–2 and Luke 1–2 are not allegories such as those that characterize Philo's exposition of the Pentateuch. But the problem of discerning where midrash and poetic imagery end and where literal claims begin in the birth narratives permits of no easy resolution. To be sure, the imagery of birth (the coming into existence of a new human being) does not immediately mesh with the idea of incarnation (the enfleshment of one already preexistent). But that is less of a problem if we recognize the metaphorical and midrashic character which such descriptions would be assumed to have within a first-century Jewish context. Whether fresh ground had in fact been broken would only become evident when the idea of virginal conception was subsequently integrated into the more powerful concept of incarnation.

Matthew, in fact, is not far off from doing just that. For not only does he make good use of the virginal conception tradition (Matthew 1-2), but he also goes beyond the earlier portrayal of Jesus as the emissary of Wisdom to a portrayal of Jesus as Wisdom herself (Matt. 11:19, 25-30; 23:34-36, 37-39). Not only so, but he also takes up the language of divine presence and depicts Jesus as "God with us" (1:23; 18:20; 28:18, 20). Here is confirmation that Wisdom was not thought of as a divine being other than God (not even the Son of God in that sense), but as God himself in his active concern for and outreach to his creation and people. It is because Jesus was seen as the complete embodiment of that concern and outreach that he could be spoken of in such terms with the function of the birth narratives used as much to underscore the point that he embodied this divine presence from the first. In this sense, at least, we can speak of a concept of incarnation in Matthew, even if it does not come to explicit expression as such.

H. John

In the Fourth Gospel there is an extraordinary concentration of christological claims. Individually they might be understood as still caught within the earlier categories and structure of thought; but together they may well be judged to express a breakthrough into a different conceptuality and a bolder claim.

The claim is posed at once in the prologue. The subject is God's Word — another way of speaking of God's self-revelation, action upon, and communication with the world of humankind, along with Wisdom and Spirit (e.g., Pss. 33:6; 107:20; Wis. 9:1-2,17; Philo, *Somn.* 1.65-69; Luke 1:2; Acts 10:36-38). So in John 1 the Word was in the beginning, was with God, and was God; all things were made through this Word (John 1:1-3). It was this Word which "became flesh" in Jesus Christ (1:14). The juxtaposing in this way of the two concepts "Word" and "flesh" is very striking. For just as John is clear that the Word belongs wholly to the realm of the divine, is *theos* (God/god), so is he clear that flesh belongs wholly to this world, transient and corruptible and antithetical to the other (1:13; 3:6; 6:63). The choice of verb, therefore, is hardly accidental, and it cannot easily be diminished in significance or rendered unwarrantably as "appear." John evidently wanted to say "the Word *became* flesh." The concept of incarnation, as distinct from indwelling or inspiration, has come to explicit expression. Jesus is being presented as the incarnation of the divine Word.

In the light of this, John's other christological emphases gain a clearer perspective. The characteristic talk of Jesus as the Son sent from the Father is there to emphasize primarily that Jesus is the self-revelation of God, the only one who can make God fully known (1:18; 6:46; 14:9). The less prominent but equally striking talk of Jesus as the Son of Man descended from heaven is used to emphasize that Jesus is the authoritative spokesman of the mystery of God (1:47-51; 3:12-13; 6:60-62). The "I am" statements no doubt deliberately echo the "I am" of Exod. 3:14 and Isa. 43:10 (particularly John 8:58); Jesus is the glory of God visible to humankind (12:41, referring to Isa. 6:1). Most striking of all is the uninhibited use of the title "God/god" to describe *Jesus* (1:18; 20:28). That the title was provocative to his fellow Jews was well known to the author (5:18; 10:33) and probably resulted within a few years in the rabbinic charge that the Christians had abandoned belief in the unity of God (early second century). This is probably sufficient evidence to confirm that the Fourth Evangelist was aware that in pushing such a developed portrayal of Jesus he was going beyond what had previously been acceptable or at least retainable within the hitherto accepted conventions of Jewish talk of God and his self-revelation. To speak of God's wisdom dwelling in Israel or embodied in the Torah was one thing; to portray the man Jesus as God's Word incarnate was something else.

The matter seems to be put beyond doubt by the way in which John ties the thought of incarnation tightly to the cross. The whole Gospel moves toward the climax of Christ's death. The glory of the Son is manifested particularly in his death (12:23-24; 13:31; cf. 21:19). The lifting up, which corresponds to his descent from heaven, is a lifting up on the cross (3:14; 12:32-33). Most striking of all is the emphasis in 6:53-58 that the flesh of the Son of Man must be chewed if it is to result in eternal life. The point of the incarnation is the death of the incarnate one (6:51). Here, too, John was probably aware that he was pushing into uncharted territory (6:60). A claim that God had revealed himself in king, prophet, sage, or righteous man could be expressed in a variety of hyperbolic language without breaching philosophic or theological conventions. But to claim that the Eternal had *become man* in order to *die* was a step beyond.

I. Conclusions

(1) It is difficult to draw a sharp line between a before and after in the emergence of the concept of incarnation. All we can say with some confidence is that before Christians began to express the significance of Jesus the concept of incarnation as such is not yet attested; whereas at the end of the first century the concept has been deliberately and provocatively put forward. Arguably, the thought is implicit already in formulations used by Paul. But whatever we make of these formulations, it does look rather as though the concept of incarnation was the outcome of what seems with hindsight to have been an inevitable and logical progression, as the first Christians found that previous ways of speaking of the revelation of God were inadequate to express the full significance of the divine revelation which was Jesus.

(2) The focal point of this being sent, coming under the law, as man, becoming flesh, in all cases seems to be the death and resurrection of Jesus. Within the New Testament there is no evidence of a concept of incarnation as itself the decisive act of salvation — flesh redeemed by being assumed. The moment of salvation remains decisively centered on the cross. At this point, incarnation and Adam christologies readily blend into each other.

(3) The recognition that Wisdom christology is the most obvious root of incarnation christology also has an important corollary, particularly when it is recalled that in Jewish thought Wisdom is not a being independent of God but is God's self-manifestation. The point is that Christ is the *incarnation* of this Wisdom/Word. To speak of *Christ* as himself preexistent, coming down from heaven, and so forth, has to be seen as metaphorical; otherwise it leads inevitably to some kind of polytheism — the Father as a person, just like Jesus was a person (Lampe, *God as Spirit*). Whereas, what a Wisdom/Word christology claims is that Jesus is the person/individual whom God's Word *became*. Even to speak of the incarnation of the Son of God can be misleading, unless the Son christology of John is seen as it was probably intended, as an expression of the same Wisdom/Word christology; otherwise, there is the danger of a too literal translation of Father-Son language once again into a form of polytheism — that very abandoning of the oneness of God of which Jews and Muslims accuse Christians. The incarnation doctrine which comes to expression in the New Testament is properly understood only if it is understood as the incarnation of God's self-revelation, in the sense as that incarnation of God himself. The issue which caused the breach with Jewish thought and with Judaism is the charge against the Johannine Jesus that "you being a man, make yourself God" (John 10:33).

3

Interpreting New Testament Christology

The history of interpretation of New Testament christology has been marked by the attempt, at best, to understand the New Testament texts within the context of changing and developing philosophical and dogmatic structures; at worst to use the New Testament to support ideas and teachings whose legitimacy and coherence were effectively unrelated to the New Testament.

In the patristic period discussion of christology returned again and again to the key texts, Prov. 8:22; John 1:14; Phil. 2:6-11; Col. 1:15; and Heb. 1:3f. Initially, when Logos christology formed the main stream of thought, the principal issue was whether the Logos was created. Prov. 8:22 was a favorite Arian verse and pointed to the equivalent interpretation of Col. 1:15 ("first-born of all creation"). Opposition to the idea of the Logos as "created" resulted in a response to Arianism at these points characteristically dependent more on dogmatic presupposition and less on exegesis — e.g., *ktizein* taken in the sense "appoint" rather than "create"; Col. 1:15 understood with reference to Christ's flesh; the *prōtotokos* of Col. 1:15 understood within the distinction between "begetting" and "creating" (Grillmeier, *Christ in Christian Tradition,* 156, 174, 182, 213). In a similar way the virgin birth narratives were soon absorbed into a larger doctrine of incarnation and ceased to have independent significance except as they contributed to a different line of dogmatic development focusing on Mary.

Still more important was John 1:14, which might seem to speak straightforwardly of incarnation ("the Logos became flesh"), but with the sense in which the Logos became flesh being precisely the issue in dispute (e.g.,

---

Grillmeier, 245, 328). In this debate the alternatives centered on a Logos-anthropos (Word-man) christology and a Logos-sarx (Word-flesh) christology. The former was typical of the Antiochene school and focused on the human Christ but left the unity of the divine and human in Christ in some question. The latter was typical of the Alexandrian school and focused on the preexistent Logos, leaving Christ's humanity in some unclarity. Thus was formulated in classic terms a tension which has been fundamental to christology from the beginning, reflecting not least the different portrayals of Jesus in Synoptic and Johannine Gospels.

When the focus was more on the issue of relationships within the Godhead, the language of Phil. 2:7 and Heb. 1:3 came to the fore. The problem was what terms like *morphē, charaktēr,* and *hypostasis* might mean (Grillmeier, 365, 374). The resolution was provided by giving *hypostasis* a new technical meaning relating to the distinctiveness of the three divine "persons" (allowing the new technical formula, one *ousia* and three *hypostases*). The solution, in other words, was not derived exegetically, but could call on Heb. 1:3 for support within a "language game" where semantic values were in transition (cf. Grillmeier, 446).

In short, as the christological and trinitarian debate became more technical, with ever more subtle refinement, it moved further and further from questions of exegesis as such and more toward a prooftexting for arguments and positions determined by the different terms and logical constraints of later debates. And so it has continued in greater or less degree since, at least to the extent that the terms of the debates have been determined by the great credal confessions hammered out in the early centuries.

Something of the same can be said of the other focus in New Testament christology — on the soteriological significance of Christ. An early powerful example of exegesis feeding theology was Irenaeus's development of Paul's Adam christology in his theory of "recapitulation." But for much of the time the theme of atonement was subordinated to what was perceived as the more important issue, the theme of incarnation — as in the classic epigram of Gregory of Nazianzus, "What has not been assumed cannot be restored" (*Ep.* 101.7). The New Testament language of sacrifice and ransom in reference to Christ's death was taken seriously, with the usual exegetical assumption being that "sacrifice" implied a theory of penal satisfaction and the image of ransom raising the question as to whether a ransom had been paid to the devil. In his classic study, *Christus Victor* (1931), G. Aulén also argued in effect for a more definitive influence of Col. 2:15. But again the momentum and thrust of the discussion usually depended more on dogmatic logic or "necessary reasons" (Anselm) than on exegesis or exposition of what was taken for granted to be the authoritative scriptural text.

In all this the hermeneutical technique of allegorizing allowed a wide range of texts to be drawn in without anything approaching an adequate exegetical or hermeneutical control. And while the Reformation brought a renewed emphasis on exegesis and on the importance of rooting doctrine firmly in the biblical text, in the area of christology the classical categories and paradigms were on the whole too firmly established to allow any real question to arise at the level of exegesis or interpretation.

With the rise of historical and biblical criticism in the post-Enlightenment period, however, the philosophical and dogmatic frameworks of interpretation soon came into conflict. The impact was first experienced in the deist polarization of historical Jesus and dogmatic Christ, with the clear presumption that the latter was no longer an acceptable hermeneutical option and that the alternative framework of rationalism or idealism or liberal optimism ipso facto provided a sounder interpretation.

The contrast between a historically rediscovered Jesus and a dogmatically determined Christ thus became the modern expression of the older tension between the humanity and divinity of Jesus (cf. the distinction between Logos-anthropos and Logos-sarx). In the modern period it has reappeared in many different forms as a hermeneutical key to the NT texts; e.g., the teacher Jesus and the Hellenized Redeemer, the historical Jesus and the Christ of faith, christology from below and from above, Jesus the Jew and Christ the Lord of the Christian mystery cult, the Jesus of Bible story and the Christ of doctrinal proposition. And it has been a factor in several important developments in biblical criticism, e.g., the emergence of Q as a non-miraculous source outflanking the problem of the miracle-performing Savior; the questioning of John's Gospel as being a document of the Christ of faith rather than a source for the historical Jesus; the evolution of form criticism of Gospels and Epistles as a way of bridging the gap between the historical reality of Christianity's beginnings and the already theologized documents of the NT.

A consistent feature of the past two centuries is the search for parallels, the assumption of the historical-critical method being that contemporary parallels in idea and idiom can be confidently expected to throw light on the biblical data. In the case of the birth narratives, for example, comparisons have been drawn with talk of demi-gods in Greek myth and of virgin mothers in Philo. In dispute is precisely the question of the distinctiveness of the Christian narratives — whether lack of an exact parallel is evidence of a new category provided by revelation and divine act, or whether a historical context in which similar ideas can be expressed is sufficient evidence of a way of conceptualizing divine interaction with the human sphere within which the thought of a virginal conception is simply a new variant of an older motif, even if the emphasis comes on the word "new." Within this larger exegetical debate the influence of Isa. 7:14 in shaping the tradition and the extent to which all or part of the narratives can be described as "midrash" are specific questions still under discussion. The most recent and thorough exegetical study by R. E. Brown *(The Birth of the Messiah)* underlines the gap which still remains at the end of the day between historical findings and dogmatic affirmation.

In the case of the historical Jesus the hermeneutical problem is equally sharp, though often not perceived to be so. To what extent is the historical method able to allow for a Jesus whose self-consciousness or claims regarding himself transcend categories currently available, or does it inevitably reinforce a polarization between historical Jesus and Christ of faith? The impact of J. Weiss and A. Schweitzer undermined the liberal Protestant portrayal of Jesus the moral teacher or social reformer and left twentieth-century research with a still uncomfortable picture of Jesus the eschatological prophet, predicting the imminent end of history, a stranger and enigma to modern susceptibilities, as well as posing awkward questions to the dogma of Christ's divinity. In more recent years awareness of social unrest in first-century Palestine and of similar structures of oppression in the twentieth century have encouraged a reexpression of the older Jesus-the-revolutionary model in terms of liberation theology. And the continuing revulsion at the horrors of the Holocaust has resulted in a restatement of Jesus-the-Jew, or even Jesus-the-Pharisee. In such cases a christology from below is followed through to coherent and logical conclusion, usually without regard to the gap it leaves between it and the Christ of faith.

The search for parallels to the concept of Christ's saving death has regularly fixed on the myth of the dying and rising god as expressed in the mystery cults of the period. And a "deemphasis" on the importance of historical reference, such as has characterized the theology of Karl Barth and the current resurgence of narrative theology, provides a larger hermeneutic within which such a historical assessment can be sustained. Otherwise the difficulty of explaining how the mythological expression of the annual cycle of fertility came to be a means of interpreting the death and resurrection of a historical individual has usually proved to be a decisive consideration against such hypotheses. A more plausible analogy/genealogy hypothesis has been perceived in the martyr theology and the motif of the suffering righteous in intertestamental Judaism, which seems to lie behind such formulations as Rom. 5:6-11. With regard to the Gospels one of the chief ongoing debates is whether the model of Suffering Servant (Isaiah 53) or Son of Man (Daniel 7) provides the most important exegetical key to the central passion statements (particularly Mark 10:45). Outside the Gospels the various disputes focusing on Rom. 3:25 characterize the range of debate — whether and to what extent there is a pre-Pauline formula to be discerned with a different theology of atonement, whether the category of sacrifice was actually promoted by the NT writers in discussing the significance of Jesus' death (this is of interest particularly among German scholars), and whether the language of "propitiation" or "expiation," of "substitution" or "representation" provides the more appropriate exegesis and interpretation (particularly among English-speaking scholars).

Within each phase of biblical criticism the resurrection narratives have come under renewed scrutiny: Which is the oldest source? How far do parallels of translation to heaven and apotheosis help explain the data? How do form-critical categories illuminate them? To what extent have the narratives of the empty tomb been determined or redacted in the light of mythological or kerygmatic considerations or by liturgical practice? The fact that belief in Jesus' resurrection was a central confession of faith from the first has been widely recognized, with 1 Cor. 15:3-8 providing the decisive evidence. So too the fact that this belief was rooted in resurrection "appearances." For those working with a narrowly defined historical method, the most obvious explanations have been in terms of hysterical visions, the conviction that Jesus' message could not die, or cognitive dissonance (the refusal to accept evident disconfirmation of earlier hopes), though all such explanations labor under the difficulty of explaining the striking differences between the pre-Easter and post-Easter proclamation. For those with a more open model of historical enquiry, however, the interpretative conundrum remains, characterized by the description of the resurrection as "eschatological event"; how to speak meaningfully within history of an event which by definition transcends or breaks out of history, an event which is utterly unique, without parallel within history, because it marks the end of history and forms a unique interface between this world and the world to come? Where the dividing line between demonstrable history and faith proclamation becomes thus elided, the only solution is to maintain the integrity of the dialogue at both sides of the point of intersection.

On any reckoning the resurrection is the definitive moment of transition from the historical Jesus to the Christ of faith and inevitably therefore stands at the center of New Testament christology as the interpretative key, however that key is formally expressed. That has also been brought home by another major line of research during the same period, that is, into the titles of Jesus — Messiah, Son of Man, Son of God, Lord, etc. This proved valuable as a descriptive exercise, but unsatisfactory in terms of providing hermeneutical keys for christology. The reason is presumably that the Christ event contributed more to the titles than vice-versa. Titles like Messiah and Son of Man proved incapable of carrying the growing weight of theological significance accorded to Jesus; *kyrios* provided an invaluable transition from pre-Easter ("sir" is its secular sense) to post-Easter (it also means "Lord"). *Logos* carried the main christological weight into the post-apostolic period, and Son of God proved the most durable title of all. But at each phase it was the burgeoning christology itself which was decisive, either leaving the unadaptable titles behind or steadily transforming the significance of the more adaptable. As labels by which to chart the progress and diverse emphases of earliest christology, titles have continuing interpretative value, but they do not themselves explain that progress or its dynamic.

While such attempts were being made to explain and interpret christology "from below," the classical creeds continued to provide a framework for those who saw the deficiencies of the historical method as decisive and who continued to interpret the biblical texts in terms of a christology "from above." Characteristic here have been the expositions of kenotic christology and Barth's christocentrism. The former, well regarded by many scholars in the late nineteenth and early twentieth centuries, had its putative hermeneutical basis in Phil. 2:7 ("he emptied himself"), though the exegetical toehold was tenuous and the debate on the meaning of *kenōsis,* as so often before, depended on dogmatic considerations well removed from the text of Philippians. Barth's theology of the Word, with its disjunction between the word of God and all human thought, came to hermeneutical expression in his early emphasis on the belief that historical criticism and exegesis are but preparatory to the task of theology and the word of proclamation. Here once again any effective historical control or check on dogma was effectively discounted. More recent attempts to provide a systematic conceptuality in theology have made greater attempts to root the theological paradigm in the New Testament, with varying degrees of success: W. Pannenberg, recognizing the crucial interface character of the New Testament accounts of Jesus' resurrection; J. Moltmann with his more dogmatically oriented focus on the cross; and E. Schillebeeckx trying to work more fully with New Testament exegesis and scholarship and finding the resolution in effect in Christian experience.

The most persistent attempt at bridging the christology-from-above/ christology-from-below divide has been the quest of the Gnostic redeemer myth, which has dominated much of twentieth-century New Testament research (particularly under the influence of R. Bultmann). Its attraction grew partly from the observation of non-Christian features in the developed form of the myth in the later Gnostic systems, suggesting the possibility of a pre-Christian form, and partly from the historical method's difficulty in handling the *novum,* the problem of explaining a historical datum which seems to make a "quantum leap" beyond anything which came before. The presupposition that already before the first century there was a developed myth of a divine figure who descended from heaven to rescue spiritual entities (fragments of light-souls) trapped within the prison of matter would certainly explain how Jesus came to be spoken of as a descending/ascending redeemer. The search for the pre-Christian myth has, however, had the character more of a wild goose chase. The hypothesis that the pre-Christian indications of the myth are fragments of an unattested whole has had to give way before the more credible hypothesis that these elements are building blocks which were later put together to form the developed myth. The dualism of the reconstructed myth fits poorly with the evolution in the Christian texts from a resurrection-centered proclamation to a concept of incarnation (docetism coming later). The key New Testament texts themselves are better explained as distinctively new developments of Hellenistic Jewish ideas of Wisdom and Adam provoked by the impact of the whole Christ event.

In fact, in a rather striking way, the interpretation of New Testament christology has come full circle, with the same texts which provided the biblical subject matter for the debates of early centuries once again at the center of hermeneutical debate, particularly John 1:14; Phil. 2:6-11; and Col. 1:15-20. As in the early centuries, other models have been taken up and tried. An angelomorphic christology can argue for exegetical support in the Son of Man motif of the Gospels and particularly in the visions of the seer of Revelation; but the same factors condemn it to the edges of the main stream of developing christology. A spirit christology (as in Lampe, *God as Spirit*) can build strongly on the category of Jesus the prophet and on such texts as 1 Cor. 15:45, but fails to take adequate account of why the category of prophet proved unsatisfactory to the evangelists and of the dynamic within New Testament christology. As the developing christology of the early centuries also bears witness, it was the New Testament's Adam christology and Wisdom/Logos christology which proved the most productive in drawing out the full significance of the Christ event. This should occasion no surprise since it is precisely the talk of divine image, common to both Adam and Wisdom, which bridges the divide between human and divine and which expresses the revelatory significance which the first Christians evidently experienced in and through Christ: Christ the archetype of humankind and the window into God.

For the same reason it is the Fourth Gospel which serves as the indispensable bridge between the historical Jesus and the Christ of dogma. For it clearly indicates that stage in Christian reflection which was still rooted in historical memory of what Jesus did and said (as more clearly expressed in the Synoptic tradition), which (like the earlier New Testament writers) still saw the primary revelatory and redemptive focus in Christ's death and resurrection as illumined by the interpreter Spirit, and which now saw the need to bring his fuller significance to expression precisely in Gospel format, but using language and categories which would have greatest impact on the writer's contemporaries and readers. To the extent that the Fourth Evangelist was successful in maintaining that threefold tension, to that extent his Gospel still provides the most important single New Testament paradigm for expounding the significance of God's revelation in Christ.

JESUS AND CHRISTOLOGY

4

The Messianic Secret in Mark

Despite the cool reception given to it by English scholarship when it first appeared, it is now abundantly evident that Wilhelm Wrede's *Das Messiasge-heimnis in den Evangelien* (1901) marked a turning point of considerable importance in the study of the Gospels inasmuch as Wrede was really the first to recognize and appreciate the theological nature of the Synoptics. His specific thesis (that the messianic secret motif in Mark has a theological rather than a historical origin) has "mark"edly influenced the researches of those who came after him, to such an extent that it is often taken for granted, a "given" in the investigation of new propositions and theses.[1] His own statement of the thesis has not escaped criticism and refinement, of course, but his main conclusion still stands as proven for the majority of continental scholars. An investigation of the messianic secret motif in Mark must therefore deal in the first place with Wrede himself, and I will begin by briefly outlining Wrede's argument.

He points first to the commands with which Jesus silences the messianic

1. For the influence of Wrede's work see, e.g., P. W. Meyer, "The Problem of the Messianic Selfconsciousness of Jesus," *NovT* 4 (1960) 122-38; N. Perrin, "The Wredestrasse Becomes the Hauptstrasse," *Journal of Religion* 46 (1966) 296-300. The continuing interest in Wrede's own thesis is illustrated by the reissue of a third edition of *Das Messiasgeheimnis* in 1963, with an English translation due shortly, and by the recent contributions of G. Minette de Tillesse, *Le secret messianique dans l'Évangile de Marc* (Paris: Cerf, 1968), which unfortunately I have so far been unable to consult; B. G. Powley, "The Purpose of the Messianic Secret: A Brief Survey," *ExpT* 80 (1968-69) 308-10; D. Aune, "The Problem of the Messianic Secret," *NovT* 11 (1969) 1-31; and R. N. Longenecker, "The Messianic Secret in the Light of Recent Discoveries," *EQ* 41 (1969) 207-15.

Originally published in *Tyndale Bulletin* 21 (1970) 92-117. Revised form of a paper given at the New Testament Study Group of Tyndale Fellowship at Tyndale House, Cambridge, July, 1969. Copyright © 1970 by Tyndale House and used by permission. A briefer version was published in *The Messianic Secret,* ed. C. Tuckett (Philadelphia: Fortress/London: SPCK, 1983) 116-31.

confessions of the demons (1:23-25, 34; 3:11f.; cf. 5:6f.; 9:20). Since the various explanations offered for the possessed individual's knowledge are unsatisfactory, we must recognize a legendary development in the tradition. When other commands to silence are also taken into consideration — to those healed miraculously (1:43-45; 5:43; 7:36; 8:26), the disciples after Peter's confession (8:30) and after the transfiguration (9:9) — as also the intention of Jesus to remain hidden (7:24; 9:30f.) and the command addressed by the crowd to Bartimaeus to be silent (10:47f.) — it becomes evident that what is being thus guarded is the messianic secret. Wrede goes on to cite other evidence, the most notable of which are the private instruction which Jesus gives to the disciples (4:34; 7:17-23; 9:28f.; 8:31; 9:31; 10:32-34; 13:3ff.) and the saying about parabolic teaching (4:10-13). On the basis of this Wrede delivers his judgment — namely that for Mark there is no historical motif in question; rather the idea of the messianic secret is a wholly theological conception. The key is Mark 9:9, when Peter, James, and John are commanded not to speak of what they have seen until the Son of man should have risen from the dead. Jesus' messiahship is and must be a secret. Only the inner circle can be let into the secret. But with the resurrection comes the revelation to all. In short, the whole is a theological construction. Jesus did not in fact claim to be Messiah during his ministry, and it was not until after the resurrection that his messianic status was affirmed by the Christian community. The messianic secret is nothing other than the attempt made by Mark to account for the absence of messianic claims by Jesus himself.

I

An analysis of Wrede's thesis reveals three principal strands: first, the isolation of a distinct motif in Mark which can be called the "messianic secret"; second, the argument that certain elements of that motif, noticeably the exorcisms, are nonhistorical, leading to the conclusion that the whole motif is the construction of Christian or Markan theology (the more recent rise of form criticism has, of course, given more depth and consistency to this argument); third, as the *raison d'être*, the complementary argument that belief in Jesus as Messiah was an Easter faith and that the messianic secret results from an attempt to read back messiahship into the life of Jesus.

(1) If this is a fair presentation of Wrede's argument, it seems to me to be open to several major criticisms. The first of these is that Wrede has narrowed the scope of the secrecy motif too much. I strongly question whether the silences commanded by Jesus in connection with the healing miracles can adequately be brought under the category of *messianic* secret. What is there about the healings that cannot be understood before the cross and resurrection

which is not *publicly* demonstrated in, for example, the healing of the paralytic before the scribes in chapter 2 or the healing of the man with the withered arm in the synagogue in chapter 3? What is there about the healing miracles which particularly marks out Jesus as Messiah? According to Mark not one of the miracles performed publicly led the spectators to conclude that Jesus was the Messiah (though see below, p. 63), while several passages indicate that their caution was often completely different. The people of Nazareth saw only the carpenter, the member of a well-known local family, despite the public knowledge of his miracles (6:1-6). Herod and others thought he might be John the Baptist resurrected or Elijah or another prophet (6:14f.; 8:28). The Pharisees judged him to be possessed by Beelzebub (3:22).[2] Moreover, the only recipient of Jesus' healing who hails him in messianic terms (10:46ff.) is not silenced by Jesus. So just what secret was being safeguarded by those commands to silence? I am not altogether surprised therefore to note that Ulrich Luz distinguishes the *Wundergeheimnis* from the *Messiasgeheimnis*, though I would hesitate to follow him in linking the former to a θεῖος ἀνήρ christology as distinct from the latter's Messiah-christology.[3] What I am more certain of is that the attempt to bring all the healing miracle commands to silence under the heading of "messianic secret" fails to carry conviction. Despite Wrede's belief that only one explanation must be applied to the so-called secrecy passages, it is highly probable that in different situations there were a variety of motives operative — and particularly in Jesus' dealings with the sick: e.g., desire for privacy and concern for the well-being of the individual being cured (cf. 1:44; 5:40; 7:33; 3:22, 26; 9:25) as well as the wish to discourage misleading ideas about himself from gaining fresh currency, and perhaps the strong sense that his destiny was completely in the hands of God.[4] In this connection it is worth noting that there are grounds for recognizing 1:21-45 as a pre-Markan block of material in whose construction one of the determining motifs was the way in which excessive publicity resulted in increasing restriction on Jesus' movement and ministry (Capernaum, country towns, desert areas — 1:21, 38, 45).

I question also whether the saying about the use of parables can be counted as part of the evidence for the messianic secret. In Mark 4:11 what

2. G. H. Boobyer, "The Secrecy Motif in St. Mark's Gospel," *NTS* 6 (1959-60) 232.

3. U. Luz, "Das Geheimnismotiv und die markinische Christologie," *ZNW* 56 (1965) 9-30. L. E. Keck further subdivides the Markan miracle material into a θεῖος ἀνήρ cycle and a distinct "strong man" cycle ("Mark 3:7-12 and the Alleged Dualism in the Evangelist's Miracle Material," *JBL* 87 [1968] 409ff.).

4. Cf., e.g., R. H. Lightfoot, *The Gospel Message of St. Mark* (Oxford: Clarendon, 1950) 37, 46; J. W. Leitch, "The Injunctions of Silence in Mark's Gospel," *ExpT* 66 (1954-55) 178f.; T. W. Manson, "Realized Eschatology and the Messianic Secret," *Studies in the Gospels,* ed. D. E. Nineham (Oxford: Blackwell, 1955) 212f.; T. A. Burkill, "Concerning St. Mark's Conception of Secrecy," *HJ* 55 (1956-57) 153, n. 2; Aune, 24f.

Jesus says is that parables conceal the mystery of the *kingdom* from οἱ ἔξω — and while I would agree that the mystery of the kingdom is closely related to the historical status and ministry of Jesus, it is not to be wholly identified with the messiahship of the earthly Jesus.[5] Besides, both 4:11 (to those who are outside *everything* comes in parables) and 4:34 (he would not speak to them except in parables) indicate that it was his *whole* ministry of word and deed which had this parabolic effect — and his whole ministry cannot be contained within the bounds of the messianic secret. In 7:17, for example, the parable whose explanation he gives to the disciples in private is his teaching about inward cleanliness. One should also note that if 4:11 (the illumination of the disciples) is interpreted in terms of the messianic secret it at once comes into conflict with passages like 9:32 (the incomprehension of the disciples).[6]

Turning to this latter theme, the obtuseness of the disciples, which is often cited as an important element in Mark's theology of the messianic secret, even this cannot be contained within its scope. I would be prepared to admit the instance of the disciples' astonishment and hardness of heart at the stilling of the storm as part of the messianic secret (6:51-52). For I certainly see messianic significance in the feeding of the five thousand, although I am not so sure that Mark wished to bring out that significance, and Mark does specifically say that the disciples were dumbfounded "because they had not seen what the miracle of the loaves meant" (so Jerusalem Bible — οὐ γὰρ συνῆκαν ἐπὶ τοῖς ἄρτοις). For the same reason I can see the justification for including the disciples' misunderstanding over the saying about the yeast of the Pharisees and of Herod with the messianic secret, although the passage is a difficult one. For once again their obtuseness is underlined by a reference to the feeding of the five thousand and the feeding of the four thousand, and the pericope ends with the words of Jesus οὔπω συνίετε; but it is impossible to bring 10:10 under the messianic secret — for what the disciples inquire of Jesus in private (εἰς τὴν οἰκίαν) is the meaning of his saying about divorce and marriage — hardly a distinctively messianic theme.[7]

Bearing in mind this diversity in the situations which demonstrate the disciples' obtuseness, it is more plausible to recognize in the motif a historical

---

5. Cf. Aune, 25.

6. T. A. Burkill's rather cavalier treatment of the point — "It is probable that the evangelist was unaware of this problem" — is no answer in view of the considerable skill which has otherwise gone into the construction of the messianic secret motif ("The Cryptology of Parables in St. Mark's Gospel," *NovT* 1 [1956] 252).

7. See also 9:34 and 10:37. P. Vielhauer also points out that the infrequency of Mark's use of χριστός shows that it is not the most important title of Jesus for Mark and calls in question the use of the expression "messianic secret" ("Erwägungen zur Christologie des Markusevangeliums," *Zeit und Geschichte. Dankesgabe an R. Bultmann,* ed. E. Dinkler [Tübingen: Mohr, 1964] 157).

reminiscence of the very natural and unexceptional slowness of unlettered men whose rigid and closed system of thought made it difficult for them to adjust to new teaching. It was not simply the difficulty of coping with new information but the impossibility of trying to assimilate that new information into a system of thought and reference which had no place for such information. The situation which would cause a computer either to admit defeat or to explode caused only confusion and incomprehension on the part of the disciples. Such a situation can be resolved only by a conversion of mind — a transformation of *Weltanschauung* — something which by all accounts did not happen to the disciples till the gift of the Spirit after Jesus' resurrection. To go to the other extreme and attribute the motif to a Markan polemic against the disciples is certainly uncalled for.[8]

I rather suspect that Wrede was misled by taking the exorcisms as his starting point. It was natural that a nineteenth-twentieth century man should fasten onto these incidents, which were to him among the most bizarre and incredible and which for that very reason gave him immediate access to the theological viewpoint of the primitive church — that is, to the way the primitive church had viewed and worked over the historical facts. No psychological argument could explain how, for example, the Gerasene demoniac came to hail Jesus as Son of the Most High God, and recourse to a supernatural explanation was unacceptable. Therefore, Wrede concluded, we are in the presence of a legendary development in the tradition which leads us straight into the heart of the messianic secret. Leaving aside the issue of demon possession and the possibility of supernatural knowledge, which I personally hold to be a far more open question than Wrede allowed, it still seems to me that Wrede's approach was methodologically suspect. For the exorcism narratives would not stand out so prominently in Mark's time. The fact is that in their manner of presentation they accord by and large with the standard pattern of exorcism stories, even to the extent of the demon using the name of the exorcist and the exorcist commanding the demon to silence,[9] and the knowledgeable reader of Mark's Gospel would see nothing out of the ordinary in Jesus' response to the demon's cry in Mark 1:25 — φιμώθητι καὶ ἔξελθε ἐξ αὐτοῦ. I recognize that there is weight to the counterargument that *Mark* understood the injunction to silence in this first exorcism in terms of 1:34 and 3:11f., which could well be taken to indicate that demoniacs regularly hailed Jesus as Son of God and that Jesus' usual response was a strong warning that

---

8. Contra J. B. Tyson, "The Blindness of the Disciples in Mark," *JBL* 80 (1961) 261-68; J. Schreiber, "Die Christologie des markusevangeliums," *ZTK* 58 (1961) 154-83; T. J. Weeden, "The Heresy that Necessitated Mark's Gospel," *ZNW* 59 (1968) 145-58.

9. T. A. Burkill, "The Injunctions to Silence in St. Mark's Gospel," *TZ* 12 (1956) 593f.; also *Mysterious Revelation: An Examination of the Philosophy of St. Mark's Gospel* (Ithaca: Cornell University, 1963) 72-78.

they should not make him known.[10] But if Mark was trying to "get over" to his readers the message of the messianic secret, the first exorcism would give no indication of it to his readers. In fact, the distinctive messianic secret motif only appears in these two summary statements, and there are no commands to silence in any of the other exorcisms where the narrative goes into any detail (5:1-20; 7:24-30; 9:14-29). I question therefore whether Wrede was right to single out the exorcisms as the decisive clue to the meaning of the secrecy theme in Mark. I might also mention here by way of support Eduard Schweizer's argument against J. M. Robinson[11] that the special theological contribution of Mark lies in his emphasis on the teaching of Jesus, not on the exorcisms which came to him in the tradition. The function of the latter is much more to illuminate and characterize the teaching of Jesus as an act of divine authority. Thus we note 1:27: the people's response to the exorcism is to say, "Here is a teaching that is new and with authority behind it. . . ."[12]

This then is my first criticism of Wrede's thesis: that it fails to do sufficient justice to the full scope of the secrecy motif in Mark. The secrecy motif is more complicated than Wrede allowed. And since those passages which give his thesis credibility are only part of a larger whole, it suggests that there is more to Mark's picture of Jesus at this point than the hypothesis of the *messianic* secret allows — a "more" which puts a question mark against that hypothesis.

(2) If the first criticism puts a question mark against Wrede's isolation of a specifically *messianic* secret, my second puts a question mark against his calling the motif "messianic *secret*." For it appears to me that Wrede did not give sufficient weight to what might be called a counterbalancing publicity-revelation theme. Of course, it is part of the messianic secret, especially as revised by Wrede's successors, that it holds in a certain tension the paradox of hiddenness and openness, of secrecy and revelation.[13] But my point is this: not only is the publicity theme quite as prominent as the theme of secrecy, but also, and more important, it seems frequently to run directly counter to the secrecy motif. After the first exorcism Mark says "his reputation spread everywhere (πανταχοῦ) through all (ὅλην) the surrounding Galilean country-side" (1:28). After the healing of the leper we are told that the leper started talking about it freely and telling the story everywhere, so that Jesus could no longer go openly into any town but had to stay outside in places where

---

10. Burkill, *Mysterious Revelation,* 63-66, 71.

11. *The Problem of History in Mark* (London: SCM, 1957) 33-42.

12. E. Schweizer, "Anmerkungen zur Theologie des Markus," *Neotestamentica* (Zurich: Zwingli, 1963) 96f. The imperfect tenses of 1:21 and the general statement of 1:27 (spirits — plural) indicate that the incident has typical significance.

13. See, e.g., G. Strecker, "Zur Messiasgeheimnistheorie in Markusevangelium," *Studia Evangelica* 3 (1964) 93f.

nobody lived. Even so, people from all around came to him (1:45). On another occasion Mark says "once again such a crowd collected that they could not even have a meal" (3:20). And far from commanding him to be silent Jesus orders the Gerasene demoniac, now cured, to "go home to your people and tell them all that the Lord in his mercy has done for you." So the man goes off and proceeds to spread throughout the Decapolis all that Jesus has done for him (5:19f.).[14] In Nazareth they certainly knew all about Jesus' miracles, were "scandalized" at him (6:2-3), and so remarkable and public were the miracles that all sorts of rumors were current about him — Elijah, a prophet, John the Baptist risen from the dead (6:14ff.; 8:28). The feeding of the five thousand was the result of an attempted escape to seclusion on the part of Jesus and his disciples, because "there were so many coming and going that the apostles had no time to eat" (6:31). And in the region of Tyre and Sidon he entered a house (εἰς οἰκίαν) and did not want anyone to know it; but it was impossible for him to be concealed (7:24). To cite but one other instance, it is certainly remarkable, if we believe that the messianic secret motif decisively shaped the material, that Bartimaeus should be allowed to be depicted as twice loudly hailing Jesus as Son of David — *and* Jesus neither rebukes him nor tells him to be silent (10:46ff.)! In view of the messianic significance of the title Son of David (12:35-37a) it is surely quite inadequate to dismiss this pericope as having nothing to do with the theory of the messianic secret, as Wrede and those who follow him do.[15]

So far as the messianic secret is concerned the publicity theme is most noticeable in the contexts where one would expect withdrawal and silence. In the healing of the paralytic Mark alone says that the proof of the miracle — his rising and walking off — happened ἔμπροσθεν πάντων — "in full view of them all" (2:12, New English Bible). And in the case of the man with the withered arm, far from performing the miracle privately, Jesus commands him ἔγειρε εἰς τὸ μέσον and there, having first drawn all eyes upon him, effects the healing (3:3ff.). It is true that there is a secrecy, or better, privacy motif in some of the healings: Jesus lets only Peter, James, and John accompany him to Jairus's house and only the parents to enter the room (5:37ff.); he takes the man who was deaf and had an impediment of speech away from the crowd and performs the miracle κατ' ἰδίαν (7:31-37); he also takes the blind man out of the village before he heals him (8:22-26). But the woman with the

---

14. The argument of Wrede (140f.) and Boobyer (230) that the command to go εἰς τὸν οἶκον σου is a command to secrecy, since οἶκος denotes a place of concealment from the public elsewhere in the Gospel (cf. 7:17a, 24b; 8:26a), does not carry conviction. οἶκος is most definitely *not* a place of concealment in 2:1ff. and 3:20; and what is more natural and ingenuous than to encourage a man to "go home" (5:19; 8:26)? See also Burkill, *Mysterious Revelation,* 91f. Note also that the connecting participle in v. 20 is καί and not δέ as in 1:45 and 7:36.

15. Wrede, 278f.; and see E. Haenchen, *Der Weg Jesu* (Berlin: de Gruyter, ²1968) 372.

hemorrhage is healed in the crowd and it is Jesus himself who draws attention to a cure which no one else had noticed. And Bartimaeus is healed in full view of the crowd. Nor surely was Mark naive enough to impose a messianic secret motif on a story like the raising of Jairus's daughter. How could the raising of a dead girl to life be kept silent when the mourning had already begun? And why is it on several occasions after Jesus gives a strict command to silence that Mark immediately goes on to tell how the news was broadcast far and wide (1:25-28, 43-45; 7:36f.)? If the messianic secret motif was added to explain why Jesus was not recognized as Messiah, and part of that motif is the command to demons and people not to tell of their cures, I am at a loss to understand what Mark was trying to achieve by adding or at least retaining the publicity sequel. For the whole point of these passages is that the secret commanded was *not* kept. The commands to silence failed, and so the so-called attempt to keep his messiahship secret also failed. If the messianic secret was a Markan theory, then these publicity passages are the *reductio ad absurdum* of that theory.[16] This publicity motif may not simply be dismissed as though it left the theory of the messianic secret unaffected.[17] On the contrary, it shows that at most we can speak of a messianic *misunderstanding,* but hardly of a messianic *secret.*

There is also a very prominent theme of revelation which should not be ignored, since it, too, runs counter to the straight messianic secret thesis. I will not enlarge upon it but simply call attention to its various facets — the authoritative claims made by the Markan Jesus for himself: to forgive sins, no less (2:10); to have a mission to call (καλέσαι) sinners (2:17); to be sovereign (κύριος) over the Sabbath (2:28); to be the one who binds the strong man (Satan) and ransacks his house (3:27); that loyalty to *him* will be the yardstick of judgment in the parousia (8:38). Again there is the teaching Jesus gives to his disciples in private about the true nature of his messiahship (8:31-33; 9:31-32; 10:32-34, 45; 14:22-25). Schweizer justifiably notes the concern with which Jesus brings God's mystery to people, especially the disciples (4:34; 7:17-23; 8:15-21, 27-33; 9:30-32; 10:32-34; cf. 5:37; 9:2; 13:3f.).[18] Finally one might call attention to such passages as the parable of the Wicked Tenants, where the Markan Jesus specifically claims a special relation of sonship and where Mark tells us that the priests and lawyers recognized that the parable was aimed at them (12:12); or again to the Bar-

---

16. My point is illustrated by Burkill's very unconvincing treatment of 1:23ff.: Mark "construes the injunction to silence in the sense of a command to secrecy, and therefore takes it for granted that the congregation does not hear what the demon says to Jesus. In other words, on the evangelist's interpretation the story is not convincing; the injunction to silence comes too late, since the secret has already been divulged" (*Mysterious Revelation,* 71).

17. Contra Strecker, 94.

18. E. Schweizer, "Zur Frage des Messiasgeheimnis bei Markus," *ZNW* 56 (1965) 3.

timaeus episode, where Jesus is twice hailed as Son of David (10:47f.), and to 15:39, where the centurion confesses that the *dead* Jesus was truly a or the Son of God. A theory of the messianic secret which does not take account of these other themes, which are just as prominent, will inevitably give a distorted picture both of the Markan Jesus and of the Markan theology.

(3) My third criticism of Wrede's thesis is that it does not give sufficient weight to the element of historicity which is firmly attached to the motif of the messianic secret. As I have already indicated, Wrede believed that Jesus did not claim to be Messiah during his life and that all messianic elements were superimposed upon the tradition. And though his successors have admitted that the tradition had a messianic stamp at an early, pre-Markan stage, they have not thereby committed themselves any more firmly to its historicity.[19] But in my opinion there are several incidents whose historicity it is almost impossible to dismiss and whose central significance has definite messianic overtones — a significance which must have been known to and intended by Jesus.

I think first of the feeding of the five thousand. As John O'Neill observes,

> we may suppose that some extraordinary event will lie behind such a miraculous narrative . . . it remains true that if Jesus did preside at a communal meal in the desert places of Galilee and Judaea, this would have had peculiar significance to his contemporaries. They would perhaps remember that Moses by praying to God was able to feed the people with manna and quail in the desert; they would perhaps be reminded of the promise that the desert would again be fruitful; and they would think of the shepherd King as they were given food in the barren places (*cf.* Pss. of Sol. 17:45). The Qumran desert community placed great emphasis on communal meals, and looked forward to the time when the Messiah of Aaron would preside and the Messiah of Israel, whom God had begotten among them, would come (1QSa 2.11-22).[20]

Even more to the point is the evidence of John 6:15 that the crowd intended to "come and seize Jesus to proclaim him king." C. H. Dodd argues, convincingly I think, for the historicity of John 6:14f.[21] Most noticeable is the

---

19. See, e.g., H. Conzelmann, "Gegenwart und Zukunft in der synoptischen Tradition," *ZTK* 54 (1957) 294f.; Strecker, 89-93; and W. Marxsen, who follow Conzelmann in arguing that it was not the nonmessianic nature of the tradition which troubled Mark but the *messianic,* i.e., the post-resurrection, kerygmatic character of the tradition (*Introduction to the New Testament* [Oxford: Blackwell, 1968] 137).

20. J. C. O'Neill, "The Silence of Jesus," *NTS* 15 (1968-69) 163f.; see also V. Taylor, "The Messianic Secret in Mark," *ExpT* 59 (1947-48) 149.

21. C. H. Dodd, *Historical Tradition in the Fourth Gospel* (Cambridge: Cambridge University, 1963) 213-16.

otherwise very odd use of ἠνάγκασεν in Mark 6:45 — Jesus had to force the disciples to put out into a difficult sea. The two independent traditions interlock and together provide a very coherent picture. The crowd sees the messianic significance of Jesus' action and is so carried away on a wave of mass enthusiasm that they attempt to make Jesus king by acclamation. The disciples themselves are caught up in the excitement, and Jesus in order to forestall the move has first to force the disciples to embark by themselves on an uninviting lake. Only then is he able to turn to the crowd and with the voice of authority to dismiss them (ἀπολύειν). He then goes off immediately by himself into the hills to pray — and it is perhaps significant that Mark only mentions Jesus praying three times and that on each of the other occasions the implication is that Jesus resorted to prayer because of temptation: temptation at the time of his early success to remain where he was so popular (1:3, 38) and temptation in Gethsemane (14:35f.). So in 6:46 there is the implication that Jesus was tempted to give way to the crowd's demands — to be the Messiah of popular conception and popular appeal and that he fled to the silence and loneliness of the hills so that quiet communion with his Father might strengthen his conviction concerning the nature of his mission and messiahship. Whether Mark was aware of the messianic significance of the story he recorded it is hard to say; but I would strongly maintain that that significance is inherent to the historical incident he records.

I think secondly of Peter's confession in Mark 8:27ff. — a passage which caused Wrede not a little difficulty.[22] Points in favor of the substantial authenticity of the pericope are: the specification and location of the place of confession (none of the traditional resurrection appearances to the Twelve took place so far north), the unique appearance of the title Χριστός addressed to Jesus by a disciple, the evidence that Jesus was *Pneumatiker,* and the total improbability of the primitive church calling Peter "Satan." Nor should we ignore the otherwise surprising insertion καὶ ἰδὼν τοὺς μαθητὰς αὐτοῦ in verse 33a, which has the ring of an authentic reminiscence, and the Jewish character of verse 33.[23] Grundmann also calls attention to the thrice-repeated ἐπιτιμᾶν and to the ἤρξατο διδάσκειν, which is not the normal Markan Semitism but indicates a particular point of time at which for the first time the repeated teaching referred to by the διδάσκειν received a concrete content.[24]

Bultmann treats the passage in his not unusual high-handed manner:

22. See A. Schweitzer, *The Quest of the Historical Jesus* (London: Black, 1910) 340; V. Taylor, "W. Wrede's The Messianic Secret in the Gospels," *ExpT* 65 (1953-54) 248.

23. SB I, 748.

24. W. Grundmann, *Das Evangelium nach Markus* (Berlin: Evangelische, [2]1959) 167 — referring to Riesenfeld, "Tradition und Redaktion im Markus-Evangelium," *Neutestamentliche Studien für R. Bultmann* (Berlin: Töpelmann, [2]1957) 160f.

Jesus obviously would not ask such a question of his disciples, since he was bound to be as informed as they were, and the original narrative *must* have contained an account of the attitude of Jesus himself to the confession he had stimulated — a response which Bultmann finds not in verses 30-33, a Markan formulation, but in Matthew 16:17-19![25] I consider that Ferdinand Hahn's description of the exchange as "a teaching conversation" is sufficient answer to Bultmann. As a good teacher Jesus takes the initiative, but does not put the answers into his pupils' mouths. In a fascinatingly minute dissection of the text Hahn goes on to reach the conclusion that Jesus originally rejected the Messiah title as such with the implication that he did so because of its popular secular-political connotations — rather unexpected support for the view that Jesus himself counseled silence about his messiahship because of the popular misconception of what it involved.[26]

Recent writers like T. J. Weeden have continued to draw particular attention to the way in which Mark's Gospel falls into two divisions, with the episode at Caesarea Philippi as the beginning of the second part.[27] While disagreeing with Weeden's acceptance of two opposing christologies in Mark — a θεῖος ἀνήρ christology and a suffering christology — there is some justification for his opinion that in 8:29 Peter makes his confession to a θεῖος ἀνήρ Christ and that Mark presents Jesus as correcting this false christology by expounding his understanding of a Messiah who must suffer. For it is a fact that for the first time Mark speaks of Jesus teaching the disciples and for the first time he speaks of suffering. The only thing I do not see is why we have to attribute this decisive development to Markan theology or postresurrection apologetic. It seems to me that what we have here is a perfectly understandable sequence of events which culminate in a turning point in Jesus' ministry. The disciples have observed at first hand Jesus' authoritative ministry of word and action. And they have slowly come to the conclusion that he is the Messiah — not the only conclusion possible, as the opinions of others show, but a conclusion which is inescapable for his closest companions. When Jesus at last brings them to the point of crystalizing their belief in open confession, he sees the time is now come to take them a further step. For their belief has been nourished almost solely on a diet of exorcisms and miracles, and the authoritative teaching they have so far heard would do little to correct a false idea of a messiahship which consists in the exercise of effective power.

25. R. Bultmann, *The History of the Synoptic Tradition* (Oxford: Blackwell, 1963) 258f., followed by E. Trocmé, *La formation de l'évangile selon Marc* (Paris: Presses Universitaires, 1963) 46, 96.

26. Hahn, *Titles of Jesus,* 223-28; cf. E. Dinkler, "Petrusbekenntnis und Satanswort: Das Problem der Messianität Jesu," *Zeit und Geschichte* (see n. 7) 127-53.

27. Weeden, 145-58; see also, e.g., A. Kuby, "Zur Komposition des Markusevangeliums," *ZNW* 49 (1958) 52-64; Burkill, *Mysterious Revelation,* 143ff.; Luz, 29.

And so they must be taught that for Jesus messiahship involves suffering. Having at last got over to them the message *that* he is Messiah, he must now explain *what kind* of Messiah. This, of course, does not exclude the possibility that Mark used this narrative in particular and intended his Gospel as a whole to combat a heretical θεῖος ἀνήρ christology, as Weeden argues. Theological editing[28] and historical reminiscences are by no means mutually exclusive factors in the preservation and development of the primitive tradition, as for example Wrede and more recently Ernst Haenchen seem to think.[29]

I see no adequate reason, therefore, for separating 8:27-30 from 8:31ff., for the two passages cohere without any mark of artificial conjunction. It is unquestionable in my opinion that Jesus saw (or at least came to see) his mission in terms of suffering, and entirely probable that he should begin to explain this to his most intimate followers at some stage in his ministry. Nor do I feel it necessary to attribute verse 30 — the command to silence — to the hand of an interpolator.[30] For it is not the Christ of Easter whom Peter confesses, or else why is he rebuked? And if it is the Christ of Jewish hope and popular expectation whom Peter hails[31] — as the rebuke requires — a pre-Easter origin cannot so readily be denied to the confession. Thus far I have the support of Hahn and Dinkler. It is with the next step that we part company. For if the confession is historical, then it seems to me that the command to silence is best explained not as part of a secondary theological motif but as a measure taken by Jesus to prevent this false idea of messiahship gaining fresh currency.[32] This misleading and dangerous half-truth must be both silenced and corrected. Hence Jesus immediately responds both negatively and positively. In this connection note particularly how closely Matthew and Luke link the injunction to silence to the subsequent passage. Luke makes it all one sentence and Matthew indicates that Peter's confession led to repeated teaching about the nature of messiahship. The evidence is very strong therefore for seeing in this passage a substantially accurate account of an actual event in Jesus' ministry — an event which is obviously of messianic significance.

28. Most noticeably the sudden appearance of the crowd caused by the Markan juxtaposition of the saying of verses 34ff. with 27-33.

29. Wrede, 115; E. Haenchen, "Die Komposition von Mk. 8.27–9.1 und Par.," *NovT* 6 (1963) 81-109.

30. The Markan style of verse 30 is no proof of its redactional origin and speaks neither for nor against the historicity of the command to silence (contra G. Stecker, "Die Leidens-und Aufersteungs-voraussagen im Markusevangelium," *ZTK* 64 [1967] 22 n. 16) since the whole pericope has a Markan stamp. It suggests rather that Mark drew the story from oral tradition (cf. Strecker, 32).

31. These are the two most plausible alternatives (see Dinkler, 131f.).

32. The other alternative — that Jesus denied the messianic title altogether (Hahn, Dinkler) — is shown to be inadequate by the other passages under consideration.

The third incident in which I believe historicity and messianic significance go together is the entry into Jerusalem. On the score of historicity
Vincent Taylor points to

> the local expressions at the beginning, the vivid character of the account,
> . . . the description of what happened, the restrained nature of the acclama-
> tion, and the strange manner in which the account breaks off without any
> suggestion of a "triumphal entry" (as in Mt.).[33]

One might also note that the actions and shouts of those with Jesus create an
impression of authenticity, because though they conform in a general way to
Zechariah 9:9 they include details which are neither necessary nor even
particularly appropriate — a fact which makes it unlikely that the narrative is
a construction of the primitive church.[34] Specially worthy of comment is the
appearance of ὡσαννα, which is firmly embedded in the Synoptic tradition
and also in John's account, but which appears nowhere else in the New
Testament — a strong indication of authenticity. I therefore find Taylor's
conclusion wholly justified: "These characteristics suggest the eyewitness
rather than the artist."[35]

As for messianic significance, we may note again that the passage caused
Wrede's theory some difficulty. As R. H. Lightfoot observed: "St. Mark's
doctrine of the secret Messiahship of Jesus is here strained to breaking
point."[36] In the words of D. E. Nineham,

> It is difficult to see why Jesus sent for the colt and entered the city on it
> unless he intended to make clear the fact of his Messiahship. Pilgrims
> normally entered Jerusalem on foot, so, as the story stands, the fact that
> Jesus deliberate procured and rode an ass makes it impossible to think of
> him as simply a passive figure in a demonstration which was none of his
> doing.[37]

The messianic associations of the Mount of Olives should also not go unob-
served. The fact is that there is no effort on the part of Jesus to keep his
messiahship secret — certainly not in Mark's narrative, for Mark's narrative,
and, I would add, the historical event, can only be construed as a clear assertion
of a kind of messiahship.

The fourth incident I want to fasten onto is the trial and condemnation

---

33. V. Taylor, *The Gospel according to St. Mark* (London: Macmillan, [2]1956) 452.
34. D. E. Nineham, *St. Mark* (London: Black, 1968) 293.
35. Taylor, *Gospel according to Mark,* 452.
36. R. H. Lightfoot, *History and Interpretation in the Gospels* (London: Hodder and
Stoughton, 1934) 121.
37. Nineham, 292.

of Jesus. That Jesus was found guilty of claiming to be king of the Jews is the testimony of all four Gospels (Mark 15:26; Matt. 27:37; Luke 23:38; John 19:19). The frequent repetition of the title in Mark 15 — verses 2, 9, 12, 18, 26, 32 — is particularly noticeable. Since it was not a title employed by the early church there can be little doubt, Bultmann notwithstanding, that we are on sure historical ground here: Jesus was crucified as a messianic pretender, because of the political connotations of the title King of the Jews.[38] But this implies that there was some basis to the charge and the condemnation — that there were substantial grounds for applying it to Jesus — that, indeed, the title was in some sense accepted by him. The historicity of the trial scene in 15:2ff. inevitably reflects favorably on the authenticity of the earlier hearing described in 14:55ff., since it can be fairly argued that the question of Pilate (15:2) is simply the Greco-Roman version of the question of the high priest (14:61) — the blasphemy charge suitably nuanced for a Roman court.[39]

Turning to that earlier hearing, the presumption is strong that Jesus did actually speak the words about building the Temple, in some form at least. Although Lohmeyer is probably correct in classifying χειροποίητον and ἀχειροποίητον as a Markan or community explanatory addition,[40] nevertheless the fact cannot be ignored that six New Testament passages testify to the saying (Mark 14:58; 15:29; Matt. 26:61; 27:40; John 2:19; Acts 6:14); and if the saying sometimes seems obscure, that speaks rather in favor of than against its authenticity.[41] Incidentally, the saying also attests to the power which was ascribed to Jesus — καταλύσω. It is not without relevance to the question we are studying that such power could be ascribed to Jesus by way of accusation — and it certainly testifies to some claim, by word or action, to messianic activity and power. As attributed to Jesus by the witnesses it can only be intended and understood messianically. The probability is high that it provided the basis of the prosecution's attack on Jesus, and Otto Betz in particular has shown how naturally an examination at that point leads on to the direct question of the high priest: "Are you the Messiah, the Son of the Blessed?"[42] for the building of the Temple belonged to the messianic age (1 En. 90:29; 4 Ezra 9:38–10:27; cf. Ezekiel 40–48; Jub. 1:17, 27f.) and the saying involves

38. See, e.g., E. Stauffer, "Messias oder Menschensohn?" NovT 1 (1956) 90f.; P. Winter, On the Trial of Jesus (Berlin: De Gruyter, 1961) 108f.; Burkill, Mysterious Revelation, 295f.; Dinkler, 148; R. H. Fuller, The Foundations of New Testament Christology (London: Lutterworth, 1965) 110; O. Betz, What Do We Know about Jesus? (London: SCM, 1968) 84.

39. Note particularly 15:32 — ὁ Χριστὸς ὁ Βασιλεὺς ᾿Ισραηλ.

40. E. Lohmeyer, Das Evangelium des Markus (Göttingen: Vandenhoeck und Ruprecht, [16]1963 [= 1937]) 326.

41. See also J. Blinzler, The Trial of Jesus (Cork: Mercier, 1959) 120.

42. Betz, "Die Frage nach dem messianischen Bewusstsein Jesu," NovT 6 (1963) 24-37; see also Blinzler, 102f.; Betz, Jesus, 87ff.; Aune, 23f.; cf. Lohmeyer, 330; Grundmann, 302; Burkill, Mysterious Revelation, 284f.

a claim to fulfil the prophecy of Nathan (2 Sam. 7:12-14) and so to be Messiah, Son of David, and Son of God. In Bultmann's opinion, however, the fact that witnesses were not called for Jesus' messianic claims as they were for his saying about the Temple is an indication that the two accusations did not belong together originally.[43] The logic behind this line of reasoning eludes me. If anything the absence of witnesses testifies to Jesus' reticence about messianic claims or to his complete failure to make an unequivocal claim, by word of mouth at least.

But if we can find no adequate reason to dispute the authenticity of the course of questioning, what are we to make of Jesus' reply to the high priest's question? It is here that Wrede's thesis breaks down completely. For however affirmative or evasive were his opening words — and we shall return to this point shortly — there is no doubt that the high priest understood the reply as a messianic claim: the high priest's tearing of his clothes was hardly prompted by the *silence* of Jesus.[44] In the words of Montefiore, "We must surely believe that the Messiahship claim was at least ventilated, and that it was resolved that Jesus was to be denounced to Pilate on that ground."[45] We need not discuss at greater length the actual saying of 14:62. Among the indications of authenticity one might mention the unique use of the motif of sitting on the right hand of God and the divergence of 14:62 from Psalm 110:1. The sitting motif is unusual, for if we take it as signifying a stage of exaltation before and apart from the parousia, then it is unique in the Synoptic tradition;[46] if, on the other hand, we take it as referring to the parousia, what evangelist would retain the ὄψεσθε other than one very faithful to his sources? In addition we have to reckon with Matthew's ἀπ' ἄρτι and Luke's ἀπὸ τοῦ νῦν, which together suggest that they were both following a non-Greek source. Further, with reference to the charge that 14:62 shows signs of a conflation of ideas which can only be postresurrection in origin, we may refer to *1 En.* 62:5, which, as F. H. Borsch has recently pointed out, brings together seeing, Son of man, and sitting in a manner very similar to that of Mark 14:62.[47] I conclude then that here we have another incident whose historicity is well grounded and whose central significance is preeminently messianic.

43. Bultmann, 270.

44. Taylor, *Gospel,* 569.

45. C. G. Montefiore, *The Synoptic Gospels* (London: Macmillan, [2]1927) I, 357.

46. H. E. Tödt, *The Son of Man in the Synoptic Tradition* (London: SCM, 1963) 39.

47. F. H. Borsch, "Mark xiv 62 and I Enoch lxii 5," *NTS* 14 (1967-68) 565-67. Although there is a very large question mark against the pre-Christian origin of the Similitudes of Enoch (37–71), the two passages in question are probably independent of each other.

II

Wrede's thesis that the messianic secret motif had a theological rather than a historical origin was based on his conclusion that certain elements of that motif were clearly *unhistorical.* We are now in a position to stand Wrede's line of reasoning on its head, for our conclusion thus far is that certain elements of that motif are clearly *historical;* that is, that the messianic character of the tradition is not the result of Mark's redaction, or of pre-Markan but post-resurrection Christian theology — it belongs to the incidents themselves. On the basis of *that* conclusion we can now present the thesis that contrary to Wrede the so-called "messianic secret" motif had a historical rather than theological origin. To argue this thesis in depth is beyond the scope of this paper, but the four incidents already examined almost constitute proof enough.

First the feeding of the five thousand. The important points which emerge here are, first, that there was abroad, in Galilee at least, a popular conception of the Messiah as a political kingly figure — the sort of king of the Jews that Pilate felt justified in crucifying; that Jesus was a Messiah of this type was the conclusion reached by those whom Jesus miraculously fed in the desert. The second important point is the evidence of how Jesus reacted against this attempt to force a false messianic role on him. He saw all too clearly how politically inflammable the Galilean crowd was. The lesson learned, or confirmed, by this effect of his display of authority would go a long way toward explaining his reticence in other situations.

With regard to Peter's confession, the interesting thing is again Jesus' reaction. Peter hails him as Messiah, and how does Jesus respond? There is certainly no question of his denying the title — but there is also no indication of his accepting it beyond the impersonal περὶ αὐτοῦ of 8:30. 8:30 is a word neither of rebuke nor of congratulation. It is a command to silence followed immediately by explicit and very pointed teaching about the nature of Jesus' messiahship. The implication is strong that Peter was little further forward than the Galilean crowd in his understanding of Jesus' messiahship. The command to silence is given not so much because Jesus' messiahship is secret, but because it is misunderstood.[48]

In the entry into Jerusalem three points call for attention. The first is that Mark carefully avoids making the messianic character of the event fully explicit. The Zechariah prophecy is not referred to; the ovation seems to come from the disciples rather than the crowd, and the cries of welcome fall short of complete messianic recognition and homage. The second is the manner of Jesus' entry: he comes as the humble king who speaks peace, not as the political king of the Jews. The third is the fact that the authorities did not

48. Cf. O. Cullmann, *The Christology of the New Testament* (London: SCM, 1959) 124f.

immediately pull Jesus in and that no reference seems to have been made to the entry at the trial — a fact which suggests that no political significance was seen or could easily be read into the entry. In short, Jesus' entry into Jerusalem was an enacted parable about the nature of his messiahship. Those whose ears were attuned to catch political overtones heard nothing. Those who looked and listened for the coming of the kingdom saw something of eschatological and messianic significance, but fell short of full understanding.[49]

In the trial of Jesus once again interest centers on Jesus' response to the questions put to him by the high priest and by Pilate. I am much impressed by the arguments in favor of the longer reading in 14:62. What scribe faced by the triumphant and unequivocal ἐγώ εἰμι would dilute it to the colorless and equivocal σὺ εἶπας ὅτι ἐγώ εἰμι? And the longer reading certainly accounts for the texts of Matthew and Luke. In that case Jesus' reply to the high priest is very similar to his reply to Pilate. To both questions — "Are you the Christ?" and "Are you the king of the Jews?" — Jesus answers in effect, "You could put it that way." He accepts the titles, but at the same time makes it clear that he does not attach the same significance to them as do his questioners (cf. John 18:33-37). These exchanges are important in that they exemplify the dilemma which must constantly have confronted Jesus — could he accept or use *simpliciter* titles which meant one thing to himself and something very different to his hearers?

The conclusions I draw from studying these passages are that Jesus believed himself to be Messiah, but that his conception of the messianic role was an unexpected and unpopular one. Because the title Messiah had such different connotations to Jesus and to those who heard him he never once used it of himself or unequivocally welcomed its application to him by others;[50] and when his actions or words seemed to encourage the to him false conception of messiahship he tried to prevent it by commands to silence. Nevertheless he did not take what might appear the easiest course — that of completely renouncing the title. He did not deny his right to the title, but attempted to reeducate his hearers in the significance of it for him. And the claims he made to messiahship and messianic authority were of a parabolic sort whose significance was there, plain for all to see whose eyes were not blinded and whose ears were not clogged by misconceptions (8:17-21).

These conclusions follow directly from the four passages we examined. But I believe that they hold true for the whole of the Markan tradition, and to round off the argument I will merely illustrate the force of this contention by drawing attention to three other motifs which shed light over the whole

49. See also Stauffer, 85ff.
50. Cf. Boobyer, 229-31; O'Neill, 159ff. For supporting arguments from rabbinic traditions concerning Jesus see Stauffer, 94-102.

Gospel. First of all, the motif of authoritative teaching and action. I refer in particular to the section 2:1–3:6. There are good grounds I think for seeing this as a pre-Markan block of material in which we are given a cameo of Jesus' whole ministry and of the impact made by his teaching on the Jewish authorities — the decision on the part of the Pharisees and Herodians to destroy Jesus is remarkably early and unproductive otherwise. In that case it is worth noticing that Mark has made no attempt to impose any of the elements of the "messianic secret" on the section. On the contrary we have four very definite claims made by Jesus to very considerable status and authority — authority to forgive sins (2:10), authority to command and call (καλέσαι) people (2:14, 17), status as bridegroom (2:19 — in the context of Old Testament thought a very pointed and meaningful metaphor) — and status and authority as Lord over the sabbath (2:27; 3:4-6). In none of these incidents could it be said that Jesus was explicitly claiming to be Messiah, but in each case there were messianic overtones — overtones which the individual seeking the truth and open to new revelation would be able to recognize.[51]

Secondly, there is the parabolic nature of Jesus' teaching, to which attention is drawn in Mark 4. I do not wish to become involved in a discussion of the significance of the ἵνα in 4:10, with its seemingly double predestinarian ring.[52] I would only draw attention again to the τὰ πάντα in 4:11: "to you has been given the mystery of the kingdom, but to those outside all things are in parables," or, as Jeremias translates, "all things are obscure." Bearing in mind 4:33f., I take the parallelism of this verse to signify that *all* Jesus' teaching was in the nature of a parable; that is, to those who had ears to hear (4:9) the parable unfolded its meaning; but to those whose ears were dulled to the note of divine authority the parable gave no light. The saying has to be read together with those of verses 21-22, as the repetition of the challenge to hear aright makes clear (4:9, 23). Jesus came to give light, and his teaching shed light enough; nevertheless that light was hidden for many, and would remain so for the time being, till either the resurrection or the parousia. I have no doubt that this double-edged quality of Jesus' teaching was his own choice. Rather than a straightforward statement of certain truths which would register on most of his hearers' understanding but make no impact on their emotions

---

51. Cf. Burkill, *Mysterious Revelation,* 134, n. 37. On the messianic nature of Jesus' teaching see Aune, 26ff. Particularly worth noticing, as underlining the marked effect of his openly displayed authority, is the amazement motif (1:2, 27; 2:12; 5:20, 42; 6:2, 51; 7:37; 9:15; 10:32; 11:18; 12:17; 15:5). In particular, 9:15; 15:5; and especially 10:32 bear witness to Jesus' tremendous presence.

52. But see J. Jeremias, *The Parables of Jesus* (London: SCM, [6]1963) 13-18; and we would do well to heed C. F. D. Moule's plea against interpreting the passage with "prosaic solemnity" (*The Gospel acccording to Mark* [Cambridge: Cambridge University, 1965] 36). Among the marks of authenticity the most noticeable is the agreement of the reference to Isa. 6:9f. with the Targum rather than the Hebrew or the LXX (see Jeremias, 15).

or their will, Jesus deliberately chose to speak in parables so that the truth thus conveyed might have maximum impact, even if only on a few.[53] Kierkegaard grasped the rationale behind Jesus' method when he wrote,

> Christianity, by becoming a direct communication, is altogether destroyed. It becomes a superficial thing, capable neither of inflicting deep wounds, nor of healing them.[54]

Thirdly, I would point to the phrase "Son of man," the self-designation preferred by Jesus, as I believe it to be. Again we enter a much-plowed field, and I will not attempt to plow a fresh furrow. Suffice it to say that the work of Geza Vermes on the one hand and of Morna Hooker on the other serve to underline how fully that phrase exemplifies the parabolic nature of Jesus' messianic claims. Vermes cites several examples of Aramaic usage which seem to support the view that *bar nash(a)* could have been used by Jesus as a circumlocution for "I" and that the phrase could have been understood by his hearers in that sense.[55] Nor can the link between the Markan Son of man and the Danielic Son of man so well forged by Hooker be easily broken.[56] In the words of Matthew Black: "No term was more fitted both to conceal, yet at the same time to reveal to those who had ears to hear, the Son of Man's real identity."[57] Here is the real vehicle of the "messianic secret."

Finally, attention should also be drawn to the parallel noted by Richard Longenecker between the Synoptic Jesus on the one hand and the Qumran Teacher of Righteousness and Simeon ben Kosebah on the other. Common features in each case include (a) external acclamation, (b) reticence on the part of the individual to speak of himself in terms used of him by others, and (c) consciousness on that individual's part of the ultimate validity of the titles employed. The basis of this common pattern Longenecker finds not in any "messianic secret" theology but in the Jewish view that "no man can be defined as a messiah before he has accomplished the task of the anointed."[58] If this is so it certainly enhances the historicity of the Synoptic picture.

In short, I believe that to speak of a messianic *secret* is misleading and unjustified. So far as Jesus' messiahship was concerned there was no secret

53. The objection that Jesus would have made it plain that he was *not* a political Messiah fails to reckon with the parabolic nature of *all* Jesus' action and teaching.

54. Cited by V. de Waal, *What Is the Church?* (London: SCM, 1969) 22.

55. G. Vermes in an appendix to M. Black, *An Aramaic Approach to the Gospels and Acts* (Oxford: Clarendon, [3]1967) 310-28; although see J. A. Fitzmyer's critical review in *CBQ* 30 (1968) 424-28.

56. M. Hooker, *The Son of Man in Mark* (London: SPCK, 1967).

57. Black, 329; see also I. H. Marshall, "The Synoptic Son of Man Sayings in Recent Discussion," *NTS* 12 (1965-66) 350f.; cf. E. Sjöberg, *Der verborgene Menschensohn in den Evangelien* (Lund: Gleerup, 1955) 126; O'Neill, 161.

58. Longenecker, 211-14, citing David Flusser.

as such, only a cautious disavowal of false views — those of the Galilean wonder-worker and of the warrior or political king of the Jews — and an equally cautious assertion and explication of his own understanding of messiahship — that of service and suffering in this world and of exaltation only after death. As to the reason for this, all the evangelists agree: Jesus was indeed Messiah during his earthly life, but his messiahship was incomplete and inevitably misunderstood during that phase. Only with the cross, resurrection, and exaltation would he enter into the fullness of his messianic office, and only then could its true nature be properly understood. John brings this out through the δοξάζειν and κρίσις motifs. Luke brings it out by developing his three-age presentation of *Heilsgeschichte*. In Matthew one sees it in the kingdom sayings, for instance in the link between the Spirit and the kingdom in Matthew 12:28: it is because and only because Jesus is the one who is empowered by the Spirit that the kingdom can be said to have come upon them and to be fully in their midst, though not yet fully realized. And in Mark it is the "messianic secret" which is the vehicle of this theme. In other words, the so-called secrecy motif in Mark is nothing other than *Mark's* method of bringing home to his readers *the programmatic nature of Jesus' messiahship*.

In conclusion, Wrede's thesis has been subjected to many criticisms in the course of its life. For example, form criticism has shown that the silencing of demons is a feature antecedent to any "messianic secret" redaction,[59] and that the privacy motif (see pp. 63-64 above) has nothing to do with the "messianic secret."[60] The conclusion that the messianic character of the tradition belongs to a primitive form of the tradition (see p. 72 above) has also reduced the form critic's confidence when it comes to pronouncing on the historical value of the tradition. Besides which it has become evident that passages like 8:30 do not provide independent evidence for the redactional nature of the secrecy motif since the more skeptical conclusions there usually depend on a prior acceptance of the Wrede hypothesis.

However, the full significance for Wrede's thesis of the post-Bultmannian quest of the historical Jesus does not seem to have been fully appreciated. For the nub of the debate is the messianic self-consciousness of Jesus and the messianic character of his ministry, not the authenticity of this messianic title or that command to silence. And the new questers have found that though they can still pronounce a confident negative judgment on the authenticity of this messianic title or that command to silence, it is almost impossible to deny that Jesus saw his mission at least to some extent in messianic terms or that his authentic

---

59. See pp. 61-62 above; also H. C. Kee, "The Terminology of Mark's Exorcism Stories," *NTS* 14 (1967-68) 232-46.

60. M. Dibelius, *From Tradition to Gospel* (London: Ivor, Nicholson, and Watson, 1934) 73f.; Bultmann, 224.

words and deeds bear an unmistakably messianic character.[61] When one adds, as one must, that Jesus' concept and practice of his mission was popular with the people but unpopular with the authorities, it becomes evident that the whole "messianic secret" thesis has been stripped of the logical consistency which bound it together and is in danger of falling apart at the seams. The "messianic secret" hypothesis in fact is now a theory searching for a rationale, and the recent attempts to defend and define its *raison d'être* in terms of an anti-θεῖος ἀνήρ polemic (n. 3) or an anti-disciple polemic (n. 8) must be pronounced inadequate. Since the "messianic secret" motif is part and parcel of the tradition itself we are at the end of the day more or less shut up to the choice between the mere "that"-ness of complete Bultmannian skepticism and a Jesus who was a secret or rather a misunderstood Messiah.

We have not been able to study all the relevant data, and I do not want to overstate my case. I would not deny, for example, that Mark may have interpreted simple commands to silence demons in terms of the "messianic secret" motif (1:34; 3:11f.) or that it is Mark's own opinion about the disciples which is being expressed in passages like 6:51-52; 14:40b. But the question is whether this interpretation and opinion expresses an understanding of the material which is essentially foreign to it, or whether it is merely developing a theme which is already native to the material. When one takes into account the complexity of the secrecy motif (which reflects the complexity of life rather than the artificial complicatedness of a theory — see for example nn. 6, 16), the counterbalancing publicity-revelation theme, the inherent messianic character of the pericope we examined, and the very strong probability which emerged from that examination that there were two understandings of messiahship at issue, I cannot but conclude that the so-called "messianic secret" originated in the life-situation of Jesus and is in essence at least wholly historical.

---

61. See, e.g., E. Käsemann, "The Problem of the Historical Jesus," *Essays on New Testament Themes* (London: SCM, 1964) 37-43; G. Bornkamm, *Jesus of Nazareth* (London: Hodder and Stoughton, 1960) 169-72, 178.

5

Messianic Ideas and Their Influence
on the Jesus of History

Introduction

Jesus was a Jew. It is inconceivable that he was not "influenced" by Jewish "ideas." This uncontroversial *a priori* conceals potentially explosive issues. In particular, it leads naturally to a whole sequence of follow-up questions. To what extent was Jesus' whole message and ministry shaped and determined by particular ideas which came to him as part of his Jewish upbringing, character, and context? To what extent was the movement which sprang from Jesus shaped and determined by these same Jewish ideas, and to what extent by other (non-Jewish) forces? Does Jesus belong more to the Judaism from which he emerged or to the Christianity which resulted from his ministry? Did Jesus inject something new and different into his ancestral faith and practice, and can he therefore be credited (or blamed) for the consequent transformation which within two or three generations led to the schism between (rabbinic) Judaism and Christianity?

Such are the wider issues with still wider ramifications which surround the more specific issue. Was Jesus influenced by current Jewish messianic ideas? Did he see himself or his ministry as the fulfillment of his people's hopes and aspirations for the future? Even this topic is huge and impossible to tackle at more than an overview level within the scope of a single paper. Nevertheless the issue is potentially of immense significance and it is important that such a summary treatment be attempted as part of the wider inquiry of this colloquy.

Reprinted by permission from *The Messiah: Developments in Earliest Judaism and Christianity,* ed. J. H. Charlesworth, 146-62. Copyright © 1992 by Augsburg Fortress.

Definitions

The terms used need to be defined with some care, lest we find ourselves arguing at cross purposes: (a) What do we mean by "messianic ideas"? Are we referring to: (i) Specific figures of whom the word "messiah" is used — in Jewish circles prior to Jesus or also in the first century C.E. as a whole? (ii) "Messiah" as redefined within earliest Christianity, not the least by drawing in other motifs and passages of the OT not previously regarded as "messianic"? (iii) The range of Jewish eschatological expectation (the "messianic age"), including expectations where no figure as such is specified, as well as the whole range of revelatory or redemptive or judgmental figures who feature within the kaleidoscope of diverse Jewish hopes and visions? In short, what can we say *might* have influenced Jesus (or any of his contemporaries) on the theme of "messiahship"? Since the issues are mutually entangled and a too narrow definition could shut off possible sources of influence too quickly, I will try to keep the inquiry as broad as possible within the constraints of the paper.

(b) "The Jesus of history" as popularly used denotes the Jesus who ministered within Palestine during the late 20s and/or early 30s of the common era — "the historical Jesus," "Jesus as he actually was." New Testament scholars sometimes disparage this more popular usage and insist on a more restricted definition — "the Jesus of history," in some antithesis to "the Christ of faith/dogma," or Jesus insofar as he may be reconstructed by the tools of historical criticism. The problem with the former is that it makes too sharp a distinction between the "before and after" of Easter; it will hardly be disputed that Jesus made a considerable impact during his ministry — that is, before Good Friday and Easter. It would be unwise to predetermine what that impact could have involved in terms of "messianic ideas" or to assume that talk of either "Christ" or "faith" before Easter is inadmissible. The problem with the latter is that methodological presuppositions may impose a grid upon the text and prevent us from including within our evidence matter which is highly relevant. For the purposes of this paper I prefer to attempt a more open-ended inquiry into what "messianic ideas" we can say with some historical probability actually did influence Jesus in his ministry and in what he said about it.

Both these areas, of context and of methodology, need some fuller exposition before we proceed. To avoid overextending this study, however, I will restrict the discussion of Jewish "messianic ideas" chiefly to those sources and Jewish writings which most probably predated or were contemporary with Jesus. This is not to deny that later documents may contain earlier traditions, but the need to demonstrate the earlier form of any tradition would involve some complex analysis and disrupt the form of the overview here offered. Besides which the undisputedly pre-Jesus traditions already provide substantial material and a relatively clear perspective on the range of options which must certainly have been "available" to Jesus and his contemporaries.[1]

What "Messianic Ideas" Were in Current Use or Available as Categories of Possible Definition at the Time of Jesus?

(a) The category of "messiah" itself.

(i) Most important here is the hoped-for Davidic or royal messiah — so designated explicitly in *Psalms of Solomon* 17 (see esp. 17:32; cf. 18:57), and *Shemoneh 'Esreh* 14, and almost certainly in view in the Dead Sea Scrolls' designation of the "messiah of Israel" (1QSa 2.12, 14, 20; also 1QS 9.11; cf. CD 12.23f.; 14.19; 19.10; 20.1).[2] This more specific language is clearly part of a richer strain influenced both by other "messiah" references with eschatological overtones (1 Sam. 2:10; Pss. 2:2; 89:51; 132:17; Dan. 9:25-26) and by specific promises regarding the Davidic dynasty — David's son/God's son (2 Sam. 7:12-14; 4QFlor 1.10-13), the royal "branch" (Jer. 23:5 and 33:15; 4QPat 3-4 and 4QFlor 1.11), and the Davidic "prince" (Ezek. 34:24 and 37:25; CD 7.20, 1QSb 5.20; 1QM 5.1; 4Q161); see also Isa. 11:1-2; Hag. 2:23; Zech. 3:8, 4; 6:12; Sir. 47:11, 22; 1 Macc. 2:57. We may conclude that these passages must have nurtured a fairly vigorous and sustained hope of a royal messiah within several at least of the various subgroups of Israel at the time of Jesus, and that that hope was probably fairly widespread at a popular level (such being the symbolic power of kingship in most societies then and since).[3] Talk of an expected "coming of the Messiah" would have been meaningful to first-century Jews and represented a major strand of Jewish eschatological expectations.[4]

(ii) "Messiah" is also used of a hoped-for *priest* figure. This is explicit in the same "messiahs of Aaron and Israel" references from Qumran (1QS 9.11, etc.) and in *T. Reu.* 6:8 (ἀρχιερεὺς χριστός) — the high priest being also

---

1. For a more extensive survey, see J. H. Charlesworth, "The Concept of the Messiah in the Pseudepigrapha," *ANRW* II.19.1 (1979) 188-218.

2. L. H. Schiffman's cautions (during the colloquy) on identifying the Messiah of Israel as Davidic are methodologically commendable, but since a clear Davidic hope is entertained in the Dead Sea Scrolls [see (i) above], and since the Messiah of Israel associated with a Messiah of Aaron (1QS 9.11) would most naturally be understood as a reference to a royal messiah [see (i) above], it is hard to know how else the "Messiah of Israel" would be understood other than as a way of designating the hoped-for Davidic branch or prince.

3. See further R. A. Horsley and J. S. Hanson, *Bandits, Prophets, and Messiahs: Popular Movements in the Time of Jesus* (Minneapolis: Augsburg, 1985), ch. 3.

4. See further E. Schürer, *The History of the Jewish People in the Age of Jesus Christ,* rev. G. Vermes, et al. (Edinburgh: Clark, 1979) II, §29.

an anointed office (Lev. 4:3, 5, 16; 6:22; 2 Macc. 1:10; cf. Ps. 84:9). But it is closely modeled on the Moses-Aaron and Zerubbabel-Joshua (Zechariah 4) dual role, with *T. 12 P.* showing a similar concern to rank the priestly figure above the royal figure (particularly *T. Jud.* 21:2-5), such as is also evident in 1QSa 2.11-22. The influence of this double expectation is indicated in the possible association of the priest Eleazar with Bar Kokhba in the leadership of the second revolt.[5] We should note also here *T. Mos.* 9:1 — the expectation regarding Taxo, "a man from the tribe of Levi." A further element which should be reckoned within the total picture is the promise of a "covenant of perpetual priesthood" made to Phinehas (Num. 25:10-13), which evidently fascinated and influenced more than one branch of early Judaism (Sir. 45:23-24; 1 Macc. 2:54; pseudo-Philo, *Biblical Antiquities* 48:1), not least the Zealots.[6]

(b) When the category of "messiah" broadens out, the first to be considered is the *prophet,* not least since anointing can be associated also with prophets (1Kgs. 19:16; Isa. 61:1-2; Joel 3:1; CD 2.12; 6.1; cf. Ps. 105:15). But beyond that, the expectation becomes diverse and unclear, with various strands or fragments evident whose relation to each other is far from clear. (i) Least problematic is the anticipated return of Elijah (Mal. 4:5; Sir. 48:9-10; see also *1 En.* 90:31; Rev. 11:3); but whether this was confined to the thought of Elijah's personal return (he had never died) or included the idea of a further prophet, Elisha-like, "in the spirit and power of Elijah" (Luke 1:17; cf. 2 Kgs. 2:15) remains uncertain. (ii) The hope of a prophet like Moses (Deut. 18:15, 18) might have been expected to generate considerable expectation, but the only clear evidence of its influence in pre-Christian Judaism comes in the Qumran testimonies (4QTestim 5-8); though we should note that according to Josephus, *Ant.* 20.97, 169-70, Theudas and the Egyptian saw themselves both as "prophet" and as successor to Moses (dividing Jordan and causing city walls to fall down). (iii) For the rest there is a scattering of evidence difficult to correlate: "the prophet" (1QS 9.11 = the Moses prophet of 4QTestim? cf. John 6:14; 7:40, 52; how different from 1 Macc. 4:46 and 14:41? cf. Josephus, *War* 6:285); the anointed one of Isa. 61:1-2 (used in 1QH 18:14-15 and 11QMelch); "a prophet" (Mark 6:15; 8:28) or "one of the old prophets risen" (Luke 9:8; cf. Matt. 16:14); Samaritan expectation focused particularly on a prophet figure, but our evidence does not enable us to reach a firm conclusion on whether such a hope was already entertained at the time of Jesus.[7]

Whether these are diverse expressions of a single broad but vague

5. Schürer, *History* I, 544.
6. M. Hengel, *The Zealots* (Edinburgh: Clark, 1989) 171-77; Schürer, *History* II, 598-606.
7. Schürer, *History* II, 513.

conviction that some prophet figure was bound to be part of any eschatological climax is impossible to say. And how this variegated expectation related to the hopes of one or more messiahs (§1.2a) is also obscure — even in the one text which mentions all three together (1QS 9:11); perhaps it was simply an expression of a similarly imprecise conviction that the three main offices in Israel's salvation history (king, priest, prophet) must surely be represented in any new age. In particular there is no indication that the idea of Elijah coming as the precursor or forerunner of another (*the* Messiah?) was already current in pre-Christian Judaism outside Christian sources (particularly Mark 9:11); the relevance and point of Mal. 3:1 is unclear (the forerunner of God?);[8] and though a forerunner role could have been claimed by the Baptist (cf. John 1:23 with 1QS 8:13-14; 9:19-20; and Mark 1:3 par.), the question both of Christian editing and of whom he might have meant by "the one stronger than me" (Mark 1:7 pars.) remains open.

(c) When we turn to OT motifs and passages which seem first to have been given a messianic significance by application to Jesus, the focus of the discussion shifts. For in this case we cannot speak properly of "messianic ideas" already abroad at the time of Jesus; though since, in the event, a messianic significance has been claimed by Christianity, we should presumably allow a category of "potentially messianic ideas" which might within the constraints of the Jewish history of revelation, tradition, and hermeneutics be candidates for application to a putative messiah. Here the whole range of interest in the suffering righteous man would have to come under consideration,[9] including not the least the "suffering servant" of Second Isaiah. It is beyond doubt that Isaiah 53 in particular played an important role in earliest Christian apologetic on behalf of a crucified Messiah (Acts 8:32-33; Rom. 4:25; 1 Pet. 2:22-25, etc.); the real question for us would be whether it was Jesus himself who first drew the passage as such, or the motif in general, into play, or whether its potential as a messianic proof text only became evident in the wake of Jesus' death.

Under this heading should also be mentioned the figure of Daniel 7, "one like a son of man." The continued fecundity of this theme in New Testament scholarship is remarkable,[10] though too much of the debate is

---

8. See the brief review of the evidence in J. Jeremias, *TDNT* II, 931f.

9. See particularly G. W. E. Nickelsburg, *Resurrection, Immortality, and Eternal Life in Intertestamental Judaism* (Cambridge: Harvard, 1972).

10. For example, R. Leivestad, "Jesus — Messias — Menschensohn: Die jüdischen Heilandserwartungen zur Zeit der ersten römischen Kaiser und die Frage nach dem messianischen Selbstbewusstsein Jesu," *ANRW* II.25.1, 220-64; B. Lindars, *The Son of Man* (Grand Rapids: Eerdmans, 1983); S. Kim, *"The 'Son of Man' " as the Son of God* (WUNT 30; Tübingen: Mohr, 1983); M. Müller, *Der Ausdruck "Menschensohn" in den Evangelien* (Leiden: Brill, 1984); C. Caragounis, *The Son of Man* (WUNT 38; Tübingen: Mohr, 1986); D. R. A. Hare, *The Son of Man Tradition* (Minneapolis: Fortress, 1990).

repetitive. I continue to see no evidence for the existence of a pre-Christian/pre-Jesus Son of Man expectation within Judaism. Daniel 7 is not itself evidence of such speculation,[11] though clearly it is a "potentially messianic" passage. The Similitudes of Enoch, which do make messianic use of Daniel 7, cannot be dated to the period before Jesus' ministry with any confidence; they appear to be making a fresh interpretation of Daniel 7 (as also *4 Ezra*); and probable influence on the Synoptic tradition is confined to the later strata. The lack of any clear confessional or apologetic identification of Jesus with "the [well-known] Son of Man" would be very surprising if such a powerful image was already in use at the time of Jesus (contrast *1 En.* 71:14, Knibb).[12] Here, too, then the question is not of influence on Jesus of already recognized and established ideas or categories. The question is rather whether an innovative use of Daniel 7 can be ascribed to Jesus himself or can be traced back only as far as the first Christians in the post-Easter Palestinian conventicles. Here, too, earliest Christian thought (including Jesus?) has to be seen itself as *part* of the development and transformation in the messianic ideas of the period, and not merely as reactive to ideas already in existence.

(d) Beyond this, the category of "messianic ideas" becomes too ill-defined to be of much use. Should we include glorification of heroes like Phinehas (Ps. 106:30-31; Sir. 45:23-24; 1 Macc. 2:54; 4 Macc. 18:12), or the idea of a human translated to heaven without death (Enoch — *Jub.* 4:23; *1 En.* 12:4; *T. Abr.* 11) or after death (Ezra and Baruch — *4 Ezra* 14:9; *2 Bar.* 13:3; 25:1, etc.) or given roles in the final judgment (Enoch, Elijah, Abel — *1 En.* 90:31; *T. Abr.* 11; Melchizedek[?] — 11QMelch)? Should we include heavenly intermediaries — angels (e.g., Dan. 10:13; Tob. 12:15; *1 En.* 9:1-3; *T. Levi* 3:5; 1QH 6.13) or the vigorous poetic imagery used of divine wisdom (e.g., Prov. 8:30; Wis. 9:4; Sir. 24:5)?[13] For myself I think not. The full spectrum of eschatological expectation within Judaism, so far as we know it, should be borne in mind, including the visions in which no recognized or potential messianic figure appears. For any or all of it could have influenced Jesus and have interacted in his teaching and ministry with more specifically "messianic ideas" to evolve a new formulation or idea. But in that case we

11. At this point I should register my cordial disagreement with colloquy colleagues M. Black and A. Yarbro Collins: I do not see the manlike figure of Dan. 7:13-14 as an "angelic representative" of Israel, but as a symbolical representation of Israel, in which the creation myth is reworked (Dan. 7:2ff.) by depicting Israel's enemies as the beasts (beastlike figures) over which humankind (the manlike figure, Israel) is given dominion.

12. See further my *Christology in the Making* (London: SCM, 1980) 67-82. My point is unaffected even if there is an emerging consensus on a pre-70 date for the Similitudes (Charlesworth), since the other evidence just indicated would still point to a post-Jesus, post-earliest Christian date for the document or its ideas coming to public attention.

13. See further chapter 20 below and my *The Partings of the Ways between Christianity and Judaism* (London: SCM; Philadelphia: TPI, 1991), ch. 10.

are talking of the eschatological or apocalyptic context of the messianic ideas more than the ideas themselves. In view of the limitations of this paper, therefore, I do not propose to go into any detail on this broader area of interest.

Methodology and Perspective

A final word of introduction must be said about the perspective from which I approach the Jesus tradition of the Synoptics, where the debate must obviously focus most intensively. Such a declaration is necessary since it is very clear from the study of the Synoptic tradition during the past sixty years that the critical tools do not of themselves provide clear verdicts on most debated passages. Agreed criteria for determining redaction simply do not exist beyond a few general principles — and when it becomes a question of distinguishing multiple layers of tradition, the argument becomes increasingly circular and the subjectivity factor unacceptably high. Probability judgment in most individual cases therefore depends on a broad presuppositional perspective bolstered by a few key examples.[14]

In my own work, not specializing on the Synoptics so thoroughly as many of my colleagues, I have become increasingly persuaded that the best *starting* point for study of the main body of the Synoptic tradition is to view it as the earliest churches' memories of Jesus as retold and reused by these churches. The importance of teachers and of tradition is well attested in the earliest documents of the New Testament (e.g., teachers — Acts 13:1; 1 Cor. 12:28; Gal. 6:6; tradition — 1 Cor. 11:2; Col. 2:6; 1 Thess. 4:1; 2 Thess. 2:15; 3:6). The Synoptics themselves conform surprisingly closely to the ancient (not modern) biography *(bios* or *vita);*[15] and the *a priori* probability that the earliest groups cherished and rehearsed the memories of the one whom they now counted as Lord *(mar,* κύριος), that is, the traditions which gave them reason for their distinctive existence, must be regarded as strong. This perspective differs significantly from the characteristically *literary* model which has exercised far too much influence on tradition-history analysis of the Synoptic tradition. The literary model envisages strata of tradition, and the task as tracing the linear descent of a tradition down through successively elaborated layers, each one dependent on the previous exemplar — much as one does in textual criticism or in tracing the history of translations of the Bible. But in *oral* transmission that model is inappropriate, for in oral tradition we have to do with themes and formulae and core material which often remains

14. E. P. Sanders, *Jesus and Judaism* (Philadelphia: Fortress, 1985), despite his trenchant criticism of his predecessors, provides a classic example.

15. D. Aune, *The New Testament in Its Literary Environment* (Philadelphia: Westminster, 1987), ch. 2.

constant while quite a wide range of variations are played on them. The point is that one variation need not necessarily lead to another; subsequent variations may be derived directly from the central theme or core. Consequently tradition history analysis seeking to penetrate back to Jesus himself need not consist solely of pressing back through different variations but can focus immediately on the more constant material. For the probability is that the more constant material is the living heart of the earliest recollections of Jesus which has maintained the vitality of the tradition in all its variant forms.

In short I see the earliest tradents within the Christian churches as preservers more than innovators, as seeking to transmit, retell, explain, inter-pret, elaborate, but not to create *de nova*. All of which means that I approach the Synoptic tradition with a good deal more confidence than many of my New Testament colleagues. Through the main body of the Synoptic tradition, I believe, we have in most cases direct access to the teaching and ministry of Jesus as it was remembered from the beginning of the transmission process (which often predates Easter), and so also fairly direct access to the ministry and teaching of Jesus through the eyes and ears of those who went about with him.

So much by way of introduction. What then of the issue itself: what messianic ideas influenced Jesus and how?

Jesus within a Context of Eschatological Expectation

We can start by noting the likelihood that Jesus would have been aware of such messianic ideas as were current at the time. The strong eschatological note which is an undeniable feature of his preaching is of a piece with the broader stream of eschatological and apocalyptic expectation which served as the seed bed within which messianic ideas flourished during the various crises of Israel's history in the two centuries prior to Jesus' ministry. No one, I think, would dispute either that Jesus' proclamation of the kingdom of God was central to his preaching, or that his remembered utterances on the subject are essentially eschatological in character. We need not even go into the still contested question of whether he saw the kingdom as a future good ("the restoration of Israel")[16] or present reality, or both, though I would have to contest any attempt to argue that Jesus saw it as a timeless symbol (and therefore, properly speaking, noneschatological).

Given this eschatological context and emphasis, it would be utterly astonishing if Jesus had not come into some sort of interaction with the

---

16. Sanders, *Jesus,* part one; Dunn, *Partings,* 47-49.

messianic ideas which thrived in that same context. Without making any prejudgment on the question of whether Jesus saw a role for himself with regard to the kingdom, it nevertheless remains highly likely that one who proclaimed the kingdom of God in the way Jesus did would be faced with the issue of how his eschatological ideas related to the other (messianic) ideas cherished by others.

Moreover we must accept that Jesus made a substantial stir, even if only for a short time, and that he gained a fair amount of publicity and/or notoriety, however local or regional — he was, after all, condemned to death for causing some sort of trouble. In such circumstances his fellow Jews (or Galileans) were bound to attempt to categorize him, to fit him into an appropriate slot in their perspective. And the available categories would have included the ones reviewed above: was he one of the looked-for anointed figures? was he a/the prophet? In other words, the tradition of popular speculation and questioning which we find in Mark 6:15; 8:28; and John 1:19-22 is just what we might have expected.

But can we be more specific? More important, can we say whether Jesus reacted to these suggestions and questions? And if so, *how* he reacted? Only thus will we be able to speak of any influence of such messianic ideas on him. We naturally start with the messianic idea most narrowly defined as such in the above review — Jesus as messiah.

Are You Messiah? A Question Jesus Must Have Faced

We can dismiss at once the second of the two messiah figures described above — the *priest* messiah. There is no indication whatsoever that this was ever canvassed as a possibility or seen as an option in the case of Jesus. Presumably Jesus was known to lack the basic qualification of belonging to the tribe of Levi, and so it was a nonstarter even for (or particularly for) those who would have regarded the priestly messiah as more significant than the royal messiah. Significantly when the attempt is subsequently made to present Jesus as high priest, it is done by using the quite different and extraordinary order of Melchizedek rather than that of Aaron (Heb. 5:7).

The picture is quite different, however, in the case of the *royal* messiah. The fundamental fact here is that Jesus was put to death as a claimant to such a role — executed as a messianic pretender for claiming to be king of the Jews (so all four Gospels — Mark 15:26 par.). Since "king of the Jews" is not a Christian title and probably caused the Christians some political embarrassment, there is a general agreement that this much at least must be historical of the passion narratives. But once that is granted, along with the fact of Jesus' crucifixion as a royal messianic pretender, a sentence carried out as a formal legal act on the authority of the Roman governor (cf. Tacitus, *Annales* 15.44.3),[17] we have established the core of the hearing before Pilate described in Mark 15:1-4. And when we press further backward to the issue of some sort of preliminary Jewish hearing, we find ourselves with an equally plausible historical core — where an accusation that Jesus said something about the destruction and rebuilding of the temple results in the question, "Are you Messiah, son of the Blessed?" (Mark 14:57-61). For it was precisely this association of ideas which the messianic prophecy (4QFlor 1.10-13) of 2 Sam. 7:13-14 would suggest — the son of David (royal messiah) who would build the temple and who would be God's son.[18] In short, the evidence is strong that at the end of his life Jesus was confronted with the question, certainly implicitly but probably also explicitly as well: Are you Messiah, son of David?

It is also unlikely that this was the first or only time in the course of Jesus' ministry that this question was put to him or the issue confronted him. Assuming that Jesus did say something about the future of the temple, on which the later accusation was based (Mark 14:58 par.; cf. esp. Mark 13:2; John 2:19; Acts 6:14), and that Jesus engaged in some sort of symbolic act in the temple (Mark 11:15-17 pars.),[19] the same correlation (Messiah = temple builder) probably occurred to him and to others (hence the subsequent accusation). Given too the excitement he engendered as a successful healer, it would be of no surprise that one such as Bartimaeus should seek to attract his attention or ingratiate himself with Jesus by hailing him as "son of David" (Mark 10:47-48 par.).[20]

The confession of Peter at Caesarea Philippi is a much contested pericope (Mark 8:27ff. par.) whose detail we can hardly enter into here. Suffice it to say its basic content carries with it a strong degree of probability: Jesus had engaged for some time in what had evidently been overall a highly successful and popular teaching and healing ministry. It would have been odd indeed if none of those who had invested their lives in following him had not asked themselves whether Jesus might be the hoped-for leader from the house of David and in due course expressed the belief or hope to Jesus himself.

To mention only one other episode. If we allow that behind the "feeding of the five thousand" (Mark 6:30ff. par.) lies the memory of some symbolic meal in the desert, such a meal would probably have evoked a very potent

---

17. See further particularly A. E. Harvey, *Jesus and the Constraints of History* (London: Duckworth, 1982), ch. 2.

18. O. Betz, *What Do We Know about Jesus?* (London: SCM, 1968) 88-89.

19. See particularly Sanders, *Jesus,* ch. 1.

20. The argument here is not dependent on an early date for the *Testament of Solomon* or for the traditions behind it; David was already regarded as a healer (ἰατρός) and exorcist in the case of Saul, as Josephus, *Ant.* 6.166-68, indicates.

mix of messianic ideas — Moses and manna, the shepherd king feeding his flock (Ezek. 34:23), perhaps the same association of eschatological banquets presided over by the messiah(s) which we find in 1QSa. It is not surprising then that John's Gospel contains the testimony that the crowd wanted to make Jesus king by force (John 6:15), which meshes well in an uncontrived way with the unexpected note in Mark's Gospel that Jesus brought the occasion to an end by *forcing* the disciples to leave by boat, *before* he dismissed the crowd. There is a strong suggestion here of a crowd caught up on a wave of messianic enthusiasm which affected also the immediate circle of Jesus' disciples. Here too, in other words, Jesus was probably confronted in effect with the same stark question, "Are you Messiah, son of David?"

This brief review of the most directly relevant evidence must suffice. In my judgment it presents us with the very strong probability that Jesus was confronted with the category of royal messiahship and was forced, whether he liked it or not, to respond to it. The more important question for us is: how did he respond? What sort of influence did the prevailing or dominant expectation regarding the royal messiah have on him?

The answer which emerges is consistent and striking. He reacted more negatively than positively to it. As a possible role model he was more hostile than welcoming to the idea of the royal messiah. The evidence can be reviewed briefly.

A basic fact is that nowhere in the Synoptic tradition is Jesus remembered as having laid claim to the title or role of messiah on his own initiative (only John 4:26). Since the earliest Christians certainly wanted to claim the title for him, the silence of the Synoptic tradition is striking: it confirms an unwillingness to retroject material beyond what Jesus was remembered as teaching back into the Jesus tradition; and since the claim to such a role was certainly a possibility for Jesus (as in principle for many first-century Jews), the fact that no such claim is remembered suggests at least an unwillingness on the part of Jesus to associate his mission with that particular role.

This inference gains strength from some of the episodes touched on above. The "feeding of the five thousand" pericope has two points of interest. First, it confirms that there was abroad, in Galilee at least, a popular conception of the messiah as a kingly, political figure — the sort of king of the Jews, we might say, that Pilate felt justified in crucifying. Second, it indicates that Jesus reacted against this role and rejected it. The lesson learned there about the inflammability of the Galilean crowd would certainly help explain Jesus' reticence in other situations.

In the Caesarea Philippi episode the earlier account of Mark shows Jesus as neither welcoming nor denying the confession of Peter (though Matthew understandably develops the tradition to give Jesus' response a warmer note — Matt. 16:17-19). The command to silence of Mark 8:30, so often taken as part of a theological motif later imposed on the tradition,[21] makes very good sense if the category "messiah" used by Peter was the same as that cherished in the *Psalms of Solomon* and among the Galileans. Since that indeed *was* what Messiah, son of David meant, the only content of the category "royal messiah" as then understood, we may assume that in any such historical confrontation this *would* have been the prospect offered to Jesus. The ambivalence of his immediate response thus becomes indicative of a certain unwillingness on the part of Jesus to entertain such a political role. And if the immediately appended teaching on the prospect of his suffering and rejection (Mark 8:31-33) belongs to the same sequence as remembered by those involved, as is certainly arguable, then we would have to begin speaking of an attempt by Jesus to redefine the category of messiahship.

Finally with the hearing and trial of Jesus the interest again focuses on Jesus' reply in each case. To the high priest's question Jesus is shown as answering "I am" (Mark 14:62). But the more weakly attested longer reading has a strong claim to originality — "You say that I am."[22] In which case it matches more closely the reply to the equivalent question by Pilate, "Are you the king of the Jews?" To which Jesus is said to have responded σὺ λέγεις (Mark 15:2). In each case, therefore, the answer probably was ambivalent — "You could say so"; "that is your way of putting it." In other words, we can see here a further indication of an unwillingness on the part of Jesus to accept the title of royal messiah, at least as understood by his questioners. For our inquiry the exchanges are important since they exemplify the dilemma which constantly must have confronted Jesus: could he accept or use categories which, however desirable in themselves, were usually understood to describe a role he did not or could not see himself as fulfilling?

In short, if the question is "Did the hope of a royal messiah influence Jesus in shaping and executing his mission?" the evidence points to a fairly negative answer. Jesus seems to have reacted against rather than to have been influenced by the idea of a royal messiah as then conceived. The only qualification we would have to add is that this title "messiah" was too potent and resonant with theological significance for it to be rejected outright. And Jesus may have attempted to redefine the content of the title in terms of the role he saw himself as filling. The first Christians were certainly in no doubt that

---

21. I refer of course to "the Messianic secret"; see ch. 4 above, on which this section of the discussion is based.

22. The longer reading explains the Matthean and Lukan versions better than the shorter:

Mark   σὺ εἶπας   ὅτι ἐγώ εἰμι
Matthew   σὺ εἶπας
Luke   ὑμεῖς λέγετε   ὅτι ἐγώ εἰμι.

And it is more likely that the equivocal longer text was abbreviated to the strong affirmation (ἐγώ εἰμι) rather than the reverse.

Jesus was Messiah and that the title had to be understood in the light of what had actually happened to Jesus ("Christ crucified"). But the extent to which we can say that the process of redefinition began already with Jesus himself depends on our evaluation of other material within the Jesus tradition which at the time of Jesus would not have been regarded as "messianic" in the stricter sense.

The Eschatological Prophet

In terms of messianic categories properly so called at the time of Jesus, the only other category of significance is that of *prophet*. Of all the categories available, it seems to have been the one which was used most often. It was evidently applied to the Baptist (Mark 11:32; Matt. 11:9; Luke 7:26); it was the category canvassed most frequently for Jesus, according to Mark 6:15 and 8:28 (cf. 14:65; note also particularly Matt. 21:11, 46 and Luke 24:19); and there seems to have been no lack of claimants to the role of prophet during that whole period (Josephus, *Ant.* 18.85-87; 20.97-98, 167-72, 188). Given the relative prominence of Jesus as preacher and healer, it is wholly to be expected that he would have been regarded by many as at least *a* prophet.

Jesus himself is remembered as accepting the designation for himself in at least some degree (see particularly Mark 6:4 par. and Luke 13:33). But more important is the evidence that he, like the Qumran sect, made use of Isa. 61:1-2 as providing a program for his mission. The primary evidence is not Luke 4:18-19, which looks too much like an elaboration of the briefer account of Jesus' preaching in the synagogue at Nazareth as recalled by Mark. It is rather the emphasis which comes out both from the first beatitude (Luke 5:20/Matt. 5:3) and from Jesus' response to the question of the Baptist in prison (Matt. 11:5/Luke 7:22) — viz. that Jesus saw one of his priorities as proclamation of the good news to "the poor."[23] If this recalls one of Jesus' own repeated assertions, as seems likely, then the implication is strong that he drew on Isa. 61:1-2 to inform his own mission. This also makes best sense of the Lukan account of Jesus' preaching in Nazareth, for Luke 4:16-30 is then best seen not as a complete fabrication by Luke but as the sort of midrashic elaboration of a basic claim made by Jesus which we would expect in the course of oral retelling of the memories regarding Jesus, with Luke of course setting it at the beginning of his account of Jesus' ministry to give it programmatic significance for his own retelling of the Jesus story.

---

23. The passages are discussed in more detail in my *Jesus and the Spirit* (London: SCM/Philadelphia: Westminster, 1975) 55-60.

Relevant here too is the fact that Jesus is remembered as having spoken on more than one occasion of his sense of commission in prophetic terms — as one "sent" by God (Matt. 10:40/Luke 10:16; Mark 9:37 par.; Matt. 15:24; Luke 4:43).[24] Also that Jesus evidently undertook what might be called a self-consciously prophetic role — both in terms of his championing "the poor" and in terms of such prophetically symbolical actions like the entry into Jerusalem, the clearing of the temple, perhaps the meal in the desert, and certainly the Last Supper.

All this is significant, for so far as the Evangelists were concerned, the category of prophet was not particularly helpful and certainly not of sufficient weight to embody the significance of Jesus. Part of the point of the Caesarea Philippi episode in all the Synoptics is that prophet categories canvassed by the crowds are less satisfactory (even that of Elijah) than the title ascribed by Peter — "You are the Messiah" (Mark 8:28-29 par.). The point of Matt. 12:41 (and Luke 11:32) is that something *greater* than Jonah is present among them. According to Luke 16:16, the time of the law and the prophets has been left behind by the new era in which the kingdom of God is preached. And most striking of all, the category of prophet, even *the* prophet, has been completely relegated by the Fourth Evangelist to the status of one of the less than satisfactory opinions of the fickle crowd (particularly John 4:19; 6:14; 7:40; 8:52-53; 9:17). The implication is plain: it is unlikely that the category of prophet was first applied to Jesus after Easter. In the wake of Easter even the category of eschatological prophet would have been regarded as inadequate to express his status and its significance. From this it follows that the attribution of a prophetic role to Jesus and the use made of Isa. 61:1-2 in describing his mission is likely to go back to the pre-Easter period; also that Jesus himself probably accepted the category of "prophet" as a more adequate description of his role (than messiah) and took Isa. 61:1-2 as at least to some extent programmatic for his ministry.

To sum up: Of the range of options within the more diverse expectation of a prophetic figure, the prophet like Moses has left least trace in the Synoptic Gospel accounts (Mark 9:7 par.; John 12:47-48; cf. Acts 3:22; 7:37). And though others may have proposed the category of Elijah for Jesus (Mark 6:15; 8:28), Jesus himself is remembered as referring that designation to the Baptist (Matt. 11:10/Luke 7:27; Mark 9:13). It is only of the less specific categories of prophet and eschatological prophet that we can speak with some confidence. But there it does seem possible to speak of an influence and a positive influence on Jesus of the Jewish expectation that a prophet figure would be involved in the last days.

24. For the prophetic significance of the claim cf., e.g., Ps. 105:26; Jer. 1:7; Mic. 6:4; Luke 4:26; 20:13.

The Suffering Righteous Man

Of those reviewed in the first section, the only other category which calls for consideration is that of potential messianic ideas, in particular the suffering righteous man. The prominence of the motif in the Psalms and the Wisdom of Solomon and the variations on it in Daniel 7 and the martyr theology of the Maccabean literature are sufficient to indicate the strong probability that wherever those of faith found themselves in a situation of oppression, the theme of the suffering righteous man would be one which proved fruitful for consolation and encouragement. Under the Roman occupation it must be judged likely therefore that this strand of theologizing was still being actively pursued in Jewish circles and was available to Jesus, or at least near to hand for Jesus to use if he so chose.

That he did so choose is strongly attested in the Synoptic tradition. Unfortunately this testimony has become for the most part inextricably bound up with the much more specific issues of whether Jesus was influenced in his own self-understanding by the suffering servant passage in Isaiah 53 and the vision of the manlike figure in Daniel 7. I say unfortunately, because the more contentious features of these more specific debates have tended to obscure the fact that both Isaiah 53 and Daniel 7 are quite properly to be seen as particular expressions and outworkings of the broader and more pervasive reflection in Jewish thought of the sufferings of the righteous.[25] It may very well be the case therefore that what we should be looking for in the Jesus tradition are indications of whether Jesus was influenced by that broader stream of Jewish theologizing; and, moreover, we should bear in mind the possibility that any use made of Isaiah 53 and Daniel 7 in particular in the Synoptic tradition is a Christian elaboration of a less specific strand within the earliest memories of Jesus' teaching. Alternatively, of course, the possibility equally should be borne in mind that it was Jesus himself who saw the value and importance of these particular crystallizations of the broader movement of thought and saw their appropriateness to his own mission.

The debate on these issues is much too complex to allow a satisfactory treatment here. I must confine myself to three observations. First, it must be judged highly likely that Jesus anticipated suffering and rejection for his message and himself — that is, that Jesus saw himself in the tradition of the suffering righteous. The expectation is clearly attested, apart from any influence of Isaiah 53 and Daniel 7, in Mark 10:38-39 par. and 14:36 par.; the facts that the prophecy of John suffering the same martyrdom was apparently not fulfilled and that the anguish of Jesus in the garden is depicted in most unmartyrlike terms (contrast Mark 14:33 with 2 Macc. 7:14) strongly suggest

---

25. See above, n. 9.

that these formulations are based on firsthand memory of what Jesus himself said. Moreover, as one who saw himself in the prophet tradition, Jesus must have anticipated the possibility of rejection, as a firm strand of tradition confirms (Mark 6:4 par.; 12:1-9 par.; Matt. 23:29-36/Luke 20:47-51; Luke 13:33; Matt. 23:37/Luke 13:34); the fate of the Baptist provided precedent and warning enough; and the opposition which Jesus roused must have confirmed the strong likelihood that he would meet a similar fate. Moreover, if Jesus did see the full consummation of the kingdom of God as imminent (Mark 1:15 par.; 9:1 par.; 13:29-30 par.; Matt. 10:7/Luke 10:9,11; Matt. 10:23), he would probably be aware of the apocalyptic expectation of a period of extreme tribulation prior to the final climax (Dan. 12:1-2; Matt. 3:7-12/Luke 3:7-9; 16-17)[26] and indeed probably shared it (cf. Mark 13:5-8, 17-20 par. with Matt. 5:11-12/Luke 6:22-23; Matt. 6:13/Luke 11:4; Mark 10:39 par., etc.). That he himself would be caught up in that extreme suffering must have been recognized as at least a real possibility. And when we add in the other strands just referred to, the probability begins to become rather strong that Jesus anticipated his own death and indeed saw it in positive terms as somehow redemptive — as an eschatologically (or messianically) intensified expression of the martyr theology which comes to expression elsewhere in 2 Macc. 7:38 and 4 Macc. 17:22. Certainly it must be judged improbable that Jesus saw his likely death as a complete defeat (otherwise he could have stayed out of harm's way), and probable that he would see it as bound up with the coming of the kingdom. The famous passage of Schweitzer, its rhetorical flourish notwithstanding, looks more and more like a justifiable restatement of Jesus' own hope and expectation — "Jesus' purpose is to set in motion the eschatological development of history, to let loose the final woes, the confusion and strife, from which shall issue the parousia and so to introduce the supra-mundane phase of the eschatological drama."[27]

All this strengthens the likelihood that behind the passages influenced more explicitly by Isaiah 53 and Daniel 7 stand utterances of Jesus himself, remembered either as expressing his expectation of suffering by himself drawing in these passages, or as expressing an expectation of rejection which was illuminated and readily elaborated by the first Christians, who themselves drew in these passages. In fact it is difficult to demonstrate use of Isaiah 53 at the earliest level of the Synoptic tradition: Luke 22:37, although found in an obviously ancient context, does look as though it has been inserted into preexisting material; Mark 10:45 is as likely to have been influenced by Daniel

---

26. Sanders notes that the "dogma" that suffering *must* precede the coming of the kingdom is difficult to document before 135 C.E. (*Jesus*, p. 124). But the idea flows directly from Daniel 7 and 12:1-2 and is already implicit in such passages as *Jub.* 23:22-31; *T. Mos.* 5-10; 1QH 3.28-36; and *Sib. Or.* 3.632-56.

27. A. Schweitzer, *The Quest of the Historical Jesus* (London: Black, 1910) 369.

7 as by Isaiah 53; and the earliest form of the cup word in the Last Supper is disputed (Mark 14:24 par.; 1 Cor. 11:25). And it is certainly arguable that behind the three Son of Man passion predictions (Mark 8:31 par.; 9:31 par; 10:33-34 par.) lie בר אנשא sayings which of themselves contained no specific reference to Dan. 7:13;[28] in which case they would quite likely have used the Jewish recognition of human frailty (as in Ps. 8:4) as the means of expressing expectation of the brevity of life and the expectation of it being soon cut off.[29] But even if our critical tools and methods do not permit firm conclusions that Jesus himself made use of (and therefore was influenced by) Isaiah 53 and Daniel 7, the probability remains strong that Jesus entertained an expectation of rejection, suffering, and death, which was of a piece in his own perspective with the suffering of the righteous man and the final eschatological tribulation and which would play a positive role therein.

Conclusion

It would seem then that we can speak of the influence of messianic ideas on Jesus in several ways. (1) Some ideas he reacted *against*. In particular, the current view of the royal messiah was one which he did not find helpful as a means of understanding or informing his mission. (2) Some he drew on and used to inform his own vision of what he had been called to. This may not be the same as saying that he applied clearly defined *roles*, let alone clearly defined *titles*, to himself. It would be more accurate to say that particular elements within a much more variegated spread of messianic ideas were taken up by him. Isa. 61:1-2 is a good case in point. (3) Even those he did respond to favorably and found inspirational or informative for his own mission he adapted and molded by his own conception of his mission. This would apply in greater or lesser degree to all the categories and motifs discussed above.

In every case, in fact, we have to avoid any impression of a fixed category which Jesus filled (or fulfilled), of a sequence of clearcut "messianic ideas" which provided the agenda for Jesus' mission. It would appear that Jesus was as much shaping the messianic ideas of the time as being shaped by them. Certainly that has to be said of the totality of the Christ-event as reflected on in earliest Christian theology; but it would be surprising if Jesus himself had not begun the process of redefining the categories either by deliberate teaching or simply by the very shape of his ministry and its un-

---

28. See P. M. Casey, *The Son of Man: The Interpretation and Influence of Daniel 7* (London: SPCK, 1980) 232-33; Lindars, *Son of Man*, ch. 4.

29. See esp. J. Bowker, "The Son of Man," *JTS* 28 (1977) 19-48.

doubted significance for many. In other words, Jesus is in no sense a tailor's dummy draped convincingly or otherwise in the robes of Jewish messianic hope. Rather he himself must be seen as part of the stream of Jewish messianic reflection and one of the most important currents within that stream during the first half of the first century C.E., broadening the stream and quite soon becoming the occasion of it splitting into two different channels.

A final point worth pondering is that the brief review of the Jesus tradition just completed has by no means encompassed the full sweep of that tradition. We have had insufficient occasion to comment on other aspects of the Jesus tradition which certainly have christological if not messianic significance. I think of the question of the unusually high degree of authority Jesus evidently claimed — as a spokesman for God who could pronounce authoritatively on the eschatological meaning of the Torah without having undergone proper training. Or of the significance of his sense of intimate sonship evidenced in his "Abba" praying to God — a lived-out "claim" to divine sonship which seems surprisingly independent of any messianic son of God claim (2 Sam. 7:14). The point is that if we are to have any hope of seeing Jesus adequately we cannot confine the discussion to the question of the influence of messianic ideas on him. That there was some such influence can be strongly affirmed, but the impact of Jesus and his own part in redefining several of these ideas have other roots as well.

6

Jesus, Table-Fellowship, and Qumran

There can be no question about the importance of the meal table as a focus of religous and social significance in the ancient Near East. J. Jeremias expresses the point well:

> to invite a man to a meal was an honour. It was an offer of peace, trust, brotherhood and forgiveness; in short, sharing a table meant sharing life. . . .[1] In Judaism in particular, table-fellowship means fellowship before God, for the eating of a piece of broken bread by everyone who shares in the meal brings out the fact that they all have a share in the blessing which the master of the house had spoken over the unbroken bread.[2]

This, what we might call the sacredness of the meal table, is often lost sight of in a Christianity where the link between sacrament and meal has been long broken and the heightened sacredness of the sacrament has resulted in a diminished religious significance for the ordinary meal. Nor is it sufficient to

---

1. The story is told of Lawrence of Arabia, who on one occasion was fleeing for his life across the desert from the Turks. As he fled he encountered a Bedouin family who had just made camp at an oasis. Invited to partake of their meal, Lawrence had scarcely dipped his hand in the communal dish when he revealed to them his plight. Without more ado his hosts struck camp and took Lawrence with them. He had eaten with them. They were one with him. Regrettably I have been unable to track down the source of this story.

2. J. Jeremias, *New Testament Theology* I: *The Proclamation of Jesus* (London, 1971) 115. He cites appropriately 2 Kgs. 25:27-30 (par. Jer. 52:31-34) and Josephus, *Ant.* 19.321. See also O. Hofius, *Jesu Tischgemeinschaft mit den Sündern* (Stuttgart, 1967) 9-13; I. H. Marshall, *Last Supper and Lord's Supper* (Exeter, 1980) 18-20; X. Léon-Dufour, *Sharing the Eucharistic Bread* (Mahwah, 1987) 35-38.

---

focus that significance in food taboos and dietary laws, much though a social anthropological perspective sharpens our awareness of dimensions we might otherwise have missed or disparaged.[3] It is much more, as Jeremias noted, that in the sharing of everyday food which is blessed before God human relationships can become an expression of the more fundamental divine-human relationship. The ideal had long since been characterized in the Greek legend of Philemon and Baucis (Ovid, *Metamorphoses* 8.613-70) and in Judaism particularly in the story of Abraham's entertaining the three heavenly visitors in Genesis 18 (Philo, *Abr.* 107-14; Josephus, *Ant.* 1.196; Heb. 13:2; *1 Clement* 10:7).[4] It is against this background that any discussion of Jesus' practice of table-fellowship has to be set.

Jesus and Table-Fellowship

The significance of table-fellowship in the ministry of Jesus has also been recognized in recent years. It is obvious from the Gospel traditions that much of Jesus' ministry took place in the context of the meal table. He is remembered as one who often was a guest at another's table (Mark 2:15-16 pars.; 14:3 par.; Luke 7:36; 10:39; 11:37; 14:1; 19:5-7), and he seems to have acted as host on a number of occasions (Luke 15:2; Mark 14:22-23 pars.; cf. Mark 6:41 pars.; Luke 24:30-31).[5] Evidently guest friendship as expressed in the shared meal was so much a feature of Jesus' ministry that it was regarded as something notorious. Fasting was typical of other religious groups, but not of the group around Jesus (Mark 2:18-19 pars.). In contrast to John the Baptist's asceticism, Jesus' enjoyment of the table was almost proverbial: "Behold, a glutton and a drunkard" (Matt. 11:19//Luke 7:34). The accounts of the meal(s) in the desert (Mark 6:30-44 pars.; Mark 8:1-10 par.)[6] and of the Last Supper (Mark 14:17-25 pars.) are best seen against this background. Against the same background Mark's repeated note that at times the demands on Jesus were so intense that he had no time even to eat (Mark 3:20; 6:31) gains an added

3. The work of M. Douglas has been particularly important here: *Purity and Danger: An Analysis of the Concepts of Pollution and Taboo* (London, 1966).

4. Also Job (Job 31:32; *T. Job* 10:1-3; 25:5; 53:3). See further G. Stählin, *TDNT* V, 17-20; SB I, 588-89; IV, 565-71.

5. If Mark 2:15-17 was formed independently before being incorporated into the sequence of controversy stories, the house would be most naturally understood as Jesus' own house (as also 2:1); see, e.g., V. Taylor, *The Gospel According to St. Mark* (New York, 1966) 204; J. Jeremias, *The Parables of Jesus* (London, 1963) 277, n. 92; Hofius, *Tischgemeinschaft*, 29, n. 42.

6. Even if the two accounts are doublets (see, e.g., J. Gnilka, *Das Evangelium nach Markus I [Mk 1–8.26]* [Neukirchen, 1978] 25-26), the fact that the tradition had so developed and diverged indicates that it was a story much retold.

poignancy, as do the Lukan accounts of renewed table-fellowship after Jesus' resurrection (Luke 24:30; Acts 1:4). According to Luke, Jesus also commended the model of itinerancy dependent on table hospitality to his disciples (Luke 10:7-8). Although Luke has chosen to highlight this feature of Jesus' ministry, the motif is sufficiently well rooted in the Synoptic tradition as a whole. The probability is that much of Jesus' remembered teaching began as "table talk" (Mark 2:17; 14:6-9; Luke 7:36-50; 10:39; 11:39-41; 14:1-24; cf. Mark 6:34).

The meal was also a feature of Jesus' *teaching,* particularly the wedding banquet with all its eschatological overtones of God's final acceptance (Mark 2:19 pars.; Matt. 22:1-14; 25:10; Luke 14:16-24; 22:30).[7] Hence, the power of the parable of the prodigal son: the welcome back to the table of celebration marks the son's acceptance as "son," the transition from death back to life again (Luke 15:23-24, 32). Hence too the seriousness of the warning in Luke 13:26-27 — to have participated in table-fellowship with Jesus is no guarantee of final salvation — and the significance of Matt. 8:11-12//Luke 13:28-29 (also Luke 12:35-37). Not least in importance is the fact that Jesus saw it as desirable that contemporary practice of table-fellowship should be determined by (and thus foreshadow) the eschatalogical banquet in character (Luke 14:13, 21).

Particularly noticeable is the extent to which Jesus' practice of table-fellowship is remembered in the Synoptic tradition as a focus of controversy. The fact that he ate with tax collectors and sinners was evidently a cause of offense (Mark 2:16 pars.; Matt. 11:19//Luke 7:34; Luke 15:2; 19:7). The Markan and Matthean traditions also record that the table practice of his group called forth critical comment by its failure to observe purity ritual (Mark 7:1-5; Matt. 15:1-2, 20). It will be no accident then that both evangelists immediately present the story of the Syrophoenician woman; it too turns very neatly on the limits and significance of table etiquette as expressing much more profound issues of mutual acceptance and of human acceptability to God (Mark 7:24-30//Matt. 15:21-28). Gentile inferiority ("dogs") to the privileged covenant relationship of Israel is characterized precisely by their unacceptability at the meal table of the chosen ("children"; cf. again Matt. 8:11-12//Luke 13:28-29).[8]

The picture provided by the Synoptics of this dimension of Jesus' ministry is therefore clear and is consistent across all four strands of the Synoptic tradition (Mark, Q, M, L).[9] If we were to summarize the evidence documented

---

7. No doubt in echo of such scriptural passages as Isa. 25:6; 54:4-8; 62:4-5; and Hos. 2:16-20. See also M. Trautmann, *Zeichenhafte Handlungen Jesu. Ein Beitrag zur Frage nach dem geschichtlichen Jesu* (Würzburg, 1980) 161-62, and those cited there.

8. See, e.g., Taylor, *Mark,* 350; Gnilka, *Markus,* 292-93.

9. M = material peculiar to Matthew. L = material peculiar to Luke. I do not envisage M and L as written sources.

above it would be in terms of the coherence between Jesus' teaching and his own lifestyle. Jesus evidently saw the fellowship of the meal table as an expression of life under the rule of God (particularly Matt. 22:2; 25:1); in his own social relationships he sought to live in accordance with his vision of the kingdom (cf. particularly Luke 6:20 with 14:13, 21). It was this lived-out vision of acceptability before God as expressed in table-fellowship which, according to the Synoptics, was one of the major causes of complaint against Jesus among some of his contemporaries.[10]

We should also note that the Synoptic tradition is inconsistent in attributing such criticism to some Pharisees in particular (but certainly not all Pharisees). The picture just sketched does not actually depend on such specific identification, but though many of the references to Pharisees in the Synoptic tradition are clearly redactional,[11] on this point the testimony is unanimous (Mark 2:16 pars.; 7:1). In filling out the context of Jesus' table-fellowship, therefore, we must look more closely at what lies behind this element in the tradition.

A Focus of Controversy with Pharisees

The Synoptic picture of Jesus' table-fellowship as something that drew fire from Pharisees has been brought into sharper focus in recent years by the work of J. Neusner. As is now well known, Neusner's study of rabbinic traditions specifically attributed to the period before 70 C.E. has produced a striking conclusion:

> Of the 341 individual Houses' legal pericopae, no fewer than 229, approximately 67 percent of the whole, directly or indirectly concern table-fellowship. . . . The Houses' laws of ritual cleanness apply in the main to the ritual cleanness of food, and of people, dishes, and implements involved in its preparation. Pharisaic laws regarding Sabbath and festivals, moreover, involve in large measure the preparation and preservation of food.[12]

10. Others who emphasize the importance of table-fellowship in Jesus' ministry include Hofius, *Tischgemeinschaft,* 16-20; N. Perrin, *Rediscovering the Teachings of Jesus* (London, 1967) 102-8; B. F. Meyer, *The Aims of Jesus* (London, 1979) 158-62; J. Riches, *Jesus and the Transformation of Judaism* (London, 1980) 104-6; Trautmann, *Zeichenhafte Handlungen Jesu,* 160-64; M. J. Borg, *Conflict, Holiness, and Politics in the Teachings of Jesus* (New York, 1984) 73-121; R. Horsley, *Jesus and the Spiral of Violence: Popular Jewish Resistance in Roman Palestine* (San Francisco, 1987) 178-80; P. Stuhlmacher, *Jesus von Nazareth — Christus des Glaubens* (Stuttgart, 1988) 49.

11. Matt. 3:7; 12:24, 38; 21:45; 22:34, though secondary redaction and sound historical information need not, of course, be mutually exclusive categories.

12. J. Neusner, *From Politics to Piety* (Englewood Cliffs, 1973) 86, being a more popular statement of his *The Rabbinic Traditions about the Pharisees before 70* (2 vols., Leiden, 1971).

Neusner also draws out two points of particular interest to this inquiry. First, that this concern to maintain ritual purity in respect of the meal table was a primary expression of Pharisees' desire to live as though they were serving as priests in the Temple — to regard, we might say, the whole land as sharing the sanctity of the Temple and thus requiring the same degree of holiness as for the Temple priest. Second, that this concern did not focus on special or ritual meals but came to expression in all meals; it was precisely in their daily life, in the daily meal table, that the test of their priestlike dedication would be proved.

The importance of Neusner's work at this point is twofold: (1) It confirms the initial assumption that the daily meal table had a significance at the time of Jesus which was much richer and deeper than typical Christian practice today. (2) It confirms in a striking way the picture of the Gospels, that table-fellowship would probably have been a sensitive issue between Jesus and many of the Pharisees. This is perhaps the most significant feature of Neusner's work: Not only has he pioneered the critical analysis of the rabbinic traditions — enabling us to gain a firmer "fix" on those traditions which go back to the pre-70 period[13] — but he has also demonstrated that the Synoptic Gospel tradition is to be regarded and used as a more valuable source for our knowledge of pre-70 *Judaism* than most of his Jewish colleagues have hitherto acknowledged.[14]

Neusner's conclusions, however, have recently come under heavy fire from E. P. Sanders.[15] Sanders's argument has two major prongs. (1) The sayings specifically attributed to the period before 70 cannot be regarded as particularly characteristic of that period, since there are numerous anonymous laws which were equally characteristic of the same period.[16] And while concern regarding the purity of the meal table can be attributed to the *haberim* (associates), it cannot be assumed that all Pharisees were *haberim*.[17] In other words, Sanders calls into question whether there was more than a small group who at the time of Jesus sought to maintain such a degree of purity at the meal table as Neusner has pointed to.

(2) Having called into question the significance of the pre-70 rabbinic traditions, Sanders also diminishes the historical value of the Synoptic tradition which seems to mesh into the former so well, specifically, the Synoptic

13. It is worth recalling at this point the warnings, e.g., of P. Alexander, "Rabbinic Judaism and the New Testament," *ZNW* 74 (1983) 237-46.

14. See G. Vermes, "Jewish Literature and New Testament Exegesis: Reflections on Methodology," *Essays in Honour of Yigael Yadin, JJS* 33 (1982) 361-76, reprinted in *Jesus and the World of Judaism* (London, 1983) 74-88.

15. E. P. Sanders, *Jesus and Judaism* (Philadelphia, 1985).

16. Ibid., 388, n. 59.

17. Ibid., 187-88.

attestation that Jesus' meal table practice aroused criticism from Pharisees. In particular, he notes the confusion between impurity and sin. Impurity merely debarred from participation in the Temple cult for the duration of the impurity; it did not constitute anyone a sinner. And since impurity only related to the Temple cult, it would not be a cause for comment outside the Temple; lack of concern for purity outside the Temple simply showed that one was not a *haber.* What Jesus was criticized for was association with *sinners* — that is, people who were generally regarded as "wicked" or "traitors." To make purity and table-fellowship the focal points of debate, therefore, is to trivialize the charges against Jesus.[18] In fact, Sanders finds no evidence of substantial conflict between Jesus and the Pharisees in respect of food and purity laws, and traditions like Mark 7:1-23 must, in his view, be discounted as later retrojections into the Synoptic tradition.[19]

I have offered a fuller critique of Sanders elsewhere,[20] and so can focus more briefly on the main points that bear upon the present discussion. (1) Although Sanders dismisses much of the Synoptic tradition as good evidence for Jesus' ministry itself, so far as it bears on the topic of our interest, he does not dispute the basic facts outlined above in "Jesus and Table-Fellowship": that Jesus was notorious for his acceptance of "sinners," and that he probably saw this as an expression of his understanding of the kingdom and of who would be members of it.[21] Sanders doubts whether this aspect of Jesus' ministry had a lasting impact on Jesus' followers. But the important point for us is Sanders's confirmation, as a historian, of this dimension of Jesus' historical ministry. What then of the more specific issue of whether Jesus was in fact criticized by Pharisees, and if so on what grounds?

(2) Despite Sanders, it must be significant that those who passed down the rabbinic traditions from the pre-70 period chose to retain the atttibution of so many of them to that period. At the very least it indicates that the purity of table-fellowship was recalled as a particular concern of the pre-70 predecessors of the rabbis. And even if Pharisees and *haberim* are not to be completely identified, the latter almost certainly constituted a significant proportion of the former,[22] so that once again the conclusion is probably sound that the purity of the meal table was a very active concern among many or most of Jesus' Pharisaic contemporaries.

18. Ibid., 177-87.
19. Ibid., 264-67.
20. J. D. G. Dunn, "Pharisees, Sinners, and Jesus," in *The Social World of Formative Christianity and Judaism,* ed. P. Borgen, J. Neusner et al. (Philadelphia, 1988) 264-89; reprinted in my *Jesus, Paul, and the Law* (London, 1990), ch. 3.
21. Sanders, *Jesus and Judaism,* 206-9.
22. "Before 70, there was probably an appreciable overlap between Pharisees and *haberim*" (Sanders, *Jesus and Judaism,* 187).

(3) Sanders completely ignores the fact that the term "sinners" had a well-established factional use within the Judaism of the time. The clear testimony of the Jewish literature which dates to the two hundred years between the Maccabean revolt and Jesus is that Judaism was fairly riven with factions. Prominent among the factional terms was the description "sinners." The factions represented by such documents as *1 Enoch* (1–5 and 81–82), or the *Psalms of Solomon,* or the sectarian scrolls from Qumran clearly saw themselves as "the righteous" and condemned those outside or opposed to their factions as "sinners" (e.g., *1 En.* 1:1, 7-9; 5:6-7; 82:4-7; *Pss. Sol.* 3, 13, 15; CD 1.13-21; 1QH 2.8-19). The point, of course, is that the term "sinners" was being used *by Jews of fellow Jews,* and being used to designate what was regarded by the members of the faction as unacceptable conduct for a devout Jew.[23] This is precisely the position reflected in the Synoptic tradition, where it is the Pharisees who are depicted as condemning those whose conduct they counted unacceptable for a righteous Jew. In short, within the context of late Second Temple Judaism, it is wholly to be expected that Pharisees would characterize those who were outside their circle and who disputed their understanding of what righteousness involved and required as "sinners."

(4) Added to this firm historical data is the sociological probability that such factions would draw clear boundaries around themselves to mark off the righteous from the sinners and that the boundaries would most probably have ritual expression. For example, in the case of *Jubilees* and *1 Enoch,* we know that the correct dating of the feasts was regarded as a crucial boundary issue (*Jub. 6:32-35; 1 En.* 82:4-7).[24] Into this background the historical Pharisees fit well. The very name "Pharisees" (probably a nickname = "separated ones")[25] indicates a desire for social distinctiveness. And one of the areas in which ritual could safeguard that distinctiveness where it might be most threatened by careless conduct would be the food used in a meal and its preparation. Despite his concern to evaluate the Synoptic data as a historian, Sanders has ignored these important dimensions of the historical context.

23. We need not identify the authors or communities behind these documents, to which we could add *Jubilees* and the *Testament of Moses.* The point is the clear intra-Jewish, factional character of the charges made. Insofar as opponents can be identified, most would accept that the likely targets of the Qumran and *Testament of Moses* attacks are the Pharisees themselves! Particularly noteworthy is the fact that the eating habits of these opponents are at the very center of the no doubt highly biased attack of *T. Mos.* 7.

24. In *Jubilees,* cf. particularly 6:35 and 22:16: to celebrate a feast on the wrong date was to "forget the feasts of the covenant and walk according to the feasts of the Gentiles" (6:35); separation from the Gentiles meant in particular not eating with them (22:16).

25. E. Schürer, *The History of the Jewish People in the Age of Jesus Christ (175 B.C.–A.D. 135),* ed. G. Vermes et al. (Edinburgh, 1979) II, 396-98.

(5) Finally, we may simply note that the Synoptic traditions cannot be dated after 70 C.E. with any probability.[26] The traditions on which Mark draws in chapters 2 and 7 must certainly be dated at the very least to the period before 70. They therefore provide the confirmation that Neusner found in them for a pre-70 group of Pharisees who regarded table-fellowship as very important and who criticized the followers of Jesus for their slackness in this respect. It is not necessary to hypothesize outright conflict between Jesus or his disciples and all Pharisees (on the contrary, Luke 7:36; 11:37; 14:1). All that is required for the Synoptic tradition to make good historical sense is that at least some Pharisees felt their own understanding and practice of covenant loyalty to be called into question and in some degree threatened by the lifestyle and message of Jesus. That would be quite sufficient to explain the kind of criticism and complaint attested in Mark (chs. 2, 7).

In short, Sanders's challenge to the mutually reinforcing picture drawn by Neusner's analysis of the pre-70 rabbinic traditions and by the Synoptic traditions must be judged to have failed. Table-fellowship was at the heart of many Pharisees' self-identity; for them Sirach's counsel, "Let *righteous* men be your table companions," would be a basic rule of life.[27] A practice of table-fellowship that rode roughshod over and called into sharp question the deeply held convictions of these Pharisees was liable to trigger a strong reaction on the part of at least some of them. Jesus' table-fellowship seems to have been just such and was evidently perceived by at least some Pharisees as a threat to their ritually expressed and maintained boundaries.[28]

It is within this context that the question of table-fellowship as understood and practiced at Qumran comes into focus.

Qumran and Table-Fellowship

The importance of the common meal for the Essenes is also beyond dispute. It was a familiar feature of Essene life long before the discovery of the Dead Sea Scrolls, since both Philo and Josephus draw attention to it. Philo comments on how developed was the common life of the Essenes in this respect:

> They all have a single treasury and common disbursements; their clothes are held in common and also their food through their institution of public meals. In no other community can we find the custom of sharing roof, life

26. Most scholars continue to date Mark to the period 64-70 C.E.; see W. G. Kümmel, *Introduction to the New Testament* (revised edition, Nashville, 1975) 98.

27. Hofius, *Tischgemeinschaft*, 16.

28. See particularly Borg, *Conflict*, 73-143.

and board more firmly established in actual practice. (Philo, *Every Good Man Is Free* 86; LCL)

In Josephus the fullest description of the Essenes comes in *War* 2.119-61. He describes their daily meal:

> After this purification[29] . . . they repair to the refectory, as to some sacred shrine *(eis hagion ti temenos)*. When they have taken their seats in silence, the baker serves out the loaves in order, and the cook sets before each one plate with a single course. Before meat the priest says a grace, and none may partake until after the prayer. When breakfast is ended, he pronounces a further grace; thus at the beginning and at the close they do homage to God as the bountiful giver of life. Then laying aside their raiment, as holy vestments, they again betake themselves to their labors until the evening. On their return they sup in like manner. . . . No clamor or disturbance ever pollutes their dwelling. . . . To persons outside the silence of those within appears like some awful mystery. . . . (*War* 2.129-33; LCL)

Later on Josephus describes the probationary period for the novice: after one year he is permitted "to share the purer kind of holy water," but he is "not yet received into the meetings of the community." After a further two years, if found worthy, he is "enrolled in the society. But before he may touch the common food *(tēs koinēs trophēs),* he is made to swear tremendous oaths" (*War* 2.138-39; LCL). Still later Josephus notes that even the expelled member still bound by his oath was "not at liberty to partake of other men's food" and so often died of starvation (*War* 2.143) and that during the war against the Romans the Essenes resolutely refused "to blaspheme their lawgiver or to eat some forbidden thing," despite horrendous torture (*War* 2.152; LCL).

The picture provided by Philo and Josephus received fairly detailed confirmation from the Dead Sea Scrolls, confirming beyond a reasonable doubt that the Rule of the Community (1QS) in particular is an Essene document. We may note especially 1QS 6.2, 4-5:

> They shall eat in common. . . . And when the table has been prepared for eating, and the new wine for drinking, the Priest shall be the first to stretch out his hand to bless the first-fruits of the bread and the new wine.[30]

The subsequent descriptions of the hierarchical character of the seating in their assemblies (6.8-9) matches Philo (*Every Good Man Is Free* 81; cf.

---

29. "The obligation to take a ritual bath, instead of merely washing the hands, implies that the Essene meal was endowed with a sacred character" (Schürer, *History,* II, 569, n. 44).

30. Translation from G. Vermes, *The Dead Sea Scrolls in English* (London and New York, 1987).

Josephus, *War* 2.150), and that of the orderly manner of their spoken contributions (6.10-11) matches Josephus (*War* 2.132). Most striking of all, the stages of novitiate are more or less just as Josephus described: a one-year's probation before the would-be member may "touch the purity of the Many"; but "he shall not touch the drink of the Many until he has completed a second year among the men of the community" (1QS 6.16-17, 20-21).[31]

It is clear from all this that the meal table was regarded by the Essenes as of particular significance; it was a feature of their common life recognized by others. Like (many of) the Pharisees, the Essenes clearly believed that the character and purity of the daily meal table were an expression of and indeed a test case for their devotion to the covenant as understood within the community. The purity rule governing their table-fellowship obviously functioned as a boundary around the community — indeed as an inner boundary, requiring not just separation from "the men of falsehood" and devotion to the covenant (1QS 5.10-11) but also a still stricter observance of purity rules than among the *haberim*.[32] Whatever the precise distinction between "the purity of the Many" and "the drink of the Many,"[33] it is clear that full participation in the common meal was reserved for the full members alone ("the Many"). Acceptance into table-fellowship was the final hurdle by surmounting which the novice became one of "the Many."

Particularly interesting is 1QSa, the Rule of the Congregation "in the last days" (1QSa 1.1). The interest for us is in two points. First, the community was expected to function in the last days in the same way as it always had, even when the Messiah of Israel was among them.

> [When] they shall gather for the common [tab]le, to eat and [to drink] new wine, when the common table shall be set for eating and the new wine [poured] for drinking, let no man extend his hand over the first-fruits of bread and wine before the Priest; for [it is he] who shall bless the first-fruits of bread and wine, and shall be the first [to extend] his hand over the bread. Thereafter the Messiah of Israel shall extend his hand over the bread. . . . (1QSa 2.17-21)[34]

---

31. See further K. G. Kuhn, "The Lord's Supper and the Communal Meal at Qumran," in *The Scrolls and the New Testament,* ed. K. Stendahl (London, 1958) 67-70.

32. Given the degree of antagonism that seems to have been cherished at Qumran against the Pharisees (see above, n. 23), it is more than a little surprising that J. Jeremias should use the Dead Sea Scrolls to illustrate Pharisaic practice (Jeremias, *Jerusalem in the Time of Jesus* [London, 1969] 259-62).

33. See further A. R. C. Leaney, *The Rule of Qumran and Its Meanings* (London, 1966) 191-95; G. Vermes, *The Dead Sea Scrolls: Qumran in Perspective* (London, 1977) 95-96; M. Newton, *The Concept of Purity at Qumran and in the Letters of Paul* (SNTSMS 53; Cambridge, 1985) 10-26.

34. Translation from Vermes, *Dead Sea Scrolls in English.* See 1QS 6.4-5, cited above.

At this point the parallel with Jesus' table-fellowship becomes obvious. As with Jesus, so also with the Essenes, the current practice of table-fellowship seems to have been seen as an expression and a foretaste of the fellowship of the future age.[35] For both groups the meal table was an eschatological symbol, an enacted conviction, commitment, and promise.

The other noteworthy feature of 1QSa is the list of those whom the community excluded from its assembly, that is, from the community of the last days, including by clear implication the common meal — an exclusions policy presumably already enacted in the life of the community at the time of Jesus.

> [3]No man smitten with any [4]human uncleanness shall *enter* the assembly of God. . . . [5]No man smitten in his flesh, or *paralysed in his feet or* [6]*hands, or lame (psh),* or *blind ('wr),* or deaf, or dumb, or smitten in his flesh with a visible *blemish (mwm)* . . . for the angels of holiness are [with] their [congregation] . . . let him not *enter* among [the congregation], for he is smitten. (1QSa 2.3-10)[36]

The passage is obviously based on Lev. 21:17–24:37:[37]

> [17]Say to Aaron, None of your descendants throughout their generations who has a *blemish (mwm)* may *approach* to offer the bread of his God. [18]For no one who has a *blemish* shall *draw near,* a man *blind ('wr)* or *lame (psh),* . . . [19]or a man who has an *injured foot* or an *injured hand.* . . . (Lev. 21:17-21)

Once again the significance is obvious: the Essenes saw themselves as a priestly community who regarded the purity regulations governing priestly service as binding on their community.[38] Here a close parallel with (many of) the Pharisees is evident: both groups sought to maintain in their daily meals a level of purity required for the Temple and its service. In the case of the Essenes, however, particularly in the closed community at Qumran,[39] the

---

35. M. Black, *The Scrolls and Christian Origins* (London, 1961) 109-11; Vermes, *The Dead Sea Scrolls: Qumran in Perspective,* 182; questioned by Marshall, *Last Supper,* 26.

36. Translation from Vermes, *Dead Sea Scrolls in English.*

37. J. A. Fitzmyer, "A Feature of Qumran Angelology and the Angels of 1 Cor 11.10," in *Essays on the Semantic Background of the New Testament* (London, 1971) 198-99.

38. See further B. Gärtner, *The Temple and the Community in Qumran and the New Testament* (SNTSMS 1; Cambridge, 1965) chs. 2 and 3; Newton, *Concept of Purity,* ch. 2, esp. pp. 34-36.

39. I have left the question of other Essene communities open; but since Qumran is the only obvious example known to us in any detail, the issues can be posed most simply and most sharply by reference to it as such.

purity norms and boundaries were intensified, and the purity of the community more tightly controlled and safeguarded.

A final point worthy of note is how frequently the Dead Sea Scrolls make a point of listing who is excluded from the community by virtue of physical defect. As well as 1QSa 2.3-10 cited above, we may add the following texts:

> [4]No man who is *lame (psḥ),* or *blind ('wr),* or crippled *(ḥgr),* or afflicted with a lasting bodily *blemish (mwm),* or smitten with a bodily impurity, [5]none of these shall march out to war with them . . . [6]. . . for the holy angels shall be with their hosts. (1QM 7.4-6)[40]
>
> Fools, madmen, simpletons, and imbeciles, the *blind* (literally, those who, being weak of eye, cannot see), the *maimed (ḥgr),* the *lame,* the deaf, and minors, none of these may *enter* the midst of the community, for the holy angels (are in the midst of it). (4QCD^b)[41]
>
> No *blind* people may enter it (the holy city and the sanctuary) all their days lest they defile the city in whose midst I dwell, for I YHWH, dwell amongst the sons of Israel for ever and eternally. (11QTemple 45.12-14)[42]

With these passages is confirmed the twin logic of Essene purity emphasis: the community saw itself as representing and maintaining the purity of the Temple, a community in whose midst God and his holy angels could dwell. Moreover, the emphasis on exclusion of all impurity, including physical blemish, was so consistently maintained that it would probably be well known outside the community.

Since this was evidently a matter of major concern for the Qumran meal table and may have been well known as such, and since Jesus seems to have reacted against the somewhat similar concerns lived out by (many) Pharisees, the remaining question is whether Jesus also knew of and reacted against the Essene practice of exclusive table-fellowship as well.

Luke 14:13, 21 — A Critique of Qumran?

Only one passage provides support for the suggestion that Jesus did indeed know of and react critically to the practice of table-fellowship which evidently characterized the Qumran community. The passage is Luke 14:12-21, which reads as follows:

40. Translation from Vermes, *Dead Sea Scrolls in English.*

41. Reference and translation from J. T. Milik, *Ten Years of Discovery in the Wilderness of Judaea,* tr. J. Strugnell (SBT 26; London, 1959) 114.

42. J. Maier, *The Temple Scroll,* tr. R. T. White (JSOTSS 34; Sheffield, 1985) 41.

¹²Jesus said to the one who had invited him, "When you give a dinner or banquet, do not invite your friends, or your brothers, or your relatives, or your rich neighbors, lest they too invite you in return, and you are repaid. ¹³But when you give a feast, invite the poor *(ptōchous),* the *maimed (anapeirous),* the *lame (chōlous),* the *blind (typhlous);* ¹⁴and you will be blessed, because they cannot repay you. . . ." ²¹. . . Then the householder was angry and said to his servant, 'Go out quickly into the streets and lanes of the city and bring in the poor and the *maimed* and the *blind* and the *lame' (tous ptōchous kai anapeirous kai typhlous kai chōlous eisage).*

The (contrasting) parallel between Luke 14 and 1QSa 2 has, of course, been recognized,⁴³ but these were only brief references. The possibility that Jesus actually had Qumran teaching and practice in mind deserves closer and more careful scrutiny.

Two points of significance emerge immediately. First, the point already noted, that the conjunction of 1QS 6.4-5 with 1QSa 2.17-21 is paralleled by the conjunction of Luke 14:13 with 14:21. In both cases there was an explicit intention that the practice of table-fellowship in the present should be determined by and express already the eschatological experience of covenant fellowship — community at table as it should be, as God intended it to be. Second, the clear implication of Luke 14:12-24 that Jesus' vision and recommendation would be surprising to contemporary etiquette and probably to some extent offensive to religious sensibilities. These observations suggest that the Jesus tradition was formulated in opposition to an alternative practice and vision, such as we see in the Dead Sea Scrolls. But whether we can say more than that depends heavily on a comparison of the two sets of lists cited previously. Those explicitly excluded according to the Dead Sea Scrolls from the meals of the community (especially from the common meal) include those specifically named in the Jesus tradition as the ones who should be invited to table-fellowship.

In comparison with the list of four groups in Luke 14, of course, the Dead Sea Scrolls lists (and Leviticus 21) are more extensive and more varied. But a close parallel is immediately evident in the case of two elements: the "lame" and the "blind." *Chōlos* is the unvarying Septuagintal translation of the Hebrew *psḥ,* and *typhlos* likewise of *'wr.* The association of the two

43. D. Barthélemy and J. T. Milik, *DJD* I (Oxford, 1955) 117; F. M. Cross, *The Ancient Library of Qumran and Modern Biblical Studies* (London, 1958) 179; "It is difficult to suppose that the parable is not told in conscious reaction to sectarian doctrine" (n. 89) — though Cross's translation of 1QSa 2.11, 13 as "the men of the name who are invited to the festival" (to bring out the parallel with Luke 14:21) was rather tendentious. M. Burrows was less confident: "No specific reference to the Qumran sect in particular is indicated, but the contrast between its attitude and that of Jesus is unmistakeable" (Burrows, *More Light on the Dead Sea Scrolls* [London, 1958] 91). Cf. A. Vögtle, *Das öffentliche Wirken Jesu auf dem Hintergrund der Qumranbewegung* (Freiburger Universitätsreden N.F. 27; Freiburg, 1958) 12-13.

categories, however, is fairly common in the Old Testament; apart from Lev. 21:18, there are Deut. 15:21 and Mal. 1:8 (in reference to sacrifice); 2 Sam. 5:6, 8, 9 and Job 29:15 (linked with "the poor" in a description of Job's righteousness); and Isa. 35:5-6 (a description of eschatological blessing). In the New Testament, apart from Luke 14:13, 21, we can list Matt. 11:5//Luke 7:22 (reference to Isa. 35:5-6); Matt. 15:30-31 and 21:14 (further descriptions of Jesus' healing ministry); and John 5:3. Consequently, the association of the two categories, the *lame* and the *blind,* cannot be said to demonstrate a specific or distinctive link between Luke 14 and the Qumran texts. Nevertheless, it may well be significant that in the various Dead Sea Scrolls lists it is these two categories which appear most regularly. If Jesus had compared or contrasted his position with Qumran, he would most probably have included some mention of the lame and the blind.

Working backward in the Luke 14 lists, the second category is *anapeirous,* "the crippled." *Anapeiros* is a variant form of *anapēros;* the former is attested also in the Septuagint manuscripts of Tob. 14:2 (*anapeiros tois ophthalmois,* "a defect of the eyes" or "an affliction of the eyes") and 2 Macc. 8:24 (*tois melesin anapeirous,* "the wretchedly wounded"), but the more common literary usage is *anapēros,*[44] which has a more general sense, denoting physical disability of an unspecific kind. A better translation, therefore, would probably be "disabled" or "seriously disabled" rather than the too-specific "crippled" and the somewhat emotive "maimed." The point, however, is that *anapeiros* would naturally offer itself as an appropriate equivalent to Hebrew *ḥgr* (cf. above 1QM 7.4 "crippled"; 4QCD[b] "maimed") or possibly also *mwm,* "blemish" (Lev. 21:17-18; 1QSa 2.5; 1QM 7.4) — since physical impairment is clearly in view in the Dead Sea Scroll texts at least — or indeed as a general word to embrace a range of physical disabilities such as featured in the Qumran texts.[45] In other words, behind Luke 14:13, 21 at this point may well lie a word that recalled or specifically alluded to the list of disabilities which Qumran was known to exclude from its community; Luke or his source saw *anapeiros* as the obvious Greek equivalent.[46]

44. The same passage is cited in Eusebius, *Praeparatio Evangelica* 13.8.3. A brief examination of the *TLG* texts quickly shows how natural it was for *anapēros* to be associated with *chōlos* and *typhlos:* Plato, *Crito* 53a (*ē hoi chōloi te kai typhloi kai hoi alloi anapēroi,* ". . . than the lame and the blind and the other cripples"); Aristotle, *Historia Animalium* 585b (*ginontai de kai ex anapērōn anapēroi, hoion ek chōlon chōloi kai typhlon typhloi,* ". . . the crippled give rise to the crippled; such as is lame to the lame, the blind to the blind"); Diogenes Laertius, *Vita* 6.33 (*anapērous elegen ou tous kōphous kai typhlous, alla tous me echontas pēran,* ". . . the deaf and the blind should not be said to be crippled, rather he who has no money bag"). See also Plutarch, *Regum* 194C; Galen, *De usu partium* 3.237; and Clement of Alexandria, *Protrepticus* 10.105.

45. *Kyllos* ("crippled, deformed") is used in a similar unspecific way and in close association with *chōlos* and *typhlos* in Matt. 15:30-31, but it is not as widely attested as *anapēros,* which was almost certainly better known to Luke.

46. I use "equivalent" deliberately since more than translation as such may be involved.

This means that three out of the four items in the Luke 14 list are closely matched by items in the typical Dead Sea Scroll lists. But what about the other item — the "poor" — which appears first on Luke's list? It is obvious that "the poor" do not feature in any of the other lists (Leviticus, Dead Sea Scrolls, Qumran), although it may be significant that Diogenes Laertius cites Diogenes redefining "the disabled" not as the deaf or blind but as "those who have no wallet" (see above). More immediately to the point, however, is the fact that "the poor" feature prominently in both Jesus' and the Essenes' teaching. In the Synoptic tradition Jesus' concern for the poor is quite marked (Mark 10:21 pars.; 12:42-43 par.; Luke 6:20//Matt. 5:3; Matt. 11:5//Luke 7:22; Luke 4:18; 14:13, 21; 16:19-31; 19:8). In the Dead Sea Scrolls "the poor" seems to have been a favorite self-designation for the sect itself (1QpHab 12.2-10; 1QM 11.9, 13; 13.14; 1QH 5.22; 4QpPs 37 1.9; 2.10 [= "the congregation of the poor"]; cf. in the singular 1QH 2.32; 3.25; 5.16, 18)[47] with only the Damascus Document (6.21 and 14.14) using it in the more common sense. Moreover, in 4QpPs 37 1.9 the motif of the messianic banquet appears in the same context.

May it be then that we should see in the Lukan inclusion of "the poor" a further allusion to the belief and practices of Qumran? Clearly, the Qumran community delighted in the self-designation "the poor." "The poor" designated the community in assembly, at the communal meal, and at the eschatological banquet. "The poor" designated their scrupulous exclusiveness from the disabled, the lame, and the blind.

Jesus, in contrast, was remembered as one who had been very open to the actual poor, the very much wider circle of those living at or below subsistence level. Jesus linked the poor equally with the disabled, the lame, and the blind as special objects of God's favor. The contrast was evident: A self-styled "poor" who lived by a scrupulous understanding of what and who were acceptable to God contrasts impressively with a Jesus who lived by an understanding of God's grace as open precisely to those excluded by Qumran. Whether it was Jesus himself who formulated it (as is quite possible), or the Lukan tradition (with its special interest in the poor), the contrast was too inviting to remain unformulated. In the Palestinian Jesus movement the table of God was open to *all* the poor, and not least to the disabled, the lame, and the blind — those specifically excluded by the self-styled "poor" of Qumran.

---

47. We need not speak of a title as such, but in some texts at least the group behind these texts clearly identified themselves with "the poor" of the biblical tradition; see further A. Dupont-Sommer, *The Essene Writings from Qumran,* tr. G. Vermes (Oxford, 1961) ad loc.; E. Bammel, *ptōchos, TDNT* VI, 897; L. E. Keck, "The Poor among the Saints in Jewish Christianity and Qumran," *ZNW* 57 (1966) 54-78.

Conclusions

We can summarize our findings very straightforwardly.

(1) Table-fellowship was an important expression of the teaching and practice of Jesus, Pharisaic *haberim,* and the Qumran covenanters. It expressed their understanding of communion with God, of the company of the kingdom, an eschatological ideal to be prepared for and lived out now.

(2) For Pharisee and Qumran Essene the measure of acceptability of such table-fellowship to God was the unacceptability at such table-fellowship of those whose attitude or actions showed them to be "sinners." In contrast, Jesus ignored, resisted, and even denounced such measuring of acceptability. His table-fellowship was notable for its acceptance of the "sinner" and tax collector. This brought him into controversy with at least some Pharisees, a controversy whose traces are still clear in the Gospel traditions.

(3) Cumulatively, it is likely that Jesus' table-fellowship would also be seen as a point of comparison and contrast with the Essene common meal — particularly as the Qumran practice and measure of acceptability were even more tightly drawn than those of the Pharisees, excluding not just "sinners" but also those physically blemished. This likelihood becomes a firm probability when the close degree of parallel between Luke 14:13, 21 and the list of those excluded from the Qumran messianic banquet is recognized. Jesus was probably aware of the strictness of the Qumran ideal and, on at least one occasion, deliberately spoke out against it. Those whom God counted acceptable were not so much the self-styled "poor" as those who actually were poor, together with the disabled, the lame, and the blind — the very ones excluded by the Qumran ideal.

In short, Jesus' table-fellowship must be seen as both a protest against a religious zeal that is judgmental and exclusive and as a lived-out expression of the openness of God's grace.

SPIRIT AND CHRISTOLOGY IN PAUL

7

2 Corinthians 3:17
"The Lord Is the Spirit"

Does Paul identify the risen Jesus with the πνεῦμα in 2 Cor. 3:17? The debate occasioned by this question is one of long standing. But so far as the present century is concerned the majority of commentators have answered it in the affirmative, albeit often with "ifs" and "buts" added in liberal measure.[1] In view, moreover, of the fact that the most recent fullscale treatment of the passage argues the affirmative case with great persuasiveness one who finds himself still unpersuaded may well consider himself justified in subjecting the question to fresh scrutiny.

The monograph just referred to is Ingo Hermann's *Kyrios und Pneuma* (1961), the first five chapters and fifty-eight pages of which are devoted to

---

1. See, for example, W. Bousset, *Kyrios Christos* (German original, 1913) 112f.; A. Plummer, *II Corinthians* (ICC; 1915) 102; E. F. Scott, *The Spirit in the New Testament* (1923) 142ff.; H. Windisch, *Der zweite Korintherbrief* (1924⁹) 123; E. Büchsel, *Der Geist Gottes im Neuen Testament* (1926) 428; C. A. A. Scott, *Christianity according to St. Paul* (1927) 258; H. W. Robinson, *The Christian Experience of the Holy Spirit* (1928) 11; A. Schlatter, *Paulus der Bote Jesu* (1934) 253; J. S. Stewart, *A Man in Christ* (1935) 309f.; R. H. Strachan, *II Corinthians* (Moffatt; 1935) 88f.; C. H. Dodd, *The Apostolic Preaching and Its Developments* (1936) 124; W. Foerster, *TDNT* III, 1091; F. Prat, *Theology of St. Paul* (1945) II, 435-41; R. Bultmann, *Theology of the New Testament* (1952) I, 124; W. D. Davies, *Paul and Rabbinic Judaism* (1955²) 196; E. Schweizer, *TDNT* VI, 417f.; N. Q. Hamilton, *The Holy Spirit and Eschatology in Paul* (1957) 6ff.; H. P. van Dusen, *Spirit, Son and Father* (1958) 66; A. Wikenhauser, *Pauline Mysticism* (1960) 81; A. M. Hunter, *Paul and His Predecessors* (1961²) 95; K. Stalder, *Das Werk des Geistes in der Heiligung bei Paulus* (1962) 51, n. 23, 53f.; P. E. Hughes, *Paul's Second Epistle to the Corinthians* (1962) 115; E. Käsemann, *Essays on New Testament Themes* (1964) 113; H.-D. Wendland, *Die Briefe an die Korinther* (NTD; 1964¹⁰) 158; H. Berkhof, *The Doctrine of the Holy Spirit* (1964) 25; W. Kramer, *Christ, Lord, Son of God* (1966) 165ff.; H. Ulonska, "Die Doxa des Mose," *Evangelische Theologie* 26 (1966) 387; D. Hill, *Greek Words and Hebrew Meanings* (1967) 278ff.

---

the elucidation of 2 Cor. 3:17. He regards this verse as the key to and sum total of all Paul's theology regarding the relation of Kyrios and πνεῦμα, and the conclusions he draws from it are the foundation for his other exegetical and theological investigations. Briefly he argues that 2 Cor. 3:17 identifies Christ and the Pneuma — an identification not in divine "substance" but in Christian experience. We experience the exalted Christ *as* Pneuma. Verse 17a is an existential, not a speculative statement. For Paul πνεῦμα is a functional concept and describes the means by which Christ is at work in the Church — the dynamic presence of the κύριος. To ask about the Trinity and the personality of the Spirit is to raise questions which would never have entered Paul's head; it robs Pauline Christology of its fullness and life and throws his whole theology into confusion. τὸ πνεῦμα is for Christians above all a reality of experience and Christ is real and present only *through* the πνεῦμα and as πνεῦμα.

Valuable as this understanding is, its exegetical basis in 2 Cor. 3:17 must be sharply questioned. Does κύριος in 17a in fact mean Christ? This question cannot be answered at once, for it depends on the answer to another question: To whom does the κύριος of verse 16 refer — to Christ (verse 14) or to Yahweh? And this in turn depends on the answer to a further question: Is verse 16 an Old Testament citation or not? The issue is therefore more complicated than it appears at first sight, and to resolve it we must examine the context in more detail.

The underlying theme which connects 2 Corinthians 3 with its context is the διακονία of the new covenant.[2] The whole of 2 Corinthians 3 itself is taken up with the contrast between the two διακονίαι, the old and the new covenants, the one epitomized by the law, the other by the Spirit,[3] the point being that the superiority of the new covenant, of which Paul is a διάκονος and which the Corinthians have themselves experienced through Paul's διακονία, in itself both validates his ministry over against that of his opponents and makes it an imperative of the first priority for Paul.

---

2. G. Kittel, *TDNT* II, 251; J. Jeremias, *TDNT* IV, 869. Note how frequently διακονία and its substantives appear in ch. 3 (verses 3, 6, 7, 8, and 9) and the way in which 4:1 gathers up the preceding argument. W. C. van Unnik shows the thematic importance of παρρησία, which relates the following midrash to the preceding context and indicates the former to be a defense of Paul's "barefacedness" as a minister of the new covenant (" 'With Unveiled Face': An Exegesis of II Cor. iii.12-18," *NovT* 6 [1963] 153-69). For other recent attempts to set this passage in its polemical life-setting see Ulonska, op. cit., 378-88.

3. Cf. M. Dibelius, "Der Herr und der Geist bei Paulus," *Botschaft und Geschichte* 2 (1956) 129. The γράμμα/πνεῦμα antithesis is not to be interpreted as a contrast between letter and spirit, that is, between the literal surface sense and the deeper spiritual sense (contra Prat, op. cit. II, 440; E.-B. Allo, *Seconde Épitre aux Corinthiens* [1956²] 95; cf. A. Richardson, *An Introduction to the Theology of the New Testament* [1958] 121f.). The antithesis is rather between the law and the Holy Spirit, the regulating principles of the old and new covenants respectively (see my *Baptism in the Holy Spirit* [1970] 135-37).

In the immediate context (verses 7-18) the theme being elaborated is the temporary nature of the διακονία of death and condemnation over against the increasingly glorious nature of the διακονία of the Spirit and righteousness. It is essential for the right understanding of these verses to realize that Paul bases his argument *throughout* this section on Exod. 34:29-35,[4] and that his argument takes the form of a Christian midrash[5] or interpretative homily on the Exodus passage. The key words in this midrash are δόξα and κάλυμμα.[6]

In verse 7 Paul indicates that he is going to use the Exodus passage as an allegory to draw out the antithesis between the two dispensations: the δόξα of Moses' face *is,* not just illustrates, the δόξα of the old covenant. Its fading indicates that the old covenant's usefulness to God is short lived. With this Paul contrasts the greater δόξα of the dispensation of the Spirit[7] — a contrast stylistically elaborated by the threefold "if . . . much more" (verses 7-11).

In verse 13 he turns again to Exodus 34, and takes up his second key word (κάλυμμα) by citing Exod. 34:33: "Moses put a veil over or on his face." But in Paul's exposition the purpose of the veil is to prevent the Israelites from seeing the fading away of the δόξα (= the temporary nature of the Mosaic law and covenant). Notice that in both these key words Paul has gone beyond, if not actually contradicted, the sense of Exodus:[8] in the latter there is nothing said about the δόξα fading away, and Moses uses the veil lest the people find the brightness too unbearable and become frightened.

In verse 14 Paul extends his interpretation to his own time: the veil is still there when the Jews read the old covenant/law, so that they still fail to recognize that the law is temporary and finished.[9] They do not recognize its temporary nature for only in Christ does it (the old dispensation with its fading splendor) finally cease.[10] Notice that the veil which blinds their minds

---

4. Note the references to the Exodus passage in verses 7, 10, 13, 16, and 18.

5. Windisch, op. cit., 112.

6. Cf. Windisch, op. cit., 115.

7. ἔσται should be taken as a logical future (Plummer, op. cit., 90f.; H. Lietzmann, *An die Korinther* [HNT; 1949⁴] 111), although the still future eschatological sense is present also insofar as the glory increases as the consummation approaches (verses 8 and 18). Cf. Windisch, op. cit., 114f.

8. Lietzmann, op. cit., 112; C. K. Barrett, *From First Adam to Last* (1962) 52f.

9. Hermann, op. cit., 35f., 46f. Verse 14 does *not* mean that they fail to understand the true meaning of the law, as though the contradiction in verse 6 was between letter and spirit. It is not a difference within the old dispensation that Paul is describing, but a difference between dispensations (*contra* Lietzmann, op. cit., 113; Prat, op. cit. II, 440).

10. The subject of καταργεῖται must be determined by the subject of the same verb in verses 7, 11, and 13 — i.e., the old dispensation in its δόξα, not the veil which hides the fact denoted by καταργεῖσθαι (cf. Lietzmann, op. cit., 113; Hermann, op. cit., 35f.; J. Schildenberger, "2 Kor. 3.17a: 'Der Herr aber ist der Geist,' " *Studiorum Paulinorum Congressus Internationalis Catholicus* [1961] I, 456; W. Schmithals, *Die Gnosis in Korinth* [1965²] 299-308; NEB; contra Kümmel, supplement to Lietzmann, 200; RSV).

is the same (τὸ αὐτὸ κάλυμμα) as that which covered Moses' face (verses 14-15).[11]

But now comes verse 16 — is it a citation from Exod. 34:34? A little thought will show that it must be. For the whole of Paul's midrashic exposition of Exodus 34 has been leading up to this point. We may even say that it is really because of Exod. 34:34 that Paul lighted on this passage in the first place. He has not taken his idea of a fading δόξα from Exodus, nor is the function he ascribes to the κάλυμμα derived from Exodus. Why then has he bothered with the Exodus passage? Moses' κάλυμμα in itself would make a useful if rather forced illustration; but Paul wants more than a mere illustration. His purpose is rather to use Exodus 34 as a buttress to support his central contrast between the covenant of law, which has been done away ἐν Χριστῷ, and the covenant of the Spirit, which is ever more glorious. Therefore his aim is to show how the removal of this veil is linked with the Spirit/law antithesis and the replacement of the latter by the former, and *to do so in terms of the passage he is using as his text.* For unless he can show from his text how the veil is removed his text has been of no real service to him.

That this reasoning is on the right lines is confirmed by four facts. First, there is the way in which he has used Exod. 34:29-35: he has taken up the word δόξα from Exod. 34:30 and elaborated it (verses 7-11); then he has taken up the word κάλυμμα from Exod. 34:33 and developed it (verses 12-14). His interpretation of these two words has been preparatory to the key sentence of Exod. 34:34, "But when he turns to the Lord the veil is removed." It is as though he said: "Consider Exod. 34:29-35 — by δόξα I understand the temporary nature of the old covenant; by κάλυμμα I understand that which blinds the Jews to this fact. With this understanding in mind observe what the text says about the way in which the veil is removed."

Second, it is the same veil (τὸ αὐτὸ κάλυμμα):[12] the veil which blinds the Jews of his own day is the same veil as that which covered Moses' face. This being so, the action which will remove the veil is the same action as that which resulted in Moses' veil being removed — same veil, same removal. Hence the key sentence in the midrash is Exod. 34:34: "When he turns to the Lord the veil is removed." We may paraphrase Paul's train of thought thus: Moses' veil hid the temporary nature of the old covenant when it was used by Moses. The same veil hides this fact from the Jew today. But the text shows

11. Not just "a veil having the same effect" (Plummer, op. cit., 99). Such an interpretation betrays a basic misunderstanding of what Paul is doing here. See Windisch, op. cit., 121.

12. The two phrases which show most clearly that Paul is using Exod. 34:29-35 as an allegory are τὸ αὐτὸ κάλυμμα and ὁ δὲ κύριος τὸ πνεῦμά ἐστιν.

that "when he turns to the Lord the veil is removed."[13] And so, having explained how he understands the terms of the Exodus passage and applied them to the sad plight of his Jewish contemporary, Paul the preacher returns triumphantly to his text to demonstrate the way of redemption revealed therein.

Third, since his midrashic exposition is not merely an illustration but an argument, he now (verse 17) ties it in with the central thrust of the passage — the contrast and replacement of the old covenant of γράμμα with the new covenant of πνεῦμα. He explains what the key sentence in Exodus 34 means in terms of his main argument: "Now the Lord of whom this passage speaks is the Spirit" (NEB). "By 'the Lord,' " says Paul, "I understand the πνεῦμα I have been talking about in verses 3, 6, and 8."[14] This is precisely parallel to his exegetical notes in his other allegories: Gal. 4:25 — τὸ δὲ Ἁγὰρ Σινᾶ ὄρος ἐστίν;[15] 1 Cor. 10:4 — ἡ πέτρα δὲ ἦν ὁ Χριστός.[16] As Moses turned to Yahweh so the way of redemption for the Jew is to turn to the Spirit. It is when he turns his attention and devotion from the γράμμα to the πνεῦμα that he will be freed from the bondage and condemnation of the law which kills and experience the liberty and righteousness of the life-giving Spirit. For it is the πνεῦμα who opens people's eyes to the bondage and fear (Exod. 34:30) of the old covenant and brings them into the liberty and boldness (verse 12) of the new.[17]

Fourth, having made his meaning clear parenthetically he brings his exposition of Exod. 34:29-35 to a glorious conclusion. As in verses 7-11 he took up the theme of δόξα from Exodus and enlarged on it, and as in 12-15 he took up the idea of κάλυμμα and enlarged on it, so now in 18 he takes up the key sentence of Exod. 34:34 and enlarges on it. This is clearly shown by

---

13. Paul deliberately does not specify the subject of ἐπιστρέψῃ so that its ambiguity might embrace both Moses and the Jews (cf. van Unnik, op. cit., 166). Schildenberger follows Allo in understanding the subject as "their (i.e., the Jews') heart" (op. cit., 457).

14. This has been a minority opinion on verse 17 in this century. See, for example, J. H. Bernard, *Expositor's Greek Testament* (1917) III, 57f.; A. E. J. Rawlinson, *The New Testament Doctrine of the Christ* (1926) 155, n. 6; V. Taylor, *The Doctrine of the Holy Spirit* (Headingley Lectures, 1937) 46; Dibelius, op. cit., 129f.; F. W. Dillistone, *The Holy Spirit in the Life of Today* (1947) 95; Kümmel, op. cit., 200; K. Prümm, "Die katholische Auslegung von 2 Kor. 3.17a in den letzten vier Jahrzehnten," *Biblica* 32 (1951) 22ff.; Schildenberger, op. cit., 456-59; van Unnik, op. cit., 165; G. S. Hendry, *The Holy Spirit in Christian Theology* (1965²) 24f.

15. Schweizer thinks that on the analogy of Gal. 4:25 we should expect τὸ δὲ κύριος (*TDNT* VI, 417f.). But an exegetical note does not require to be introduced by τό. See Gal. 3:16 (καὶ τῷ σπέρματί σου, ὅς ἐστιν Χριστός) and 1 Cor. 10:4. The neuter τό of Gal. 4:25 has been dictated by the neuter ὄρος, just as in Gal. 3:16 the ὅς following σπέρμα has been determined by the gender of Χριστός.

16. That Paul says "The rock was (ἦν) Christ" and not "is (ἐστίν) Christ" is not significant. In 1 Cor. 10:1-5 the figures in the allegory lie wholly in the past, and he makes no attempt to extend any of them into his own time — as he does in Gal. 4:25 and 2 Cor. 3:14.

17. The law is so much to be equated with death and slavery for Paul that in the Spirit/law antithesis the keynote of the Spirit is life and liberty (Gal. 4–5).

the continuity of thought between 16 and 18,[18] and by the fact that the veil is considered once again in relation to the face.[19] The passage thus expounded demonstrates clearly the contrast between the old and the new covenants. When Moses removed the veil from his face he beheld and shone with the glory of the Lord — only his reflected glory faded, and this fading splendor which is hidden from its members is the mark of the old covenant. But Christians, on the other hand, those who have responded to Paul's ministry of preaching and have entered the new covenant through the Spirit by turning to the Lord (in terms of the present argument = the Spirit), behold and reflect the glory of the Lord with unveiled faces. And in so doing they are transformed more and more into his likeness from one degree of glory to another (cf. Gal. 4:19; Phil. 3:21). "All this comes," says Paul, rounding off both his exposition and his argument, "from the Lord of Exod. 34:34, who in our experience is the Spirit."

This appears to me to be the interpretation which emerges most naturally from the passage; but in order for it to be sustained there are three major objections which it must meet: (a) verse 16 is not a citation of Exod. 34:34; (b) κύριος is Christ; (c) the understanding and role of πνεῦμα involved in the above interpretation is un-Pauline.

(a) Hermann argues that verse 16 is not a citation from Exodus but a free play with a well-known idea from the Old Testament. His case rests on a comparison between 16 and the LXX of Exod. 34:34 —

2 Cor. 3:16 — ἡνίκα δὲ ἐὰν ἐπιστρέψῃ πρὸς κύριον, περιαιρεῖται τὸ κάλυμμα.

Exod. 34:34 — ἡνίκα δ' ἂν εἰσεπορεύετο Μωυσῆς ἔναντι κυρίου λαλεῖν αὐτῷ περιηρεῖτο τὸ κάλυμμα ἕως τοῦ ἐκπορεύεσθαι.

He notes the following differences: εἰσεπορεύετο has been replaced with ἔπιστρέψῃ and the middle περιηρεῖτο with the passive περιαιρεῖται; the phrases λαλεῖν αὐτῷ and ἕως τοῦ ἐκπορεύεσθαι are omitted; the subject of the Exodus sentence has disappeared; the action is transferred from the past to the present (or future — Windisch).[20] On the basis of these alterations

18. Dibelius, op. cit., 129, n. 3. The fact that verse 18 joins directly on to 16 is one of the reasons why Schmithals takes 17 as an exegetical gloss (together with the last clause of 18) added to the letter by Paul's Gnostic opponents in Corinth!

19. The application of Exod. 34:34 is slightly different therefore from the application of 34:33, but the difference is insignificant for Paul's overall meaning.

20. But to take verse 16 as forward-looking is to forget that for Paul the dispensation of the Spirit is already present and operative; Christians are living in the eschatological "Now" (6:2).

Hermann concludes that it is hardly possible to describe 16 as a citation of Exod. 34:34.

However, Hermann fails to reckon with the fact that verses 7-18 are a Christian midrash on Exodus 34, and so he does not realize that 16 is a pesher text. Without becoming too involved in this subject we may say that in the New Testament's use of the Old Testament there are two major types of pesher:[21]

(i) Where the Old Testament passage is cited, often at some length and is followed by an exposition in which words and phrases are repeated and interpreted;

(ii) Where the interpretation or commentary has been written into the text, modifying the textual form if necessary; or, more fully, where a text is interpreted of and applied to a certain situation in the light of some new revelation or from a new revelational standpoint, and both altered in detail and modified in sense in accordance with that interpretation and revelation.[22]

The first type is the true pesher, with which the Dead Sea Scrolls have made us familiar (see particularly the Commentary on Habakkuk). The best examples within the New Testament are Rom. 10:5-9 and Heb. 10:5-10. See also Rom. 9:7-8 (τοῦτ' ἔστιν); 2 Cor. 6:2; Eph. 4:8-11; Heb. 2:6-9; 3:7-19.[23] The second type is not properly a pesher, if we make the Qumran pesher the determinative use;[24] and it could be argued that it stands as much, if not more, in the line of the interpretative translations of the Targum (and frequently the LXX).[25] But we may say that "pesher" as the title of the second type is a legitimate (Christian) extension of its use — for even in the first type the text cited has often been tendentiously modified prior to its exposition (cf. Heb. 10:5),[26] and (ii) is just an extension of this — a choosing of the most suitable text among possible variants and a modifying of the text as necessary to

21. "Pesher" means, of course, "exposition" or "interpretation" (see, e.g., Eccles. 8:1; Dan. 2:4).

22. This understanding of "pesher" was popularized by K. Stendahl, *The School of St. Matthew* (1954, [2]1968), following W. H. Brownlee, and applied by E. E. Ellis to Paul in *Paul's Use of the Old Testament* (1957); see also "A Note on Pauline Hermeneutics," *NTS* 2 (1955-56) 127-33.

23. See S. Kistemaker, *The Psalm Citations in the Epistle to the Hebrews* (1961) 81-86.

24. B. Gärtner, "The Habakkuk Commentary (DSH) and the Gospel of Matthew," *Studia Theologica* 8 (1955) 12, among others, has objected to Stendahl's use of the word "pesher" for the formula quotations in Matthew.

25. A striking example is the Targum on Isaiah 52:13–53:12, where the translation has been so framed as to rule out a Christian interpretation; see *The Targum of Isaiah,* ed. J. F. Stenning (1949).

26. Gärtner, op. cit., 13.

embody the interpretation and convey the meaning intended. In any case, it could equally well be argued that "pesher" can properly be used for a text which is interpreted, whether the interpretation is embodied in the text itself or stands outside.

The best example of this form of pesher is probably Matt. 27:9-10, where the details of Zech. 11:13 have been greatly altered, probably in some combination with Jer. 32:6-9, to fit with the events surrounding Judas's death, as Matthew understands them.[27] Matt. 2:23 is another good example, where Samson is taken as a type of Jesus and the pesher text is established by a play on ναζιρ(αῖον) (Judg. 13:5) and נֵצֶר (Isa. 11:1).[28] In Acts two less striking examples are Acts 1:20 and 4:11. In the Pauline literature see Rom. 12:19; 1 Cor. 15:54-55; Eph. 4:8.[29] A pesher quotation may, like Matt. 27:9-10, involve a combination of texts (Matt. 21:5, 13; Rom. 9:33; 11:8; 1 Cor. 2:9; 2 Cor. 6:16-18; Gal. 3:8; Heb. 10:37-38), or like Matt. 2:23 involve the development of a text which has no real parallel (Luke 11:49; John 7:38; Rom. 11:35; Eph. 5:14; cf. Jas. 4:5). It may be that the text does not need to be altered, even though the interpretation is quite different from the sense originally intended (Rom. 1:17; 10:18). And it may well be that different interpretations are applied to the same passage (compare Heb. 2:13's use of Isa. 8:17-18 with Rom. 9:33 and 1 Pet. 2:8's use of Isa. 8:14-15).

Paul's treatment of Exod. 34:34 is quite in accord with this pesher technique and takes no more liberty with the sense than many of these other examples. The textual alterations and omissions are those and only those which are required to bring the text into line with the interpretation and exposition Paul has drawn from the passage.[30] In particular, in 2 Cor. 3:16 Paul alters the historic tense (εἰσεπορεύετο) to a conditional or frequentative clause (ἐπιστρέψῃ) in order to show how (at any time in the future) the veil may be removed. NEB's (pesher) translation is superb and excellently conveys Paul's meaning: "However, as Scripture says of Moses, 'whenever he turns to the Lord the veil is removed.' Now the Lord of whom this passage speaks is the Spirit."

(b) As noted at the outset, the majority of exegetes in this century have taken κύριος of verse 17 = Christ. Kümmel and Schildenberger, despite taking κύριος in 17a as a reference to the κύριος (= Yahweh) of 16, join the rest in interpreting the κύριος 17b as Christ. And κύριος in 18 is likewise usually

---

27. Cf. Stendahl, op. cit., 120-26, 196ff. That modifications have been made is best shown by the very awkward μοι which is left.

28. Cf. E. Schweizer, "Er wird Nazoräer heissen," *Neotestamentica* (1963) 51-55.

29. Ellis also refers to Rom. 10:11; 11:26; 1 Cor. 3:20; 15:45a.

30. Indeed, the textual modifications are no more drastic than those in many of Paul's "straight" quotations (Rom. 3:10-12, 14, 15-17; 9:9, 17, 25, 27-28; 10:15, 20 [clauses in reverse order]; 11:3; 1 Cor. 1:31; 14:21).

referred to Christ. The chief reason for this interpretation is that κύριος for Paul, with only few exceptions, means Christ. The Jew of Paul's time removes the veil not by turning to Yahweh but by turning to Christ,[31] who, after all, has already been referred to in this connection (verse 14).

This interpretation, however, must be rejected. κύριος in verse 16 is Yahweh, as we have shown; and 17a explains who this κύριος is in terms of the present argument. While κύριος in Paul does usually refer to the exalted Christ, in Old Testament citations κύριος is almost always Yahweh.[32] Moreover, Nigel Turner has pointed out that normally ὁ κύριος (with article) is Christ, while κύριος (without article) is Yahweh.[33] In this case, as Turner suggests, the definite article with κύριος in 17 will be anaphoric, that is, it takes up the immediately preceding reference to κύριος (no article) = Yahweh, and becomes virtually demonstrative: this κύριος (of Exod. 34:34) is the Spirit.[34]

It is not enough, therefore, to say that in Paul ὁ κύριος usually equals Christ and must do so in verse 17. The determinative factor in such discussions is the context, and the context here is that of a Christian midrash on an Old Testament passage where κύριος = Yahweh. Not only so, but the immediate context (verses 16-18) is dominated by the Exod. 34:34 citation. On both occasions in verse 17 κύριος refers back to the Yahweh of 16,[35] for 17b is as important as 17a in relating the exposition of Exodus 34 to the theme of law and Spirit, death and life, condemnation and righteousness, bondage and liberty.[36] Likewise in 18 κύριος (no article) is the Yahweh of the Exodus passage,[37] for

31. Hermann, op. cit., 39. Cf. Prat, op. cit. II, 437.

32. See W. Foerster, *TDNT* III, 1086f. Thus Rom. 4:8; 9:28, 29; 10:16 (κύριε); 11:3 (κύριε is added to the LXX); 11:34; 15:11; 1 Cor. 2:16; 3:20; 10:26; 14:21; 2 Cor. 6:17-18; 8:21; 2 Thess. 1:9; 2 Tim. 2:19 (LXX reads ὁ θεός). In Rom. 10:13; 1 Cor. 1:31; and 2 Cor. 10:17, Paul may well intend the primary reference to be to the exalted Christ; but it is significant that in the last two of these three cases the text is much modified, and ἐν κυρίῳ does not occur in this form in the LXX.

33. But κύριος has the article in Rom. 15:11; 1 Cor. 10:26; and 2 Thess. 1:9, of the references in n. 32 above.

34. N. Turner, *Grammatical Insights into the New Testament* (1965) 127. See his discussion of anaphora in *Grammar of New Testament Greek* III (1963) 172ff.

35. It would just be possible to follow Kümmel and Schildenberger and to see in Paul's use of κύριος something of the variety of use already observable in this chapter with ἐπιστολή and κάλυμμα, but to refer the κύριος in 17b to Christ is to postulate an unnecessary confusion of thought.

36. As Galatians 4–5 and Romans 7–8 show clearly, these are all related concepts in Paul's mind, so that Schmithals is quite wrong when he maintains that 17b is foreign to the context and that ἐλευθερία is left entirely up in the air (303f.). Turner suggests reading οὐ instead of οὗ ("not" instead of "where") so that κυρίου is separated from πνεῦμα and linked to ἐλευθερία, and we have the translation: "But the Spirit is not independence of Yahweh" (*Insights*, 128). This is both unnecessary and unconvincing. There is even less warrant for J. Héring's conjectural emendation (*Second Epistle of S. Paul to the Corinthians* [1967] 26f.).

37. *Contra* Kümmel, op. cit., 200f.; Schildenberger, op. cit., 460.

18 takes up and enlarges on 16: it is the Lord to whom Moses turned from whom the glory comes, the Lord who in terms of Paul's argument here is the Spirit. We might well paraphrase the final clause of 18: "Such is the influence of the Lord, who, as we have already said, is Spirit."[38]

(c) The final criticism we must consider is that the role given to the Spirit in this interpretation is one wholly foreign to Pauline theology. By translating "Yahweh is the Spirit" we make an identification which Paul never makes and put the Spirit in the place of Christ. Indeed Schmithals thinks it self-evident that Paul would have said ὁ δὲ κύριος ὁ Χριστός ἐστιν. That is to say, he would have identified the Yahweh of Exod. 34:34 with Christ; but that he should identify Christ and the Spirit is for Schmithals out of the question, since Paul always "clearly distinguishes" the two.[39]

The fact is, however, that the central antithesis in this chapter is between the law and the Spirit, not between the law and Christ. In the comparison with Judaism the Spirit is the decisive factor; as the law was the regulating principle and motivating power of the Old Covenant, so it is with the Spirit in the New Covenant.[40] And the πνεῦμα which Paul equates with Yahweh is the πνεῦμα of the preceding verses. Only as an attempt to relate Exod. 34:34 to his main theme can verse 17 be properly understood; otherwise it is no more than "a superfluous Christological digression."[41]

Hermann is quite right at this point — Paul is talking in terms of experience and the πνεῦμα is a functional concept.[42] Paul's experience of the old covenant was of death, condemnation, and bondage; but his experience of the new covenant was of life, righteousness, and liberty. The Spirit for Paul was above all a reality of experience — an experience of miraculous power (1 Thess. 1:5; Gal. 3:5; 1 Cor. 2:4-5; Rom. 15:19), of moral transformation (2 Thess. 2:12; 1 Cor. 6:9-11; Rom. 8:13), of enlightenment (1 Cor. 2:12), of joy (1 Thess. 1:6), of love (Gal. 5:22; Rom. 5:5), of sonship (Gal. 4:6; Rom. 8:15-16), etc., so that the manifest presence of the Spirit determined whether one was a Christian or not (Rom. 8:9).[43] It was by receiving the Spirit that Paul entered into the dispensation of the Spirit, and through the Spirit that he

---

38. See Plummer, op. cit., 108, and Windisch, op. cit., 129f., for the various possible renderings of κυρίου πνεύματος. Windisch and Wendland, op. cit., 160, prefer the sense "Lord of the Spirit." Hermann suggests that there is a duality of meaning intended: both "the Lord who is the Spirit" and "Lord of the Spirit" (op. cit., 55). The majority of commentators seem to take the phrase in the sense of 17a.

39. Schmithals, op. cit., 299f.

40. Cf. Schildenberger, op. cit., 452.

41. Kümmel, op. cit., 200.

42. Hermann, op. cit., 28-31, 49ff., 57. Cf. Büchsel, op. cit., 428; Strachan, op. cit., 89f.; Windisch, who speaks of a "dynamic identification" (op. cit., 124); Hamilton, "For purposes of communicating redemption the Lord and the Spirit are one" (op. cit., 8).

43. See also my *Baptism in the Holy Spirit*.

experienced the life and liberty of the new covenant. He experienced God by the Spirit. He experienced the exalted Christ through the Spirit. This does not mean that they are identical in all their functions (far less their "beings"), as though, for example, the Spirit had been crucified and raised from the dead. It only means that they are identical in experience. Only so can we explain such passages as Rom. 8:9-11; 1 Cor. 6:17; 12:4-6 — because the Spirit *is* the Spirit of Jesus (Rom. 8:9; Gal. 4:6; Phil. 1:17): Christ lives in us by the Spirit (Gal. 2:20), and our transfiguration into his image is the ἁγιασμός of the Spirit (cf. Gal. 4:19; 2 Cor. 3:18).[44]

This is not to deny the unusualness of the formulation. But no interpretation of this passage escapes that charge, and the formulation here is determined by the context and the type of exposition employed by Paul. Schildenberger also reminds us that the teaching it expresses is genuinely Pauline, the uniqueness of the expression notwithstanding: "The Spirit is the Unveiler, the Revealer" (1 Cor. 2:10, 12; 12:3; cf. Eph. 1:18).[45] When we bear these facts in mind it does not seem odd that Paul should speak of the Lord of the Exodus quotation in terms of the Spirit who gives life, brings liberty, and transforms into the image of God in a way that Moses of old never knew.

44. M. Bouttier, *En Christ* (1962), has pointed out that on balance Paul prefers to speak of Christians ἐν Χριστῷ and of the Spirit ἐν ἡμῖν, rather than the reverse (see also C. F. D. Moule, *The Phenomenon of the New Testament* [1967] 24ff.).

45. Schildenberger, op. cit., 459f.

8

Jesus — Flesh and Spirit
An Exposition of Romans 1:3-4

How did the primitive church understand the relation between Jesus and the Spirit? In the Pauline literature, 1 Cor. 15:45 apart, there is no more important passage on this subject than Rom. 1:3-4:[1]

> . . . περὶ τοῦ υἱοῦ αὐτοῦ
> τοῦ γενομένου ἐκ σπέρματος Δαυειδ κατὰ σάρκα,
> τοῦ ὁρισθέντος υἱοῦ Θεοῦ ἐν δυνάμει κατὰ πνεῦμα
> Ἰησοῦ Χριστοῦ τοῦ κυρίου ἡμῶν.

It is now generally recognized that Paul has taken over an earlier statement, presumably known also to his Roman readers, and so a guarantee of Paul's "good faith." The decisive pointers are: the parallelism of the phrases, with the combination of participial and relative clauses characteristic of such formulas, the Semitically styled and untypically Pauline emphasis on Jesus' descent from David, the primitive "adoptionist"-like ring of ὁρισθέντος,[2] the singular occurrence in Paul of the phrase υἱοῦ Θεοῦ ἐν δυνάμει, the almost unique Semitic form πνεῦμα ἁγιωσύνης,[3] and the absence of any mention of the cross, elsewhere so central to Paul's theology.[4]

---

1. I have shown in chapter 7 above that 2 Cor. 3:17 is not directly relevant.
2. Note the parallels in the other formations of the kerygma, particularly Acts 2:36; 10:42; 12:33; 17:31; Heb. 1:5.
3. The only exact verbal parallel is *T. Levi* 18:11; but note also Isa. 52:10f.; Ps. 51:11. In the Qumran literature see 1QS 3.7; 4.21; 8.16; 9.3; 1QH 7.6; 9.32; 12.12; 14.13; 16.7, 12; 1QSb 2.24; CD 2.12; 5.11; 7.4; cf. 1QH 8.12.
4. See, e.g., A. M. Hunter, *Paul and His Predecessors* ([1]1940, [2]1961) 24f.; G. Bornkamm, "Das Bekenntnis im Hebräerbrief," *Theologische Blätter* 21 (1942), reprinted in *Studien zu Antike*

More disputed is the question of how much Paul has added. There is a firm consensus that the closing phrase Ἰησοῦ Χριστοῦ τοῦ κυρίου ἡμῶν falls into this category; it is unmistakably Pauline (Rom. 1:7; 5:1, 11, 21; 7:25; 13:14; 15:6, 30; 1 Cor. 1:2f., etc.). Similarly there is a more or less firm consensus that Paul added the initial reference to "the Son" to counteract the suggestion of adoptionism in the second clause.[5] There is less agreement with regard to ἐν δυνάμει and the κατὰ σάρκα/κατὰ πνεῦμα ἁγιωσύνης antithesis. Some think ἐν δυνάμει is a Pauline addition, whether to soften the adoptionism of ὁρισθέντος υἱοῦ Θεοῦ ... ἐξ ἀναστάσεως νεκρῶν and complement the περὶ τοῦ υἱοῦ αὐτοῦ,[6] or on the ground that it spoils the antithetic parallelism of the clauses.[7] However, Ferdinand Hahn argues that "the concept of a sonship of superior degree" implied in the juxtaposition of τοῦ υἱοῦ αὐτοῦ and υἱοῦ Θεοῦ ἐν δυνάμει is "hardly conceivable within the pattern of Pauline Christology" and concludes that ἐν δυνάμει is a constituent part of the original formula.[8] As for the κατὰ σάρκα/κατὰ πνεῦμα antithesis, this too has been widely regarded as a Pauline interpolation, particularly at an earlier stage in the discussion, as being Paul's attempt to give sharper definition to the confession.[9] But Schweizer has forcefully replied that whereas Paul uses the antithesis to contrast humanity in the power of sin with humanity ruled by the Spirit (above all Rom. 8:4f.), the κατὰ here must be understood as "in the sphere of" rather than "in the power of."[10] More recent commentators

---

und Urchristentum (1963) 199, n. 25; E. Schweizer, "Röm. i.3f. und der Gegensatz von Fleisch und Geist vor und bei Paulus," *Evangelische Theologie* 15 (1955), reprinted in *Neotestamentica* (1963) 180; idem, *Erniedrigung und Erhöhung bei Jesus und seinen Nachfolgern* ([1]1955; English translation 1960; [2]1962), 8e; W. Kramer, *Christ, Lord, Son of God* (1966) 108; O. J. F. Seitz, "Gospel Prologues: A Common Pattern?" *JBL* 83 (1964) 266; B. Schneider, "Κατὰ Πνεῦμα Ἁγιωσύνης," *Biblica* 48 (1967) 370f. Already in 1914 Johannes Weiss had noted with reference to Rom. 1:3f. that "the harsh construction . . . shows clearly enough that two different modes of thought have collided at this point" (*Earliest Christianity* I [1937, 1959] 119).

  5. Bultmann, however, suggests the original formula ran as follows:

(Jesus Christ) the Son of God,
Come from the seed of David,
Designated Son of God in power by his resurrection from the dead

(*Theology of the New Testament* I [1952] 49).

  6. Schweizer, *Neotestamentica*, 180; K. Wegenast, *Das Verständnis der Tradition bei Paulus und in den Deuteropaulinen* (1962) 71; Kramer, op. cit., 110; R. H. Fuller, *The Foundations of New Testament Christology* (1965) 165.

  7. C. K. Barrett, *The Epistle to the Romans* (1957) 18; for the same reason Barrett also regards ἐξ ἀναστάσεως νεκρῶν as an interpolation. In terms of parallelism Barrett certainly has the best prima facie case.

  8. *The Titles of Jesus in Christology* (1963, English translation 1969) 247.

  9. See especially Bultmann, *Theology* I, 49f.; N. A. Dahl, "Die Messianität Jesu bei Paulus," *Studia Paulina* (J. de Zwaan FS; 1953) 90; O. Michel, *Der Brief an die Römer* ([10]1955, [12]1963) 38; O. Kuss, *Der Römerbrief* (1957) 8; and now A. Sand, *Der Begriff "Fleisch" in den paulinischen Hauptbriefen* (1967) 161; see also E. Linnemann (n. 11 below).

  10. Schweizer, *Neotestamentica*, 181, 185, 187; *Erniedrigung*, 8e; *TDNT* VI, 416f.; VII, 126f.

have generally accepted both this translation or its equivalent and the corollary that the antithesis is pre-Pauline.[11]

This brings us to the heart of the matter. Is Schweizer justified in drawing such a clear line of distinction between the Pauline use of the antithesis elsewhere and its occurrence here? The question is fundamental to the correct exegesis of Rom. 1:3f., and its resolution will tell us much about the christology of the primitive church and of Paul.

Before taking up this question, however, there is a more basic methodological issue which must be settled. Most recent christological studies of this passage have attempted to penetrate back to the pre-Pauline form and theology of the text before commenting on Paul's use and understanding of it. The pre-Pauline significance becomes the control which enables us to determine how much or how little Paul has added to, modified, or subtracted from the original form. This procedure is more suspect and speculative than necessary and detracts from the weight of the conclusions reached. The fact is, putting it in more general terms, that we can never be so certain about the earlier form of a saying or pericope as we can about the form in which it has come down to us. We can never be so certain about its earlier context as we can about its present context. And since exegesis and interpretation depend to a crucial degree on form and context, this means that we can never be so sure of a saying's original or earlier meaning and significance as we can about its present meaning and significance in the mind of evangelist or letter-writer.[12] This being so, the *present* form and meaning of the saying must serve as a control for and test of the more speculative hypotheses aimed at uncovering

---

11. Barrett, *Romans*, 18; F. J. Leenhardt, *The Epistle to the Romans* (1961) 35f.; Hahn, *Titles*, 247, 249f.; Kramer, op. cit., 109; Fuller, *Foundations*, 165f., 187; D. Hill, *Greek Words and Hebrew Meanings* (1967) 280; less certainly H. Conzelmann, *An Outline of the Theology of the New Testament* (1969) 77. Schneider is sure that κατὰ πνεῦμα ἁγιωσύνης is pre-Pauline, but less sure for κατὰ σάρκα (p. 369). More recently E. Linnemann, "Tradition und Interpretation in Röm. i.3f.," *Evangelische Theologie* 31 (1971) 264-75, has suggested this improbable reconstruction of the Pauline *Vorlage:*

πιστεύω εἰς Ἰησοῦν,
τὸν γενόμενον ἐκ σπέρματος Δαυίδ,
τὸν ὁρισθέντα υἱὸν Θεοῦ
ἐν δυνάμει πνεύματος ἁγιωσύνης
ἐξ ἀναστάσεως νεκρῶν.

As we shall see, it is unnecessary to argue that Paul made such alterations and unlikely that he did so.

12. This line of reasoning applies of course primarily to sayings which have no precise parallel elsewhere in the records of the early church and whose earlier form and meaning must be discovered by digging behind the one text or passage which preserves it. In other words, it applies more to Mark, John, Paul, etc., than it does to Matthew and Luke, who use Mark as a source and where Q can often be reconstructed with a high degree of probability by comparing Matthew and Luke. It need hardly be added that I am speaking in relative terms here — "more certain," "less certain." We can never be absolutely certain that any exegesis is correct.

the earlier form and its significance — the limiting factor always being: Could Paul or the Evangelist *reasonably* be expected to have derived his form and understanding of the saying from the proposed earlier form and understanding? It necessarily follows that *the first task of the exegete and student of Christian origins is the uncovering of the meaning of the saying in the form and context in which it has come down to us.* Only when we are reasonably confident at this point do we have an adequate control for our investigations into the tradition history of that saying. The quite proper understanding of redaction criticism as a task subsequent to form criticism, tradition criticism, and source criticism must not become the illogical corollary that the exegete should start his investigations at some uncertain point lost in the mists of the past when he has before him the concrete reality of the present text. So, for example, any attempt to recover the historical Jesus, or any part of his life, must start with the Gospel portrayals of him and is dependent on them and to a considerable, often decisive, degree controlled by them.

So with our present passage. The hazard of starting our investigations at a point prior to Paul is clearly highlighted by the disagreement over the earlier form of the saying (particularly in relation to ἐν δυνάμει and the σάρξ/πνεῦμα antithesis) and by the fact that the κατὰ σάρκα/κατὰ πνεῦμα antithesis itself is so peculiarly Pauline.[13] No, the primary object must be to discover what *Paul* understood by the saying. Only then can we begin to ask whether and how he has adapted and molded the earlier formula. And only then will we be able to determine the significance of Rom. 1:3f. for our understanding of the development of early christology in relation to the Spirit. This is now our task.

I

There are two major arguments in favor of Schweizer's interpretation of the σάρξ/πνεῦμα antithesis. First, in normal Pauline usage κατὰ σάρκα has a distinctly pejorative ring,whereas here, according to Schweizer, κατὰ σάρκα can hardly "describe the life of one who trusts in his own possibilities and capabilities or is mastered by them, in contrast to another who trusts in God's Spirit or is mastered by him."[14] Second, the form and order of the verbs in Rom. 1:3f. and the parallel with 1 Tim. 3:16 (also 1 Pet. 3:18) indicate that

---

13. Cf. J. A. T. Robinson, *The Body* (1952) 22, n. 2, citing E. Käsemann, *Leib und Leib Christi* (1933) 103; Linnemann, "Tradition," 265.
14. *Neotestamentica*, 185, and earlier H. Lietzmann, *An die Römer* (⁴1933 = ⁵1971) 25; cf. Sand, op. cit., 161.

we have here a temporal sequence. The γενομένου clause therefore signifies Jesus' earthly existence in the sphere of the flesh, followed by his installation as Son of God in the heavenly sphere. Contrary to earlier exegesis, which referred κατὰ πνεῦμα to Jesus' earthly existence as well — where πνεῦμα was usually taken as a description of Jesus' divine nature or human spirit distinguished "from that of ordinary humanity by an exceptional and transcendent Holiness"[15] — what we have here is a two-stage christology, the two stages being before and after the resurrection.[16]

Both these arguments are open to criticism. The first makes too sharp a distinction within Paul's use of σάρξ, and the second fails to appreciate the full significance of Paul's understanding of the σάρξ/πνεῦμα antithesis.

It is my contention that Paul does not and would not understand κατὰ σάρκα in a neutral sense. On the contrary, it has here its usual "bad connotation."[17] Paul's use of σάρξ cannot be neatly classified into separate categories and pigeonholes, as is done for example by W. D. Davies into "places where 'flesh' has a physical connotation" and "places where 'flesh' has a moral connotation."[18] σάρξ in Paul has a "spectrum" of meaning, and individual uses are often less like a point in the spectrum and more like a range of meaning within the spectrum.

(a) At one end of the spectrum there is the more or less neutral usage, denoting the physical body, or physical relationship or kinship, without any negative connotation — so Rom. 11:14; 1 Cor. 6:16; 15:39; Eph. 5:29, 31; Col. 2:1; cf. 2 Cor. 7:1.

The meaning then broadens out in two closely interrelated directions.

(b) First, and still with primary reference to the physical, σάρξ embraces the typically Semitic thought of weakness: 1 Cor. 15:50, where σάρξ καὶ αἷμα cannot inherit the kingdom of God precisely because it is perishable and mortal; 2 Cor. 7:5, where the σάρξ is characterized as that which is subject to affliction and weariness; Gal. 4:13f., "the weakness of the flesh"; cf. 1 Cor.

15. W. Sanday and A. C. Headlam, *The Epistle to the Romans* ([5]1902) 9. More recent exponents include M.-J. Lagrange, *Épître aux Romains* ([1]1914, [6]1950) 7; F. Prat, *La Théologie de saint Paul* II (1923) 513; A. Feuillet, "Le plan salvifique de Dieu d'après l'Épître aux Romains," *Revue Biblique* 57 (1950) 338; J. Bonsirven, *Theology of the New Testament* (1963) 230. See also Kuss, op. cit., 6ff.

16. See n. 6 above. For earlier expressions of the "two-stage" interpretation see G. Smeaton, *The Doctrine of the Holy Spirit* (1882, reprinted 1958) 72, referred to by F. F. Bruce, *The Epistle of Paul to the Romans* (1963) 73; G. Vos, *The Pauline Eschatology* (1930) 155, n. 10; also W. Manson, "Notes on the Argument of Romans (Chapters i–viii)," *New Testament Essays: Studies in Memory of T. W. Manson* (1959) 153; J. Murray, *The Epistle of Paul to the Romans* I (1960) 7ff.

17. *Contra* Schweizer, "The Concept of the Davidic 'Son of God' in Acts and Its Old Testament Background," *Studies in Luke-Acts*, ed. L. E. Keck and J. L. Martyn (1966) 192, n. 4.

18. W. D. Davies, "Paul and the Dead Sea Scrolls: Flesh and Spirit," *The Scrolls and the New Testament*, ed. K. Stendahl (1957) 163.

7:28. The range of meaning broadens still more in other passages where this physical weakness gathers up into itself the further thought of moral inadequacy and imperfection: σάρξ is not only weak by reason of being physical; its weakness also means that it is unable to achieve righteousness and that it has *nothing* in which to glory (Rom. 3:20; 1 Cor. 1:29; Gal. 2:16); the law is unable to achieve its object precisely because of the weakness of the flesh (Rom. 8:3), so that those ἐν σαρκί are by virtue of that very fact incapacitated and unable to please God (Rom. 8:8); hence Paul's condemnation of the Judaizers (Gal. 6:12f.) and the need for the σάρξ to be destroyed (Rom. 8:3; 1 Cor. 5:5; Eph. 2:14; Col. 1:22); cf. 2 Cor. 7:1. Closely related is the understanding of σάρξ as the sphere of sin's operations, the instrument of sin (Rom. 7:18, 25; 8:3; cf. 7:5) — a usage which merges into the sense of σάρξ as itself a source of corruption and hostility to God (Rom. 8:5, 7, 12; 13:14, Gal. 5:13, 24; 6:8; Eph. 2:3; Col. 2:11, 13, 18, 23). In all these passages σάρξ has broadened out in meaning well beyond the sense of the merely physical: it signifies all in humanity that makes for mortality and corruption; it is what is human insofar as humans are in the world and belong to the world and are determined by the world.[19] Yet at the same time, the fuller meaning always involves and revolves round the physical — human spiritual and physical weakness are all of a piece; humans' moral corruption and hostility stems largely from their physical appetites and passions and their indulgence of them.

(c) Second, this broadening out of the meaning of σάρξ from the simply physical to include the sense of weakness, inadequacy, corruptibility, etc., carries with it also a further dimension — viz., σάρξ as standing in contrast to a superior realm, mode of being, or pattern of conduct. Thus in Gal. 1:16 "flesh and blood" is not simply humankind, but humankind in contrast to God as a source of apostolic authority (cf. Eph. 6:12). Similarly in Gal. 2:20, the life lived "in the flesh" is not simply physical, everyday existence; that has been superseded, as the "I who live" has been superseded by the "Christ who lives in me." Likewise in Philem. 16, Onesimus is to be a brother not merely ἐν σαρκί, but also ἐν κυρίῳ — the latter being the more significant and determinative relation (cf. Col. 2:5). That the weakness of σάρξ is part and parcel of this inferiority, and vice versa, is clear enough by implication, and 2 Cor. 10:3; 12:7 only make this close interconnection of meaning more explicit: 10:3, where ἐν σαρκί signifies both weakness and inferiority; 12:7, where the "thorn in the flesh" is precisely a weakness set in contrast to the abundance of revelations from God and power of God.

As the idea of σάρξ's physical weakness merges over into the sense of

19. Cf. W. G. Kümmel, *Man in the New Testament* (1963) 62f; J. A. T. Robinson, *The Body*, 19-21.

its imperfection and corruption, so the sense of physical contrast merges into that of spiritual antithesis between the two modes of existence. Rom. 6:19 — the weakness of their flesh poses the constant danger of their abandoning their service of righteousness and resorting to their old slavery to sin; 2 Cor. 4:11 — the life of Jesus manifested in the mortal σάρξ is equivalent to the antithesis between the inner person which is being renewed every day and the outer person which is wasting away (cf. Col. 1:24); Phil. 1:22, 24 — life ἐν σαρκί stands in sharp contrast to being σὺν Χριστῷ, "which is far better." The antithesis becomes most apparent when σάρξ, as not only mortal but defective, disqualifying, and destructive, is set against the life-giving πνεῦμα — Rom. 2:28; 8:6, 9; Gal. 3:3; 5:16, 17, 19; Phil. 3:3, 4; cf. Eph. 2:11.[20]

Again σάρξ has broadened out beyond the merely physical; but not so as to leave the physical behind — for the antithesis between flesh and Spirit comes to its sharpest point again and again precisely when the emphasis is placed on the physical, the external, the ritual.[21]

(d) Paul's use of κατὰ σάρκα in particular demonstrates the same breadth of meaning, but is mainly negative in significance. Only in one passage does it seem to be free of depreciatory overtones: 1 Cor. 10:18 — "Consider Israel κατὰ σάρκα. . . ."

The other occasions in which κατὰ σάρκα describes physical kinship with Israel appear on the surface to be equally neutral; but in fact they are set in contexts of antitheses which give the phrase deeper resonance. Thus in Rom. 4:1, where Abraham is described as "our forefather κατὰ σάρκα," the context shows that the sense of purely physical ancestry shades over into that of "on the human level" — that is, the merely human level (of law and works) as opposed to the spiritual (κατὰ πνεῦμα) level of grace and faith. For one thing the phrase is used, in diatribe style, as an objection to Paul's exposition of justification by faith; the devout Jew's appeal to physical descent from Abraham is an integral part of his defense of justification by works. And for another, Paul meets this argument by citing Abraham as a witness on *his*

---

20. Paul never quite says that σάρξ itself is evil, only that in its weakness and corruptibility it is the ready instrument of sin and that life lived only "on that level" is bound for death. Both Paul and Qumran, though influenced by Hellenistic thought, stop short of the distinctively Hellenistic idea of the flesh as evil (Davies, "Flesh and Spirit," 162, 165; see also pp. 146-47 below).

21. According to D. E. H. Whiteley, "Gal. v.19f. makes it clear that when 'flesh' is used in a moral sense it does not necessarily have any physical meaning, since most of the sins ascribed to the lower nature (sarx) could well be practised by a disembodied spirit" (*The Theology of St. Paul* [1964] 39). Although it is a fair point in the context of Whiteley's discussion, such a curtailment in σάρξ's range of meaning would hardly occur to Paul. Indeed in the Galatian situation it cuts quite against the grain of his thought, since it is integral to his argument that σάρξ is used with its full range of meaning — see particularly 3:3; 6:12f. As H. W. Robinson notes, "In any moral conflict, the lower element will tend to be identified, in whole or in part, with physical impulses . . ." (*The Christian Doctrine of Man* [³1926] 111, see also p. 115).

behalf: both Abraham's own justification and his fatherhood are primarily in terms of grace (κατὰ χάριν), not of works or physical relationship (4:4, 16). By way of immediate response Paul goes on in verse 2: "If Abraham was justified by works, he has something to boast of, but not πρὸς Θεόν" — where there is probably an implied contrast between κατὰ σάρκα and πρὸς Θεόν.[22]

In Rom. 9:3 κατὰ σάρκα again denotes physical descent and kinship, but again there are distinct overtones that this physical relationship is wholly inferior to relationship through the Spirit and promise — as 9:8 and the similarly themed Gal. 4:13 make clear by setting physical descent in open antithesis to sonship διὰ τῆς ἐπαγγελίας. This context of antithesis in Romans 9 cannot but reflect on the other occurrence of κατὰ σάρκα in that chapter: verse 5 — "from them [the Israelites] comes ὁ Χριστὸς τὸ κατὰ σάρκα." Here κατὰ σάρκα is obviously a qualification. Paul does not of course deny that the Christ is an Israelite, but he implies that there is more to the Christ who has come than his descent from Israel; that which is of decisive significance about him is *not* his physical descent. As with Abraham in Rom. 4:1, any emphasis on Christ's relationship κατὰ σάρκα is inevitably negative since it obscures the central message of the gospel. So here Paul, having mentioned the Christ's descent from Israel, immediately goes on to depreciate such descent — (verses 6-8) "it is not the children of the flesh who are the children of God, but the children of the promise are reckoned as descendants."

κατὰ σάρκα in the later Pauline literature is also used in a broader sense of human relationships — that of slave to master — but on both occasions (Eph. 6:5; Col. 3:22) in more or less explicit contrast to the more basic and important (spiritual) relationship of earthbound Christian to heavenly Master, the Lord Christ (Eph. 6:6-9; Col. 3:2–4:1).

Elsewhere the phrase broadens out more explicitly into the moral realm. In the reference to "not many wise κατὰ σάρκα" (1 Cor. 1:26) the context is precisely that of contrast between merely human wisdom and the wisdom of God, a wisdom of a totally different order (1:25). In 2 Cor. 1:17; 5:16 κατὰ σάρκα denotes a merely human attitude, inferior and inadequate, because it lacks the superior insight and deeper concern of the perspective κατὰ πνεῦμα. In 2 Cor. 10:2f. the ideas of moral weakness and this-worldly imperfection are combined. And in 2 Cor. 11:18 and particularly Rom. 8:22f. κατὰ σάρκα becomes positively immoral and wrong — "if you live κατὰ σάρκα, you will die."

(e) Finally, there are the three other passages which put the antithesis most explicitly and sharply. Gal. 4:29 contrasts two types of people — the Jew, born κατὰ σάρκα, with the Christian, born κατὰ πνεῦμα. While Rom. 8:4f. contrasts two types of conduct — life lived κατὰ σάρκα with life lived κατὰ πνεῦμα.

22. See also Robinson, *The Body,* 23 and n. 1.

Two important conclusions follow from this survey of Paul's use of σάρξ.

(a) First, the fact that σάρξ represents a range of meaning rather than a number of discrete points means that the full range of meaning often lies in the background, even when the immediate emphasis is more narrowly defined in a particular context. Thus, on the one hand, even when σάρξ seems to have left the physical connotation behind, there is still, embedded in the context, the idea of flesh as the purely physical, whether in terms of ritual or relationship — for it is precisely in these rituals and relationships that the fleshly attitude comes to its clearest and grossest expression, as, for example, the Galatians references make clear.

Conversely, regularly when Paul speaks of human σάρξ or about humankind in terms of its physical relationships, the overtones of the fuller spectrum are not far below the surface. This helps to explain Paul's attitude to marriage in 2 Corinthians 7: the physical *relationship* can never simply be that; it means also concern about worldly affairs (τὰ τοῦ κόσμου — 7:33f.), which is equivalent to an *attitude* κατὰ σάρκα (cf. 2 Cor. 1:27; also 1 Cor. 1:20 — σοφία τοῦ κόσμου — with 1:26 — σοφοὶ κατὰ σάρκα). It explains too why Paul can so rarely talk of physical kinship among Jews in neutral terms — for it is precisely this physical relationship with Abraham, Jacob, and David which was the cause of the Jewish rejection of the gospel: it was this physical kinship in which they boasted and put their trust, and salvation depended not on a gospel of grace and faith but on the reception of a physical sign. The Jewish concept of election identified race with religion. Paul's rejection of that strict identity, and his recognition that election was by grace not race, meant that he could seldom think of these racial ties without thinking also of that other, more important relationship of gospel and Spirit, on which the bulk of Israel had turned its back. This comes through again and again in various passages in Romans.

(b) Second, because σάρξ regularly encompasses such a wide range of its spectrum of meaning it often has a depreciatory significance not apparent on the surface. This is particularly true of the phrase κατὰ σάρκα. With only one exception (out of 28 occurrences, not including Rom. 1:3) κατὰ σάρκα is always a phrase of contrast and antithesis. The contrast becomes explicit in the open κατὰ σάρκα/κατὰ πνεῦμα antithesis, but it is present elsewhere. And in all these cases κατὰ σάρκα stands on the negative side of the contrast denoting inferiority or inadequacy and usually bearing a distinctly pejorative, somewhat derogatory note as well, sometimes with the added implication of blameworthiness. Again it is in the explicit κατὰ σάρκα/κατὰ πνεῦμα antithesis that the pejorative note sounds most clearly.

Moreover, this applies to the phrase denoting sarkical relationship (kinship κατὰ σάρκα) as well as to that denoting sarkical attitude (conduct κατὰ σάρκα). It is *not* the case that the former is neutral and only the latter depreciated. For, as we have seen, the two hang together, the meaning of the latter often based in the former, the meaning of the former regularly spilling over into the latter. Hence both carry the note of inferiority and stand on the negative side of a depreciatory antithesis.[23] The other attempt to distinguish sarkical relationship from sarkical attitude by the phrases ἐν σαρκί and κατὰ σάρκα (2 Cor. 10:3) also fails. In Rom. 7:5; 8:8f. ἐν σαρκί embraces the full range of meaning of σάρξ, and in Rom. 8:5; Gal. 4:29 (in the application of the allegory) κατὰ σάρκα is used in a similarly all-embracing way.

In short, a simple distinction between physical and moral and between neutral and pejorative uses of σάρξ will not do. It holds only rarely.

If we turn again to Rom. 1:3f. in the light of these conclusions, what do we find? Remembering that our concern is with *Paul's* understanding of the finished formula, *it must be judged highly probable that for Paul κατὰ σάρκα in Rom. 1:3 carries its normal note of depreciation.* For one thing, the physical relationship is precisely that which elsewhere in Romans is Israel's stumbling block — the foundation of its vanity, the source of its faith in works-righteousness, and the cause of its rejecting the gospel. And, for another, κατὰ σάρκα here stands in open antithesis with κατὰ πνεῦμα and so could hardly lack a pejorative significance in Paul's mind.[24]

It may be thought incredible by some that Paul should refer to Jesus' descent from David in a somewhat derogatory manner. But the fact is that the early church appears to have been in two minds about the value of claiming Davidic sonship for Jesus. The Palestinian church was in no doubt about its importance, as the oldest tradition and its popularity in Matthew's Gospel indicate.[25] And in the Jewish context where Messiah was expected to be a successor of David this is wholly understandable. But outside Palestine, in the Hellenistic communities, the identification of Jesus as Son of David seems to have been more of an embarrassment and hindrance than a glad and central affirmation.[26]

This conclusion is strongly suggested by the following facts:

(a) Paul never uses the title of his own accord, even in his exposition of the true significance of Jesus to Jewish readers or to converts under pressure

---

23. Bultmann's distinction between κατὰ σάρκα modifying substantives and κατὰ σάρκα modifying verbs (p. 237) can hardly be pressed, as he clearly recognizes (p. 238) and as his wider discussion of σάρξ indicates (pp. 234ff., particularly 236f.).

24. Cf. the Johannine use of σάρξ in reference to Jesus (John 1:14; 6:51-56, 63); see my "John vi — A Eucharistic Discourse?" *NTS* 17 (1970-71) 331f.

25. Cf. Hahn, *Titles*, 240-46.

26. Linnemann's distinction between "descended from David" and "Son of David" amounts only to a splitting of hairs (op. cit., 267ff.). See Schweizer's reply in *Evangelische Theologie* 31 (1971) 276; also I. H. Marshall, "The Divine Sonship of Jesus," *Interpretation* 21 (1967) 101.

from Jewish sources.[27] Even in the kerygma in Acts, where the audience addressed is usually Jewish, the title receives no prominence (Acts 2:30; 13:23); indeed Acts 2:29 may reflect a reaction against a too Jewishly conceived Davidic messiahship. Certainly with the Epistle of Barnabas the repudiation of Davidic sonship has become explicit and unequivocal (*Barn.* 12:10).

(b) The famous pericope Mark 12:35-37 is, to be sure, not an attempt to refute the description of Messiah as Son of David; but nevertheless it is evidence of some embarrassment within the Christian community about the title: they do not deny it, but neither do they particularly wish to affirm it. It must rather be set alongside the more important title κύριος and so corrected and replaced by the latter. It may also be significant that in Mark "on the only occasion where Jesus is addressed as υἱὲ Δαυίδ, the speaker of these words is described as 'blind,' a condition from which he is 'saved' by his faith in Jesus whom he proceeds to follow 'in the way' (x.46-52)."[28] Moreover, we may note that whereas Mark leaves the connection between the entry into Jerusalem and the Davidic kingdom vague, no doubt deliberately, it is precisely Matthew who makes the crowd's acclamation an explicit recognition of Jesus as "Son of David" (Matt. 21:9).

(c) Equally relevant is the manner in which the Fourth Evangelist handles the title. Reference to Davidic descent as an attribute of the Christ appears only once, and that on the lips of the fickle, wavering crowd (7:42). John himself never affirms it of Jesus, and he clearly regards the crowd's understanding of the Christ as totally inadequate. For one thing, the fact that it is the opinion of the *crowd* itself denotes, as one of John's dramatic conventions, an understanding of Jesus which falls misleadingly short of the truth to a dangerous degree; this dramatic effect is best displayed in reference to the title "prophet" (4:19; 6:14; 7:40). And for another, in the continuation of the scene into chapter 8 Jesus denies that the Jews know his origin (8:14). However right or wrong such knowledge, it is irrelevant (cf. 7:28). Such evaluations of the Christ are false because they are κατὰ τὴν σάρκα (8:15) — a striking parallel to Rom. 1:3.

Why the identification of Jesus as Son of David was so treated in the Hellenistic church is not entirely clear — most probably because it was too peculiarly Jewish to permit its easy translation into the wider world. The Jewish hope of a messianic son of David was expressed in strongly political and so nationalistic terms: the son of David was expected to introduce a political kingdom and effect a this-worldly salvation.[29] However amenable this was to the gospel of the Palestinian church it cannot but have been an

---

27. Though in the wider Pauline corpus cf. the formulistic 2 Tim. 2:8.
28. Seitz, op. cit., 266.
29. Hahn, *Titles,* 242ff.

embarrassment outside Palestine. In short, since both Mark and John, and perhaps Luke, treat Jesus' Davidic sonship in a somewhat pejorative fashion as a wholly inadequate and defective understanding of Jesus, it should occasion no surprise that Paul reacts to the title in similar manner.

Our conclusion thus far is therefore that "in the sphere of" as a translation of κατὰ (σάρκα) is too vague and colorless an interpretation of Paul's thought and that Rom. 1:3 in Paul's intention can hardly be understood as a neutral reference to an acceptable christology. On the contrary, as elsewhere in Paul, κατὰ σάρκα carries with it overtones from its fuller range of meaning and is intended pejoratively. Paul does not affirm the Davidic sonship of Jesus without qualification. He does not deny it either, but he makes it clear that to describe Jesus as "born of the seed of David" is a dangerously defective and misleading half-truth.

II

If Schweizer's interpretation of κατὰ σάρκα is inadequate the same is true of his interpretation of the κατὰ σάρκα/κατὰ πνεῦμα antithesis. As a sharp distinction within Paul's use of σάρξ is not possible, so too it is impossible to take the σάρξ/πνεῦμα antithesis so completely outside the normal Pauline soteriological contrast of flesh and Spirit.

Paul's soteriology at this point can be summarized fairly briefly. Humanity in itself, in Adam, is σάρξ and σάρκινος/σαρκικός, with all that that implies in terms of the range of meaning already demonstrated. A person becomes a Christian, "in Christ," by receiving the Spirit of Christ, the Holy Spirit.[30] But this does *not* mean that the person thereby ceases to be σάρξ and ἐν σαρκί. At this point many commentators miss the way and misunderstand Paul. Thus, for example, E. Brandenburger, in the most recent study of the terms flesh and Spirit, writes that in Paul

> Sarx and Pneuma appear as mutually exclusive spheres of power . . . : either one is in the sphere of power opposed to God ἐν σαρκί, or in the sphere of power which brings salvation ἐν πνεύματι (Rom. 8:8f.). More precisely: believers were once in the Sarx, but now find themselves in contrast in the realm of the Pneuma. The change of state [*Befindlichkeit*] may be thought of as a "being set free from" or "transfer" (Gal. 1:4; Col. 1:13).[31]

30. See my *Baptism in the Holy Spirit* (1970).
31. E. Brandenburger, *Fleisch und Geist: Paulus und die dualistische Weisheit* (1968) 45f.; cf., e.g., Lietzmann, *Römerbrief,* 79f.; C. H. Dodd, *The Epistle to the Romans* (1932) 116f.; A. Nygren, *Commentary on Romans* (1952) 316.

Two misinterpretations run together here. One is that ἐν σαρκί and ἐν πνεύματι are successive states — the convert moves out of one into the other. The second, more fundamental error is that these spheres wholly absorb a person, so that he or she is either entirely in the flesh or else entirely in the Spirit.

Paul, however, sees the Christian as living in "the overlap of the ages." Where the Christian once was only in Adam, now he is in Christ *as well;* where once the Christian lived only in the power of the σάρξ, now he experiences the power of the πνεῦμα *as well.* We should not make the mistake of taking Paul's metaphors of liberation, transfer, crucifixion, death and burial, etc., too literally without reference to his fuller thought. The Christian has indeed entered the new sphere of power (πνεῦμα), but not entirely; he still belongs to the old sphere of power (σάρξ) at the same time — *simul peccator et justus.* He is still bound to the world by the body of flesh, with *all* that that involves. And the Christian will not leave the σάρξ behind until his redemption is complete, when the *body* is redeemed as well and enters the realm of Spirit as a σῶμα πνευματικόν. This is why the Spirit already received is only the ἀρραβών and ἀπαρχή of complete salvation. The incompleteness of the Christian's salvation is precisely because he is still a person of flesh and blood, still bound up with the σάρξ ἁμαρτίας. The time will come when "the change of state" will be complete, when the old nature has been once and for all put off and put to death (Rom. 8:17ff.; 2 Cor. 4:16–5:5), when the image of Christ is fully formed in σῶμα as well as πνεῦμα (2 Cor. 3:18; Gal. 4:19; Phil. 3:21), but in the interval between Pentecost and parousia the Christian belongs to both camps and cannot escape the tension and warfare involved (Rom. 8:12f.; Gal. 5:17). The alternative proposed by Brandenburger is an idealistic, docetic soteriology which does scant justice to the realism of Paul's thought.

It is true, of course, that in his moral exhortations Paul presents κατὰ σάρκα and κατὰ πνεῦμα as two opposing, alternative, and mutually exclusive modes of conduct (Rom. 8:4ff.). But the striking fact is precisely that he has to exhort *Christians not* to live κατὰ σάρκα (8:12f.) — the possibility of conducting life on that level is always open to the Christian and is an ever-present danger. Why so? — simply because the Christian is human, and as such *cannot help living on the level of the σάρξ at least to some extent.* The Christian lives in the world and cannot help being determined by the world. The danger is not that he returns from a total existence ἐν πνεύματι to a partial existence ἐν σαρκί, but that he abandons the tension of the warfare between σάρξ and πνεῦμα and returns to an existence *exclusively* κατὰ σάρκα. This duality of existence both in flesh and in Spirit at one and the same time is implied by a verse like Gal. 2:20 and comes to clearest expression in Rom. 7:25b and 8:10. Gal. 2:20 — although "it is no longer I who live, but Christ who lives in me," nevertheless I still "live in the flesh"; the tension of living in the overlap of the ages is precisely that of having to express the life of the Spirit *in and through* the body of death (Rom. 8:10). Rom. 7:25b — after expressing the frustration inevitably involved in living in "this body doomed to death," Paul does *not* go on to imply that deliverance from it is achieved *before* the resurrection of the body. Rather he affirms with calm realism that the Christian living as he still does in this world is inevitably a person of divided loyalties — serving the law of God with the mind, while *at the same time* he serves the law of sin with his flesh.[32] The body of flesh is doomed to death and is steadily wasting away (2 Cor. 4:16), but it is not yet dead and raised again; the πνεῦμα has not yet brought the σῶμα under its sway (σῶμα πνευματικόν), and until that time the Christian lives both ἐν σαρκί and ἐν πνεύματι, experiencing both death and life (Rom. 8:12f.; 2 Cor. 4:10-12; Phil. 3:10f.; Col. 1:24). He must minimize the extent of the flesh's control and power, and must maximize the extent of the Spirit's (Rom. 8:12f.), but until the Spirit reclaims the body the Christian can never wholly escape the domain and influence of the σάρξ.

In short, a straightforward two-stage soteriology (from σάρξ to πνεῦμα) is over-simple: the two stages overlap. A *three-stage* soteriology would be the more accurate shorthand description of Paul's thought at this point — flesh, flesh and Spirit, Spirit. Similarly, to pose κατὰ σάρκα and κατὰ πνεῦμα as mutually exclusive options for conduct is over-simple: the Christian lives on both levels at one and the same time.

Paul's soteriology in terms of σάρξ and πνεῦμα must have influenced his christological use of the same terms. In particular it is highly probable that Paul's understanding of Rom. 1:3f. reflects his soteriology of flesh and Spirit: that is, that κατὰ σάρκα, κατὰ πνεῦμα in Rom. 1:3f. denote not successive and mutually exclusive spheres of power, but modes of existence and relationships which overlap and coincide in the earthly Jesus.

(a) The principal justification for this claim is the fact that in Paul's view the Christian's experience of flesh and Spirit is patterned on Christ's. Not only did Jesus come as man (Phil. 2:8), in the precise likeness of sinful flesh (ἐν ὁμοιώματι σαρκὸς ἁμαρτίας — Rom. 8:3),[33] but his resurrection is the ἀπαρχή of the general resurrection (1 Cor. 15:20ff.), so that the resurrection of the body as σῶμα πνευματικόν is in fact the transformation of the body of flesh into a body of glory like that of Christ (1 Cor. 15:44f.; Phil. 3:21). It follows that for Paul the earthly Jesus was the prototype of and example to

---

32. The attempt to excise 7:25b as a gloss (R. Bultmann, "Glossen im Römerbrief," *Theologische Literaturzeitung* 72 [1947] 198f.; G. Zuntz, *The Text of the Epistles* [1953] 16; cf. Leenhardt, *Romans,* 200) or to treat it as transposed from an original position between verses 23 and 24 (Moffatt translation; Dodd, *Romans,* 114f.; K. E. Kirk, *The Epistle to the Romans* [1937] 208) lacks all manuscript support and totally misunderstands Paul's thought.

33. For this sense of ὁμοίωμα see my *Baptism,* 142f.

the Christian caught in the overlap of the ages — for it can hardly be argued that in Paul's mind Jesus' experience of the Spirit only began with the resurrection.[34] This is not as clear as it might be since Paul says so little about the historical Jesus. But two elements in his thought make it clear enough.

The first is the link between the Christian's experience of the Spirit and his sense of sharing in Christ's sonship and inheritance (Rom. 8:15ff.; Gal. 4:6f.). Sonship for Paul is clearly a function of the Spirit (πνεῦμα υἱοθεσίας, τὸ πνεῦμα τοῦ υἱοῦ αὐτοῦ), and the ἀββά cry of the Christian son was almost certainly recognized as a reproduction of Jesus' own experience of sonship (Mark 14:36).[35] Paul probably knew and accepted the "Q" tradition, reproduced in Matthew and Luke, that Jesus' experience of the Spirit at Jordan sealed Jesus' sense of sonship and equipped him for his mission. Certainly the play on Χριστός and χρίω in describing the Christian convert's reception of the Spirit in 2 Cor. 1:21f. strongly implies that Paul recognized the parallel between Jesus' experience at Jordan and conversion. The historical Jesus like the Christian experienced both the "flesh of sin" and the Spirit of God.[36]

Second, there is the strand of *imitatio Christi* firmly embedded in Paul's thought — Rom. 15:2f.; 1 Cor. 4:17; 11:1; 2 Cor. 8:8f.; Gal. 1:10; Eph. 4:20, 32–5:2; Phil. 2:5-8; Col. 2:6; 1 Thess. 1:6; also Rom. 13:14; Eph. 4:24. For Paul "every Christian is pledged to an attempted ethical conformity to Christ; the imitation of Christ is part and parcel of Paul's ethic."[37] The fact that Christ stands as an example to the Christian caught as he is in the tension and conflict of flesh and Spirit indicates clearly enough that in Paul's view Christ too was caught in the same overlap of the ages. As he had come to victory through the suffering which being in the flesh involves, so the Christian must welcome suffering as a stage on the way to glory (Rom. 8:17; Phil. 3:10f.; Col. 1:24). As he had made an end of sin in the flesh, so must the Christian by the power of the Spirit (Rom. 8:3f.). The disciple looks not only to the exalted Jesus for the power/Spirit to pursue his course, but also to the historical Jesus for the example of one who has already won through to total victory.

(b) That Paul sees in Rom. 1:3f. the prototype of the Christian living both κατὰ σάρκα and κατὰ πνεῦμα is borne out by two facts. First, there is the twofold use of υἱός. Without the first υἱός the simple two-line formula in the pre-Pauline form favored by Schweizer (see n. 6 above) is best understood

---

34. 1 Cor. 15:45 does *not* imply that the relation between Jesus and the Spirit began at the resurrection, only that it was consummated then, when Jesus became σῶμα πνευματικόν, as the context makes clear — that is, when the *totality* of his being was "taken up into the life of the Spirit" (M. E. Dahl, *The Resurrection of the Body* [1962] 81). See also n. 42 below.

35. See particularly J. Jeremias, *The Prayers of Jesus* (1967) 54-65.

36. Note the significance, if correct, of Michel's suggestion that in Rom. 1:3f. we have an old baptismal confession (*Römerbrief,* 39). It implies the recognition that the baptizand enters into the same tension between the flesh and Spirit which Jesus experienced after Jordan.

37. W. D. Davies, *Paul and Rabbinic Judaism* (1948, [2]1955) 147.

as affirming that Jesus only became Son of God at and by his resurrection.[38] But with the addition of the first υἱός it becomes obvious that Paul refers Jesus' sonship to the whole formula — pre- as well as post-resurrection. In the former stage the sonship has to be expressed through the flesh; only in the latter stage is it sonship ἐν δυνάμει.[39] We have here a striking parallel with Paul's understanding of the Christian's sonship, for it too falls into the same two stages — the adoption which comes with the Spirit of adoption (Rom. 8:15) and the full adoption in glory which awaits the redemption/resurrection of the body (Rom. 8:23). Sonship in *both* stages is clearly a function of the Spirit: insofar and only insofar as a person is controlled and directed by the Spirit, to that extent he is a son (Rom. 8:14); only with the resurrection of the body (σῶμα πνευματικόν) does the Spirit assume full control. The parallel between Rom. 1:3f. and 8:15, 23 is too close to admit any doubt that the sonship of *Jesus* in the first stage is likewise a function of the Spirit.

Second, there is the use of ἐξ ἀναστάσεως νεκρῶν, instead of ἐξ ἀναστάσεως <u>αὐτοῦ</u> or ἐξ ἀναστάσεως <u>ἐκ</u> νεκρῶν. The reading in the text is not to be taken as an abbreviated form of the fuller formula[40] but as a deliberate reference to the general resurrection of the dead expected at the end of the age (cf. Acts 26:23). "For Paul the resurrection of Christ is the beginning of the resurrection of the dead."[41] This expression at once calls to mind the fact of the overlap of the ages; for it is precisely because the Christian lives between the resurrection of Christ and the general resurrection that he experiences both flesh *and* Spirit — Spirit, because he has received the Spirit of the risen Christ, flesh, because the power of the resurrection has not yet extended to his body to redeem and raise it from the dead. The implication is strong therefore that in Paul's mind was the thought that as Jesus' resurrection is the forerunner of the final resurrection, so Jesus in the flesh is the forerunner of the Christian

---

38. That ὁρισθέντος signifies appointment and installation and not merely the declaration or revelation of a previous appointment is shown particularly by M.-E. Boismard, "Constitué Fils de Dieu (Rom. i.4)," *Revue Biblique* 60 (1953) 5-17. It is probably drawn from the adoption formula of Ps. 2:7 (L. C. Allen, "The Old Testament Background of (ΠΡΟ)'OPIZEIN in the New Testament," *NTS* 17 [1970-71] 104).

39. Cf. F. Büchsel, *Der Geist Gottes im Neuen Testament* (1926) 403; W. Grundmann, *TDNT* II, 304; O. Cullmann, *The Earliest Christian Confessions* (1949) 55; idem, *The Christology of the New Testament* (1959) 235, 292; D. M. Stanley, *Christ's Resurrection in Pauline Soteriology* (1961) 163ff.; Schneider, op. cit., 361ff. ἐν δυνάμει is usually and rightly taken with υἱοῦ Θεοῦ rather than ὁρισθέντος, although as Kuss, op. cit., 6, and Hahn, *Titles,* 249, point out, there is no essential difference either way in the net result.

40. Contra Lietzmann, *Römerbrief,* 25; Hahn, *Titles,* 249.

41. Nygren, *Romans,* 50. See also M. Dibelius, "Glaube und Mystik bei Paulus," *Botschaft und Geschichte* II (1956) 103; Michel, *Römerbrief,* 40; Kuss, op. cit., 6; S. H. Hooke, "The Translation of Rom. i.4," *NTS* 9 (1962-63) 370f.; Schneider, op. cit., 365; cf. H.-W. Bartsch, "Zur vorpaulinischen Bekenntnisformel im Eingang des Römerbriefes," *Theologische Zeitschrift* 23 (1967) 329-39.

caught between the ages. As the Christian lives in the overlap of flesh and Spirit so did Jesus.[42]

In short, we have in Rom. 1:3f. a reference to Christ parallel to the reference to Christians in 1 Cor. 15:49. Both at first glance seem to indicate two mutually exclusive stages following one upon the other, whereas in Christians the image of the man of heaven is already in process of being formed even while they still bear the image of the man of dust (2 Cor. 3:18; 4:16), and in the case of Christ he lives κατὰ πνεῦμα even while his existence is still κατὰ σάρκα.

III

It is entirely probable therefore that the κατὰ σάρκα/κατὰ πνεῦμα antithesis of Rom. 1:3f. not only describes two distinct and successive phases in the life of Jesus separated by the resurrection, but refers also to the pre-resurrection life of Jesus as a life lived both according to the flesh and according to the Spirit. Insofar as Jesus lived on the level of the flesh, was bound and determined by the weakness and inadequacy of the human condition, allowed worldly considerations to determine his conduct, he was merely Son of David and no more — Messiah indeed, but a disappointing, ineffective, irrelevant Messiah, whether judged in terms of Jewish expectations or in terms of the Christian Gentile mission. But insofar as Jesus lived on the level of the Spirit, refused to allow merely human considerations, fleshly suffering, or Jewish expectations to determine his course or deter him from his chosen ministry, he manifested that he was indeed Son of God, and thereby proved his right to be installed as Son of God in power as from the resurrection of the dead.[43]

It is clear therefore that Paul understands the formula of Rom. 1:3f. in terms of a two-stage christology: but at *both* stages Jesus is Son of God, and at *both* stages his sonship is determined by the Spirit and by Jesus' response to the Spirit. This point is of considerable importance for understanding the relation of Jesus to the Spirit. In Paul's view the sonship of the earthly Jesus

42. It is doubtful whether a two-stage christology was ever held apart from the tradition of Jesus being anointed as Messiah *and* Son of God at Jordan; that is, apart from some belief that the ages overlapped in the Jesus of history, a belief which in its kernel almost certainly went back to Jesus (cf., e.g., G. Bornkamm, *Jesus of Nazareth* [1960] 51); see also n. 16 above and pp. 150-51 below.

43. The primary significance of ἐξ is probably temporal (Lietzmann, *Römerbrief,* 25; Barrett, *Romans,* 20; Hahn, *Titles,* 250f.), although one is tempted to see in it a deliberate ambiguity, perhaps, as Lagrange suggests, something less than causal and more than temporal (*Romans,* 8, followed by Kuss, op. cit., 6).

was constituted by the Holy Spirit. He was Son of God because the Holy Spirit was in him and because he lived in obedience to that Spirit.[44]

It will be recognized that this exegesis is to a certain degree a return to the older interpretation represented by Sanday and Headlam. But there is a significant difference. Whereas Sanday and Headlam recognized that "the antithesis of σάρξ and πνεῦμα requires that they shall be in the same person," they shrank from identifying the πνεῦμα with the Holy Spirit for that very reason.[45] Instead πνεῦμα ἁγιωσύνης was identified in terms of later dogmatic thought with the divine nature in Christ, or with the human spirit of Jesus. Now it is no doubt true that the σάρξ/πνεῦμα antithesis has been the root of the two-natures doctrine in later dogma (Loofs).[46] But the niceties of third-, fourth-, and fifth-century controversies and formulations must not be allowed to determine our interpretation of Paul or to force us into a clear-cut distinction between Jesus and Holy Spirit where it does not exist in Paul. πνεῦμα ἁγιωσύνης is unquestionably to be taken as a Semitic form for "Holy Spirit."[47] And this simply means that Jesus' possession and experience of the Spirit is what Paul called Jesus' sonship and what later dogma has called his divinity. The "deity" of the earthly Jesus is a function of the Spirit, is, in fact, no more and no less than the Holy Spirit.[48]

This line of interpretation would not, however, justify us in describing the Jesus of Paul as the "first Christian," as though his experience of the Spirit was entirely on a par with the Christian's. For there is a uniqueness in the relationship between Paul's Jesus and the Spirit which cannot be repeated. This uniqueness comes through in a passage like Col. 1:19, where πλήρωμα

44. Those who in recent years have accepted that κατὰ πνεῦμα refers also to the earthly Jesus include Hunter, op. cit., 25f., taking up a suggestion by T. W. Manson; J. M. Robinson, *A New Quest of the Historical Jesus* (1959) 52f.; W. C. van Unnik, "Jesus the Christ," *NTS* 8 (1961-62) 108f.; Hill, op. cit., 280, n. 4; and especially P. Althaus, *Der Brief an die Römer* (NTD; [6]1932, [10]1966); cf. Nygren, *Romans,* 53f.; Leenhardt, *Romans,* 37. Schneider argues "that in primitive N.T. usage πνεῦμα ἅγιον as distinguished from πνεῦμα used alone, was specific for the Spirit of Pentecost" (op. cit., 380; cf. O. Procksch, *TDNT* I, 104). I question whether such a distinction was made by or was meaningful to the primitive church. But even if it was, Rom. 1:3f. would simply underline that the early church looked back on the historical Jesus in the light of the Spirit of Pentecost and that for the early church it was precisely the Spirit which they themselves experienced which had dwelt so fully in Jesus. See further below.

45. Sanday and Headlam, *Romans,* 9. Though see W. Bousset, *Kyrios Christos* ([2]1921) 125, n. 2. Later commentators, as we have seen, have tended to argue in the reverse direction.

46. J. N. D. Kelly, *Early Christian Doctrines* ([2]1960) 38; W. Pannenberg, *Jesus God and Man* (1968) 119.

47. Procksch, *TDNT* I, 114f., contra L. Cerfaux who takes πνεῦμα ἁγιωσύνης as "the spirit of sanctification" (*Christ in the Theology of St. Paul* [1958] 315).

48. This is not to say that Paul would have so expressed himself in the context of the christological and trinitarian controversies of later centuries, or that dynamic or modalistic monarchianism (H. B. Swete, *The Holy Spirit in the Ancient Church* [1912] 96-101; Kelly, *Early Christian Doctrines,* 115-23, 140) was an appropriate development of Paul's thought. See pp. 144-45 below.

may be a description for the Holy Spirit filling the earthly Jesus in unique measure,[49] and particularly in 1 Cor. 15:45 and in the Pauline descriptions of the Holy Spirit as the Spirit of Christ, the Spirit of the Son, the Spirit of Jesus Christ (Rom. 8:9; Gal. 4:6; Phil. 1:19). Jesus from being a man under the direction of the Spirit, Son of God κατὰ πνεῦμα, becomes by virtue of his resurrection Son of God in full power of his sonship, that is, in full power of the Spirit. The personality and the role of Jesus expand and swallow up the less well-defined personality and more restricted role of the Spirit. Jesus becomes the Spirit (1 Cor. 15:45) and the Spirit becomes the Spirit of Jesus. It is not that Jesus usurps the role of the Spirit. Rather we have to say that in Paul's view, whereas the earthly Jesus was ruled by the power of the Spirit, now the Spirit becomes the executive power of the exalted Christ. "What the πνεῦμα ἁγιωσύνης is for Christ's own person, the πνεῦμα ζωοποιοῦν is for humanity" (F. C. Baur). The uniqueness of Jesus was not that he was the first to possess the Spirit in a distinctive (Christian) way, but that he was uniquely "full of the Spirit" and that he impressed his character and personality on the Spirit, so that thereafter the mark of the Spirit was his inspiration of an acknowledgment of the Lordship of Jesus and his reproduction of the character of Jesus in Christians (1 Cor. 12:3; 2 Cor. 3:18). In short, to express the point in an epigram, if the Spirit gave Jesus his power, Jesus gave the Spirit his personality.

If doubt is expressed about the validity of this interpretation of Paul's thought in view of his belief in the preexistence of Jesus,[50] I have to reply: first, that the idea of preexistence does not enter into the thought of Rom. 1:3f. Neither κύριος nor Son of God presupposes it, as verse 4 makes clear — τοῦ ὁρισθέντος υἱοῦ Θεοῦ . . . ἐξ ἀναστάσεως νεκρῶν. It is inappropriate therefore to speak of a three-stage christology in this passage.[51] Only two stages are apparent. Second, and more generally, the preexistence of Jesus is an inaccurate description of the Pauline theology. In Paul the only really explicit references to preexistence come where Paul identifies Jesus with preexistent Wisdom (1 Cor. 8:6; Col. 1:15ff.; cf. 1 Cor. 1:24, 30). Strictly speaking it is Wisdom alone which is preexistent. The earthly Jesus was not preexistent: Jesus was the *man* that Wisdom *became* (so also, probably, Phil. 2:6f.; cf. John 1:14). Thus, on the one hand, one can affirm of Jesus what one affirms of Wisdom. But on the other, what one affirms of Jesus is not necessarily true of preexistent Wisdom, only of incarnate Wisdom. Hence Paul can apply the language of Wisdom to Jesus, just as we can make the

---

49. Cf. G. Münderlein, "Die Erwählung durch das Pleroma. Bemerkungen zu Kol. i.19," *NTS* 8 (1961-62) 272.

50. Cf. P. Stuhlmacher, "Theologische Probleme des Römerbriefpräskripts," *Evangelische Theologie* 27 (1967) 382f.; Linnemann, op. cit., 275.

51. *Contra* Stuhlmacher, "Theologische Probleme des Römerbriefpräskripts," 382f. Hunter's threefold division of the text is rather different (op. cit., 25f.).

perfectly sensible statement today that "the Prime Minister studied economics at Oxford." But the relation of the man Jesus to the Spirit of God was not that of preexistent Wisdom.[52]

Third, Paul's understanding of the earthly Jesus was not primarily an extension forward in time of his belief in Wisdom as preexistent. Rather the preexistence of Jesus — Wisdom, incarnate — is an extension backward of his understanding of the *exalted* Jesus. Paul's understanding of the historical Jesus was rooted primarily in his knowledge, from the tradition, of the real man Jesus of Nazareth and secondly in his own experience of the Spirit. The concept of preexistence arose from reflection on this Jesus now exalted in the context of Hellenistic thought and with the categories of Hellenistically influenced Wisdom literature. As the transformation from earthly Jesus is to be explained in terms of the Spirit, so the transformation from preexistent Wisdom to historical Jesus is to be explained presumably in terms of a realistic kenosis christology (Phil. 2:7).[53]

IV

So much for Paul's understanding of the formula in Rom. 1:3f. One question remains. Is Paul's interpretation of the formula different from that intended by those who framed it? Has he significantly altered the formula?

In my opinion it is likely that Paul clarified the nature of the two stages expressed in the original two clauses by prefacing them with περὶ τοῦ υἱοῦ αὐτοῦ. But it is very probable that he made no further alteration, apart from adding the last five words, and that his understanding of the formula was of a piece with a widely held christology in the primitive church.

(a) It is possible that Paul added ἐν δυνάμει to balance the insertion of the first υἱός. Similarly the conclusion that κατὰ σάρκα/κατὰ πνεῦμα fits easily into the range of Paul's use and thought could be taken as support for the view that these words were added by Paul. But both suggestions must be judged unlikely. The phrase υἱοῦ Θεοῦ ἐν δυνάμει is unusual in Paul, although, as we have seen, the underlying thought is consonant with his christology. And there is no conceivable reason why Paul should introduce the unique

---

52. See also pp. 150-51 below.
53. I must therefore express my dissatisfaction with K. L. Schmidt's claim that in Rom. 1:4 "the appointment of Jesus (Christ) as what he is to be must be equated with what he already is from the very beginning of the world, from all eternity in God's decree" (*TDNT* V, 453). Not only is his exegesis of ὁρισθέντος inadmissible, but he fails completely to realize the significance of the second stage of such a three-stage christology (preexistent Wisdom, the man Jesus, the exalted Lord).

semitism πνεῦμα ἁγιωσύνης. An origin in Jewish (though non-Palestinian) Christianity is clearly indicated.

Moreover, while the addition of the first υἱός makes no essential alteration to a formula already containing ἐν δυνάμει, the insertion of both would significantly alter the meaning of the sentence. The same is obviously true if Paul added the σάρξ/πνεῦμα antithesis. Since Paul is clearly using the formula as an introduction card testifying that he shares the common faith by his affirmation of a widely acknowledged confessional statement, and not throwing down the gauntlet of his own distinctive faith, it would equally clearly defeat that aim if he subjected a familiar and respected formula to too much alteration.

It follows that the original form of the sentence was more or less as we find it here, apart from the opening and closing phrases.

(b) Is Paul's interpretation of these words different from that intended by those who framed it and accepted by those who used it? In particular, is Schweizer justified in arguing for the more or less neutral sense "in the sphere of flesh/Spirit" for the pre-Pauline stage?

The answer is a fairly clear-cut negative. The fact is that *when we are dealing with the σάρξ/πνεῦμα antithesis or its equivalent in pre-Pauline literature, the ideas of "neutrality" and "spheres of power" do not go together.* Where flesh and spirit have a more neutral connotation (and it is never entirely neutral) they denote actual beings or that which essentially constitutes and characterizes actual beings (Num. 16:22; 27:16; *1 Enoch* 15:8; see also Judith 10:13; *Pss. Sol.* 16:14). And where the antitheses can appropriately be described in terms of "spheres of power," as in dualistic wisdom, the more neutral significance has been lost in open opposition and hostility.[54] With what is probably the closest biblical parallel, Isa. 31:3, we stand somewhere in the middle, neither neutral nor hostile. Indeed what we have is the same sort of derogatory contrast between that which is mere σάρξ and that which is πνεῦμα with which we are familiar from our study of Paul.[55]

The closest parallels, however, are to be found in the Qumran literature. Not only has "flesh" a very similar breadth of meaning to that found in Paul and signifies "the realm where ungodliness and sin have effective power," but just as in Paul so in Qumran, "the 'neutral' use of 'flesh' is completely embedded (in) and overshadowed by the loaded meaning."[56] Even more

54. See Brandenburger, op. cit., 65-68, 75, and *passim* in the section on Philo (pp. 123-221).

55. For the negative range of σάρξ see also Esther 4:17ᵖ; Wis. 7:1f.; Sirach 17:31; 28:5; 40:8; 4 Macc. 7:13.

56. K. G. Kuhn, "New Light on Temptation, Sin and Flesh in the New Testament," *The Scrolls and the New Testament,* ed. K. Stendahl (1957) 107 — see more fully pp. 101-7; also Davies, "Flesh and Spirit," 161f.; J. Licht, "The Doctrine of the Thanksgiving Scroll," *Israel Exploration Journal* 6 (1956) 10f.

striking is the fact that Qumran dualism does not divide humankind simply into two distinct groups belonging to two mutually exclusive spheres of power; instead, as with Paul, the *believer* experiences the dualism *within himself,* whether expressed in the antithesis of flesh and election[57] or of the two spirits dwelling in him.[58]

If anything, then, the immediately comparable material in non-Christian pre-Pauline writings suggests that Paul's understanding of the σάρξ/πνεῦμα antithesis was more widely rooted in Hellenistic Jewish Christianity, as in Hellenistically influenced Judaism generally; and Schweizer's attempt to drive a wedge between the σάρξ/πνεῦμα contrast in Rom. 1:3f. and the rest of Paul must be judged a failure.

While we have still to bring other Christian passages under scrutiny the probability is gaining strength that Paul's interpretation of the Rom. 1:3f. formula was precisely that of Hellenistic Jewish Christianity — for it is certainly to that context that the formula belongs, as the almost unique Jewish form πνεῦμα ἁγιωσύνης and the Hellenistic embarrassment over Jesus' Davidic sonship[59] indicate. This probability is still more strengthened by the likelihood that Paul quotes the formula where he does as proof that he stands within and fully shares the faith of the wider church. Since Paul understood the formula in the way indicated or at least was most liable to be understood in this way (as his commentators demonstrate) *he must have shared the faith of the wider church at this point also.* If the wider church understood the formula as a mere neutral, spatial, temporal contrast, and if Paul read it as a pejorative, moral antithesis, then he did *not* share the faith of the wider church, and his use of the formula as an earnest of good faith was misleading, not to say deceptive. The more logical conclusion is that Paul quotes a formula which expresses not only his faith but the faith of the wider church.

(c) Within early Christian literature the most often cited parallel to Rom. 1:3f. is the early Christian hymn contained in 1 Tim. 3:16, particularly the first two lines:

---

57. "The believer therefore belongs to both groups: inasmuch as he is man, that is, inasmuch as he sins, he is *'flesh of sin';* inasmuch as he is 'the elect of God' (by strength of the 'spirit of truth' which dwells in him and determines his deeds according to predestination) he belongs to the 'eternal community' . . ." (Kuhn, "New Light," 103).

58. P. Wernberg-Møller, "A Reconsideration of the Two Spirits in the Rule of the Community (IQSerek iii.13–iv.26)," *Revue de Qumran* 3 (1961-62) 422-24, 432; J. Pryke, " 'Spirit' and 'Flesh' in the Qumran Documents and Some New Testament Texts," *Revue de Qumran* 5 (1964-65) 350f. See also A. A. Anderson, "The Use of 'Ruah' in IQS, IQH and IQM," *Journal of Semitic Studies* 7 (1962) 300f.; A. R. C. Leaney, *The Rule of Qumran and Its Meaning* (1966) 37. Cf. the rabbinic doctrine of the good and evil impulse in humans (Davies, *Paul and Rabbinic Judaism,* 17-35).

59. See pp. 135-37 above.

ὃς ἐφανερώθη ἐν σαρκί
ἐδικαιώθη ἐν πνεύματι.

Without entering into the debate concerning the origin and meaning of the hymn,[60] we may simply note that here too Schweizer finds strong support for his interpretation of Rom. 1:3f. The first line describes the early life of Jesus as an epiphany in the sphere of flesh; the second refers to his vindication in the sphere of spirit and is equivalent to entry into the divine sphere.[61] But here too we must demur.

Certainly there is a stronger prima facie case for recognizing a broader, more general use of the contrast, but once again there is the grave danger of narrowing the meaning of σάρξ and πνεῦμα too much. ἐν σαρκί in first-century Christian literature can often designate a person's fleshly existence, but it is always with a particular reference to *that person's* flesh as an individual.[62] That is to say, ἐν σαρκί denotes *mode* of being rather than *sphere* of being. It is more probable therefore that the first line of the hymn means that Jesus was manifested as a man of flesh, that is, as an ordinary and real human being — as the closest parallels (1 John 4:2; 2 John 7; cf. Rom. 7:3) strongly suggest.

Similarly ἐν πνεύματι in its regular use has a more specific reference, describing individuals not in the *sphere* of πνεῦμα, but as determined or inspired by πνεῦμα.[63] As always in these phrases πνεῦμα refers to a spirit possessing or controlling a person, not the human spirit. Apart from a few references to demon possession, ἐν πνεύματι in the literature of our period refers to possession by the Holy Spirit. So here.[64] In that case, and assuming that the ἐδικαιώθη refers to Jesus' resurrection-exaltation,[65] we can hardly

60. R. H. Gundry, "The Form, Meaning and Background of the Hymn Quoted in I Timothy iii.16," *Apostolic History and the Gospel,* ed. W. W. Gasque and R. P. Martin (F. F. Bruce FS; 1970) 203-22, surveys recent work on the hymn very thoroughly. More recent are the too brief comments of J. T. Sanders, *The New Testament Christological Hymns* (1971) 15ff., 94f.

61. *Erniedrigung,* 8q; see also "Two New Testament Creeds Compared: I Corinthians xv.1-5 and I Timothy iii.16," *Current Issues in New Testament Interpretation,* ed. W. Klassen and G. F. Snyder (O. A. Piper FS; 1962), reprinted in *Neotestamentica* (1963) 125f.; *T.W.N.T.* vii.138. He is followed by G. Holtz, *Die Pastoralbrief* (1965) 90f., and Fuller, op. cit., 218. Linnemann, however, thinks the parallel here and in 1 Pet. 3:18 is not close enough (op. cit., 265).

62. See particularly Rom. 2:28; 7:5; 8:3, 8f.; 2 Cor. 10:3; Gal. 2:20; Eph. 2:11; Phil. 1:22; 3:3f.; Col. 2:1; Philem. 16; 1 Pet. 4:2; 1 John 4:2; 2 John 7.

63. E.g., Matt. 22:43; Luke 2:27; John 4:23f.; Acts 19:21; Rom. 8:9; 1 Cor. 14:16; Eph. 2:22; 4:18; Rev. 1:10; 17:3. The closest parallel to line 2 is 1 Cor. 6:11 — ἐδικαιώθητε . . . ἐν τῷ πνεύματι τοῦ Θεοῦ ἡμῶν.

64. Cf., e.g., C. K. Barrett, *The Pastoral Epistles* (1963) 65; contra Gundry, op. cit., 211.

65. So most commentators — contra Gundry, op. cit., 213f., who refers line 2 to the vindication of Christ during and by the *descensus ad infernos* in spirit-form between death and resurrection (cf. 1 Pet. 3:18ff.).

understand the ἐν πνεύματι as a description of the mode of being which *follows* the vindication — since no Christian would have thought of the *exalted* Jesus as empowered, possessed by the Spirit. The more probable interpretation is that ἐν πνεύματι describes not the sphere or mode of being into which Jesus entered, but the mode of being which was the *cause* of Jesus' vindication.[66] He was manifested as (a man of) flesh; he was vindicated as (a man of) Spirit. In other words, it appears that here too there is the implication that σάρξ and πνεῦμα overlap in the earthly Jesus and that his exaltation was somehow due to his unique possession of the Spirit and brought about by the Spirit.[67] That we are back once more with the same sort of christology as we found in Rom. 1:3f. is confirmed by the contrast between the two modes of being implied in the use of ἐδικαιώθη and in the antithesis ἐν σαρκί/πνεύματι (cf. Rom. 2:28; 7:5; 8:8f.; Phil. 3:3f.).[68]

(d) The other parallel to Rom. 1:3f. frequently cited is 1 Pet. 3:18 — Christ θανατωθεὶς μὲν σαρκὶ ζωοποιηθεὶς δὲ πνεύματι. We need not linger over this passage. It is tempting to take the πνεύματι as a simple instrumental dative — giving us the only explicit affirmation in the NT that Jesus was raised from the dead by the direct agency of the Spirit.[69] But the NT's coyness about this affirmation and the fact that the parallel σαρκί cannot be taken instrumentally militates against this interpretation. The more plausible suggestion is that both σαρκί and πνεύματι are datives of reference. In which case it looks rather as though we are back in the same sort of christological thought which finds more formalized expression in Rom. 1:3f. and 1 Tim.

66. Cf. J. Jeremias, *Die Briefe an Timotheus und Titus* (NTD; [8]1963) 24. Schweizer's attempt to equate "vindicated in Spirit" with "enter into the divine sphere" is unconvincing, since the parallel references from the NT period and before "carry only the meaning of vindication, not entry into the divine sphere" (Gundry, op. cit., 210). Against the similar suggestion of M. Dibelius and H. Conzelmann, *Die Pastoralbriefe* (HNT; [4]1966) that δικαιοῦσθαι here refers to "the entry into the divine sphere, the sphere of δικαιοσύνη" (p. 50), see R. Deichgräber, *Gotteshymnus und Christushymnus in der frühen Christenheit* (1967) 134, n. 3.

67. A local sense for ἐν should not be pressed here (Deichgräber, *Gotteshymnus,* 136, n. 3). In such phrases ἐν can often have an ambiguity which English's choice of "in," "by," or "with" cannot convey (see, e.g., 1 Cor. 6:11); and here the poetic parallel lies in the word and sound rather than an exact and precise meaning, something which poetic form frequently prevents anyway.

68. The more negative meaning of σάρξ should not be pressed so far as to confine the reference to Jesus' crucifixion (contra Stanley, op. cit., 237; A. R. C. Leaney, *The Epistles to Timothy, Titus and Philemon* [1960] 61). Similarly Schneider's attempt to refer line 1 to "the glorious appearance of the risen Christ" (op. cit., 367, 384f., following A. Descamps and J. Dupont) is an unjustified narrowing of the meaning.

69. That πνεύματι means (Holy) Spirit rather than human spirit (Gundry, op. cit., 211) or divine nature (E. G. Selwyn, *The First Epistle of St. Peter* [[2]1947] 197) is indicated by the regular description elsewhere in the NT of the Spirit as the "life-giver" (John 6:33; Rom. 8:11; 1 Cor. 15:45; 2 Cor. 3:6), by the presence of the regular flesh/Spirit antithesis, and by the parallel with Rom. 1:3f. and 1 Tim. 3:16. Cf. W. J. Dalton, *Christ's Proclamation to the Spirits: A Study of I Peter iii.18–iv.6* (1965) 33, 124-34; Schneider, op. cit., 367f.

3:16. Jesus was put to death as flesh: it was because he was flesh that death was possible, indeed necessary, for him. But he was brought to life as Spirit: it was because he possessed the Spirit, because the Spirit wrought in him and on him, that ζωοποίησις followed death.[70]

Once again the vague sense of "in the sphere of" advocated by Schweizer[71] takes too little account of the individualistic reference of σάρξ and πνεῦμα. It was not σάρξ in general which was destroyed in Christ's death, but *his* σάρξ in particular. Any generalized sense in σάρξ here is focused upon the particular σάρξ of Jesus. Likewise πνεύματι signifies not the "sphere of the Spirit" but the Spirit which possessed Jesus and which was instrumental in his resurrection. In the parallel verse 1 Pet. 4:6 there is of course no thought of overlap between σάρξ and πνεῦμα, because the possibility of living πνεύματι is offered to those who are already put to death σαρκί, but in the σάρξ/πνεῦμα antithesis it is the particular reference to the individuals who died and their *mode* of existence rather than the sense of *spheres* of existence which is the more prominent thought. They were condemned and died because they were flesh, and they lived solely on the level of the flesh. The purpose of the proclamation is that they might live by the power of the Spirit, that is, share in the actualization of the Christian hope, the whole redeemed person alive and living by the Spirit of God.[72]

(e) It remains simply to point out that the form of christology uncovered in Rom. 1:3f. and 1 Tim. 3:16 and at least reflected in 1 Pet. 3:18[73] is more widely held within the NT. In particular it is related to the so-called "messianic secret" in Mark, and it is clearly present in the more fully developed three-stage or programmatic christology of Luke-Acts. As I have demonstrated elsewhere,[74] the interaction between Jesus and the Spirit is the decisive element in this christology. In the first stage Jesus is the *creation of the Spirit* (Luke 1:35). In the second he is the uniquely anointed *Man of the Spirit* (Luke 3:22; 4:18; Acts 10:38). Only in the third does he become *Lord of the Spirit* (Acts 2:33). In each case the changeover from one stage to the next (Jordan,

---

70. B. Reicke speaks of "the intimate subjective meaning/function" of πνεύματι here (*The Disobedient Spirits and Christian Baptism* [1946] 106f.). However, that the overlap of the two stages in the "two-stage christology" was not fully recognized here is perhaps indicated by the parallel in 4:6 (cf. Deichgräber, *Gotteshymnus,* 173).

71. *Neotestamentica,* 185, 187; *TDNT* VI, 417; cf. F. W. Beare, *The First Epistle of Peter* (1947) 143; Fuller, op. cit., 219; J. N. D. Kelly, *The Epistles of Peter and of Jude* (1969) 151; Schneider, op. cit., 368.

72. πνεύματι in 4:6 cannot have the same meaning as πνεύμασιν in 3:19, since it is precisely *escape* from their existence as πνεύματα ἐν φυλακῇ which life πνεύματι offers them.

73. Schneider also cites 1 Corinthians 15 as a parallel (op. cit., 365f.). But there the direct contrast is between πνεῦμα and ψυχή, and it sets in antithesis two different men, first Adam and last Adam (verse 45), and two different bodies, σῶμα ψυχικόν and σῶμα πνευματικόν. The κατὰ σάρκα/κατὰ πνεῦμα antithesis in Rom. 1:3f. has a different connotation.

74. "Spirit and Kingdom," *ExpT* 82 (1970-71) 38f.

exaltation, Pentecost) is effected by a transformation in the relationship between Jesus and Spirit. What is to be noted in our present study is that the
second stage consists precisely in the sort of overlap between σάρξ and
πνεῦμα,[75] between kingdom present and kingdom still future, between already
and not yet, which we found both in Paul's soteriology and in the christology
of Rom. 1:3f. Jesus' anointing by the Spirit at Jordan is an indispensable
prerequisite not merely of his earthly ministry but also of his resurrection and
exaltation. It was because the old aeon (of Israel and law) was seen to overlap
with the new aeon (of Spirit) in the earthly Jesus that the early church's
experience of the Spirit could be linked with and attributed to the exalted
Jesus. More briefly, it was because the historical Jesus was recognized as the
unique Man of the Spirit that the exalted Jesus could be acclaimed as Lord
of the Spirit. That is to say, Jesus' exalted life in terms of the Spirit (κατὰ
πνεῦμα, ἐν πνεύματι, πνεύματι) was recognized to be continuous with his
earthly life in terms of the Spirit (κατὰ πνεῦμα, ἐν πνεύματι, πνεύματι), the
latter being the necessary presupposition for the former.[76]

The same sort of christological thinking also underlies the Fourth
Gospel's talk of the Spirit as the ἄλλος παράκλητος. Jesus is the incarnation
of the λόγος; the author might almost as appropriately have said "of the
πνεῦμα," or "of σοφία." Present with his disciples once as incarnate Logos,
uniquely anointed with Spirit (1:33; 3:34; 6:27), he continues to be present
with his disciples as Spirit — the same Spirit. Here again the idea of an overlap
between Jesus' earthly existence and the disciples' experience of the ascended
Jesus is integral to the christology and is expressed in terms of the Spirit.

V

In conclusion, what we have seen in Rom. 1:3f. and these other passages is
the early church's attempt to formulate the relation between the historical
Jesus and the exalted Jesus: how could they express their faith concerning
both Jesus as they knew him to have been from the tradition and eyewitness
accounts, and the Jesus they now worshiped? That it was the same Jesus was
to them self-evident; but how to explain both the continuity and the transformation? The answer which the early theologians found was the Spirit. Jesus'
relation to the Spirit explained both the continuity and the difference. And it

---

75. Cf. L. Legrand, "L'arrière-plan néo-testamentaire de Lc. i.35," *Revue Biblique* 70
(1963) 181ff.

76. This being so, the parallels cited by Schneider from Acts (op. cit., 370-76) must be
understood in terms of our interpretation rather than of his.

is this *continuity and difference between historical and exalted Jesus in terms of the Spirit* which finds expression in Rom. 1:3f. and the other passages examined.

At its simplest this conviction is expressed in the belief that the Spirit which dwelt in Christians was the Spirit of Jesus (Acts 16:7; Rom. 8:9; Gal. 4:6; Phil. 1:19; 1 Pet. 1:11, John's *other* Paraclete). But underlying this language is the more difficult thought that somehow the Spirit which inspired Jesus has become wholly and exclusively identified with him — although only Paul expresses it so boldly: "the last Adam became a life-giving Spirit" (1 Cor. 15:45).[77] That the transformation from Spirit *inspiring* Jesus to Spirit *of* Jesus took place at the resurrection of Jesus was axiomatic. But to express both this transformation and the continuity more clearly was exceedingly difficult, and it is obvious that the early church was content not to explore further in this direction. This is why their writings shy away from the unequivocal affirmation that Jesus was raised *by* the Spirit (cf. Rom. 1:3f.; 1 Tim. 3:16; 1 Pet. 3:18; also Rom. 6:4; 8:11; 1 Cor. 6:14; 2 Cor. 13:4) — although it would appear to be the logical corollary to the twin propositions that the resurrection of Christians will be by the Spirit (Rom. 8:11) and that Christ's resurrection is the ἀπαρχή of Christians' resurrection (1 Cor. 15:20, 44f.).[78] But it was precisely *in and by the resurrection* that Jesus fully "took over" the Spirit, ceased to be a man dependent on the Spirit, and became Lord of the Spirit. Hence the early church's coyness at this point. It is for the same reason that we find in some passages, particularly John 19:30 and Heb. 9:14,[79] as well as 1 Tim. 3:16[80] and 1 Pet. 3:18,[81] an inevitable, sometimes deliberate ambiguity between Christ's Spirit and the Holy Spirit — precisely because the Spirit which empowered Christ from Jordan onward was now wholly identified with Christ as his Spirit, the Spirit of Christ. The complexity of this relationship and the first Christian theologians' reserve in speaking of it also means that the charge of adoptionism cannot be laid against them, if only for no other reason than its oversimplification and overdefinition in an area where the early church humbly acknowledged its inability to define and clarify the more than human.[82]

In short, the failure (if that is the correct word) of the early church to investigate more thoroughly the relation between Christ and the Spirit and its transformation at his resurrection is measured by its failure to achieve greater

---

77. See also Hermas, *Sim.* 11:1. See further ch. 9 below.
78. See especially N. Q. Hamilton, *The Holy Spirit and Eschatology in Paul* (1957) 12-15.
79. See n. 49 above.
80. Cf. J. N. D. Kelly, *The Pastoral Epistles* (1963) 90f.
81. Cf. H. Windisch, *Die katholischen Briefe* (HNT; 1911) 68.
82. Cf. Schweizer, *T.W.N.T.* viii.368; see also the earlier objection by A. E. J. Rawlinson, *The New Testament Doctrine of the Christ* (1926) 265-69.

clarity of expression in passages like Rom. 1:3f. But despite their ambiguity and enigmatic quality, these formulations nevertheless express a clear enough faith in the Jesus who once lived himself κατὰ πνεῦμα, whose resurrection transformed their relationship, and who now directs his disciples by the same Spirit, his own Spirit.

9

1 Corinthians 15:45 —
Last Adam, Life-Giving Spirit

How did Paul relate his present experience of the exalted Lord to the historical person Jesus? This is one of the key problems in Pauline christology and soteriology. And probably no other verse in the Pauline corpus poses the question more abruptly and more sharply than 1 Cor. 15:45:

οὕτως καὶ γέγραπται,
Ἐγένετο ὁ πρῶτος ἄνθρωπος Ἀδὰμ εἰς ψυχὴν ζῶσαν·
ὁ ἔσχατος Ἀδὰμ εἰς πνεῦμα ζωοποιοῦν.

For in this verse Paul seems to say not only that the central, constitutive element of the corporate Christian life is the experience of God's Spirit; but also that Jesus can be fully and adequately understood in terms of this Spirit. Not only is the earthly Jesus lost in the shadows behind the exalted Lord, but the exalted Lord seems to be wholly identified with the Spirit, the source of the new life experienced by believers.

It is unfortunate that the theological implications of this passage have not been more fully investigated in recent years, and that commentators seem to have been concerned more with the origins of Paul's ideas than with their place in his overall theology. It is to this task — the elucidation of 1 Cor. 15:45 in its context within Pauline theology — that we now turn. I offer it to Professor Moule, my *Doktorvater,* as a small token of appreciation with warmest greetings and regards.

Originally published in *Christ and Spirit in the New Testament,* ed B. Lindars and S. S. Smalley, 127-41. Copyright © 1973 by Cambridge University Press and reprinted by permission.

I

We take up first the exegesis of 1 Cor. 15:45 in its immediate context. As in most of the letter, Paul is here addressing his Gnostic opponents at Corinth. As part of their superior knowledge and higher wisdom it appears that they have denied the resurrection of the dead (15:12). That is, presumably, they denied that their spiritual state was incomplete; already they were mature, already full, already reigning (3:1f.; 4:8; cf. 10:1-12); they were already experiencing resurrection life in their experience of the Spirit; they had no place for a still future resurrection.[1] Above all, they denied that full redemption came through resurrection of the *body;* on the contrary, for a Gnostic salvation would be wholly independent of the body; if anything was awaited as still future it would be release *from* the body. In short, they denied both the somatic and the future eschatological character of the resurrection.[2]

In refutation Paul argues first for a resurrection that is still future: as Christ's resurrection followed his death, so believers can look forward to resurrection after death (15:13-23) (or transformation of σῶμα at the parousia — 15:51f.); he then goes on to argue for a resurrection of the body — not the same body, though one in some degree of continuity with the present body (15:35-50).[3]

The contrast between first Adam and last Adam occurs in the course of this latter argument. Paul justifies his belief in the resurrection body by contrasting the scriptural description of humankind's creation (Gen. 2:7) with the mode of existence now enjoyed by the risen Christ. Humanity was created ψυχὴν ζῶσαν; Christ has become πνεῦμα ζωοποιοῦν. Or in other words, humanity was created σῶμα ψυχικόν; Christ became σῶμα πνευματικόν. The order of events is clear — first psychical then spiritual — the one from dust, the other from heaven. As the man made of dust is the pattern of psychical humans, so the man from heaven is the pattern of spiritual people; that is, as earthly existence is an embodiment of ψυχή, σῶμα ψυχικόν, so resurrection existence is an embodiment of σῶμα πνευματικόν.

What has not been sufficiently realized in many expositions is the central significance of verse 45 in Paul's argument. The fact that verse 45 can be

---

1. Cf. 2 Tim. 2:18; *2 Clement* 9:1; Polycarp, *Philippians* 7; Justin, *Apology* 1.26.4; *Dialogue* 80; Irenaeus, *Adversus Haereses* 1.23.5; 2.31.2; *Acts of Paul and Thecla* 14; Tertullian, *De Resurrectione Carnis* 19.

2. H. von Soden, *Sakrament und Ethik bei Paulus* (Marburg, 1931) 23, n. 1; H. D. Wendland, *Die Briefe an die Korinther* (NTD 7; Göttingen, 1932, [10]1964) 125; Kümmel in H. Lietzmann and W. G. Kümmel, *An die Korinther* I/II (HNT 9; Tübingen, [4]1949) 192f.; W. Schmithals, *Die Gnosis in Korinth* (Göttingen, [2]1965) 147ff.; C. K. Barrett, *The First Epistle to the Corinthians* (London, 1968) 347f.; J. H. Wilson, "The Corinthians Who Say There Is No Resurrection of the Dead," *ZNW* 59 (1968) 90-107.

3. Kümmel, 194f.; M. E. Dahl, *The Resurrection of the Body* (London, 1962) 94.

treated as a parenthesis[4] and the recognition that Paul's main concern throughout this passage is anthropological rather than christological[5] obscures how basic is the assertion of verse 45 to Paul's whole case. The series of contrasts of verses 42-44 have in themselves proved nothing, but were designed to lead up to the key antithesis of verse 44 between σῶμα ψυχικόν and σῶμα πνευματικόν, and the key statement, εἰ ἔστιν σῶμα ψυχικόν, ἔστιν καὶ πνευματικόν.

This simple affirmation is a classic example of Paul's apologetic skill. He appears to have taken over the ψυχικός/πνευματικός antithesis from his Gnostic opponents.[6] But he subtly transposes it into his own terms, σῶμα ψυχικόν and σῶμα πνευματικόν. Such a use of σῶμα would normally have been unacceptable to the Gnostics and his argument would have fallen to the ground, for σῶμα in the general usage of the time in reference to the human person means physical body and is not distinguished from σάρξ — that is, in Gnostic thought it stood together with σάρξ and ψυχή in denigratory contrast to πνεῦμα.[7] But Paul introduces a distinction between σάρξ and σῶμα which outflanks the Gnostics' position and leaves them open to Paul's counterattack. He accepts the Gnostic antithesis ψυχικός/πνευματικός and stands side by side with them in affirming that "σάρξ καὶ αἷμα cannot inherit the kingdom of God" (15:50). But he affirms also that pneumatic existence is a form of existence, neither physical/fleshly nor incorporeal. There are many kinds of σώματα, heavenly as well as earthly, nonfleshly as well as fleshly (15:40). So there is a σῶμα ψυχικόν and there is a σῶμα πνευματικόν. In short, Paul is combating the Gnostics on their ground, but in his terms.[8] Given Paul's distinction between σῶμα and σάρξ and their own distinction between ψυχικός and πνευματικός, they are bound to accept the fuller Pauline distinction between σῶμα ψυχικόν (bodily existence vivified and determined by ψυχή) and σῶμα πνευματικόν (bodily existence vivified and determined by πνεῦμα).

The crucial step in Paul's argument is the next one — for now he must clarify and establish the *relation* between these two σώματα. And this he does in verses 45-49, where verses 46-49 are his exposition of verse 45. Verse 45 in other words is not the proof of verse 44b, contrary to common opinion;

4. A. E. J. Rawlinson, *The New Testament Doctrine of the Christ* (London, 1926) 129, n. 1.

5. R. Scroggs, *The Last Adam* (Oxford, 1966) 85, 87; Barrett, 376.

6. R. Reitzenstein, *Die hellenistischen Mysterienreligionen* (Leipzig/Berlin, [3]1927) 74; J. Weiss, *Der erste Korintherbrief* (Göttingen, [10]1925) 371ff.; R. Bultmann, *Theology of the New Testament* I (London, 1952) 174; E. Brandenburger, *Adam und Christus* (Neukirchen, 1962) 74f.; R. Jewett, *Paul's Anthropological Terms* (Leiden, 1971), 340-44, 353f.

7. See E. Schweizer, *TDNT* VII, 1025-57.

8. Cf. H. Clavier, "Brèves Remarques sur la Notion de Σῶμα Πνευματικόν," in *The Background of the New Testament and Its Eschatology: Studies in Honour of C. H. Dodd,* ed. W. D. Davies and D. Daube (Cambridge, 1954) 360; Jewett, 266f.

verse 44b needs no proof as such, since it is common ground with Paul's opponents. As the καί, not γάρ, indicates, Paul here takes the argument one stage further: "Moreover as Scripture says, 'The first man Adam became a living soul; the last Adam a life-giving spirit.' " In other words *he identifies the two kinds of* σώματα *with Adam and Christ.* Once this position is gained he has the upper hand over the Gnostics; and the rest of the argument flows irrefutably on. If Christ is the type of σῶμα πνευματικόν, then it is an eschatological, heavenly mode of existence which can be achieved only as Jesus achieved it, after death, or at the parousia. Everything therefore hangs on verse 45. The question obviously arises, Can Paul's assertion in verse 45 bear the heavy weight Paul puts on it?

Verse 45 is introduced by Paul as a scriptural quotation, and the whole verse stands under the οὕτως γέγραπται — including verse 45b, as the absence of δέ indicates.[9] Of course Gen. 2:7, to which Paul refers, reads only καὶ ἐγέντετο ὁ ἄνθρωπος εἰς ψυχὴν ζῶσαν. Verse 45 must therefore be understood as Paul's pesher or midrash on Gen. 2:7. But how does Paul achieve this exegesis? It is unlikely that the only justification is the rabbinic hermeneutical principle of inferred antithesis.[10] It is possible but unnecessary to assume that he is reworking a rabbinic midrash on Gen. 2:7.[11] And it is probable that he is consciously aware of the Adam or Primal Man speculation which was current in his day (see below). But as with all Paul's midrashim, the exegesis of Gen. 2:7 in verse 45 is drawn principally from Paul's own understanding of Christ and the gospel (cf. 1 Cor. 9:8-10; 2 Cor. 3:7-18; Gal. 3:8; 4:21-31).[12] This is clearly indicated by Paul's insertion of πρῶτος (and Ἀδάμ) into the Gen. 2:7 clause. The understanding of "the man" in Gen. 2:7 as πρῶτος Ἀδάμ is determined by Paul's understanding of Jesus as ἔσχατος Ἀδάμ. In other words, the point and force of the citation of Gen. 2:7 lies not in the actual Genesis passage itself, but in the contrast between that Adam and the last Adam — a contrast drawn from Paul's own understanding of Christ.

Paul must play his trump card, Christ, at this point — for the argument up to and including verse 44b has in fact proved nothing against the Gnostics. Only in the case of Christ does the relation between σῶμα ψυχικόν and σῶμα πνευματικόν become evident — their disjunction and temporal sequence. Only by reference to Christ can Paul hope to prove that spiritual embodiment is not something already enjoyed by the believer in the here and now, but a mode of existence which lies the other side of death and resurrection.

9. Cf. Weiss, 373ff.; H. Conzelmann, *Der erste Brief an die Korinther* (Göttingen, 1969) 337f.

10. Best exemplified in Matt. 5:43.

11. Scroggs, 86f.; cf. C. F. Burney, *The Aramaic Origin of the Fourth Gospel* (Oxford, 1922) 46.

12. See J. D. G. Dunn, *Baptism in the Holy Spirit* (London, 1970) 126.

This brings us to the crux of the debate and the heart of Paul's theology. For Paul's whole case at this critical point rests on two assumptions. The first is that the exalted Jesus is *known* to possess a spiritual body. The second is that the exalted Jesus has a *representative* capacity in this mode of existence. Without these two assumptions Paul's case fails. But how well grounded are they for Paul? We will examine them in turn.

II

As Adam became εἰς ψυχὴν ζῶσαν, so Christ became εἰς πνεῦμα ζωοποιοῦν. Clearly πνεῦμα ζωοποιοῦν means also or at least includes the idea of σῶμα πνευματικόν — otherwise the citation would not really be relevant; as Adam's existence as ψυχὴ ζῶσα means a bodily existence vivified and determined by ψυχή, so the risen Christ's existence as πνεῦμα ζωοποιοῦν means a bodily existence vivified and determined by πνεῦμα. But the reason why Paul writes πνεῦμα ζωοποιοῦν is not simply to achieve an aesthetically pleasing parallel with ψυχὴ ζῶσα, for that could have been achieved as well by writing πνεῦμα ζῶν. The principal reason is that Paul wishes to ground his assertion about the spiritual embodiment of the risen Christ *in the experience of the believing community*. Hence he characterizes Jesus not simply as πνευματικός but as πνεῦμα, not simply as ζῶν, but as ζωοποιοῦν.[13] In other words, *the believer's experience of the life-giving Spirit is for Paul proof that the risen Jesus is σῶμα πνευματικόν*.

πνεῦμα ζωοποιοῦν cannot be understood except as a reference to the spiritual experience of the early believers. It is one of the chief merits of the *religionsgeschichtliche Schule* that it demonstrated so clearly the experiential basis of early theologizing. πνεῦμα denotes neither a theological dogma nor an idealized *Zeitgeist* but a spiritual experience — an experience of being taken hold of by a mysterious power, of being overwhelmed or inspired or directed or moved by a supernatural force.[14] "Geist ist die göttliche, überirdische Macht. . . . Die Wurzel seiner [Paul's] πνεῦμα-Lehre liegt also in der Erfahrung des Apostels" (Gunkel, pp. 79, 82). In many cases in early Christianity this experience of πνεῦμα was marked by ecstatic phenomena (Acts 2:4, 33; 8:18; 10:46; 19:6; 1 Cor. 1:5, 7; Gal. 3:5; Heb. 2:4); in others by a strong emotional content (Rom. 5:5; 1 Thess. 1:6; κράζειν — Rom. 8:15f.;

---

13. "Non solum vivit, sed etiam vivificat" (Bengel); cf. Schweizer, *TDNT* VI, 420.
14. See particularly H. Gunkel, *Die Wirkungen des heiligen Geistes* (Göttingen, 1888); H. Weinel, *Wirkungen des Geistes und der Geister im nachapostolischen Zeitalter* (Freiburg im Breisgau, 1899).

Gal. 4:6); sometimes it was an experience of liberation (Rom. 8:2; 2 Cor. 3:17; Gal. 5:18), sometimes of intellectual illumination (2 Cor. 3:16ff.; Eph. 1:17f.; Heb. 6:4); and so on.

Notice particularly the attribution of ζωοποίησις to πνεῦμα in John 6:63 and 2 Cor. 3:6. For John Christianity was essentially a matter of "having life" (20:31) — that is, the experience of sheer exuberant vitality, like a stream of running water (7:38) or a well bubbling up within (4:14). So new and fresh was this experience of life that it could be spoken of in terms of birth or creation (3:3ff.; 20:22 — ἐνεφύσησεν). And this experience John not merely attributes to the Spirit (3:5f. — ἐκ πνεύματος) but actually *identifies* with the Spirit (4:10 — τὴν δωρεὰν τοῦ Θεοῦ;[15] 7:39; 20:22 — λάβετε πνεῦμα ἅγιον). *(Holy) Spirit is the name John gives to the experience of new life* — τὸ πνεῦμά ἐστιν τὸν ζωοποιοῦν (6:63). Likewise for Paul, the experience of life which set him free from the law of sin and death and from the dispensation of condemnation and death was the Spirit (Rom. 8:2, 10; 2 Cor. 3:7-9); 2 Cor. 3:6 —

> τὸ γὰρ γράμμα ἀποκτείνει
> τὸ δὲ πνεῦμα ζωοποιεῖ.

Hence in 1 Cor. 15:45 πνεῦμα ζωοποιοῦν can only refer to the early believers' experience of new life.

The significant factor, however, is that Paul identifies the risen Jesus with this life-giving Spirit; Jesus himself is the source of these experiences of Spirit, or to put it the other way, the experience of life-giving Spirit is experience of the risen Jesus. Moreover, and this is the crucial point, this experience constitutes for Paul proof that Jesus is risen from the dead and exists as σῶμα πνευματικόν. How so? Because for Paul that which distinguishes Christian experience of πνεῦμα from comparable experiences in other religions is precisely its Christ-relatedness, its Jesus-content. Paul was of course well aware that similar pneumatic phenomena were present in other sects, when worshipers "would be seized by some irresistible power" (NEB), "irresistibly drawn . . . toward dumb idols" (JB — 1 Cor. 12:2).[16] It is precisely for this reason that at the beginning of his discussion of the spirituals or spiritual gifts (chs. 12–14) he stresses the distinctive feature of the spiritual experience of those "in Christ" — not more exalted experiences, or experiences of a totally different order, but experiences which are centered on Christ. The test case he gives here is an inspiration which recognizes the exalted

---

15. J. D. G. Dunn, "A Note on δωρεά," *ExpT* 81 (1969-70) 349-51.

16. See particularly E. R. Dodds, *The Greeks and the Irrational* (Berkeley, 1951) 64-101; W. F. Otto, *Dionysius Myth and Cult* (Bloomington, 1965).

status of Jesus as Κύριος — only that power is God's Spirit which inspires a person to confess "Jesus is Lord" (1 Cor. 12:3).

This Jesus-content of early Christian experience is even more marked in the believer's assurance of sonship, when the Spirit cries within and through him "ἀββά" (Rom. 8:15f.; Gal. 4:6). For this experience reproduces what had hitherto been the unprecedented and unique spiritual experience of Jesus himself.[17] The intimate ἀββά-relationship with God which until then only the historical man Jesus had enjoyed was now experienced by those "in Christ," so that they could think of themselves not only as adopted sons of the Father and heirs of God, but also as *fellow* heirs with Christ (Rom. 8:17). In consequence of such experiences they believed not only that their relationship with God was patterned on Jesus' but also, as we shall see below, that their whole character was being transformed into the image of Christ.[18] Such experiences they could only attribute to the risen Jesus acting upon them through the Spirit; there was a spiritual power moving in them which they could describe equally well as "Christ in me" or "the Spirit in me,"[19] or, most striking of all, as "the Spirit of Christ" (Rom. 8:9), "the Spirit of his Son" (Gal. 4:6), "the Spirit of Jesus Christ" (Phil. 1:19). The "intensive feeling of personal belonging and of spiritual relationship with the exalted Lord," which Bousset rightly calls the "dominant" note in Paul's piety,[20] Paul on several occasions likens to the intimacy of a marriage relationship; most striking is 1 Cor. 6:17 — as physical union means oneness of flesh, so union with the Lord means a oneness of Spirit.[21]

It was this Jesus-relatedness, this Jesus-content in their spiritual experience which constituted proof for the early believers that it was the exalted Jesus who was acting upon them — Jesus had become πνεῦμα ζωοποιοῦν.

---

17. J. Jeremias, *The Prayers of Jesus* (London, 1967) 54-65; *New Testament Theology* I: *The Proclamation of Jesus* (London, 1971) 63-68.

18. Professor Moule expressed this point well when he wrote: "The diffused and little defined and fitfully manifested Spiritual presence of God (viz. as we meet it in the Old Testament) becomes sharply contracted to a 'bottle-neck' so as to be defined and localized in Jesus of Nazareth; God who formerly spoke at various times and in many different fragments has now spoken to us in one who is a Son. But the pattern, thus contracted to a single individual, widens again, through his death and resurrection, to an indefinite scope, though never again to an undefined quality. However widely diffused, however much more than individual, it bears henceforth the stamp of the very character of Christ" ("The Holy Spirit in the Church," an unpublished lecture [1963] quoted by E. M. B. Green, *The Meaning of Salvation* [London, 1965] 175f.).

19. Rom. 8:10; Gal. 2:20; Eph. 3:17; Rom. 8:9, 11; 1 Cor. 3:26; 6:19, etc. Cf. 1 Cor. 12:6; Phil. 2:13; Col. 1:29; Eph. 3:20.

20. W. Bousset, *Kyrios Christos* (Göttingen, [6]1967) 104; English translation (New York, 1970) 153.

21. Note also Gunkel's comment on Paul's conversion: "The first pneumatic experience of Paul was an experience of Christ" (p. 99) — a suggestion which may help to explain the ἐν ἐμοί of Gal. 1:16.

That is, he was the source of the power of new life which moved in and through them. The fact that Paul does not have to argue the point indicates that this type of experience was fairly general among believers, and perhaps particularly among the Gnostics. Thus the affirmation of verse 45b is one which would be both understood and accepted by the Gnostics at Corinth. It is in the implied, but in the context of Paul's argument, inevitable, corollary that the punch comes — for existence as πνεῦμα ζωοποιοῦν means also existence as πνευματικόν. In short, the nature of the believing community's experience of Spirit enables Paul to affirm that Jesus has become πνεῦμα ζωοποιοῦν and therefore also σῶμα πνευματικόν.

III

The second assumption which underlies verse 45b is that Jesus has a representative capacity in his existence as πνεῦμα ζωοποιοῦν. The idea of Jesus as representative man comes to expression in several places in Paul's writings (notably Rom. 5:12-21; 1 Cor. 15:20ff.; Phil. 2:7f.;[22] cf. Heb. 2:5-18). Paul probably introduces the idea into 1 Corinthians 15 partly at least because his Gnostic opponents were influenced by the speculation concerning the Primal Man current at that time — as is shown particularly by Philo[23] and the Hermetic writings,[24] not to mention the apocalyptic concept of the heavenly (son of) Man.[25] This external evidence, taken in conjunction with verse 46,[26] certainly indicates that Paul was aware of some sort of Gnostically influenced speculation about Jesus as Man, although the more elaborate divine *Urmensch* theses of Käsemann and Brandenburger both lack adequate foundation and are unnecessary to explain Paul's theology or argument at this point.[27]

22. R. P. Martin, *Carmen Christi: Philippians 2:5-11* (Cambridge, 1967) 207-11.

23. *De Opificio Mundi* 134; *Legum Allegoriae* 1.31f.; W. D. Davies, *Paul and Rabbinic Judaism* (London, [2]1955) 44-52. Though see also Scroggs, 115-22.

24. *Poimandres* 12-17; R. Reitzenstein, *Poimandres* (Leipzig, 1904) 81-116; though see also C. H. Dodd, *The Bible and the Greeks* (London, 1935) 145-62. Cf. J. M. Creed, "The Heavenly Man," *JTS* 26 (1925) 113-36.

25. Dan. 7:13f.; *1 Enoch* 48:2f.; 69:26-29; 71:14-17; 2 Esdras 13; J. Weiss, *Earliest Christianity* (New York, 1937, reprinted 1959) 485f.; Rawlinson, 122-27; J. Jeremias, *TDNT* I, 142f.; O. Cullmann, *The Christology of the New Testament* (London, 1959) 166-70; W. G. Kümmel, *Die Theologie des neuen Testaments* (Göttingen, 1969) 139. Though see also Brandenburger, 131-35; R. H. Fuller, *The Foundations of New Testament Christology* (London, 1965) 233f.

26. J. Moffatt, *The First Epistle of Paul to the Corinthians* (London, 1938) 263; J. Héring, *The First Epistle of Saint Paul to the Corinthians* (London, 1962) 178; Cullmann, 167ff.; J. Jervell, *Imago Dei* (Göttingen, 1960) 258ff.; Brandenburger, 74ff., 155ff.; Barrett, 374f.; Jewett, 353.

27. The discussion is conveniently summarized and well assessed by Jewett, 230-36.

However, what is all too often lost sight of in these debates is the fact that Paul's assertion here is again based on the believer's *experience. The community's experience of the exalted Jesus as* πνεῦμα ζωοποιοῦν *is what enables Paul to affirm the representative significance of Jesus' resurrection and resurrection body.* Paul's affirmation of the representative significance of Jesus' risen state is not based merely on the belief that postmortem existence must be somatic — for then he could have said merely, the last Adam became εἰς πνεῦμα ζῶν. It is the Christian's experience of life as coming from the exalted Jesus which is determinative. Nor is he building on the foundation of a (Gnostic) identity between Jesus and the Primal Man, for it is precisely that equation which Paul severs in verse 46: Jesus is ἔσχατος Ἀδάμ, not πρῶτος Ἀδάμ; it is the *risen* Jesus who is the image of God, not any *Urmensch,* let alone the first Adam.[28] Nor is he simply drawing out corollaries from the sense of corporate oneness "in Christ" which the worshiping assembly experiences, although that is undoubtedly important for Paul and probably contributes to his thinking here. The primary focus of his thought at this point however is the believer's experience of the life-giving Spirit. How so? Because in this experience the believer finds himself being steadily transformed to become like Christ. *Paul's own experience of the life of the Spirit bearing the imprint of Jesus' character and conforming him to that image is the ground on which Paul asserts the representative significance of Jesus' risen humanity.*

We enter here the deepest waters of Paul's Christ-mysticism. Paul's experience as a believer is not merely of new life; it is also of decay and death. Although the Spirit is life διὰ δικαιοσύνην, the body is dead διὰ ἁμαρτίαν (Rom. 8:10). The believer knows the life of the Spirit, but he has to express it through the body of death (Rom. 7:24f.; 8:13; 2 Cor. 4:11f.). Day by day he is being "inwardly renewed," but at the same time his "outward humanity is in decay" (2 Cor. 4:16). The suffering this involves is a necessary preliminary to glory — suffering to death is the way to glory (Rom. 8:17). The significant feature of this death-life experience is that for Paul *both the death and the life are Christ's* — it is the outworking of Christ's death and risen life. Hence the perfect tenses in Rom. 6:5; Gal. 2:19; 6:14: the believer's experience is that of having been knit together with the ὁμοίωμα of Christ's death; not only does he experience the life of Christ within but there is also a dimension to his experience which can be described as a state of having been crucified with Christ — still hanging there! So, too, the significance for Paul of his suffering is that it is a suffering *with Christ* (Rom. 8:17), a sharing in Christ's own suffering (2 Cor. 1:5). Paul can even think of his suffering as

---

28. Adam in Paul is always fallen man; only "the resurrected and exalted Christ is the perfect realization of God's intent for men" (Scroggs, 91, 100; cf. Jervell, 263-68).

a continuation and completion of Christ's (Col. 1:24). Most striking of all is Phil. 3:10f., where Paul expresses his longing to know Christ more fully, that is, to experience not just the power of his resurrection, but to share his sufferings, and so be more and more conformed to his *death;* only in this way will he attain the resurrection of the dead.

Integral to this whole train of thought of course is Paul's experience of Christ as Spirit. For the Spirit is the ἀρραβών of full redemption (2 Cor. 1:21; Eph. 1:14); that is to say, the experience of the Spirit is the first installment, the beginning of the process of life and death which leads up and into the "heavenly habitation" of the resurrection body (2 Cor. 5:5).[29] Or in equivalent terms, the Spirit is the ἀπαρχή, the beginning of the full harvest of the resurrection body, so that the groaning and frustration of life in the present body of death is an expression of hope rather than of despair (Rom. 8:23f.).[30] It is this death-life motif which lies behind Paul's talk of the continuing Christian experience as one of more and more being transformed into the image of Christ through the Spirit (2 Cor. 3:18; Col. 3:10; cf. Rom. 8:29; 12:2; 13:14; 2 Cor. 4:4; Col. 1:18) — the process of the full personality of Christ coming as it were to birth in the believer with all the birthpangs which that involves (Gal. 4:19), a process which only ends when "the body belonging to our humble state" is transfigured to become like Christ's glorious resurrection body by the power of the Spirit (Phil. 3:21; Rom. 8:11). That this whole train of thought is in Paul's mind in 1 Cor. 15:45 is clearly indicated by verse 49, with its talk of believers coming to "bear the image of the man of heaven" as something still future (φορέσομεν).[31] What verse 45 affirms is that this transformation into the image of the last Adam is the outworking of the life-giving power of the last Adam, a power which believers already experience.

It is to be noted that at no stage does Paul give way to the Gnostic views: that a fully matured Christian experience and state can be achieved here and now, and that the body is wholly evil. He recognizes that the full flowering of the life of Christ in him involves the experience of death as well as of life; he shares Christ's risen life through the Spirit, but not fully; there is still a future-ness in Christian experience, a not yet; he is in process of being transformed into the image of Christ, but he does not yet fully bear that image;

29. Cf. C. F. D. Moule, "St Paul and Dualism: The Pauline Conception of Resurrection," *NTS* 13 (1966-67) 106-23.

30. Cf. E. Käsemann, "The Cry for Liberty in the Worship of the Church," *Perspectives on Paul* (London, 1971) 122-37. Notice also the use of παθεῖν in Gal. 3:4: believers ἔπαθον the Spirit and his δυνάμεις.

31. As most commentators agree, φορέσομεν is undoubtedly to be read rather than φορέσωμεν (contra Héring, 179; Scroggs, 110); otherwise we have a Gnostic exhortation, not an anti-Gnostic affirmation. The believer lives his present life ἐν ἀσθενείᾳ, ἐν φθορᾷ (verses 42f.).

the Spirit is only the ἀρραβών and ἀπαρχή of a life fully vivified and determined by the Spirit, that is, of the σῶμα πνευματικόν; otherwise "hope" would be a meaningless concept (Rom. 8:24f.).[32] At the same time Paul's talk of decay and death does not express a dualistic pessimism with regard to the body. For the full outworking of the Spirit's life-giving power is precisely the σῶμα πνευματικόν. The experience of decay and death of the body is a sign of hope not of pessimism, for it is the converse side of the coming to be of the spiritual body (2 Corinthians 4:7–5:5). The point is that it is the experience of Christ as πνεῦμα ζωοποιοῦν which assures Paul that the present experience is only a foretaste, a process of coming to be of the full life of the Spirit, the full character of Christ — which assures Paul that Christ's glorified state is not an isolated or individual occurrence, but the beginning of a new kind of humanity. As (Christ) the life-giving Spirit is the ἀπαρχή of the resurrection body, so Christ (the life-giving Spirit) is the ἀπαρχή of the harvest of resurrected humans.

To sum up, the nature of Paul's spiritual experience, with its distinctive Jesus-content and Jesus-character, enables, even requires, Paul to understand it not only in terms of the risen Christ, but also in terms of a Christ whose risen state is archetypal for believers' future state. Hence if Adam is the type of psychic existence, then Christ, the risen Christ, is the type of pneumatic existence. This experience of πνεῦμα ζωοποιοῦν now implies σῶμα πνευματικόν because that is the inevitable end result of a process already under way, the process of being transformed into the image of Christ by his Spirit. In short, verse 45b constitutes proof because Paul's experience of the πνεῦμα ζωοποιοῦν convinces him that the exalted Jesus has a spiritual, somatic existence and that in that mode of existence he is the pattern and forerunner of a new humanity.

As we have already noted, the argument of verses 46-49 flows on directly from the assertion of verse 45. If the Gnostics have appreciated the full force of that one pregnant phrase, they cannot deny the rest, for verses 46-49 merely spell out the principal implications in verse 45b. Verse 46: the life-giving Spirit they all experience is the *risen* Jesus, the *last* Adam; the πνεῦμα ζωοποιοῦν, the σῶμα πνευματικόν, does not precede the ψυχὴ ζῶσα, the σῶμα ψυχικόν, it succeeds it — only after the decay and death of the latter does the former come into existence. Verses 47f.: the last Adam has *pneumatic* existence — it is in his risen

---

32. Reitzenstein, *Mysterienreligionen,* 333ff., and Bousset, though not without justification, nevertheless seriously misinterpret Paul and leave him with no reply to the Gnostics at this point (so, too, A. Schweitzer, *The Mysticism of Paul the Apostle* [London, 1931] 167, 220). Paul does *not* regard the "present Christian standing" as one of "perfection" *(Vollkommenheit);* on the contrary, Phil. 3:8-14. Nor does he believe that "the natural being has completely died in him [the pneumatic Christian]" (Bousset, 118, 122; English translation, 170, 174). On the contrary, Rom. 8:13; Col. 3:5; Eph. 4:22.

existence, as the heavenly man,[33] σῶμα πνευματικόν, that he represents a new humanity; "as we have borne the image of the man of dust (and still do), so we shall bear (φορέσομεν) the image of the man of heaven" — "such is the influence of the Lord who is Spirit" (2 Cor. 3:18).

IV

It remains simply to underline some of the christological corollaries which follow from Paul's experience-based christology.

(a) Paul identifies the exalted Jesus with the Spirit — not with a spiritual being (πνεῦμα ζῶν) or a spiritual dimension or sphere (πνευματικόν), but with the Spirit, the Holy Spirit (πνεῦμα ζωοποιοῦν). Immanent christology is for Paul pneumatology; in the believer's experience there is *no* distinction between Christ and Spirit.[34] This does not mean of course that Paul makes no distinction between Christ and Spirit. But it does mean that later trinitarian dogma cannot readily look to Paul for support at this point. A theology which reckons seriously with the ἐγένετο of John 1:14 must reckon just as seriously with the ἐγένετο implied in 1 Cor. 15:45b.

Moreover, if christology is the key to Christianity, then the teeth of that key are not only the historical Jesus and the kerygmatic Christ but also the life-giving Spirit. The new "Quest" and interest in the "titles of majesty" must not detract attention from the further dimension of christology — "Christ in me, the hope of glory."[35] In the debate between those who seek to ground an understanding of faith in the historical Jesus and those who start from "the kerygma," the *experiential* basis of early Christianity must not be ignored. People believed in Jesus as Christ and Lord because they experienced a to them supernatural vitalizing power — a power whose character, if Paul is to be our guide, directed them to the conclusion that Jesus was its living source. Paul's understanding of the exalted Christ emerged out of his experience of the Spirit, not vice versa.[36]

(b) The antithesis in verse 45 and the context of verse 45 make it clear that Jesus *became* Last Adam at his resurrection. As the first Adam came into

33. There may well be an allusion to the parousia here (Barrett, 375f.; D. M. Stanley, *Christ's Resurrection in Pauline Soteriology* [Rome, 1961] 126), making a smoother movement in thought from Christ's resurrection to that of believers.

34. 2 Cor. 3:17 should not be cited as a parallel; see chapter 7 above; contra particularly I. Hermann, *Kyrios und Pneuma* (Munich, 1961).

35. "This certainty of the nearness of Christ occurs far more frequently in Paul's writings than the thought of the distant Christ 'highly exalted' in Heaven" (A. Deissmann, *Paul* [London, ²1927, reprinted 1957] 140).

36. Cf. Gunkel, 100. The same is true to a significant degree of his understanding of the earthly Jesus; see chapter 8 above.

existence (ἐγένετο) at creation, so the last Adam (as such) came into existence (ἐγένετο) at resurrection (1 Cor. 15:20-22; Rom. 8:29; Col. 1:18). For Paul "the resurrection marks the *beginning* of the humanity of the Last Adam."[37] Christ's role as "second man" does not begin either in some preexistent state[38] or at incarnation.[39] The "man" of Phil. 2:7f., "that one man" of Rom. 5:15ff., strictly speaking is not identical with the "last Adam" of 1 Cor. 15:45. It was not by incarnation that Christ became the image of God or sanctified humanity. On the contrary, in incarnation he took on the flesh of the first Adam, *sinful* flesh, *fallen* humanity, and by his death he destroyed it — dust to dust (Rom. 8:3; 2 Cor. 5:14).[40] For Paul the last Adam is precisely the "man" who *died,* who brought to an end the "old man," destroyed sin in the flesh, in order that the "new man" might come to be. The contrast in verse 45 is between death and life, not between two stages of evolution (1 Cor. 15:22). In short, the new humanity stems from the resurrection; only those participate in the last Adam who participate in the life-giving Spirit; their hope of fullness of life, σῶμα πνευματικόν, is real only because Jesus has become πνεῦμα ζωοποιοῦν.

(c) In terms of the modern debate and of our opening question the significant feature to emerge from our study is that although Paul thinks almost exclusively in terms of the present Jesus experienced now as Spirit, he does not thereby ignore or deny the relevance of the historical man Jesus. For it is precisely the Jesus-, that is, the historical Jesus-content and Jesus-character of the present experience of Spirit which is the distinctive and most important feature of the experience. Christ has become Spirit, *Christ is now experienced as Spirit* — that is true. But it is only because *the Spirit is now experienced as Christ* that the experience of the Spirit is valid and essential for Paul. The centrality given to the experience of the exalted Lord does not deny the relevance and importance of the historical Jesus for Paul; on the contrary it reinforces it, by binding the historical Jesus and the exalted Lord together in the single all-important experience of the life-giving Spirit. It is the *continuity* between earthly Jesus and exalted Lord, denoted by the clause ὁ ἔσχατος Ἀδὰμ εἰς πνεῦμα ζωοποιοῦν, which is the key to Paul's thought here and to much of his christology and soteriology as a whole.

---

37. Scroggs, 92 (my emphasis); see also F. Büchsel, *Der Geist Gottes im Neuen Testament* (Gütersloh, 1926) 406f.; Kümmel, 195; Jervell, 258ff.; Hermann, 61f.; Conzelmann, 341f.

38. Contra Weiss, *Korintherbrief,* 376; W. L. Knox, *St Paul and the Church of Jerusalem* (Cambridge, 1925) 134; Moffatt, 263; W. Manson, *Jesus the Messiah* (London, 1943) 186, 189.

39. Contra Cullmann, 166ff.; Wendland, 136; Héring, 179; F. W. Grosheide, *The First Epistle to the Corinthians* (London, 1953) 388.

40. Irenaeus's "recapitulation" theory completely misinterprets Paul at this point (Bousset, 348-60; English translation, 437-50), as do most incarnation-based soteriologies (see, e.g., A. R. Vidler's study of F. D. Maurice, *Witness to the Light* [New York, 1948] 29-57; R. C. Moberly, *Atonement and Personality* [1901] 86-92). "It is only in virtue of resurrection that He became the archetype and head of a new race" (H. R. Mackintosh, *The Doctrine of the Person of Jesus Christ* [Edinburgh, 1912] 69). See also n. 28 above.

PAULINE CHRISTOLOGY

10

Jesus Tradition in Paul

How much did Paul know about Jesus? How much did Paul want to know about Jesus or think it necessary to know about Jesus? These questions have been a burning point in New Testament research for the last two hundred years, with the issue sharpened successively in the latter half of the period by repeated variations on the contrast between the Jesus of history and the Christ of faith and on the "Paul was the real founder of Christianity" theme. The largest consensus still maintains that Paul knew or cared little about the ministry of Jesus apart from his death and resurrection, though the theological corollaries of that conclusion are less often pursued.[1]

The reasons are not hard to find. Paul's letters express only the most basic knowledge of Jesus apart from the eschatological turning point of Good Friday and Easter (Rom. 1:3; Gal. 4:4; 2 Cor. 10:1; 1 Cor. 11:23-26). And apart from 1 Cor. 7:10-11; 9:14; and 11:23-25, he never refers to Jesus' teaching as such or cites Jesus as his authority for his own emphases. So the basis for the consensus is clear.

There is, however, the further question as to whether there are *echoes* of Jesus tradition in Paul's letters, particularly in his parenesis, and if so whether Paul was aware that he was echoing utterances of Jesus. This also involves a long-standing debate[2] and one into which we must venture as our

1. But see S. G. Wilson, "From Jesus to Paul: Contours and Consequences," in P. Richardson et al., ed., *From Jesus to Paul: Studies in Honor of F. W. Beare* (Waterloo: Wilfrid Laurier University, 1984) 1-21. According to Wilson: "Few would now deny that Paul's interest in the person and teaching of Jesus is minimal" (6-7).

2. See details in D. C. Allison, "The Pauline Epistles and the Synoptic Gospels: The

first priority, both in terms of the a priori plausibilities of the case, and by scrutinizing a sample of the evidence itself. But even if we could draw the firm conclusion from such data that Paul *did* after all know a good deal more of the Jesus tradition than his specific attribution at first suggests, the puzzle still remains: why did Paul not cite Jesus as his authority on more occasions, since an exhortation attributable to Jesus would presumably carry more weight with his readers? This will have to form a further topic for reflection.

1. A Priori Plausibilities

It must surely be considered highly likely that the first Christian communities were interested in, not to say highly fascinated by the figure of Jesus. Even for any who were converted from mystery cults, the very bare form of the kerygmatic outline such as we find in 1 Cor. 15:1-8 would be hardly satisfying, since cultic myths, and so also the corresponding initiation rites, were usually a good deal more elaborate and complex.[3] And however much or little the kerygma was seen as equivalent to such myths, the fact remains that the Jesus who was featured in the kerygma had lived and ministered for a number of years within the lifetime of the first generation of converts. Given the universal curiosity in the prominent or hero figure which is as evident in ancient writings as it is today, it would be surprising if those who claimed to have put their faith in this Christ were not a little curious about the character and content of his life and ministry prior to his death.[4]

Pattern of the Parallels," *NTS* 28 (1982) 1-32, and F. Neirynck, "Paul and the Sayings of Jesus," in A. Vanhoye, ed., *L'Apôtre Paul* (BETL 73; Leuven: Peeters, 1986) 265-321. In recent literature note particularly J. Piper, *"Love your Enemies:" Jesus' Love Command in the Synoptic Gospels and the Early Christian Paraenesis* (SNTSMS 38; Cambridge University, 1979), esp. 102-19; P. Stuhlmacher, "Jesustradition im Römerbrief. Eine Skizze," *TBei* 14 (1983) 24-50; D. Wenham, "Paul's Use of the Jesus Tradition: Three Samples," in D. Wenham, ed., *The Jesus Tradition outside the Gospels* (Gospel Perspectives 5; Sheffield: JSOT, 1985) 7-37; J. Sauer, "Traditionsgeschichtliche Erwägungen zu den synoptischen und paulinischen Aussagen über Feindeliebe und Wiedervergeltungsverzicht," *ZNW* 76 (1985) 1-28; A. J. M. Wedderburn, ed., *Paul and Jesus: Collected Essays* (JSNTSS 37; JSOT, 1989); M. Thompson, *Clothed with Christ: The Example and Teaching of Jesus in Romans 12.1–15.13* (JSNTSS 59; JSOT, 1991); T. Holtz, "Paul and the Oral Gospel Tradition," in H. Wansbrough, ed., *Jesus and the Oral Gospel Tradition* (JSNTSS 64; JSOT, 1991) 380-93. An earlier version of this essay appeared as "Paul's Knowledge of the Jesus Tradition: The Evidence of Romans," in K. Kertelge et al., eds., *Christus Bezeugen. Festschrift für Wolfgang Trilling* (Leipzig: St. Benno, 1989) 193-207.

3. As is indicated, e.g., in the famous wall paintings in the "villa of mysteries" at Pompeii. It should be remembered that the "mysteries" included public rites and processions as well as secrets for the initiates; see A. J. M. Wedderburn, *Baptism and Resurrection: Studies in Pauline Theology against Its Graeco-Roman Background* (WUNT 44; Tübingen: Mohr, 1987) 98; also idem, "Paul and the Story of Jesus," in Wedderburn, ed., *Paul,* 161-89.

4. Note for example the degree of biographical interest evident in Dio Chrysostom in the

This basic plausibility is further strengthened by the sociological insight that the emergence of a new sect or religious community was bound to depend in one degree or other on the formulation and preservation of the sacred tradition by which it defined itself in distinction from other related or similar movements or groupings.[5] Certainly the kerygma of the death and resurrection of Jesus would be at the heart of this sacred tradition. But again it would be surprising if early congregations who placed themselves under the name of Christ were not concerned to learn and cherish what was known about this Christ, to rehearse it in their communal gatherings for worship, to draw on it in instruction of new converts, and to use it in discussion with those outside the group (in polemic or apologetic) and for the wisdom it provided them in the ethical and practical problems of their own common and individual lives.

The evidence which we have is wholly consistent with this a priori picture and confirms its strong credibility. I have in mind the emphasis which we find, not least in Paul's letters, on teaching and tradition. It is clear from such passages as 1 Thess. 4:1 (παρελάβετε παρ' ἡμῶν τὸ πῶς δεῖ ὑμᾶς περιπατεῖν . . .); 2 Thess. 3:6 (περιπατοῦντος μὴ κατὰ τὴν παράδοσιν ἣν παρελάβοσαν παρ' ἡμῶν); 1 Cor. 11:2 (καθὼς παρέδωκα ὑμῖν τὰς παρα-δόσεις κατέχετε); 15:3 (παρέδωκα ὑμῖν ἐν πρώτοις, ὃ καὶ παρέλαβον . . .); and Col. 2:6 (ὡς οὖν παρελάβετε τὸν Χριστὸν Ἰησοῦν τὸν κύριον, ἐν αὐτῷ περιπατεῖτε) that Paul saw it as part of his own responsibility in founding a church to bequeath it with the traditions which belonged to the new movement[6] and which marked it out from synagogue, collegium, and mystery cult. These would no doubt include the traditions which he himself had learned when he "got to know" Peter in Jerusalem, three years after his conversion (Gal. 1:18), a "getting to know" which must surely have included "getting to know" Peter's role as Jesus' leading disciple during Jesus' ministry in Galilee.[7]

The central role of teachers in the congregation from which Paul began his apostolic work (Acts 13:1) points to the same conclusion. Even in the more charismatically structured churches of Paul the importance of teaching was taken for granted from the first (1 Cor. 12:28), and "teacher" seems to have been the first ministry to develop toward a de facto professional status (Gal. 6:6). This must mean that the first Christian congregations, as we would expect, recognized the need to maintain and pass on their characteristic and

life and teaching of Diogenes, or, on the Jewish side, in Jeremiah preserved (by his disciples) in "The Words of Jeremiah" (= canonical Jeremiah).

5. The emergence of the Pentateuch can be explained in such sociological terms.

6. See BAGD, παραδίδωμι 3; παραλαμβάνω 2g.

7. See further J. D. G. Dunn, "The Relationship between Paul and Jerusalem according to Galatians 1 and 2," *NTS* 28 (1982) 463-66; idem, "Once More — Gal 1.18: ἱστορῆσαι Κηφᾶν," *ZNW* 76 (1985) 138-39; both reprinted in *Jesus, Paul and the Law: Studies in Mark and Galatians* (London: SPCK; Louisville: Westminster, 1990) 108-28.

distinctive traditions (what other functions would "teachers" fulfill?). In an oral community the treasury of sacred tradition and of tried and tested wisdom would have to be largely entrusted to those whose special gift or responsibility it was to retain and retell the tradition and wisdom on behalf of the community.

Nor do we have to look far for examples of that tradition. For it is there in our Synoptic Gospels. As is now becoming more clearly recognized, the Gospels themselves *do* display a biographical interest in Jesus — not in terms of modern biography, but in terms of ancient biography. That is to say, they display a didactic concern to portray the character of their subject matter by recounting things he did and said.[8] To cite a variety of examples, Matthew 5–7 is clearly structured for ease of instruction and learning; here is a body of Jesus' teaching, collected together because of its continuing relevance to the churches. Luke was clearly determined to portray Jesus as an example of one who lived by prayer (Luke 3:21; 5:15; 6:12; 9:18, 28-29, etc.). And Mark itself can be regarded quite properly as an example of the way a teacher presented the Jesus tradition in oral form.[9]

The same interest is evident in much of the earlier forms of the material used by the Evangelists, even when it was serving other functions as well, as for example in the earlier blocks of material which we find in Mark's Gospel (2:1–3:6; 4:35–5:43, etc.)[10] It would, of course, be ludicrous to assume that all the Pauline congregations were wholly ignorant of such material until they received their copy of Mark's Gospel. As the variant forms of tradition between the three Synoptics clearly enough indicate, there must have been different versions of much if not all of the Markan material circulating round a wide range of churches before Mark took the step of gathering it into a "Gospel." It would be utterly astonishing then if the congregations to which Paul writes did not possess their own stock of Jesus tradition, much of which he would himself probably have supplied.

Moreover, when we press the form-critical point about the oral nature of the tradition behind the Gospels, it is hard to escape at least two firm conclusions. First, that Jesus was remembered from the first, inter alia, as himself a teacher of parable and wisdom.[11] And second, that this character of teaching-worth-cherishing, because of its content and the authority of its originator, is integral to the tradition itself (however much it may have been elaborated in the course of transmission). It would be simply ridiculous to

8. See further D. E. Aune, *The New Testament in Its Literary Environment* (Philadelphia: Westminster, 1987) 17-76; R. A. Burridge, *What Are the Gospels? A Comparison with Graeco-Roman Biography* (SNTSMS 70; Cambridge University, 1992).

9. T. P. Haverly, *Oral Traditional Literature and the Composition of Mark's Gospel* (Ph.D. dissertation, Edinburgh, 1983); against W. H. Kelber, *The Oral and the Written Gospel* (Philadelphia: Fortress, 1983).

10. See H. W. Kuhn, *Ältere Sammlungen im Markusevangelium* (Göttingen: Vandenhoeck und Ruprecht, 1971).

11. See the various essays in Wansbrough, ed., *Jesus and the Oral Gospel Tradition*.

ignore such material when inquiring into the teaching which teachers must have been responsible for in the earliest churches.

In short, the a priori plausibility outlined above is strongly confirmed by the evidence of our earliest documentation and by the character of the gospel tradition. But is it confirmed by specific evidence within the Pauline letters? To address this question must be our next task.

2. Echoes of Jesus' Teaching in Paul

There is little point in rehearsing the debate on whether allusions to Jesus tradition are present in the Pauline letters. It never succeeded in achieving a widespread consensus in the past and is hardly likely to do so now. The traditional form of the debate is well represented in Victor Furnish's brief review of the question. He recalls that at the beginning of the century Alfred Resch claimed to have found no fewer than 925 parallels with the Synoptic Gospels in nine Pauline letters.[12] Furnish himself, however, could find only eight convincing parallels to the Synoptics in the ethical teaching of Paul (Rom. 12:14, 17; 13:7; 14:13-14; 14:14; 1 Thess. 5:2, 13, 15).[13] That there can be such a disparity at once tells us how subjective the whole exercise has been and still is.[14]

The discussion, of course, has not been merely repetitive. For example, Dale Allison was able to argue on the basis of a clustering of allusions that Paul knew three collections of sayings — the sources behind Mark 9:33-50; Luke 6:27-38; and Mark 6:6b-13 par.[15] And more recently Michael Thompson has attempted a more scientific analysis by setting out a sequence of criteria for recognizing an allusion or echo — including verbal or conceptual or formal agreement, common motivation, dissimilarity to Greco-Roman and Jewish traditions, presence of dominical or tradition indicators, and presence of other dominical echoes in the immediate context; though he too accepts that "in most cases the judgment of the scholar is subjective."[16]

12. A. Resch, *Der Paulinismus und die Logia Jesu in ihrem gegenseitigen Verhältnis untersucht* (TU 12; Leipzig: Hinrichs, 1904).

13. V. P. Furnish, *Theology and Ethics in Paul* (Nashville: Abingdon, 1968) 53-54; see further Allison, "The Pauline Epistles and the Synoptic Gospels," 10, who notes the same texts most frequently cited as containing "firm echoes," with 1 Cor. 13:2 replacing 1 Thess. 5:13 in Furnish's list, and with bibliography in n. 47.

14. For an in-between example see A. M. Hunter, *Paul and His Predecessors* (London: SCM, 1961) 47-51.

15. See n. 2 above; for a critique see Neirynck, "Paul and the Sayings of Jesus," 281-306.

16. Thompson, *Clothed with Christ,* 30-36 (quotation from p. 31); he acknowledges his indebtedness to R. B. Hays, *Echoes of Scripture in the Letters of Paul* (London and New Haven: Yale University, 1989) 29-32. Note also the distinction between *Entsprechung* ("correspondence") and *Kontinuität* ("continuity") offered by Wedderburn, "Introduction," in Wedderburn, ed., *Paul,* 13.

It would seem, in fact, as though we have reached something of an impasse in the debate as carried out in traditional terms, and little would be gained by going round the mulberry bush yet once more with a "fresh" analysis of the same material. On individual passages there is little genuinely fresh to be said, and the result would not change the complexion of the debate or its broad outcome.

Nevertheless, the very fact of the debate and the range of opinion arising from it are of significance. For the character of the debate is itself a reflection of the character of the evidence; the inconclusiveness of the debate reflects the inconclusiveness of the evidence. All are agreed that Paul does cite or refer to dominical tradition at two points at least (1 Cor. 7:10-11; 9:14).[17] All are agreed that there is a further group of passages in Paul which look very much as though they contain allusions to or echoes of Jesus tradition.[18] And all are agreed that there is a further group of passages of indeterminate dimensions where there is at least some similarity of theme or wording with elements of the Jesus tradition. In other words, there *is* a degree of consensus — on the character of the evidence within the Pauline letters.

One could indeed plot a graph of Pauline parenesis containing echoes of the Jesus tradition, peaking at the two or three clear citations, broadening out to the small number which are widely regarded as containing allusions or echoes, and with a still larger base of possible allusions merging imperceptibly into the still larger mass of Pauline parenesis. Horizontal lines could then simply mark out the various "cut-off" points where different individuals have recognized more or less likely allusions to or echoes of the Jesus tradition.

To appreciate the force of this observation (the character and differing strengths of the putative allusions) some documentation is called for before we reflect on its further significance. We begin with a sample of the strongest candidates and then as it were "slide" gently down the graph.[19]

(a) One of the most convincing examples would, by general consent, be Rom. 12:14. Certainly, the echo of the saying of Jesus preserved in Luke 6:27-28 and Matt. 5:44 seems fairly clear.

Romans	*"Bless those who persecute you, bless* and do not curse"
Matthew	"Love your enemies . . . *bless* those who *curse* you"
Luke	"Love your enemies and pray for *those who persecute you*"

---

17. Others include 1 Thess. 4:15-17, but it is better understood as a prophetic utterance rather than a dominical saying; see J. D. G. Dunn, *Jesus and the Spirit* (London: SCM; Philadelphia: Westminster, 1975) 230; cf. N. Walter, "Paul and the Early Christian Jesus-Tradition," in Wedderburn, *Paul,* 66-67.

18. Neirynck is one of the most skeptical; see further below, p. 185.

19. In the following quotations *italics* indicate the parallel features.

That this was, at least in some degree, a distinctively Christian teaching is indicated by two factors. (1) The sense for εὐλογέω as "bless" is characteristically and distinctively Jewish rather than Greek, where it would more naturally mean "speak well of, praise, eulogize."[20] (2) But the thought of returning blessing for cursing is something of an advance on the more typical *lex talionis* assumption of Jewish covenant faith that God would curse those who cursed his people (Gen. 12:3; 27:29; Num. 24:9; 1QS 2.1-10; 10.17-21). Matt. 5:43-44 puts the claim to distinctiveness more strongly.

Moreover the saying is hardly Pauline in formulation (Paul nowhere else uses καταράομαι, "curse"), and has echoes elsewhere (1 Cor. 4:12; 1 Pet. 3:9; *Did.* 1:3). Clearly the sentiment that abuse should be met by blessing quickly became an established part of Christian response to persecution. Since the testimony of the Jesus tradition is clear that Jesus was remembered as saying something to this effect, it would be somewhat perverse to look for a different source of this distinctively Christian teaching. And since it is only in the Lukan and Romans form that we have the contrast drawn between "blessing" and "cursing," the most obvious corollary is that it was indeed Jesus who provided the decisive moral impetus for the conduct here commended, and that the form known to Paul was expressed somewhat along the lines of the Lukan version.

That Jesus was remembered as having said something along these lines would therefore seem hard to dispute. The variation between the Pauline and Gospel forms is no greater than the variation between the Lukan and Matthean forms. The fact that Jesus' exhortation was remembered in different versions simply indicates that the Jesus tradition was not yet in a finally fixed form, but could be adapted to different settings.

A second widely accepted example is Rom. 14:14. "I know and am persuaded in the Lord Jesus that nothing is profane (οὐδὲν κοινόν) in itself." There is a strong likelihood that the conviction so strongly asserted here is dependent in some measure at least on the saying of Jesus as given in Mark 7:15: "there is nothing outside a person . . . which is able to defile him" (οὐδέν ἐστιν . . . ὃ δύναται κοινῶσαι). The issue is made more complex by the fact that a "weaker" form of the saying appears in Matt. 15:11 and *Gospel of Thomas* 14, and in view of the surprising unwillingness of the earliest community of Jesus' disciples in Jerusalem to follow what, according to Mark 7:15, was unequivocal teaching (cf. Acts 10:14; 11:2-3; Gal. 2:12). It is best resolved by assuming both that Jesus' original words had been more ambiguous than Mark represents (closer to Matthew's version) and that Mark 7:15 *and* Rom. 14:14 demonstrate the use made of the saying and interpretation

---

20. See details in H. W. Beyer, *TDNT* II (1964) 754-63.

given to it when the question of clean and unclean foods emerged as a central issue in the Gentile mission.[21]

We should perhaps also note the emphatic use of ἐκεῖνος in the final clause of the verse: "to the one who reckons something profane, to that person it is profane" (ἐκείνῳ κοινόν). The point is that such a use of ἐκεῖνος here and in v. 15 is unusual in Paul, but may just be a further indication that Paul knew and was drawing on, consciously or unconsciously, the tradition preserved in Mark 7:15, 18-20, where in 7:20 a similar emphasis is given to what comes forth from a person as the defiling agent: "that is what defiles a person" (ἐκεῖνο κοινοῖ).

(b) As examples which are also frequently cited, but which are slightly more problematic, we may refer to 1 Cor. 13:2 and 1 Thess. 5:2 and 13.

1 Cor. 13:2	"if I *have* all *faith* so as to move (μεθιστάναι) *mountains*"
Matt. 17:20	"if you *have faith* . . . you will say to this *mountain,* 'Move from here to there and it will move (μεταβήσεται).'"

The greater remoteness of Mark 11:23 ("Whoever says to this *mountain,* 'Be taken up and thrown into the sea,' and does not doubt in his heart but believes . . ."), and the possibility that there was a (Jewish) proverbial expression to the same effect reduces the strength of the case here.[22] On the other hand, one might well ask whether it is more likely that Paul echoes a well-known proverb (whose attestation is all a good deal later than Paul) or that his formulation reflects the force of a well-known saying of Jesus about the efficacy of faith.

1 Thess. 5:2, 4	"You yourselves *know* well that the day of the Lord is coming like a *thief* in the night . . . you are not in darkness that the day will surprise you like a *thief*"
Matt. 24:43	"*Know* this that if the householder had known at what watch the *thief* was to come, he would have watched."

Here the wording is still less close, but the imagery is closely similar. We should further note that Jesus was remembered as speaking in terms of similar

---

21. This case is argued in detail in J. D. G. Dunn, "Jesus and Ritual Purity: A Study of the Tradition History of Mark 7.15," in *À Cause de L'Évangile. Melanges offerts à Dom Jacques Dupont* (Paris: Cerf, 1985) 251-76, reprinted in my *Jesus, Paul and the Law,* 37-60; cf. Walter, "Paul and the Early Christian Jesus-Tradition," in Wedderburn, ed., *Paul,* 71-72; Thompson, *Clothed with Christ,* 185-99; contrast Neirynck, "Paul and the Sayings of Jesus," 306-8.

22. See esp. C. K. Barrett, *1 Corinthians* (London: Black, 1968) 301.

urgency on more than one occasion, or (alternatively expressed) that the Jesus tradition has preserved similar warnings elsewhere: Matt. 24:43 is parallel to Luke 12:39, and may therefore be reckoned a Q saying; and Mark 13:33-37 preserves a scatter of such warnings, which also have further parallels in Matt. 24:42 (where the wording more closely approximates to 1 Thess. 5:2 — *"you* do not *know* at what *day* your *Lord is coming"),* in the parable of the wise and foolish girls (Matt. 25:13), and in Luke 21:34-36. Moreover, 2 Pet. 3:10 has language precisely similar to 1 Thess. 5:2 ("the day of the Lord will come like a thief"), and Rev. 3:3 and 16:15 have combined the force of 1 Thess. 5:2 and the Gospel warnings in a saying of Jesus himself ("I will come like a thief and you will not know at what hour I will come upon you"; "I am coming like a thief"). The most obvious deduction to draw from all this is that there was a well-known tradition in at least many churches of Jesus having given such a warning and that Paul reflects this knowledge in his formulation in 1 Thess. 5:2.

1 Thess. 5:13	"live at peace among yourselves" (εἰρηνεύετε ἐν ἑαυτοῖς)
Mark 9:50	"live at peace with one another" (εἰρηνεύετε ἐν ἀλλήλοις)

Here again we should note a certain parallel with Matt. 5:9 ("Blessed are the peacemakers") and the fact that Paul echoes the same exhortation in Rom. 12:18: "If possible, so far as it depends on you, live at peace with everyone" (μετὰ πάντων ἀνθρώπων εἰρηνεύοντες), and to some degree in 2 Cor. 13:11: "live in peace" (εἰρηνεύετε). The ideal itself is a widely cherished one (e.g., Sir. 6:6; *Epictetus* 4.5.24), and that inevitably raises a suspicion as to the source of Paul's exhortations. But even so, Christians in affirming it on their own part would be more likely to recall that Jesus had so encouraged his first disciples and thus to cite him (were the need to arise) as their authority for it.[23]

(c) Three examples of passages which fall outside the strongest group of eight or nine can be cited from my own work on Romans.

Romans 13:9: "You shall love your neighbor as yourself," as the summation of the law. The issue here can easily be obscured by the debate as to whether this is a distinctively Christian assertion. In fact it could equally well be described as Jewish. For example, the famous episode about Hillel summing up the Torah in the negative form of the golden rule (*b.* Shabbath 31a)

---

23. Oddly enough, although Allison ("The Pauline Epistles and the Synoptic Gospels," 13-15) makes a good case for the thesis that Paul knew the pre-Markan collection of logia incorporated by Mark at 9:33-50, he makes no mention of the possible link here with Mark 9:50, which would add further strength to his thesis.

indicates clearly enough that the thought of focusing the whole law in a single command was quite acceptable within a large sweep of Judaism. And according to *Sipra Lev.* §200 (on 19:18) Rabbi Aqiva used to speak of Lev. 19:18 as "the greatest principle in the Torah."[24]

At the same time we have to note that the teaching was particularly characteristic within earliest Christianity, with Lev. 19:18 the passage in all the Pentateuch most frequently cited by New Testament writers (Mark 12:31 par; 12:33; Matt. 5:43; 19:19; here; Gal. 5:14; Jas. 2:8). And if we ask where the impetus came for such a focusing on Lev. 19:18 in Christian parenesis the answer is most likely to be Jesus. Paul would no doubt be well aware that such a sentiment as Hillel's was in no sense an exemption from the rest of the law. Whereas his own use of Lev. 19:18 was a way of relativizing the rest of the law so that some could be set aside. The Jesus who was recalled in the Synoptic tradition as sitting loose to the sort of laws which Paul is about to discuss in Romans 14 (cf. Mark 2:23–3:5 par.; 7:1-23 par.) would be the obvious source for his summary treatment of the law. Not that either used Lev. 19:18 to relativize *all* the law (cf. after all Rom. 13:9a with Mark 10:19); but it is just the degree of relativizing which Paul here commends for which he could expect his readers to find support in the Jesus tradition.[25]

Romans 14:17: "The kingdom of God does not consist of eating and drinking, but in righteousness, peace, and joy in the Holy Spirit." Kingdom language is not common in Paul, and where it does occur it usually does so in formulaic talk of "inheriting the kingdom" (1 Cor. 6:9-10; 15:50; Gal. 5:21) or with similar future eschatological reference (1 Thess. 2:12; 2 Thess. 1:5). The only close parallel is 1 Cor. 4:20. This suggests that the category of "the kingdom of God" lay near to hand in the common Christian tradition. Paul chose to make little use of it, but could take it up as an obviously familiar concept when it was appropriate to do so. The obvious source of this traditional usage was Jesus, since it is clear beyond dispute from the Synoptic tradition that proclamation of the kingdom of God was a characteristic feature of Jesus' preaching and that the metaphors and emphases he used in connection with it marked out that preaching as distinctive.

Moreover, unusually for him, Paul's usage here reflects a central emphasis in the Jesus tradition — that God's eschatological rule was already being manifested in the present, particularly in Jesus' exorcisms (Matt. 12:28 = Luke 11:20) and table fellowship (Luke 14:12-24 = Matt. 22:1-10). Two points of contact are noteworthy.[26] (1) In both cases it is the powerful activity of the Spirit

---

24. See further I. Abrahams, *Studies in Pharisaism and the Gospels: First Series* (Cambridge: Cambridge University, 1917) 18-29.

25. See also Thompson, *Clothed with Christ,* 121-40.

26. These are insufficiently recognized by G. Haufe, "Reich Gottes bei Paulus und in der Jesustradition," *NTS* 31 (1985) 467-72.

which is presented as the manifestation of God's (final) kingly rule. The thought in fact is very much of a piece with the eschatological tension so characteristic of Paul's thought, where the Spirit is understood precisely as the first installment in the present of the inheritance which is the future kingdom (1 Cor. 6:9-11; Gal. 4:6-7; also Eph. 1:13-14). In both the Jesus tradition and Paul the Spirit's present activity is an experience already of the kingdom whose consummation is not yet.[27] (2) The remembrance that Jesus likened the kingdom to a banquet does not run counter to the disclaimer in Rom. 14:17. On the contrary, Jesus' parable of the banquet was remembered as a protest against the sort of restrictions on table fellowship which characterized Pharisees (and Essenes) (cf. Luke 7:34-39 with 14:12-14; and Luke 14:13 with 1QSa 2.3-9).[28] Paul here is making precisely the same sort of protest — against a measuring of what is acceptable to God in terms of rules governing eating and drinking.

Romans 16:19. The unusualness of the formulation in Paul, and the similarity in emphasis and intent to a distinctive feature of the Jesus tradition, together point more strongly than has usually been appreciated to the conclusion that Paul here was dependent in substantial measure on a community memory of Jesus' preaching and enacting of the kingdom.[29]

Rom. 16:19	"I want you to be wise (σοφούς) in regard to what is good and innocent (ἀκεραίους) in regard to what is bad."
Matt. 10:16	"Be wise (φρόνιμοι) as serpents and innocent (ἀκέραιοι) as doves."

The sentiment is not distinctively Christian in character, and is typical of a general exhortation of practical wisdom familiar not least in Jewish circles. However, it may be significant that the word "innocent" here occurs in biblical literature only in these two passages and in the similar exhortation in Phil. 2:15. The best explanation is likely to be that Paul has drawn on the combined heritage of Jewish wisdom, as added to by one who was also cherished as a teacher of wisdom by the first Christians (as evidenced by the Q material); but the evidence has hardly been sufficient to persuade most commentators.[30]

(d) With this last example our slide down the graph of plausible allusions is already almost at the point where any distinctive echo of the Jesus tradition

27. See further J. D. G. Dunn, "Spirit and Kingdom," *ExpT* 82 (1970-71) 36-40 (= ch. 10 in *The Christ and the Spirit* II: *Pneumatology*); also idem, *Jesus and the Spirit*, 310-11.

28. See further below, pp. 183-84.

29. See also A. J. M. Wedderburn, "Paul and Jesus: The Problem of Continuity," in Wedderburn, ed., *Paul*, 101-15; Thompson, *Clothed with Christ*, 200-207.

30. But see Hunter, *Paul and His Predecessors*, 50; and M. Black, *Romans* (NCBC; London: Oliphants; Grand Rapids: Eerdmans, 1973) 184.

is becoming almost inaudible. The echo is still fainter in cases like 1 Thess.
5:6 and 16:

1 Thess. 5:6	"So then, let us not sleep as others do, but let us keep awake (γρηγορῶμεν) and be sober"
Matt. 24:42	"Keep awake (γρηγορεῖτε) therefore" (cf. Luke 21:34-36)
1 Thess. 5:16	"Rejoice (χαίρετε) at all times"
Luke 10:20	"Rejoice (χαίρετε) that your names have been written in heaven"

At most one can say in such a case that the number of possible allusions
within a few verses (1 Thess. 5:2, 4, 6, 13, 15, 16) strengthens the possibility
that Paul's parenesis at this point was shaped by patterns and emphases of the
Jesus tradition. That is to say, the presence of stronger allusions may just be
sufficient to carry with them other weaker allusions (weaker in terms of the
actual evidence). The fact that similar clusters of allusions can be detected
(Rom. 12:14, 17, 21;[31] 13:7,[32] 9; 14:13,[33] 14, 17, 18, 15:1, 2[34]) may strengthen
the case somewhat. Conversely, Allison's argument suggests at least the possibility that Paul made use of clusters of Jesus tradition.

Allison also cites the work of B. Fjärstedt,[35] whom he criticizes for
building too much on the coincidence of words between 1 Cor. 3:10-14 and
Luke 6:48-49 and between 1 Corinthians 4 and Luke 12:35-48 (25 shared
words and expressions). But when one who is as sympathetic to the enterprise
as Allison concludes that the sum of Fjärstedt's lists is still zero, we may be
sure that we are near the bottom of the graph.[36]

---

31. With 12:17, 21 cf. again Matt. 5:43-48 = Luke 6:27-28, 32-36; and see my "Paul's
Knowledge," 201. Cf. Walter in Wedderburn, *Paul,* 56; Thompson, *Clothed with Christ,* 90-110.
32. With 13:7 cf. Mark 12:17 par. (note Luke 22:25). See also, e.g., W. Sanday and A. C.
Headlam, *Romans* (ICC; 5th ed., Edinburgh: Clark, 1902) 371; C. H. Dodd, *Romans* (MNTC;
London: Hodder and Stoughton, 1932) 205; H. W. Schmidt, *Römer* (THKNT 6; Berlin: Evangelische, 1963) 221-22; C. E. B. Cranfield, *Romans* (2 vols., ICC; Edinburgh: Clark, 1979) II,
669-70; Stuhlmacher, "Jesustradition," 248; Thompson, *Clothed with Christ,* 111-20. Allison
notes that the sequence of 13:7, 8-10 is paralleled by the sequence Mark 12:13-17, 28-34 par.
("The Pauline Epistles and the Synoptic Gospels," 16-17), though a misprint of Luke 10 for
Luke 20 exaggerates the closeness in the case of Luke.
33. With Rom. 14:13 cf. Matt. 7:1 = Luke 6:37 and Mark 9:42 = Matt. 18:6; see discussion
in Thompson, *Clothed with Christ,* 161-84. Romans 13:7 and 14:13 are two of the eight or nine
widely accepted allusions (see above, p. 173).
34. On Rom. 14:18 and 15:1-2, see my "Paul's Knowledge," 204-5 and below, pp. 181-83;
also C. Wolff, "Humility and Self-Denial in Jesus' Life and Message and in the Apostolic Existence
of Paul," in Wedderburn, ed., *Paul,* 145-60, here 154-56.
35. B. Fjärstedt, *Synoptic Traditions in 1 Corinthians: Themes and Clusters of Theme
Words in 1 Corinthians 1-4 and 9* (Uppsala: Theologiska Institutionen, 1974).
36. Allison: "The Pauline Epistles and the Synoptic Gospels," 6-8.

3. Allusions to Jesus as Example in Paul

For the sake of completeness we should mention the further possibility that Paul was influenced by the Jesus tradition not only in respect of Jesus' teaching but also in regard to his conduct or lifestyle. Any appeal to the example of Jesus would, of course, imply a presupposition on Paul's part that his readers knew characteristic episodes from Jesus' ministry as well as characteristic teaching. We have already noted that the Gospels display a biographical interest in Jesus' behavior as much as in his teaching. And passages like Rom. 6:17;[37] 8:15-16;[38] 2 Cor. 8:9;[39] 10:1; Gal. 1:18;[40] and Phil 2:5[41] strengthen the a priori likelihood that Paul would have shared a similar interest.

The most striking instance, however, may well be Rom. 15:1-5. There is no doubt that Paul appeals to the example of Jesus here: ". . . let each of us please his neighbor . . . for Christ did not please himself . . ." (vv. 2-3). The appeal is not to incarnation[42] but primarily to Christ's denying himself by submission to the cross (2 Cor. 8:9; Phil. 2:5-8). This is confirmed by the appeal to Scripture, Paul continuing, "but as it is written, 'The reproaches of those who reproach you have fallen on me.' " The quotation is verbatim from the LXX of Ps. 69:9 (LXX 68:10). As one of the most powerful cries of personal distress in the psalter, it naturally commended itself to the first Christians as one of those Scriptures rendered prophetically luminous in the light of Jesus' suffering and death. And so we find it quoted frequently in the New Testament, the most explicit allusions usually with direct reference to Christ's passion and the events surrounding it (Mark 15:23, 36 par.; John 2:17; 15:25; 19:28-29; Acts 1:20).

At the same time it is also probable that the reference is not exclusively to Jesus' death and included also the thought of the character of his ministry as a whole. Here the case can be made by reference to the immediate context of 15:2-3.

The thought of Jesus as example is probably present already in v. 1: "we, the strong, ought to support the weaknesses of those who are without

---

37. See my *Romans* (2 vols., WBC 38; Dallas: Word, 1988) I, 343-44; also my "Paul's Knowledge," 196-97.

38. See my *Romans* I, 453-54; also "Paul's Knowledge," 197-98, where I also cite Rom. 13:14. So also Walter, "Paul and the Early Christian Jesus-Tradition," in Wedderburn, ed., *Paul,* 59.

39. See my *Christology in the Making* (London: SCM; Philadelphia: Westminster, 1980; 2nd ed., 1989) 121-23.

40. See above n. 7.

41. See, e.g., the review of discussion in P. T. O'Brien, *Philippians* (NIGTC; Grand Rapids: Eerdmans, 1991) 253-66.

42. H. Lietzmann, *Römer* (HNT 8; 5th ed., Tübingen: Mohr, 1971) 119.

strength." Outside the context of the present discussion (14:1–15:6), the only other passage where Paul speaks of people as "weak" in the letter is 5:6. The thought in fact is closely parallel, of someone else acting with responsible concern for the "weak" — there Christ, here "the strong" (οἱ δυνατοί). The implication is fairly obvious that Christ is the model of such concern — a parallel perhaps strengthened by the description of the exalted Christ as the Lord who "has power/strength" (δυνατεῖ) to uphold his servant (14:4). The reference of 5:6, of course, was again to Christ's death; and of 14:4 to the exalted Christ. But again it may be judged unlikely that Paul would neatly separate the character of Jesus' ministry in death and exaltation from that of his prior ministry or of his ministry as a whole.

This a priori inference is strengthened by his use of the word βαστάζειν, "carry, bear, support."[43] For one thing it may well carry an allusion to Isa. 53:4 ("Surely he has borne our griefs and carried our sorrows"), since βαστάζειν was probably in current use to translate "borne" in that passage, at least in the translations known to the early Christians, as Matt. 8:17 demonstrates.[44] Here, too, the primary thought in the earliest Christian apologetic use of Isaiah 53 would be of Christ's death. But Matt. 8:17 is itself proof of the a priori inference just drawn: that such a passage could be referred also to Jesus' healing ministry quite naturally and without any thought of it being inappropriate so to do.

And for another the thought seems to be much the same as in Gal. 6:2 ("Bear [βαστάζετε] one another's burdens"), where Paul continues, "and thus fulfill the law of Christ." "The law of Christ" is most naturally understood by reference to the "fulfilled law" of Gal. 5:14 ("You shall love your neighbor as yourself"[45]), since Jesus' summarizing of the law by reference to Lev. 19:18 would presumably be well enough known among the Christian churches, as Paul's own use of it (Rom. 13:8-10; Gal. 5:14) suggests.[46] Paul was certainly recalling that use in Rom. 15:2, since the word "neighbor" occurs elsewhere in Paul only in the two passages which cite Lev. 19:18 (Rom. 13:9-10; Gal. 5:14).

So the further similarity between Gal. 6:2 and Rom. 15:1, 3, 5 suggests that Paul here was following a familiar line of exhortation.

---

43. The sense "bear patiently, endure, put up with," suggested by BAGD and used by several modern English translations is too weak: a call for tolerance at this point would be an anticlimax following the strong counsel of 14:13-21.

44. βαστάζειν becomes more prominent in the later Greek versions of the Old Testament, and is used by Aquila in Isa. 53:11.

45. See particularly H. Schürmann, " 'Das Gesetz des Christus' (Gal. 6:2). Jesu Verhalten und Wort als letzgültige sittliche Norm nach Paulus," in J. Gnilka, ed., Neues Testament und Kirche (R. Schnackenburg FS; Freiburg: Herder, 1974) 282-300.

46. See above, pp. 177-78.

| Rom. 13:8-10 | love your neighbor | Gal. 5:14 | love your neighbor |
| Rom. 15:1-2 | bear with failings of
weak and please the
neighbor | Gal. 6:2 | bear one another's
burdens and so fulfill
the law of Christ |

In both cases the implication is strong that Paul was making an appeal to Jesus' ministry, referring to the character of his loving concern which both his teaching and example had brought to such clear expression, as, we may assume, his readers would be aware from their own knowledge of the Jesus tradition.

The overtone that Jesus serves as example for the conduct commended is probably continued in v. 5: "to live in harmony among yourselves in accordance with Christ Jesus" (κατὰ Χριστὸν Ἰησοῦν). As the equivalent κατά phrase elsewhere indicates, the phrase here probably refers primarily to the will of Christ (Rom. 8:4-5; 2 Cor. 11:7).[47] But once again it would be somewhat forced to exclude a reference also to the example of Christ as encapsulated in the various Jesus traditions possessed by all of the earliest Christian congregations.[48] Christ has just been evoked as an example in v. 3, and, as we have seen, there are several echoes of such Jesus tradition in the preceding exhortation (14:13-14, 17-18; 15:1-2). And in other similar κατά phrases the double thought of "modeled on and obedient to" seems likewise implicit: Col. 2:8 follows 2:6: "as you received the traditions concerning Christ (παρελάβετε τὸν Χριστὸν τὸν κύριον), so walk in him," and in Eph. 4:24 the thought, of course, is of "the new person" as modeled in accordance with the image of God (cf. Col. 3:10) = Christ (cf. Rom. 13:14; 2 Cor. 3:18; 4:4, 6).

What emerges from this brief discussion is the interesting likelihood that a central feature of Paul's parenesis was determined by a combination of Jesus' teaching and example — the two elements of the Jesus tradition (words and deeds) mutually reinforcing one another, as we might expect.[49]

Another possibility of a similarly combined influence of Jesus' words and conduct has recently been suggested by both my colleague A. J. M. Wedderburn and, independently, myself.[50] This is the suggestion that Paul's attitude to Gentile "sinners" was influenced by an awareness of Jesus' self-chosen mission "to call sinners" (Mark 2:17). The case here is more allusive

---

47. W. Michaelis, *TDNT* IV (1967) 669, n. 18; E. Käsemann, *Romans* (London: SCM, 1980) 383; Cranfield, *Romans,* 737.

48. So, e.g., Sanday and Headlam, *Romans,* 393; M. J. Lagrange, *Romains* (ÉBib; Paris: Gabalda, 1950) 344.

49. See also Thompson, *Clothed with Christ,* 208-36.

50. A. J. M. Wedderburn, "Paul and Jesus: Similarity and Continuity," in Wedderburn, ed., *Paul,* 117-43, here 124, 130-43; Dunn, *Jesus, Paul and the Law,* 101.

(further down the graph), but the cumulative weight is nevertheless quite impressive.

We might note, first of all, that Paul combined stress both on Jesus' Jewishness and on the effectiveness of his ministry with regard to Gentiles (Rom. 15:8-9; Gal. 4:4-7; note the interplay of "we" and "you"). This is significant when we also recall how little contact Jesus is remembered as having with Gentiles within the Synoptic tradition.

Second, the fact that Paul talks of "Gentile sinners" when the issue is acceptable practice of table fellowship (Gal. 2:11-15) cannot but recall the fact that Jesus was remembered precisely as one who ate with "sinners" (Mark 2:16-17; Matt. 11:19 = Luke 7:34). If the Jesus tradition is historical at this point (and few question it) and if Paul did indeed use the same language when rebuking Peter over what in Paul's eyes must have appeared as an equivalent issue, it is hard to imagine that no echo of the Jesus tradition was heard or intended at this point.[51]

Thirdly, we have already noted[52] that in Rom. 14:14 and 17 there are probably echoes of Jesus' teaching. Both, we should point out, in relation to the same set of interrelated questions: what may observant Jews eat and so also with whom may they eat? And both reflect the more open attitude of Jesus in respect of food, at least as remembered in the Markan form of the tradition (Mark 7:15, 19), and in respect of the significance of the kingdom for present conduct (Matt. 11:19; Luke 14:7-24).

If all this lies in the background of such Pauline passages, it would also help explain what still seems something of a conundrum for most exegetes: how it was that the appearance of Jesus to Paul on the Damascus road should point Paul so immediately to a mission to Gentiles (most explicitly Gal. 1:15-16 — note the "in order that"). The most obvious answer is probably that the memory of Jesus' lax attitude to "sinners" was part of the underlying offense of the Jesus movement which stirred Paul's persecuting wrath, especially as he saw it translated into outreach to Gentiles (at least by the Hellenist Christian Jews). Consequently the recognition and acknowledgment of Jesus on the Damascus road would have carried with it the immediate implication that the Jesus who had been friend of "sinners" must also wish to "call" Gentile sinners.[53]

All this is, of course, highly speculative, and to talk of clear echoes of

---

51. Peter no doubt disagreed that the two issues were equivalent. For the logic of Peter's position, see, e.g., my *The Partings of the Ways between Christianity and Judaism* (London: SCM; Philadelphia: Trinity Press International, 1991) 132-33; also my *Galatians* (BNTC; London: Black, 1993) 141-42.

52. See above, pp. 175-76, 178-79.

53. For a fuller attempt to explicate the rationale of Gal. 1:15-16, see again my *Partings*, 119-24; also *Galatians*, 65-67.

or allusions to the Jesus tradition would be to push the evidence too hard. Nevertheless there are lines of connection here which should not be ignored and which constitute a further reminder of the character of the range of evidence relevant in this discussion.

4. The Influence of the Jesus Tradition

Why then did Paul not cite Jesus as his authority for so many of the points of exhortation discussed above? Most would regard his failure to do so as a decisively critical weakness in any attempt to argue for allusions to Jesus tradition in Pauline parenesis. This consideration has weighed very heavily with two recent contributions to the debate.

Nikolaus Walter tries to grasp the nettle by noting that, whatever allusions to the teaching of Jesus may be present in Paul's letters, there is no indication of a consciousness on Paul's part that they were allusions.[54] The argument, if followed through, would suggest that the Synoptic-like traditions used in the early churches were not remembered as stemming from Jesus, or at least that the early churches did not think it necessary to retain the attribution of them to Jesus in their corporate memory. That would seem an odd conclusion to be forced to, given the fact of the Synoptic Gospels, which presumably constitute contrary evidence in themselves — that is, that such traditions were remembered as explicitly attributable to Jesus and that from such traditions Mark and the others were able to compile their Gospels.

At about the same time Frans Neirynck made a similar observation: that in the Pauline letters, apart from 1 Cor. 7:10-11 and 9:14, "there is no certain trace of a conscious use of sayings of Jesus. Possible allusions to gospel sayings can be noted on the basis of similarity of form and context but a direct use of a gospel saying in the form it has been preserved in the synoptic gospels is hardly provable."[55] The final clause of this quotation, however, is a reminder that Neirynck's real concern is whether the Pauline letters provide evidence of a pre-Synoptic Gospel or of Q or pre-Q collections. In such a discussion the degree of similarity to the actual wording of the Synoptic parallels must be a decisive consideration. Whereas for us the more productive question is whether such "allusions" within Paul, together with the Synoptic parallels, constitute evidence of a Jesus tradition which was remembered and reused in different forms.

---

54. Walter, "Paul and the Early Christian Jesus-Tradition," in Wedderburn, ed., *Paul,* 56, 78.

55. Neirynck, "Paul and the Sayings of Jesus," 320.

Sandy Wedderburn has suggested a further possibility: that Paul did not cite Jesus explicitly as authority because the teaching of Jesus was largely, at that time and in Paul's eyes, "in enemy hands," in that it was being used by his opponents, whereas Paul was more concerned to maintain his own independence.[56] This might help explain Paul's reticence in a case like Rom. 14:14,[57] but not in all cases; and an appeal to "opposition" teaching by allusion would seem to be open to the same objection as an explicit appeal.[58]

The real problem in all this, as the contributions of Walter and Neirynck show, is that the issue is being posed in a too narrow or onesided way. If the question is asked: Did Paul allude to or echo Jesus' tradition? then the discussion is soon forced down the lines marked out by Walter and Neirynck. But should we not rather be asking: Given such similarity and such differing degrees of similarity between a number of Paul's exhortations and elements within the Jesus tradition, what does that tell us about the influence of the Jesus tradition on Paul's parenesis? And further: Given the character of these allusions/echoes, what does that tell us about the way that influence worked? Such questions are deserving of more consideration than they have so far been given.

One conclusion which follows almost immediately from the variation between the Pauline material reviewed above and the related Jesus tradition is that the Jesus tradition was not yet set in fixed and unyielding forms. Rather it was *living* tradition, tradition which was evidently adaptable to different needs and diverse contexts. This character of the Jesus tradition was already sufficiently obvious from the variations contained *within* the Synoptic Gospels themselves. But its relevance to the present question has been too little recognized. In fact the variations between Paul's usage and that of the Synoptics are more or less of the same order. So we can speak quite appropriately of pneumatic tradition, or of charismatic usage of the tradition,[59] or of targumic paraphrase[60] of the tradition. The point being that it was cherished not merely as something said two or three decades earlier, but as a living word; not merely as a relic of a dead leader, but as still expressing the will of the living Lord.[61] And the force of each saying must have depended as much on its appropriateness to the situation addressed by the apostle as on the fact that both writer and reader knew that its original authority for Christian congregations

56. Wedderburn, "Problem of Continuity," in Wedderburn, *Paul*, 100-101.
57. See above, pp. 175-76.
58. See also Thompson, *Clothed with Christ*, 73-76.
59. Dunn, *Unity and Diversity in the New Testament* (London: SCM; Philadelphia: Westminster, 1977; 2nd ed., 1990) 69, 77-79.
60. As do O. Michel, *Römer* (KEK; 13th ed., Göttingen: Vandenhoeck und Ruprecht, 1966) 386; and H. Schlier, *Römerbrief* (HTKNT; Freiburg: Herder, 1977) 379, in reference to Rom. 12:14.
61. See further my study, *The Living Word* (London: SCM; Philadelphia: Fortress, 1987).

stemmed from Jesus as recalled by both in the Jesus tradition which they shared originally.

We are not entirely in the dark on this matter, for we know how Paul used and how his thinking was influenced by his other great source of authority — the Old Testament, or to be more precise, the Scriptures of his ancestral faith and earlier training. Here, too, an obvious parallel (influence of Scripture, influence of Jesus tradition) has been often neglected because of an issue focused too narrowly or approached only from one side. Of course the parallel is not exact, because Paul makes so many explicit citations from his Scriptures. On the other hand, we should note that Paul shows the same freedom in his handling of the Scriptures[62] as he does in his explicit references to the Jesus tradition (1 Cor. 7:10-11; 9:14).[63] More to the point here, however, there are also riches of allusion and echo which have only recently begun to be explored in a systematic way. Here credit must be given above all to Richard Hays, who has been able to demonstrate from the four major letters of Paul (Romans-Galatians) how many such echoes there are in his writing, without recognition of which the text would lose much of its spring and the argument its force.[64]

Some examples from my own work on Romans may be appropriate. One comes early on in Rom. 1:19-32, where, as has often been noted, Paul echoes the language of Wisdom 13–15, even though he nowhere cites it precisely. A second is the use of Deut. 30:11-14 in Romans 10. The passage is quoted, of course, but appreciation of the full significance of that quotation for Paul and his readers requires some awareness of the influence of Deuteronomy 30 within diaspora Judaism, as evidenced, for example, by the LXX of Deuteronomy 30, by Philo's use of the passage, and by reference to Deut. 30:7 in Jewish tomb inscriptions.[65] And for a third we might note that in Rom. 12:15-21 Paul echoes themes of traditional Jewish wisdom,[66] even though he cites specifically only Deut. 32:35 and Prov. 25:21.

It should be evident in all this that we are witnessing established or hallowed tradition which had become so much part of Paul that it influenced him from within, not just from without. Its influence, in other words, is to be recognized at the level of shaping thought, not so much as an external authority

---

62. See D. A. Koch, *Die Schrift als Zeuge des Evangeliums* (Tübingen: Mohr, 1986), esp. 102-98.

63. Walter, "Paul and the Early Christian Jesus-Tradition," in Wedderburn, ed., *Paul,* 68-74.

64. Hays, *Echoes.* For an earlier list of allusions and parallels see E. E. Ellis, *Paul's Use of the Old Testament* (Grand Rapids: Eerdmans, 1957) 153-54.

65. For details, see my *Romans* II, 603-5.

66. 12:15 (Sir. 7:34); 12:16 (Prov. 3:7; Isa. 5:21); 12:17 (Prov. 3:4); 12:19 (Lev. 19:18; Deut. 32:35); 12:20 (Prov. 25:21-22); 12:21 (*T. Benj.* 4:3).

whose authority can be called on only by formal citation. Moreover, Paul would almost certainly expect his readers to recognize some at least of the allusions to and the echoes of well-known themes, since, in the examples just cited, his indictment in Rom. 1:19-32 depends on their recognition that this is standard Jewish polemic against idolatry and sexual immorality, the validity of his use of Deut. 30:11-14 in Romans 10 depends on an already widespread perception of the universal application of the word, and in Rom. 12:9-21 he would presumably not want to be thought of as giving wholly fresh advice.

The same we may observe is probably true of the already traditional kerygmatic and confessional formulas which Paul seems to use on frequent occasions. Here the parallel is closer. For, on the one hand, there is a similar imbalance between the very few explicit citations of such formulas (notably 1 Cor. 15:3-4) and the more frequent allusions (Rom. 1:3-4; 3:25-26; 4:24-25; 8:11, 34; 10:9; 14:9, 15; 1 Cor. 1:13; 6:14; 8:11; 15:12, etc.).[67] And, on the other, there is a similar debate among contemporary scholars as to whether the latter should be designated as "pre-Pauline formulas" in the first place.[68] The double parallel is not accidental; it reflects the same character in the material. In this case, too, similarities in wording suggest a degree of interdependence best explained in terms of a speech pattern ingrained by frequent usage, the natural reflex of a habitual worshiper and indefatigable preacher and teacher.[69] Here, too, Paul would presumably expect his readers to recognize such echoes for what they were, even though the level of his explicit argument does not appear to depend on such recognition.

In both cases what we are actually witnessing is the language of community discourse. We must imagine Christians who were steeped in the language and thought forms of the (Jewish) Scriptures (the only Scriptures they had), and who had been deeply impressed, their whole lives transformed and shaped afresh, by the message of Jesus. In communities bonded by such common experience and language there is a whole level of discourse which consists of allusion and echo. It is the very fact that allusions are sufficient for much effective communication which provides and strengthens the bond; recognition of the allusion/echo is what attests effective membership of the group. Who has never belonged to a community where "in-jokes" and code allusions or abbreviations both facilitated communication between members of the group and left outsiders at best able to function only on the surface of the exchange without recognizing implications and ramifications obvious to the insiders? A community which can communicate only by citing explicit

---

67. See W. Kramer, *Christ, Lord, Son of God* (London: SCM, 1966); K. Wengst, *Christologische Formeln und Lieder des Urchristentums* (Gütersloh: Mohn, 1972).

68. Notably questioned by M. D. Hooker.

69. Cf. also the "liturgical reflex" in passages like Rom. 1:25 and 9:5.

chapter and verse has no depth to it. And the same assuredly applies in the case of early Christian communities' store of Jesus tradition.

In other words, what we find in the Pauline parenesis in terms of echoes of/allusions to the Jesus tradition is just what we would expect. It would be surprising were it otherwise. The traditions of Jesus, no doubt well taught by the first Christian apostles and teachers, would have been treasured, meditated on, given prominent place in the reshaping of life and conduct consequent upon baptism. Such traditions would have entered into their own thinking and quite quickly have begun to shape their own language as well as their lives, and so also to shape their discourse one with another.[70] The letter of James provides another clear example of the same phenomenon.[71]

Here, then, emerges a surprising answer to our question, "Why was Jesus not cited explicitly as authority for the exhortations which drew on the Jesus tradition?" The answer is that to force, as it were, the web of allusion and echo into the open may strengthen the explicit authority of a particular exhortation,[72] but it also weakens the bonding effect of the web of shared discourse. In communities of shared discourse allusions can be all the more effective because they trigger off wider associations and communal memories whose emotive resonance gives added motivation to the looked for response.[73]

In short, in each case (Old Testament, church tradition, and Jesus tradition), and particularly in the case of the Jesus tradition, whose form was not yet finally fixed, what we see before us in passages like those discussed above is evidence of the Jesus tradition shaping Pauline parenesis at the level of his own thought processes, and no doubt intended by him to be recognized as derived from or indebted to the common memory of what Jesus had said and done — a celebration and reaffirmation by means of their common discourse of their shared indebtedness to their common Lord.

---

70. That Romans has such a high proportion of such allusions is significant, since Paul could not have passed on such traditions to the Roman believers himself. He must have been able to assume, nevertheless, that the churches in Rome, or elsewhere, had been furnished with a stock of Jesus (and kerygmatic) tradition similar to that which Paul himself drew on. This tells us much about the breadth and relative fixedness of the Jesus tradition passed on to new churches.

71. Notably Jas. 1:5, 17 (Matt. 7:7, 11); Jas. 1:6 (Matt. 21:21); Jas. 1:22-23 (Matt. 7:21, 24-27); Jas. 4:12 (Matt. 7:1); Jas. 5:12 (Matt. 5:34-37).

72. In fact, however, in the two most cited cases (1 Cor. 7:10-11; 9:14-15), Paul quotes a word from the Lord in order to *qualify* it!

73. Hence the weakness of Furnish's observation: "One must record with some surprise the fact that the teaching of the earthly Jesus seems not to play a vital, or at least as obvious, a role in Paul's concrete ethical instructions as the Old Testament" (*Theology and Ethics in Paul,* 55).

11

Paul's Understanding of the Death of Jesus as Sacrifice

The thesis put forward in what follows is that Paul's understanding of Jesus' life as having representative significance is the key which opens up to us his understanding of the significance of Jesus' death. Or to put the point in more technical shorthand: Paul's Adam christology is integral to his theology of Jesus' death as atoning sacrifice. The claim in essence is hardly a new one. It has been familiar in systematic theology in one form or another, as we might say, from Irenaeus ("theory of recapitulation")[1] to Pannenberg.[2] But it has been largely ignored or overshadowed in recent decades in New Testament scholarship, with the principal exception of M. D. Hooker,[3] and deserves more attention than it has received. Independently of Hooker I had developed my own version of the thesis[4] and now re-present it in an updated version.

Jesus as Representative Man

The fact that Paul tells us next to nothing about the historical Jesus has always been at the heart of one of the most intractable problems in New Testament

---

1. J. N. D. Kelly, *Early Christian Doctrines* (2nd ed., London: Black, 1960) 170-74.
2. W. Pannenberg, *Jesus God and Man* (London: SCM, 1968) 260-69.
3. M. D. Hooker, "Interchange and Atonement," *BJRL* 60 (1977-78) 462-80; idem, "Interchange in Christ," *JTS* new series 22 (1971) 349-61; idem, "Interchange and Suffering," in *Suffering and Martyrdom in the New Testament,* ed. W. Horbury and B. McNeil (Cambridge: Cambridge University, 1981), 70-83.
4. Dunn, "Paul's Understanding of the Death of Jesus," in *Reconciliation and Hope,* ed. R. J. Banks (L. L. Morris FS; Exeter: Paternoster, 1974) 125-41.

Originally published in *Sacrifice and Redemption: Durham Essays in Theology,* ed. S. W. Sykes, 35-56. Copyright © 1991 by Cambridge University Press and reprinted by permission.

theology and Christian origins — the relation between the gospel of Jesus and the theology of Paul. The discontinuity between the two had been stressed by Liberal Protestantism and by the history-of-religions school, particularly W. Heitmüller and W. Bousset.[5] And although R. Bultmann[6] shared many of their conclusions, he did attempt to demonstrate a significant element of continuity between Jesus and Paul. More recently the probable influence of particular sayings of Jesus on Paul has been highlighted,[7] and a link is still possible along the lines of *imitatio Christi* (1 Cor. 11:1; Eph. 4:20; Col. 2:6; 1 Thess. 1:6). Perhaps we should also mention that at the other end of the spectrum Paul's apparent lack of knowledge of the historical Jesus has been made the main justification for a further attempt to revive the nevertheless thoroughly dead thesis that the Jesus of the Gospels was a mythical figure.[8]

What does not seem to have been adequately appreciated is that for Paul the Jesus of history is integral to his soteriology: it is of vital significance for Paul that Jesus actually lived and died in history. Paul calls men not to take up some timeless ideal, not merely to believe in a divine being contemporary with him, but to believe in the Jesus who lived and died and now lives again. The contemporary Christ is one and the same as the Jesus of history. If it is not the same Jesus, then his gospel falls in ruins. It is the Jesus of history now exalted who challenges presumptuous and self-indulgent man; it is the presence here and now of the Jesus who lived and died which brings men to the crisis of decision. Paul's soteriology therefore hangs on the wholeness of his christology;[9] separation of the Jesus of history from the Christ of faith does not characterize Paul's soteriology, it destroys it.

5. W. Heitmüller, "Zum Problem Paulus und Jesus," *ZNW* 13 (1912) 320-27; W. Bousset, *Kyrios Christos* (2nd ed., Nashville: Abingdon, 1970 [German original 1921]).

6. R. Bultmann, "The Significance of the Historical Jesus for the Theology of Paul," in *Faith and Understanding: Collected Essays* (London: SCM, 1969) 220-46; idem, "Jesus and Paul," in *Existence and Faith* (London: Fontana, 1960) 217-39.

7. D. M. Stanley, "Pauline Allusions to the Sayings of Jesus," *CBQ* 23 (1961) 26-39; H. Riesenfeld, "Parabolic Language in the Pauline Epistles," in *The Gospel Tradition* (Oxford: Blackwell, 1970) 187-204; D. L. Dungan, *The Sayings of Jesus in the Churches of Paul* (Oxford: Blackwell, 1971); C. K. Barrett, "I Am Not Ashamed of the Gospel," in *New Testament Essays* (London: SPCK, 1972) 116-43; D. C. Allison, "The Pauline Epistles and the Synoptic Gospels: The Pattern of the Parallels," *NTS* 28 (1982) 1-32; D. Wenham, "Paul's Use of the Jesus Tradition: Three Samples," in *The Jesus Tradition outside the Gospels* (Gospel Perspectives 5; Sheffield: JSOT, 1985) 7-37.

8. G. A. Wells, *The Jesus of the Early Christians* (London: Pemberton, 1971).

9. Cf. A. E. J. Rawlinson, *The New Testament Doctrine of the Christ* (London: Longmans, 1926), chapter 5; W. D. Davies, *Paul and Rabbinic Judaism* (1st ed., London: SPCK, 1948) 41-42, 49-57; M. Black, "The Pauline Doctrine of the Second Adam," *SJT* 7 (1954) 170-79; D. E. H. Whiteley, "St. Paul's Thought on the Atonement," *JTS* new series 8 (1957) 242-46; R. Scroggs, *The Last Adam: A Study in Pauline Anthropology* (Oxford: Blackwell, 1966) 92-112; A. J. Hultgren, *Christ and His Benefits: Christology and Redemption in the New Testament* (Philadelphia: Fortress, 1987).

Why is this so? Because for Paul the earthly Jesus was not significant primarily for what he *said* or *did* during his life, but for what he *was*. And what he *did* by his death and resurrection gains its significance for salvation primarily from what he *was*. The key idea which runs through Paul's christology and binds it to his soteriology is that of solidarity or *representation*. To adapt the words of Irenaeus, *Jesus became one with man in order to put an end to sinful man in order that a new man might come into being. He became what man is in order that by his death and resurrection man might become what he is.*

The most sustained expositions of Jesus' representative significance come in Rom. 5:12-21 and 1 Cor. 15:20ff., 45-49. In both instances Jesus is compared and contrasted with Adam. The point of the comparison and contrast lies in the representative significance of the two men. "Adam" means "man," "humankind." Paul speaks about Adam as a way of speaking about mankind. Adam represents what man might have been and what man now is. Adam is man, made for fellowship with God, become slave of selfishness and pride. Adam is sinful man. Jesus, too, is representative man. He represents a new kind of man — man who not only dies but lives again. The first Adam represents physical man *(psychē zōsa, sōma psychikon)* — man given over to death; the last Adam represents pneumatic man *(pneuma zōopoioun, sōma pneumatikon)* — man alive from the dead.

Now it is clear from the 1 Corinthians passage that Jesus only takes up his distinctively last Adam/man role as from the resurrection; Christ is eschatological Adam/man, "the firstfruits of those who have fallen asleep"; only in and through resurrection does he become life-giving Spirit.[10] How then can we characterize his representative function in his life and death? The answer seems to be that for Paul the earthly Jesus represents *fallen* man, man who though he lives again is first subject to death. Adam represents what man might have been and by his sin what man is. Jesus represents what man now is and by his obedience what man might become. This is most clearly expressed in four passages:

(a) Rom. 8:3: "What the law could not do, because it was weakened by the flesh, God has done — by sending his own Son in the very likeness of sinful flesh *(en homoiōmati sarkos hamartias)*. . . ." *Homoiōma* here as elsewhere in Paul means a very close likeness, a mirror image. In Rom. 1:23 its use with *eikōn* must signify an intensifying of the idea of likeness/image,

---

10. See chapter 9 above; Dunn, *Christology in the Making* (London: SCM, 1980; 2nd ed. 1989). R. P. Martin has recently contested this interpretation by arguing that the passage alludes to "Christ's pretemporal existence" rather than to his eschatological state (*The Spirit and the Congregation: Studies in 1 Corinthians 12–15* [Grand Rapids: Eerdmans, 1984]), an interpretation I find very odd. The whole topic is the resurrection body, and the logic is that Christ, the first resurrected person, sets the pattern for the rest, just as Adam set the pattern for humankind in this age (cf. Rom. 8:29; Phil. 3:21). Martin's rejoinder to me (*Carmen Christi: Philippians 2:5-11 in Recent Interpretation and in the Setting of Early Christian Worship* [2nd ed., Grand Rapids: Eerdmans, 1983] xxi) falls under the same critique.

otherwise the phrase *en homoiōmati eikonos* is merely tautologous — perhaps, indeed, an example of the Semitic tendency to give added force to an idea by repeating it.[11] Thus: "changed the glory of the incorruptible God into what was *nothing more than* the image of corruptible man. . . ." In Rom. 5:14: "death reigned from Adam to Moses even over those who did not sin *in just the same way* as Adam *(epi tō homoiōmati tēs parabaseōs Adam).*" In Rom. 6:5 the "likeness of Christ's death" does not mean baptism nor the death of Christ itself but the converts' experience of death to sin and life to God beginning to work out in themselves, which Paul characterizes as a sharing in Christ's death and so as an experience which is the mirror image and actual outworking of Christ's own death to sin within the present age (6:10).[12] So in Rom. 8:3 *en homoiōmati sarkos hamartias* must mean "in the very form of sinful flesh."[13]

But is Paul saying then that Jesus became guilty of sin? No! As is generally recognized, *sarx* in Paul is not evil, otherwise he could not use it in a neutral sense, or speak of it being cleansed (2 Cor. 7:1).[14] Flesh is not evil, it is simply weak and corruptible. It signifies man in his weakness and corruptibility, his belonging to the world. In particular it is that dimension of the human personality through which sin attacks, which sin uses as its instrument (Rom. 7:5, 14, 18, 25) — thus *sarx hamartias.* That is to say, *sarx hamartias* does not signify *guilty* man, but man in his *fallenness* — man subject to temptation, to human appetites and desires, to corruption and death. The "sinful flesh" is nothing other than the "sinful body" (Rom. 6:6), the "body doomed to death" (Rom. 7:24).

Thus in Rom. 8:3 Paul is saying simply that God sent his Son in the very form of fallen man, that is, as representative of fallen humanity. *Homoiōma* in other words does not distinguish Jesus from sinful flesh or distance him from fallen man, as is often suggested; rather it is Paul's way of expressing Jesus' *complete identity* with the flesh of sin, with man in his fallenness.[15] So far as Paul was concerned, Jesus had to share fallen humanity, sinful flesh, otherwise he could not deal with sin in the flesh. It was only because he shared

11. Cf. J. H. Moulton and W. F. Howard, *A Grammar of New Testament Greek* II: *Accidence* (Edinburgh: Clark, 1929) 419-20.

12. Dunn, *Baptism in the Holy Spirit* (London: SCM, 1970) 142-43.

13. See further Dunn, *Romans* (Word Biblical Commentary; Dallas: Word, 1988), on Rom. 6:5 and 8:3.

14. H. W. Robinson, *The Christian Doctrine of Man* (3rd ed., Edinburgh: Clark, 1926) 114-15; W. D. Stacey, *The Pauline View of Man* (London: Macmillan, 1956) 162; E. Schweizer, *TDNT* VII, 135.

15. Cf. P. Althaus, *Der Brief an die Romer* (10th ed., NTD 6; Göttingen: Vandenhoeck, 1966); C. K. Barrett, *The Epistle to the Romans* (London: Black, 1957); O. Kuss, *Der Römerbrief* II (Regensburg: Pustet, 1959); R. Jewett, *Paul's Anthropological Terms* (Leiden: Brill, 1971) 150ff.

man's sinful flesh that his death was "a sacrifice for sin" and so served as God's act of judgment on sin in the flesh (see further below, pp. 198-205).

(b) Gal. 4:4-5: "When the fullness of time had come, God sent forth his Son, born of woman, born under the law. . . ." The point is the same here. "Born of woman" was a familiar phrase in Jewish ears and denoted simply "man" (Job 14:1; 15:14; 25:4; 1QS 11.20-21; 1QH 13.14; 18:12-13, 16; Matt. 11:11). "Born under the law" likewise denotes the human condition, specifically that of the Jew (cf. 1 Cor. 9:20; Gal. 4:21), but of the Jew in a state of tutelage and bondage which is typical of humankind generally in its fallen enslavement under the "elemental spirits" (Gal. 4:3, 9). It was only by virtue of his identity with the human condition in its enslavement that Jesus could (by his death and resurrection) "redeem those under the law" and enable them to share his sonship by adoption (Gal. 4:5-7; cf. Rom. 8:15-17).[16]

(c) Phil. 2:7-8. It is very likely that the Christ-hymn of Phil. 2:6-11 uses an Adam christology, patterning the description of Christ on the well-established strand of Jewish reflection on Adam and his fall, but in such a way as to show how Jesus corrected the pattern. Adam, made in the image of God, sought equality with God and became man as he has been ever since, enslaved to corruption (cf. Rom. 8:18-21) and the elemental spirits (cf. Gal. 4:3), subject to death by virtue of his disobedience (cf. Rom. 5:15-19). Christ, likewise in the form of God, refused to grasp at equality with God, but chose nevertheless to embrace the lot of man, accepting his condition of enslavement (Phil. 2:7), and submitting himself to death as an act of obedience rather than the consequence of disobedience (Phil. 2:8).[17]

In particular we might simply note the two lines:

en homoiōmati anthrōpōn genomenos
kai schēmati heuretheis hōs anthrōpos.

This is the only other occurrence of *homoiōma* in Paul; Jesus became the very likeness of men; he became just what men are. Indeed, he came *hōs anthrōpos,* that is, not just as one man among many, but *as man,* as representative man[18] — man, who, be it noted, is immediately described as subject, obedient to death.

(d) 1 Cor. 15:27: Paul explicitly quotes Ps. 8:6 — "He has put all things in subjection under his feet" — and refers it to the exalted Christ. Since Ps. 8:4-6 was widely used in the early churches as a testimonium to Christ (Mark 12:36 pars.; Eph. 1:22; Phil. 3:21; Heb. 2:6-9; 1 Pet. 3:22), it is probable that

16. See further Dunn, *Christology in the Making,* 40-42.
17. See further ibid., xvii-xix, 114-19.
18. Cf. Martin, *Carmen Christi,* 109-10.

Paul had the whole passage in mind.[19] That is to say, it is probable that Paul understood Ps. 8:4-6 with reference to Jesus in the same way as did the writer of the Epistle to the Hebrews. Jesus was the man who fulfilled the destiny God had originally intended for man.[20] Man had been made "lower than the angels," but had not yet been crowned with glory and honor and granted Lordship over all things. But in contrast, Jesus *had* fulfilled that destiny. He, too, was man "for a short while lower than the angels," but had now been crowned with glory and honor "because he suffered death" (Heb. 2:9). That this train of thought is in Paul's mind in 1 Cor. 15:27 is likely in view of the explicit Adam christology in the immediate context of the quotation. In other words, Jesus entered his role as New Man only after living and suffering as Man. Adam had missed his destiny because of sin and his destiny had become death (1 Cor. 15:21-22). Only after Jesus lived out that destiny (death) and through it created a new destiny (resurrection) could the original destiny be fulfilled. Only by his living out the destiny of Adam could the destiny of the Last Adam become a reality.

Space prohibits an elaboration of this aspect of Paul's theology — that *for Paul Jesus in his life and death is representative man, representative of fallen man — by living out that fallenness to the death and overcoming it in resurrection he becomes representative of new life, of new man.* It must suffice to refer briefly to other passages where the same christology is reflected: Rom. 1:3 — as man he lives, like man, *kata sarka* — through flesh, and to some extent anyway, in terms of flesh;[21] Rom. 6:9-10 — as man of flesh, like men, he is subject to death. In short, as representative man he shares the weakness and corruptibility of man's flesh; as representative man he knows the power of the powers, sin, and death, which enslave men. "Christ dies the death of the disobedient, of sinners" (Rom. 5:6, 8; 2 Cor. 5:21).[22]

We might mention also Paul's use of the title *Christos*. It is frequently assumed that Paul uses the title quite conventionally and adds nothing to it.[23] This is not, however, true. And the way in which Paul does use it is of special interest for us. For, on the one hand, he links it firmly to Jesus in his death: the Christ is the Crucified One (1 Cor. 1:23 and 2:2; Gal. 3:1). And, on the other, it becomes the chief vehicle for Paul's expression of Christ's represen-

---

19. Cf. C. H. Dodd, *According to the Scriptures* (London: Nisbet, 1952) 32ff., 120ff., 126; B. Lindars, *New Testament Apologetic* (London: SCM, 1961) 50ff., 168.

20. C. K. Barrett, *The First Epistle to the Corinthians* (London: Black, 1968); F. F. Bruce, *1 & 2 Corinthians* (London: Oliphants, 1971); Dunn, *Christology in the Making,* 108-11.

21. See ch. 8 above.

22. G. Delling, "Der Tod Jesu in der Verkündigung des Paulus," in *Apophoreta,* (E. Haenchen FS; Berlin: Töpelmann, 1964) 85-96.

23. For example, R. Bultmann, *Theology of the New Testament* I (London: SCM, 1952); O. Cullmann, *The Christology of the New Testament* (London: SCM, 1959); R. H. Fuller, *The Foundations of New Testament Christology* (London: Lutterworth, 1965).

tative capacity, the solidarity of believers with the risen Christ: he is baptized in the Spirit *into* Christ (Rom. 6:3; 1 Cor. 12:13; 2 Cor. 1:21; Gal. 3:27); he has died *with* Christ, is crucified *with* Christ, his life is hid *with* Christ in God, and so on (Rom. 6:3-4, 8; 8:17; Gal. 2:19-20; Eph. 2:5; Phil. 1:23; Col. 2:20; 3:1, 3; 1 Thess. 5:10); his present life in all its aspects is lived *in* Christ (for example, Rom. 6:11; 8:39; 1 Cor. 15:22; 2 Cor. 5:17, 19; Gal. 2:4; Phil. 2:1; Col. 1:28; 1 Thess. 2:14); he is a member of the *body* of Christ (Rom. 12:5; 1 Cor. 12:12, 27, etc.); Christ is the offspring of Abraham to whom the promise has been made, and all who identify themselves with Christ are counted as Abraham's children (Gal. 3:16, 26-29). The two distinctively Pauline emphases in Paul's use of *Christos* cannot be unrelated. *Christ is representative man precisely as the Crucified One.*[24]

2 Cor. 5:14 now becomes clearer as one of the most explicit expressions of Paul's understanding of Jesus as representative man — "one man died for all; therefore all humankind [*hoi pantes*] has died." When we talk of Christ as representative man we mean that what is true of him in particular is true of men in general. When we say Adam is representative man in his fallenness, we mean that *all men* are fallen. So when Paul says Christ died as representative man he means that there is no other end possible for men — all humankind dies, as he died, as flesh, as the end of sinful flesh, as the destruction of sin. Had there been a way for fallen man to overcome his fallenness and subjection to the powers, Christ would not have died — Christ as representative man would have shown men how to overcome sinful flesh. His death is an acknowledgment that there is no way out for fallen men except through death — no answer to sinful flesh except its destruction in death. "Man could not be helped other than through his annihilation."[25] Only through death does the New Man emerge in risen life. In other words, if we may follow the train of thought a little further, Christ's identification with fallen men is up to and into death. But there it ends, for death is the end of fallen men, the destruction of man as flesh — Christ died, all died. Beyond death he no longer represents all men, fallen man. In his risen life he represents only those who identify themselves with him, with his death (through baptism), only those who acknowledge the Risen One as Lord (2 Cor. 5:15). Only those who identify themselves with him in his death are identified with him in his life from death. Hence it is a mistake to confine the "all" of 5:14 to believers.[26] The "all" of

24. See further Dunn, *Jesus and the Spirit* (London: SCM/Philadelphia: Westminster, 1975) 324-38; and for further material where Adam christology provides the basic structure of the thought see also Black, "The Pauline Doctrine of the Second Adam"; Scroggs, *The Last Adam.*

25. Barth, cited in G. C. Berkouwer, *The Triumph of Grace in the Theology of Karl Barth* (Grand Rapids: Eerdmans, 1956) 135.

26. Pace R. P. Martin, *2 Corinthians* (Word Biblical Commentary; Waco: Word, 1986).

4:14-15 are not identical with "the living" of 5:15. Jesus' representative capacity before resurrection (sinful flesh — Rom. 8:3) is different from his representative capacity after resurrection (spiritual body — 1 Cor. 15:44-45). All die. But only those "in Christ" experience the new creation (2 Cor. 5:17).[27] In short, as Last Adam Jesus represents only those who experience life-giving Spirit (1 Cor. 15:45).

Jesus' Death as a Sacrifice

We must now attempt to view Jesus' death through Paul's eyes from another angle and then bring the two viewpoints together to give us a fuller picture of Paul's thinking about the cross. I refer to Paul's understanding of Jesus' death in terms of cultic sacrifice. The idea of blood sacrifices and of divine-human relationships being somehow dependent on them is so repellent to post-Enlightenment man that many commentators have instinctively played *NB* down or ignored this side of Paul's theology. E. Käsemann, for example, reacts against undue emphasis being given to the idea of sacrificial death by firmly denying that Paul ever definitely called Jesus' death a sacrifice, and sums up: "The idea of the sacrificial death is, if anything, pushed into the background."[28] Similarly G. Friedrich, in one of the most recent studies of the topic, goes out of his way to play down any sacrificial significance in the passages we are about to cite.[29] An examination of Paul, however, makes it difficult to escape the conclusion that Käsemann and Friedrich have fallen into the trap of making Paul's language less foreign and less distasteful and so have missed both the offense of Paul's thought and its point.[30]

In Rom. 3:25 *hilastērion* cannot have any other than a sacrificial reference. Since the word is used so often in the LXX for the lid of the ark, the "mercy seat," the only real debate has been whether it should be understood as *place* or *means* of expiation/propitiation — the latter ("means") being probably the more appropriate (cf. 4 Macc. 17:22; Josephus, *Antiquities*, 16.182; Gen. 6:16 Symmachus).[31] And even if the verse is a quota-

27. Cf. Hooker, "Interchange and Atonement," 479; "Interchange and Suffering," 71.
28. E. Käsemann, *Perspectives on Paul* (London: SCM, 1971) 42-45; cf. M. Hengel, *The Atonement* (London: SCM, 1981) 45-46.
29. G. Friedrich, *Die Verkündigung des Todes Jesu im Neuen Testament* (Neukirchen-Vluyn: Neukirchener, 1982) 47, 66, 70-71, 75, 77.
30. See particularly P. Stuhlmacher's critique of Friedrich in "Sühne oder Versöhnung," in *Die Mitte des Neuen Testaments,* ed. U. Luz and H. Weder (E. Schweizer FS; Göttingen: Vandenhoeck, 1983) 291-316, especially 297-304.
31. See L. Morris, "The Meaning of ἹΛΑΣΤΗΡΙΟΝ in Romans III.25," *NTS* 2 (1955-56) 435-43; K. Kertelge, *Rechtfertigung bei Paulus* (Münster: Aschendorff, 1967) 55-57; H. Schlier,

tion,[32] Paul gives it such a central place in a key passage of his exposition
that it must be very expressive of his own thinking; indeed in such a case
one quotes from an earlier text or source because it puts the point as well
as or better than one can oneself.

The attempt has sometimes been made to see as the immediate background of Rom. 3:25 the martyr theology which finds its clearest expression
in 4 Macc. 17:21-22, where *hilastērion* is used to describe the atoning significance of the Maccabean martyrs' deaths.[33] This is certainly possible. But two
qualifications are necessary. First, martyr theology is itself an application of
sacrificial metaphor; the reason why the death of the martyrs can be thought
to carry such weight of atonement is because their death can be seen as a kind
of sacrifice. Indeed in Diaspora Judaism martyr theology is sacrificial precisely because it served as one of the substitutes for the sacrificial cult in
faraway Jerusalem.[34] Second, in Rom. 3:25 the *hilastērion* is presented by
God himself. This thought is not present in Jewish martyr theology but is
quite common in connection with the sacrificial cult in the Old Testament.[35]
Thus, whether or not Paul was consciously alluding to martyr theology here,
it is most likely that the primary reference to his metaphor was to Christ's
death as cult sacrifice.[36]

Rom. 8:3: "God sent his Son in the very likeness of sinful flesh and for
sin *(peri hamartias)*"; the New English Bible translates the last phrase "as a
sacrifice for sin." And this is wholly justified since *peri hamartias* is regularly
used in LXX to translate the Hebrew *hatta'th* (sin offering — e.g., Lev. 5:6-7,
11; 16:3, 5, 9; Num. 6:16; 7:16; 2 Chron. 29:23-34; Neh. 10:33; Ezek. 42:13;
43:19; in Isa. 53:10 it translates the Hebrew *'asham,* guilt offering).[37] It is

Der Römerbrief (Freiburg: Herder, 1977); otherwise B. Janowski, *Sühne als Heilsgeschehen*
(Neukirchen-Vluyn: Neukirchener, 1982) 350-54; A. J. Hultgren, *Paul's Gospel and Mission*
(Philadelphia: Fortress, 1985) 55-60.

32. See, e.g., P. Stuhlmacher, "Recent Exegesis on Romans 3:24-26," in *Reconciliation,
Law, and Righteousness: Essays in Biblical Theology* (Philadelphia: Fortress, 1986) 94-109;
S. K. Williams, *Jesus' Death as Saving Event* (Missoula: Scholars, 1975) 5-19; B. F. Meyer,
"The Pre-Pauline Formula in Rom. 3.25-26a," *NTS* 29 (1983) 198-208.

33. E. Lohse, *Martyrer und Gottesknecht* (2nd ed., Göttingen: Vandenhoeck, 1963) 152
n. 4; D. Hill, *Greek Words and Hebrew Meanings* (Cambridge: Cambridge University, 1967)
41-45; Williams, *Jesus' Death as Saving Event,* 248.

34. Lohse, *Martyrer und Gottesknecht,* 71.

35. Cf. Kertelge, *Rechtfertigung bei Paulus,* 57-58; idem, "Das Verständnis des Todes
Jesu bei Paulus," in *Der Tod Jesu. Deutungen im Neuen Testament,* ed. Kertelge (Freiburg:
Herder, 1976) 114-36.

36. Cf. Kuss, *Römerbrief,* 165-66.

37. See particularly N. T. Wright, "Adam in Pauline Christology," *SBLSP* 1983, 359-89;
U. Wilckens, *Der Brief an die Römer* II (Evangelisch-katholischer Kommentar zum Neuen
Testament 6; Zurich: Benziger, 1980); O. Michel changed his mind in favor of this view in the
fifth edition of his commentary (*Der Brief an die Römer* [5th ed., Göttingen: Vandenhoeck,
1977] 251).

likely that Paul drew the words from this background as a deliberate allusion, since otherwise the phrase is unnecessarily vague.[38] Some commentators object that such a reference confuses Paul's thought at this point,[39] although Paul is well known for his mixed metaphors (see, for example, Rom. 7:1-6; Gal. 4:1-6, 19). But is the charge just? The logic of Paul's thought is, in fact, quite straightforward: the sin offering was just what the law provided to cover the unwilling sins which Paul has been lamenting in chapter 7.[40] And when Paul says that God sent his Son *peri hamartias* ("in order that the just requirement of the law might be fulfilled in us . . ."), does he not include the law of the sin offering as part of "the just requirement of the law"?

1 Cor. 5:7: Paul explicitly states, "Christ, our paschal lamb, has been *sacrificed.*" It is frequently remarked that "the Paschal victim was not a sin-offering or regarded as a means of expiating or removing sins."[41] However, the Passover is already associated with atonement in Ezek. 45:18-22, and this link was probably already firmly forged in the double association of the Last Supper with the Passover and with Jesus' "blood poured out [*ekchunnomenon*] for many," which we find in the Synoptic traditions (Mark 14:24 pars.), where the language is unavoidably sacrificial and signifies atonement.[42] The same tendency to run together different metaphors and descriptions of Jesus' death so that old distinctions are blurred and lost is clearly evident elsewhere in the early churches (1 Pet. 1:18-19; John 1:29), and Paul's language in 1 Cor. 5:7 and elsewhere hardly suggests that it was otherwise with him.

2 Cor. 5:21: "God made him into sin, him who knew no sin." The antithesis "made into sin"/"sinless," makes it difficult to doubt that Paul had in mind the cult's insistence on clean and unblemished animals for the sacrifices.[43] A more specific allusion to the Day of Atonement's scapegoat is probable.[44] Perhaps there is also an allusion to the suffering servant of Isaiah

---

38. Among others Barrett *(Romans)* thinks that Paul means nothing more precise than Gal. 1:4 — Jesus Christ gave himself "for our sins" *(hyper tōn hamartiōn).* But LXX in Ezekiel usually uses *hyper* instead of *peri* in reference to the sin offering, and Paul may well regard *peri hamartias* and *hyper tōn hamartiōn* as equivalent phrases. In the mind of a Jewish Christian could "for our sins" have any other reference than to the cult? The NEB has, quite rightly, "Jesus Christ, who sacrificed himself for our sins."

39. For example, A. Schlatter, *Gottes Gerechtigkeit* (Stuttgart: Calwer, 1935) 257; Lohse, *Martyrer und Gottesknecht,* 152, n. 6; Friedrich, *Die Verkündigung des Todes Jesu im Neuen Testament,* 68-71.

40. N. T. Wright, "The Meaning of *peri hamartias* in Romans 8.3," in *Studia Biblica 1978* III (*Journal for the Society of the New Testament* Supplement 3; Sheffield: JSOT, 1980) 453-59.

41. G. B. Gray, *Sacrifice in the Old Testament* (Oxford: Oxford University, 1925) 397.

42. J. Jeremias, *The Eucharistic Words of Jesus* (revised ed., London: SCM, 1966) 222ff.

43. R. J. Daly, *Christian Sacrifice* (Washington: Catholic University of America, 1978) 237, 239.

44. H. Windisch, *Der zweite Korintherbrief* (Göttingen: Vandenhoeck und Ruprecht, 1924).

53;[45] but this should not be seen as a way of lessening the sacrificial allusion, since Isaiah 53 itself is studded with sacrificial terminology and imagery, and the role of the Servant cannot be fully understood apart from the sacrificial background of his death.[46]

Similarly the several passages in which Paul uses the phrase "in or through his blood" cannot be understood except as a reference to Christ's death as a sacrifice (Rom. 3:25; 5:9; Eph. 1:7; 2:13; Col. 1:20). Again attempts have been made to avoid the full offensiveness of the allusion.[47] But the emphasis on blood can hardly have come from the tradition of Jesus' death since it was not particularly bloody,[48] and must be drawn from the understanding of Jesus' death in terms of cult sacrifice.[49] Likewise Paul's talk of Jesus' death as "for sins" (Rom. 4:25; 8:3; 1 Cor. 15:3; Gal. 1:4) or "for us," and so on (Rom. 5:6-8; 8:32; 2 Cor. 5:14-15, 21; Gal. 2:20; 3:13; Eph. 5:2, 25; 1 Thess. 5:9-10) probably reflects the same influence, even if, in the latter case, it is mediated through martyr theology.[50]

Paul's Theology of Atoning Sacrifice

Granted then that Paul sees Jesus' death as a sacrifice, what light does this throw on Paul's understanding of Jesus' death? The obvious way to answer the question is to enquire into the Old Testament or Jewish theology of sacrifice. But here we run into a considerable problem. For, as is well known, there is no clear rationale in Judaism concerning sacrifice. No doubt the sacrifices were very meaningful to the pious and penitent worshiper in Israel.[51] But just what the essence of atonement was for the Jew remains an unsolved riddle. "It seems necessary to admit that we do not know or understand what the Old Testament and 'Judaism' really believed and taught about the mystery of expiating sacrifice."[52]

On the other hand, in view of the passages cited above, particularly Rom.

---

45. Cullmann, *Christology of the New Testament,* 76; J. Jeremias, *The Servant of God* (revised ed., London: SCM, 1965) 97, n. 441; Bruce, *1 and 2 Corinthians;* V. P. Furnish, *II Corinthians* (Anchor Bible; Garden City: Doubleday, 1984); Martin, *2 Corinthians.*

46. V. Taylor, *The Atonement in New Testament Teaching* (3rd ed., London: Epworth, 1958) 190; M. Barth, *Was Christ's Death a Sacrifice?* (Edinburgh: Oliver and Boyd, 1961) 9-10.

47. E.g., those cited in Davies, *Paul and Rabbinic Judaism,* 232ff.

48. E. Schweizer, *Erniedrigung und Erhöhung bei Jesus und seinen Nachfolgern* (2nd ed., Zurich, 1960) 74.

49. For example, Taylor, *Atonement,* 63-64; Davies, *Paul and Rabbinic Judaism,* 236; Lohse, *Martyrer und Gottesknecht,* 138-39; Barth, *Was Christ's Death a Sacrifice?* 7.

50. H. Riesenfeld, *TDNT* VIII, 507-16; cf. Delling, "Der Tod Jesu," 87.

51. H. H. Rowley, *Worship in Ancient Israel* (London: SPCK, 1967), chapter 4.

52. M. Barth, *Was Christ's Death a Sacrifice?* 13.

3:25 and 8:3 and 2 Cor. 5:21, it seems likely that Paul himself had a fairly well-defined theory of sacrifice. Moreover, whereas rabbinic thought may already have begun to play down the importance of sacrifice and to recognize other means of expiation,[53] Paul seems to retain an important place for the category of sacrifice in describing the effect of Jesus' death.[54] This, too, suggests that, however obscure Jewish theology was, or at least now appears to our perception, Paul himself could give a fairly clear exposition of atoning sacrifice. One possible way forward, therefore, is to read back Paul's understanding of sacrifice by correlating the two conclusions we have already reached — that Paul thinks of Jesus dying both as representative man and in terms of cultic sacrifice — and by examining the sacrificial ritual in their light. The exercise is necessarily speculative, but it may help to illuminate Paul's understanding of Jesus' death.

(a) First, we note that the *sin* offering, like Jesus' death in Rom. 8:3, was intended to deal with sin. In some sense or other, the ritual of killing the sacrifice removed the sin from the unclean offerer. Now it is true that the sin offering dealt only with inadvertent or unwilling sins — according to Old Testament ritual there was no sacrifice possible for deliberate sins. But at the same time the fact that a death was necessary to compensate for even an inadvertent sin signifies the seriousness of even these sins in the cult. The others were too serious for any compensation to be made. In such cases the sinner's own life was forfeit — no other life could expiate his sin.[55]

(b) Second, as Jesus in his death represented man in his fallenness, so presumably Paul saw the sin offering as in some way representing the sinner in his sin. This would probably be the significance for Paul of that part of the ritual where the offerer laid his hand on the beast's head. Thereby the sinner identified himself with the beast, or at least indicated that the beast in some sense represented him;[56] that is, represented him as sinner, so that his sin was somehow identified with it, and its life became forfeit as a result — just as Christ, taking the initiative from the other side, identified himself with men in their fallenness (Rom. 8:3) and was made sin (2 Cor. 5:21).

It is by no means universally held that this was the generally understood meaning of the act. The laying of a hand on the head of the beast is sometimes given a far less significant role — simply indicating ownership or signifying

---

53. Davies, *Paul and Rabbinic Judaism,* 253-59; Lohse, *Martyrer und Gottesknecht,* 21ff.

54. Cf. Barth, *Was Christ's Death a Sacrifice?* 33.

55. R. de Vaux, *Studies in Old Testament Sacrifice* (Cardiff: University of Wales, 1964) 94-95.

56. G. Nagel, "Sacrifices," in *Vocabulary of the Bible,* ed. J. J. von Allmen (London: Lutterworth, 1958) 275-80, here 279; Rowley, *Worship in Ancient Israel,* 133; H. Gese, *Essays on Biblical Theology* (Minneapolis: Augsburg, 1981) 105-6; Daly, *Christian Sacrifice,* 100-106; Janowski, *Sühne als Heilsgeschehen,* 199-221; O. Hofius, "Sühne und Versöhnung. Zum paulinischen Verständnis des Kreuzestodes Jesu," in *Versuche, das Leiden und Sterben Jesu zu verstehen,* ed. W. Maas, (Munich: Schnell und Steiner, 1983) 25-46, here 35-36.

the readiness of the offerer to surrender that which belonged to him.[57] But this hardly seems an adequate explanation of the importance attached to this action in the detailed instructions of Leviticus 4. And if that was all the action meant we would have expected it to be repeated in all sacrifices, non-bloody ones as well, whereas, in fact, it only occurs in the case of sacrifices involving blood. Again, where the same action is used outside the sacrificial ritual, identification seems to be the chief rationale. Thus, in Num. 27:18, 23 and Deut. 34:9, Moses lays hands on Joshua, thereby imparting some of Moses' authority to him, that is, conveying some of himself in his role as leader to Joshua, so that Joshua becomes in a sense another Moses. In Num. 8:10, the people lay their hands on the Levites so that the Levites become their representatives before the Lord, in particular taking the place of their firstborn. Finally, in Lev. 24:14, hands are laid on a blasphemer prior to his execution by stoning. The whole people performs the execution, but only those who witnessed the blasphemy lay their hands on his head. This suggests that they do so to identify themselves with the blasphemer insofar as by hearing the blasphemy they have been caught up in his sin.[58]

The only place where the significance of laying hands on an animal in cultic ritual is explained is Lev. 16:21, where the high priest lays both his hands on the second goat in the Day of Atonement ceremony — thereby explicitly laying the sins of the people on the head of the goat. Of course, it was the first goat which was sacrificed as a sin offering, whereas the second goat was not ritually killed, only driven into the desert (and left to die). But were the two layings-on of hands seen as quite distinct and different in significance? In the most recent full-scale treatment B. Janowski would so argue against those who have understood them to bear the same significance.[59] But is the transfer of sin and identification with the animal *as sinner* as different as Janowski suggests? Is it not more likely that the two goats were seen as part of the one ritual, representing more fully and pictorially what one goat could not? Perhaps, indeed, part of the significance of the Day of Atonement ritual was that the physical removal of the sins of the people out of the camp by the second goat demonstrated what the sin offering normally did with their sins anyway — sin offering and scapegoat being taken as two pictures of the one reality.[60] This is certainly the implication of Mishnah *Shebuoth* 1:7:

57. See particularly W. Eichrodt, *Theology of the Old Testament* I (London: SCM, 1961) 165, n. 2; de Vaux, *Studies in Old Testament Sacrifice*, 28, 63; cf. E. Schillebeeckx, *Christ: The Christian Experience in the Modern World* (London: SCM, 1980) 487.

58. Cf. D. Daube, *The New Testament and Rabbinic Judaism* (London: Athlone, 1956) 226-27.

59. Janowski, *Sühne als Heilsgeschehen*, 219-20, disputes with P. Volz, R. Rendtorff, and K. Koch.

60. U. Wilckens, *Der Brief an die Römer* I (Evangelisch-katholischer Kommentar zum Neuen Testament 6; Zurich: Benziger, 1978) 237.

> R. Simeon says: As the blood of the goat that is sprinkled within (the Holy
> of Holies) makes atonement for the Israelites, so does the blood of the
> bullock make atonement for the priests; and as the confession of sin recited
> over the scapegoat makes atonement for the Israelites, so does the confes-
> sion of sin recited over the bullock make atonement for the priests.

And a similar merging is already implied in the Temple Scroll from Qumran,
where the same formula is used for both sin offering and scapegoat (cols.
26-27). Rom. 8:3 and 2 Cor. 5:21 strongly suggest that Paul, too, had in mind
such a composite picture of Jesus' death as sacrifice.

Against this view, that the sin offering was thought to represent the
offerer, it has been argued that if the beast became laden with the offerer's
sin it would be counted as unclean and so could not be used in sacrifice.[61]
But does not this objection miss the point? The animal must be holy, wholly
clean, precisely so that priest and sinner may be certain that its death is *not
its own,* that it does not die for any uncleanness of its own. Only a perfect
beast can represent sinful man; only the death of a perfect animal can make
atonement for imperfect man.

Alternatively the argument has been put that the sin offering could not
embody sin since the priests ate the meat left over from some of the sin
offerings. Since they could not eat contaminated flesh, the sacrifice could not
have been contaminated by sin.[62] But again this seems to miss a key point —
namely that the life of the animal was regarded as its blood (Lev. 17:10-12;
Deut. 12:23). The priests did not, of course, eat the blood. On the contrary,
the blood was wholly used up in the ritual. Indeed, the blood played a more
important role in the sin offering than in any other sacrifice.[63] And the sprinkling of the blood "was regarded as the essential and decisive act of the
offering up";[64] "it is the blood, that is the life, that makes expiation" (Lev.
17:11). Thus, since the life *is* the blood, so the *life of the sacrifice was wholly*
used up in the ritual. The equivalence between the life of the man and the life
of the beast lay in the *blood* of the victim, not in the whole victim. And, since
the blood was wholly used up, the use made of the carcass did not affect its
role as sin offering; that role was completed in the blood ritual.

(c) Third, if we extend the line of reasoning in the light of Rom. 8:3
and 2 Cor. 5:14, 21, the conclusion follows that Paul saw the death of the
sacrificial animal as the death of the sinner *qua* sinner, that is, the destruction

---

61. Eichrodt, *Theology* I, 165, n. 2; Nagel, "Sacrifices," 378.

62. Eichrodt, *Theology* I, 165, n. 2; de Vaux, *Studies,* 94.

63. R. de Vaux, *Ancient Israel* (London: Darton, 1961) 418; *Studies,* 92; Daly, *Christian Sacrifice,* 108.

64. A. Büchler, *Studies in Sin and Atonement* (Jews' College Publications 2; London: Humphrey Milford, 1928) 418-19.

of his sin. The manner in which the sin offering dealt with sin was by its death. The sacrificial animal, identified with the offerer in his sin, had to be destroyed in order to destroy the sin which it embodied. The sprinkling, smearing, and pouring away of the sacrificial blood in the sight of God indicated that the life was wholly destroyed, and with it the sin of the sinner. One can hardly fail to recognize what we may call the sacrificial chiasmus or "interchange":[65]

> By the sacrifice the *sinner* was made *pure* and *lived free of that sin;*
> by the sacrifice the *pure* animal *died.*

And we can hardly fail to fill out the rest of the second line by adding:

> By the sacrifice the *pure* animal was made *impure* and *died for that sin —*

by its death destroying the sin. That this is wholly in accordance with Paul's thought is made clear by 2 Cor. 5:21, the clearest expression of the sacrificial chiasmus/interchange:

> For our sake God made the *sinless one* into *sin*
> so that in him *we* might become the *righteousness* of God.

So too Rom. 8:3:

> [God] condemned *sin* in the flesh [of *Jesus*]
> in order that the *just requirement of the law* might be fulfilled in *us.*

So too Gal. 4:4-5:

> God sent forth his *Son,*
> A   born of woman,
> B   born *under the law,*
> B   in order that he might redeem those *under the law,*
> A   in order that we might receive the *adoption.*

So too Gal. 3:13, although here the metaphor is not directly sacrificial:

> *Christ* redeemed us from the *curse* of the law
> having become a *curse* for *us.*

In short, *to say that Jesus died as representative of fallen man and to say that Jesus died as sacrifice for the sins of men is for Paul to say the same thing.* Jesus' death was the end of fallen man, the destruction of man as sinner.

65. See Hooker (n. 3 above).

But only those who, like the offerer of old, identify themselves with the sacrifice may know the other half of the chiasmus and interchange, the life of Christ beyond the death of sin, the righteousness of God in Christ.

Paul's *Theologia Crucis*

We cannot go further into Paul's soteriology in this essay. But since his understanding of the *process* of salvation also falls under the heading of a "theology of the cross," we should simply note the extent to which the above exposition is confirmed thereby. I have developed the point elsewhere[66] and need only summarize it here.

For Paul, union with Christ in his death is not a once-for-all event of initiation now past and gone for the believer. Despite the aorist tenses of Rom. 6:3-4, Paul also uses perfect tenses (Rom. 6:5; Gal. 2:19-20; 6:14): identification with Christ in his death is a *process* as well as an *event*. The event is more precisely to be defined as the event which sets the process in motion. The believer has been nailed to the cross of Christ, and is still hanging there! This is simply a vivid way of saying that the death of "the old nature," of "the body of sin" is not accomplished in an instant. Rather it is a lifelong process, only completed in the resurrection of the body (Rom. 8:17-23; 2 Cor. 4:7–5:5). Only then will the union with Christ in his resurrection be complete (Rom. 6:5-8). In the between-time of the present, the process of salvation is the outworking of Christ's death as well as of his life, a sharing in his sufferings as well as in the power of his resurrection (Rom. 8:10-11; 2 Cor. 4:10; Phil. 3:10-11). Unless this two-sidedness of Paul's soteriology is appreciated Paul's soteriology is bound to be misunderstood.[67]

It is this soteriology which we can now see to be wholly consistent with and indeed consequential upon Paul's understanding of Jesus' death as a representative and sacrificial death of sinful humankind. One side of the process of salvation is the *destruction* of the sinner *qua* sinner, of man in his belongingness to this age, as determined by the desires and values of this age, "the old man." And this, if we are correct, is what the sin offering accomplished ritually or sacramentally. It is precisely by identification with Christ in his death as a *sacrifice* that the process of the dying away of the believer in his dependence on this age can be accomplished; only so can the *destruction* of the sinful flesh, the body of death, be accomplished without destroying the

---

66. Dunn, *Jesus and the Spirit,* 326-38.
67. See further Dunn, "Paul's Epistle to the Romans: An Analysis of Structure and Argument," *ANRW* II/25/4 (1987) 2842-90, here 2858-64; idem, *Romans,* 301-3.

believer at the same time. In short, the rationale of sacrifice as expounded above is integral to Paul's whole gospel.[68]

Conclusions and Corollaries

This recognition of the representative and sacrificial character of Jesus' death confirms the central importance of the death of Jesus in Paul's understanding of how God's saving purpose actually works. Jesus' death as sacrifice is not an incidental throwback to Paul's pre-Christian faith which can be discarded without affecting his theology as a whole. Sacrifice is not merely one metaphor among many which can be set aside without loss in favor of more pleasing metaphors, such as "reconciliation." It *is,* of course, a metaphor, but one which goes so much to the heart of Paul's understanding of the death of Jesus and sheds so much light on Paul's understanding of the process of salvation that to set it aside would be to close an important window into Paul's theology.

Since Jesus' death as sacrifice is such an important category for Paul's thought we should take special care to ensure that the key words used to describe it reflect Paul's emphases as closely as possible. Otherwise there is a real danger that Paul's theology as a whole will be skewed and the concerns which the very metaphor was intended to express will be misunderstood. This seems to me still to be a danger in the continued insistence on the part of some scholars that the words "propitiation" and "substitution" are fundamental terms in any restatement of Paul's theology.[69]

(a) *Propitiation.* Should we translate *hilastērion* in Rom. 3:25 as "propitiation" or "expiation"? The debate was reinitiated by C. H. Dodd more than fifty years ago by his rejection of all propitiatory significance for the *hilaskesthai* word group in the LXX.[70] The most effective response came from L. Morris and made unavoidable some retreat at least from Dodd's overstate-

---

68. N. T. Wright criticizes my treatment of Adam christology in *Christology in the Making* (1st ed., 111-13) as "a bare exemplarist view: Jesus is the pattern to show people how to attain to the new sort of humanity." "It is not clear, from this account, why the cross should have been necessary at all" (Wright, "Adam in Pauline Christology," 388). I find this caricature astonishing since it has completely ignored the references made in the passage criticized to an earlier version of the present chapter ("Paul's Understanding of the Death of Jesus"). I do not expound the wholeness of Paul's theology in every treatment of a Pauline theme. The coherence of my exposition of Paul's understanding of Jesus' death and resurrection as saving events should be clear to anyone who has read my *Jesus and the Spirit,* 326-38.

69. E.g., G. E. Ladd, *A Theology of the New Testament* (Grand Rapids: Eerdmans, 1975) 427-33.

70. C. H. Dodd, "Atonement," in *The Bible and the Greeks* (London: Hodder and Stoughton, 1935) 82-95.

ment.[71] Particularly important was Morris's reminder that context as well as individual usage must always be considered.

Nevertheless, in view of the larger understanding of Jesus' death which we have gained above, and without neglecting the context, "expiation" does seem to be the better translation for Rom. 3:25. The fact is that for Paul *God is the subject of the action;* it is God who provided Jesus as a *hilastērion.* And if God is the subject, then the obvious object is sin or the sinner. To argue that *God* provided Jesus as a means of propitiating *God* is certainly possible, but less likely. For one thing, regularly in the Old Testament the immediate object of the action denoted by the Hebrew *kipper* is the removal of *sin* — either by purifying the person or object, or by wiping out the sin; the act of atonement "cancels," "purges away" sin. It is not God who is the object of this atonement, nor the wrath of God, but the sin which calls forth the wrath of God.[72] So, for example, 2 Kgs. 5:18: Naaman prays, "May *Yahweh* expiate [*hilasetai*] your servant"; Ps. 24:11: "For the honor of thy name, O Lord, expiate [*hilase*] my wickedness"; Ecclus. 5:5-6:

> Do not be so confident of pardon [*exilasmou*]
>   that you sin again and again.
> Do not say, "His mercy is so great,
>   he will pardon my sins, however great [*exilasetai*]."

And for another, if we have indeed gained an insight into Paul's understanding of the rationale of sacrifice, then it follows that for Paul the way in which Christ's death cancels out man's sin is *by destroying it* — the death of the representative sacrifice as the destruction of the sin of those represented, because it is the destruction of man's sinful flesh, of man as sinner. The New English Bible therefore correctly translates Rom 3:25: "God designed him to be the means of expiating sin by his sacrificial death."

On the other hand, we must go on to recognize that a secondary and consequential result of the destruction of a man's sin in the sin offering is that he no longer experiences the wrath of God which his sin called forth. At this point we must give weight to Morris's reminder that this section of Romans follows immediately upon the exposition of God's wrath "against all ungodliness and wickedness of men" (Rom. 1:18). Almost inevitably, therefore, the action of God which makes righteousness possible for men does involve the

---

71. L. Morris, "The Use of ἱλάσκεσθαι etc. in Biblical Greek," *Expository Times* 62 (1950-51) 227-33; idem, *The Apostolic Preaching of the Cross* (London: Tyndale, 1955), chapters 4-5; see also R. R. Nicole, "C. H. Dodd and the Doctrine of Propitiation," *Westminster Theological Journal* 17 (1955) 117-57; Hill, *Greek Words,* 23-36.

72. Dodd, "Atonement"; Schlatter, *Gottes Gerechtigkeit,* 145; F. Büchsel, *TDNT* III, 314ff., 320ff.

thought that wrath need no longer apply to them. As C. K. Barrett notes, "It would be wrong to neglect the fact that expiation has, as it were, the effect of propitiation: the sin that might have excited God's wrath is expiated (at God's will) and therefore no longer does so."[73]

But we must be clear what we mean by this. As Rom. 1:18-32 shows, God's wrath means a process willed by God — the outworking of the destructive consequences of sin, destructive for the wholeness of man in his relationships.[74] Jesus' death therefore does not propitiate God's wrath in the sense that it turns an angry God into one who forgives; all are agreed on that point of exegesis. But, in addition, it is not possible to say, as some do, that Jesus' death propitiates God's wrath in the sense of turning it away. The destructive consequences of sin do not suddenly evaporate. On the contrary, they are focused in fuller intensity on the sin — that is, on fallen humanity in Jesus. In Jesus on the cross was focused not only man's sin, but also the wrath which follows upon that sin. The destructive consequences of sin are such that if they were allowed to work themselves out fully in man himself they would destroy him as a spiritual being. This process of destruction is speeded up in the case of Jesus, the representative man, the *hilastērion,* and destroys him. The wrath of God destroys the sin by letting the full destructive consequences of sin work themselves out and exhaust themselves in Jesus. Such at any rate seems to be the logic of Paul's theology of sacrifice.

This means also that we must be careful in describing Jesus' death as penal, as a suffering the penalty for sin. If we have understood Paul's theology of sacrifice aright, the primary thought is the *destruction* of the malignant, poisonous organism of sin. Any thought of *punishment* is secondary. The wrath of God in the case of Jesus' death is not so much retributive as preventative.[75] A closer parallel may perhaps be found in vaccination. In vaccination germs are introduced into a healthy body in order that by destroying these germs the body will build up its strength. So we might say the germ of sin was introduced into Jesus, the only one "healthy"/whole enough to let that sin run its full course. The "vaccination" seemed to fail, because Jesus died. But it did not fail, for he rose again; and his new humanity is "germ-resistant," sin-resistant (Rom. 6:7, 9). It is this new humanity in the power of the Spirit which he offers to share with men.

(b) *Substitution.* As we have to seek for a sharper definition of *hilastērion*

---

73. Barrett, *Romans,* 78.

74. See particularly S. H. Travis, *Christ and the Judgment of God: Divine Retribution in the New Testament* (Basingstoke: Marshall Pickering, 1986); also Morris, *Apostolic Preaching,* 161-66; D. E. H. Whiteley, *The Theology of St. Paul* (Oxford: Blackwell, 1964) 61-72.

75. Cf., for example, H. H. Farmer, "The Notion of Desert Bad and Good," *Historisches Jahrbuch* 41 (1943) 347-54; C. F. D. Moule, "The Christian Understanding of Forgiveness," *Theology* 71 (1968) 435-43.

than "propitiation" affords, so that of the two words "expiation" seems more able to bear that fuller meaning, so we must examine "substitution" to check whether it is the best word to describe Paul's theology of the death of Christ. For many, "substitution" is perhaps the key word in any attempt to sum up Paul's thought at this point. It is significant that D. E. H. Whiteley's whole discussion of the death of Christ in Paul's theology is framed with reference to this question (with chiefly negative conclusions).[76] Both Morris and D. Hill argue from 4 Macc. 6:29; 17:21 that the idea of "substitution" is involved in the thought of Rom. 3:24-25 — that for Paul Jesus' death was substitution-ary.[77] And Pannenberg gives the word "substitution" a central role in his exposition of the meaning of Jesus' death, though he does take care to speak of "inclusive substitution."[78] So, too, for Morris, 2 Cor. 5:14, 21 can hardly be understood except in substitutionary terms — "the death of the One took the place of the death of the many."[79] This is a very arguable case, and it certainly gains strength from the theology of sacrifice outlined above — for there it would be quite appropriate to speak of the death of the sacrifice as a substitutionary death.

Nevertheless, although "substitution" expresses an important aspect of Paul's theology of atonement, I am not sure that Paul would have been happy with it or that it is the best single word to serve as the key definition of that theology. The trouble is that "substitution" has two failings as a definition: it is too one-sided a concept, and it is too narrow in its connotation.

"Substitution" is too *one-sided* because it depicts Jesus as substituting for man in the face of God's wrath. But we do no justice to Paul's view of Jesus' death unless we emphasize *with equal or greater weight* that in his death Jesus also substituted *for God* in the face of man's sin — "God was in Christ reconciling the world to himself" (2 Cor. 5:19). In other words, "sub-stitution" shares the defects of "propitiation" as a description of Jesus' death. It still tends to conjure up pagan ideas of Jesus standing in man's place and pleading with an angry God. "Substitution" does not give sufficient promi-nence to the point of primary significance — that God was the subject: God provided Jesus as the *hilastērion;* God sent his Son as a sin offering; God passed judgment on sin in the flesh; God was in Christ reconciling the world to himself — "*God in Christ.* No thought is more fundamental than this to St. Paul's thinking."[80] Our earlier exposition of Paul's theology of Jesus as

76. Whiteley, *Theology,* 130-48.

77. Morris, *Apostolic Preaching,* 173; Hill, *Greek Words,* 75-76; cf. J. Jeremias, *The Central Message of the New Testament* (London: SCM, 1965) 36.

78. Pannenberg, *Jesus: God and Man,* 263-64.

79. L. Morris, *The Cross in the New Testament* (Exeter: Paternoster, 1965) 220.

80. Taylor, *Atonement,* 75; the point is strongly reiterated by Wilckens, *Brief an die Römer* I, 236-37, and Hofius, "Sühne und Versöhnung."

Man suggests that a much more appropriate word is *representation:* in his death Jesus represented not just man to God but also God to man. And while "substitution" is an appropriate description of Paul's theology of sacrifice, it is perhaps more definite than our knowledge of Paul's thought, and the sacrificial ritual, permits; whereas, in discussing Paul's view of sacrifice, "representation," the identification of the offerer with his sacrifice, was a word we could hardly avoid. So here, "representation" gives all the positive sense of "substitution" (a positive sense I by no means deny) which the context requires, while at the same time bringing in the other side of the equation which "substitution" tends to exclude.

"Substitution" is also too *narrow* a word. It smacks too much of individualism to represent Paul's thought adequately. It is true, of course, that Paul can and does say Christ "loved me and gave himself for me" (Gal. 2:20). But his more typical thought is wider. For as we have seen, in Paul's theology Jesus represents *man,* not just a man, on the cross. Christ died as man, representative man. As Adam represents man so that his fallenness is theirs, so Jesus represents fallen man so that his death is theirs. The point is that he died not *instead of* men, but *as* man, "he died for all, therefore all have died" (2 Cor. 5:14). That is to say, fallen men do not escape death — any more than they escape wrath: *they die!* Either they die their own death without identifying themselves with Christ; or else they identify themselves with Christ so that they die his death — his death works out in their flesh. And only insofar as it does so do they live (Rom. 7:24-25; 8:10-13, 17; 2 Cor. 4:10-12; Phil. 3:10-11; Col. 1:24).[81] Either way *fallen humanity cannot escape death;* resurrection life, the life of the Spirit, lies on the other side of death, his death. Jesus' death was the death of the old humanity, in order that his resurrection might be the beginning of a new humanity, no longer contaminated by sin and no longer subject to death (Rom. 6:7-10). In short, Jesus dies not so much as substitute in place of men, but as man, representative man.[82]

As I implied at the beginning of the second section, an emphasis on Paul's theology of Jesus as representative man and of his death as sacrifice for sin increases the strangeness of Paul's gospel to the twentieth century. But if we can only do justice to Paul's theology by highlighting these aspects of it, then this is unavoidable. Indeed it is necessary to face up squarely to this strangeness and not balk at it, for only by tracing out the warp and woof of Paul's thought will we begin to understand its overall pattern; and only by thinking through his mind, so far as we can, will we be able to reinterpret his

---

81. See further Dunn, *Jesus and the Spirit,* 326-38; cf. Delling, "Der Tod Jesu," 91-92; R. C. Tannehill, *Dying and Rising with Christ* (Berlin: Töpelmann, 1966).
82. So also Hooker, "Interchange in Christ," 358; idem, *Suffering and Martyrdom,* 77.

thought to modern humankind without distorting its character and central emphases.[83] I do not suggest that that reinterpretation is easy, and to undertake it requires a much fuller investigation of the other side of Jesus' death — the life of the Spirit (Rom. 8:1ff.), the life-giving Spirit (1 Cor. 15:45). But that is another story.

83. For examples of such an attempt, see J. Knox, *The Death of Christ* (London: Collins, 1959), chapter 6; Moule, "Christian Understanding of Forgiveness."

12

How Controversial Was Paul's Christology?

1. Introduction

It is Christian belief in Jesus and particularly in the significance of Jesus which most clearly marks out Christianity from all other religions, including its two close relations, Judaism and Islam. Christology, in other words, marks the natural fault line and main breach between Christianity and Judaism in particular. A natural corollary to this indisputable fact is the inference that this must have been true of christology more or less from the first. Already with the first christological claims, Jew and Christian, including not least Christian Jew, were bound to have been at loggerheads. But is the corollary well founded?

The deduction that Christian claims for Jesus were a bone of contention from the first can, of course, find ready support within the New Testament. The Gospel traditions are united in recounting how Jesus was rejected by the Jewish authorities in being handed over to the Romans for execution. And Paul in particular notes how "Christ crucified" was "a stumbling block to Jews and folly to Gentiles" (1 Cor. 1:23). Later on he castigates his opponents in Corinth, probably influenced in at least some degree by the Christian Jews of Jerusalem and Palestine, for preaching "another Jesus" (2 Cor. 11:4).[1] And his talk of Christ as having become accursed (by the law) probably echoes some early internal Jewish polemic against the attempts by the earliest Christian Jews to interpret Jesus' death in a positive way (Gal.

---

1. On Paul's opponents in 2 Corinthians see, e.g., V. P. Furnish, *2 Corinthians* (AB 32A; Garden City: Doubleday, 1984) 49-54.

3:13).[2] An obvious conclusion to draw from these texts is that already by the time of Paul the claims made for Christ by the first-generation Christians were highly controversial and made a breach with Judaism unavoidable.

The conclusion is reinforced by those who argue that the distinctive features of christology were already present in Jesus' own self-understanding or that the most decisive developments in christology had already taken place within the first generation of Christianity. Influential here has been M. Hengel's claim that "more happened in this period of less than two decades than in the whole of the next seven centuries, up to the time when the doctrine of the early church was completed."[3] If that is actually true, notwithstanding the tremendous developments in christological thought from the second century onward and the tremendous deepening of the breach between Christianity and Judaism which took place during that period, then once again it is hard to see how Paul's christology in particular could have avoided being highly controversial.

Congruent with Hengel's thesis is the more recent restatement of the older view that the payment of divine honors to and worship of Jesus was an early feature of christology which must have been sufficient of itself to cause a breach with monotheistic Judaism.[4] Here again the argument is in effect that the decisive make-or-break issues were already being posed during the time of Paul's ministry and writings. Indeed, it can hardly mean other than that Paul himself, the most important and controversial of the early principal figures in Christianity's expansion and self-definition, played an active role in sharpening the issues which focused in christology. On this reckoning, the split between Christianity and Judaism over christology was all over bar the shouting by the time Paul disappeared from the scene, with only the *i*s to be dotted and the *t*s crossed for the full extent of the divisions to become clear to all.

But again we have to ask, is this an accurate reconstruction of the course of events? The impression given in Acts is that while Christian preaching of Jesus and the resurrection caused some embarrassment, it was not a make-or-break issue (cf., e.g., Acts 5:34-39; 23:6-9). The first real make-or-break issue seems to have been what was perceived as the Hellenists' attack on the temple (Acts 6–7). Not unnaturally, it was the more immediate political and economic

2. See, e.g., G. J. Brooke, "The Temple Scroll and the New Testament," in G. J. Brooke, ed., *Temple Scroll Studies* (JSPSup 7; Sheffield: JSOT, 1989) 181-99, here 181-82, with bibliography in n. 3.

3. M. Hengel, *The Son of God* (London: SCM, 1976) 2 (italicized in Hengel's text); see, e.g., I. H. Marshall, *The Origins of New Testament Christology* (Leicester: Inter-Varsity, 1976).

4. See, e.g., various contributors to H. H. Rowdon, ed., *Christ the Lord: Studies in Christology Presented to Donald Guthrie* (Leicester: Inter-Varsity, 1982); L. W. Hurtado, *One God, One Lord: Early Christian Devotion and Ancient Jewish Monotheism* (Philadelphia: Fortress, 1988).

reality embodied in the temple as well as its power as a religious symbol which proved the more sensitive and explosive issue.[5] Paul himself recalls persecuting the church not out of disdain for the church's christology, but out of "zeal" for the law (Gal. 1:13-14; Phil. 3:6). And subsequently in Paul's own mission and writings the crucial issue vis-à-vis the parent faith (Judaism) seems uniformly to have been the law (as in Galatians and Romans, the two Pauline letters in which the tensions between the gospel and traditional Judaism come most clearly to the fore).[6] Nor should we forget the findings of recent research in the Corinthian epistles to the effect that social issues, as much if not more than doctrinal issues, were at the heart of the problems confronting Paul there.[7]

So the question that arises is to what extent was christology an issue between Paul and his opponents? Was Paul's christology quite so controversial as the usual reconstructions of the Pauline controversies argue and as such texts as those cited above seem to imply? We can only answer this question by looking afresh at the key christological motifs in Paul.

2. Jesus as Messiah

So far as the question of this essay is concerned, the most striking feature of Paul's christology at this point is the degree to which Messiah/Christ has become virtually a proper name for Paul — "Jesus Christ," or "Christ Jesus," with "Christ" having a titular significance ("the Christ") only rarely. The bare statistics are almost sufficient to make the point on their own (confining the sample to the undisputed Paulines).

Christ Jesus/Jesus Christ	68
+ Lord	43
Christ (without article)	112
the Christ	46

That is, of some 269 occurrences of "Christ" only 46 (17%) speak of "the Christ." Moreover, in a high proportion of the 46 instances, the presence of the definite article is dictated by syntactical convention;[8] W. Grundman accepts a titular significance in only seven of these cases (Rom. 9:5; 15:3, 7; 1 Cor. 1:13;

---

5. See further my *The Partings of the Ways between Christianity and Judaism* (London: SCM/Philadelphia: Trinity Press International, 1991), chs. 3 and 4.

6. See my *Partings*, ch. 7.

7. See Furnish, *2 Corinthians*, 53.

8. Cf. BDF §260(1).

10:4; 11:3; 12:12),[9] and F. Hahn adds a further six (Rom. 9:3; 1 Cor. 10:9; 2 Cor. 11:2; Gal. 5:24; Phil. 1:15, 17).[10] Even if one or two more should be drawn in (Rom. 14:18), the disproportion between Paul's use of "Christ" with the definite article and without is still striking. Perhaps most striking of all is the fact that the fuller name Jesus Christ/Christ Jesus never has the definite article in Paul; Paul never says "Jesus, the Christ," or "the Christ, Jesus."

The situation is clear: the title ("the Christ") has been elided into a proper name, usually with hardly an echo of the titular significance. That must mean that the claim, or rather the argument, that Jesus is the Christ was no longer an issue for Paul. To call Jesus "Christ" was not a controversial assertion in the context in which Paul was writing. Had it been so Paul must have argued the point or defended the claim. But nowhere does he do so, or apparently feel the need to do so.

Here is an astonishing fact, but its astonishing character has been dulled for modern students of the New Testament because it has been so familiar for such a long time. We know that the claim of Jesus as Messiah was a controversial matter during Jesus' life — at least toward the end, since evidently it was the political character of the claim which provided the justification for Jesus' execution (Mark 14:61-64; 15:2, 26, 32 pars.).[11] We also know that the claim subsequently became decisive in the final break with the synagogue mirrored in John 9:22.[12] But at the time of Paul or in the context of Paul's mission the question of whether Jesus was indeed the Christ seems not to have been an issue.

The same point emerges from a glance at the earlier formulae which Paul cites. In particular, in Rom. 1:3, a passage where Paul seems to be at pains to cite something on which all were agreed as a sign of his "good faith,"[13] Jesus' Davidic pedigree can be simply taken for granted. It was evidently noncontroversial across the spectrum of early Christianity and could thus be used in a formula which united all who believed in Jesus. Subsequent creedal formulae were the result of tremendous controversy and political infighting in later centuries. But there is no trace of that here.

What is to be made of this? It can hardly be concluded that Paul was simply operating (in the diaspora) far away from where the controversy actually still raged, or that the controversy would have been so meaningless to Greek-speaking Gentiles that it lost all point in the Gentile mission. For

---

9. *TDNT* IX, 541.

10. *Exegetisches Wörterbuch zum Neuen Testament,* ed. H. Balz and G. Schneider (Stuttgart: Kohlhammer, 1980-83) III, 1159.

11. See, e.g., A. E. Harvey, *Jesus and the Constraints of History* (London: Duckworth, 1982), ch. 2; M. de Jonge, *Christology in Context: The Earliest Christian Response to Jesus* (Philadelphia: Westminster, 1988) 208-11.

12. On John 9:22 see particularly the line of exegesis established by J. L. Martyn, *History and Theology in the Fourth Gospel* (Nashville: Abingdon, 1979), ch. 2.

13. See, e.g., my *Romans* (WBC 38A; Dallas: Word, 1988) 5-6.

the Jewish and Gentile missions were by no means distinct in the diaspora, as Galatians and Romans again remind us. The issues of Jewish conviction and hope were by no means marginal among the early Gentile-dominated churches, as we shall see in a moment. And in Paul's letters we hear clear echoes of other matters of controversy between Paul and his Palestinian and Jewish interlocutors (principally regarding the law). Nor can it mean that an earlier controversy had already died down, especially if the messianic hope was so central to and significant for Jewish self-understanding.

The more obvious answer is that the identification of Jesus as Messiah was not after all so controversial as a point of issue between Christian Jews and their fellow Jews. For one thing, Jewish eschatological hope was not consistently messianic in character as has traditionally been assumed. M. de Jonge has been among those who have reminded us how diverse was Jewish expectation and indeed how diverse were the hopes for an anointed one or anointed ones.[14] Perhaps we should ask, therefore, whether the messianic status accorded to Jesus was any more controversial than the significance accorded to the Teacher of Righteousness at Qumran or to Phinehas by the Zealots or to bar Kokhba in the second Jewish revolt. Or whether the claim of the first Christians to find Jesus and his fate foreshadowed in the prophets was perceived as a threat to Jewish identity and hope or simply as an invitation to recognize the wealth of meaning in their common Scriptures (cf. particularly Acts 17:11). The answer seems to be that it was quite possible to put forward Jesus as candidate for messianic status without thereby undermining Jewish identity and the alternative (whether competing or complementary) expressions of Jewish hope.

This conclusion is probably borne out by other indications. For example the name by which the new movement was known within Judaism: "the Way" (Acts 9:2; 19:9; 22:4, 22) or "Nazarenes" (24:5). It was as those who followed a particular pattern of life or teaching or who followed Jesus the Nazarene that the first Christian Jews were known among their fellows, not because their claim that this Jesus was Messiah made them so distinctive. On the other hand, the title "Christians" *(Christianoi)* is precisely not a Jewish title, but a Latin formation *(Christiani),* coined no doubt by the Antioch authorities who heard this word as characterizing this new group, without fully understanding its significance — followers of "Christ," Christ's people, a political rather than a theological designation — like *Herodianoi,* Herodians, those who identified themselves with the cause of Herod.[15]

---

14. M. de Jonge, "The Earliest Christian Use of Christos: Some Suggestions," *NTS* 32 (1986) 321-43, here 329-33; also idem, *Christology in Context,* 166-67.

15. This point has been made by E. A. Judge in a paper presented at the New Testament Conference in Sheffield (September, 1991) and to the New Testament Seminar in Durham (December, 1991). He cites the further parallel of the "Augustiani" who demonstrated on Nero's behalf (Tacitus, *Annales* 14.15.5).

So, too, Paul can list "the Christ" (one of his few titular usages) as the chiefmost of Israel's blessing (Rom. 9:5) without any sense or hint that this was a blessing different in character from the other blessings ("the adoption, the glory, and the covenants, the law, the service, and the promises"), or that the Christians had somehow stolen the title from Israel.[16] And subsequently he can reexpress the Jewish hope in nonmessianic terms, indeed in unspecifically Christian terms, as hope for "the deliverer" to "come out of Zion" (Rom. 11:26). The fact that the Christians believed that the Messiah had already come was of less significance at this point than the common hope for the still future coming of the Messiah.

In short, it would appear that the claim to Jesus' messiahship could be contained within the spectrum of competing claims which were a feature of the closing decades of Second Temple Judaism.

What then about 1 Cor. 1:23 — "Christ crucified, a stumbling block to Jews"? To which we might add Rom. 9:32-33 — "They [Israel] have stumbled over the stone of stumbling; as it is written, 'Behold, I place in Zion a stone of stumbling and a rock of offense. . . .'" Also Gal. 5:11 — "the stumbling block of the cross." Clearly there was something offensive to Jewish sensibilities about the Christian claims regarding Christ. But equally clearly the offense lay more in his death, the manner of it (cf. again Gal. 3:13), than in the attribution to him of the Messiah/Christ title. Or to be more precise, the offense lay not in the fact that messiahship was attributed to someone, but primarily in the fact that it was attributed to one who had been crucified. I must therefore turn to this aspect of Paul's teaching as the second main area of inquiry.

Before I do so, however, I should clarify what the stumbling block consisted of. At first it might seem that it was the very claim made by some of their number which was offensive to the majority of Jews. But when we look at Paul's use of the metaphor elsewhere a rather different picture emerges.

Paul uses the same metaphor in 1 Corinthians 8 and Romans 14 when talking about the problem posed to some Christian Jews by the fact that Christian Gentiles (and other Christian Jews) ate food prohibited to devout Jews by law and tradition (idol meat and "unclean" food). "If food is a cause of my brother's stumbling, I will never eat meat, lest I cause my brother to stumble" (1 Cor. 8:13). "It is right not to eat meat or drink wine or do anything that makes your brother stumble" (Rom. 14:21). What was the stumbling block? As with 1 Cor. 1:23, first impressions might be misleading. At first

---

16. It is the self-evidently Jewish character of the reference to "the Christ" here which makes it so hard to believe that Paul or his Roman readers would have taken the following benediction as addressed to anyone other than the one "God over all" (see further my *Romans*, 528-29).

sight it appears that it was the simple fact that the "strong" felt free to eat which was so offensive to the "weak"; the more scrupulous would have been offended simply at the sight of other believers eating what was unacceptable to them. But on closer inspection it becomes clear that the only offense Paul had in mind was when the weak actually ate the idol meat or unclean food in spite of a bad conscience (1 Cor. 8:10; Rom. 14:23). In other words, the stumbling block was not merely the strong sense of disagreement or distaste on the part of the "weak" for the actions of the "strong," but the action of actually joining in a practice of which they did not approve.

The parallel can be drawn at once with 1 Cor. 1:23. The offense for most Jews was not simply the message of a crucified Messiah, the fact that some other Jews (and Gentiles) believed and preached that Jesus, crucified and all, was Messiah.[17] It was the prospect of accepting that claim for themselves which was the stumbling block. They stumbled not over the beliefs of others, but at the challenge to share that belief for themselves. If we now link this back into the picture already drawn, it becomes evident that there was a much higher degree of tolerance among most Jews for the messianic claims (at least) of the first Christians. They found the thought of accepting these claims for themselves offensive and stumbled over them. But that did not mean they could not entertain the thought with some equanimity that other Jews held such beliefs. In the sectarian atmosphere of late Second Temple Judaism there must have been some such degree of *de facto* tolerance for the competing claims of the diverse groups among Jews as a whole. Disputes regarding the law and the temple were far more serious. Disagreement regarding the messianic status, or otherwise, of Jesus was evidently not a matter of such central concern.

3. Jesus' Death as Atonement

It is generally recognized that the cross stands at the center of Paul's gospel. We need think only of such passages as 2 Cor. 5:14-21 and Gal. 2:19–3:1, as well as those cited earlier.[18] From this it is easy to deduce, and again particularly from 1 Cor. 1:23 and Gal. 3:13, that it was the proclamation not so

17. This is the usual way of taking 1 Cor. 1:23; e.g., G. D. Fee, *1 Corinthians* (NICNT; Grand Rapids: Eerdmans, 1987): "To the Jew the message of a crucified Messiah was the ultimate scandal" (p. 75).

18. For recent detailed treatments see particularly K. Grayston, *Dying, We Live: A New Inquiry into the Death of Christ in the New Testament* (London: Darton, Longman and Todd, 1990), ch. 2; C. B. Cousar, *A Theology of the Cross: The Death of Jesus in the Pauline Letters* (Minneapolis: Fortress, 1990).

much of Jesus as *Messiah,* but of Jesus as Messiah *crucified* which would have been so offensive to Paul's fellow Jews. It would be the significance claimed for Jesus' death, not least as validated by the resurrection, which would have been so controversial among more traditionally minded Jews. But again we must ask whether this conclusion represents a wholly rounded view of Paul's teaching on the subject.

The most striking feature here is the degree to which Paul's theology of the death of Christ is contained in pre-Pauline, that is, already traditional, formulae. This is clearest of all in the letter in which Paul works out the theology of his gospel at greatest length — Romans. It is generally agreed that Rom. 3:21-26 is the theological heart of the exposition. And it is also widely agreed that the core of that passage is an earlier formulation reworked by Paul.[19] What is noteworthy, and too little noticed by commentators, is the brevity of the treatment. It is an astonishing fact indeed that after two full chapters of carefully argued indictment, building up to the devastating climax of 3:9-20, Paul can resolve the dilemma thus posed in the space of a mere six verses, and by means of citing an established description of Jesus' death. Evidently the solution he was proposing was so uncontroversial that there was no need for him to argue it in any detail. Evidently it was a way of understanding the death of Jesus which was widely shared among the earliest Christian churches — by Christian Jews as well. Some would argue that Paul has subtly shifted the terms of the formula he uses in Rom. 3:25-26.[20] But any shift could itself hardly have been controversial, otherwise the point of citing the formula in the first place (to demonstrate common ground with his readers and other Christians) would have been self-defeating. And the more controversial a shift in emphasis, the more Paul would have had to argue for or to defend it. The most widely agreed shift is the addition of "through faith" in v. 25.[21] And Paul does proceed to argue for that emphasis (3:27–5:1); but that is not properly speaking a christological issue, more one regarding the relation of faith to the law, as the elaboration itself makes plain (3:27–4:16).

Moreover, we should note that there are many elements of conscious controversy in Romans, as Paul's frequent use of the diatribe indicates (2:1-5, 17-29; 3:27–4:2; 9:19-21; 11:17-24). And the chief interlocutor in most of these cases is one whom Paul characterizes as a typical "Jew" (2:17), where it is clear that it is not just (or not at all) the Christian Jew whom Paul has in mind, but his fellow countrymen generally. Paul was in no doubt that there were features of his gospel which would cause offense among his fellow Jews.

---

19. See, e.g., my *Romans,* 163-64, and those cited there.

20. So, e.g., P. Stuhlmacher, *Der Brief an die Römer* (NTD 6; Göttingen: Vandenhoeck und Ruprecht, 1989) 55-56; see others in my *Romans,* 175.

21. See those cited, e.g., by B. F. Meyer, "The Pre-Pauline Formula in Rom. 3.25-26a," *NTS* 29 (1983) 198-208.

What is striking here, however, is that the death of Christ does not feature in any of these diatribes; Paul does not resort to the diatribe when referring to the cross as such. Again the implication is clear. The basic understanding of the death of Christ, as widely agreed among the early Christians generally, including, presumably, those Christian Jews resident in Palestine, was not a matter of particular controversy between Christians and Jews.

Much the same seems to be true of Paul's other main documentation of the controversy between Jew and Christian — Galatians. It opens with what once again appears to be a common formula indicating the significance of Christ's self-sacrifice (Gal. 1:4).[22] And once again we have to deduce that Paul cites the formula in the introduction precisely because it indicated common ground, precisely because it was noncontroversial — and this in a letter where, more than any other, Paul was conscious of the tensions between faith in Christ and the traditional Jewish heritage. Controversy there was in plenty, but, as the whole letter shows clearly, the controversy focused entirely on the law. The cross was caught up in that, as Gal. 3:13 indicates. But here, too, the brevity of the reference indicates that the controversy centered more on the law than on the cross. That Christ hanging on the tree could be called "accursed" by the law (Deut. 21:23) was actually common ground between Jew and Christian (cf. Acts 5:30; 10:39). The real dispute was whether that fact said anything at all about Gentiles and the law.[23]

The evidence here is remarkably like the evidence considered above in relation to Jesus as Messiah. In both cases there is a taken-for-granted quality in Paul's references. In both cases that could indicate an earlier controversy which had already died down, with results so conclusive that they could be assumed rather than argued for. But given the time scale and continuing points of tension between Jew and Christian throughout that period such a conclusion is hardly justified. The only other obvious conclusion is that the Christian claims were in themselves not, or not yet, a matter of controversy. Even when Christians themselves would see the controversial matters as direct corollaries of their understanding of Jesus' death (Rom. 3:27ff.; Gal. 3:14ff.), the christology as such was more the calm at the center of the storm than the center of the storm itself.

The point at which we might have expected a breach to open up on this front between the first Christians and the rest of Judaism is the attribution to Jesus' death of significance as a sacrifice, particularly if it carried the implication that, in consequence, the temple sacrifices were no longer necessary.

---

22. K. Wengst, *Christologische Formeln und Lieder des Urchristentums* (Gütersloh: Gütersloher Verlagshaus, 1972) 56-57.

23. Gal. 2:21 has to be understood in light of 3:13; see my *Jesus, Paul and the Law: Studies in Mark and Galatians* (London: SPCK/Louisville: Westminster, 1990) 230-32, 249, and n. 34.

This is certainly the conclusion drawn by the writer to the Hebrews, and the polemical character of his exposition is clear (Heb. 8:1–10:18). But in Paul, once again it is significant that his theology of Jesus' death as sacrifice is contained almost wholly in already traditional formulae (Rom. 3:25; 4:25; 8:32; 1 Cor. 15:3; Gal. 1:4; 1 Thess. 5:9-10), or in passing reference (Rom. 8:3; 1 Cor. 5:7), or in allusive references to Christ's "blood" and to his death "for sins" or "for us" (Rom. 5:6-9; 2 Cor. 5:14-15, 21; Gal. 2:20; 3:13).[24] So much so that several have argued that Paul himself did not entertain a theology of Christ's death as sacrifice,[25] or that at least the center of his own gospel lies more in the concept of reconciliation than in atonement.[26] Neither deduction is justified. What is characteristic and central to someone's theology need not be distinctive; what is fundamental can also be shared, and as shared, little referred to; what is axiomatic is often taken for granted. The more appropriate conclusion is, once again, that Paul did not need to elaborate the point because it was common ground, shared with other Christian Jews, and as thus shared consequently noncontroversial.

It is not to be denied that there is something of a historical problem here whose solution is far from clear. When was it that early Christian understanding of Jesus' death as a sacrifice became a make-or-break issue within Judaism? It is frequently assumed that it was a factor of significance more or less from the first — even already in Jesus' own teaching. As soon as Jesus' death was seen as a sacrifice for sins, the implication would be widely understood that in consequence there was no need for other sacrifice. Jesus' death made sacrifice and temple of no continuing relevance.[27] This was certainly the case for Hebrews, as already indicated. But was it so from the first among the infant Christian movement in Jerusalem?

A crucial consideration here must be the fact that the earliest Christians stayed on in Jerusalem and evidently continued to attend the temple at the hour of sacrifice (Acts 3:1). It would no doubt be they who also preserved Jesus' teaching about the conditions for acceptable sacrifice in the temple (Matt. 5:23-24) — presumably because the teaching was of continuing relevance, that is, because they continued to offer sacrifice in the temple. Since Jerusalem was the temple, the holy mount of Zion, it would be primarily for the temple that any Jews would stay in Jerusalem. Or to put the point the

---

24. See chapter 10 above.

25. E. Käsemann, *Perspectives on Paul* (London: SCM, 1971) 42-45; G. Friedrich, *Die Verkundigung des Todes Jesu im Neuen Testament* (Neukirchen-Vluyn: Neukirchener, 1982) 47, 66, 70-71, 75, 77.

26. See particularly R. P. Martin, *Reconciliation: A Study in Paul's Theology* (London: Marshall, Morgan and Scott/Atlanta: John Knox, 1981).

27. See particularly the discussion by M. Hengel, *The Atonement: The Origins of the Doctrine in the New Testament* (London: SCM, 1981), ch. 2.

other way round, it is certainly hard to envisage a group who were at fundamental odds with the temple and its sacrificial cult staying on in Jerusalem,
or a group who made controversial claims regarding the cult, being allowed
to stay in Jerusalem as undisturbed as the continuing Christian community
evidently were (until the approach or outbreak of the Jewish revolt at least).
We know of two groups who did make such controversial claims regarding
the temple (the Qumran Essenes and the Christian Hellenists) and we know
how things worked out for them. They either chose to leave Jerusalem and
center their work elsewhere, or they were forced to do so.[28]

It is hard to avoid the conclusion that whatever the first Christians believed
and taught about Jesus' death, it was not sufficiently controversial in character
for them to feel the need to abandon the temple. And that presumably was the
teaching which we find encapsulated in the formulae which Paul echoes on so
many occasions. Even in the case of Paul's own potentially more controversial
views of Jesus' death, or at least the certainly more controversial corollaries, Paul
himself, according to Acts, was able to join in the temple ritual, including the
offering of sacrifice toward the end of his career (Acts 21:26). If Acts provides
an accurate record of Paul's final days at this point (and why not? — cf. 1 Cor.
9:19-21), that must mean that even Paul himself did not think of his christology
in its implications for the cult as particularly controversial. It is true, still
according to Acts, that Paul's tactic or compromise on his last visit to Jerusalem
failed (Acts 21:27ff.); but the breaking point had nothing to do with christology,
it was rather, once again, all to do with Paul's known openness to and involvement with Gentiles and consequent breach of the law (Acts 21:28).

So the question still remains: how controversial was Paul's understanding of the death of Jesus in the eyes of his fellow Christians and other Jews?

The position can be better understood when it is realized that the death
of a Jew of some public significance on a cross was nothing very unusual in
that period, [29] and also that there were other Jewish deaths which were seen
as having significance in terms of sacrifice.

In the first case, we may recall, in particular, that in the previous century
no less than about 800 Jews were crucified by Alexander Jannaeus in the
center of Jerusalem. What is of special interest here is that the episode is
recalled in the Dead Sea Scrolls, in 1QpNah. 1.6-8. The interest focuses in
two points. One is that the victims are described as "those who seek smooth
things" — usually taken as a reference to the Pharisees (regarded as opponents
by the Qumran writers).[30] The other is that their execution ("hanged alive on

---

28. See further my *Partings,* ch. 4.
29. Details in M. Hengel, *Crucifixion* (London: SCM, 1977) 26, n. 17.
30. See, e.g., E. Schürer, in G. Vermes and F. Millar, ed., *The History of the Jewish People in the Age of Jesus Christ* (Edinburgh: Clark, 1973) I, 224 and n. 22.

the tree") recalls Deut. 21:23, just as is the case with Acts 5:30 and 10:39. It is likely, then, that Deut. 21:23 was used to invoke a curse on various Jews who had been crucified as part of the intra-Jewish polemic between different Jewish factions during this period.[31] And since so many Jews had fallen victim to this barbaric Roman form of execution, it is quite possible that such polemic was regarded as a piece of exaggerated rhetoric and "mud-slinging" more than a serious point of real critique.[32] The implication would then be as before — that the death of Jesus on the cross allowed a good deal of cheap propaganda by the propagandists among the Jewish factions hostile to the followers of the Nazarene. But otherwise the death of Jesus on a cross would not have been seen as a matter of major substance or in itself an occasion for controversy for the majority of the first Christians' fellow Jews.

If anything, indeed, the death of Jesus at the hand of the Romans gave his death a potential significance in terms of martyr theology. We know that the Maccabean martyrs were a focus of a good deal of reflection in such terms (2 Maccabees 7; 4 Maccabees 6–18). Moreover, their deaths could be spoken of in sacrificial terms (cf. particularly 2 Macc. 7:37-38; 4 Macc. 17:21). This is the theology Paul echoes in Rom. 5:6-8 — Christ as the one who gives his life willingly on behalf of others.[33] The language in 4 Macc. 17:21 is in fact the same as that used in the pre-Pauline formulation in Rom. 3:25 *(hilastērion),*[34] and the language of reconciliation is used in 2 Macc. 7:33 (cf. 8:29) in a way not altogether dissimilar to that in 2 Cor. 5:18-20. Here again, then, the implication must be that to see Jesus' death in sacrificial and martyr terms was not a claim which would necessarily cause much controversy within Second Temple Judaism.

In short, despite its importance for Paul's theology, it would appear that his christology of the cross was not particularly controversial, either as between Paul and his fellow Jews who believed Jesus to be Messiah, or indeed

---

31. Cf. Hengel, *Crucifixion,* 84-85.

32. This remains true despite Hengel's observation that "the cross never became the symbol of Jewish suffering; the influence of Deut. 21:23 made this impossible. So a crucified messiah could not be accepted either. . . . the theme of the crucified faithful plays no part in Jewish legends about martyrs" (*Crucifixion,* p. 85). Since so many loyal Jews had been subjected to this cruelest of punishments, including Jews on different sides of the various factional divisions, it would have been impossible for crucifixion to be used as a fully fledged weapon of polemic against a particular individual who had been crucified, without it being turned against the users. The comparative silence in our sources (to which Hengel draws attention) simply reflects these sensitivities.

33. See my *Romans,* 254-57.

34. D. Hill, *Greek Words and Hebrew Meanings: Studies in the Semantics of Soteriological Terms* (SNTSMS 5; Cambridge: Cambridge University, 1967) 41-48; S. K. Williams, *Jesus' Death as a Saving Event: The Background and Origin of a Concept* (Missoula: Scholars, 1975) 76-90.

as between Paul and those more traditional Jews with whom he maintained
debate and argument.

4. The Divine Significance of Jesus

Here controversy seems inevitable. The argument seems to be straightforward.
As soon as Jesus was seen as a heavenly figure, that must have begun to put
an unbearable strain on infant Christianity's Jewish credentials. And particularly when he was seen as a heavenly figure with divine significance, ranked
together with God in Christian piety and devotion; that must have been highly
controversial and unacceptable to the fundamental axiom of Jewish monotheism.[35] But was it so? We know that such claims became unacceptable to
the Jewish authorities reflected in John's Gospel, making a breach with the
synagogue unavoidable: "This was why the Jews sought all the more to kill
him, because he . . . called God his own Father, making himself equal with
God" (John 5:18); "It is not for a good work that we stone you but for
blasphemy; because you, being a man, make yourself God" (John 10:33). But
such texts certainly reflect a later situation than that of Paul.[36] In contrast,
what is striking once again is the total absence of any indication that Paul's
christology of exaltation was a sticking point with his Jewish (Christian)
opponents. "Christ crucified" was controversial, as we have seen; but we
have no indication that Christ exalted was seen as a problem for Jews as a
whole.

I have already dealt with the key evidence elsewhere and can thus
prevent this essay becoming too long by summarizing it briefly.[37] The point
is simply that the idea of a particular historical individual being exalted to
heaven, particularly a hero of the faith, was by no means strange to late Second
Temple Judaism. The hope of resurrection was shared with Pharisees (Mark
12:18-20; Acts 23:6), and the suggestion that a particular individual had been
raised from the dead could apparently be entertained outside Christian circles
(Mark 6:14; Luke 9:8). Enoch and Elijah were thought to have been translated
to heaven (Gen. 5:24; 2 Kgs. 2:11), and the righteous expected to be numbered
with the sons of God/angels (Wis. 5:5, 15-16). Enoch was also thought to
have been transformed by his translation to heaven (*Jub.* 4:22-23; *1 Enoch*
12–16; *2 En.* 22:8), and Moses to have been made "equal in glory to the holy
ones (angels)" (Sir. 45:2).

35. See again those cited in nn. 3 and 4 above.
36. This judgment reflects the broad consensus; see, e.g., my *Partings,* 220-29.
37. For more detailed treatment see particularly *Partings,* ch. 10.

We cannot even say that the claim that a historic figure was now participating in divine functions would have been regarded as especially controversial and unacceptable in Jewish circles. Enoch and Elijah were both thought to have a part to play in the final judgment (*1 En.* 90:31; *Apocalypse of Elijah* 24:11-15). In one of the Dead Sea Scrolls Melchizedek seems to have been depicted as the angelic leader of the holy ones who execute judgment on Belial and his host (11QMelch 13-14). And in *Testament of Abraham* 11 and 13 Adam and Abel are depicted in similarly exalted roles. Nor should we forget that the Twelve and the saints generally are also said to have a share in the final judgment according to Matt. 19:28/Luke 22:30 and 1 Cor. 6:2-3. Or that power to bestow the Holy Spirit was attributed by the Baptist to the Coming One (Mark 1:8 par.) and by Simon Magus to Peter (Acts 8:17-20).

How much more than this was being claimed by hailing Jesus as Lord? The echoes of Joel 2:32 in Rom. 10:13 and of Isa. 45:23 in Phil. 2:10 are undoubtedly of tremendous significance in christology. But the question still persists. How controversial was the attribution of lordship to the exalted Christ? Paul after all speaks of God as "the *God* and Father of our *Lord* Jesus Christ" (e.g., Rom. 15:6; 2 Cor. 1:3; 11:31): even Jesus as Lord has God as his God. The climax of the celebration of Christ's lordship is "the glory of God the Father" (Phil. 2:11). And the climax of Jesus' own rule over all things is to be Jesus' own subjection "to the one who put all things under him, that God may be all in all" (1 Cor. 15:25-28). Evidently there was in all this nothing so threatening to traditional Jewish belief in God, nothing so controversial as to have left any mark of controversy between Paul and his fellow Jews or Christian Jews in particular. The same is true of Paul's characteristic "in Christ" language.[38] Quite what his fellow Jews made of this incorporative and Adam christology is far from clear. But they have left no record of any criticism of Paul on the subject.

The Wisdom language used of Jesus, as is generally agreed, in 1 Cor. 8:6 and Col. 1:15, 20[39] leaves the same impression. Whether Jewish Wisdom writers already conceived of divine Wisdom as a "hypostasis" or simply as a vigorous personification for divine action, the point remains the same. The use of such language in reference to Jesus does not seem to have crossed a critical boundary in Jewish eyes. The fact that Wisdom had already been identified with the Torah in such circles (Sir. 24:23; Bar. 4:1) is clear enough indication of how relaxed the Jewish Wisdom writers were on the subject. If the identification of a book with divine Wisdom could be taken easily in their

---

38. Cf. M. Casey, *From Jewish Prophet to Gentile God: The Origins and Development of New Testament Christology* (Cambridge: Clarke/Louisville: Westminster, 1991) 129-31.

39. See now J. Habermann, *Präexistenzaussagen im Neuen Testament* (Frankfurt: Lang, 1990), chs. 3 and 5.

stride, would the identification of a man in a similar way be any more puzzling or controversial? Paul himself evidently had no difficulty whatsoever in affirming the one lordship of Christ in such Wisdom terms in the very same breath as he affirmed the *Shema,* the fundamental Jewish axiom of the oneness of God (1 Cor. 8:6). Once again, where we would expect at least one indication that this christology was controversial, had that been the case, we find absolutely no hint or suggestion of it. Even to speak of Jesus in the language of preexistent Wisdom was not particularly controversial in Jewish ears.

What then about the association of Jesus as Lord with the Lord God in greetings and benedictions (as for example in Rom. 1:7 and 1 Thess. 3:11-13)? And what of the devotion and prayer to Jesus?[40] The most relevant point here probably has to be that the devotion to Christ seems to have been contained within the constraints of Jewish monotheism. It consists more of hymns *about* Christ than hymns *to* Christ (especially Phil. 2:6-11 and Col. 1:15-20), more of prayer *through* Christ than prayer *to* Christ (Rom. 1:8; 7:25; 2 Cor. 1:20; Col. 3:17). At the time of Paul, therefore, should we speak, as does Pliny fifty or so years later, of Christians reciting a hymn "to Christ as to a god" (Pliny, *Ep.* 10.96.7); or is the parallel more that of veneration offered to and through the Virgin and the saints in the still later church? Even after Paul, Judaism could encompass the thought of Enoch or the Messiah as fulfilling the role of the man-like figure in the vision of Daniel 7 (*1 Enoch* 37–71; 4 Ezra 13:32),[41] that is, one who takes the throne beside God and who can thus in some degree be associated with God in devotion and in the bestowal of blessing as well as in judgment. Within the "broad church" of that range of Judaism, how controversial would have been Paul's attribution of divine agency to the exalted Jesus, how controversial would have been the degree of devotion which he offered? Once again a crucial consideration must be the absence of any protest within the sphere of Paul's mission — no consciousness of Paul's part that he was transgressing some clearly drawn line; no suggestion that other Jews must have found such language and devotion repugnant; in a word, no hint of controversy.

If we were to broaden out the discussion to Paul's interaction with the wider Hellenistic world (rather than just traditional Judaism) the range of discussion would be different, but the outcome would not. Thus, in 1 Corinthians 1–2 the issue is more one of what counts as "wisdom" than of christology as such; the earlier attempts to demonstrate a counter-christology maintained by Paul's opponents have not been successful.[42] As for 1 Corinthians 15, there is

---

40. See again particularly Hurtado, *One God, One Lord,* 11-15, 99-114.

41. The tradition that Rabbi Akiba thought the second throne of Dan. 7:9 was for (the son of) David is found in *b. Ḥagigah* 14a and *b. Sanhedrin* 38b.

42. So particularly U. Wilckens, *Weisheit und Torheit* (Tübingen: Mohr, 1959).

certainly controversy over the resurrection — that is, the (future) resurrection of believers, whereas the belief that Jesus had already been raised seems to have been common ground (15:5-12). In each case, as in 1 Corinthians 10–11, the christology could be assumed; it was what the different opinions within Corinth made of these common emphases in christology which caused the controversy.

In 2 Cor. 11:4 Paul does speak of "another Jesus" and again there is clear evidence of sharp controversy, as serious as that voiced in Galatians. But in this case the "other Jesus" seems to be Paul's way of describing what he regards as an exaggerated emphasis on the resurrected and exalted Christ; or to be more precise, the implications of such an emphasis for concepts of apostolic ministry (2 Corinthians 10–13). In contrast, it is Paul who calls for the stress to be laid elsewhere — on the cross, on the Christ crucified in weakness; not as a way of defending a distinctively different christology (as we have already seen, the fact of Christ's death was part of the faith common to all Christians at that time) but as a way of justifying a different model of apostleship, not over christology as such.[43]

So I could continue. The issue in 1 (and 2) Thessalonians is not christological (the belief in the parousia is common ground), but chronological (how soon will it happen). There is no apparent christological issue in Philippians at all. And in Colossians, speculation about the status of Jesus within the heavenly sphere may be implied, but whether we can speak of "false teachers" and "opponents" is far from clear.[44]

In general, within the context of Hellenistic syncretism it is not apparent that the initial claims made by the first Christians for Christ would have been so controversial. A society which could cater for "many gods and many lords" (1 Cor. 8:6) would not be particularly put out or nonplussed by the earliest christological affirmations. In fact, it was only toward the end of the first century and the beginning of the second that Christian assertions of the lordship of Christ seem to have become a matter of controversy and persecution. But that was because of the political challenge which these Christian claims were seen to pose. To affirm the lordship of Jesus was now to deny the lordship of Caesar and thus to challenge the empire which Caesar represented. To sing or speak to Jesus "as to a god" had the unacceptable corollary that the local temples were being deserted and the sacrificial rites neglected, with potential hazard for the civic and political constitution of the communities

---

43. "It is not even clear that this verse [2 Cor. 11:4] warrants the identification of 'Christology' as the basic difference between Paul and his opponents in Corinth . . . since nowhere else in 2 Corinthians is Christology taken up as a topic in and for itself, not even in 3.7-18, 4.4-6, 9-14, [and] 5.14-19, where the real theme is the nature of Paul's apostolic service" (Furnish, *2 Corinthians*, 501).

44. See particularly M. D. Hooker, "Were There False Teachers in Colossae?" in *From Adam to Christ: Essays on Paul* (Cambridge: Cambridge University, 1990) 121-36.

involved. Prior to that, however, the points of tension were not particularly christological as such, but simply the fact that in the eyes of the Roman intelligentsia Christianity was merely another example of a "pernicious superstition" imported from the Middle East.

5. Conclusions

This essay has been an attempt to bring more clearly into focus the extent to which christology was at the center of earliest Christian controversy and dispute with others. Its findings say nothing to disturb the centrality of christology for Christianity in general or even to question that christology inevitably was (and is) the cutting edge of Christian theology and its distinctive claims. It simply draws attention to the fact that the fundamental christological claims do not seem initially to have created as much disagreement or to have provoked as much hostility as we would have expected. Nor have I any wish to deny that it was christology which became the absolutely crucial factor in the final parting of the ways.[45] However, it does seem that initially the foci of controversy seem to have been elsewhere (the temple, the law).

Perhaps it is inevitable that it was the issues which impinged most immediately on daily practice which became the points of tension. In the same way, in the period prior to Jesus' ministry, the various messianic (and non-messianic) expectations of the various strands of Second Temple Judaism seem to have functioned simply as part of the rich tapestry of first-century Judaism. In these cases, too, the disagreements which touched the different groups most directly were those relating to temple, festivals, and Torah. Perhaps it is simply a reflection of how human dialogue works, that the course of debate begins with the more immediate points of disagreement and only thereafter presses back behind these more obvious issues into the underlying presuppositions. That was certainly how the christological debates themselves progressed in the subsequent centuries. Be that as it may, it does not appear that the christological claims made by Paul were initially seen as particularly controversial in themselves.

---

45. Precisely the contrary — see my *Partings*, chs. 11-12.

13

Pauline Christology
Shaping the Fundamental Structures

In an influential monograph, Martin Hengel maintained that more developments in christology happened within the period of Paul's ministry than in the whole of the next seven centuries.[1] Hengel's claims may be exaggerated,[2] but they are truthful enough to underline the importance of Paul's treatment of christology and the extent to which subsequent Christian understanding of Christ has been dependent on Paul's formulations, like it or not.

How should we characterize and sum up Paul's contribution to this theme so crucial to Christian theology? What are the central emphases in this Pauline christological thought that has had such an important role in shaping Christian thinking?

The answer cannot be found in what Paul tells us about Jesus' ministry prior to Good Friday and Easter. It is well known that Paul says next to nothing about Jesus' life, apart from its final suffering. And although it is possible to detect in Paul's ethical exhortations an influence of the Jesus-tradition — both Jesus' example and his own teaching, which is stronger than is usually acknowledged[3] — Paul makes no attempt to focus his christology on the pre-Good Friday Christ.

---

1. M. Hengel, *The Son of God* (London: SCM, 1976), esp. 2 and 77.

2. See my *Christology in the Making* (London: SCM, 1980, 1989) 351, n. 1; also *The Partings of the Ways* (London: SCM, 1991), chs. 9-11. I apologize for referring so often in what follows to my own work, but in a summary treatment it seems to be the simplest way to document both the detailed exegesis on which claims are based and the other secondary literature with which I dialogue.

3. See, e.g., discussion in A. J. M. Wedderburn, ed., *Paul and Jesus: Collected Essays* (JSNTSS 37; Sheffield: JSOT, 1989), and M. B. Thompson, *Clothed with Christ: The Example and Teaching of Jesus in Romans 12.1–15.13* (JSNTSS 59; Sheffield: JSOT, 1991).

Originally published in *Christology in Dialogue,* ed. R. F. Berkey and S. A. Edwards (Cleveland: Pilgrim, 1993) 96-107.

What then of Christ's death? One thinks immediately of key texts such as Rom. 3:24-26 and 2 Cor. 5:21. While such texts lie close to the heart of any Christian doctrine of atonement, a notable feature of Paul's treatment of Christ's death is the extent to which he relies on what are generally agreed to be earlier formulations (e.g., Rom. 3:24-25; 4:25; 8:34; Gal. 1:4; 2:20).[4] Paul did not seem to have much new to say about the death of Christ. For example, in Romans, after the lengthy indictment of 1:18–3:20, the response of 3:21-26 seems very brief, and presumably could be so brief because the understanding of the death of Christ encapsulated there could be taken as common ground between Paul and even those churches he had never visited before. Of course he preached "Christ crucified" and recognized that a crucified Messiah constituted a scandal for most of his Jewish peers (1 Cor. 1:23; 2:2; Gal. 3:1), but already the issue seems to be an echo of an older, intra-Jewish debate, with Paul able to take the messiahship of Jesus so much for granted that "Christ" functions for the most part as a quasipersonal name throughout his letters. This is not to deny that the cross was very much at the center of Paul's gospel, but if we are looking for the points at which Paul made his own contribution to christological thought, we probably will have to search elsewhere.

What then of Christ's resurrection and exaltation? One thinks at once of the fact that "Lord" is Paul's favorite title for Christ precisely because Christ's resurrection and exaltation are the vital presuppositions of his lordship. Yet here, too, the most relevant word may be "presuppositions," because, once again, the key statements that "explain" Christ's lordship seem to be pre-Pauline formulas that Paul inherited (Rom. 1:3-4; 10:9-10; Phil. 2:9-11).[5] And even where resurrection is at the heart of the discussion (1 Corinthians 15), it is not the resurrection of Jesus, either its facticity or its nature, that is at issue (15:3-8, 12-19). In other words, Christ's resurrection and exaltation can hardly be ignored as essential starting points of Paul's christology, but they themselves do not provide its central thrust. Essential foundations, no doubt, but for the Pauline superstructure we have to inquire further.

These considerations should not be perceived as polemical or unduly radical. I am not denying the central importance of Christ's death and resurrection behind and within Paul's theology. But if we focus our attention on them we run the risk of stopping short at where Paul started. The traditional emphasis on these undeniably foundational elements of all Christian theology may obscure Paul's further contribution, which was to integrate the already

---

4. See particularly part 1 in W. Kramer, *Christ, Lord, Son of God* (London: SCM, 1966); K. Wengst, *Christologische Formeln und Lieder des Urchristentums* (Gütersloh: Gütersloher, 1972).

5. See those cited in n. 4.

established axioms of Christ's atoning death and eschatological resurrection into an overarching christological schema, and thus to secure the significance of these individual elements within a larger theological framework.

Christ and Adam

We start with what Paul clearly sees as the Adamic significance of Christ, a significance for the history and salvation of humankind equivalent to that of the (mythical) Adam. *Adam* began the history of humankind and thus sums it up. In particular, in accordance with a doctrine of human fallenness that Paul can again assume (e.g., Wis. 2:23-24), Adam sums up humankind in its mortality and submissiveness to human appetite and selfish desire. In Adam, all die; death is the end for all who share human traits and family likenesses. *Christ,* in contrast, opens up the possibility of a new beginning — a humanity no longer enslaved by its animal nature, no longer subservient to selfish desire, and no longer fearful of death. In Christ, all shall be made alive (1 Cor. 15:22).

At first this seems a thin strand indeed out of which to construct one of the principal load-bearing beams in the superstructure of Pauline christology. The Adam/Christ parallel comes to clear expression in only two passages in the Pauline letters, Rom. 5:12-21 and 1 Cor. 15:20-22, 44-49. But these passages are more significant than at first appears and make explicit what is more frequently implicit elsewhere.

For one thing, the passages constitute two of the most distinctive Pauline elaborations of his two foundational axioms — Christ's death and resurrection. He characterizes the death of Christ in a sequence of striking, epigrammatically concise antitheses as the counterbalance (and more than counterbalance) of Adam's sin — the death that was an act of obedience outweighing the death that was the punishment of disobedience (Rom. 5:15-19). The resurrection of Christ he characterizes in the epigram already cited as the definitive answer to the last enemy, death: Christ's resurrection does not make any difference to the fact that all die, but it does give hope of life beyond death. The last Adam who became life-giving Spirit is a more powerful representative figure than the Adam who became a living soul (1 Cor. 15:22, 45).

Thus it also becomes clear that it is precisely as last Adam that Christ has undone the damage wrought by Adam, that in a figure equivalent in significance to Adam the remedy to the cancer of human sin is presented. Paul repeatedly reverts to the language and imagery of Genesis 2–3 in what is his most sustained indictment and description of the human condition: a humanity that has refused to rely on God and give God due glory (Rom. 1:19-25); a humanity that has lost out on the glory initially given to Adam

(3:23); a humanity that has fallen victim to the enticing deception of sin (7:7-12); a humanity that shares in the consequent futility and subjection to decay (the opposite of glory) of the cosmos as a whole (8:19-23). The significance of this Christ is that he has made possible the restoration of that same glory to humanity by himself receiving a glory which he seeks to share with others (Rom. 8:29-30; 2 Cor. 3:18–4:6; Phil. 3:21).6

In a series of insightful studies, Morna Hooker has shown how far the Adam/Christ parallel extends in Paul in terms of what she calls "interchange in Christ."7 Adam exchanged his share in divine glory for slavery to sin and death. Christ changed places with this Adam, sharing Adam's subjection to sin and death in order that Adam might experience Christ's victory over sin and death. The pattern of interchange is most obvious in passages referring to Christ's death (Rom. 8:3; 2 Cor. 5:21; 8:9; Gal. 3:13; 4:4; Phil. 2:6-8). But it embraces the whole of Jesus' life: it was because his life had a representative character that his death could have the same character (Rom. 8:3; Gal. 4:4; Phil. 2:6-8). Because of this Adamic character of Christ's entire ministry, Paul thinks of the process of salvation as a sharing in Christ's sufferings, a becoming like him in his death (as in Rom. 8:17; 2 Cor. 1:5; 4:10-12, 16-18; Phil. 3:10-11). Hooker shows how the pattern of interchange extends even into ethical exhortation (e.g., Rom. 13:14; 15:1-3).8 At all events, an ethical dimension in Adam christology is very clear in Col. 3:9-11 (and also Eph. 4:22-24).

To an extent not usually appreciated, Adam christology also embraces the thought of Christ's resurrection and exaltation. More striking still, it includes the affirmation of the lordship of Christ. This becomes clear in the way Paul and his contemporaries freely ran together Ps. 110:1 (the key text validating Christ's lordship) and Ps. 8:4-6 (the key text for Adam christology): in appointing Christ as Lord (Ps. 110:1), God had put all things under his feet (Ps. 8:6; 1 Cor. 15:25-27; Phil. 3:21; Eph. 1:20-22; also Heb. 1:13–2:8; 1 Pet. 3:22). In other words, the exaltation of Christ as Lord was also the fulfillment of the divine purpose in creating humanity; the lordship of Christ is the completion of the lordship of Adam. The Creator's program, which broke down in Adam, has been "run through" again in Christ and achieved its original goal. Those "in Adam" share in the tensions of a fractured creation; those "in Christ" (will) share in the fulfillment and completion of God's purpose for creation as a whole.9

---

6. On these passages, and Rom. 5:12-21 above, see my *Romans* (WBC 38; Dallas: Word, 1988).

7. Collected in M. D. Hooker, *From Adam to Christ: Essays on Paul* (Cambridge: Cambridge University, 1990).

8. "Interchange in Christ and Ethics," *Journal for the Study of the New Testament* 25 (1985) 3-17; also in *Adam to Christ,* ch. 4.

9. See more fully my *Christology,* ch. 4.

This last thought links us into one of the most pervasive (it occurs more than eighty times) and characteristic motifs in Paul's writings — the understanding of believers as "in Christ." A frequent variant is "in the Lord," and correlated phrases include "into Christ" (e.g., Gal. 3:26-28), "through Christ" (e.g., Rom. 5:1), "with Christ" (e.g., 2 Cor. 4:14), and "the body of Christ" (e.g., 1 Cor. 12:27). It is no accident that there is a cluster of such phrases in Rom. 6:1-11 — that is, immediately following the exposition of Christ in Adam terms in Rom. 5:12-21 — because the "in Christ" language is a natural outworking of Adam christology. The idea of Christ as in some sense a "corporate" person[10] is part and parcel of Adam christology. So, too, is the thought of Christ as the eldest of a new family of God, the firstborn of (the new) creation (Rom. 8:29; Col. 1:18). In his parallel to and contrast with Adam, Christ provides an alternative template for humanity.

Adam christology can thus be seen to form an extensive feature in Paul's theology. More important, it provides an integrating framework both for Paul's christology and for his entire gospel. In expressing the significance of Christ, more than any other christological motif, Adam christology embraces Christ's entire life and ministry: Christ as sharing with the Adamic fallenness of humanity; Christ as exchanging the death of sin for the death of obedience leading to life; Christ as fulfilling the divine purpose for humanity through his resurrection and exaltation to lordship. In broader terms, Adam christology embraces the entire scope of salvation: the eschatological significance of Christ's actions as introducing a new and final epoch in God's dealings with humanity, which sees the final goal in terms of the fulfillment of the original purpose; an individual salvation, which is a conformity to the last Adam's suffering and death with a view to the future full conformity to his resurrection; a corporate salvation, which sees the embodiment of the divine ideal of humanity only in a community of faith; a cosmic salvation, which does not seek to escape the material and bodily but looks for the salvation of humanity as part of a redeemed creation.

Not all these themes are unique to Paul. The Philippians hymn is probably pre-Pauline (Phil. 2:6-11), and one of the clearest expositions of Adam christology is to be found outside Paul (Heb. 2:5-18). Nevertheless, several of the extended features outlined above are both characteristic of and distinctive to Paul. And the use of Adam christology to provide such an overarching and integrating framework is certainly to be attributed to Paul. As such, Adam christology must be counted as one of the central emphases in Pauline christological thought, an essential part of Paul's contribution to Christian theology.

10. See particularly C. F. D. Moule, *The Origin of Christology* (Cambridge: Cambridge University, 1977), ch. 2.

Christ and Wisdom

The theme of Christ and Wisdom is even less evident in Paul than that of Christ and Adam. It is explicit in only one passage, 1 Cor. 1:24 and 30: "Christ the power of God and the wisdom of God"; "Christ Jesus, whom God made our wisdom." But to anyone familiar with the Jewish wisdom tradition, it is also evident in 1 Cor. 8:6 and Col. 1:15-17. In both passages Paul speaks of Christ's role in a relation to creation in terms that, in Jewish thought, were most characteristically used for the personification of divine wisdom (as in Prov. 3:19; 8:22, 25; Sir. 24:9; Wis. 7:26).[11] And anyone who was aware of the way in which Deut. 30:12-13 was related to divine wisdom in Jewish reflection (as in Bar. 3:29-30) would recognize that Paul was playing with an identification of Christ and Wisdom in Rom. 10:6-8. Even so, the theme, explicit or immediately implicit, is brief. Why then single it out as one of the leading edges of Pauline christology? The answer lies not only in the fact that the ramifications of the Christ-Wisdom association are far-reaching in Paul's own theology, but, still more, in the fact that Paul's identification of Christ and Wisdom constitutes the first statement of a motif that was to become the principal focus in the burgeoning christology of the next two centuries.

The female figure of divine wisdom was familiar in religious thought of the ancient Middle East as one of the chief ways of expressing belief in the divine care and fruitful provision for creation. Particularly in the myth of Isis the ancients expressed their convictions about the cycle of life and death and their dependence on the natural cycle of fertility. The wisdom writers of Israel had domesticated this widespread belief in divine wisdom, the key to success in life but hidden from human eyes, by identifying her with the Torah (Sir. 24:23; Bar. 3:9–4:4). In passages such as 1 Cor. 8:6 and Col. 1:15-17, the first Christians in effect were doing the same thing, identifying this divine wisdom with Christ. Where Jewish wisdom writers said to the wider world, "Here in the Torah is the divine wisdom on which you depend and which you seek," Paul and the first Christians could express the significance of their gospel in similar terms: "Here in Christ is the sum and epitome of the divine wisdom by which the world was created and is sustained." In making this identification between Christ and Wisdom, Paul and the first Christians were using a theme that constituted a major element in the ancient Mediterranean world's search for meaning and a major element in Jewish diaspora apologetic.

Note the specific twist that Paul gave to this line of Christian apologetic: his initial and, as we have seen, only explicit identification of Christ and Wisdom comes in 1 Corinthians 1. Here Paul shows that he was well aware of the ancient world's thirst for wisdom, whether in terms of human cleverness

---

11. For this and the supporting data for what follows, see my *Christology*, chs. 6 and 7.

and rhetorical sophistication, or in terms of human perception of what is a fitting outworking of the divine purpose of salvation. Such human estimates of how divine wisdom comes to expression within human society Paul challenges boldly and bluntly with the cross. Christ is the measure of divine wisdom; and by that Paul means not the Christ of creation or the Christ of exaltation, but Christ crucified (1 Cor. 1:22-24). The significance of this Wisdom-Christ spans all of time, from creation (1 Cor. 8:6) to new creation (Col. 1:15, 18); but the cross is the midpoint that symbolizes the character of the whole. Thus Paul anchors this major theme in the religious self-understanding of the ancient world firmly in Christ, and stamps the whole with the gospel of the cross.

At the same time, the identification of Christ and Wisdom provides a crucial vehicle for expressing the divine, or more than human (more than Adamic, we may say) significance of Christ, which was a feature of christology from the beginning. Because Wisdom, in Jewish thinking at least, was a way of speaking of the one *God's* care and provision for God's creation, the identification of Christ with this Wisdom becomes a powerful way of expressing *God's* care for God's people and provision for their salvation (most clearly in Wisdom 10–11). Hence it provides an even more potent description of Christ's significance than speaking of God's putting forward Christ as a means of atonement (Rom. 3:25), or even of God in Christ as "reconciling the world to himself" (2 Cor. 5:19), which could be interpreted simply in terms of divine inspiration rather than pushing toward the thought of incarnation (as becomes clear later in John 1:14). So, too, the affirmation of Christ as divine wisdom can be seen as an alternative to speaking of Christ as proof of the divine faithfulness to all God's promises (2 Cor. 1:20) and thus plugs into one of the central themes of Romans — God's faithfulness to God's promises to Abraham and Israel (1:17, 25; 3:3-7, 25; 4; 9:6; 15:7-13).[12]

The Wisdom-Christ identification also gives us the clue to how Paul can speak so boldly about the divine significance of Christ in language that seems at first to threaten the Jewish axiom of monotheism that he shared. Jewish talk of Wisdom could be almost as bold, but it was clearly understood as simply a way of expressing the one God's care for creation and provision for God's people (as Wisdom 10–19 shows). Although the exalted Christ shares in God's lordship as object of devotion and source of divine blessing (as in Rom. 1:7 and Phil. 2:9-11), Paul does not understand this as any sort of

---

12. The point is more obscure for us than it would be for readers familiar with Old Testament and LXX thought, because in Romans the single theme of divine faithfulness is spread among the several variations of the same theme — God's faithfulness, God's truth, and God's righteousness; see, e.g., my *Romans,* 41, 44, 63, 132-33, 135-36, etc.

compromise with or even redefinition of his faith in God as one (e.g., Rom. 3:30; 1 Cor. 8:6); Christ as divine wisdom is the Wisdom of the one God and in no way an alternative, far less competing, source of authority (1 Cor. 3:23; 11:3; 15:24, 28). Even in the later Titus 2:13, Jesus Christ is thought of as the glory of God, that is, the visible manifestation of God's majesty, rather than as (another) God alongside the one God. By formulating the divine significance of Christ in wisdom language, Paul was able to retain the already burgeoning christology within the constraints of the Jewish monotheism that remains axiomatic for Christian theology.[13]

Paul's Wisdom christology thus serves as a fundamental and integrating structure in Pauline theology similar to that afforded by Adam christology. It secures the continuity of the Christian epoch not only with creation (as does the Adam theme) but also with Israel (both Jewish and Christian wisdom writers are speaking of the same Wisdom). It provides an apologetic theme of tremendous power in the ancient world indicating the universal significance of Christ. In Paul in particular it becomes stamped with the theology of the cross, preventing any Docetic divorce between the human and the divine in Christ. And it holds together the strongest assessments of the divine significance of Christ and his work within the framework of the common Jewish/Christian conviction that God is one. It is precisely for these reasons that Wisdom (or equivalently expressed, Logos-Word) christology became the mainstream of classic christological reflection leading up to the third and fourth-century creeds.[14] The character of christology stamped on it by Paul's development of Wisdom christology determined its future.

Here, too, we cannot speak of exclusively Pauline contributions. With Col. 1:15-20, as with Phil. 2:6-11, we are probably dealing with a pre-Pauline formulation; and Heb. 1:1-3 is as manifestly a wisdom formulation as anything in Paul. Nevertheless, as with Adam christology, our clearest and earliest expressions of Wisdom christology come from Paul: several of the emphases are distinctive of Pauline theology; and the range of his theological writings enables us to see how widespread are the ramifications of Wisdom christology. Here, too, Wisdom christology must be counted as one of the major emphases in Pauline christological thought, and his reworking of it an essential part of Paul's contribution to Christian theology.

---

13. See my *Partings,* chs. 10-12.

14. See, e.g., J. N. D. Kelly, *Early Christian Doctrines* (London: Black, 1960), chs. 4 and 5.

Adam-Christ-Wisdom

All that remains is to point out the importance of the fact that Paul called in not just the (mythical) figure of Adam to illuminate the significance of Jesus and his work, but also the (mythical) figure of divine Wisdom. He found it necessary to use *both* integrating frameworks, not simply one or the other.

We can talk of the *complementarity* of the two themes and frameworks. At this earliest stage, we may say, both the character of the Christ event and the theological traditions available to fill out its significance pushed christology, as expressed by Paul, in a double direction. One highlighted what might be summarized as the humanity of Christ, the other the divinity of Christ. But it was not the significance of Christ as such, or of Christ in himself, that was perceived to be at stake, but the significance of Christ in relation to humankind and to God. In Adam christology we are speaking about *humanity,* not about the humanity of Christ; and in Wisdom christology we are speaking about *deity,* not about the deity of Christ.

This doubly representative significance of Christ comes to expression in these christologies. Christ as Adam shows us what God intended humanity to be. Christ as Wisdom shows us what God is like in God's creating, sustaining, and saving concern for all creation. The recognition that *both* are integral to christology, as Paul clearly demonstrates, prevents christology from degenerating either into an idealist or exemplarist christology or into a Docetic or Gnostic christology. Holding *both* together, in the terms that Paul was already providing, ensured that classic christology always had the shape of an ellipse, held in place by its twin foci, rather than a circle spinning off into a christocentric humanism (Christ only as ideal humanity) or a christocentric theism (Christ alone as God for us).

On the other hand, we have to talk of the *overlapping* character of the two emphases. In Paul's theology this comes out both in the conception of Christ as the image of God and, once again, in the thought of Christ as *Lord.* The latter, we have noted, can be referred both to Christ's Adamic role as crown and head of creation (1 Cor. 15:25-27) and to Christ as the one Lord in his wisdom role as divine agent in creation (1 Cor. 8:6). Christ as Lord thus represents both God's purpose for the humankind God created and the lordship of God in that act of creation. Paul does not allow the thought of Christ's lordship to spin free from the lordship of God (as 1 Cor. 15:28 makes abundantly clear). In the concept of Christ as Lord, Paul is able to hold together the divine significance of Christ, particularly in view of his resurrection, and the oneness of the creator God.

Similarly, in the Pauline letters we find that the *image of God* is referred both to Christ's Adamic role and to Christ's wisdom role. As to the former, we may think of Rom. 8:29: the son is the image to which, as "firstborn among many brothers," Christians are being conformed. Or 1 Cor. 15:49: as believers have borne the image of the first, earthly Adam, so they will bear the image of the last, resurrected Adam. As to the latter, the most obvious example is Col. 1:15: "He is the image of the invisible God" through whom all things were created. In 2 Cor. 3:18–4:4 the thought is both of believers being transformed into God's image and of Christ as embodying the image of God; is this Adam or Wisdom? In Col. 3:10, is Christ the image of God as Adam or Wisdom?

The point is that the concept of the image of God can be used both for Adam *and* for Wisdom. It can denote both the image on the rubber stamp and the image that the stamp puts on the page; it can be used both for the agency used in creation and for that which is created. It is in this overlapping role that it is referred to Christ. Christ as bearing the divine image is the One who bridges the gap between creator and creation. In this supreme mediatorial role the two central strands of Pauline christology overlap and intertwine. Christ as the image of God, even more than Christ as Lord, is the nodal point at which the two great arcs of Pauline christology intersect and which thus prevents them from falling apart into a mutually destructive dichotomy.

In Christ as Adam and Christ as Wisdom we find the two major integrating themes of Pauline christology, themes that integrate the other emphases of Pauline christology and complement and overlap with each other in such a way as to provide the basic framework for all future christology.

CHRISTOLOGY IN ACTS

14

ΚΥΡΙΟΣ in Acts

It is a curious fact that the use of the term κύριος in Acts has received so little attention both in christological studies of the NT and in commentaries on Acts itself. The surprise is occasioned partly by the fact that the term occurs more in Acts than in any other NT writing (though, of course, Acts and the Gospel of Luke are the two longest texts in the NT). Moreover, it is used as a title for Jesus more than any other title in Acts, apart from the name Jesus; this remains true, however several disputed usages (whether they refer to Jesus or to God) are resolved.[1] Not only so, but the character of Acts (a late first-century document describing the beginnings of Christianity), with its balance between speeches attributed to the chief actors in Christianity's beginnings and Luke's[2] own narrative, provides a unique opportunity to check whether any diversity or development of usage can be detected across the period covered from the first beginnings to the time of composition.

---

1. "The most frequently used title for Jesus in Luke-Acts" (J. A. Fitzmyer, *The Gospel according to Luke 1-9* [AB 28; Garden City, 1981] 200-201). J. C. O'Neill, "The Use of *KYRIOS* in the Book of Acts," *SJT* 8 (1955) 155-74, counts 137 occurrences in all, including variants, and excluding the 4 "secular" occurrences (157-58).

2. I will speak of "Luke" as the author of Acts for convenience sake — indicating my acceptance of the consensus that Luke-Acts was written by the same person, probably during the last two decades of the first century. No more specific assumption is necessary for the present paper.

Originally published in *Christus als die Mitte der Schrift,* ed. C. Landmesser et al. (O. Hofius FS). Copyright © 1997 Walter de Gruyter and Co. and used by permission.

241

I

When we sample major works of reference written over the past two or three generations, however, the interest in this topic and its potential for shedding some light on earliest christology is fairly minimal. One of the fullest treatments is the brief analysis of H. J. Cadbury (3.5 pages),[3] which still provides the best starting point for the present study. He noted the narrative use of κύριος in the Gospel and observed that in Acts "ὁ κύριος has become a fixed surrogate for Jesus and is not a conscious title." He pointed out the relative insignificance of the vocative κύριε: "it is much the same as 'sir.'" And he paid particular attention to the brief confessional assertion in 10:36: οὗτός ἐστιν πάντων κύριος. The accompanying commentary contains a number of judicious notes: in particular, on 1:24 the authors observe that the name of Jesus is invoked elsewhere in Acts (9:14, 21; 22:16; 7:59, 60; 14:23), showing that he was regarded by his followers as able to help them, but then they add, "but it is doubtful whether they [these passages] prove that he was prayed to in the same way as God";[4] and at 9:17 they observe that whereas in 9:17 Ananias is sent by "the Lord Jesus," in 22:14 Ananias comes with a message from "the God of our Fathers," with Jesus referred to not as "the Lord" but as "the Righteous One."[5]

In contrast, we may note first the sequence of christological studies. W. Bousset pauses over κύριος in Acts only long enough to dispute the idea that Acts proves a pre-Hellenistic use of the title: "it even appears likely that the occurrence of κύριος in the first half of Acts can be used as a means for precisely distinguishing the reworking done by Luke from the older sources which he used."[6] W. Foerster's comments on the usage in Acts are scattered across the nine pages of his *TDNT* article. His most significant observations are that the usage in Acts confirms that the κύριος title in the NT is related to Jesus' resurrection,[7] and that 14 (out of 18 non-Pauline NT) references to ὁ κύριος (ἡμῶν) Ἰησοῦς occur in Acts and probably reflect the "missionary character" of Acts.[8] O. Cullmann's use of the Acts material is restricted to his argument that the conviction of 2:36 goes back to "the very earliest church," in support of his thesis that the "original confession" was "Jesus is Lord." He adds: "It is probably no accident that in this passage the title Κυριος

---

3. H. J. Cadbury, "The Titles of Jesus in Acts," in F. J. Foakes-Jackson and K. Lake, eds., *The Beginnings of Christianity* I: *The Acts of the Apostles* V (London, 1933) 359-62.

4. K. Lake and H. J. Cadbury in Foakes-Jackson and Lake, *Beginnings* IV, 15 (also 86).

5. Ibid., 104.

6. W. Bousset, *Kyrios Christos* (Nashville, 1970) 125, citing his "Der Gebrauch des Kyriostitels als Kriterium für die Quellenscheidung in der ersten Hälfte der Apostelgeschichte," *ZNW* 15 (1914) 141-62.

7. W. Foerster, κύριος, *TDNT* III, 1089 and 1094 (referring in the latter to 2:36 and 10:36).

8. Foerster, 1092.

comes *before* the title Christ; Jesus can be designated Messiah-King only in view of his invisible lordship as κυριος."[9] F. Hahn's treatment is more or less limited to a brief discussion of 2:36 and 10:36 in exposition of his thesis that reference to the exalted Jesus as κύριος belongs to the Hellenistic Jewish Christian stage of christological development, with its "quite characteristic" "adoptionist" emphasis.[10]

When we turn to the larger commentaries the picture is much the same. E. Haenchen provides a brief listing of the κύριος references which he thinks refer to Jesus in his Introduction, but his comments on individual passages are usually brief: for example, on 7:59 — "the Lord Jesus, who here takes the place of God (cf. Luke 23:46)"; and on 10:36 — "Hence πάντων is meant personally. Jesus is Lord of all, Jews and Gentiles. Cf. Rom. 10:12."[11] H. Conzelmann notes the issue whether 2:36 stems from tradition or from Luke himself, and that in 10:36 "πάντων κύριος ist eine Wendung der hellenistischen, kosmologischen Religion,"[12] but says little more. In his excursus on the christology of Acts, G. Schneider, like Haenchen, simply lists the references which use κύριος of Jesus, pausing only to distinguish those which appear in the Missionsreden from those outside the Missionsreden.[13] His main point of emphasis is that Jesus is clearly ranked under God, as seen particularly in the heilsgeschichtlich function which God assigned to him; this excludes any idea that Luke thought in terms of a preexistence of Christ, but Luke's portrayal equally cannot be described as an "adoptionist" christology.[14] A. Weiser does not seem to add anything of weight to the discussion,[15] and R. Pesch says next to nothing on the subject beyond a brief comment on 2:36, but offers insightful opinion on disputed κύριος references at several points.[16]

In English language commentaries, F. F. Bruce and L. T. Johnson show little interest in the christological issues.[17] C. K. Barrett in his superbly detailed treatment, however, is notable for his willingness to read the early κύριος passages with a strongly christological content. Against the stream he refers 1:24 to Jesus. He has no doubt that 2:21 refers to Jesus. 2:36 is an

9. O. Cullmann, *The Christology of the New Testament* (London, 1959) 207, 216-17.

10. F. Hahn, *The Titles of Jesus in Christology* (London, 1969) 106-7. Similarly R. H. Fuller, *The Foundations of New Testament Christology* (London, 1965) 184-86.

11. E. Haenchen, *The Acts of the Apostles* (Oxford, 1971) 92, n. 3, 293, 252, n. 4.

12. H. Conzelmann, *Die Apostelgeschichte* (HNT 7; Tübingen, 1963) 30, 65.

13. G. Schneider, *Die Apostelgeschichte* (HTKNT 5; Freiburg, 1980, 1982) I, 333, n. 8. But Schneider is assuming his previously more detailed study (see below n. 26).

14. Schneider I, 334-35; see also on 2:36 (I, 276-77).

15. A. Weiser, *Die Apostelgeschichte* (ÖTKNT 5; Gütersloh/Würzburg, 1981, 1985) 95, 268. Similarly G. Schille, *Die Apostelgeschichte des Lukas* (THKNT; Berlin, 1983).

16. R. Pesch, *Die Apostelgeschichte* (EKK 5; Zürich/Neukirchen-Vluyn, 1986).

17. F. F. Bruce, *The Acts of the Apostles* (Grand Rapids/Leicester, [3]1990); L. T. Johnson, *The Acts of the Apostles* (Sacra Pagina 5; Collegeville, 1992). Contrast the brief notes of Fitzmyer, *Luke*, 202-3.

expression of "unreflecting Christology, not yet submitted to such theological criticism as Paul was able to provide. He who shares the throne of God shares his deity; and he who is God is what he is from and to eternity — otherwise he is not God. This truth, evident as it is, was not immediately perceived. . . ." The reference of 5:9 ("the Spirit of the Lord") and 5:19 ("an angel of the Lord") is uncertain. "The fear of the Lord . . . now refers to, or gains some definition from, the Lord Jesus."[18]

The only real exceptions to the minimal interest in Luke's κύριος language are a few specialist studies.[19] J. C. O'Neill analyzes the use of κύριος by speaker (Peter, Stephen, Paul), other direct speech, and narrative. He notes that most of the ambiguous readings come in the narrative sections, concludes that most of them refer to Jesus, and draws the odd conclusion from 9:17 that "Jesus was the Lord God's Name."[20] C. F. D. Moule responds to Conzelmann's "assertion of Luke's promiscuous use of titles,"[21] by arguing that Luke did make a distinction between before and after resurrection by restricting κύριος on the lips of human observers to the postresurrection context.[22] Against Moule, D. L. Jones argues that Luke makes "no distinction between the earthly and the exalted Lord . . . he is Lord even before his birth"; "the resurrection only confirmed and vindicated him in that role." In addition, Jones maintains that the repeated phrases used by Luke in Acts ("the word of the Lord," "added to/turning to/believing in the Lord," and "the name of the Lord") all consistently refer to Jesus.[23] E. Franklin critiques Moule to similar effect. Both ὁ κύριος and κύριε express the language of faith and commitment to the exalted one; but in resurrection "Jesus does not become other than what he was before."[24] Finally the article on which Schneider drew for his commentary, makes a careful analysis of all κύριος uses in Luke and Acts. He separates out those which can be referred without dispute either to

18. C. K. Barrett, *Acts* I (ICC; Edinburgh, 1994) 103, 139, 152, 270, 284, 474.

19. Otherwise, I. H. Marshall, *Luke: Historian and Theologian* (Exeter, 1970), makes only brief comments (166); R. F. O'Toole, *The Unity of Luke's Theology: An Analysis of Luke-Acts* (Wilmington, 1984), concentrates on refuting the claims that Luke has an "absentee christology" in Acts — "Activity of the Risen Jesus as Lord" (40-43); R. L. Brawley (*Centering on God: Method and Message in Luke-Acts* [Louisville, 1990]) has a brief analysis of Luke's usage (126).

20. O'Neill, 159-66, 167, 164-65.

21. Referring to Conzelmann, *The Theology of St. Luke* (New York, 1961) 171, n. 1; cf. Acts 8.

22. C. F. D. Moule, "The Christology of Acts," in *Studies in Luke-Acts,* ed. L. E. Keck and J. L. Martyn (P. Schubert FS; Nashville, 1966) 159-85 (here 160-61, 171-72).

23. D. L. Jones, "The Title *KYRIOS* in Luke-Acts," *SBLSP 1974,* II, 85-101 (here 96, 93, 94-95).

24. E. Franklin, *Christ the Lord: A Study in the Purpose and Theology of Luke-Acts* (London, 1975) 49-55, here 52-54. He draws particular attention to Acts 20:17-35, where "the designation [of Jesus as Lord] is found most frequently" (53).

God or to Jesus and subjects the remaining disputed fourteen verses[25] to closer analysis, in which he is able to make firm deduction as to reference. His conclusion is that there is no "Vermischung" in the use of κύριος in Luke-Acts, since reference is either to God or to Jesus each time.[26]

All this seems a remarkably modest amount to glean from such a large sample of data, and suggests that a little more scrutiny and reflection may be fruitful.

II

A complete survey of uses of κύριος in Acts is the appropriate place to start. In the following table the columns are numbered thus:[27]

1. vocative
2. anarthrous
3. articular
4. narrative
5. speeches (not conversation)
6. OT
7. God
8. Jesus — [1]the Lord Jesus, [2]the Lord Jesus Christ
9. Ambiguous

	1	2	3	4	5	6	7	8	9
1:6	x							x	
1:21					x			x[1]	
1:24	x						x		
2:20		(x)			x	x	x		
2:21		(x)			x	x	x		
2:25			x		x	x	x		
2:34			x		x	x	x		
2:34			x		x	x		(x)	
2:36		x			x			x	
2:39		x			(x)		x		

25. Acts 2:21; 2:47; 5:9; 5:14; 8:22, 24; 9:31; 11:23, 24; 13:2; 13:10; 14:3; 15:40; 16:15.
26. G. Schneider, "Gott und Christus als ΚΥΡΙΟΣ nach der Apostelgeschichte," in *Begegnung mit dem Wort*, ed. J. Zmijewski and E. Nellessen (H. Zimmermann FS; Bonn, 1980) 161-73 (here 171).
27. The attribution to column 9 in particular is at this stage provisional.

	1	2	3	4	5	6	7	8	9
2:47			x						x
3:20			x		x		x		
3:22		(x)			x	x	x		
4:26			x		x	x	x		
4:29	x				x		x		
4:33				x				x¹	
5:9		(x)							x
5:14			x	x				x?	
5:19		x							x
7:31		x			x	(x)	x		
7:33			x		x	(x)	x		
7:49		x			x	x	x		
7:59	x							x¹	
7:60	x							x?	
8:16			x	x				x¹	
8:22			x						x
8:24			x						x
8:25			x	x					x
8:26		x		x					x
8:39		x		x					x
9:1			x	x				x	
9:5	x			x				x	
9:10			x	x				x	
9:10	x			x				x	
9:11			x	x				x	
9:13	x			x				x	
9:15			x	x				x	
9:17			x	x				x	
9:27			x	x				x	
9:28			x	x				x	
9:31			x	x					x
9:35			x	x					x
9:42			x	x					x
10:4	x			x					
10:14	x								
10:33			x	(x)			x?		
10:36		x			x				x
11:8	x								
11:16			x		x			x	
11:17			x		x			x²	

	1	2	3	4	5	6	7	8	9
11:20			x	x				x[1]	
11:21			x	x					x
11:23			x	x				x?	
11:24			x	x				x	
12:7		x		x					x
12:11			x?	x					x
12:17			x	x					x
12:23		x		x			x		
12:24 v.l.			x	x					x
13:2			x	x					x
13:10			x?	(x)					x
13:11		x		(x)					x
13:12			x	x				x	
13:44 v.l.			x	x					x
13:47			x	(x)		(x)	x		
13:48 v.l.			x	x					x
13:49 v.l.			x	x					x
14:3			x	x				x	
14:23			x	x				x	
15:11			(x)	x				$x^{1/2}$ v.l.	
15:17			x		x	x	x		
15:17		x			x	x	x		
15:26			x					x[2]	
15:35			x	x					x
15:36			x	x					x
15:40 v.l.			x	x					x
16:14			x	x					x
16:15			x	(x)				x	
16:16	masters								
16:19	masters								
16:30		x pl							
16:31			x	(x)				$x^{1/2}$ v.l	
16:32 v.l.			x	x					x
17:24			(x)		x	(x)	x		
18:8			x	x				x	
18:9			x	x				x	
18:25			x?	x				x	
19:5			x	x				x[1]	
19:10			x	x					x
19:13			x	x				x[1]	

	1	2	3	4	5	6	7	8	9
19:17			x	x				x^1	
19:20			x	x					x
20:19			x		x			x	
20:21			x		x			$x^{1/2}$ v.l.	
20:24			x		x			x^1	
20:28 v.l.			x		x				x?
20:32 v.l.			x		x				x?
20:35			x		x			x^1	
21:13			x	(x)				x^1	
21:14			x	(x)					x
22:8	x			(x)				x	
22:10	x			(x)				x	
22:10			x	x				x	
22:19	x			(x)				x	
23:11			x	x				x	
25:26	Caesar								
26:15	x			(x)				x	
26:15			x	x				x	
28:31			x	x				$x^{2/1}$ v.l.	

III

On the basis of this data we can draw some conclusions immediately.

a) The vocative use of χύριε is unspecific as to the status accorded to the one addressed. It is certainly used in prayer (1:24; 4:29) and certainly used in prayer or invocation to the exalted Jesus (7:59, 60). But it is also used in address to an angel (10:4) and an unknown heavenly voice (10:14; 11:8). This helps clarify the significance of Paul's address to the voice which addresses him on the Damascus road. In that context it cannot be regarded simply as a polite form of address,[28] since from the first the address is to a glorious heavenly being. But since the initial use is a question, "Who are you, Lord?" it can hardly be taken as a confession of Jesus' lordship.[29]

---

28. Cadbury, "Titles of Jesus in Acts," 360.

29. This may refer to all the uses of χύριε in the repeated accounts of the episode (9:5, 10, 13; 22:8, 10; 26:15) — "unknown apparitions" (Foerster, *TDNT* III, 1086), but not, presumably 22:19 (*pace* Fitzmyer, *Luke*, 203). In 16:30 it is Paul and Silas who are so addressed. Contrast Franklin, *Christ the Lord:* "the vocative is given the full significance of *ho kurios*" (52).

b) Leaving aside genitival phrases for the moment (πνεῦμα κυρίου, ἄγγελος κυρίου, χεὶρ κυρίου), the only anarthrous uses which undoubtedly refer to Christ are 2:36 and 10:36, which highlights the distinctiveness of these two passages.

c) The division between speeches and conversation is not a very precise one. But in the above categorization an interesting feature does emerge: in most of the set speeches κύριος is almost always God (2:20, 21[?], 25, 34a; 3:20, 22; 4:26; 7:31, 33, 49; 15:17; 17:24); but in 10:36; 11:16-17; and 20:19-35 the reference is uniformly to the exalted Jesus. At the same time, we have to observe that most of the former are scriptural quotations or allusions (2:20, 21, 25, 34; 3:22; 4:26; 7:31, 33, 49; 15:17; 17:24), and none of the latter. The fact that the preponderance of κύριος = God references in speeches are derived from Scripture prevents us from making any deduction about age or development in usage. But it also highlights the significance of two verses in particular. One is 3:20, where it is clearly the Lord God referred to: "turn again . . . that the Lord may send the Christ appointed for you, Jesus." The uniqueness of this usage supports the case for seeing primitive tradition at this point.[30] The other is 2:21, to which we shall return below.

d) It is also possible to clarify some of the ambiguities indicated (on a first reading) in column 9. "The spirit of the Lord" should almost certainly be understood as the spirit of God: 5:9 could be taken as parallel to 16:7; but 8:39 looks as though it is part of the parallel with Elijah (2 Kgs. 2:16)[31] which features in the Philip sequence.[32] The "angel of the Lord" likewise (5:19; 8:26; 12:7, 11, 23; cf. 7:35; 10:3; 27:23).[33] Similarly "the hand of the Lord" evokes strong scriptural echoes (11:21 = 2 Sam. 3:12 LXX; 13:11 = 1 Sam. 7:13; 12:15).[34] Also "the fear of the Lord" (9:31), evoking a powerful scriptural motif,[35] "the ways of the Lord" (13:10), similarly evoking scriptural echoes,[36] and "the will of the Lord" (21:14), a traditional formulation ("may the will of God be done").[37] So too "the word of the Lord" (8:25; 12:24 v.l.;

---

30. See particularly J. A. T. Robinson, "The Most Primitive Christology of All?" *Twelve New Testament Essays* (London, 1962) 139-53; R. F. Zehnle, *Peter's Pentecost Discourse* (Nashville, 1971).

31. Pesch, *Apostelgeschichte,* 294.

32. F. S. Spencer, *The Portrait of Philip in Acts: A Study of Roles and Relations* (JSNTSS 27; Sheffield, 1992) 135-41.

33. Barrett is uncertain regarding 5:19 (284), but since "ἄγγελος κυρίου is a very common OT expression . . . (it) will probably have its OT sense here" (422). "ἄγγελος κυρίου (nach LXX) ist bei Lk immer er Engel Gottes. Engel Christi kennt er nicht" (Conzelmann, *Apostelgeschichte,* 41).

34. Haenchen, 366, n. 1; Pesch, *Apostelgeschichte* II, 25. Note also Luke 1:66.

35. G. Wanke and H. Balz, *TDNT* IX, 201-3, 216.

36. Haenchen, 400, n. 3 — "a blend of Prov. 10.9 . . . and Hosea 14.10." Pesch II, 25 refers also to Sir. 39:24.

37. See, e.g., BAGD, θέλημα; G. Schrenk, *TDNT* III, 53-54. O'Toole, however, takes 21:14 as a reference to the risen Lord, citing as proof the commission referred to in 20:24 (*Unity,* 42-43).

13:44 v.l.; 13:48 v.l.; 13:49 v.l.; 15:35, 36; 16:32 v.l.; 19:10, 20), not least since it seems to be equivalent to "the word of God" (8:14; 13:5, 7, 46; 17:13; 18:11, and all the v.l.).[38] Yet it would appear that "the name of the Lord" should usually be referred to Jesus,[39] as also "the teaching of the Lord" (13:12), particularly if taken as an objective genitive, which seems most natural.

Moreover, when we turn from genitival phrases to those where κύριος is the object, there is a greater inclination to refer it to Christ. Talk of "turning to the Lord" (9:35; 11:21), "believing in the Lord" (9:42; 11:17; 16:15, 31; 18:8; 20:21), "added to the Lord" (5:14; 11:24), "disciples of the Lord" (9:1), "remain in the Lord" (11:23) and "committed to the Lord" (14:23) presumably all hang together. And several of the phrases are directed to the Lord Jesus (Christ) specifically (11:17; 13:12; 16:15, 31; probably 18:8; 20:21). Yet, at the same time, it is notable that several of the phrases have "God" parallels: "turn to God" (14:15; 15:19; 26:18, 20); "believed God" (16:34); "remain in the grace of God" (13:43); "commit to God" (20:32; cf. Ps. 31:6).

e) Some passages, however, remain hard to categorize finally. For example, 1:24: who is the "Lord who knows the hearts of all"? Most assume on the basis of 15:8 that a reference to God would be taken for granted.[40] And the continuation of the usage in postapostolic Christianity is persuasive.[41] But the only "Lord" so far mentioned in the text is Jesus (1:6, 21) and others remain unpersuaded.[42] In 2:47 "the Lord" seems to be in syntactical contrast with the preceding mentioned "God," and the correlation with the "added to" language just mentioned would seem to suggest that Jesus is in view. But Schneider argues that 2:47; 5:14; and 11:23, 24 all refer to God, citing Deut. 1:11 (LXX).[43] Similarly with 8:22 and 24: is it to God or to Jesus that prayer is to be offered regarding Simon? The only "Lord" mentioned in the preceding context is Jesus (8:16), but in 8:25 "the word of the Lord" probably has God in mind (cf. 8:14).[44] An intriguing reference is 13:2, with its talk of "worshiping (λειτουργέω) the Lord." Context does not help much here, but those who raise the issue mostly come down on the side of κύριος = God here.[45]

---

38. Contrast O'Neill, 168-70; Jones, 94.
39. See above n. 23.
40. Foerster, Haenchen, Conzelmann, Weiser, Schneider.
41. Haenchen, *Apostelgeschichte*, 162, n. 8.
42. Lake and Cadbury, O'Neill, Barrett.
43. Schneider, "Gott," 168.
44. Schneider, "Gott," 168-69, again argues for a God reference, comparing Acts 5:1-10 and 13:10f. (χεὶρ κυρίου); also Pesch, *Apostelgeschichte*, 277.
45. Haenchen notes that "Luke has borrowed an expression of special solemnity from LXX" citing 2 Chron. 5:14; 13:10; 35:3; Judith 4:14; Joel 1:13; 2:17; Ezek. 40:46; 44:16; 45:4; Dan. 7:10 (*Acts,* 395 and n. 3). Schneider follows Haenchen and notes also the traditional worship context (fasting and praying).

In 14:3 and 15:40 should the unspecified Lord to whom "grace" is attributed be the Lord Jesus (15:11), or God, in accordance with the more regular phrase, "the grace of God" (11:23; 13:43; 14:26; 20:24; cf. 20:32)? Finally, in 16:14, who opened Lydia's heart? On one side could be cited 2 Macc. 1:4. But on the other could be cited Luke 24:45. 16:15 does not help too much since, as we have just seen, "faithful to the Lord," while more likely to refer to Jesus, does have 16:34 as an alternative parallel.[46]

IV

In the light of all this what can be said about the significance of Luke's use of κύριος in Acts?

a) A striking feature, too little noted, is that Luke uses κύριος so frequently for God in his own narrative section. In Paul, the significance of whose use of κύριος has been subjected to endless analysis, the rule is generally recognized: κύριος denotes κύριος Ἰησοῦς except in scriptural quotations (where the reference may still be primarily to Jesus in two or three occasions). So, for Paul, simply to speak of "the Lord" is to speak unequivocally of Christ. Luke, writing later, observes no such rule or practice. It was still as natural for him to speak of "the Lord," or to have his characters so speak, and thereby to denote God.[47]

b) Still more striking is the way Luke can vary his usage within the same context. The most remarkable sequence is 2:20-36, where God is presumably the reference in 2:20, 25[48] and certainly in 34a, while Christ is clearly in view in 2:34b and 36. In 2:21 "the Lord" is the Yahweh of Joel 2:32, and the echo of Joel 2:32 in 2:39 suggests that "the Lord" of 2:21 is "the Lord our God" of 2:39. On the other hand, the same verb in 22:16 presumably speaks of a "calling upon the name (of Christ)" (cf. particularly 9:14, 21), and those who respond to Peter's Pentecost sermon are baptized "in the name of Jesus Christ" (2:38).[49] In the light of Rom. 10:13 it can hardly be doubted that such a reference of a κύριος = Yahweh text to the exalted Christ (2:36) was possible and accepted in earliest Christianity. If that is what has happened

46. Schneider is happy to refer 16:14 to God, but 16:15 to Jesus ("Gott," 163, 171).

47. Usually in a genitival phrase, but note 12:17 and 13:47.

48. Barrett, 138, argues that Luke understands "the day of the Lord" (2:20) as the day of the Lord Jesus (1 Cor. 1:8; 2 Cor. 1:14; Phil. 1:6, 10; 2:16). But in 2:25 it is the speaker (David, foreshadowing the Messiah) who sees "the Lord," who can therefore only be God, who raised Jesus from the dead (2:27-32).

49. Note also the other "name of the Lord" references in Acts — 8:16; 9:28; 15:26; 19:5, 13, 17; 21:13. Those who think Jesus is the referent in 2:21 include Haenchen, 179; Schneider, "Gott," 167-68; *Apostelgeschichte* I, 270; Barrett, 139.

in this case also (2:21), it should be noted that it is already a step beyond 2:36. 2:36, after all, was quite understandable in the light of 2:34 (Jesus had been designated the second κύριος of Ps. 110:1). But to imply that this exalted Lord was now the one on whom the first inquirers were to "call" in place of Yahweh (at Yahweh's behest) would seem to be a major christological development, analogous to Rom. 10:9-13 and Phil. 2:9-11. Since the application of Yahweh texts to the exalted Christ is usually seen as marking a major development in early christology, 2:21 should be given more weight than has usually been the case.[50] At any rate, we should note that Luke had no inhibition both in citing what some have regarded as an "adoptionistic" formula (2:36) and in implying that the exalted Christ would now be fulfilling functions previously the prerogative of the one God, all within a few verses of each other, and in what he presented as the first missionary speech of the infant church.

Other examples are 10:33 followed soon by 10:36. In the former, Cornelius presumably refers to God; he has not yet heard of Jesus. But in the latter we have the most striking κύριος Ἰησοῦς reference in Acts. Or 13:10-12, where on the above discussion the first two references would be most naturally taken in reference to God, but the last in reference to Christ. We noted above the problems in deciding with regard to 16:14 and 15. Similarly with 16:31 and 32, the former specified as Jesus, but the latter a strongly attested "word of God" reference (ℵ* B). Also 21:13 and 14. However such issues are resolved, it is evident that Luke was content either to vary his use of κύριος within the same narrative or to leave it ambiguous.

c) What do we deduce from this? Luke clearly thought of both God and Jesus as κύριος. Unlike Paul, he did not make any effort to distinguish the one God and Father from the one Lord Jesus Christ (1 Cor. 8:6).[51] But that does not mean that he thought of them as two equal κύριοι, or casually mixed them up, or saw them in some sophisticated pretrinitarian way as expressions of the one θεὸς καὶ κύριος. The care that Luke took in his use of κύριος in the Gospel[52] and the weight of 2:36 and 10:36 (whether old tradition or insertions) indicates his awareness of the significance of the title as used of Jesus.

Probably 2:34 is the best clue. Luke, I would suggest, simply took as his starting point the well-established Christian reading of Ps. 110:1. That enabled him to speak both of God as Lord and of Jesus as Lord within the same breath. The same text made clear the relationship of the two lordships:

---

50. Cf. Hahn, *Titles,* 108; see also, e.g., M. Hengel, *The Son of God* (London, 1976) 77-80; P. Pokorný, *The Genesis of Christology* (Edinburgh, 1987) 75-76.

51. Note also the regular formula in the Pauline letters: "the God and Father of our Lord Jesus Christ" (Rom. 15:6; 2 Cor. 1:3; 11:31; Col. 1:3; Eph. 1:3, 17; 1 Pet. 1:3).

52. Moule.

Jesus had been given lordship by the Lord God (2:36). That also meant that when both were spoken of as κύριος within the same context there need be no confusion, for the lordship of Jesus was a derivative lordship, but as derived from the Lord God it was in effect an expression of God's lordship. This is presumably why within the same sequence (2:21, 39) there need be no confusion or misunderstanding about "calling upon the Lord" since, as referred to Jesus, this was part of the authority as κύριος which God had bestowed on the exalted Jesus.[53]

The conclusion we draw from this may be that Luke was rather naive in his readiness to continue speaking in such a confusing way. Why did he not, like Paul, give more thought to the relation of God to the exalted Christ? But it would probably be fairer to see his usage as indicative of an unreflective stage in early christology, where both the belief in the supreme God was unquestioned and the belief that Jesus was Lord had become an established and distinctive Christian confession. Both could be assumed and asserted without provoking tortuous theological reflection or agonized questionings. This was the level of firm and uncomplicated faith which, according to Acts, lay behind Christianity's earliest and most decisive expansion. It is a reminder to us, not least, that Christ can be Lord, at the center of both Scripture and faith, without in any sense challenging the lordship of God.

---

53. Cf. the brief comments of Marshall, *Luke,* 166; Franklin, *Christ the Lord,* 54.

CHRISTOLOGY IN THE MAKING

15

M. Wiles on *Christology in the Making* and Responses by the Author

Reflections on James Dunn's *Christology in the Making*

Maurice Wiles

James Dunn's *Christology in the Making* (London: SCM, 1980) is a valuable survey of the main New Testament evidence that needs to be taken into account in any reflection about the doctrine of the incarnation. His expressed aim is "to let the NT writers speak for themselves, to understand their words as they would have intended, to hear them as their first readers would have heard them" (p. 9). The book combines, with greater success than most theologians can command, scholarly erudition and clarity of expression. Moreover, in the difficult matter of the assessment of evidence, he seems to me to show good judgment and a sure touch.[1] It ought to be required reading for all those who want to take part in the continuing debate about christology and incarnation.

What he brings out time and again in the earlier chapters of the book is how the meaning of the words that most naturally springs to the mind of the modern reader is unlikely to have been the meaning intended by the author or understood by the first readers. I give just two examples, "Phil. 2:6-11 certainly seems on the face of it," he writes, "to be a straightforward statement contrasting Christ's pre-existent glory and post-crucifixion exaltation with his earthly humiliation" (p. 114). But when the Philippian hymn is seen against

---

1. New Testament specialists will no doubt have many particular criticisms to raise, which fall outside my competence or concern here. Frances Young's review in *Theology* (July 1981, pp. 303-5) embodies a number of such criticisms within the context of a general commendation of the book.

Originally published in *Theology* 85: 92-98, 326-30, 360-61. Copyright © 1982 by SPCK and used by permission.

the background of an Adam christology, he goes on to argue, the (to us) natural incarnational understanding of it ceases to be the most plausible interpretation of its original intention. So too with that other famous christological hymn in Col. 1:15-20: "the thought is not of Jesus himself as there in the beginning, despite what seems to us the 'obvious' meaning of the language used. . . . A Wisdom christology does not assert that Christ was a pre-existent being" (p. 212). This negative emphasis should not for a moment be allowed to suggest that Dr. Dunn does not see these Adam and Wisdom christologies as "high" christologies; he most emphatically does. But he is equally clear that they do not directly express belief in a preexistent personal divine being who has become incarnate in Jesus.

This careful evaluation of the New Testament evidence which might on the face of it seem to suggest a belief in the personal preexistence of Christ but which in Dr. Dunn's view does not makes his handling of the most overtly incarnational writing in the New Testament, namely the Fourth Gospel, of particular interest. For here in John 1:14 he does find "an explicit statement of *incarnation*, the first and indeed only such statement in the New Testament" (p. 241).[2] How is this explicit statement to be understood on the basis of Dr. Dunn's expressed objective of getting at the meaning the author intended to convey to his original readers?

Dr. Dunn believes that the prologue embodies "a Logos poem which originally had an existence independent of the Gospel" (p. 239), and regards it as methodologically important "to keep . . . discussion of John's use of it in relation to his Gospel" (p. 349). The poem incorporates two important features that seem to go beyond anything asserted in earlier tradition. In the first place the Logos here is eternally preexistent. It did not come to be; it was not "created," not even as the first of created beings like the Wisdom of Prov. 8:22; it *was* in the beginning. And secondly it did not simply enter into a man; it *became* flesh (pp. 240-41). What do these new developments imply? The first does not appear to be of great significance in this context. For if we understand Logos in the poem as "God's utterance," and like Wisdom, "a personification of God's own activity" rather than a personal divine being, then it is natural enough to speak of it as eternally coexistent with God. And it is in those terms that Dr. Dunn does understand it (pp. 243, 210). The second,

---

2. As a footnote appended to this phrase, Dr. Dunn says: "So Wiles is inaccurate when he affirms 'the incarnation, in its full and proper sense, is not something directly presented in Scripture' (*Myth*, ed. Hick p. 3)." But on p. 1 of that article I had defined a narrower sense of incarnation which affirms "that Jesus of Nazareth is unique in the precise sense that, while being fully man, it is true of him, and of him alone, that he is also fully God, the Second Person of the co-equal Trinity." In *that* sense I believe my initial statement to be accurate and not in conflict with Dr. Dunn, for whom incarnation does not necessarily involve even a preexistent divine being, let alone a coequally divine one (see *Christology in the Making* [London: SCM, 1980], p. 212).

with its identification of the Logos with an individual human person, is more striking. But except for its bolder form of linguistic expression, it does not add much to what was already implicit in the earlier Wisdom christologies (pp. 243-44). In Dr. Dunn's judgment the identification of the Logos with a human person asserted in v. 14 is not to be seen as requiring the Logos prior to v. 14 to be understood as personal (p. 349). If that is right, as I believe it to be, the Logos poem taken by itself does not mark any decisive step beyond earlier formulations.

But when the Logos poem is incorporated into the Gospel as a whole the situation is very different. For John equates the Logos of the poem with the Son of God of his own gospel tradition (p. 244). He does not even leave open the loophole that Marcellus of Ancyra was later to exploit of restricting the preexistence of this Logos-Son to his Logos aspect only. He is clearly preexistent also as Son. As Dr. Dunn rightly puts it, "for the first time in earliest Christianity we encounter in the Johannine writings the understanding of Jesus' divine sonship in terms of the personal preexistence of a divine being who was sent into the world and whose ascension was simply the continuation of an intimate relationship with the Father which neither incarnation nor crucifixion interrupted or disturbed" (p. 59). So he concludes "only with the Fourth Gospel can we speak of a full-blown conception of Christ's personal pre-existence and a clear doctrine of incarnation" (p. 258). Finally, he reminds us of the immense historical significance of this Johannine christology. "Without the Fourth Gospel all the other assertions we have been looking at would have been resolvable into other more modest assertions. The history of christological controversy is the history of the Church's attempt to come to terms with John's Christology — first to accept it and then to understand and re-express it" (pp. 249, 250).

If this is a sound historical reconstruction, as I judge it to be, how are we to evaluate it? Dr. Dunn's purpose is a strictly historical one, but he very properly offers us clues to his own evaluative judgments. "It is," he writes, "a lasting testimony to the inspired genius of the Fourth Evangelist that he brought together the Logos poem and the Father-Son Christology in such a definitive way" (p. 249). Certainly no one can doubt the historical effectiveness of the Fourth Evangelist's achievement. But are we right to see it as an act of inspired genius? And if we are, what are the implications of so seeing it? One might, for example, want to claim that it represents a brilliant setting of the scene for a single inspired but idiosyncratic work of the historical imagination, yet at the same time to question the appropriateness of its subsequent role of providing guidelines for all future christological reflection.

Hesitations of this kind are reinforced for me by a warning to modern christologians given by Dr. Dunn himself in the concluding section of his book. He warns us, as he did in an earlier book,[3] against trying to put together all the diverse christological approaches of the New Testament into one single whole. "Modern Christology . . . should not insist on squeezing all the different NT conceptualizations into one particular 'shape,' but it should recognize that from the first the significance of Christ could only be apprehended by a diversity of formulations which though not always strictly compatible with each other were not regarded as rendering each other invalid" (pp. 266-67). But is it unreasonable to suggest that what he warns us against is just what the Fourth Evangelist has done? The original Son of God christology carried no implication of preexistence; the original Logos/Wisdom christology was not conceived in personal terms. Each by itself can speak forcefully and fruitfully of the significance of Jesus. What the Fourth Evangelist has done is, in Dr. Dunn's language, to complete a "backward extension of the Son of God language" (p. 256) and to present "the Logos-Son no longer as the impersonal (even if personified) utterance of God but as the Son of God conscious of his existence with the Father before the world was made" (p. 258). And these he has then brought together in a form that Dr. Dunn regards as the successful synthesis of an inspired genius, but which I am suggesting might equally validly be seen as an example of that "squeezing . . . different NT conceptualizations into one particular shape," against which Dr. Dunn has put us on our guard. Bringing different conceptualizations together is not, of course, wrong in itself. But it is always necessary to test the way in which such bringing together is done. Moreover the fact that the bringing together occurs in this case in a work that itself falls within the New Testament canon does not exempt it from the necessity of such testing. And when the Fourth Gospel is looked at with this question in mind, the result is hardly reassuring. The "backward extension of the Son of God language" does not simply enhance the status of that language but *radically alters it.* The Johannine Son who prays to his Father for the sake of the bystanders (John 11:41-42) or in full consciousness of a preexistent glory in the presence of the Father (John 17:5) is a very different Son of God from the Markan Son praying to his Father in the Garden of Gethsemane (Mark 14:36). These "docetic" tendencies in the Johannine picture of Jesus, to which attention has frequently been drawn, are clear indications that the Fourth Evangelist has not avoided the *distorting effect* that so easily arises when earlier distinct conceptualities are squeezed into one particular shape.

Now that we are in a better position than most of our forebears were to see something (even if still only a little) of the way in which the christology of the Fourth Gospel developed, how ought we to regard it in the context of our own attempts at christological affirmation? Many Christian scholars of

---

3. J. D. G. Dunn, *Unity and Diversity in the New Testament* (London: SCM, 1977) 226-27.

unimpeachable christological orthodoxy have already wholly abandoned the view directly presented in the gospel of Jesus as a "Son of God conscious of his existence with the Father before the world was made."[4] But they are much more inclined to hold on to the idea of a personally preexistent Christ, even though on Dr. Dunn's evidence such a view only appears within the New Testament in the self-conscious form of the Johannine Christ. Dr. Dunn warns that "the subsequent dominance of the Johannine presentation should not blind us to the diversity of christological formulation which is a feature of the first-century writings" (p. 265). But we will only be able to act on that warning (as I believe we should) if we are prepared to adopt a much more critical attitude toward that Johannine presentation. For if *personal* preexistence is anything more than a highly pictorial way of saying the same thing as the earlier "impersonal (even if personified)" Wisdom christologies, then it cannot coexist with the other christological formulations. It is bound in the long run to distort and to devour them. So if modern christology is to draw positively on the rich variety of approaches that contemporary New Testament scholarship is increasingly drawing to our attention, it needs to distance itself at least one stage further than it has yet done from the legacy of the Fourth Evangelist's synthesis and its dominant influence on all subsequent christological thought.

Some Thoughts on Maurice Wiles's "Reflections"

I am grateful to Professor Wiles for his perceptive account of my study. His chief point is that my warning against "squeezing different NT conceptualizations into one particular shape" can actually be used as a criticism against one of the New Testament writers themselves — the Fourth Evangelist. Consequently modern christology must try to get behind the distorting effect of John's christology to an earlier, less distorted/distorting conceptuality — this I take to be the thrust of his last sentence.

This critique and challenge, while not without some justification, is in the end unfair to John. If I may put it so, it is the dogmatic John who is thus criticized and challenged, not the historical John.

We should not exaggerate the size of the step John took. My strong impression at the end of the study was that John was part of a wider and developing movement of thought, that in the second half of the first century

---

4. This point emerged very clearly in the debate about *The Myth of God Incarnate*. See my "A Survey of Issues in the *Myth* Debate," in M. Goulder, ed., *Incarnation and Myth* (London: SCM, 1979) 4.

A.D. the thought of the ancient world was expanding to embrace in particular the concept of personal preexistence. We see this in the developing talk of the Son of man in both Jewish and Christian writings, in the burgeoning angelology of Jewish apocalyptic and Jewish mysticism, in the emergence of the "two powers heresy" rejected by rabbinic Judaism, in the developing language of predestination and election in Christian and Jewish writings, as well as in the Wisdom and Logos christology of Paul, Hebrews, and John. However much we may see John's christology as a "radical alteration" from our perspective in time, it is hardly so within the historical context of the late first century A.D.

For example, "Son of God" was not a clear cut concept with well defined boundaries — it simply denoted the fact or claim that someone stood in a close or favored relation with God. So it had precisely the sort of elasticity which John was able to make use of, and his use can be described as a "radical alteration" only with difficulty. Moreover J. A. Bühner has recently shown that the great bulk of John's Son of God christology can be readily understood against the background of Jewish speculation about prophetic commissioning. And the opening of the first epistle of John shows how closely continuous is the Johannine Word christology with the earlier theology of the word of proclamation.

Again, we should not overestimate the significance of the category of preexistence in any critique of John — something that can easily happen since it rings so strangely in modern ears. The development of the language of preexistence seems to have been one of the major elements in the much broader development of thought in which John played a leading role. And while John's application of it to Jesus was distinctive, it was not the idea of preexistence itself which marked John out. The rabbis could subsequently speak of various preexistent entities, not least of the Torah, and there is language from first-century Jewish writings which is not so very dissimilar in talk of the Son of man and of Moses.

The chief problem confronting Jewish-Christian thought at this point was rather the threat to *monotheism*. Elsewhere in the broader developing trajectory rabbinic Judaism concluded that speculation concerning the Son of man (and Enoch) had transgressed monotheism. Is John's christology open to a similar criticism? The answer depends largely on how John's combination of Logos language and Son of God christology should be interpreted. I would suggest that an affirmative answer can be given only if John's concept of personal preexistence is interpreted in terms of our modern idea of personality. Or in historical terms, only if John's christology is interpreted in terms of the Gnostic redeemer myth. Moreover I would like to suggest that Wiles's criticism of John is only valid against such an *interpretation* of John. But in fact it was such an interpretation of John which the early church *rejected*. This it seems to me is in part at least the significance of the dominance of Logos christology in the second and third centuries: in effect they interpreted John's Son of God categories by means of his Logos christology, and by thus identifying the redeemer with the creative energy of God they thereby demonstrated their intent to remain within the bounds of monotheism. As I have pointed out elsewhere, it is this monotheistic interpretation of John which finally won the day against the more Gnostic syncretistic use of John, so that when the Son of God language became the major christological motif from Nicaea onward it is the Logos-Son who is in view, the Johannine Son of God understood in the light of the Johannine Logos and not the Johannine Son of God understood as an expression of the Gnostic redeemer myth, as a redeemer who is not also creator.

In other words, I would judge it unfair to level a criticism against John which was made with reference to later stages of christological discussion when categories were much more sharply defined and alternatives more clearly distinguished. The point is that John was at the vanguard of a developing way of thinking, when categories were being framed and explored and not yet precisely defined. John's language and conceptualization set out the parameters for the subsequent debate, but his words and images should not be read with an anachronistic rigidity.

In short, the synthesis John achieves cannot fairly be said to "distort" the categories taken up, and to claim that he has "radically altered" the language used is a criticism directed more against the Gnostic interpretation of John than against John himself.

I would not wish to deny that John's christology does pose questions and problems to twentieth-century conceptuality, but I doubt whether the answer is to regret the fact that John's christology was ever framed in that way or to "distance" ourselves from it. Rather, I would suggest, we need to take more serious account of the dynamic within earliest christology which resulted in John's christology. I refer to the dynamic set up by the recognition that Jesus provides a definition of God as well as of what is human, the dynamic between Wisdom christology and Adam christology, if you like, which is there as much in Paul (however undeveloped) as it is in John. It is that dynamic which caused Christian thinking to reexpress Jewish monotheism in terms of Jesus while still affirming "God is one," and which has to be taken more fully into account in modern christology — otherwise we distance ourselves not just from John but from all the major Christian thinkers of the first as well as of subsequent centuries.

Christology — The Debate Continues

Dear Maurice,

I am glad the common ground is so substantial and am happy to continue the discussion since I am sure it will help clarify my own thinking.

I realized of course that the issue of monotheism was not the main thrust of your article, but I brought it to the fore precisely because I believe you did not give it enough prominence in your "Reflections." And this I suspect is true of most analyses of developments in christology over the first century or two of Christian thought. The impression I retain from my earlier studies in early Church theology is that the chief patristic debates really begin with the apologists, and the New Testament writings and apostolic fathers are viewed from that later perspective, their texts quarried and discussed in the light of these later debates about the teaching of Arius, etc. The implication usually is that the main stream of Christian thought was moving inexorably toward a full trinitarian statement and that the importance of the earlier contributions was the extent to which they foreshadowed and prepared for the later crucial definitions or redefinitions of key concepts.

My point however is that there is an *earlier* context of equally or even more crucial significance and that to view the New Testament and early second-century material only from the later perspective is to miss that earlier context and so to misconstrue the material's significance in what was its primary context. That context is of a movement of thought seeking self-understanding initially within Judaism and then in dialogue primarily with rabbinic Judaism, but at the same time still part of a broader stream flowing from Judaism before A.D. 70 and including strong strains of apocalyptic and mystical tradition. Within *that* context the chief issue, so far as you and I are now concerned, is monotheism and whether this new movement focusing on Messiah Jesus could remain within Jewish monotheism and properly lay claim to the heritage of Jewish monotheism. It seems to me therefore that the second-century apologists are better understood as the latter stages of *that* debate than as precursors of the trinitarian debate proper. As you will be aware, this is not the only area in earliest Christian thought and Christian origins where the *Jewishness* of its context has been astonishingly underplayed or misunderstood.

When viewed within the whole sweep of thought from Paul onward, therefore, the transition from Logos christology to Son christology at Nicaea is better seen as marking the transition from a debate oriented to the question of monotheism to one oriented to the question of the internal relationships within the Godhead. Expressing my point in too summary fashion, I would want to put it this way: it was only when Christianity had been able to establish itself sufficiently as a monotheistic faith through its Logos christology (without having to resort to the more obvious alternative of some form of adoptionism) that it was able to switch the focus of its attention to a definition of its monotheism as trinitarian monotheism. Where this point begins to bite on our discussion is that Logos language was not well adapted to describing relationship, not at least where the description is endeavoring to clarify what *distinguishes* the partners in the relationship from each other. Logos terminology is more fitted to expressing continuity between, the sameness of the partners — and this is true whether we mean Logos as rational thought and spoken word or Logos as the self-expression of God. This of course is precisely why the Logos christology of the pre-Nicene period is best seen as an expression and defense of Christian monotheism and why it had to be superseded when the object became the clearer definition of relationships within the unity of the Godhead.

The bearing of all this on the christology of the Fourth Gospel will I hope be fairly obvious. (1) Exegesis of John's christology has to see part of its primary context as what may be loosely called the debate between different heirs of Second Temple Judaism on the crucial question of monotheism — how far could one go in conceiving/speaking of God in revelation and redemption without transgressing the fundamental Jewish belief in God as one? The question in this case is whether John's Logos-Son was stretching Jewish monotheism beyond the limits acceptable within the broad stream of Judaism after A.D. 70. (2) Consequently also John's Son language should *not* be interpreted as though the Nicene and post-Nicene question of *relationship* was in view, but should be interpreted within the context of the earlier issue of monotheism. Which is to say John's Son language is best seen as an expression of his Logos christology, that is, as a way of elaborating and illustrating the continuity and sameness which the word Logos expressed in itself. The fact that John already brings together the two principal categories of the pre- and post-Nicene stages of the subsequent debates should not confuse us into assuming that the post-Nicene questions or interests were already present to John. John speaks as a Jewish-Christian monotheist trying to explore (among other things) how Jesus/"the Christ event" has illumined and clarified the Jewish understanding of God.

It is against this late first-century broad Jewish background that John's language of preexistence and in particular his presentation of Christ's consciousness of preexistence has to be understood. It was a way of elaborating the primary Logos category, of documenting and explaining in a sequence of different discussions the continuity between the invisible Father and the visible Christ: for example, the judgmental and illuminating impact of the Son is the judgment and illumination of the Logos of God. As other strands of Judaism presented the Torah as preexistent in order to claim its continuity with and sameness as the archetypal purposes of God, so John presents Christ as preexistent. And since Christ was a conscious being, and not an inanimate object like a scroll, it is a natural extension of the same parabolic logic to present Christ as conscious of his preexistence. But the purpose of the language was not to develop a definition of relationship between Father and Son as "two distinct persons," but rather to eliminate any thought of discontinuity between the invisible Father and the revelation of Christ. Jesus' consciousness of preexistence in John therefore does not seem to me to be such a significant step or "radical alteration" as you claim. Given the logic of Logos language as a way of speaking about God's self-revelation, and given its natural extension in the concept of preexistence when that language is applied to an entity within human experience, then consciousness of preexistence is simply a further and equally natural extension when the concept of the preexistent Logos of God is applied to a self-conscious being.

It is an understanding of John along these lines, that is, within the context of late first-century Jewish and Jewish-Christian exploration of the limits of Jewish monotheism, to which I refer when I spoke of "the historical John." By "the dogmatic John" I refer particularly to the Johannine Son-conscious-of-preexistence language taken out of that context and put to the service of post-Nicene concern about the internal relationships of the trinity ("a free-floating concept in their dogmatic constructions" is not the way I would put it, but I see what you mean). That becomes open to criticism precisely when it ignores the context of John's monotheism expressed most clearly in the Logos prologue. And post-Nicene use of John's Son language becomes open to criticism precisely insofar as it ignores or forgets the first stage of the christological debate, the debate about monotheism stage, precisely when it understands the Son other than as the *Logos*-Son. But the chief misappropriation of John's Son language along these lines was by the Gnostics. John's Son language, when freed from its context as illustration of the Jewish Logos in application to Christ, became vulnerable to pressures toward pluralism (polytheism or multiplicity of emanations). And *that* interpretation of John had in effect already been defeated by the Logos christology *before* the Son category became dominant in the post-Nicene period. That is to say, the Son of Nicene orthodoxy *was* essentially the Logos-Son. The leading exponents of that orthodoxy were presumably for the most part fully conscious that they were operating within the constraints of monotheism — a consciousness always to be borne in mind when interpreting the Son language of Nicene orthodoxy. In effect, then, I am questioning the extent to which "Son-conscious-of-preexistence" was "a free-floating concept" within traditional trinitarian orthodoxy. I suspect the criticism here is more appropriate to modern commentators on patristic theology who have failed to appreciate the lasting significance of the monotheistic stage of the debate not least on the meaning of the categories used.

Here I should perhaps try to respond to your description of John as a work of "dramatic irony." "Dramatic irony" I take to be a writer's exploitation of a difference between the character's understanding of his own words and the fuller understanding which the reader has because he is able to see the larger context. I am uncertain how well that applies to John's preexistence language. Certainly it can be used in reference to other elements in John, particularly his "signs" (including the footwashing, the blood and water from Jesus' side, etc.). The reader would be aware of their fuller significance. But the difference between Jesus' talk of preexistence and the readers' understanding of it is not quite of that order. Do you mean then the irony of the readers' awareness that it was the man Jesus of Nazareth, the Messiah, who is shown as saying such things? Or the "irony" between John's intended use (Logos-Son) and later use as a "free-floating concept" free of the Logos and more susceptible to pluralistic interpretation? And is your "distancing" yourself then an attempt to get back to "the historical John," or to the historical Jesus behind the Johannine Christ? If the former, my comments of the previous paragraph become more relevant. If the latter, I refer back to my first response, particularly the last paragraph. Or perhaps I have missed your point. Either way I would welcome more clarification.

A few final thoughts on the concept of *personal* preexistence. I am very conscious of my lack of philosophical equipment here, but what I am trying to argue is that John's concept of personal preexistence need only be a problem for us either when we presuppose a polytheistic or emanatory model for God, or when we presuppose a model definition of "person." As to the former, the point is that early Christian thought rejected these models and opted to stay firmly within a monotheistic framework. Within that framework the language of Jesus' personal preexistence has to be understood in the same way as, say, Philo's wide-ranging talk of the Logos in personal terms: that is, as a way of expressing the personality of God, the personal nature of God's interaction with his creation. In other words, early Christian thought rejected the idea of the Son as another person (in *our* sense of "person") other than the Father, the invisible God. As to the latter, what we must constantly recall is that in this whole debate we are dealing all the while with the mindset of the ancient world, which found no difficulty in conceiving of power/energy extended or dispersed throughout time and space as *personal* (divine Wisdom is a very good example). Within the Christian tradition we have felt uncomfortable about trying to hold onto such a way of thinking except in reference to God — and even then with some discomfort! But there we have been left no choice by the constraints of our tradition, our experience, and our logic. What the basic understanding of Christ in terms of the Logos-Son is saying at this point is that our understanding of God as *personal* and of the character of that personality gains its greatest clarification and clearest definition from the person of Christ. In the last analysis the development of Logos christology and Nicene orthodoxy is the attempt to explore and defend the logic of that claim.

I have gone on long enough, and am probably well out of my depth, but swimming strongly I hope.

Yours sincerely,
Jimmy

Christology Yet Once More:
A Further Letter to Professor Wiles

Dear Maurice,

Many thanks for your letter of April 19. I found your elaboration of my suggested analysis of stages in the development of early Christian thought about God and Christ helpful. Presumably the fact that modalism was such a serious option at the end of the second century is a further confirmation that the decisive issue at the earlier stage was *monotheism:* modalism is an improper corollary drawn from the assertion that Christianity is still monotheist (in the tradition of Jewish monotheism), despite its pulling apart from Judaism; modalism is one possible but inadequate way of spelling out *Logos* christology. I am less competent to comment on your criticisms of Nicene orthodoxy, though speaking personally I have found also helpful Lonergan's observation that the Nicene Creed is better seen as a heuristic statement than a finished definition.

However, returning to the (for me) more familiar territory of John's Gospel, on which our discussion has focused, I do agree that everything hangs on how the Gospel is read. John, it seems to me, has been the victim of too many harsh cross-examinations, where he has been forced to answer the questions of his interrogators rather than being allowed to bear his own witness in his own terms. "Tell us about the historical Jesus," urges one interrogator. "Tell us about the Gnostic Redeemer myth," insists another. "Tell us about the inner relationships of the true God," requires a third. But what if John was concerned with *none* of these things? What if he *was* simply following the logic of Wisdom/Logos christology in reference to Jesus the Christ, elaborating the idiom of preexistence in a vivid and dramatic way? (there is no question that John has a developed sense of the dramatic). He would have thought he was simply elaborating the earliest statements of Christian monotheism, but in the event he used language which left his presentation not a little vulnerable to interpretation in the direction of the Gnostic redeemer myth. In that case his, too, is a heuristic statement and is open to criticism (in the same way that Nicene orthodoxy is open to criticism) for using language which could be so interpreted. But, as I suggested in *Christology* (pp. 264f.), perhaps this is an inevitable characteristic of statements which explore the frontiers of our thinking and conceptuality in a challenging way.

John seems vulnerable to criticism therefore because *for us* preexistence in particular is a more significant factor than it was for John. So *we* see the emergence of a concept of personal preexistence, expressed by John in a "self-consciously incarnate Jesus" (to use your phrase), as a step of some magnitude. Whereas for John it was probably simply a not unnatural elaboration of earlier Wisdom imagery, for us, aware as we cannot help being of the later debates (*agenētos* or *agennētos,* etc.), it has a degree of epochal significance. Now if the meaning of a writing is the meaning it has actually had over subsequent centuries, then John's presentation forms that kind of watershed — "the dogmatic John." And I would not deny that this dogmatic John has misled not a few believers into what is in effect a kind of bi-theism or tri-theism. But if the primary meaning of a writing is the meaning intended by the writer (as I want to maintain), then John (the historical John) is less vulnerable to that kind of criticism. I need not labor the point since we seem to be in closer agreement regarding it than at first appeared.

May I attempt a kind of brief summing up? The primary claim which John certainly makes is that Jesus shows us what God is like, more clearly and definitively than anything or anyone else: the continuity between the self-expression of God and Jesus is one of complete identity in the incarnation. But does John simply fill out that prologue assertion with the developing preexistence idiom applied reflectively and with midrashic elaboration to episodes and sayings of Jesus' life, or does he actually say something *more,* requiring belief that Christ was himself preexistent and that Jesus was self-consciously incarnate as a historical fact? Even if the hermeneutical answer to this question is more disputed, at least his primary claim is clear enough, however *we* try to restate it.

Many thanks for initiating the discussion. It has helped clarify my own thinking at several points.

With regards and greetings,

James Dunn

16

In Defense of a Methodology

Of all that I have written over the past ten to fifteen years, nothing has provoked such vigorous reaction as *Christology in the Making*.[1] Whether it is that christology is such a central subject for Christian faith, or that I managed to touch some raw nerves, or that I may possibly even have stimulated some fresh lines of inquiry, I am not sure. It is not that the book drew a particularly noteworthy selection of reviews: perhaps predictably, criticism ranged from imputations that I had been too critical to accusations that I had not been critical enough. But reviews are rarely long enough for any critique to be developed or firmly grounded, and though I quite often reply to them personally any fuller response would probably be unfair to most reviewers. But *CiM* has also had the good fortune, or misfortune (I am not sure which), to provoke a fair amount of more detailed response, both in periodical articles and in some recent books which have devoted several pages to critiques of *CiM*. An author who feels he has been unfairly handled in a book review may be best advised to fume quietly to himself or to confine his rejoinder to personal correspondence. But if such fuller critiques have missed key points, despite being fuller, an author may be forgiven for finding it difficult to restrain himself.

This is the position I find myself in and I am grateful to the editor for permitting me to "blow off steam" in what follows. I have in fact been able to respond already to the principal attack on one flank (that in effect I was not critical enough).[2] But criticisms have fallen even thicker and faster on the other flank and these in turn do require some sort of response. I have in mind

1. London: SCM/Philadelphia: Westminster, 1980, subsequently *CiM*.
2. Ch. 18 below.

Originally published in *ExpT* 95: 295-99. Copyright © 1983 by T. & T. Clark and used by permission.

three publications in particular whose critiques, not all from the same perspective, nevertheless share the same basic flaws. These are R. G. Gruenler, *New Approaches to Jesus and the Gospels* (Baker, 1982), especially pp. 88-107, several contributions to the Donald Guthrie Festschrift, *Christ the Lord,* ed. H. H. Rowdon (Inter-Varsity, 1982), and A. T. Hanson, *The Image of the Invisible God* (SCM, 1982), especially chapter 3.

In all three cases basically the same point is made: that my hesitations in tracing the emergence of a clear doctrine of the incarnation of Christ are unfounded; the preexistence of Christ was already clearly in the mind of Paul in several passages; and some would have little or no hesitation in tracing a clear understanding of Christ's "divinity" back to the earliest days of Christianity or to Jesus himself. In each case I have the same complaint: they have not taken seriously enough what I regard and repeatedly stressed to be basic axioms of exegetical method. What I have in mind can be summed up in two phrases — "historical context of meaning" and "conceptuality in transition." Unless these principles are taken with full seriousness a proper exegesis is rendered impossible.

Historical Context of Meaning

To achieve a proper exegesis of a New Testament text we must ask what the writer intended his first readers to hear — that also means, what he could have expected his readers to understand by the language he used, given the way words and concepts were understood individually and in combination within the broader context of thought at that time and within the particular context of the situation in which or for which the text was written. Only when we have some reasonably clear idea of the context of meaning in which the New Testament texts were initially understood can we have any hope of recognizing the distinctive and unique features of these texts which caused them to be treasured and preserved. Let me illustrate this with three examples.

(a) Several contributors to the Guthrie Festschrift argue in effect that Jesus was regarded as divine from very early on because as exalted he was recognized to have divine status and/or because he exercised divine functions. A crucial exegetical question, ignored by them all, however, is: How would this sort of language have been understood in a historical context where similar language was already being used of previous heroes of the faith — notably Enoch and Elijah, but also others, including Abel, Moses, and possibly Melchizedek? For example, Josephus indicates that speculation could be entertained as to whether Moses had been taken or had returned to "the deity" (*Ant.* 3.96f.; 4.326). According to Luke, the Palestinian crowd could readily entertain the notion that Herod Agrippa had been apotheosized into a god (Acts 12:22). The role of Enoch (Gen. 5:24) as one not merely translated to heaven but also transformed into a heavenly being and exercising a role in judgment had already become the subject of much speculation by the time of Jesus (*Jub.* 4:22-23; *1 En.* 12–16; *2 En.* 22:8; *T. Abr.* 11). In recent years we have become aware of the mysterious Melchizedek figure mentioned in one Dead Sea scroll who also is envisaged as a divine being acting at heavenly judge (11QMelch 10). Nor should we ignore the fact that Jesus himself seems to have envisaged the twelve as involved in dispensing the final judgment (Matt. 19:28/Luke 22:30; cf. 1 Cor. 6:2). And within a few decades both Ezra and Baruch were being numbered among those who had been taken up from earth to be preserved in heaven for the consummation (4 Ezra 14:9; *2 Baruch* 13:3; 25:1, etc.).

My question to the contributors to the Guthrie Festschrift is this: How would the language used of Jesus in the middle decades of the first century have been understood when not so very different language was already current in reference to others? If thought of apotheosis, of exaltation, of other individuals exercising such a divine prerogative as judgment, were already being entertained in the first half of the first century, how significant and how distinctive would talk of Jesus' exaltation and heavenly session have seemed to those already familiar with such ideas? My point should not be misrepresented. I am not attempting in any way to diminish or explain away the distinctiveness of the Christian claims for Jesus — such imputations of a hidden agenda to undermine traditional beliefs I find deeply hurtful. Rather my concern is precisely to clarify what *was* the distinctiveness, the real, the historical distinctiveness of these Christian claims. And if the result is that the Christian distinctives as initially formulated appear to be less clearcut, or at a further remove from the fuller christological dogmas of subsequent centuries, that may only be a truer reflection of how Christian thought actually developed, and as such should help us to a clearer perception of the historical link between Jesus of Nazareth and the Christ of dogma. Whereas any attempt to exegete key christological texts by abstracting them from their historical context is almost bound to misconceive the significance of the claims actually being made for Jesus in these earliest years of Christianity and to oversimplify the truth of these claims.

(b) A. T. Hanson's entertaining attack misunderstands several points and in the end descends to point-scoring and in dismissing my findings in the chapter on "Wisdom" manages to ignore completely the issue of first-century context of meaning on which my conclusions entirely turned. It really will not do to speak simply of the "obvious meaning" of a text without reference to the historical context. Obvious — but to whom? It is certainly not a priori obvious that what is "obvious" to us now was equally "obvious" in the context of first-century Hellenistic Judaism. In the event it may prove to be so; but it certainly cannot be assumed. So, in a context where typological or even allegorical interpretation would have been familiar (the identification of what the scriptural text spoke of with a current, eschatological reality), is it really "obvious" "the rock was Christ" (1 Cor. 10:4) refers to the preexistent Christ " 'in, with and under' that rock as the supernatural source of drink" (Hanson, p. 72)? Likewise, to ignore so completely the fact that my discussion of Col. 1:15-20 depends on its Wisdom content and on the significance of the Wisdom allusions within the first-century context of meaning is really to undermine the value of his own critique. Professor Hanson later on shows that he is by no means unaware of the Wisdom background to Col. 1:15-20, but in his critique of *CiM* he plays too much the part of a man who thinks he can win the marathon by joining the race over the last two miles!

Writing with regard to the same text in the Guthrie Festschrift, J. F. Balchin falls prey to the same seductive line of reasoning. "The vast majority of scholars have recognized . . . the plain meaning here is that Christ preexisted the creation of the world . . ." (Rowdon, ed., p. 125; also I. H. Marshall in Rowdon, ed., p. 9). But my question is ignored: Was it equally "plain" to the hymn-writer and its first users, to Paul and his first readers? It may have been, and I have no wish to force the evidence in any direction whatsoever — despite several reviewers' assumption that I was determined to prevent certain meanings emerging. But if writers like ben Sira and Philo used similar language in reference to Wisdom and the divine Logos, without thinking of Wisdom and Logos as "divine beings" or as anything other than a way of speaking of God's immanence, then the search for "plain meaning" has to take that into consideration as a decisive factor in exegesis. Would Paul's readers, whose thought moved within that world of conceptuality, not simply assume that the hymn was speaking of Christ in the same way — especially in view of the more "adoptionist"-like emphasis of the second part of the hymn, which critics have conveniently ignored (*CiM,* pp. 191-93)? The suggestion is certainly open to debate in terms of the first-century context of meaning; but it certainly cannot be treated so dismissively as Balchin and Marshall do.

(c) Most disturbing of all is Gruenler's attempt to preempt the exegesis of various Synoptic texts by application of what he describes as a "phenomenological analysis," which evidently allows the text to be treated in almost total disregard for its historical context. This somehow justifies him in arguing from Jesus' use of "abba" in prayer to God and from Jesus' reference to the Spirit in a passage like Matt. 12:28 that Jesus claimed to be "on a parity with *Abba* and *Pneuma,*" and that he "felt himself equal to God." "And if he is aware of being equal to God, is he also aware of his pre-existence" (pp.

93-95)? What sort of exegesis is this? Is it not even relevant to ask whether that line of argument would have been meaningful to Jesus' contemporaries? What about the adequately well attested fact that there were one or two other charismatic figures active in the Judaism of this period who also addressed God in a similarly intimate manner, quite probably also using "abba" (*CiM*, p. 15)? What does the "phenomenology of persons" say about the prophet who first uttered Isa. 61:1f.: "The Spirit of the Lord God is upon me . . ."? Why, one might wonder, does Gruenler find it so threatening to recognize the prophetic categories which formed one remarkably resilient strand of first-century christology and which must therefore have been of continuing importance and significance for the first Christians (*CiM*, pp. 137-41)? The roots of christology within Jesus' own ministry and teaching have to be eased from the soil of the Synoptic Gospels with much, much more care. Gruenler, by claiming far more than the texts allow, when set within their original context, puts the whole endeavor in disrepute and only succeeds in setting back the task of demonstrating the historical probability that the high christology of subsequent years is continuous with and rooted in Jesus' own self-assertion and self-understanding.

I might simply add that his initial charge, that I rule out of consideration Jesus' own self-understanding as a starting assumption, I regard as a piece of disinformation not worthy of Gruenler's scholarship. That the historical Jesus did not think or speak to himself as a preexistent being is, of course, an exegetical conclusion. An introductory description of the ground actually covered by the investigation should not be read as though it were an original "game plan" for the investigation. As Gruenler must know, the Preface is usually the last thing to be written!

The revived interest in the Bible as literature provides an attractive temptation to abandon or disparage original context of meaning — as though it inevitably meant shutting the text up in the distant past, as though a text severed from historical context can float freely across the stream of time to speak with its own logic to today. The trouble is that a free-floating text severed from its historical context remains floating above history, its meaning to be determined more or less arbitrarily by the context of whoever pulls it to earth to use it. The only defensible check against imposing one's own meaning on a text is the meaning intended by the person whose text it is by virtue of creation or formulation. But that means setting the New Testament writings as wholly as possible within their own first-century context. When we have begun to understand a New Testament text in the sense originally intended, with the force it initially exerted, then we begin to appreciate why it was preserved to become Scripture, and we free it to speak with its proper force. To be thus subservient to the text of the New Testament is fundamental to all teaching and preaching of the New Testament.

Conceptuality in Transition

As is well known, the task of translating from one language to another is never simple. The problem is that words are not single points of meaning, so that each point in one language will have a precise equivalent in the other. Words rather have a range of meaning, and the ranges of meaning of words most nearly equivalent in two languages never fully coincide. In addition, each culture and subculture will have its own patterns and structures, allusions and overtones, idioms and taken-for-granteds which do not match across the boundaries of culture. When we add the dimension of time, the position becomes even more complex, since words change meaning, fresh concepts emerge and develop, others degenerate or disappear, and so on. The consequence is that to ask after historical context of meaning in another culture and age involves a careful locating of words and ideas within the *movement* of the thought of the time. The difficulty of entering empathetically into the thought forms even of Victorian Christianity for late-twentieth-century Christians, or of prewar Nazi Germany for postwar Europeans, is sufficient example of what I mean.

The point is that the first century of our era was no exception. On the contrary, a relatively short span of decades saw the emergence of a whole new religion of international significance (Christianity itself), not to mention the emergence of rabbinic Judaism as the enduring form of the Jewish religion. On any count, all this must have involved a substantial movement of thought, a shaping of concepts and remolding of categories. We can see something of this in the way the concept "Messiah" became particularized (for Christians) by reference to Jesus, redefined by reference to his death, and transformed into a proper name (Jesus Christ). The phrase "the son of man" probably moved from being an indefinite personal reference (somewhat like "one") to a title with apocalyptic significance, to a theological assertion of Christ's humanity. We know that the Christian doctrine of the Trinity evolved over a lengthy period with key words gaining special significance. We can trace with considerable confidence the great burgeoning in the use of Father-Son imagery to describe Jesus' relationship to God as we move from Mark and Q through Matthew to John, or the greater freedom with which Christian writers spoke of Jesus as "God" as we move through the first century and beyond to Ignatius, or the neat transition in Wisdom christology as we move from Q to Matthew (*CiM,* pp. 197-206), or the tremendous blossoming in Jewish angelology in the "intertestamental" period. So we can, even from our perspective about two millennia later, actually see thought in movement, the development of faith, conceptuality in transition. The finding of development in earliest christology is hardly a mere assumption on my part, as some reviewers have suggested: the a priori likelihood is confirmed by good evidence.

However, the task of locating any particular text within such a movement of thought is very difficult. With only occasional access to what must, in the nature of things, have been a much more complex process, we can never be sure whether, for example, some text is an early foreshadowing of a later theme, or constitutes evidence that the theme was already well developed, or indeed whether the text itself is actually later. We have become properly sensitized to the dangers here in one of the debates which have dominated twentieth-century scholarship on early Christianity — the origins of Gnosticism. And New Testament scholars have become accustomed to recognize elements in the New Testament writings which became important to Gnosticism but which in the New Testament writing itself should be described at most as "gnostic" or "proto-gnostic," if the word is to be used at all.

CiM was an attempt to sensitize those concerned with the origins of christology to the same dangers (dangers to proper exegesis, that is). The danger of reading what may have been an early formulation of a theme in the light of its full development in subsequent decades. The danger of reading a text whose terms of reference were in process of transition as though the transition was already complete. Unless we locate ourselves within the *limited horizons* of a particular writer, so far as that is possible, seeing no further than he saw, we cannot achieve a proper exegesis. Unless we wrestle seriously with the phenomena of *conceptuality in transition* we will never escape the danger of reading a text anachronistically.

So I still find myself asking with regard to several Pauline texts: How did Paul intend his words to be understood, given his primarily Jewish mode of thought and the limitations of his own particular horizon? Did he think and speak so clearly of Christ's preexistence as now seems obvious to us from our hindsight perspective? For example, with Gal. 4:4, given the context of meaning outlined in *CiM* (pp. 38-44), and despite Marshall (Rowdon, ed., p. 7) and Hanson (pp. 59-62), I still ask whether Paul did not intend to speak simply of Jesus as one who stood in uniquely intimate relation to God, sent by God with eschatological commission, a person to bring people into similarly intimate relation, a Jew to redeem his fellow Jews. In the case of 1 Cor. 15:44-49 I remain puzzled at Hanson's insistence that "the man from heaven" (v. 47) must refer to Christ as preexistent (pp. 63f., 80), when the whole context has in view the resurrection body and Christ as the first to be raised and as thus providing a pattern for the final resurrection — he is the heavenly man as all the resurrected will be heavenly people (v. 48), that is, by virtue of resurrection (v. 45; cf. Rom. 8:11; Phil. 3:20f.). Even with 2 Cor. 8:9, and once again despite Hanson's dismissive comments, I hardly think the matter is so clearcut as he believes (p. 65). In a letter (or letters) which work(s) regularly with contrasts between weakness leading to death and spiritual treasure and glory, it would not be at all surprising if Paul refers to Christ's weakness and death under the imagery of poverty in contrast to the richness of his intimate *abba* relationship with God, to which the Pauline churches were no stranger (Rom. 8:15-7; Gal. 4:6-7). Historical context must be allowed to determine the probabilities of exegesis more than rhetoric.

I have had to duck more brickbats regarding Phil. 2:6-11 and Col. 1:15-20 than any other texts. Disagreement over exegesis I do not mind. But failure to take into account the considerations which weighed most heavily with me I find harder to excuse. So I simply have to refer my critics back to the not undetailed deliberations which elaborated the likely context of meaning of these passages and posed with some care the conceptuality in transition point. If, for example, Adam christology was as significant a factor in earliest Christian thinking, as I believe I demonstrated, and if it provides the principal context of thought for the Philippian hymn, as I still believe, then the extent to which the Adam language and parallel inform the wording of the hymn needs to be given more consideration than either Marshall or Hanson allows. In particular, what would a Jewish Christian, familiar with the implied contrast between Adam before his fall (Gen. 1:27 — image of God) and fallen Adam (Gen. 5:3 — begetting a son in his own image), make of the contrast between "form of God" and "form of men," "form as a man" (Phil. 2:6-7)? I still remain doubtful as to whether he would have seen an assertion of preexistence necessarily involved in the latter — even though I am sure it was not long before the passage was read that way.

Balchin puts his finger on an important point when he asserts with great conviction that Paul's readers must have understood Col. 1:15-17 as talk of Christ's preexistence: "The dangerous implications would have been obvious to Paul's monotheistic countrymen" (Rowdon, ed., p. 125). Now we know that a threat to Jewish monotheism was perceived by the rabbis, not least from Christian claims regarding Christ — but our evidence indicates that the threat only emerged at the end of the first century and beginning of the second century (cf. particularly John 5:18; 10:33).[3] So far as we can tell, it was only Paul's attitude to the law which put him in bad odor with his countrymen. Even though monotheism was a fundamental axiom of Jewish faith, Paul was never attacked for calling monotheism in question. The obvious deduction from this is that Paul's Wisdom christology was *not* read in the way Balchin suggests. On the contrary, the evidence rather supports my suggestion: that Col. 1:15-20 was *not* read as ascribing preexistence to Christ as such, initially at least. Is this not precisely a classic case of conceptuality in transition — a formulation which gathered meaning and significance to it as Christian understanding of Christ grew and which itself played an important part in that growth of understanding? It would be pleasant to see the actual thesis dis-

3. See ch. 21 below.

cussed rather than the particular suggestions as to how it bears on a passage like the Colossian hymn so cavalierly dismissed.

I do not need to discuss all the points in dispute between *CiM* and these various writers. I am not concerned to defend every exegetical observation I offered. My concern here is more to defend the methodological considerations from which they were derived — particularly those summed up in the phrase "historical context of meaning" and "conceptuality in transition." Of course I may not be reading the context aright, or may be misreading the pace of transition. But that is where I would prefer the argument to focus — on such key issues as the status of the Wisdom figure in pre-Christian Judaism, and on the significance of the same language when first used of Christ.

One final reflection. Few critics seem to recognize the opposite danger — of reading the talk of preexistence in respect of Christ ("a preexistent Being") in a way which actually threatens Christian monotheism. If my investigation made me aware of anything, it is of the very tight course which has to be steered between the Scylla of underestimating the divine in Christ and the Charybdis of undermining Christianity as a monotheistic faith. In steering too wide of the former, more than one self-styled "orthodox" christology has come to grief on the latter. If my exegesis is at all on the right lines, it shows that the writers of the New Testament were a good deal more sensitive to both dangers than they are usually credited with. It also suggests that they would not altogether welcome some of the ways in which their words are read by those who think to defend them!

17

Some Clarifications on Issues of Method
A Reply to Holladay and Segal

I am grateful to Carl Holladay for doing me the honor of using my *Christology in the Making (CiM)* as an occasion to raise some very important methodological issues, and I welcome the opportunity to respond both to him and to Alan Segal's review. Since Segal also presupposes Holladay's critique I will focus primarily on the latter.

Holladay gives a clear and, for the most part, accurate summary of the argument of *CiM*. But he also makes three major criticisms. (a) *CiM* creates a methodological tension between history and theology which it leaves unresolved (p. 65). It looks "more like an exercise in dogmatics based on historical-critical examination of certain canonical texts" (p. 78). (b) "It fails to conceive the world of late antiquity with sufficient breadth, and insufficiently recognizes the extent of interaction between religious traditions within that world" (p. 78). (c) It depends too much on establishing a clear chronology of traditions and writings, "and the result is that the evidence is often forced into a chronological Procrustean bed" (p. 73). "The proper methodological question here is . . . whether the nature of the evidence allows any *termini* to be established with the degree of precision he needs" (p. 78).

As it happens I strongly agree with the main thrust of the methodology Holladay outlines. So much am I in agreement, in fact, that I find a good deal of his critique puzzling and misdirected. The two main points of my counter-critique are: (1) that Holladay, and to some extent Segal also, has misrepre-

Originally published in *Christology and Exegesis: New Approaches*, ed. R. Jewett, *Semeia* 30: 97-104. Copyright © 1985 by Scholars Press and used by permission. Reference is made throughout to C. Holladay, "New Testament Christology: A Consideration of Dunn's *Christology in the Making*," and A. Segal, "Pre-existence and Incarnation: A Response to Dunn and Holladay," pp. 65-82 and 83-95 in the same volume of *Semeia*.

sented the task I set myself in *CiM,* and (2) that he has missed one important qualification which I made in describing my own methodology. I will attempt to pick up other points of criticism from both Holladay and Segal *en passant.*

I

My concern in *CiM* was to trace from "inside," so far as that is possible, the evolution of thought within earliest Christian circles by which the Christian doctrine of incarnation came to expression. The only a priori assumption I made was that there was some evolution, whether an application or adaptation of an already current conceptuality to Jesus, or an evolution within the first century C.E. period itself in which Jesus and/or the first Christians may or may not have played a significant role. It was just that process which I sought to clarify. The points of reference, the texts to be clarified, are the first-century Christian writings — a limited aim, I freely admit (though it engaged me for more than 350 pages). To attempt to trace the history of relevant ideas across the complete spectrum of the Hellenistic and Mesopotamian worlds from say 150 B.C.E. to 100 C.E., using all the available resources of literature, papyrology, art, and epigraphy, is a much vaster task. And however desirable it may be (a "systematic investigation of comparable notions in the world of late antiquity" [p. 78]), it was not the task I set myself. My task was simply that of New Testament exegesis — the attempt to understand the New Testament writers' words as they would have intended, to hear them as their first readers would have heard them. All this I hope I had made sufficiently clear in my introductory statements (*CiM,* 9-10, 13).

In other words, *CiM* was *not* intended as a study of the beginnings of christology as a whole, as Segal seems to think (nor do I find his reformulation of the issue on pp. 84-85 helpful). Nor was there any assumption of a doctrinal uniformity on these points in primitive Christianity — despite Segal's repeated criticism to that effect (my *Unity and Diversity in the New Testament* is usually criticized for overemphasizing the *diversity* of first-century Christianity!). Nor do I think I fall into Tiede's "circular argument" (referred to by Holladay, p. 80), since I did not start by assuming clearly defined christological categories in the New Testament but rather set out to discover how the Christian doctrine of incarnation, whose distinctiveness certainly became more and more clearly defined over the first four centuries of our era, first began to emerge as a distinctive teaching. And the technique followed I would prefer to describe as a survey of current options (categories or concepts) which might be used and/or adapted to make sense of Jesus rather than "a modified titular approach" (Holladay, p. 66), which is appropriate to only two or three chapters of *CiM.*

The task I set myself requires, of course, a very sensitive ear to the first-century context of meaning. I stressed this too, repeatedly (*CiM*, index, "context of meaning"). "To understand the language of the NT in its original intention involves asking where that language came from, what its background was, how it was being understood in the wider usage of the time . . ." (*CiM*, 10). It is here that Holladay's methodological objective and my own are in substantial agreement. I am sure that my ear is still not sensitive enough, that I am not sufficiently immersed in the thought world of late antiquity to catch all the overtones and "taken-for-granteds" which even the moderately well informed would have heard in any statement of the time. But, for better or worse, a clear conclusion did emerge from my study — viz., that the primary context of meaning for most of the key New Testament texts is Hellenistic Judaism. Motifs and conceptuality such as we find expressed in the Roman poets may be part of a much broader background, but such influence as they did exert was mediated through the more proximate world of Hellenistic Judaism, and not, so far as I can tell, directly.

To describe that finding as "an unmistakable bias against pagan traditions" (Holladay, p. 76) is unjustified and potentially mischievous. If the principal "source" and context of earliest Christianity is Judaism (both Palestinian and Hellenistic Judaism), a conclusion to which I find myself increasingly driven, then it is hardly surprising if an investigation of its origins is "conspicuously one-sided" in the proportion of space devoted to "Jewish background." And both Holladay and Segal seem to have confused the point that when I occasionally speak of "popular superstition" it is not intended as a Christian (or Judaeo-Christian) critique of paganism. The critique referred to initially was that of Seneca and Lucian. Plutarch's account of the different ways in which the Osiris myth was demythologized at that time would have served equally well (*De Iside et Osiride* 32ff.); and I acknowledged an equally popular piety within first-century Christianity but concluded that the expressions in the New Testament must be regarded as rather sophisticated (*CiM*, 18, 251f.), though I do not recall using the phrase "respectable sophistication" which Holladay attributes to me (p. 77).

It is unfortunate that so much of Holladay's criticism seems to be directed against the way I set out chapter 2 (13-22) in *CiM*. That was little more than a preliminary and summary statement to illustrate the dimensions of "the first century context of meaning," to indicate the chief areas requiring more detailed analysis, and to show that the title "Son of God" was used with such a broad sweep of reference in the ancient world that its application to Jesus tells us little in and of itself. Even here, I simply have to deny the charge that I was working with a set of "inflexible" categories and "consistently" classified my material as "Jewish" and "Graeco-Roman" (Holladay, pp. 73, 76). It is a factually inaccurate description. And it is a rather serious misrepresentation of the subsequent important discussion of the influences bearing on the language of "wisdom" and "word" which the first Christians inherited in chapters 6 and 7. How anyone can describe, for example, my necessarily brief analysis of Philo's *logos* concept as involving a "sharp dichotomy" between Jewish and Greco-Roman influences which "are never seen to have merged, or even interacted, in any genuine sense" (Holladay, p. 73) remains a puzzle to me. To criticize *CiM* for insufficient breadth in its range of material examined and for insufficient depth of exposure to the world of late antiquity in its totality is one thing. But, when Holladay claims that *CiM* "radically divorce[s] early Christianity from its environment" (p. 76), I think he must have some other book in mind, since my concern throughout *CiM* was to trace the process by which the characteristic Christian view of Christ emerged *within* its environment; and every chapter repeatedly attests the interaction of Christian thought (the New Testament texts) with that environment. That I see that environment primarily as Palestinian and Hellenistic Judaism may provoke the charge that the environment is too limited, but in *CiM* there is nothing of the rigid compartmentalization between Christian, Jewish, and Greco-Roman which Holladay seems to find and which I would criticize as fiercely as he, if it were there. Which brings me to my second point.

II

The chief weakness of Holladay's critique is that he has failed to note the important qualification I made in describing the task of exposing the first-century context of meaning (*CiM,* 14). And since the methodology of *CiM* cannot be fully appreciated apart from that qualification, much of his critique misses the target. The qualification can be summed up in the phrase "limited horizons." By this I mean that it is very easy for us today to envisage that world of late antiquity in *too* broad and unified a sense and to fail to appreciate how similar sounding motifs and conceptions would often carry different overtones and "taken-for-granteds" in cultures and traditions heavily influenced by their own more limited, more national or domestic, cultural context. However far we may think the Hellenization of Jewish thought and religion had already developed by the first century C.E., in Palestine as well as the Diaspora of course, we can hardly deny the distinctive features which continued to mark out that thought and religion within the Mediterranean and Mesopotamian worlds. Nor should we discount, as a methodological a priori, the inevitable corollary that these Jewish distinctives must have modified in one degree or another the ideas, concepts, and language which Jewish writers drew from the common pool of the ancient world.

I also had in mind a second aspect of the "limited horizons" point: viz., that in tracing the evolution of any new motif or idea it is important *not* to read the process of evolution from the perspective of its end, as though that were the only and necessary outcome, which could therefore be discerned as already present implicitly at the earlier stages of the evolution. If our concern is to understand a text in the way its author and first readers would have understood it, then it would be methodologically improper to read that text as it was read 300, 200, 100, or even 50 years later. Now I have no illusions regarding the very great difficulty of this task, of getting back within the limited horizons of particular writers in particular contexts — it may even be impossible beyond specific details. But that is the experiment I undertook.

The difficulty of the task lies in locating particular writings, let alone their motifs, within sufficiently defined dates and locales. And here Holladay is quite right to raise the issue of chronology, as other reviewers have. So let me try to restate the nature of my experiment. I simply asked the question: If, as a working hypothesis, we take the consensus dates for the most relevant documents, what can we deduce from them for the currents and movements of thought which we find in the New Testament texts? And to my surprise (I kid you not), as the study proceeded, a rather striking phenomenon began to emerge, a broad movement in patterns of conceptuality in the middle and second half of the first century, most prominent in Christian writings, which so far as consensus dates go may well have given the lead, but also in other streams of Judaism, particularly apocalyptic and mystical Judaism, and in the emergence of beliefs about the early Gnostic redeemer figures. In other words, it became my own thesis that there was a broader movement, with different traditions interacting in ways that are not always evident on the surface (*CiM*, 259-61), contrary to Holladay's critique. And my suggestion that Christian thought was in the vanguard of that movement is much more tentative than Holladay recognizes, based in large part on the simple observation that the earliest firmly datable documents in which such conceptuality (individualized Son of man, uniquely incarnate Wisdom/Logos) comes to unequivocal expression are Christian. The methodological point about conceptuality in transition and limited horizons is an important aspect of *CiM* which remains valid even if the date sequence of the relevant documents remains finally obscure, though my particular suggestion hardly requires a second-century date for the Similitudes of Enoch, as Segal insists (p. 93).

Holladay notes that "if any genuine conceptual or historical analogue were found to be prior to the Christian formulation of the doctrine of the incarnation, the whole thesis would collapse" (p. 80) — as though that were a criticism of my method. But of course! That is the nature of a truly historical investigation. Such an analogue would become part of the evidence which would have to be reassessed accordingly — just as our picture of pre-70 Judaism has had to be reassessed in the light of the Dead Sea Scrolls. The question I was examining was precisely whether there was something prior to first-century christology which could be called a "genuine conceptual or historical analogue" to the doctrine of the incarnation. My conclusion: that so far as the evidence is concerned, the most plausible hypothesis is that the Christian idea of incarnation emerged in the second half of the first century particularly through the use of wisdom language in reference to Christ. I am gratified that Segal is able to endorse that conclusion as far as he does (Segal, p. 93), though I was surprised that he should think I was advocating "a single historical development of the material" (p. 94), despite my explicitly drawing attention to the diversity of christological formulation in the New Testament writings (CiM, 265-67).

It was the attempt to attune myself to an emerging pattern of conceptuality as it emerged, to follow a train of thought in transition as new formulations came to expression, which explains the line of approach to such key texts as Phil. 2:6-11 and Col. 1:15-20, for which I have been most heavily criticized by reviewers generally. It is not that I have any dogmatic ax to grind; Segal misconceives the point of my quotation from *Unity and Diversity* on *CiM*, 6, and consequently distorts the logic of my discussion (Segal, pp. 83-84). Nor is it the case conversely, that I was "keen to delay" the formulation of the idea of incarnation as such until as late as possible (which would have been a piece of illogical perversity on my part), as Holladay seems to think (p. 74). It was simply that I asked the questions: If Phil. 2:6-11 is so dominated by Adam theology as it appears to be, how would its first readers have understood it? If Col. 1:15-20 is chiefly determined by the category of Jewish Wisdom, and Wisdom was understood within Jewish circles as a way of speaking about God's immanence, what meaning would these verses have had for the first Christian congregations who used them, how would they have understood this identification of Christ as divine wisdom? And my answers tried to take the methodological point about conceptuality in transition and limited horizons as strictly as I could. I am certainly open to the possibility that I have been overstrict in the application of that principle. But I would find it easier to accept the charge from those who recognize the transitional nature of so much of the evidence and who acknowledge the opposite danger of reading too much into a text, where the overtones and "taken-for-granteds" are those of a later perspective.

It is because of such considerations that I find myself at odds at several points with both Segal and Holladay. Segal seems to think that I argue for a Jesus who hinted at his own preexistence and who thought of himself in titular terms as the Son of God (pp. 83, 86). This I find surprising in view of the careful and cautious treatment in *CiM* (26-33) where I draw out what the evidence seems to indicate — a distinctive and even, properly speaking, unique sense of sonship on the part of Jesus — but stress that the evidence does not permit us to say any more with confidence (Segal also ignores my response to Morton Smith on the *abba* question — *CiM*, 27f.). And the assertion that I want "to place everything of importance to christology in Jesus' self-consciousness" (Segal, p. 89) misses the whole point about categories and conceptualities in transition (the careful conclusions drawn on *CiM*, 253-54, hardly warrant the jibe "a catalogue of guesses"). I am equally surprised at Holladay's dismissal of my suggested exegesis of Gal. 4:4-5 as "particularly forced and rendered impossible by the language of verse 6" (p. 74) — but "impossible" is too sweeping a condemnation, surely! I can make my point most simply by asking: What would a Jewish reader have made of similar statements about God sending Elijah on his original mission to Israel and subsequently sending the spirit of Elijah? That the original sending was "from heaven" would hardly be a necessary deduction.

Another aspect of the same methodological issue is the problem of knowing whether and when we should presuppose the existence of earlier versions of the same tradition behind a written tradition preserved for us. This must be the case in at least some instances. But how are we to know? I mean, how are we to know when we have no evidence either in the text itself or in related strands of an earlier formulation of the same tradition? And why should we assume that the written tradition is the "final form" of the tradition, when it is equally possible that a particular text before us was actually the catalyst to a new tradition (albeit using older elements) and that it was preserved precisely because of its ground-breaking character? The principle of "limited horizons" may cut quite deeply. Holladay needs to give more weight to Segal's claim that the first Christians *created* exegetical traditions to make sense of their "historical experience of a dying and reviving messiah" (Segal, pp. 91-92), a claim with which I am in considerable sympathy, as I hope my treatment of such passages as Genesis 2–3; Deut. 6:4; Ps. 2:7; 8:4-6; and Dan. 7:13f., not to mention the whole Wisdom tradition, demonstrates. I did not give enough weight to Psalm 110 or to the title "Lord," in Segal's view, but I explained the reason for that partly in *CiM* (271-72, n. 33) and partly in the early conclusion that the first thought of Christ's preexistence was unlikely to have been a deduction from his exaltation or simply a retrojection of his resurrected state back before his earthly ministry (*CiM*, 63; contrary to Segal, p. 85). In this context, I might simply add, I have no problem with Segal's advocacy of the current social scientific understanding of myth (Segal, pp. 90-91); my point in *CiM* (262-63) was merely that to speak of "the myth of God incarnate" *simpliciter* takes too little account of the extent to which both Jewish Wisdom and Christian writers had effectively demythologized the wisdom imagery they actually used.

III

A final thought on "the unresolved tension between history and theology" (Holladay's first point of criticism). Why should it be assumed that a tension has to be resolved? That tension is present in the New Testament texts and cannot be resolved without doing damage to one or the other aspect (in Segal's terms the tension set up by Christianity's hermeneutical use of the biblical text to understand its historical experience [p. 88]). Nor do I (speaking personally) want to "resolve" that tension in my own study of these texts. I want my study to be as thoroughly historical as it can be, but a merely antiquarian study of the New Testament texts as part of the world of late antiquity, while fascinating for many, would hardly justify the time and energy still poured into it in our universities and seminaries. And however theological I want to be in the questions I put to these texts, a dogmatic use of them which ignores questions of authorial intention and context of meaning I for one have certainly no wish to defend. It is precisely the interaction between the two dimensions of the text, and the two dimensions of the theologian's concern for the text, which gives the whole dialogue of exegesis and interpretation its dynamic, exciting, and perpetually challenging character.

I have not been able to take up all the points raised by Holladay and Segal. I agree with Segal that I should have paid more attention to angelology and regret that Christopher Rowland's work in particular appeared too late for me to take properly into account. And I regret that I missed the work of J. Z. Smith to which Holladay refers on p. 81. I am grateful to them for these and other helpful comments, and above all for stimulating me to clarify my thinking a little further on such important issues of method.

18

Foreword to the Second Edition of
Christology in the Making

The need for a further printing of *Christology in the Making* provides a welcome opportunity to add a fresh Foreword. The opportunity is welcome for several reasons. Not least because it enables me to underline a feature of my writing which perhaps should have been given a clearer expression before this. That is, that I regard any writing (and lecturing) which I do as part of an ongoing dialogue. While striving to put my thoughts and insights in as finished a form as possible, I have never presumed I was giving the final word on a subject. Writing helps me to clarify my own thinking; but my hope is also to help clarify the particular issues and considerations most relevant to these issues for others. Naturally I seek to find answers to my questions and offer up my own conclusions. But not in any attempt to bully readers into agreement: more with the objective of provoking them to respond, to join in the dialogue, in the hope that out of the continuing and larger dialogue a clearer and fuller picture will emerge — for myself as well as for others engaged in the dialogue. *Christology* was itself part of a dialogue on the subject of earliest christology and the doctrine of the incarnation in particular, and certainly provoked a number of responses in reviews, articles, and subsequent monographs. But a dialogue which ends with a single statement and various replies is no dialogue. And with eight years now passed and the first wave (or should I say ripple?) of interest now subsided it is probably just about the right time to attempt to carry forward the dialogue a stage further.

I am glad to make the attempt for three further reasons. First, it is clear from a number of these responses that the objectives and methodology of *Christology* have been often ignored or misunderstood. This suggests that a

---

Originally published in *Christology in the Making* (London: SCM, [2]1989; Grand Rapids: Eerdmans, 1996) xi-xxxix. Copyright © 1989 by SCM and used by permission.

brief restatement of these objectives and methods is desirable and might help promote a fuller understanding and a better dialogue than we have so far achieved. Second, as part of the ongoing dialogue, I naturally wish to respond to my critics — to point out where they have, in my view at least, misperceived my intentions, disregarded key factors which ought to be determinative in the exegesis of important New Testament passages, or shown too little awareness of the historical context out of which such texts came. There are also, of course, weaknesses in my own presentation, which have come to light as a result of the dialogue, as I had hoped, and which I am happy to acknowledge. And third, my own understanding of the meaning and significance of the New Testament data has not, of course, remained static since 1980. The dialogue has helped clarify and crystallize fuller insights into the beginnings of chris-tology, particularly in the area of Johannine christology, and into the continuing considerable importance of what happened in that period for subsequent theology and for Christianity's knowledge and understanding of God.

I

The starting point of *Christology in the Making* was the unassailable observation that the New Testament documents cover an intense period of innovation and/or development in what we now call "christology." Before Jesus, "christology" either did not exist, or existed, properly speaking, only in different forms of "messianic expectation." At the end of that period an advanced and far-reaching christology is already in place, which does not hesitate to speak of Jesus as "God." Before Jesus appeared on the scene we can speak of a wide range of speculation within early Jewish thought about God and particularly about his means of interacting and communicating with his creation and his people. At the end of that period there is a clearly articulated Christian view that much or most of that speculation has come to focus in Jesus Christ in a complete and final way.

In other words, the New Testament covers a period of development and itself constitutes in some measure that development. There is presumably no dispute here. The task I set myself, then, was simply to trace out, as best as possible, the course of that development, without assuming that it was a regular or even development,[1] and without predetermining whether it was an organic

---

1. Some reviewers have criticized me for an over-confident scheme of development based on inevitably uncertain dating of documents. I should make it clear therefore that for the most part I take as my working hypothesis consensus dating for the relevant documents; the only significant dispute would be over the Similitudes of Enoch, though even here my tentative suggestion of a late first-century A.D. date is one which commands wide support — see, e.g., Hurtado (below n. 26), 149, n. 8, and 150, n. 17. See below n. 40 and my response (n. 41); also below n. 81.

development (tree from seed) or an evolutionary development (mutation of species). And the dialogue which has ensued has been most fruitful when it has been clearly perceived that the issue under discussion is about *how quickly* that development proceeded, not about *whether* it happened. I had and have no doubts that "christology" developed very fast indeed, under the massive stimulus of the Christ event (his ministry seen in the light of his death and resurrection). My question was, and is, whether it developed quite so quickly as, for example, Hengel has argued in his influential and otherwise wholly excellent little study on *The Son of God*.[2]

In particular, with the debate about *The Myth of God Incarnate*[3] still very much alive (1978-79), it seemed both wise and desirable to focus this analysis on the emergence of the Christian doctrine of incarnation. Here, too, some kind of development had to be assumed. Whether or not we can properly speak of a concept of "incarnation" already in the thought world of the time, Greco-Roman or Jewish, and if so, in what sense, was obviously one of the questions which required scrutiny. In *Christology* I attempt to avoid prejudging the issue by declining to define the concept of "incarnation" too closely at the start: the word itself indicates with sufficient clarity the area under investigation — some form of "enfleshment" or embodiment — and any narrower definition might have put "off limits" potentially fruitful lines of inquiry.[4] But even so, some form of development must be presupposed — at the very least from a non-Christian (or not yet Christian) concept of "incarnation" to a specifically Christian one, if not from more diverse envisagings of divine embodiment and revelation to the specifically Christian concept of God incarnate in definitive and final form in Christ.

Here again the issue as it was envisaged at the time of writing and as it has come to sharper focus in the ensuing dialogue is the speed of development. There was no question in my mind that the doctrine of incarnation comes to clear expression with the New Testament — certainly at least in a sense which clearly foreshadows the further growth or evolution to the full-blown doctrine of the historic Christian creedal statements. On almost any reckoning, John 1:14 ranks as a classic formulation of the Christian belief in Jesus as incarnate God. Assuming then, as most do, that John's Gospel is one of the latest documents in the New Testament, the question was whether John 1:14 is best understood simply as a variation on an already well formed conception of incarnation or as itself a decisive step forward in the organic

---

2. M. Hengel, *The Son of God: The Origin of Christology and the History of Jewish-Hellenistic Religion* (London: SCM, 1974). It was a particular pleasure that C. F. D. Moule took the point so well in his *JTS* 33 (1982) 258-63 review (p. 261).

3. J. Hick, ed., *The Myth of God Incarnate* (London: SCM, 1977).

4. One of the criticisms levelled at *Christology* was this failure to define the key term. I have attempted to a more careful delineation in chapter 2 above.

growth or evolution of the Christian doctrine. Not whether, but how quickly the (or a) Christian doctrine of incarnation comes to expression within the period and range of Christian teaching spanned by the New Testament documents — that was the question.

Given that (on the basis of John 1:14) we can speak of the "New Testament doctrine of incarnation" and therefore of canonical authority for the doctrine, the question as posed might seem to smack too much of idle academic curiosity. Does it matter whether Jesus believed himself to be "the incarnate Son of God"? Does it matter whether Paul, and other New Testament writers, mark an earlier stage in the development toward the full-blown Christian doctrine, or even stages in diverse developments and trajectories? Others might answer in the negative: it does not matter. For myself it does. It matters what Jesus thought about himself. For if we can uncover something at least of that self-understanding, and if it differs markedly from subsequent Christian doctrine of Christ, then we have discovered a serious self-contradiction at the heart of the Christian doctrine of incarnation itself. For we then have to admit that the doctrine of God submitting himself to the full rigors of historical existence is not after all accessible to historical inquiry. This has been a fundamental issue at the heart of christology in fact from the beginning but most pressingly over the past two hundred years. It will not go away. It matters, too, whether Paul had a doctrine of incarnation. For the Pauline letters are the only New Testament writings which belong indubitably to the first generation of Christianity. And the later we have to postpone the emergence of the Christian doctrine of incarnation the more real becomes the possibility that the doctrine is the product not of organic growth ("development" as from seed to plant), but of grafting a different growth on to the earlier (non-incarnation) stock, or of transmutation into a different species (by "Hellenization," philosophization, or whatever). Besides which, it should matter to Christian theology what Paul, the first great Christian theologian and most influential of all Christian theologians, thought and taught on the subject. Apart from anything else, if there is a clear continuity between the earlier and the later christological formulations, a right understanding of Paul may well help us to a right understanding of the later texts. So I make no apologies for posing the question of how and how quickly the Christian doctrine of the incarnation emerged and developed in the first two or three generations of Christianity.

So much for the chief objective of *Christology in the Making*. As to the *method* of pursuing this objective, that can be most simply focused in two phrases — "historical context of meaning" and "conceptuality in transition." I had hoped that the first of these two in particular would have been clear in *Christology* itself.[5] But evidently not, and it became necessary to spell them out

---

5. See *Christology in the Making*, index, "Context of meaning."

with greater explicitness in "In Defense of a Methodology."[6] Here it must suffice to repeat the central consideration in each case, which, to be sure, follows as a more or less immediate corollary from what has just been said above.

By "historical context of meaning" I have in mind the task of trying to hear the words of the text as the writer of these words intended those for whom he wrote to hear them. That I continue to regard as the primary exegetical (though by no means the only hermeneutical) task confronting the New Testament scholar. Our only real hope of achieving that goal is by setting the text as fully as possible into the historical context within which it was written — both the broader context of the cultural, social, linguistic etc. conditioning factors of the time, and the narrower context of the immediate circumstances of writer and readers which must have determined in greater or less degree the choice of themes and formulation of the writing. In all this the text *by itself* cannot provide sufficient check on what we hear it saying; for there are so many allusions and taken-for-granteds which depend on the fact that the document is a *historical* document (a document of a particular time and place in history), which would be wholly apparent to writer and reader of the time, and on which much of its meaning depends, but which are now hidden from us by our remoteness from that historical context. The text *does* provide the check; but it is only the text set *within its historical context* which can do so adequately.

If then it is legitimate, as it surely is, to distinguish, for example, what Jesus said about himself from what subsequent believers said about him, or between what Paul intended to say and what later Christian theology made of his words, it is important and necessary for the exegete to undertake that difficult task of getting behind subsequent interpretation and later context to the original intention behind these words within their original context. Apart from anything else, the very fact that these words were preserved and cherished is indication enough that their original impact was significant and substantial. It cannot be unimportant for Christian theology to uncover as far as possible that original "word of God" encounter which provided the decisive impulse toward their being reckoned in due course as holy Scripture.[7]

The character of historical process and the implication of "development" is that meaning changes and that language even while remaining the same gathers to itself new meaning. Here the problem of relativity is as serious for historical study as it is for scientific study. We the observers do not occupy a fixed point from which to observe other fixed points in time and space. We

---

6. Reprinted as chapter 17 above. In other discussions, including *New Testament Theology in Dialogue,* ed. with J. Mackey (London: SPCK, 1988) 16, and *The Living Word* (London: SCM, 1988) 11-12, I have put the same point in terms of the "limited horizons" of the biblical writer (as of anyone writing within history). See also below n. 49.

7. See further my *Living Word* (above n. 6).

are caught within the flux of history, as were those to whom we look back. To abstract the New Testament documents from history is not to exempt them from the problem of relativity; it simply makes them historical vagrants and mercenaries, vulnerable to anyone who takes them over. But to set them within their original historical contexts underlines and brings to focus the problem of relativity for the exegete. At least we can get some sort of "fix" on the problem. For we can take cognizance of the relative character of our own (twentieth-century) context; and by study of the first-century period we can gain some overall impression of the social, cultural, intellectual flux from within which the New Testament writings emerged, and which they bring to expression in their own terms. In other words, the problem of historical relativity is itself relative to the nature of the subject matter under investigation and the amount of information available to us relating to both the subject matter and its historical context.

All this I try to encapsulate in the phrase "conceptuality in transition." I use "conceptuality" for the obvious reason already noted that words change in meaning even when the words themselves remain unchanged. The task of historical exegesis requires a recognition that important concepts will often be in transition. They may be on their way to becoming something else, something slightly but perhaps significantly different in the meaning they are heard to express. This will be all the more likely in the case of documents (e.g., Paul's letters) which were recognized to have more than merely occasional significance from the first, and especially where they deal with a subject (christology) of particular and growing significance for the movement (Christianity) within which these documents first emerged. For not all concepts are in transition to the same degree; conceptuality in transition is also a relative phenomenon. It is this fact which gives us some hope both of recognizing the more volatile concepts and of gaining at least a relative "fix" on them through correlating them with the less volatile concepts. In short, the task of tracing out the development of the Christian doctrine of the incarnation may not be quite so difficult as at first appeared.

If then we bring together the task of historical exegesis, the problem of historical relativity, and the fact of christology developing in or into a concept of incarnation, it becomes an inescapable part of that task to try to get inside the process of development. Here the important work is "inside." To trace the course(s) of developing christology from *outside* is comparatively easy, especially when we allow ourselves to see the end from the beginning and read the intermediate stages in the light of that end. But genuinely to locate oneself *within* the process, and genuinely to take seriously the fact of conceptuality in transition, is to limit oneself to the possibilities available at the time of writing, to take a stand within the inevitably limited horizon of writer and readers, who did not and could not know how the words written were going to be taken and understood in subsequent years and decades. This is *not* to say that subsequent understanding of a text should be debarred from contributing to a historical exegesis of that text. As a general rule one may assume a continuity between earlier and later understandings within a community which cherished the text. In which case the understanding which evolved must be able to illuminate the understanding from which it evolved. But it does mean that subsequent understanding should not be used as a grid to predetermine the scope of exegesis, to limit or elaborate what the text within its original context was intended or heard to say simply by reference to the subsequent understanding. Evaluation of the legitimacy of subsequent interpretation is in large part the responsibility of the subsequent generation, but partly also depends on the meaning of the text intended by the person whose text it primarily is, the one who wrote it — always allowing for the fact that contexts of meaning change and words and concepts evolve, and such evaluation has to take all that into account. If scripture is to have a continuing critical (canonical) role, that depends in part at least on allowing the meaning intended by Paul etc., and heard by those for whom they wrote, to exercise a critical function in relation to the use subsequently made of what they wrote.[8] This must suffice as a restatement of the objectives and methodology of *Christology*. I wish I could feel confident that any further dialogue about *Christology* or the issues it deals with would take account of these stated objectives and methodology. But experience so far has not been very encouraging. Nevertheless, may the dialogue continue.

II

In attempting to take the dialogue further it becomes necessary to respond to those who have offered criticism of *Christology in the Making*. This is both a welcome and an unwelcome task: welcome because it allows me to clarify my position on disputed points, to set the record straight where appropriate, to restate the most pertinent concerns in controverted passages, and to acknowledge fresh indebtedness on issues which required more analysis than they received in *Christology;* unwelcome because it means having to express some sharpness of disagreement and counter-criticism in a public forum with several whom I count as good friends and with whom I would much rather have out such points of dispute in private, at least in the first instance.[9]

---

8. See further my "Levels of Canonical Authority," *HBT* 4 (1982) 13-60, reprinted in *Living Word* (above n. 6) 141-92.
9. Regrettably the dialogue has been almost exclusively an English-language dialogue.

I have in mind, first of all, those alluded to earlier — those who have failed, in my view, to take account of the methodological points elaborated above. For instance, several critics and exegetes seem to have thought that a straightforward appeal to the "obvious" or "plain meaning" of the text was sufficient response to my discussion of such passages as Col. 1:15-20.[10] But "obvious" to whom? "Plain" in what context? Obvious to *us*, who look back to the text with the much developed hindsight of nearly two millennia. But the question is surely whether that understanding of the text was equally as obvious to *the original author and readers*, equally obvious when the text is set into the context within which it was framed. Where we are attempting to locate an original insight or statement within a process of developing conceptuality, that is surely a necessary and important question for historical exegesis.

For example, the talk of God sending his Son in Gal. 4:4 and Rom. 8:3. Anyone reading these texts in the light of the similar sounding and prominent Johannine formula would naturally understand Paul (or the formulation he draws on) to imply a sending from heaven.[11] But given (1) that John's formulation may well belong to his more developed (and later) christology, (2) that talk of God sending could be used equally for the commissioning of a prophet as of the sending of an angelic being from heaven,[12] and (3) that the thrust of the passage is directed to Jesus' mission of redemptive death, I still find myself asking whether the formula would have been intended or initially heard to carry with it the inevitable implication of the preexistence of the Son. Even the emphasis in both passages on the Son's humanity (to use later terminology) may not be sufficient to clinch the point (sent his Son as a man),[13] for the force of the intermediate phrases in both instances is to point up the significance of the Son's *death,* not the mode of his being sent. So Gal. 4:4 may quite properly be paraphrased: God sent his Son, a typical human

10. See, e.g., J. F. Balchin, "Paul, Wisdom and Christ," in *Christ the Lord: Studies in Christology Presented to D. Guthrie* (Leicester: Inter-Varsity, 1982) 204-19 (here particularly p. 215); D. Hagner, *Reformed Journal* 32 (1982) 19-20; A. T. Hanson, *The Image of the Invisible God* (London: SCM, 1982), especially ch. 3; L. Morris, "The Emergence of the Doctrine of the Incarnation," *Themelios* 8/1 (1982) 15-19, though in much more measured tone (here p. 19); Moule (above n. 2), 260.

11. Cf., e.g., Hanson (above n. 10), 59-62; I. H. Marshall, " 'Incarnational Christology' in the New Testament," in *Christ the Lord* (above n. 10) 7-8; C. E. B. Cranfield, "Some Comments on Professor J. D. G. Dunn's *Christology in the Making* with Special Reference to the Evidence of the Epistle to the Romans," in *The Glory of Christ in the New Testament: Studies in Christology in Memory of G. B. Caird,* ed. L. D. Hurst and N. T. Wright (Oxford: Clarendon, 1982) 271.

12. See *Christology in the Making,* 38-39. Contrast R. T. France, "The Worship of Jesus: A Neglected Factor in Christological Debate?" in *Christ the Lord* (above n. 10) 34 — "The idea of Jesus' 'being sent' . . . inevitably implies his pre-existence"; similarly R. P. Martin, "Some Reflections on New Testament Hymns," in the same volume, p. 48.

13. See above n. 11.

being,[14] a Jew, that he might redeem Jews, and that we (human beings) might become sons (note the a b b a structure). And the point of the equivalent phrase in Rom. 8:3 ("in the likeness of sinful flesh and as a sacrifice for sin") is not to emphasize the Son's humanity so much as to emphasize the degree of his identification with *sinful* humanity, so that his death might function as a sin offering and effective condemnation of *sin*.

Another example is 1 Cor. 15:44-49. It is clear that several of my critics simply take it for granted that "the man from heaven" (15:47) must and can only be understood in terms of Christ's preexistence.[15] This, I must confess, I find astonishing. For the whole thrust of the argument in context is focused on the resurrection and is built on a sequence of parallel contrasts — physical/ spiritual, earthly/heavenly, first man/second man — where it is clear enough that the second half of each contrast refers to the resurrection state. This includes the description of the second man as "from heaven," for it is precisely his heavenly image which provides the pattern for the resurrection state of others (15:49). Paul has already made this clear earlier in the same chapter: Christ in his resurrection is the "firstfruits of those who have fallen asleep"; *as risen* he is the archetype of resurrected humanity (15:20-23). And in the immediate context Paul has been at some pains (for whatever reason) to insist that the spiritual does *not* precede the psychical (15:46). Hence in relation to (first) Adam, Christ is *last* Adam (15:45). It would throw his argument into complete confusion if he was understood to mean that "the *second* man from heaven" was actually the preexistent one, and therefore actually first, *before* Adam. In the other key texts I am more hesitant, with more open questions than firm answers. But here I must say there does not seem to be much room for dispute. And if commentators can read such a clearly eschatological/ resurrection text as a reference to Christ's preexistence it simply underlines the danger we run in this most sensitive of subjects of reading the text with the presuppositions of subsequently developed dogmas and of failing to let the context (in this case the context of the argument itself) determine our exegesis.

The dialogue has probably been more fierce over the christological hymns, Phil. 2:6-11 and Col. 1:15-20, than anywhere else. It is clear from comment and conversation that some regard the questions I pose and suggestions I make in relation to these texts as insubstantial and wholly implausible, if not absurd, if not perverse.[16] I am mildly surprised at this and wonder if

14. See *Christology in the Making*, 40.

15. Hanson (above n. 10), 63-64, 80; R. P. Martin, *The Spirit and the Congregation: Studies in 1 Corinthians 12–15* (Grand Rapids: Eerdmans, 1984) 153-54.

16. Several have characterized the exegesis offered as "minimizing" or "minimalist" or "reductionist" — e.g., T. Weinandy, *TS* 42 (1981) 293-95, here 295; Hagner (above n. 10), 19; C. Stead, *Religious Studies* 18 (1982) 96; L. Sabourin, *Religious Studies Bulletin* 3 (1983) 113;

the weight of my questions and tentativeness of my suggestions have been adequately appreciated. (For those who think the meaning "obvious," alternative suggestions may be tiresome and irritating and deserve to be dismissed as quickly as possible.) But perhaps I can try once more and focus on the heart of the exegetical issues as I see them.

In the case of Phil. 2:6-11 it still seems to me that of all the contexts or paradigms of thought within which the text may be read in the endeavor of historical exegesis (Son of God, Servant, Wisdom, Gnostic redeemer myth), the one which provides the most coherent and most complete (the claim is relative) reading is Adam christology.

v. 6a　　— in the form of God (cf. Gen. 1:27);[17]

v. 6b　　— tempted to grasp equality with God (cf. Gen. 3:5);[18]

v. 7　　— enslavement to corruption and sin — humanity as it now is (cf. Gen. 2:19, 22-24; Ps. 8:5a; Wis. 2:23; Rom. 8:3; Gal. 4:4; Heb. 2:7a, 9a);[19]

v. 8　　— submission to death (cf. Wis. 2:24; Rom. 5:12-21; 7:7-11; 1 Cor. 15:21-22);

vv. 9-11 — exalted and glorified (cf. Ps. 8:5b-6; 1 Cor. 15:27, 45; Heb. 2:7b-8, 9b.[20]

Others may "fit" better at individual points; but I still await a demonstration of another paradigm which "fits" so well over all. Nor do I think it enough to attempt a rebuttal by showing how poorly the paradigm actually fits the

---

and R. G. Hamerton-Kelly in *Virginia Seminary Journal* (December 1983), 29-30. "The height of implausibility . . . a crude adoptionism" — Hanson (above n. 10), 74-75. B. Demarest thinks that "exegetical and theological fidelity have been sacrificed on the altar of scholarly novelty" (*Journal of the Evangelical Theological Society* 25 [1982] 108). Contrast the sympathetic reviews by H. Wansbrough in *The Tablet* 7 (1981) and D. Senior in *CBQ* 44 (1982) 320-22, and more qualified criticism by D. M. Smith on the same point, in *Interpretation* 37 (1982) 293.

17. The case for recognizing the synonymity of *eikon* and *morphē* is conveniently summarized by Kim (below n. 51), 200ff.

18. A reference to Gen. 3:5 still seems to me to shed most light on this disputed phrase. In the recent most thorough discussion of the debate by N. T. Wright, "*harpagmos* and the Meaning of Philippians 2.5-11," *JTS* 37 (1986) 321-52, no real consideration is given to the factors which weighed most heavily with me (see *Christology in the Making,* 116 and 311, n. 73). Cf. Wanamaker (below n. 21), 187-88.

19. Despite Marshall (above n. 11), 6, v. 7 seems to make sufficient sense as an elaboration of the contrast of Adam's fallen state — including the recapitulative "And being found in form as man" (see further *Christology in the Making,* 117-18).

20. The interweaving of Ps. 8 and Ps. 110:1 is a feature of Adam christology as we find it in Paul; see *Christology in the Making,* 108ff. I thus find surprising the judgment of L. J. Kreitzer, *Jesus and God in Paul's Eschatology* (JSNTSS 19; Sheffield: JSOT, 1987) 224f., n. 72, that vv. 9-11 "breaks the mould of any Adamic motif." Contrast Fossum (below n. 60), 293-97 (particularly p. 296). Kreitzer has, however, taken the "context of meaning" point (p. 247, n. 104).

case of Jesus.[21] As I tried to make clear in *Christology*,[22] the Philippians hymn is an attempt to read the life and work of Christ through the grid of Adam theology; the points of stress within the hymn are there simply because the "fit" is not exact or precise (though still closer than other suggested paradigms). It is the Adamic *significance* of Christ which the hymn brings out, of his life and death and exaltation (as in Romans 5, 1 Corinthians 15, and Hebrews 2), not necessarily a chronological parallel phase by phase. This is why it still seems to me an open question as to whether the hymn contains any thought of preexistence, *other than the preexistence involved in the paradigm* — that is, the metahistorical character of the Adam myth. The point of the hymn is the epochal significance of the Christ-event, as determinative for humankind as the "event" of Adam's creation and fall, with the question of preexistence rather more an irrelevance and distraction than a help to interpretation.[23] It is because Christ by his life, death, and resurrection has so completely reversed the catastrophe of Adam, has done so by the acceptance of death by choice rather than as punishment, and has thus completed the role of dominion over all things originally intended for Adam, that the paradigm is so inviting, and so "fitting" in the first place.

With Col. 1:15-20 the issues of "context of meaning" and "conceptuality in transition" become most acute. Hopefully, for the purposes of continuing the dialogue, it can be accepted that the language used of Christ in this hymn is determined by the application of Wisdom categories to him, or by the identification of Christ with Wisdom if you like. This claim was

---

21. As in the most thorough recent attempt to refute the Adam christology exegesis, by C. A. Wanamaker, "Philippians 2:6-11: Son of God or Adamic Christology?" *NTS* 33 (1987) 179-93; here pp. 182-83. In such a brief response I must, regrettably, confine myself to the specific point at which Wanamaker has criticized my *Christology in the Making*. Wanamaker's suggestion (192, n. 14) that I have changed my mind on the subject of Adam christology fails to appreciate that *Christology* at this point deals with the full sweep of Adam christology, including the stage prior to Christ's exaltation in which his Adamic role is one of identification with fallen Adam ("sinful flesh," Rom. 8:3 and Gal. 4:4) prior to his role as "last (= resurrected) Adam" (1 Cor. 15:45). Likewise L. D. Hurst, "Re-enter the Pre-existent Christ in Philippians 2:5-11," *NTS* 32 (1986) 449-57, has not really taken my point that the language including the aorists is drawn from the Adam story and gains its force by relation to (and contrast with) that story. If the language has point as a *contrast* to the Adam tale, it does not require a precise one-to-one reference to Christ's life or elements therein. More general characteristics can then be gathered into language whose form is determined primarily by the Adam reference, Christ's story told in the "shape" of Adam's in order to show how the damage was undone.

22. *Christology in the Making*, 119-20.

23. It might be pointed out that a Jesus who makes an Adamic choice is more of a model for Christian behavior (Phil. 2:1-13) then a preexistent Christ; but that would be to broaden the discussion beyond what is appropriate here. I suspect the same is true of 2 Cor. 8:9. R. P. Martin, *2 Corinthians* (WBC 40; Dallas: Word, 1986) 263, rejects my line of inquiry cursorily but does not engage with the considerations which still seem to me to carry some weight; here I may simply refer to chapter 16 above, pp. 276-77.

documented in sufficient detail in *Christology*[24] and is not the issue in dispute. The issues are twofold: What was the understanding of Wisdom within Judaism prior to this use of it in reference to Christ? And what is the significance of its use in reference to Christ?[25]

On the first I remain persuaded that the Wisdom figure in pre-Christian Jewish writing functions within the context of Jewish monotheism and would be understood by the great bulk of Jews as poetical description of divine immanence, of God's self-revelation and interaction with his creation and his people; it was a way of speaking of divine agency rather than of a divine agent distinct from God in ontological terms. I do not want to become embroiled in debate on this particular issue here, since it would become too involved and since the case set out in *Christology* I regard as still sound.[26] Let it suffice to say that this is at least a plausible context of meaning for the Colossian hymn; that is to say, it is at least quite likely that in reading Col. 1:15-20 Paul and his readers had in mind the understanding of Wisdom as a vivid personification of God's immanence.

But if that *was* the context of meaning, then how would the hymn have been understood? *Not* as an identification of Jesus with a divine being or agent independent of or distinct from God. But more likely in parallel to the way ben Sira and Baruch identified Wisdom with the Torah (Sir. 24:23; Bar. 4:1) — that is, as a way of expressing the divine significance of Jesus, that the Creator God had revealed himself and his divine wisdom in and through Jesus as nowhere else. But this is where the difficulty of locating the text within a developing "conceptuality in transition" becomes so difficult. With Col. 1:15-20 are we still at the beginning of the transition from poetic personification to Jesus understood as "God," or are we already some way into the transition? Some think the answer obvious: it is Christ, Jesus Messiah, to whom is attributed a role in creation. But is that so clear? Or is this basically a further

24. *Christology in the Making,* 165-66, 189-93.

25. Since there seems to have been some confusion on the point, may I simply note: I do not question that the Colossian hymn speaks of the preexistence of Christ; my question is what that means; my answer, that it is the preexistence of Wisdom which is attributed to Christ.

26. *Christology in the Making,* 168-76. I am encouraged by support on this point from L. W. Hurtado, *One God, One Lord: Early Christian Devotion and Ancient Jewish Monotheism* (London: SCM/Philadelphia: Fortress, 1988) ch. 2, particularly pp. 46-48. Hurtado criticizes particularly Fossum (below n. 60) at this point, but his reference to Fossum is incorrect. Equal criticism can, however, be leveled at A. J. Hultgren, *Christ and His Benefits: Christology and Redemption in the New Testament* (Philadelphia: Fortress, 1987) 7, who fails to appreciate the richness and vigor of the poetical imagery used by the Jewish wisdom writers. Nor am I sure what R. H. Fuller, "The Theology of Jesus or Christology? An Evaluation of the Recent Discussion," *Semeia* 30 (1984) 105-16, means by his distinction of Wisdom as "an aspect within the very being of God" (109). I agree, of course, that the Wisdom language invites resolution in terms of some kind of distinction in God, but that it was *perceived* to do so, experienced as a possible embarrassment for monotheism, is something which only emerged later — partly, I would suggest, as a result of using the language of a historical person, Jesus.

example of the vigorous poetic imagery of Wisdom applied to Jesus? The fact that the language could be used of Jesus without any perceived threat to monotheism is surely significant here (cf. 1 Cor. 8:6).[27] As also the fact that the same hymn goes on to speak of "God in all his fullness choosing to dwell in Christ" and of his preeminence being the consequence of his resurrection (Col. 1:18-19).[28]

I hope I am not being perverse or unnecessarily awkward. But it does still seem to me that there are legitimate questions here. I do not advocate my suggested exegesis as though that is necessarily the correct one, even as historical exegesis. But it surely cannot be simply dismissed or ruled out of order by anyone who recognizes the relevance and importance of the "context of meaning" and "conceptuality in transition" issues and who allows the possibility that Jewish understanding of Wisdom had not yet moved beyond the character of poetic personification.

Probably the most striking example of failure to take account of historical context of meaning is the assumption made by several critics that the exaltation of Jesus would have been understood to carry with it the clear implication of Christ's divine status and preexistence.[29] Such an assumption seems to ignore completely the fact that in the Judaism of the time several historical figures were being spoken of in terms of exaltation and of exercising functions hitherto attributed to God alone without similar implications being drawn — for example, Enoch, Elijah, Abel, Moses, and possibly Melchizedek. The issue is more complex, as we shall see later. All I ask here is whether it is so clear as some evidently think that talk of Jesus' exaltation and sharing in God's judgment would *ipso facto* carry with it thought of Christ's divinity and preexistence. After all, Jewish writing toward the end of the first century could still speak of Ezra and Baruch being taken up from earth to heaven

---

27. Balchin (above n. 10) follows the logic of "the plain meaning" by arguing that "The dangerous implications would have been obvious to Paul's monotheistic countrymen" (p. 215). He has no evidence for the assertion. On the contrary, it is the lack of such evidence and the fact that language like Col. 1:15ff. could be used of Christ without any sense of threat to Jewish monotheism at that stage, which continues to reinforce my serious doubts that "the plain meaning" is the meaning first intended and understood. Similarly with D. Brown, *The Divine Trinity* (London: Duckworth, 1985), who criticizes me for ignoring "the possibility that Paul may have attributed pre-existence to Christ without realizing all its implications" (p. 157). But implications as perceived by whom and when? Implications are as relative as the language and concepts used.

28. These latter points have not been addressed by critics who have assumed my questions and suggestions could be answered simply by reference to the first half of the hymn. See also my *Dialogue* (above n. 6), 54-64. Similar points could be made with reference to Heb. 1:3-4, but my exegesis of that passage has not drawn much fire, and see now L. D. Hurst, "The Christology of Hebrews 1 and 2," in *The Glory of Christ* (see above n. 11), 151-64.

29. In chapter 16 above, p. 271, I refer particularly to several contributors to the Guthrie Festschrift (above n. 10). See also Cranfield (above n. 11), 274.

without any such implications crossing the horizon (4 Ezra 14:9; *2 Bar.* 13:3, etc.). And the (final?) saying of Q could envisage the twelve participating in final judgment, where it would be ridiculous to read in any idea of them thereby being understood as divine (Matt. 19:28/Luke 22:30; cf. 1 Cor. 6:2). So too the argument that Jesus is divine because he forgave sins or pronounced them forgiven (Mark 2:5-10) must reckon with similar authority being exercised by his disciples (according to John 20:23).[30] Even in the case of the exalted Jesus dispensing the Spirit (Acts 2:33), it has to be recalled that this function of Christ is understood by Luke as fulfillment of the Baptist's expectation of an unknown (but apparently not divine)[31] coming one (Acts 1:5; Luke 3:16).[32]

More recently a critic boldly asserts that the term "Son of God" and the concept of "preexistence" belong together in the New Testament ("the two cannot be separated").[33] As a description of Johannine christology this is a wholly legitimate summary, but as a general description of "New Testament christology" it begs far too many questions and ignores the range of meaning and application for language of divine sonship in Jewish as well as the wider thought forms of the times.[34] Still more striking is the claim: "The idea of apotheosis was acceptable to pagans of the centuries before and after Christ, but to one who has lived in the light of the OT can it be anything but a nonsense?"[35] This has point only if we take "apotheosis" in a strict sense. But the plain fact is that there were not a few Jews at the time of Jesus to whom the concept of apotheosis, or at least transformation into heavenly being, was by no means a nonsense. We need not depend on the disreputable case of Herod Agrippa (Acts 12:22). Enoch and Elijah had both been taken to heaven according to OT tradition (Gen. 5:24; 2 Kgs. 2:11), and speculation regarding Enoch gave a major emphasis to the idea of such a transformation (*Jub.* 4:22-23; *1 En.* 12–16; *2 En.* 22:8). Similarly with regard to Adam in

30. For the wilder arguments of R. Gruenler, *New Approaches to Jesus and the Gospels* (Grand Rapids: Baker, 1982), which do not warrant the title "exegesis," I must be content simply to refer to my response in chapter 16 above, pp. 273-74. Equally implausible is the argument of P. B. Payne, "Jesus' Implicit Claim to Deity in His Parables," *Trinity Journal* 2 (1981) 3-23, that because Jesus in his parables used imagery which in the OT refers to God he meant it to refer to himself and therefore thought of himself in some sense as God — a double non-sequitur. However, since it is not, properly speaking, part of the dialogue with *Christology in the Making,* I will simply refer to my brief comments on it in chapter 2 above (p. 38).

31. "The thong of whose sandals I am not worthy to untie" (Luke 3:16) presumably indicates a difference in status of degree rather than of kind; to deny, as though thinkable, what would be regarded as unthinkable (the comparability of status of a human being and a divine figure) would be a mark of impiety, not of humility.

32. *Pace* M. M. B. Turner, "The Spirit of Christ and Christology," in *Christ the Lord* (above n. 10), 168-90 (particularly 182-83).

33. K. Runia, *The Present-Day Christological Debate* (Leicester: Inter-Varsity, 1984) 93.

34. See, e.g., *Christology in the Making,* ch. 1.

35. Cranfield, "Comments" (above n. 11), 275.

the *Testament of Abraham* 11, not to mention Isaiah in the (probably Christian) *Ascension of Isaiah* (particularly 9:30). In 2 Macc. 15:13 Jeremiah appears in a vision as one "distinguished by his gray hair and authority, and of marvelous majesty and authority." And according to Josephus there was speculation as to whether Moses had been taken or had returned to the "the deity" (*Ant.* 3.96f; 4.326).[36] This is the historical context within which emerged the particular claims of christology (arising out of the resurrection of Christ). To disregard that context so completely leaves any argument which does so without exegetical credibility and undermines any Christian apologetic using such an argument.

If some have failed to grasp the method used in *Christology in the Making* and what it means for exegesis, others seem to have misunderstood its objective. In one case[37] the brief review description fits quite well a principal emphasis of my earlier *Unity and Diversity in the New Testament*.[38] But it bears little resemblance to *Christology*. So much so that I am still not sure which of the two volumes the reviewer intended to describe.[39]

Much more serious and damaging has been the double critique of Carl Holladay, first in his *JBL* review, and then in a followup article in *NovT*.[40] I have already replied in some detail[41] and will have to refer those interested in a more detailed response to that article with its regrettably necessary somewhat forthright counter-critique. Here I will confine myself to one of Holladay's main points, which has been echoed more recently by Hurtado.[42] The charge is (in Hurtado's terms) that I arbitrarily and incorrectly ignored the pagan religious traditions of the Greco-Roman period, a charge to which I am vulnerable particularly because I dated the emergence of the Christian doctrine of the incarnation late in the first century C.E., when there would

36. See further Hurtado (above n. 26), 56-63.

37. G. L. Bray, "Recent Trends in Christology," *Themelios* 12/2 (1987) 52-56 (here p. 53).

38. *Unity and Diversity in the New Testament* (London: SCM, 1977).

39. L. E. Keck, "Toward the Renewal of New Testament Christology," *NTS* 32 (1986) 362-77, warns that "inquiring who first spoke of Christ's pre-existence is no substitute for trying to understand what doing so entails" (p. 374). I should not assume, however, that this is aimed at my *Christology*, since one of my concerns throughout is precisely "to understand what" use of preexistence language for Christ "entails."

40. *JBL* 101 (1982); "New Testament Christology: A Consideration of Dunn's *Christology in the Making*," *NovT* 25 (1983) 257-78, reprinted in *Christology and Exegesis: New Approaches*, ed. R. Jewett, *Semeia* 30 (1984) 65-82 (I cite the title as given in the *Semeia* volume). The contribution by A. Segal in the same volume, "Pre-existence and Incarnation: A Response to Dunn and Holladay," 83-95, presupposes Holladay's critique, is also weakened by a less than adequate appreciation of the scope and objective of *Christology in the Making* (83-85), and fails to appreciate the nuances of a "conceptuality in transition" ("Dunn wants to place everything of importance to christology in Jesus' self-consciousness," 89).

41. Chapter 18 above.

42. *One God* (see above n. 26), 6.

have been several decades during which Christian thinking in this area could have been directly influenced by pagan cults and myths.

Were the point simply that I had not provided anything like a thorough investigation of what we may call here simply "pagan parallels," it is, of course, wholly accurate. But that was *not* my objective. Nor was I attempting some grandiose overview of how divine-human interaction was conceived in the world of antiquity.[43] However desirable such an overview, it is not in my competency to provide it. My concern in *Christology* was, and is, much more limited: to trace the emergence of the Christian idea of incarnation *from inside* (not the emergence of the concept of "incarnation" per se); to follow the course of development (whether organic or evolutionary), as best as possible, whereby the concept of Christ's incarnation came to conscious expression in Christian thought.[44] As a student of the New Testament, not unnaturally, it was primarily an exegetical task I set myself — the task of exegeting the most important New Testament passages on the subject.

That involved no "bias against pagan traditions"[45] — another charge I found puzzling and misdirected.[46] On the contrary, chapter 2 draws on such traditions to demonstrate how broadly consistent within Greco-Roman as well as Jewish circles was the context of meaning of the key concept "son of God." And I find it difficult to understand how Holladay could accuse me of radically divorcing early Christianity from its environment[47] when the discussion of (probably) the most important chapters, 6 and 7, is very much about a Hellenistic-Jewish *sophia* and *logos* speculation which demonstrated to what considerable degree Hellenistic Judaism was part of and indebted to the broader Hellenistic thought world. At this point I really did begin to wonder

43. "It makes no concerted effort at systematic investigation of comparable notions in the world of late antiquity" (Holladay, 78).

44. I can see now that my italicization of the final sentence of §3.5 of *Christology in the Making* (p. 22) may have been misleading on this point; and for this I apologize. The aim of §3 should have been clear, however (it is repeated in the next sentence). The summary of §32.1 (*Christology,* 351-53) would probably reinforce the misunderstanding, but is intended, of course, as a summary of the study actually carried out. Readers should therefore note that the first of the agenda questions asked on pp. 5-6 of *Christology* is more circumscribed than at first appears by the fact that I regard the primary context for earliest Christianity as Judaism, including Hellenistic Judaism. See also chapter 2 above.

45. Holladay (above n. 40), p. 76.

46. Perhaps I should repeat that my occasional reference to "popular superstition" was not intended as a Christian "put-down" (a similar criticism is made by F. M. Young in *Theology* 84 [1981] 304), but as an echo of a common attitude among intellectuals in the Greco-Roman world. Cf. for example G. W. Bowersock, "Greek Intellectuals and the Imperial Cult in the Second Century A.D.," in *Le culte des souverains dans l'Empire Romain* (Geneva, 1973) 179-206: "As far as can be told, in the age from Augustus to Constantine, no person in the Roman empire addressed a prayer to a monarch, alive or dead" (p. 180); "Domitian's claim to be *deus* was a genuine outrage" (p. 199). Note also *Christology in the Making,* 251-52.

47. Holladay (above n. 40), 76.

whether Holladay had some other book in mind, since the book he was criticizing seemed to bear so little resemblance to what I wrote, or whether he had read much beyond chapter 2![48]

"Context of meaning," of course, does not imply that every religious attitude, practice, and form wherever expressed in the ancient world may have had equal influence on earliest Christianity. It hardly needs arguing that there will have been a more immediate context of meaning within the much broader context of meaning. In the case of Christianity that more immediate context is certainly Judaism, including Hellenistic Judaism. This is quickly and fully borne out by each of the lines of inquiry pursued in the chapters of *Christology in the Making*. I do not mind confessing that it was principally because the emergence of the Christian doctrine of incarnation, as expressed in the New Testament texts, found such ready and such complete explanation within that context (however the exegetical issues of texts like Col. 1:15-20 are resolved) that it seemed unnecessary and superfluous (not least given the length of the book) to look further.[49] In such study as I made of the broader context I found no cause even to suspect that there might have been any other or more direct influence.[50] Nor have I had my attention drawn, by Holladay or Hurtado, to any other more direct influence from "pagan cults and myths" (that is, other than through Hellenistic Judaism). I am certainly open to persuasion on the subject and would willingly discuss potentially significant texts like Justin, *Apologia* 1.20-22. But so far no one has tried to persuade me — by documented evidence at least.

A major problem about having to complete a manuscript and go to press is that new items of major relevance come to hand in the period between the completion of the manuscript and its publication. Reviewers, if they so choose, can then indulge in some point-scoring by observing that the later volume has not taken note of the earlier publication. Thankfully I did not suffer too much on that account. Alternatively there are books which appear after one's own but which propose alternative theses or marshal other material of such relevance to one's own discussion that one cannot but regret having been unable

48. According to his *JBL* review (above n. 40), "Non-NT texts from Jewish and Greco-Roman backgrounds are treated, but only indirectly" (pp. 610-11). I accept the reference to Greco-Roman texts as fair comment. For the rest, words fail me!

49. In chapter 16 above, pp. 275-78, I express the point in terms of the "limited horizons" of the first Christian writers in contrast to the unlimited overview possible to us of later generations. The point is well taken by P. R. Keifert, "Interpretive Paradigms: A Proposal Concerning New Testament Christology," *Semeia* 30 (1984) 203-14 (here 206-7). See also above n. 6.

50. The preliminary survey summarized in *Christology in the Making*, 19-22, provided little encouragement to look in another direction. Of course I took fully into account the main hypothesis of the past two or three generations — viz., the Gnostic Redeemer myth (see the index of *Christology*).

to take fuller account of them before letting one's own manuscript go. But such is the nature of the dialogue by article and book, and the possibility of continuing the dialogue here at least enables me to make some amends in at least two cases.

I have in mind first S. Kim's *The Origin of Paul's Gospel.*[51] Kim's thesis provides a welcome reassertion of the importance of Paul's conversion, or shall we say simply, Damascus road experience, as a central and formative influence on Paul's theology. The only trouble is that he "goes over the top." For he not only maintains that central features of Paul's christology and soteriology were derived from the Damascus road event, but he is even prepared to argue that they were formed to a considerable extent in that event itself. Where this bears on the discussion of my *Christology* is in the considerable amount Kim builds on the "image" language of 2 Cor. 4:4. Paul not only recognized Christ to be "the image of the invisible God," but also as "the em-bodi-ment [*sic*] of the divine glory"; and the experience must immediately have led Paul to Dan. 7:13, because he too had seen a heavenly figure "like a son of man" just as Daniel did.[52] But the logic is not entirely sound. Others saw visions of glorious figures (angels, Enoch, Adam, etc.) without the corollary of divinity being drawn, as we have already noted. And Kim's treatment of Dan. 7:13 takes no account of the considerations which proved decisive for me in chapter 3 of *Christology.*[53] Even with the "image" language itself (2 Cor. 4:4) it is by no means so clear that the thought is of (divine) Wisdom rather than of (human) Adam, given that the context has in view a growing Christian conformity to that image (2 Cor. 3:18), which seems to tie in much more closely to the Adam christology of Rom. 8:29 and 1 Cor. 15:45-49. Kim in fact seems to be in some danger of amalgamating a number of different motifs into another of those twentieth-century constructs (like the Gnostic Redeemer myth or the "divine man") so beloved of scholars looking for a source for earliest Christian theology. Without for a moment denying that the Damascus road encounter was a formative factor of the first significance in shaping Paul's theology, or that there is a very complex interrelation between the different motifs just mentioned, I remain unpersuaded by Kim's attempt to concertina such major developments in first-century christology into that single event.[54]

51. *The Origin of Paul's Gospel* (WUNT 2/4; Tübingen: Mohr, 1981).
52. Kim (above n. 51), 226, 227, 251.
53. Of course Kim did not have *Christology in the Making* to hand either. But it is somewhat surprising that in his later monograph, *"The 'Son of Man'" as the Son of God* (WUNT 30; Tübingen: Mohr, 1983), he pays no attention whatsoever to *Christology,* or, much more important, to the discussion by M. Casey, *The Son of Man: The Interpretation and Influence of Daniel 7* (London: SPCK, 1980).
54. See further my critique of Kim in "'A Light to the Gentiles': The Significance of the Damascus Road Christophany for Paul," in *The Glory of Christ* (see above n. 11) 251-66.

My principal regret with regard to *Christology* is that I had been unable to take proper account of the work of Christopher Rowland. I should have been alive to his Cambridge Ph.D. thesis (1974),[55] as Kim was, but his 1979 and 1980 articles[56] only reached me when the manuscript was complete and at proof stage (in pre-word-processor days that meant a text incapable of significant revision), and the major publication which emerged from his thesis did not appear till 1982.[57] This meant that I also failed to give enough attention to an important strand in Jewish apocalyptic and merkabah mysticism in which visions of a glorious archangel are prominent.[58] The point is that the christological issue can no longer be posed simply in terms of whether Christ was thought of as an angel.[59] Nor is it simply a question of whether the exalted Jesus was seen in angelomorphic terms, as is clearly the case in the vision of Rev. 1:13-16. The importance of Rowland's work has been to raise the question as to whether there was already in pre-Christian Judaism some kind of bifurcation in the conception of God. In particular, the similarity in description between Ezek. 1:26 (God) on the one hand, and Ezek. 8:2 and Dan. 10:5-6 (a glorious angel) on the other, suggests as one possibility a readiness on the part of at least some to envisage a merging, or transfer, of divine attributes between God and a grand vizier angel, or a "splitting in the way in which divine functions are described."[60] All this would make excellent sense as the context of meaning of Rev. 1:13-14, with its merging of features from the Ezekiel 1 and Daniel 10 visions as well as from both figures of the Dan. 7:9-14 vision ("one like a son of man," *and* ancient of days — hair like pure white wool).[61]

As should be already clear, I have found this whole line of investigation very fruitful, and it has continued to influence my own further studies in the area of earliest christology, as I shall indicate in the next section. A full discussion of Rowland's and Fossum's work is beyond the scope of this chapter, but a few brief comments are probably in order. Three main questions arise. (1) How significant is it that the clearest evidence of influence from this strand of Jewish conceptuality comes in Revelation — itself one of the latest of the New Testament writings? Does it indicate a very early stage in

55. *The Influence of the First Chapter of Ezekiel on Jewish and Early Christian Literature.*
56. See *Christology in the Making,* 392.
57. *The Open Heaven: A Study of Apocalyptic in Judaism and Early Christianity* (London: SPCK, 1982).
58. I. Gruenwald, *Apocalyptic and Merkabah Mysticism* (Leiden: Brill, 1980), also reached me too late; as also R. Bauckham, "The Worship of Jesus in Apocalyptic Christianity," *NTS* 27 (1980-81) 322-41.
59. Hurtado (above n. 26), 73, justifiably criticizes me on this score.
60. Rowland, *Heaven* (above n. 57) 94-113 (here p. 96). See also J. E. Fossum, *The Name of God and the Angel of the Lord* (WUNT 36; Tübingen: Mohr, 1985).
61. The feature is consistent with others in Revelation — particularly the fact that the Lamb shares the throne (7:17; 22:1) and that both the Lord God and the soon coming Christ call themselves "Alpha and Omega" (1:8; 22:13).

developing christology, or another expression of the very vigorous movement of thought in this area which seems to have characterized both Jewish and Christian understanding of divine self-revelation particularly in the decades following the disaster of A.D. 70?[62] (2) How much of the similarity of language used of glorious figures who appear in apocalyptic and mystical visions is due to the fact that there was, perhaps inevitably, a limited stock of imagery available for such descriptions? In other words, may it not be that the similarity of language betokens nothing more than a common dependence on a limited number of traditional formulas or hallowed phrases used in the literary description of such visions, "a cliche-like description of a heavenly being"?[63] To what extent in these descriptions was there a deep reflection on the being of God, rather than conformity to a genre pattern? I do not pretend to know the answers to these questions, but I do think they have to be asked, and if necessary left open.[64] The last question raises another line of questioning. (3) Does the language used in these visions, or the appearance of an angel "in whom God's name dwells," really signify a bifurcation in God within the conceptuality of pre-Christian Judaism?[65] Can we, should we, recognize some sort of diversification within the divine unity, a kind of "binitarianism" already in Jewish thought before christology as such emerged? Alternatively expressed, is Rev. 1:13-14 simply a further expression of the sort of thing that had been happening for some time in Jewish apocalyptic and mysticism, or does it mark some new stage or departure or quantum leap, in that this language was now being used of one who had lived on earth within living memory? The question is similar to that which has to be posed with regard particularly to the figure of Wisdom in pre-Christian Judaism. And I suspect the answer is the same: that for Jews sensitive of the need to maintain their monotheism within a polytheistic world, such language was not perceived as a threat to their fundamental confession that "The Lord our God is one Lord" (Deut. 6:4).[66] It is to Hurtado's credit that he has seen and discussed the issue so

---

62. See *Christology in the Making*, §3. Fossum (above n. 60) assembles the material for his discussion from such a broad canvas of time and context that it is very difficult to draw him into a dialogue on development and on conceptuality in transition.

63. W. Zimmerli, *Ezekiel 1* (Hermeneia; Philadelphia: Fortress, 1979) 236, cited by Hurtado (above n. 26), 76.

64. Cf. Bauckham (above n. 58): "the glory of all angels to some extent resembles the glory of their Maker" (327).

65. E.g., in *Apoc. Abr.* the angel Jaoel, "a power by virtue of the ineffable name that dwells in me" (10:9) and described in the same sort of powerful imagery (11:2), is also noted as worshiping God (17:2, 6ff.).

66. Rowland argues the parallel with Jewish Wisdom speculation the other way: "What we have here is the beginning of a hypostatic development similar to that connected with divine attributes like God's word and wisdom" (*Heaven,* above n. 57, p. 100). But I suspect that Jewish monotheists would have found the talk of "hypostatic development" meaningless and denied what it attempts to affirm.

much in these terms, and I find myself very much in sympathy with his main conclusions.[67]

We will have to return to the subject below. But perhaps we may conclude here by simply noting that the angelomorphic description of the exalted Christ, which is certainly a feature of Revelation and which certainly came to powerful lasting expression in the Byzantine Pantocrator, does not seem otherwise to have provided the high road for developing christological thought in the intervening period.

III

Since the first edition of *Christology* my understanding of the beginnings of christology has itself developed and become further clarified — not least as a consequence of having had to interact with the critical responses discussed above. The value of dialogue is in part that it forces dialogue partners to sharpen their insights, to reformulate points which have miscarried or been misunderstood, and to tackle issues which they had previously left fuzzy. But in part also that it requires revision of previously inadequate formulations and opens the mind to fresh insights and to alternative or complementary or fuller perspectives. This I regard as the value and necessity of the collegial enterprise of scholarship and, if it does not sound too pretentious, of the common search for truth. In the present case I can briefly indicate three developments in my own understanding of "Christology in the Making" which should now be incorporated into *Christology in the Making* to provide a more complete and up-to-date expression of my views.

It soon became clear to me that I had given too little attention to John's Gospel. I had been too easily content to conclude that with John 1:14 the idea of incarnation had been clearly expressed, so that after a careful study of that verse in context there was little need for a fuller investigation of John's Gospel. The decisive step had been taken, and as a New Testament investigation the study of the emergence of the doctrine of incarnation was more or less complete. The question is certainly raised as to how the Fourth Evangelist held together the Wisdom/Logos christology of the Prologue and the Son of God christology of the rest of the Gospel,[68] but left hanging. That is obviously unsatisfactory, and the lingering dissatisfaction on this point, compounded with the sharpened perspective provided by Gruenwald and Rowland, pointed the way forward.[69]

---

67. Hurtado (above n. 26), ch. 4, with critique of Rowland and Fossum on pp. 85-90.
68. See *Christology in the Making,* 244-45.
69. What follows is a summary of the main line of argument in chapter 21 below.

Part of the context of meaning of the Fourth Gospel is provided by the visionary and speculative concerns of Jewish apocalypse and mysticism. At this period there was considerable interest in the possibility of gaining heavenly knowledge through visions and ascents to heaven. Such ascents are attributed to Enoch, Moses, Abraham, Adam, Levi, Baruch, and Isaiah.[70] And the practice of merkabah mysticism, particularly the desire to experience for oneself a mystical ascent to or revelation of the throne of God, is too well attested for the first-century period to be ignored.[71] A similar concern is reflected in the Fourth Gospel: both in the repeated inquiry as to Jesus' origin — the Evangelist's answer, of course, is "from heaven" (see particularly 6:41-42; 7:27-29, 42, 52; 8:23; 9:29; 19:9) — and in the distinctively Johannine emphasis on Jesus as the revealer of heavenly knowledge, both as the Son of Man who has come down from heaven (3:12-13; 6:61-62) and the Son of God sent from heaven (1:17-18, 49-51; 3:10-13, 32; 7:16-18, etc.). John's objective at this point is clearly to focus such yearnings on Jesus: he alone has seen God and can thus make him known (1:18); the true Israelite will recognize that the Son of man is the only link between heaven and earth (1:47-51); "no one has ascended into heaven but he who descended from heaven, the Son of man" (3:13); "he who comes from heaven is above all and bears witness to what he has seen and heard" (3:31-32); no one has seen the Father except he who is from God; he has seen the Father" (6:45-46); etc. Here the language of divine agency[72] is centered on Christ in an exclusive way as a major point of Christian polemic, apologetic, or evangelism.

What also becomes clear is that John is using this complex of motifs in order to present Jesus as the self-revelation of God. The exclusiveness of the claim made for Christ's revelatory significance means that he also transcends such other claimants to heavenly knowledge and divine agency by the uniqueness of his relationship with the Father and by the closeness of continuity between the Father and the Son. He and the Father are one (10:30). To see him is to see the Father (12:45; 14:9). He embodies the glory of God (1:14; 12:41). He utters the divine "I am" (particularly 8:28, 58; 13:19). The Son's obedience to the Father is not so much a way of expressing his subordination to God, as though that were already an issue; it is more a way of expressing the authority and validity of the Son's revelation of the Father, the continuity between the Father and the Son (5:17; 10:28-29; 14:10).[73]

But this is simply to elaborate in other terms what the Prologue says by

---

70. Details in chapter 20 below, p. 359.

71. Details in chapter 20 below, pp. 359-61.

72. See particularly J. A. Bühner, *Der Gesandte und sein Weg im 4. Evangelium* (Tübingen: Mohr, 1977).

73. Cf. particularly M. L. Appold, *The Oneness Motif in the Fourth Gospel* (WUNT 1; Tübingen: Mohr, 1976).

means of its Wisdom/Logos language: as the incarnate Logos Jesus is the self-expression of God, God's own "self-exegesis" to his human creatures (1:18); as the Son of God he reveals the Father. In other words the question left hanging at the end of the brief study of John's Gospel in *Christology* about the relation between the Wisdom/Logos christology of the Prologue and the Son of God christology elsewhere in the Gospel can be resolved. *Not* by concluding that they are two divergent and incompatible christologies, but by recognizing that in the Fourth Evangelist's hands they are mutually complementary. Behind the Son language of John is not a concern to distinguish Jesus from God, by subordination or however. It is not a concern with relationship between the Father and the Son in that sense. The concern is rather to make clear that the Son is the authentic, the only authentic representation of God to humankind. He is God's wisdom/self-revelation incarnate. "The Fourth Evangelist really did intend his Gospel to be read through the window of the prologue."[74] To avoid confusion, therefore, it would be better to speak of the Johannine Christ as the incarnation of *God,* as God making himself known in human flesh, not as the incarnation of the Son of God (which seems to be saying something other).[75]

It also becomes clear from John's Gospel, to a degree I had not appreciated when I wrote *Christology,* that the main issue at that period was monotheism. Was Christianity a monotheistic faith from the beginning?[76] The question arises precisely because the development of christology was part of (a) broader movement(s) of thought within the Judaism of the first century and early second-century period. As we can now see, such reflection about translated patriarchs, glorious angels, and heavenly wisdom was bound, sooner or later, to put severe strain on Jewish monotheism, on the fundamental Jewish belief in the oneness of God. But when did that strain become apparent, and when did it become severe? I still see no evidence from the period prior to the end of the first century that Jews in general, including Christian Jews, perceived it as a threat to their monotheistic faith; and I am delighted to find Hurtado in agreement.[77] Patriarchs were glorified, not deified; the glorious

74. Chapter 20 below, p. 370. P. Schoonenberg uses this as a springboard for further theological reflection in his Bellarmine Lecture, "A Sapiental Reading of John's Prologue: Some Reflections on Views of Reginald Fuller and James Dunn," *Theology Digest* 33 (1986) 403-21.

75. For Matthew I may refer to an important thesis of one of my postgraduates, David Kupp, *Matthew's Emmanuel* (Cambridge: Cambridge University, 1996).

76. Hence the title of the article which was my first attempt to reorder the findings of *Christology in the Making* as a way of answering this question — "Was Christianity a Monotheistic Faith from the Beginning?" (chapter 20 below). The importance of the issue came home to me particularly in my debate with M. Wiles (chapter 15 above).

77. This, indeed, is one of Hurtado's main theses (above n. 26). In distinction from my *Christology in the Making* he limits his discussion to "the very first few years of Christianity, when it was thoroughly dominated by Jews and functioned as a sect of ancient Judaism" (p. 6). That is a description which actually takes us more or less up to the end of the first century, at

angel forbade worship or joined in the worship; Wisdom was domesticated as Israel's Torah. Similarly in Paul: Jesus is Lord, but God is still his God ("the God and Father of our Lord Jesus Christ"); his super-exaltation is "to the glory of God the Father" (Phil. 2:11); he can be confessed as mediator in creation in the same breath as the confession that God is one (1 Cor. 8:6); he is divine Wisdom, firstborn from the dead, indwelled by God — all in one hymn (Col. 1:15-20).[78] All this makes me question whether it is historically justified to speak of a binitarianism or bifurcation in the conception of God in Jewish thought in the period prior to the end of the first century A.D. Here again the "conceptuality in transition" point needs to be taken with all seriousness. We may say where certain trends were leading — or, to be more accurate, where certain trends in the event led. That tells us nothing of the self-understanding involved at the different stages within these trends. And the crucial point for us is that at no time prior to the end of the first century, so far as we can tell, was there any sense of mutual incompatibility or self-contradiction within the Jewish and earliest Christian understanding of God and of the various forms of divine agency.

It is equally clear, however, that such strains were becoming apparent at the end of the first century. 4 Ezra 8:20-21 seems to be directed against claims to be able to see God and describe God's throne; the rabbinic polemic against angelology probably goes back to our period; there are explicit cautionary notes concerning the chariot chapter in the Mishnah; and the apostasy of Elisha ben Abuyah in recognizing a second divine power in heaven, thus denying the unity of God, is remembered as a notorious episode from this period in rabbinic tradition.[79] Here too, however, the most striking attestation comes in the Fourth Gospel. For it is precisely the Johannine claim that Jesus, as the incarnate self-revelation of God, can himself be called "God" which evidently proved unacceptable to "the Jews" of John's time (John 5:18; 10:33).[80]

---

least so far as the New Testament documents themselves are concerned. So far as I can see, it was only when monotheism was perceived to have become an issue that the final split between Christianity and *rabbinic* Judaism became inevitable and unavoidable.

78. Contrast again Balchin (above n. 27).

79. Details in chapter 21 below, pp. 360-61.

80. I am not really persuaded by Hurtado's argument that the Christian mutation of the ancient understanding of divine agency had a "binitarian shape" more or less from the first (above n. 26, pp. 99-114). For all that there was praise, invocation, acclamation of the exalted Christ from very early on, it is less clear that we can speak of *worship* of Christ as such prior to, significantly, the Fourth Gospel (John 20:28) and Revelation (Rev. 5:8, 11-14, etc.). The earlier devotional practices were evidently not yet seen as a qualification, or threat to monotheism; that presumably means that they were still understood by Christian and other Jews as within the bounds of what was acceptable — a transmutation under way, to be sure, but whether already deserving the description "binitarian" is another question. That apart, I naturally welcome Hurtado's emphasis on the importance and theology-generative character of the earliest Christians' religious experience (114-24, particularly 121), conducive as it is to the main theme of my *Jesus and the Spirit* (London: SCM, 1975).

It would appear then that the period between the Jewish revolts (A.D. 70-132) saw an escalation or intensification in Jewish (including Jewish-Christian) reflection on knowledge of God and divine agency — including talk of glorious angels bearing the divine name, the quest for heavenly ascent and vision of the divine throne, further speculation about the manlike figure in Daniel 7,[81] and the developing Christian devotion to Jesus and reflection on the divine significance of Jesus.[82] The rabbis in the post-70 decades began to see this exploration of the limits of acceptable monotheism as no longer acceptable, as increasingly a threat to the unity of God. And this seems to have been a major factor in their successful attempt to define Judaism much more tightly and to draw a much tighter boundary round Judaism thus redefined. What needs to be remembered here, however, is that what was thereby excluded or put under heavy suspicion was not simply emerging Christianity but also these other strains of apocalyptic and mystical Judaism. The Christian assessment of Jesus by John belongs within a broader spectrum of Judaism, where such exploration of ways of conceptualizing God's self-revelation was acceptable and not perceived as a threat to God's oneness. But it also belongs to that transition of conceptuality and understanding where the strongest voices within Judaism were beginning to see such theological and spiritual innovation as just such a threat.

At the same time it has to be made clear that the Fourth Evangelist himself would not have shared that view. He evidently continued to believe, as those before him, that such reflection was consistent with Jewish monotheism. Even such talk applied to one who had been alive just sixty or seventy years ago need not be seen as a threat to God's unity. If this thesis is correct it brings to focus several points of considerable importance. A make-or-break issue between emerging rabbinic Judaism and emergent Christianity was the significance attributed to Jesus, in particular the conviction on the part of the rabbis that Christian claims for Jesus were now becoming too much of a threat to the primary Jewish confession that God is one. Within the post-70 context of broader Jewish speculation the exclusive claims made particularly by the Fourth Evangelist and his circle were seen as too adventurous or too irresponsible to be tolerated; it had to become a choice between living as a Jew and affirming such claims for Christ. John himself, however, saw the claims he expressed as simply a focusing of these other speculations on Jesus and as no more a threat to monotheism than they had been previously. His chris-

81. I include here not only 4 Ezra 13, but also John's Gospel and Revelation, and probably *1 En.* 37–72; the degree to which the Son of man speculation of the Similitudes of Enoch "fits" within the other Son of man speculation which we know belongs to that period strongly suggests that *1 En.* 37–72 should likewise be dated to this period — that is, post 70 (see above n. 1).

82. Is it significant that at about the same time the emperor Domitian caused outrage by claiming to be *deus* rather than *divus* (see Bowersock, above n. 46, 198-99)?

tology was still essentially an elaboration of Wisdom christology — Christ as
the embodiment (incarnation) of God's self-revelation.[83]

If there is anything in this then it has important corollaries for our
understanding of the continuing development of christology in the period
following John, and indeed for our understanding of the classic doctrines of
God and Christ. The first great christological battle of the Christian period
was not over docetism (Ignatius) or modalism (Tertullian); it was over monotheism. The issue was whether in applying such earlier speculation about
divine revelation to Christ, and thus developing it further, Christianity had
moved beyond the bounds of acceptable diversity within Jewish monotheism
— whether, in a word, Christianity was still after all a monotheistic faith. As
we have just noted, the dominant Jewish view was that Christianity had lost
this struggle; it had succumbed to an unacceptable view of God; it was no
longer monotheistic; it believed that there were two divine powers in heaven;
it was (together with other Jewish subgroups) now a Jewish heresy. But in
Christian eyes the battle which the Fourth Gospel represents was a victory
for monotheism — for monotheism redefined, but monotheism nonetheless.
Christ was the incarnate Logos, a self-manifestation of God, the one God
insofar as he could make himself known in human flesh — not the incarnation
of a divine power other than God. Christianity was still monotheistic; the only
difference was the belief that this God had manifested himself in and as human
flesh; this Jesus now provided a definitive "window" into the one God; he
was (and is) "God" as the self-manifestation of God, not as one somehow
other than God.

It is of crucial importance to Christianity that this issue was the first
major christological dispute to be resolved, that Christianity, at least as represented by John, faced up to this challenge to its self-understanding and
resolved it within a monotheistic framework. The claim, of course, is still
disputed by both Jews and Islam, for whom Christianity is irretrievably polytheistic, or at least bitheistic or tritheistic — believing in two or three gods.
But in the face of the temptation to abandon monotheism and the charges that
it had done so, Christianity continued to maintain that its belief in Christ
amounted only to an accommodation within earlier monotheistic faith, or,
more precisely, a fuller appreciation of monotheism in the light of God's
self-revelation in Christ. This battle over monotheism has been largely lost
sight of in studies of the early christological debates, partly because it falls

---

83. Against Wiles, then (see chapter 15 above, pp. 261-63, 265-67), I want to emphasize,
more than I do in *Christology in the Making,* the continuity between the Fourth Evangelist's
christology and both what preceded John — here I am close to J. A. T. Robinson, "Dunn on
John," *Theology* 85 (1982) 332-38 — and the "orthodox" christology which built on John. But
see also M. Wiles, "Person or Personification? A Patristic Debate about Logos," in *The Glory
of Christ* (above n. 11) 281-89.

awkwardly into the gap between the New Testament and the patristic era, and partly because it was regarded as having been already won and settled by the subsequent apologists.[84] That presumably is why the first internal debates which capture the attention in the second and third centuries are those which take for granted the deity of Christ (docetism and modalism), and why Logos christology is the high road of developing Christian orthodoxy.

The importance of this issue (Christianity as monotheistic) having been faced and won is, not least, that it enables us the better to understand the later developments in christological dogma. For it was only at Nicea that the hitherto dominant Logos christology gave way to the dominance of Son of God language. With Logos christology the emphasis is essentially the same as that in John's Gospel — on the *continuity* between the Father and the Son, since the Son is the Word, the self-expression of God. With that emphasis having become established beyond peradventure, that is, christology as an expression of Christian monotheism, the debate could move on to the tricky question of the *relationship* between the Father and the Son. But this is a shift of emphasis, not any kind of abandoning of the monotheistic position already so firmly established. The point can often be lost sight of (like the earlier debate about monotheism) and attention be focused too quickly on the awkwardness and, to our eyes, artificiality of the Nicene and subsequent creedal formulations. And an emphasis on Christ as the Son, independent of that earlier Logos christology, can easily become in effect an expression of the very bitheism or tritheism of which Judaism and Islam accuse Christianity. It is of crucial importance for a right appreciation of Christian orthodoxy, therefore, to bear in mind that Father/Son trinitarian language has to be read and understood *within the context of Christian monotheism.* If the creedal Son of God language is not understood as an expression of Logos christology, it is misunderstood.[85]

A final point of importance is the bearing of all this back on the interpretation of the same key New Testament christological texts which provided the focus of *Christology in the Making* and which have been so much at the center of the continuing dialogue. What the dialogue soon brought home to me with increasing strength is the serious danger to Christian monotheism unperceived by several at least of my critics. The importance of setting these texts within the historical context of meaning and of recognizing conceptuality in transition is indicated by the correlative recognition that these developments

84. I have in view the internal debates within Christian self-understanding. The Jewish-Christian option of Jesus as prophet or adoptionism was regarded (no longer) as a viable option for Christian faith and treated as a heresy. That is, options which might have made possible the continued unity of Jew and Christian were dismissed in mutual recrimination and in charge and countercharge of heresy.

85. The point is developed in chapter 15 above, pp. 264-69.

in earliest christology took place within and as an expression of Jewish-Christian monotheism. In contrast, the too quick resort to the "obvious" or "plain" meaning actually becomes in some cases a resort to a form of bitheism or tritheism. So, for example, the assumption that the Logos of John 1:1 can be substituted by "Christ,"[86] or the argument that Col. 1:15 would have been intended by Paul as a description of Christ, that is, of Jesus Messiah.[87] In contrast, classic orthodoxy is that Jesus Christ is he whom the Word of God *became* in the incarnation. The mistake, or so it seems to me, is the equivalent of treating "person" in the trinitarian formula ("one substance, three persons") as "person" in the sense that we now understand "person," or, more to the point, in the way that Jesus of Nazareth was a person. If the preexistent Word of God, the Son of God, is a person in that sense, then Christianity is unavoidably tritheistic.[88] And if we take texts like Col. 1:15ff. as straightforward descriptions of the Jesus who came from Nazareth, we are committed to an interpretation of that text which has broken clearly and irrevocably from monotheism. Likewise if we assume that the Father/Son language of John's Gospel has in view more the relationship between the Father and the Son (of Nicene and post-Nicene concern) than the continuity of Logos christology (of pre-Nicene concern) we lose sight of the primary monotheistic control which prevents such language slipping into polytheism.

Not for the first time, then, I find that a careful exegesis of scripture, which takes the text with full seriousness in its historical context and which has seemed to some an abandoning of cherished orthodoxies, is actually more faithful to scripture, and in this case to trinitarian orthodoxy, than some of those who have leveled such criticisms. The ironic fact is that disregard for questions of context of meaning and conceptuality in transition has in some cases resulted in the defense or affirmation of a christology at odds with that of the later creeds. What has been understood as a defense of orthodoxy against the apparent reductionism of *Christology in the Making,* has become, irony of ironies, a statement which subsequently would have been regarded as heresy.

Well now, that should be enough for the moment to provoke another round of dialogue — if anyone bothers to read this. Let us hope so, for I still do not regard this as in any sense a final word on the subject and am quite confident that I have still much to learn in this whole area. The first round of debate has been personally highly profitable in instructing, correcting, and enlarging my own theological thinking. I look forward to the next round with keen anticipation.

---

86. *The Living Bible* translation.

87. Marshall does not hesitate to speak of Christ as a "pre-existent Being" (above n. 11, 9, 13) or as "a personal agent of creation alongside the Father" (*Trinity Journal* 2 [1981] 245).

88. This point was brought home to me by G. W. H. Lampe, *God as Spirit* (Oxford: Clarendon, 1977) 135-36. In the same connection Schoonenberg (above n. 74) refers to K. Rahner, *The Trinity* (New York: Herder, 1970) 105-15.

19

Was Christianity a Monotheistic Faith
from the Beginning?

I

Students of the New Testament will be familiar with the influential hypothesis from the first half of this century usually known as the Gnostic redeemer myth. This was the thesis, associated particularly with the name of R. Bultmann, that already in the pre-Christian period there was a widely held belief in a divine figure who came down from heaven and assumed human form in order to redeem the souls trapped within human bodies.[1] They will also be aware that while Bultmann's thesis has come under heavy attack and is not widely held today,[2] there are those who still attempt to argue for it, though usually in a substantially modified form.[3] My purpose in this paper is to draw attention to one of the side effects of this whole debate, an important side effect which has not been given the attention it deserves. For it is my belief that the quest of the Gnostic redeemer myth within pre-Christian traditions, and the debate thereby stirred up, have *together* confused the history of christology's beginnings,

---

1. The clearest schematic statement is in R. Bultmann, *Theology of the New Testament* I (London: SCM, 1952) 166f.

2. See, e.g., W. Manson, *Jesus the Messiah* (London: Hodder and Stoughton, 1943) 174-90; C. Colpe, *Die religionsgeschichtliche Schule* (Göttingen, 1961); J. Munck, "The New Testament and Gnosticism," in *Current Issues in New Testament Interpretation,* ed. W. Klassen and G. F. Snyder (O. A. Piper FS; San Francisco: Harper and Row, 1962) 224-38; E. Yamauchi, *Pre-Christian Gnosticism* (London: Tyndale, 1973); and below n. 14.

3. See K. Rudolph, "Stand und Aufgaben in der Erforschung des Gnostizismus" (1964), reprinted in *Gnosis and Gnostizismus,* ed. K. Rudolph (Darmstadt, 1975) 510-53, particularly 547-49, and those cited below in nn. 9-12.

A lecture delivered to the Faculty of Theology, University of Aarhus, Denmark, in March 1981, originally published in *SJT* 35: 303-36. Copyright © 1982 by T. & T. Clark and used by permission.

particularly in the key issue of Christ's relation with God. Although principally concerned with soteriology, the discussion roused by the hypothesis of the Gnostic redeemer myth has raised the question of Christianity's *theology* (in the narrower sense of that term). In other words, it forces students of Christian origins to ask *whether Christianity began as a departure from Jewish monotheism, whether Christianity was in fact a monotheistic faith from the beginning*.

The question arises because in the most striking expressions of the Gnostic redeemer myth, which we find in developed form in the second century, the redeemer is presented as a heavenly being distinct from God. In the Naasene hymn, for example, it is Jesus himself who appeals to God:

> Therefore send me, Father;
> Bearing the seals I will descend,
> I will pass through all the Aeons,
> I will disclose all mysteries,
> I will show the forms of the Gods
> And the hidden things of the holy way,
> Awaking knowledge, I will impart.[4]

Again, in the *Song of the Pearl,* the central character is the son of the king who is sent to Egypt to fetch a pearl, but who eats their food and forgets who he is, sinking into a deep sleep, and who has to be roused and recalled to his true identity before he can accomplish his mission.[5] Similarly in the *Ascension of Isaiah,* the Most High, the Father of the Lord, is heard speaking "to my Lord Christ, who shall be called Jesus: 'Go and descend through all heavens; descend to the firmament and to that world. . . . And thou shalt become like to the form of all who are in the five heavens.' " Isaiah then witnesses the descent of the Lord and his progressive transformation, which hides his true identity, till he becomes Mary's newborn child who "sucked the breast like a baby, as was customary, so that he would not be recognized."[6]

The point is this: if there was such a myth of a heavenly redeemer figure already in existence and widely known before Christianity, then *one of the most crucial steps in earliest christology was the identification of Christ with this figure.* If pre-Christian thinking had already embraced the thought of a divine redeemer other than God himself, then the almost inevitable conclusion is that the Christian idea of Christ's divinity resulted from

---

4. Hippolytus, *Refutatio* 5.10, following the translation in W. Foerster, *Gnosis* I (London: Oxford University, 1972) 282.

5. *Acts of Thomas* 108-13 (Foerster, *Gnosis* I, 355-58).

6. *Ascension of Isaiah* 10–11 in E. Hennecke, *New Testament Apocrypha* II, ed. W. Schneemelcher, tr. and ed. R. McL. Wilson (London: Lutterworth, 1965) 659-61. See also, e.g., Clement of Alexandria, *Excerpta ex Theodoto* 1.1, and the *Paraphrase of Shem* among the Nag Hammadi codices.

the equation of Christ with this divine redeemer. Christ could be thought of as not simply a resurrected prophet, not simply an ascended hero, but as that individual whose intervention from heaven was widely anticipated. That is to say, the deity of Christ in its earliest formulation was nothing other than the heavenly status of a being already conceived of as distinct from God. It is not necessary to clarify how precisely the relation between God and the redeemer was conceptualized at this earliest stage (the later Gnostic systems are of course much more elaborate); it is sufficient for us to note how exceedingly difficult it would have been for a Christianity which identified Christ with this heavenly redeemer to retain its christology within a mono-theistic framework.

A crucial question for Christian theologians therefore is whether there was indeed something like the Gnostic redeemer myth already in circulation in the first half of the first century A.D. and whether earliest christology was influenced by it to a significant degree, whether thought of Christ as divine emerged by equating Jesus with this heavenly figure. Bultmann and those who have followed him in the quest of the Gnostic redeemer myth have no doubt as to the answer.

> According to these (Gnostic) concepts the Redeemer appears as a cosmic figure, the pre-existent divine being, Son of the Father, who came down from Heaven and assumed human form and who, after his activity on earth, was exalted to heavenly glory and wrested sovereignty over the spirit powers to himself. It is in this conception of him that he is praised in the pre-Pauline Christ-hymn which is quoted in Phil. 2:6-11. This "mythos" is also briefly alluded to in II Cor. 8:9 . . . lurks behind I Cor. 2:8 . . . is the subject of Eph. 4:8-10. . . .[7]

Similarly, behind the Fourth Gospel lies "the Gnostic myth . . . of a pre-existent divine being, which in its metaphysical mode of being is equal to God . . . ," in which the Father and the Son are two separate persons, and in which talk of the Son's preexistent relation with the Father "was originally taken literally."[8] To be sure, Bultmann believes that John had freed himself from this mythology even while retaining its language, but even so it is hard to avoid the conclusion that the attempt to incorporate the language of the Gnostic myth into a monotheistic framework must have put severe strain upon that framework.

Those who follow Bultmann continue to argue in similar terms. For example, K. Wengst draws on the *Song of the Pearl* to illuminate Phil. 2:6-11:

7. Bultmann, *Theology* I, 175.
8. R. Bultmann, *John* (London: Blackwell, 1971) 251-53.

The redeemer abandons his original divine mode of being, betakes himself
into the humiliation of the human situation before finally returning . . . to
his divine position. . . . Phil. 2 has taken over this schema.[9]

S. Schulz argues that "the absolute personification" of the Logos in the
Johannine prologue must "go back to the speculation about intermediary
beings in Hellenism influenced by Gnosis."[10] And J. T. Sanders speaks more
cautiously of "an emerging mythical configuration" and a "tendency to hypostatize divine qualities" as the historical religious background of the several
New Testament christological hymns.[11]

Even those who would distance themselves from Bultmann's thesis find
that the Gnostic redeemer myth debate has influenced the language and categories available to them. Indeed it is not a little ironical that some who seek
to offer alternative hypotheses of christology's beginnings find themselves,
perhaps despite themselves, talking of mythical figures, divine agents,
heavenly redeemers, and intermediary beings. For example, F. H. Borsch
rejects the thesis of a pre-Christian belief in a divinity descended from heaven
to become a humble human being, but he hypothesizes in its place a much
more diffuse myth of a Man who is variously first man, royal man, and
heavenly man.[12] F. Young maintains that

> the descent of heavenly beings to intervene in earthly affairs, often to render
> assistance, is clearly a feature of both pagan and Jewish legend, and certainly
> pre-dates both the New Testament and the earliest traces of a Gnostic
> descending redeemer.[13]

And M. Hengel, despite his scathing dismissal of the Gnostic redeemer myth
hypothesis,[14] nevertheless agrees that "Jewish wisdom speculation has a
mythological background," and commends the older talk of Bousset and
Gressmann about the "whole host of intermediary beings" who "forced their
way in between God, who had become distant from the world, and man."[15]

The issue, I trust, is plain. If room had indeed been made within pre-
Christian Judaism for some such mythical figure or intermediary being, and

---

9. K. Wengst, *Christologische Formeln und Lieder des Urchristentums* (Gütersloh, 1972)
154.

10. S. Schulz, *Johannes* (NTD; 1972) 28.

11. J. T. Sanders, *The New Testament Christological Hymns* (Cambridge: Cambridge
University, 1971) 96.

12. F. H. Borsch, *The Son of Man in Myth and History* (London: SCM, 1967) 251f.

13. F. Young in *The Myth of God Incarnate*, ed. J. Hick (London: SCM, 1977) 112.

14. M. Hengel, *The Son of God* (London: SCM, 1976) 33-35.

15. M. Hengel, *Judaism and Hellenism* (London: SCM, 1974) I, 155, citing W. Bousset
and H. Gressmann, *Die Religion des Judentums im späthellenistischen Zeitalter* (HNT 21; [4]1966)
319.

this heavenly redeemer was not merely of angelic rank clearly subordinate to God, then Jewish monotheism was already under strain,[16] and the identification of the resurrected and exalted man, Jesus of Nazareth, with this heavenly redeemer must have increased that strain immeasurably, so much so that Christianity's claim to be a monotheistic faith is put in question from the start. Two important issues therefore force themselves upon us. First, was there in pre-Christian Judaism a concept of a heavenly redeemer, an individual figure, conceived of in such terms of divinity that Judaism's monotheism was thereby threatened? And second, did earliest Christian thinking about Christ take up or accelerate that threat so that Christianity's own claim to be a monotheistic religion is undermined at foundation level? To answer them we must look first at the various figures suggested by Bultmann and others, either as evidence of the pre-Christian Gnostic redeemer myth itself, or as evidence within Judaism of the sort of thinking out of which the Gnostic redeemer myth grew. We will then be in a position to assess, secondly, the impact of that pre-Christian Jewish thought upon the earliest Christian understanding of Christ.

II

What evidence do we have of belief in *heavenly redeemer figures and intermediary beings in pre-Christian Judaism?*
  a) *Glorified heroes.* B. Lindars has argued that in pre-Christian Judaism

apocalyptic thought embraces the concept of an agent of God in the coming judgment, who may be a character of the past reserved in heaven for this function at the end time. . . . The identification of Jesus with this figure is fundamental to widely separated strands of the New Testament.[17]

The two most obvious candidates for such speculation were Enoch and Elijah: they had both been taken to heaven without experiencing death (Gen. 5:24; 2 Kgs. 2:11), and therefore presumably could still play a role in the body on earth. A belief in the return of Elijah certainly goes back as far as Mal. 4:5f. ("Behold, I will send you Elijah the prophet before the great and terrible day of the Lord comes . . ."), and it certainly became a regular

---

16. Unlike some of their successors, Bousset and Gressmann at least recognized the consequences of their findings for our understanding of Jewish monotheism: "Wir sehen den Monotheismus von allerei Rankenwerk umzogen. Und dieses Rankenwerk ist nicht ganz ungefährlich. Hier und da beginnt es den reinen Gottesglauben zu überwuchern" (*Religion,* 319)

17. B. Lindars, "Re-enter the Apocalyptic Son of Man," *NTS* 22 (1975-76) 52-72 (here p. 54).

element in Jewish expectation both before and after Christ (Sir. 48:10; *1 En.* 90:31; Mark 6:15 par.; 8:28 pars.; 9:11f. par.; John 1:21; Rev. 11:3; 4 Ezra 6:26; *Sib. Or.* 2.187-89; Justin, *Dialogue* 8.4; 49.1; *Apocalypse of Elijah* 24:11-15).[18] But there is no hint or suggestion in all this that Elijah was a glorified or more than human figure or had become a divine being by virtue of his translation to heaven.[19] If he is to return to this world, the presumption is that he will be just as he was when he left. Hence it is John the Baptist's manifest likeness to Elijah in manner and physical appearance (haircloth, leather belt — Mark 1:6; 2 Kgs. 1:8) which prompts the identification of the two (Matt. 11:7-11/Luke 7:24-8).[20]

Enoch drew more varied speculation. In *Jub.* 4:23 his translation to heaven is understood as a restoration to humankind's primeval glory: "he was taken from among the children of men, and we conducted him into the garden of Eden in majesty and honor." In heaven his role is to record human sins — hence his title "scribe of righteousness" (*Jub.* 4:23; *1 En.* 12:4; *T. Abr.* 11). His participation in the final judgment is assumed in *1 En.* 90:31 in association with Elijah, and later in association with Abel (*T. Abr.* 11).[21] In the course of this speculation his translation to heaven came to be conceived in more glorious terms: he is identified with the Son of man in the Similitudes of Enoch (*1 En.* 71:14 — see below); he is stripped of his earthly garments and appears like the angels in *2 En.* 22:8 (cf. *Ascension of Isaiah* 9:8f. — like Abel and all the righteous); he becomes Metatron, the Prince of the Presence, in *3 Enoch* 3–16. But such speculation takes us well beyond the earliest Christian period.[22] Even the Similitudes cannot with any confidence be dated

18. See further J. Jeremias, *TDNT* II, 931-34, 936. Mark 15:35f. also reports the speculation of the crowd around the cross as to whether Elijah would come and rescue Jesus. This may be an early hint of the later rabbinic legends of Elijah's frequent interventions on earth (L. Ginzberg, *The Legends of the Jews* [Jewish Publication Society] IV [1913] 202-35; VI [1928] 325-42), but it is not clear whether Mark's tradition presupposes such legends or that such an intervention was at that time conceived of as a real possibility.

19. Cf. C. H. Talbert, *What Is a Gospel?* (London: SPCK, 1978) 49f., n. 80.

20. Since the Baptist *is* identified with Elijah (see below), but is *not* thought of as having preexisted before his birth or as having descended from heaven full grown, it may be doubted whether the hope of Elijah's return actually envisaged the personal return of the historical figure. Did this earlier stage of Elijah speculation envisage simply the raising up of another prophet "in the spirit and power of Elijah" (Luke 1:17), a prophet like Elijah = a prophet like Moses? And is this partly the reason for the appearance of just these two in the account of the transfiguration (Mark 9:2-8 pars.)?

21. Following the destruction of Jerusalem in A.D. 70 speculation that particular heroes from the past were being kept in heaven until the end of the age was extended to include others, particularly Ezra and Baruch (4 Ezra 14:9; *2 Baruch* 13:3; 25:1; 43:2; 46:7; 48:30; 76:3). It is probably significant that they were remembered more as scribes (like Enoch) than as prophets.

22. The Jewish *Vorlage* of *2 Enoch* may go back before A.D. 70 (J. H. Charlesworth, *The Pseudepigrapha and Modern Research* [SBL Septuagint and Cognate Studies 7; 1976] 103f.), but *3 Enoch* 3–16 is certainly much later — P. S. Alexander, "The Historical Setting of the Hebrew Book of Enoch," *JJS* 28 (1977), dates it between ca. A.D. 450 and ca. 850 (pp. 164f.).

early enough to have influenced first Christian thinking about Christ (see below). In the certainly pre-Christian documents Enoch, like Elijah, is just a man taken to heaven.[23]

Of other heroes from the past only Moses and Melchizedek need detain us.[24] Philo speaks of Moses leaving this mortal life for immortality "summoned thither by the Father, who resolved his twofold nature of soul and body into a single unity transforming his whole being into mind, pure as the sunlight" (*Mos.* 2.288). This sounds like apotheosis or deification, but only if we take it out of the context of Philo's Platonic worldview. Within that context it described Moses' transition from the perceptible, material world to the world of eternal realities, the ideal realm of pure rationality. That is to say, it is what will happen to souls generally (*Quaes. Gen.* 3.11), but preeminently to Moses because he is, for Philo, the supremely wise man (*Sacr.* 8-10), "mind at its purest" (*Mut.* 208).[25] There is no threat to Jewish monotheism here. Josephus also reports speculation on the part of some that Moses "had been taken back to the deity" (perhaps an allusion to Philo?), but it is a speculation which in Josephus's view is ruled out by the report of Moses' death in Deut. 34:5f. (*Ant.* 3.96f.; 4.326).[26]

As for Melchizedek, the fragmentary text from Qumran certainly seems to use the name for a heavenly being, probably an archangel (*"elohim"* — 11QMelch 10). But it is by no means clear that a reference to the Melchizedek of Genesis 14 is intended — the reference to Genesis 14 in the Genesis Apocryphon gives no hint of such a speculation centering on that Melchizedek (1QapGen 22.14-7; cf. *Jub.* 13:25), and no reference to Ps. 110:4 has so far been discovered in the Dead Sea Scrolls. Since the name Melchiresha (king of wickedness) was also coined by Qumran covenanters, it is quite likely that the name Melchizedek (king of righteousness) was formed in the same way,

23. See also H. Odeberg, *TDNT* II, 557f.

24. Jeremiah's appearance in a dream (2 Macc. 15:12-16) was probably understood simply as a dream's recalling of figures from the past (Jeremiah is described better as dignified and venerable than as glorified and exalted; and Onias appears as well). Matt. 16:14 may imply speculation about the possible return of particular prophets, but alternatively may simply be a way of expressing the belief that Jesus was a prophet in the line of Elijah, Jeremiah, and John the Baptist. Cf. J. Jeremias, *TDNT* III, 219-21.

25. See further C. H. Holladay, *Theios Aner in Hellenistic Judaism* (SBL Dissertation Series 40; 1977), ch. III, particularly p. 163, n. 287. Philo's treatment of Moses is usefully collocated and summarized in the index to *Philo* in the Loeb Classical Library, vol. X, 379-90. On Philo's application of Exod. 4:16 and 7:1 in reference to Moses ("You shall be to him (Aaron) as God"; "I will make you a God to Pharaoh") see Holladay, *Theios Aner,* 108-55.

26. Despite his death, Moses is associated with Elijah in the account of the transfiguration (Mark 9:2-8 pars.). Presumably then the idea was that they had both become like angels (according to Luke they "appeared in glory" — Luke 9:31) and could at least visit the earth. Cf. Rev. 11:3-12. But see also J. D. G. Dunn, *Christology in the Making* (= *CiM*) (London: SCM, 1980) 277, n. 63, 304, n. 141.

without any intended reference to the figure of Genesis 14.[27] Nonetheless on one quite possible interpretation of the text we have a (probably) pre-Christian Jewish writer envisioning the exaltation of the mysterious figure Melchizedek to archangel status. What this means for Jewish monotheism will depend on how we assess the angelology of pre-Christian Judaism, a subject to which we must now turn.

To sum up for the moment, however, there is no clear evidence that pre-Christian Jewish understanding of God was in any degree influenced or affected by speculation concerning the fate and future role of any of the great saints or heroes of the faith from the past.

b) *Angels*. If we are thinking of intermediary figures between God and humans the most obvious candidates are angels. In fact, within the biblical and intertestamental traditions that is precisely what angels are — intermediary beings, lesser beings who execute God's will. From earliest times we have "the sons of God" who are members of the heavenly council under Yahweh the supreme God (Gen. 6:2, 4; Deut. 32:8; Job 1:6-12; 2:1-6; 38:7; Pss. 29:1; 89:6; *1 En.* 13:8; 106:5). Presumably, as Israel's conception of Yahweh developed into a cosmic monotheism, this was one of the chief ways of absorbing the gods of other nations into their system — that is, by regarding them simply as members of Yahweh's heavenly council.[28] Thus in the much more elaborate angelology of the intertestamental period we have angels who have authority under God over the various nations (Dan. 10:13, 20; *Jub.* 15:31f; *1 En.* 89:59-65; 90:20-5; *T. Levi* 5:6; *T. Dan* 6:1f; *Ass. Mos.* 10:1), as well as angels who control the forces of nature (wind, seasons, stars) (*Jub.* 2:2f.; *1 En.* 75:3; 80:6; 82:10-20; 1QH 1.10f.).[29]

With such a "population explosion" in the heavenly host it is not surprising that a concept of leading angels within an angelic hierarchy emerges, with Michael, Gabriel, Raphael, and Sariel, Uriel, or Phanuel as the most prominent of the archangels (Dan. 8:16; 9:21; 10:13; Tob. 12:15; *1 En.* 9:1f; 20:1-8; 1QM 9.15; 4 Ezra 5:20). These are also called "angels of the presence" (*Jub.* 1:27, 29; 2:2, etc; *T. Levi* 3:5; *T. Jud.* 25:2; 1QH 6.13), presumably because they are depicted as forming Yahweh's inner council. As such they are able to make intercession on behalf of Israel (Tob. 12:15; *1 En.* 9:3; 99:3; 104:1; *T. Levi* 3:5; 5:6f; *T. Dan* 6:2). As such, too, they can act as

---

27. See J. T. Milik, *"Milkî-ṣedeq et Milkî-reša"* dans les anciens écrits juifs et chrétiens," *JJS* 23 (1972) 126-37; G. Vermes, *The Dead Sea Scrolls in English* (Harmondsworth: Pelican, ²1975) 253, 260.

28. See, e.g., G. von Rad, *TDNT* I, 78; T. H. Gaster, *Interpreter's Dictionary of the Bible* I, 131.

29. See, e.g., H. B. Kuhn, "The Angelology of the Non-Canonical Jewish Apocalypses," *JBL* 67 (1948) 217-32; D. S. Russell, *The Method and Message of Jewish Apocalyptic* (London: SCM, 1964) ch. IX.

captain of the Lord's hosts in the cosmic battle against Israel's enemies and the hostile angels (Dan. 10:13, 20f.; *Jub.* 48:9-19; *Ass. Mos.* 10:2; Rev. 12:7-9). It is such a role that Melchizedek fills in the Qumran document touched on above, with "Melchizedek" (king of righteousness) serving as another name for Michael, also called "the Prince of Light," "the angel of truth," and "the great angel" (1QS 3.20, 24; CD 5.18; 1QM 13.10; 17.6).

This whole conception of an angelic hierarchy is clearly modeled on the oriental court, and the authority and status given to Michael, for example, would not be seen in Jewish eyes as a threat to their monotheism. On the contrary, the more servants and councilors attributed to Yahweh the greater *his* majesty as the one true God supreme over all. And though of course angels, in their role of Yahweh's messengers, did visit earth, such visitations were for that sole purpose; there is nothing here that provides a recognizable antecedent to the Gnostic redeemer myth.

There is, however, one angelic figure who deserves a little more attention — "the angel of the Lord." In the earlier stages of Jewish thought it is clear enough that the angel of the Lord is simply a way of speaking about Yahweh himself. For example, in the theophany of the burning bush he who appears to Moses is described both as "the angel of the Lord" and as "the God of Abraham, Isaac, and Jacob" (Exod. 3:2-6); and in Judg. 2:1 "the angel of the Lord" says "I brought you up from the land of Egypt — I will never break my covenant with you." The most obvious explanation of this language is that it was an early, still unsophisticated attempt to speak of God's presence and activity on earth without resorting to even less sophisticated anthropomorphism or abandoning belief in God's holy otherness.[30] Here then is a conceptualization of God and of God's immanent activity among his people which might seem to pose a potential threat to Israel's emerging monotheism — an angelic being who is Yahweh (cf. Exod. 14:19f. with 14:24) and who yet can be distinguished from Yahweh (cf. Exod. 14:19 with 23:20, 23 and 33:2 with 33:3). Perhaps this is why the idea of the angel of the Lord disappears from the later stages of pre-Christian Jewish thought, and when it appears in the birth narratives of Matthew and Luke it is as "*an* angel of the Lord" (Matt. 1:20; 2:13, 19; Luke 1:11; 2:9) — that is, presumably, simply one of the angels of the presence, whom Luke in fact names as Gabriel (Luke 1:19, 26).

There is another strand of Jewish thought, however, which takes up something that was said of the angel (of the Lord?) who went before Israel in their wilderness wanderings — Exod. 23:20f.: "I send an angel before you. . . . Give heed to him. . . . *For my name is in him.*" In the *Apocalypse of Abraham* we meet an interpreter angel Jaoel, "a power in virtue of the

30. See further *CiM*, 150f.

ineffable Name that is dwelling in me" (*Apoc. Abr.* 10).[31] And subsequently in the Merkabah mysticism of *3 Enoch,* Metatron, the Prince of the Presence, is called "the lesser Yahweh" (*3 Enoch* 12:5) — again with specific reference to Exod. 23:21 ("for my name is in him" — cf. *b. Sanh.* 38b). As we shall see shortly, this mystical speculation on Metatron does come to be regarded as a threat to Jewish monotheism by the rabbis. What may be significant then is the fact that there is evidence of Merkabah mysticism already at Qumran (4QS1 40.24),[32] so that some merging of the idea of the angel of the Lord in whom is Yahweh's name with Melchizedek is just possible — though the relation of the two documents within the Dead Sea Scrolls is far from clear and the divine title used for Melchizedek is *elohim* (11QMelch 10). It may even be that something of the sort has to be traced back to Ezekiel himself, whose vision of the chariot-throne (Ezekiel 1) is the basis of the later Merkabah mysticism. For in Ezek. 8:2 the description of the angel is remarkably like that of God himself in 1:26f.[33] But if that is the case, then we are dealing with a thin strand of esoteric mysticism within Judaism which touched the Qumran community, but so far as we now can tell only became more widely influential from the late first century A.D. on.

In short, in the intertestamental period Jewish apocalyptic readily conceived of angelic hosts in heaven marshaled by an angelic hierarchy, whose number and majesty served not to threaten Yahweh's sovereign authority but to enhance it. Such intermediary figures neither threaten Jewish monotheism nor provide much of a model for belief in a particular redeemer in heaven. The very early idea of the angel of the Lord as a manifestation of Yahweh is soon abandoned, and, insofar as it reappears in Merkabah mysticism, that is a form of Judaism which influenced at most a small esoteric circle in the period of Christian beginnings. Here the attempt to describe the glorious

31. The *Apocalypse of Abraham* is generally dated to about the end of the first century A.D. (see Charlesworth, *Pseudepigrapha and Modern Research,* 68f.).

32. See J. Strugnell, "The Angelic Liturgy at Qumran," *Vetus Testamentum Supplements* 7 (1959) 318-45; text also in Vermes, *Dead Sea Scrolls,* 211-13. Strugnell dates the work as pre–50 B.C. G. G. Scholem suggests that the beginnings of Merkabah mysticism may go back to the Essenes (*Major Trends in Jewish Mysticism* [London: Thames and Hudson, 1955] 43). Cf. Sir. 49:8.

33. C. Rowland, "The Vision of the Risen Christ in Rev. 1:13ff.: The Debt of an Early Christology to an Aspect of Jewish Angelology," *JTS* 31 (1980) 1-11 (here 4f.). It is doubtful, however, whether the language of Dan. 10:5f. is deliberately dependent on Ezek. 1:26f. to a significant extent. The differences between Ezekiel's vision of "a likeness as it were of a human being" with a bronzelike top half and firelike bottom half (Ezek. 1:26f.) and Daniel's vision of "a man clothed in linen" with a beryllike body and bronzelike arms and legs (Dan. 10:5f.) are more significant than what may be no more than accidental or unconscious echoes of Ezekiel's complete vision (against Rowland, 3f.). And though *1 En.* 14:18-23 shows some possible influence from Ezekiel 1, it is hardly clear that 14:21 is intended to indicate "that God resembled human form" (against C. Rowland, "The Visions of God in Apocalyptic Literature," *JSJ* 10 [1979] 137-54, here 141). But see the later response on pp. 305-7 above.

figures who appear to the visionary may seem to threaten Jewish mono-theism, though we may note also that the more serious the threat the less readily can they be conceived as angelic intermediaries, still less as agents of redemption.

　c) *The Son of Man.* No other figure has aroused so much interest in the area of our inquiry as the figure of Daniel's vision —

> and behold, with the clouds of heaven there came one like a son of man, and he came to the Ancient of Days and was presented before him. And to him was given dominion and glory and kingdom. . . . (7:13f.)

The view of S. Mowinckel, "that the Jewish conception of 'the Man' or 'the Son of Man' is a Jewish variant of (a widespread) oriental, cosmological, eschatological myth of Anthropos,"[34] was very popular in the heyday of the quest of the Gnostic redeemer myth. And in the most recent contribution to the debate A. J. B. Higgins repeats the still popular view that "in Dan. 7 we have in all probability a corporate interpretation of an older concept of an individual, transcendent agent of redemption."[35]

　It is certainly probable that Daniel's vision has some background in myth. A vision which contrasts beast-like figures arising out of the sea (primeval chaos) with a human-like figure presented to God almost certainly echoes the accounts of creation — humankind as the crown of creation given dominion over the beasts and birds (Gen. 1:26f; 2:19f). And there are interesting parallels with a postulated Canaanite myth in which the ancient god abdicated in favor of a younger[36] — although we can hardly think that Daniel intended his vision to represent the human-like figure taking over from the Ancient of Days! But in Daniel itself the meaning of the vision is quite clear. The contrast between the beast-like figures and the human-like figure represents symbolically the ferocious hostility of the nations against Israel and Israel's ultimate vindication and triumph over them. The beast-like figures are specifically interpreted as Israel's enemies, and in the interpreta-tion it is repeatedly stated that what was given to the human-like figure is given to the saints of the Most High (Dan. 7:18, 22, 27). The vision is fully explained in these terms (the human-like figure as a symbolical representa-tion of the saints of the Most High), and there is nothing to suggest that Daniel thought of the "one like a son of man" as a specific individual (an

---

34. S. Mowinckel, *He that Cometh* (Oxford: Blackwell, 1956) 425.

35. A. J. B. Higgins, *The Son of Man in the Teaching of Jesus* (Cambridge: Cambridge University, 1980) 12. For others who support this view see Higgins, 3.

36. See particularly J. A. Emerton, "The Origin of the Son of Man Imagery," *JTS* 9 (1958) 225-42; C. Colpe, *TDNT* VIII, 415-19. But see also A. J. Ferch, "Daniel 7 and Ugarit: A Reconsideration," *JBL* 99 (1980) 75-86.

angel, the Messiah?). Nor is there any need to postulate a myth about the first man (Primal Man, Anthropos myth) in order to make complete sense of the passage.[37]

It is true, however, that at a later stage Daniel's vision is interpreted in Jewish circles as a description of a particular individual, the Messiah, and that this heavenly figure seems to be thought of as preexistent.[38] I am thinking here of course of the Similitudes of Enoch (*1 En.* 37–71) and 4 Ezra 13. But here we should note several points. First, in both writings the suggestion that the human-like figure of Daniel's vision is a specific individual, the Messiah, is made as though it were a fresh interpretation of Daniel's vision: *1 En.* 46:1-2 —

> And there I saw one who had a head of days, and his head (was) white like wool (Dan. 7:9); and with him (there was) another, whose face had the appearance of a man (Dan. 7:13). . . . And I asked one of the holy angels . . . about that Son of man, who he was, and whence he was, (and) why he went with the Head of Days. And he answered me and said to me, "This is the Son of Man who has righteousness and with whom righteousness dwells. . . ."

Similarly with 4 Ezra 13:1-3 —

> After seven days, I dreamed a dream in the night; and behold, a wind arose from the sea and stirred up all the waves (cf. Dan 7:1-2). And I looked, and behold, this wind made something like the figure of a man (Dan. 7:13) come up out of the heart of the sea (cf. Dan. 7:3). And I looked, and behold, that man flew with the clouds of heaven (Dan. 7:13); and wherever he turned his face to look, everything under his gaze trembled. . . .

In other words, here we have evidence that Daniel's vision was subsequently interpreted as speaking of a particular heavenly individual, the Messiah. But the freshness of each interpretation tells strongly against the view that both writings were drawing on an already established interpretation of Daniel 7 in angelic or messianic terms. The very fact that the Similitudes speak regularly of "that son of man" (of Dan. 7:13) and 4 Ezra speaks of "the man coming up from the heart of the sea" shows that "Son of man" was not yet a title

---

37. See more fully *CiM*, §9.1. And for further details in what follows see §§9.2 and 9.3. See also particularly P. M. Casey, *The Son of Man: The Interpretation and Influence of Daniel 7* (London: SPCK, 1980).

38. Though the identification of Enoch as the Son of man in *1 En.* 71:14 probably implies that the preexistence of the Son of man in the Similitudes is an ideal rather than a real preexistence — denoting God's purpose "from the beginning" that Enoch should play a decisive role in the final judgment (see *CiM*, 296, n. 64).

and that there was no clear "Son of man concept" already formulated for these writers to draw on.[39]

Second, the dating of both documents makes it very uncertain whether we can use them as evidence of Jewish speculation prior to the initial impact of Christianity. 4 Ezra is dated by general acceptance in the period following A.D. 70. And though the Similitudes are often taken as pre-Christian, this must remain very doubtful. The evidence of the Dead Sea Scrolls is that the works of the Enoch cycle were popular at Qumran.[40] The complete absence of the Similitudes, a work which would hardly have been offensive to the Qumran covenanters, cannot but suggest therefore that it was not yet written by the time the Qumran library was closed finally and forever (A.D. 68).[41] It would be unwise therefore to use a document which seems to be offering a fresh interpretation of the Danielic vision and which cannot be dated before A.D. 70 with any assurance as evidence either for a pre-Christian Jewish Son of man concept in particular or for a more diffuse pre-Christian belief in a heavenly redeemer figure.

There is, however, a strong possibility that Daniel's vision played a part in that development within early Merkabah mysticism, which the rabbis condemned as threatening their monotheism.[42] In a mystical contemplation of the throne of God (Ezekiel 1) it was probably inevitable that attention would sooner or later focus on the thrones (plural) mentioned in Dan. 7:9. The question would naturally arise, Who sat on the other throne(s)? Akiba answered: David[43] — an interpretation dangerous enough to be accused by one rabbi of "profaning the Shekinah" (*b. Sanh.* 38b). But one of his contemporaries, Elisha ben Abuya, is said to have been overwhelmed by the majesty of this second figure (Metatron) and to have cried, "Indeed there are two divine powers in heaven!" (*3 Enoch* 16:3; cf. *b. Ḥag.* 15a) — thereby detracting from the glory and honor which is God's alone. What is of particular interest for us is that Enoch is caught up in this speculation. He is identified with Metatron in the Palestinian Targum (Pseudo-Jonathan on Gen. 5:24) and in *3 Enoch* 4, as he was already identified with "that son of man" in the

39. The fact that the Son of man's role is one of judgment (*1 En.* 45:4; 49:2-4; 52:6-9; 55:4; 61:8f.) tells us nothing at this point, since involvement in judgment is a feature of all such speculation about the end (see, e.g., above regarding Enoch, Elijah, and Abel).

40. Fragments of eleven separate manuscripts have been found; see particularly J. T. Milik, *The Books of Enoch: Aramaic Fragments of Qumran Cave 4* (Oxford: Oxford University, 1976).

41. A post-A.D. 70 date is argued for by, among others, M. Black, M. A. Knibb (editor of the recent critical text of *1 Enoch*), B. Lindars (below n. 63), J. T. Milik, and G. Vermes (see *CiM,* 79).

42. See particularly A. F. Segal, *Two Powers in Heaven: Early Rabbinic Reports about Christianity and Gnosticism* (Leiden: Brill, 1977).

43. Perhaps thinking of 1 Chron. 29:23 — "Solomon sat on the throne of the Lord as king instead of David his father."

Similitudes of Enoch (*1 En.* 71:14). So too the portrayal of the angel Jaoel, in whom is Yahweh's name, in the *Apocalypse of Abraham,* may reflect a similar willingness to stretch the categories of divinity more than rabbinic Judaism could bear.[44]

It is clear enough then that in at least some Jewish circles there developed a form of visionary mysticism which drew on earlier speculation about Enoch, about particular angels, and about Daniel's vision of "one like a son of man" being presented to God in the heavenly throne room and that this speculation soon came to be seen by those formulating rabbinic Judaism as a threat to their monotheism. However, all the documentation and historical characters involved (Akiba, Elisha) belong to a period stretching from the end of the first century through the first half of the second century A.D. Whether they influenced second-century Christian thinking about Christ is open to question, but they can hardly be credited with influencing first-century christology. If anything it was the Christian use of Dan. 7:13 in reference to Christ which provided part of the stimulus for the Jewish mystical speculation and which provoked the rabbis to such vigorous rejection of it.[45]

d) *Adam.* We need mention Adam only briefly. One variation of the later Gnostic redeemer myth is the Primal Man myth — the belief that the redeemer is the first man or original heavenly man. The search for traces of such a first man-redeemer figure in pre-Christian Jewish sources is, however, a complete failure, particularly once the human-like figure of Daniel's vision falls out of the reckoning.[46] Adam is indeed an object of speculation in Jewish literature before Christianity and in rabbinic literature of the Christian era, but never as a redeemer or savior.[47] He could be thought of naturally as "the image of God" (Gen. 1:26; Sir. 17:3; Wis. 2:23); he is honored as the first patriarch (Sir. 49:16) and as pattern for man in the age to come (*1 En.* 85–90); he can be called an "angel" (*2 En.* 30:11; cf. *1 En.* 69:11). But none of this is ever seen as any sort of infringement on the prerogatives or status of God. The only foothold which some questers of the Gnostic redeemer myth have been able to find in pre-Christian Jewish sources is Philo's distinction between heavenly man and an earthly man, which seems to come out of his exposition of Genesis 1–2 (*Leg. All.* 1.31, 53f.; *Opif.* 134; *Quaes. Gen.* 1.4). However, once again we must recall Philo's

---

44. Note the rabbinic polemic against angelology, which probably goes back to this same period; see P. S. Alexander, "The Targumim and Early Exegesis of 'Sons of God' in Genesis 6," *JJS* 23 (1972) 60-71.

45. Segal, *Two Powers,* has shown that the earliest form of the heresy was more Christian in character than Gnostic — that is, it envisaged two complementary rather than opposing powers.

46. E.g., Mowinckel discusses "this oriental, cosmological, eschatological myth of Anthropos" under the heading of "the origin of the conception of the Son of Man" (*He that Cometh,* 420-37).

47. See particularly R. Scroggs, *The Last Adam* (Philadelphia: Fortress, 1966) ix-xxiii.

Platonic worldview. In that context Philo's "heavenly man" is nothing more than the heavenly counterpart of earthly man, a bloodless idea, a blueprint man who has neither cosmological nor soteriological functions.[48] There is certainly no evidence here of Gnostic influence or of a pre-Christian redeemer myth, or of a threat to Jewish monotheism.

e) *Sophia and Logos.* In the post-Bultmannian phase of the quest for pre-Christian traces of the Gnostic redeemer myth the most promising investigations have focused on what Schulz calls "speculation about intermediary beings" and Sanders describes as the "tendency to hypostatize divine qualities." The reference here is to Jewish talk of "the name of God," "the glory of God," and so on, but particularly the Wisdom of God and the Word of God.[49] When, for example, Wisdom is spoken of as God's "master workman" (or "little child" — Prov. 8:30), or described as "wisdom that sits by your throne" (Wis. 9:40), when Wisdom praises herself in such terms as Sir. 24:5, "alone I have made the circuit of the vault of heaven and have walked in the depths of the abyss," or when the Word is depicted as leaping down from Heaven as a stern warrior "into the midst of a land that was doomed" (Wis. 18:15), then it is not difficult to conclude that they are being regarded as intermediary beings distinct from but closely related to God. And certainly there can be little doubt that the prominence particularly of Sophia in later Gnostic thought, especially Valentinianism, owes not a little to the Jewish Wisdom concept.[50]

At this point, however, we need to pay more attention than history of religions researchers have in the past to the judgment of rabbinic specialists. For they have been telling us for some time that these concepts (name, glory, wisdom, word) are not to be understood within Jewish writings as "intermediary beings" introduced as it were to mediate between God, conceived of as remote and distant, and his creation. On the contrary, these so-called "intermediary beings" are better understood as ways of asserting the transcendent God's *nearness* to his creation, his involvement with his people. They are ways of speaking about *God* in his relation to the world; they serve to express his immanence without compromising his transcendence.[51] As A. M. Goldberg puts it forcefully:

---

48. See particularly, A. J. M. Wedderburn, "Philo's 'Heavenly Man,' " *NovT* 15 (1973) 301-26.

49. Wisdom of God and Word of God are largely overlapping concepts, often virtually synonymous (see particularly Wis. 9:1-2; and cf. Ps. 33:6 with Prov. 3:19; Philo, *Fuga* 97 with 108f.; and *Somn.* 2.242 with 245).

50. See G. C. Stead, "The Valentinian Myth of Sophia," *JTS* 20 (1969) 75-104; G. W. Macrae, "The Jewish Background of the Gnostic Sophia Myth," *NovT* 12 (1970) 86-101.

51. See, e.g., G. Dalman, *The Words of Jesus* (Edinburgh: Clark, 1902) 229-31; G. F. Moore, "Intermediaries in Jewish Theology," *HTR* 15 (1922) 41-85; SB II, 302-33; E. E. Urbach, *The Sages: Their Concepts and Beliefs* (Jerusalem, 1975) ch. III; E. P. Sanders, *Paul and Palestinian Judaism* (London: SCM, 1977) 212-15.

The Shekinah is not and indeed cannot be an intermediary being, because the term Shekinah always designates the immediately present God. In contrast to the angels the Shekinah is the exact opposite of an intermediary being; it is no "power of God detached from God," no "personified abstraction."[52]

J. Marböck has taken the point when he concludes his study of wisdom in ben Sira:

The Wisdom of God . . . is in ben Sira not to be conceived as an intermediary being between God and creation or as an hypostasis. Wisdom in accordance with the kaleidoscope of metaphors is to be taken rather as a poetic personification for God's nearness and God's activity and for God's personal summons.[53]

The clue to a correct interpretation is to recognize the vigor of the Jewish poetic imagery at this period — what Marböck alludes to when he talks of "the kaleidoscope of metaphors." Hebrew poetry was well accustomed to use vivid apostrophes and personifications, for example to speak of "steadfast love and faithfulness" meeting, of "righteousness and peace" kissing each other (Ps. 85:10), to call on the Lord's "arm" to awake and put on strength (Isa. 51:9), to teach him dread deeds (Ps. 45:4), to talk even of "injustice" dwelling in tents and "wickedness" stopping its mouth (Job. 11:14; Ps. 107:42). The Wisdom and Word imagery is all of a piece with this — no more distinct beings than the Lord's "arm," no more intermediary beings than God's righteousness and God's glory, but simply vivid personifications, ways of speaking about God in his active involvement with his world and his people.[54] The same holds true even for Philo in his admittedly much more elaborate conceptualization of the Logos. In the end of the day the Logos for Philo is the rational energy of God in the act of creating and sustaining the universe (particularly *Opif.* 16-24), all that may be known of God even for the purest

---

52. A. M. Goldberg, *Untersuchungen über die Vorstellung von der Schekhinah in der frühen rabbinischen Literatur* (Berlin, 1969) 535f. (against P. Volz, *Der Geist Gottes* [Tübingen, 1910] 169).

53. J. Marböck, *Weisheit im Wandel. Untersuchungen zur Weisheitstheologie bei ben Sira* (Bonn, 1971) 129f.

54. See more fully *CiM,* §23. The much suggested alternative, halfway between person and personification — viz. "hypostasis" (see those cited in *CiM,* 325, n. 21) — is a doubly anachronistic importation of a nineteenth-century misunderstanding of a key technical term from the trinitarian controversies of the third and fourth centuries A.D. "The statement that hypostasis ever received 'a sense midway between "person" and "attribute," inclining to the former' is pure delusion, though it is derived ultimately from Harnack" (G. L. Prestige, *God in Patristic Thought* [London: SPCK, 1952, ²1964] xxviii). See further *CiM,* 174 and n. 42. For the meaning of *hypostasis* see R. E. Witt, "Hypostasis," *Amicitiae Corolla,* ed. H. G. Wood (J. R. Harris FS; London, 1933) 319-43; Prestige, *God,* ch. IX.

mind (e.g., *Somn.* 1.65f., 68f.; *Post.* 16-20).[55] In other words, Philo simply elaborates the same basic insight of earlier Jewish wisdom, that God in himself is unknowable, but has made himself known in, through, and as his wisdom and rational power; which is to say that the Wisdom of God and Word of God in Jewish thought are simply God insofar as he reveals himself to humans and insofar as he may be known by humans.

In all this it is not to be disputed that many of the images and words used to describe Sophia and Logos were drawn from the wider religious thought of the time — the parallels with the worship of Isis in particular have caught many scholars' attention.[56] But this is *not* to say that Yahwism inevitably became syncretistic through incorporating motifs from Isis worship. Israel's writers were well able to take over and domesticate the myths of polytheism and put them to the service of their monotheism. They had done so with the myth of the sea dragon representing primeval chaos, making it serve as a picture of the final conflict between Israel and her enemies (Isa. 27:1; Jer. 51:34-37; Ezek. 29:3f.; Daniel 7).[57] So here too they took over attractive and usable features in the cults of surrounding paganism and put them to serve their own monotheism. If the other cults had their seductive female figures, so had Israel (particularly Prov. 1:20-33; 8:1-35; 9:1-6).[58] And if any found the Jewish idea of a God without form too difficult and wanted a more tangible focus for their faith, where else need they look than the Torah — there preeminently was God's wisdom (Sir. 24:23, 25; Bar. 3:36–4:4; cf. Wis. 6:18; Philo, *Migr.* 130; *Virt.* 62-65). Nor should we at once jump to the conclusion that they thereby deified the Torah; even when the rabbis later talk of the Torah as preexistent that is simply a way of stressing the unsurpassable importance of the Torah as the revelation of God.[59]

In the Sophia and Logos imagery of pre-Christian Judaism therefore we find no thought of a real individual being, a heavenly redeemer in any sense (beyond that of literary personification) independent of the one God — it is Yahweh himself who alone is the Savior (e.g., Sir. 51:1; Wis. 16:7; Philo, *Mut.* 56).[60] Nor is there any real threat to Israel's monotheism in the poetic license of Israel's Wisdom tradition. There is a tension between the conviction of Yahweh's transcendence and the perception of his immanence, but that was present in Hebrew thought of God from a very early stage (cf. the angel of

55. See more fully *CiM*, §28.3.

56. See particularly B. L. Mack, *Logos and Sophia* (Göttingen, 1973) *passim*.

57. M. D. Hooker, *The Son of Man in Mark* (London: SPCK, 1967) 20f.

58. Cf. 4Q184 and 4Q185 (Vermes, *Dead Sea Scrolls,* 255-59).

59. The seven preexistent things include the Torah, the throne of glory, the sanctuary, the name of the Messiah, and repentance (*b. Pes.* 54a; *b. Ned.* 39b; Targum Pseudo-Jonathan Zech. 4:7); see SB I, 974f.; II, 334f.

60. See G. Fohrer and W. Foerster, *TDNT* VII, particularly 1012-15.

the Lord); the tension was not first introduced by the subsequent personification of divine wisdom. Any problem which we today may see for Israel's
monotheism in this and other personifications is the result more of our unfa-
miliarity with the vigor of the Wisdom tradition's poetic imagery than of the
imagery itself.

f) To sum up this first section of our inquiry. We have been looking for
traces in pre-Christian Judaism of a concept of a heavenly redeemer figure
conceived in such terms of divinity as to constitute a threat in some degree
to Judaism's monotheism. What have we found? First we have found no real
concept of a heavenly redeemer other than God himself. We hear of glorified
heroes of the faith, one of whom was expected to return as herald of the end,
others to act as witnesses in the final judgment. We hear of angelic intermediaries, some of whom make short-term visits to earth as messengers of God,
others who intercede for the saints or direct the angels in cosmic conflict, and
the mysterious Melchizedek who shares in the judgment of the nations. We
know that at some stage the Messiah was identified with the human-like figure
of Daniel's vision, though we cannot be confident that that step was taken
before the first generation of Christianity. And the Sophia-Logos imagery is
simply a way of speaking of God's own activity in creation, revelation, and
salvation. Material there may be in all this which the subsequent Gnostic
speculation could and did use. But there is no trace of anything which could
be called a Gnostic redeemer myth or even a close approximation to it.

Second, such threat as there was to Jewish monotheism came from two
directions. One was the language of personification used to speak of the
transcendent God's involvement in his world and with his people. But that,
so far as we can tell, in the pre-Christian period was kept under control and
would not have been perceived as a threat to their monotheism by the writers
within the Wisdom tradition. The other was speculation about a being other
than God (a human being, though not Adam, gods of other nations, angels,
the Messiah) who comes to be thought of as so much like God, sharing in his
glory and his functions, that he might be mistaken for God, or for a second
divine power in heaven. This too did not amount to any real threat to Jewish
monotheism, except in one strand of esoteric mysticism — a speculation involving the ancient idea of an angel in whom Yahweh had put his name, the
human-like figure and the empty throne(s) of Daniel's vision, and the translated Enoch. This potentially explosive mixture was already active in the early
decades of the second century A.D., but whether the elements had been brought
together much before that must be considered doubtful.

III

We can now turn to the second question asked at the beginning: did earliest Christian thinking about Christ take up any of this pre-Christian language in such a way as to undermine Christianity's own claim to stand in continuity with Judaism's monotheism? Did Christianity begin as a truly monotheistic religion? In view of our findings in the preceding section we can rule out some of the possible factors quite quickly.

a) The *heroes of the past* provided only limited models for earliest christology and did so in ways that are not particularly relevant to our inquiry. It is possible that John the Baptist thought of the one whose coming he predicted as Elijah (cf. Mal. 3:2f.; 4:5 with Matt. 3:7-12/Luke 3:7-9, 16f.),[61] but such an equation is not an element in any extant christological reflection, where the identification of the Baptist himself as Elijah is clearly established (Mark 1:2; 9:11-13 par.; Matt. 11:10/Luke 7:27; Matt. 11:14; Luke 1:16f., 76). Jesus is presented as the eschatological prophet (e.g., Luke 4:18; Matt. 11:5/Luke 7:22; Acts 10:38), and not least as the prophet like Moses (Acts 3:22; 7:37; Mark 9:7 pars.; John 7:52; 12:47f.) forecast long before (Deut. 18:15, 18f.), but never as Moses *redivivus*.[62]

In view of the earlier discussion the two more interesting figures at this point are Enoch and Melchizedek. As to the former, there is no suggestion whatsoever that Jesus was ever linked with Enoch in earliest Christian thought.[63] With Melchizedek there is at least something to grasp hold of. For in the letter to the Hebrews Christ is repeatedly designated "a priest for ever, after the order of Melchizedek" (Ps. 110:4; Heb. 5:6, 10; 6:20; 7:3, 17, 21). However, Melchizedek's role in Hebrews is limited to providing a pattern of priesthood which is not confined to the line of Aaron and which belongs to a different plane from the Aaronic priesthood. There may well be some influence from Platonic idealism at this point — the Melchizedek of Genesis 14 as a glimpse of the real priesthood, prefiguring the ideal heavenly priesthood of Christ, beside which the Aaronic priesthood is but an imperfect and now redundant shadow.[64] But there is no hint of any influence from the

---

61. Cf. J. A. T. Robinson, "Elijah, John and Jesus: An Essay in Detection," *NTS* 4 (1957-58) 236-81; R. E. Brown, "Three Quotations from John the Baptist in the Gospel of John" (1960), *New Testament Essays* (London: Chapman, 1965) 138-40; otherwise Jeremias, *TDNT* II, 936f.

62. See further *CiM*, §19.1 and above n. 26.

63. R. Otto's suggestion that Jesus' self-understanding and expectation was influenced by or patterned on the exaltation of Enoch to be Son of man (*The Kingdom of God and the Son of Man* [London: Lutterworth, 1938] 237) depends on a firm pre-Christian date for the Similitudes of Enoch and otherwise is without foundation. See the more measured judgment of B. Lindars, "Jesus as Advocate: A Contribution to the Christology Debate," *BJRL* 62 (1979-80) 490f.

64. On Hebrews' Platonic character see *CiM*, 52-54.

Qumran Melchizedek: Melchizedek is merely a pattern and is not depicted as still exercising his priesthood in heaven;[65] Christ is not identified with Melchizedek; and any suggestion that Christ was an angel, even a superior angel, would have been resolutely rejected by the writer to the Hebrews (Hebrews 1–2).[66] The significance of Christ's priesthood as an eternal priesthood follows more from the author's opening Wisdom christology than from his understanding of Melchizedek (see below).

In short, the model of the glorified hero seems to have played no discernible role in shaping earliest christology. Christ was not identified with any particular figure from the past, nor was thought of his exaltation modeled on the translation or final ascension of any earlier saint. It is possible that belief in his future return and role in judgment was in part determined by then current beliefs about Elijah and Enoch, but otherwise it would appear that the model of the glorified hero was ignored or passed over as inadequate to express even the earliest Christian belief about the risen Christ.

b) Similarly with Jewish *angelology*. It evidently did not occur to Luke, for example, to identify the angel Gabriel with the Son of God to be born to Mary (Luke 1:26-38). And where there is some hint that in one or two instances the exalted Christ was being compared to or thought of as an angel, the reaction of the New Testament writers is clearly and emphatically hostile — "To what angel did God ever say, 'You are my son; today I have begotten you' . . . ?" (Heb. 1:5ff.; cf. Col. 1:15-20 and 2:8-10 with 2:18). Thought of him as an intermediary figure in the sense that angels were intermediary figures was also inadequate and where even considered was quickly rejected.[67] Only in the case of the *Apocalypse of John* is it possible to argue that there was some influence from Jewish angelology on earliest christology, and to that possibility we must return in a moment.

c) We must say a little more about Jesus as *the Son of man*. Since the evidence reviewed earlier tells against the thesis that there was a Son of man concept in pre-Christian Judaism, we cannot say that in this phrase Jesus was being identified with such a figure. This conclusion is confirmed by the absence of confessional or polemical phrases like "Jesus is the Son of man." For where a title or name had been current in Jewish eschatological expectation we find just such identification formulas — "You are the Messiah" (Mark 8:29), "Can this be the Son of David?" (Matt. 12:23), "Are you Elijah?"

---

65. Despite 7:3 — "neither beginning of days nor end of life" — phrases best understood as exegesis of the silences of Gen. 14:18-20 using the rabbinic principle "what is not in the text, is not" (SB III, 694f.).

66. See particularly F. L. Horton, *The Melchizedek Tradition* (Cambridge: Cambridge University, ²1976) 167-70.

67. See further A. Grillmeier, *Christ in Christian Tradition* I: *From the Apostolic Age to Chalcedon (451)* (London: Mowbray, 1975) 46-53; Dunn, *CiM*, §20.3.

(John 1:21).[68] If then there had been a widespread belief in a heavenly redeemer figure known as the "Son of man" and Jesus had been identified or identified himself with that figure, some such identification formula would inevitably have been in use. The total absence of such a formula identifying Jesus as the "Son of man" (of popular eschatology) within the New Testament documents confirms that whatever the phrase meant in reference to Jesus it did not identify him with a particular heavenly being known as the Son of man.

Where the Synoptic Evangelists' use of the phrase alludes to Daniel's vision (Mark 13:26 pars.; 14:62 pars.; Matt. 24:44/Luke 12:40; Matt. 10:23; 16:28; 25:31; Luke 18:8), it is then simply a case of Jesus or the first Christians taking over the Danielic imagery to describe Christ's exaltation and/or return on the clouds of heaven. And since in Daniel the "one like a son of man" is a symbolical representation of the saints of the Most High and is not confused with Yahweh (the Ancient of Days), the reference of the phrase to Christ does not actually say anything about Christ's being divine and neither aggravates nor clarifies the issue of monotheism.[69] He is to sit on the other throne (cf. Dan. 7:9) at God's right hand (Mark 14:62; cf. Acts 7:56); but as we shall see in a moment, that is a privilege accorded to the last Adam. He is to judge the nations (Matt. 25:31; cf. Luke 12:8f.); but that is a role which his disciples and the saints will share (Matt. 19:28/Luke 22:30; 1 Cor. 6:2f.). And the belief in his return is at this point not so very different from the pre-Christian expectation of Elijah's return (cf. Mal. 3:1-3; Acts 3:20f.). It is true that in the Fourth Gospel the idea of the Son of Man's preexistence emerges (John 3:13; 6:62; cf. 1:51), but we shall have to leave this point until we can set it within the context of the Fourth Gospel.

One other passage, however, does require closer scrutiny — the description of the exalted Christ in the vision of Rev. 1:13-16. Here "one like a son of man" is described also as having "a golden girdle," hair "white as white wool," eyes "like a flame of fire," feet "like burnished bronze," and a voice "like the sound of many waters." We should note first the direct use of Dan. 7:13 without any apparent dependence on or knowledge of the Gospels'

---

68. Contrast John 12:34 — "Who is this 'Son of Man'?"

69. According to the LXX of Dan. 7:13 (manuscripts 88 and 967) the one like a son of man came "*as* the Ancient of Days" rather than "*to* the Ancient of Days." Perhaps a very early scribal error *(hōs* for *heōs)* (J. A. Montgomery, *Daniel* [ICC; Edinburgh: Clark, 1927] 304). But perhaps a more deliberate modification (see the discussion by J. Lust, "Daniel 7:13 and the Septuagint," *ETL* 54 [1978] 62-69 — I owe this reference to my colleague Dr. P. M. Casey), which may just reflect something of the same Jewish speculation at the end of the first century A.D. to which we have already referred (note that second-century Thedootion translates *heōs).* The seer of Revelation could have known the reading (see below), but the use of the phrase "the Son of man" in the Gospels stems directly from the Aramaic and shows no knowledge of or influence from the Greek, and the Evangelists' usage is confined to reworking and developing the Jesus-tradition itself.

usage[70] — a direct use of Daniel's vision in fact more like what we find in the Enoch cycle than in the Gospels. More striking is the merging of the description of the Ancient of Days ("hair like pure wool" — Dan. 7:9) with the description of the angel of Dan. 10:5f. (golden girdle, eyes like flaming torches, arms and legs like the gleam of burnished bronze, sound of his words like the noise of a multitude), with an allusion to the visions of Ezekiel (the sound of the living creatures' wings like the sound of many waters — Ezek. 1:24; the sound of the glory of the God of Israel's coming like the sound of many waters — Ezek. 43:2).[71] Here it would appear we have the kind of blurring of distinction between Yahweh, the one like a son of man, a glorious angel, and the glory of God which we found also in Judaism at about the same period,[72] and which the rabbis in the early second century A.D. condemned as a threat to their monotheism.[73] Could it be that the seer of Revelation belongs to or was influenced by that strand of esoteric Judaism which practiced Merkabah mysticism? Could we even conclude that it was precisely the sort of vision which the seer of Revelation describes in chapter 1 of his apocalypse that the rabbis saw as a threat to their monotheism? If so, we have a type of early christology which may eventually have achieved a popular expression in the Byzantine Pantocrator but which did not provide the high road for christological thought in the intervening period, perhaps precisely because it put too much strain on early Christian monotheism.

d) With the hypothesis of a pre-Christian Primal Man myth discounted, *Adam* christology might seem irrelevant to our present inquiry, since almost by definition Christ as last Adam is Christ as man, eschatological man, man as God intended him to be, but man — Christ as model of a new humanity, elder brother of a new family who will bear the image of God undefaced by disobedience, but man. Such a christology is certainly present in Paul (Rom. 8:29; 1 Cor. 15:21f., 47-49; 2 Cor. 3:18–4:6; Phil. 3:21; Col. 3:10), and particularly in Heb. 2:6-18, where Christ is presented as the only one to have fulfilled God's purpose for man as set out in Ps. 8:4-6:

What is man that you are mindful of him?
You made him a little less than the angels,
 and crowned him with glory and honor;
And you set him over the work of your hands,
 having put all things in subjection under his feet.

70. The definite article, universal in the Gospels ("the Son of man"), is absent here.
71. Cf. Rowland, "Vision of the Risen Christ." See also now R. Bauckham, "The Worship of Jesus in Apocalyptic Christianity," *NTS* 27 (1980-81) 322-41.
72. Revelation is usually dated toward the end of the first century A.D. (see, e.g., W. G. Kümmel, *Introduction to the New Testament* [London: SCM, 1975] 466-69).
73. See also the references collated in R. H. Charles, *Revelation* (ICC; Edinburgh: Clark, 1920) I, cxif.

The Adam parallel, however, becomes relevant as soon as we realize the significance of these last two lines — Adam christology includes the thought of lordship over creation; only Christ has been crowned with glory and honor (Heb. 2:9); only Christ has had all things put in subjection under his feet (1 Cor. 15:25; Eph. 1:22; Phil. 3:21; 1 Pet. 3:22). It becomes relevant as soon as we further realize that this is precisely what is predicted of Christ as *kyrios* (Lord): Ps. 110:1 — "The Lord says to my Lord: 'Sit at my right hand, till I make your enemies your footstool.'" In these same texts Christ's lordship is proclaimed by conflating Ps. 110:1 with Ps. 8:6, that is by conflating the idea of messianic lordship (Mark 12:35-37) with the idea of humanity's dominion over the rest of creation.[74] That is to say, in the claim that Christ is "Lord of all" Adam christology and *kyrios*-christology are one and the same.

The point is that *kyrios* is a title which in several passages, particularly in Paul, carries heavy overtones of divinity. As is well known, Paul refers several OT passages which speak of *kyrios* Yahweh to *kyrios* Christ — notably Rom. 10:13, "Everyone who calls upon the name of the Lord (Yahweh, Christ) will be saved" (Joel 2:32), and Phil. 2:10, where Second Isaiah's fiercely monotheistic assertion of universal worship to Yahweh becomes an assertion of universal worship to Christ (Isa. 45:21-23).[75] However, the problem which this causes for monotheism is eased as soon as we realize that for Paul the *kyrios* title functions most often as a way of distinguishing Christ from the one God. This we see clearly in the repeated phrase "the *God* and Father *of* our *Lord* Jesus Christ" (Rom. 15:6; 2 Cor. 1:3; 11:31; Eph. 1:3, 17; Col. 1:3); also in 1 Cor. 8:6, where Christ is professed as one Lord alongside the *Shema*'s profession of the one God; and most notably in 1 Cor. 15:24-28, where Christ's lordship in terms both of Ps. 110:1 and Ps. 8:6 climaxes in the Son's own subjection to God the Father, "that God may be all in all." Even the Philippians hymn must be mentioned here; for in my judgment it is an expression of Adam christology, so that Phil. 2:10 is best seen as a confession of Christ's lordship as (last) Adam,[76] where, Paul makes it plain, all creation acknowledges Christ's lordship "to the glory of God the Father" (2:11).

It would seem then that Adam and *kyrios* christology as statements of Christ's cosmic lordship are best understood, not as any sort of threat to the unity of God or as a diffusion of the one God's sovereignty over creation, but rather in terms of God's purpose to share his authority as Creator with humanity, the crown of his creation, the image of God destined from the first to share in his fuller glory. In short, the exalted Christ is Lord over all (perhaps

---

74. See more fully *CiM*, §14.2.

75. See further A. W. Wainwright, *The Trinity in the New Testament* (London: SPCK, 1962) ch. 5.

76. *CiM*, §15.1.

even "god over all" — Rom. 9:5[77]) not so much as a right of godhood, but more as an authority given by God to the firstborn of a new race of resurrected humanity, not only as representing God before humankind but also as representing humankind before God.

e) Finally, what of *Sophia* and *Logos* christology? There is no doubt that some of the most profound christological assertions in the first century A.D. were made in terms drawn from the imagery and language used for the personified Wisdom and Word of God in pre-Christian Judaism. In particular it is this language which enabled the first Christians to relate Christ to the act of creation. Christ is not only thought of as Lord over creation; it is also said of him that "all things (came about) through him" (1 Cor. 8:6), that "in him all things were created" (Col. 1:16), that "he is the radiance of God's glory, the stamp of his nature" (Heb. 1:3). All this sort of language is very familiar to us from the Jewish wisdom tradition and from Philo as description of the Wisdom and Word of God.[78] But, as we saw earlier, Sophia and Logos in the pre-Christian Jewish tradition are simply attempts to speak of God, of God in his relation to creation and to those who seek him; the Wisdom of God, the Word of God is God in his self-revelation.

When such language is used of Christ then, what does it mean? Does it mean any more than when the Torah was identified as the Wisdom of God? That is to say, is it simply a way of asserting that Christ in his life, death, and resurrection so embodied and expressed God's wisdom that we need look no further for our definition of God and our understanding of his purposes (see particularly 1 Cor. 1:22-24, 30)? Was it simply a way of asserting that Christ has superseded the Torah as the focus and norm of divine wisdom? Such a case is certainly arguable. Even the language of preexistence can then be simply conceived as a way of expressing continuity between God's creative power and his saving purpose in Christ: it is the same God, the same power, the same wisdom that created all things and was active in and through Christ. Likewise with the prologue to John's Gospel. The language of the first verses would be familiar to anyone who knew Philo or the Wisdom tradition (John 1:1-11).[79] The decisive advance would then be that the creative and illuminating utterance of God was said to have *become* flesh, to have become human, Jesus Christ (1:14) — which would be a powerful way of asserting that Christ embodied the fullness of grace and truth more than the Torah ever did or could (1:17), embodied the self-revelation of God in a full and final way (1:18).

Yet at the same time there is a crucial difference between Judaism's

---

77. See the brief discussion in *CiM*, 45, with further bibliography in the notes.
78. See *CiM*, 165-66.
79. *CiM*, 164f., 241f.

identification of divine wisdom with the Torah and Christianity's identification of Sophia-Logos with Christ. For the Torah in the end of the day is a book, an impersonal object, and no matter how exalted became the description and assessment of the Torah, it can never really become a threat to monotheism. But Christ was a man, a human being. That of course is one important reason why he provides a better definition of God — a person can better embody the personal God's self-revelation. But to attribute to a *man* Wisdom's role in creation, to assert that a *human being* is God in his self-revelation, that is bound to have some repercussions for monotheism. After all, the reason we could conclude that the talk of Sophia and Logos in pre-Christian Judaism was *not* a threat to Jewish monotheism was simply that Sophia was a personi-fication, not a person, and Logos was the personification of God's immanence, not a personal being other than God himself. But now the impersonal Wisdom is identified as the exalted Christ, the personification Logos is identified as the man Christ Jesus, and Christianity may seem thereby to be committed to a belief in two divine beings, two powers in heaven — God himself and Sophia-Christ. Was this not to put an unbearable strain on earliest Chris-tianity's monotheism?

The exegetical answer seems to be that the first Christians were to some extent conscious of this danger.[80] Thus when Paul attributes Wisdom's role in creation to Christ in 1 Cor. 8:6, he has already prefaced it with the strong Jewish confession that God is one. Thus he must mean that the creative and redemptive role of Sophia-Christ is nothing other than the creative and re-demptive activity of this one God. That is to say, insofar as we can speak of the preexistence of Christ, the deity of Christ at this point, it is the preexistence and deity of the one God acting in and through Christ of which we are actually speaking. Christ is divine in no other sense than as God immanent, God himself acting to redeem as he did to create. In Col. 1:15-20, on the other hand, it is important not to take the first half of the hymn in isolation from the second half, for each half is evidently saying the same things but in complementary ways. The first half speaks of Christ as the creative agency and purpose of Wisdom — the activity of God in creation is identified as Christ, whereas the second half attributes Christ's preeminence over creation to the fact that "God in all his fullness was pleased to dwell in him" and to act through him (1:19f.). In other words, it is not enough to say that Christ is simply an inspired prophet or glorified hero; rather he is incarnate Wisdom, the embodied fullness of God's self-expression. But also excluded thereby is the idea that he is a god other than the God of creation, a divine being other than the God of Israel; rather he *is* the God of creation, or more precisely, he embodies the outreach of the one God in its most tangibly personal (i.e.,

---

80. For the following passages see the fuller exposition in *CiM*, §§24.2, 24.5, and 25.3.

somatic) form (Col. 2:9). Likewise with Heb. 1:2f., he who is described as God's Son, as agent in creation, is also described as the radiance of God's glory, and subsequently as the Son who learned obedience and who was made perfect through what he suffered, thus becoming qualified for his appointment as High Priest (2:9-18; 5:5-10). That is to say, Hebrews similarly asserts that that of God which is most visible to humans has become visible in and as Christ, that is, in the suffering Christ, the last Adam, perfected through suffering. In other words, the deity of Christ is God himself reaching out to humans through Christ to offer his costly forgiveness.

It is in the Fourth Gospel that the tension becomes most acute. At first it seems if anything to have slackened, for the prologue does not speak properly of Christ till v. 14. Unlike the passages just looked at we have no statement of the form, "Christ through whom all things were created." Prior to v. 14 the thought is primarily of the Logos. It is the utterance of God that John calls "God." It is God's word through which all things came to be. Christ is not the Logos *per se;* he is the Logos *become flesh*. We may quite properly say that the personified Logos, the impersonal Logos first became personal in the incarnation. But at the same time in the body of the Gospel we have regular talk of the Son of God, who is conscious of having preexisted with the Father before his entry into the world (e.g., John 6:38; 8:23, 38; 10:36; 16:28; 17:5, 24). No wonder Bultmann thought there was at the back of this something significantly different from Judaism's earlier theology of the word;[81] it is not altogether surprising that the Johannine discourses provided the greatest scope for Bultmann's reconstruction of the pre-Christian Gnostic redeemer myth.[82] Here if anywhere in the earliest Christian sources we have one who is conscious of having enjoyed a personal pre-existence with the Father prior to his life on earth, one who like the king's son in the *Song of the Pearl* remembers his true status and identity even while on earth.

Yet here, too, it must be important to retain a proper balance between the different parts of the Gospel, between the prologue and the rest, between the christology of the prologue and the christology of the discourses. After all, it can hardly be accidental that the Logos christology, which reappears nowhere else in the Gospel, is set as the preface to the whole. The intended implication presumably is that the Logos christology is the doorway or window into the rest, that we must interpret the Son of God christology in the light of the Logos christology. In this case by preexistent Son John means preexistent Logos; that is to say, the Son is not another divine power but is

---

81. Bultmann, *John,* 21f.
82. As Bultmann himself acknowledged (see R. H. Fuller, *The New Testament in Current Study* [London: SCM, 1963] 136 and n. 1).

the immanent presence of him who alone is God from all eternity. Hence the emphasis on the unity of Father and Son (particularly 10:30); hence the numinous character of the repeated "I am" (particularly 8:58);[83] and hence above all the emphasis that to see the Son is to see the Father (particularly 12:45; 14:9). For as the Logos is the self-manifestation of God, so the Logos-Son incarnate as Jesus Christ makes God seeable.

What we seem to have in the Fourth Gospel therefore is not a taking over of an earlier myth of a divine redeemer distinct from God, but rather a fresh creation — a creative molding of categories and language from prophet christology, Son of Man christology, and Sophia-Logos christology. From prophet christology is derived talk of the Son being sent.[84] From the tradition of Jesus' own words comes talk of the Son of man. From the Sophia-Logos christology emerges the idea of preexistent presence with God. Consequently in the composite christology the Logos is the Son, the Son is sent into the world, the Son of man descends from heaven. But is this so very different from pre-Christian Judaism's talk of divine wisdom? The imagery is bolder; it is used with respect to one who was a human being on earth. But is it any more of a threat to Jewish monotheism than the Jewish Wisdom or the Philonic Logos? It is true of course that the Gnostics were subsequently able to use John's composite christology as part of their own syncretism; John's christology became one of the major building blocks in Gnostic speculation, a crucial stimulus toward the Gnostic redeemer myth as such.[85] But it is very doubtful if John would have approved this use. More significant is the fact that emerging orthodoxy worked primarily in terms of a Logos christology, a christology which identified the redeemer with the creative agency of God — thereby deliberately choosing to stay within the bounds of Jewish monotheism. It is this monotheistic interpretation of John which finally won the day against the more Gnostic syncretistic use of John, so that when the Son of God language became the major christological motif from Nicea onward it is the Logos-Son who is in view, the Johannine Son of God understood in the light of the Johannine Logos (as John intended) and not the Johannine Son of God understood in terms of the Gnostic redeemer myth, as a redeemer who is not also creator.

83. E. L. Miller, "The Christology of John 8:25," *TZ* 36 (1980) 237-65, suggests that 8:25 has the sense "I am the One at the Beginning, which is what I keep telling you," which would forge a strong link between 1:1 and 8:58.

84. Cf. particularly J. A. Bühner, *Der Gesandte und sein Weg im 4. Evangelium* (Tübingen, 1977); E. Schillebeeckx, *Christ: The Christian Experience in the Modern World* (London: SCM, 1980) 313-22.

85. See further J. D. G. Dunn, *Unity and Diversity in the New Testament* (London: SCM, 1977) §64.

IV

If earliest christology had consisted simply in one or other of the elements examined above there would be no difficulty in asserting Christianity's monotheistic status. The idea of the glorified hero never provided more than a partial model for the first Christians' assessment of the exalted Christ. And where the term "Son of Man" did give more scope, its reference to the glorified Christ was not so very dissimilar to the role in judgment attributed to Enoch in the early stages of the Enoch cycle. As last Adam the risen Christ was himself thought of primarily as a pattern for a new humanity; even as Lord his lordship over creation was of a piece with the dominion over all things which God had originally intended for Adam. In all this Christ stands more on the side of creation than of creator. The christologies are not modeled on earlier ideas of a heavenly redeemer, and though Christ himself in his exaltation can now properly be called a heavenly redeemer figure he is so as representative man, not as a second god.[86]

Alternatively the first Christians also identified Christ as God's creative wisdom, as the Word of God become flesh — that is, they recognized God acting in and through Christ, they saw God in and through Christ, they understood God more clearly because they understood him in terms of Christ. In other words, Sophia and Logos were not thought to be heavenly beings distinct from God, and Christ identified as Sophia-Logos incarnate was not thought of as being distinct from God. Rather as Sophia-Logos was a way of expressing the one God's immanent presence in the world, so Christ as Sophia-Logos was understood as the focus and clearest expression of that presence, the presence of God himself.

The one model most firmly rejected within earliest Christianity was that of angelology. Where the possibility of developing a systematic identification of Christ with an archangel was even considered it was dismissed. That is to say the model which might have opened the door to a systematic christology which set Jesus at the head of an angelic hierarchy or series of evolutionary emanations in Gnostic fashion, was precisely that model on which the first Christians turned their backs.[87] There was, however, one strand within apoc-

---

86. I am less convinced than C. F. D. Moule, *The Origin of Christology* (Cambridge: Cambridge University, 1977), particularly ch. 2, that the incorporative inclusive categories which Paul uses to speak of believers' relationship to Christ ("in Christ," "the body of Christ," etc.) take us beyond an Adam christology and "conceive of Christ as any theist conceives of God" (94f., 138f.). Paul does after all speak of Jesus as representative man prior to his resurrection, in his life and death (Rom. 8:3; 2 Cor. 5:14; Gal. 3:16; Phil. 2:7f.).

87. Contrast Justin, *Apologia* 1.6.2, and Athenagoras, *Legatio* 10.5, where a readiness to draw in angelology to enrich their doctrine of God has laid them open to the charge of "crypto-polytheism" (Loofs) — see the recent discussion by W. R. Schoedel, "A Neglected Motive for Second-Century Trinitarianism," *JTS* 31 (1980) 356-67.

alyptic which shows the influence of Merkabah mysticism, where the vision of the exalted Christ merged elements of earlier visions of Yahweh with earlier visions of a glorious angel. But this made no lasting impact on either Christianity or Judaism; it was rejected by rabbinic Judaism but tolerated within Christianity — a visionary ambiguity which was unacceptable to strict Jewish monotheism was evidently not so unacceptable to Christianity's redefined monotheism (see again n. 45).

The problems of consistent expression arose, however, when these somewhat different christologies were brought together, to be plaited into a single strand — when the idea of Christ as Adam-Lord had to be meshed into the idea of Christ as Sophia-Logos — when the belief in one who represents humankind to God had to be merged with the belief in one who represented God to humankind. To put it another way, there is no final problem with the idea of Christ's preexistence — Christ's preexistence is the preexistence of Sophia-Logos, the preexistence of an impersonal personification for the outreach of the personal God. But it is more difficult to handle the idea of Christ's *post*existence, for this is the continuing existence not of an impersonal personification but of a person, Jesus of Nazareth. He who worshiped and prayed to God is seen himself as God's self-expression. The God who is God of our Lord Jesus Christ is also God in and through Christ as God to us. Even his return as Savior is "the appearing of the glory of our great God" (Tit. 2:13).[88]

To state it thus is about as far as we can go without passing beyond the bounds of the New Testament and of my own competence. But at least two points of importance for our understanding of the subsequent debates have emerged from this analysis and are worth drawing attention to in closing. First, we can see that the complexity of the subsequent debates is already determined by the first century's attempts to assess and express the significance of Christ. The complexity of the subsequent debates was not simply the result of translating first-century language into the categories of Hellenistic philosophy. More important, it was the first Christians' recognition *both* of the reality of God in Christ *and* that Christ was wholly one with them, a man among humans, that determined the course of future orthodoxy. Second, the constraints and limitations within which the subsequent debaters found they had to work were already there more or less from the beginning. The fact that he is already conceived as Adam, as he who even as Lord acknowledges the one God to be his God — that fact ruled out the modalist and Sabellian options from the start. At the same time, because he *is* Sophia-Logos and is not simply

---

88. Cf. V. Hasler, "Epiphanie und Christologie in den Pastoralbriefen," *TZ* 33 (1977) 193-209, particularly 199-201; L. Oberlinner, "Die 'Epiphaneia' des Heilswillens Gottes in Christus Jesus. Zur Grundstruktur der Christologie der Pastoralbriefe," *ZNW* 71 (1980) 192-213, particularly 197-202.

a man who became Sophia-Logos (rather Sophia-Logos became him), the adoptionist option is also ruled out. That is to say, the exalted Christ is not any more divine than the earthly Jesus — he is Sophia-Logos from the start, God comes to expression in and through him as much in his life and suffering and death as in his resurrection and exaltation. Still less is he to be conceived as a second divine being in heaven, a second power, or first in a sequence of emanatory powers — the Gnostic option is even more firmly excluded. And because as Sophia-Logos he is God himself in his outreach to the world, even Arianism is in effect already excluded. The sophisticated distinctions of the later debates are of course not yet formulated, sometimes arbitrary, sometimes artificial as they may now appear to us. Nevertheless the point remains that within the context of the philosophic categories of these early centuries distinctions and definitions of that sort were bound to emerge, if only because the testimony of the first Christians and of the New Testament writers left them no choice. Because the man Jesus was from the first at the center of Christianity, Christianity had to redefine its monotheism. But because it was the one God of Jewish faith whom those first Christians recognized in and through this Jesus it was a redefinition and not an abandoning of that monotheism. It is thus a fundamental insight and assertion of Christianity that the Christian doctrine of the trinity is but a restatement of Jewish monotheism.[89]

89. In an already too lengthy paper I cannot go into the role of Spirit christology in all this. Suffice it to say that just as the assessment of Christ in terms of Sophia-Logos leads to a redefinition of Jewish monotheism in what we might call a "binitarian" direction, so the recognition that Spirit christology was not simply a variant on Sophia-Logos christology created an internal tension and dynamic in earliest christology which resulted inevitably in a fully triadic formulation. See further my *CiM*, ch. V; also "Rediscovering the Spirit (2)," *ExpT* 94 (1982) 9-18.

20

Let John Be John
A Gospel for Its Time

1

There are several reasons that the Fourth Gospel is distinctive, even unique, among the New Testament documents. One is that it is more difficult in the case of John than with any other New Testament writing to speak of an "author." With every other New Testament document we can talk confidently of an "author," of the one who was more or less exclusively responsible for the words and sentiments of our texts as they now stand. We can set the goal of exegesis as the uncovering of the *intention* of the author, and pursue that goal as a meaningful and viable objective. But with John the concept of a single author, or of a document written from start to finish over one short period, becomes problematic. It is not simply that the history of traditions and/or sources *behind* John is obscure (the Fourth Gospel is not alone in this). It is rather that the stages of composition of the Gospel itself are difficult to recover, and the relative importance of each stage for the final product difficult to determine. To what extent have the theology and character of the Fourth Gospel been decisively stamped on the material at an *earlier* stage in the process — whatever that "earlier stage" might be — traditions or sources utilized, or an earlier edition of our present Gospel? Or, putting the same question from the other end of the process: how much of the Gospel is properly to be defined as "redactional"? And if we must speak of a redactor, to what

---

Originally published in *Das Evangelium und die Evangelien. Vorträge vom Tübinger Symposium 1982,* ed. P. Stuhlmacher (Tübingen: Mohr, 1982) 309-39 = *The Gospel and the Gospels,* ed. P. Stuhlmacher (Grand Rapids: Eerdmans, 1991) 293-322. Also delivered in modified form as one of the Wilkinson lectures at Northern Baptist Theological Seminary, Lombard, Illinois, in November 1982.

extent has he determined the character and theology of what we now have?[1] The still vigorous debate on such questions shows how difficult New Testament scholarship has found it to achieve a firm orientation toward the Fourth Gospel.[2] In the present essay we shall speak of "the Fourth Evangelist" to denote whoever put the Gospel into its present form without prejudice to the question of what and how much is more appropriately described as "redactional."

Another distinctive feature of John's Gospel is the way in which, more than any other New Testament writing, John has served as a bridge between the beginnings of Christianity in Jesus and the orthodox faith which achieved definition at Nicea and which has provided the dogmatic basis of Christianity ever since. John is written about Jesus, about his ministry of word and sign in Judea and Galilee, and its traditions are certainly rooted in greater or less degree in the earliest memories of that ministry. At the same time, John's Gospel brought together the key categories which dominated the subsequent developing debates on christology (Logos and Son of God), and the Gospel has provided a portrayal of Jesus which has served as probably the chief inspiration and textbook for centuries of Christ-centered apologetic and piety.

It is presumably these two elements of John's distinctiveness which have caused scholarship such difficulty in locating the Fourth Gospel within early Christianity. By this I do not refer simply to the difficulty of placing the Fourth Gospel within the time scale of early Christianity and within the geography of the eastern Mediterranean — the problem of date and place of composition. I am referring to the larger *problem of setting John within its historical context* — the difficulty of illuminating the cultural and theological situation(s) which called for this complex document to be written, the difficulty of determining to what extent such cultural and theological influences have shaped the Gospel, whether at an earlier or later stage in composition.

I emphasize this for two reasons. First, in my view the task of clarifying the historical context as much as possible is crucial for exegesis: the more

---

1. Cf. H. Thyen, "Aus der Literatur zum Johannesevangelium," *TR* 39 (1974) 252: "A large part of the scholarly controversies concerning the interpretation of the fourth Gospel depends on whether one understands its standpoint to be that of the basic document or of the redaction."

2. See the review of the debate in R. Kysar, *The Fourth Evangelist and His Gospel* (1975), Part One; R. Schnackenburg, "Entwicklung und der Stand der johanneischen Forschung seit 1955," *L'Évangile de Jean: Sources, rédaction, théologie,* ed. M. de Jonge (BETL 44; 1975). See also R. A. Culpepper, *The Johannine School* (SBLDS 26; 1975). Worth pondering is the caution of R. E. Brown, *The Community of the Beloved Disciple* (1979) 28: "The tendency among some scholars, especially in Germany, to see an opposition between the Johannine evangelist and his sources, and thus antithetical phases of community life in the pre-Gospel period, is in my judgment almost certainly wrong."

fully and sympathetically we can enter into the historical context of a writing, the more likely we are to understand that writing, its character and theology, to perceive the intention of the one(s) who determined that character and theology. So with John in particular, only by uncovering its historical context can we hope to hear it as the first readers were intended to hear it, the allusions and nuances as well as the explicit teaching. Second, the task of clarifying the tradition-process behind John, of illuminating both the continuities and the discontinuities with the earliest forms of the gospel, depends to a considerable extent on our achieving such a successful exegesis of John. Only when we have learned to recognize what the concerns of the Fourth Evangelist were in writing his Gospel will we be in a position to recognize whether these concerns have influenced his use of pre-formed material. Only when we have a clear grasp of what is Johannine can we hope to distinguish what is pre-Johannine in any systematic way. Of course, it by no means follows that the categories "Johannine" and "pre-Johannine" are mutually exclusive, that distinctive Johannine motifs are the *creation* of the Fourth Evangelist. But if we find that some of the motifs have been formulated to address the particular historical situation in which and to which the Gospel was written, we will be in a better position to determine the extent to which these motifs have shaped or molded the material used.

Consequently *the task of setting John in its historical context must be given a place of priority* in any inquiry into the gospel and the Fourth Gospel. Unfortunately it is a task which has often been ignored, or which has been pursued without sufficient care.[3] In both cases, because the historical context has not been clarified, John has been *mis*understood, the Fourth Gospel has not been heard in its own terms, John has not been allowed to be John. Let me say a little more on this as a way of explaining my own approach to John and his Gospel.

2

The task of contextualizing the Fourth Gospel and its message has been seriously ignored and misconceived in two directions — by reading John as though it belonged either to a *later* context or to a very *early* context.

2.1. The interpretation of John in the light of later developments is actually the classic reading of John. The fact that the Fourth Gospel played such a crucial role in the development of christological and trinitarian dogma up to and beyond Nicea has resulted in generations of scholarship reading

---

3. Cf. K. Wengst, *Bedrängte Gemeinde und verherrlichter Christus* (1981) 29-32.

John in the light of these subsequent debates.[4] In particular, it has been all too easy to assume that the Athanasian and post-Nicene concern to define the *relation* between the Father and the Son was already the Fourth Evangelist's concern. How natural, with a Gospel which speaks so much about God as Father and Jesus as the Son, simply to take it for granted that the Evangelist too was wrestling with the problem of how to conceptualize and define the relationship between the first two persons of the Godhead. But that is something exegesis cannot simply assume. The use of the Fourth Gospel within subsequent dogmatics, quite legitimate within its own terms, is *not* the key to a historically contextualized exegesis. If exegesis has the task of hearing John speak in its own terms and in its own time, so far as that is possible, then we exegetes must be prepared to speak on John's behalf if we see his Gospel being "hijacked" forward in time. For only when we have let John be itself and heard its message as its first readers heard it, so far as that is possible, only then will we be in a position to evaluate also the way in which John was used in the subsequent debates. Here not least we must be prepared to let John be John, for the dogmatic use of John too must justify itself by at least some reference to the meaning intended by the Fourth Evangelist.

2.2. Somewhat surprisingly the classic *religionsgeschichtliche* treatments of the Fourth Gospel cannot be exempted from the same criticism at this point. Although rightly motivated as attempts to understand John's Gospel against the religious context of its time, their pursuit of the phantom of the pre-Christian Gnostic redeemer myth threw their whole endeavor off course. What emerged in the event was John set against and interpreted within the context of Mandaism and the later Gnostic systems.[5] The same criticism applies, though with less force, to those who have attempted to sustain a different or modified version of the Bultmann thesis — to locate John some way along a "gnosticizing trajectory."[6] We cannot criticize those who see the Fourth Gospel simply as a stepping stone toward Nicene orthodoxy without criticizing also those who see the Fourth Gospel simply as a stepping stone

---

4. T. E. Pollard begins his *Johannine Christology and the Early Church* (SNTSMS 13; 1970), by citing F. C. Conybeare: "If Athanasius had not had the Fourth Gospel to draw texts from, Arius would never have been confuted." But he goes on to note "that if Arius had not had the Fourth Gospel to draw texts from, he would not have needed confuting" (13).

5. See, e.g., the criticisms of W. A. Meeks, "The Man from Heaven in Johannine Sectarianism," *JBL* 91 (1972) 45: "Bultmann's synthetic myth is heavily dependent on the terminology of the Fourth Gospel; there is hardly any single document other than John in which all the elements of the 'gnostic redeemer myth' listed by Bultmann in his 1923 article are integrally displayed."

6. See particularly J. M. Robinson, "The Johannine Trajectory" (1968), in J. M. Robinson and H. Koester, *Trajectories through Early Christianity* (1971) 232-68; L. Schottroff, *Der Glaubende und die fiendliche Welt* (1970); S. Schulz, *Johannes* (NTD 4; 1972), e.g., 28, 211; W. Langbrandtner, *Weltferner Gott oder Gott der Liebe: Der Ketzerstreit in der johanneischen Kirche* (BBE 6; 1977).

toward Gnosticism. To show how John was *used* by different factions from the second century onward is no answer to the question, What was the message John was intended to convey to its *first* readers? The *"dogmatic"* or the *"heretical"* John may in the event tell us very little about what we might call the *"historical"* John. To postulate a vague "gnosticizing" context for John may make meaningful sense of some elements in John, but only at the expense of ignoring such firmer indications of a historical context which makes better sense of the whole, as we shall see. Even Käsemann, who attempts manfully to elucidate the Fourth Gospel from its own internal logic and who in fact succeeds in grasping much of John's central thrust,[7] cannot in the event escape from his early *religionsgeschichtliche* perspective, and ends by accusing John of "gnosticizing tendencies" and "naive docetism," which the Church declared "orthodox" in error.[8]

A methodological point of some importance emerges from all this. I mean that the New Testament exegete should never forget that it is possible to presume too *broad* a historical context for a New Testament document as well as too *narrow* a context. The twentieth-century student of first- and second-century religion in the eastern Mediterranean (or of third- and fourth-century patristic thought, for that matter) may be as much hindered as helped by the breadth of his or her historical knowledge. The context within which the student sets a document like the Fourth Gospel, consciously or unconsciously, may be far too wide, both in time and in geographical extent. He or she may detect wide-ranging influences and tendencies which were not actually factors in the understanding of the writer(s) and the first readers. It is as important for an exegete to remember the *limited horizons* of particular documents, as it is to appreciate the much more diverse currents within the broader milieu. A bird's-eye view of the whole scene, desirable as it is, will not facilitate a close encounter with a particular author on the ground. To the extent then that German scholarship on the Fourth Gospel has been dominated by the Bultmann-Käsemann debate on John 1:14,[9] to that extent it is vulnerable to the criticism of treating the Fourth Gospel anachronistically, of asking the right questions, but against too broad a background. Here too we must attempt to let John be John.[10]

7. See below, n. 94.

8. E. Käsemann, *The Testament of Jesus* (1968).

9. According to Thyen (n. 1), 50: the "Interpretationsmodelle" of Bultmann and Käsemann "limit Johannine studies to a corner."

10. On this whole subject cf. particularly the wisely cautionary comments of W. A. Meeks, "'Am I a Jew?' — Johannine Christianity and Judaism," *Christianity, Judaism and other Greco-Roman Cults: Studies for Morton Smith*, ed. J. Neusner (1975) I, 163-85, and Wengst's concise critique of some of the above theses in *Bedrängte Gemeinde* (n. 3), 12-22. My own *Christology in the Making: An Inquiry into the Origins of the Doctrine of Incarnation* ([1]1980) is in fact an exposition of the very important "limited horizons" point.

3

If John has been read too quickly as though it belonged to a later context, an alternative tendency has been to read the Fourth Gospel as far as possible within the context of Jesus' own ministry in the late 20s or early 30s.

3.1. Most serious here has been the attempt to argue that the Fourth Gospel is more or less strictly historical from start to finish. Not simply particular elements (like geographical notes) and particular traditions (like those about the Baptist) are historical, but the narratives as such were intended as historical descriptions of actual events in Jesus' life. Not simply individual sayings within the Johannine discourses, but the discourses as a whole were intended to document what Jesus actually said during his life on earth. On this view, everything John presents Jesus as doing or saying, Jesus must actually have done, must actually have said in more or less the words reported. Only if exegesis proceeds on this presupposition can we be faithful to the intent and meaning of the document as Scripture. Such would be the thrust of conservative scholars who try to push the recognition of historical tradition in John to its fullest extent.[11]

We should pay heed to such attempts, for not only is their concern to emphasize the historical character of John's Gospel as of crucial importance in itself, but they also represent a substantial body of belief at the popular level. We need, for example, only recall the multitudinous ecumenical pronouncements which take their justification from the prayer of Jesus in John 17 ("that they may be one even as we are one" — v. 22) — apparently on the grounds that this was a dominical word. Probably no issue marks off the bulk of New Testament scholarship so sharply from the piety of the pews than the issue of how the Fourth Gospel should be understood. A New Testament scholarship which is concerned to be heard also by "the ordinary believer"[12] cannot be unconcerned at the way in which the Fourth Gospel is expounded in so many churches today. For if it is a mistake to assume that the discourses of John are more or less a transcript of what Jesus actually said during his ministry in Galilee and Judea, and if preaching on that basis is misleading the people, then those of us who are concerned to exercise a teaching ministry in the church cannot escape the obligation of correcting that mistake. Despite

---

11. See, e.g., L. Morris, *Studies in the Fourth Gospel* (1969) ch. 2; idem, *The Gospel according to John* (NICNT; 1971) 40-49; D. A. Carson, "Historical Tradition in the Fourth Gospel: After Dodd, What?" *Gospel Perspectives* II, ed. R. T. France and D. Wenham (1981) 83-145; G. Maier, "Johannes und Matthäus — Zwiespalt oder Viergestalt des Evangeliums," ibid., 267-91; cf. the older work of E. Stauffer, *Jesus and His Story* (1960) 149-59.

12. I do not imply that scholars have neglected this concern; see, e.g., E. E. Ellis, *The World of St. John* (1965); A. M. Hunter, *According to John* (1968); S. S. Smalley, *John: Evangelist and Interpreter* (1978).

the desire to be true to Scripture, such expositions are not being true to John. They are *imposing* a context and an intention *on* John, not allowing an exegesis which is mindful of historical context to elucidate the questions of intention and meaning. They are not letting John be John.

3.2. What of our concern to trace the traditions behind the Fourth Gospel, the continuities of the gospel within and behind the Fourth Gospel? It is a concern which I certainly share. If John's Gospel cannot be shown to have firm roots in the history of Jesus Messiah, the value of John *is* significantly diminished; not least its role as a bridge between the beginnings of Christianity and the subsequent christological dogmas is undermined at one end.

Moreover, I am confident that the Fourth Gospel does draw on good tradition at many points. I think, for example, of the topographical notes (Aenon near Salim, the pools of Bethzatha and Siloam, a town called Ephraim, etc.), and the parallel traditions (particularly regarding John the Baptist, the calling of the disciples, the cleansing of the temple, the healing miracles and the feeding of the five thousand, and the passion narrative). At such points John can quite justifiably be said to supplement the Synoptics, whether by design or simply because the traditions utilized by John were fuller at various points.[13] I think too of how particular verses central to the themes of various Johannine discourses can be paralleled by individual sayings in the Synoptic tradition (e.g., John 3:3, 5, another version of Matt. 18:3/Mark 10:15; John 5:19 and 10:15, possible variants of Matt. 11:27; John 6:53, drawing on the tradition of the Last Supper; John 10:1-5, a development of the parable of the lost sheep in Matt. 18:12-13; John 13:20, parallel to Matt. 10:40) and how even the striking "I am" formula in John can be paralleled to some extent by Mark 6:50 (cf. 14:62). In all this the definitive work of C. H. Dodd still stands as a landmark in Johannine study.[14] It has been and will be supplemented at individual points.[15] But it is hard to imagine its main findings being overthrown or their overall balance being much altered.

I also consider it highly probable, in the light of John 19:35; 20:2-9; 21:24, that the source and validator of this earlier tradition was the historical individual

---

13. Despite recent restatements of the view that John knew and used one or more of the Synoptics, I find the evidence not wholly persuasive. See, e.g., the review of the discussion by Kysar (n. 2), 54-66. Since then note particularly F. Neirynck, "John and the Synoptics," *L'Évangile de Jean* (n. 2) 73-106; C. K. Barrett, *John* (²1978) 15-18, 42-46; Mgr. de Solages, *Jean et les Synoptiques* (1979); D. M. Smith, "John and the Synoptics: Some Dimensions of the Problem," *NTS* 26 (1979-80) 425-44; J. Becker, "Aus der Literatur zum Johannesevangelium," *TR* 47 (1982) 289-94.

14. C. H. Dodd, *Historical Tradition in the Fourth Gospel* (1963).

15. See particularly the sequence of studies by B. Lindars, *Behind the Fourth Gospel* (1971); idem, *The Gospel of John* (NCBC; 1972), esp. 46-54; idem, "Traditions behind the Fourth Gospel," *L'Évangile de Jean* (n. 2), 107-24; idem, "John and the Synoptic Gospels: A Test Case," *NTS* 27 (1980-81) 287-94; idem, "Discourse and Tradition: The Use of the Sayings of Jesus in the Discourses of the Fourth Gospel," *JSNT* 13 (1981) 83-101.

described as "the beloved disciple," though I am less certain of the extent to which the beloved disciple has been idealized.[16] So too it must be considered probable, in the light of John 4, that Samaritans were involved in the history of the Johannine community; though I am much less certain that we can use the different *emphases* within the Gospel's christology as evidence of different *stages* in the development of the same Johannine community.[17] All in all, then, there are sufficient indications from within the Gospel itself that the Fourth Evangelist's clearly implied concern to preserve and reproclaim the truth of Jesus and the "testimony" of those who were with Christ "from the beginning" (15:27; 16:13) is to be taken with all seriousness.

My point, however, is that it is difficult to advance the discussion about such issues until the historical context of the Fourth Gospel itself has been clarified, until, in other words, we know whether we have to discount (for the purposes of tracing historical tradition) certain emphases as belonging to the latest stage of the tradition history. Not only so, but it is worth bearing in mind that a tradition-historical investigation, precisely because it is more concerned with the points of similarity and contact with the Synoptic tradition, may well pay too little attention to the Johannine *distinctives,* particularly the theological features which give John its distinctive character.

If, in addition, the inquiry is directed toward demonstrating the historical trustworthiness of the earlier tradition, that may detract still further from the Gospel itself by strengthening the hidden assumption or implied inference that John's Gospel is "authentic" or "authoritative" only in proportion as it draws on historical tradition: the more we can show the Fourth Gospel to have been dependent on tradition which goes back to the 30s, the more we value it. For all that a legitimate concern is involved here: What if John's Gospel was *not* intended primarily as a supplement to one or more of the other three? What if John's Gospel was not intended to serve as a source of *historical* information about Jesus in his ministry on earth?[18] In that case an inquiry

16. See particularly H. Thyen, "Aus der Literatur zum Johannesevangelium," *TR* 42 (1977) 213-61; Brown (n. 2), 31-34; M. de Jonge, "The Beloved Disciple and the Date of the Gospel of John," *Text and Interpretation,* ed. E. Best and R. McL. Wilson (M. Black FS; 1979) 99-114.

17. See Brown (n. 2), 25-28, in discussion with alternative reconstructions particularly of J. L. Martyn, "Glimpses into the History of the Johannine Community," *L'Évangile de Jean* (n. 2) 149-75, reprinted in J. L. Martyn, *The Gospel of John in Christian History* (1978) 90-121. See also U. B. Müller, *Die Geschichte der Christologie in der johanneischen Gemeinde* (SBS 77; 1975); G. Richter, "Präsentische und futurische Eschatologie im 4. Evangelium" (1975), in *Studien zum Johannesevangelium,* ed. J. Hainz (1977) 346-82, esp. 354-81; Langbrandtner (n. 6), esp. 117-20.

18. Cf. Lindars, "Discourse and Tradition" (n. 15), 83: "Although . . . the sayings tradition is the only source of the discourses in the strict sense, the meaning and purpose of the discourses are not dictated by the sayings, but relate closely to the conditions of Johannine Christianity at the time when the evangelist is writing, probably late in the first century."

which sought to *vindicate* John by demonstrating the historical roots of his tradition would in fact be missing the point, *John's* point. Here too it may be more important even for our present purposes to insist, let John be John!

It will be clear by now that I wish to tackle the whole question of *Traditionsgeschichte* with reference to John from the *other* end — by attempting to understand the finished product of the Fourth Gospel in its own terms, within its own context. Where other approaches are more obvious and more attractive with regard to the other Gospels, by virtue of their high degree of similarity of form and content, with the Fourth Gospel it is the *distinctiveness* of John which we must come to terms with in the first instance. The more we can clarify the Johannine distinctives, the reasons for any discontinuities and their theological significance, the better position we will be in to highlight the points of similarity and continuity. By hearing the Gospel according to *John* clearly we may hear the gospel according to all four Evangelists more clearly too.

4

Two observations provide our point of departure. Having achieved a preliminary "fix" on John we will be able to "spiral in" to gain a closer look at the Fourth Gospel within its historical context.

4.1. First, in attempting to let John be John, I make no apology for focusing on *John's christology*. For one thing, the stated *aim* of the Gospel as it now stands gives first place to christological claims: "these things are written that you may believe that Jesus is the Christ, the Son of God . . ." (20:31). We need not decide here whether this is an evangelistic aim for a Gospel written to nonbelievers, or, as is more probable, a didactic aim to strengthen the faith of those who have already believed, at least in some measure.[19] Either way the first objective of the Evangelist is christological — so to present Jesus in his Gospel that his readers may believe the Christian claim expressed in the formulation, "Jesus is the Christ, the Son of God."

For another, it is abundantly apparent that most of the Johannine *distinctives* come to clearest expression in John's christology. Certainly we can find many Synoptic-like traditions in the Johannine discourses; but it is the thoroughgoing portrayal of the Son sent from the Father, conscious of his preexistence, the descending-ascending Son of man, making the profoundest claims in his "I am" assertions, which both *dominates* John's christology *and* distances it most strikingly from the Synoptic tradition. Bultmann after all did

---

19. See, e.g., Wengst (n. 3), 33-36, and those cited by Meeks (n. 10), 180, n. 64.

have a point when he insisted that any attempt to solve the "Johannine puzzle" must begin with John's portrayal of Jesus as the descending-ascending redeemer[20] — a rock on which many a thesis regarding John has come to grief. If we can reach a clearer understanding of these Johannine distinctives, we will be in a better position both to distinguish the historical roots of John's tradition and to evaluate the Johannine elaboration of that tradition.

We can also learn the same lesson from what we might call *the points of sensitivity* in the Gospel, the points at which an effort is evidently being made to clarify some confusion or to counter opposing views. These points obviously tell us something about the situation to which such polemic or apologetic is addressed — a subject to which we must return shortly. For the moment, all we need note is how consistently these points of sensitivity focus on the Christian claims concerning Christ — for example, the repeated contrast with John the Baptist in the first three chapters, with the Baptist being deliberately set over against the Christ as his inferior (1:6-9, 15, 20; 3:28-31);[21] the way in which older battles over the law and the sabbath have become christological battles (particularly chs. 5, 7, and 9);[22] the dramatic unfolding of the mounting *krisis* in the middle section of the Gospel, where the point of *krisis* particularly for the wavering crowd is consistently the status of Jesus (7:12-15, 25-27, 31, 40-44, 52; 8:12, 25, 48, 53; 9:16-17, 29-33; 10:19-21, 24, 33; 11:27; 12:34);[23] or the way in which the Evangelist depicts the disciples' faith in the Christ going from initial confidence through crisis and clarification to the climactic confession of Thomas, "My Lord and my God" (1:41, 45, 49; 6:68-69; 14:5-11; 20:28).

The christological claim is at the heart of the Fourth Gospel, including not least the distinctively Johannine elements of that claim. Clearly then it is the reason for and rationale of this christological claim which we must illuminate if we are to have any hope of understanding the good news as preached by John.

4.2. Second, in attempting to set John within its historical context, it is *the context of late first-century Judaism* which must have first claim on our attention. This view has been well argued several times and has won increasing support during the past twenty years, so that I need do little more than rehearse its main outline. The factors of greatest significance are John's references to "the Jews" and his use of the word ἀποσυνάγωγος (9:22; 12:42; 16:2).

"The Jews" feature regularly in the Fourth Gospel as the opponents of

---

20. See the references in Meeks (n. 5), 44.

21. W. Wink, *John the Baptist in the Gospel of Tradition* (SNTSMS 7; 1968) ch. V.

22. See particularly S. Pancaro, *The Law in the Fourth Gospel* (NovTSup 42; 1975).

23. It was C. H. Dodd's masterly exposition of this theme in his *The Interpretation of the Fourth Gospel* (1953), 345-89, which first stirred my interest in John as a work of theology in my student days.

Jesus. In this role they appear as a single coherent group. More important, in this role they are evidently the official representatives of Judaism, the religious authorities who determine matters of faith and polity for the people (1:19; 5:16; 9:18; 18:12; 19:31; even Jews fear "the Jews" — 7:13; 9:22; 19:38; 20:19). In this role, in fact, "the Jews" are often more or less synonymous with the Pharisees (cf. 1:19 and 24; 7:1 and 32; 8:13 and 22; 9:13 and 18; 18:3 and 12), and, most striking of all, with "the world" in its hatred of Jesus (cf. particularly 8:21-47 with 15:18-25).[24] As for ἀποσυνάγωγος, the significance particularly of 9:22 is that it seems to presuppose a formal decision made by Jewish authorities to excommunicate Jews from the synagogue on the sole ground that they confessed Jesus to be the Messiah.[25]

The prominence and character of this tension between Jesus and "the Jews" point the exegete firmly toward a mainly Jewish context for the Fourth Gospel, somewhere after the destruction of Jerusalem in A.D. 70. (1) The sharpness of the breach between Jesus and "the Jews" and the sustained vehemence of the polemic in the middle section of the Gospel is matched elsewhere in the New Testament only in part, even when we include Matthew 23. (2) The breach evidently centered on the Christian confession of Jesus as Messiah. And although Jesus was, of course, crucified as a messianic claimant,[26] there is *no* indication that in the intervening years the confession of Jesus as Messiah was regarded as a "make or break" issue between Jewish Christians and the leaders of Judaism.[27] There *were* issues which brought Jew and Christian to blows (particularly the temple and the law). But in Jerusalem itself, and probably also in areas of the Christian mission controlled from Jerusalem, Jews who believed Jesus to be the Messiah were apparently undisturbed (and even highly regarded) in the period prior to the Jewish revolt.

---

24. See, e.g., E. Grässer, "Die antijüdische Polemik im Johannesevangelium," *NTS* 11 (1964-65) 74-90; R. E. Brown, *John 1-12* (AB; 1966) lxxi; Wengst (n. 3), 37-44. That the Fourth Evangelist also uses the phrase in a broader, less polemical way does not diminish the force of this point; see, e.g., most recently, F. Hahn, " 'Die Juden' im Johannesevangelium," in *Kontinuität und Einheit,* ed. P. G. Müller and W. Stenger (F. Mussner FS; 1981) 430-38. On the irony of John 19:15 ("We have no king but Caesar") see particularly W. A. Meeks, *The Prophet-King: Moses Traditions and the Johannine Christology* (NovTSup 14; 1967) 76-78.

25. See particularly J. L. Martyn, *History and Theology in the Fourth Gospel* (1968, ²1979) ch. 2, whose main thesis that the Evangelist presents a two-level drama (an *einmaliges* event during Jesus' earthly lifetime, and the situation facing his own community) has been widely accepted.

26. In recent literature see particularly O. Betz, "Probleme des Prozesses Jesu," *ANRW* 2/25/1 (1982) 565-647, esp. 633-37; A. E. Harvey, *Jesus and the Constraints of History* (1982), ch. 2.

27. See particularly Martyn (n. 25), 45-51; B. Lindars, "The Persecution of Christians in John 15,18-16, 4a," in *Suffering and Martyrdom in the New Testament,* ed. W. Horbury and B. McNeil (1981) 48-69, here 49-51; against J. A. T. Robinson, *Redating the New Testament* (1976) esp. 272-74, and Carson (n. 11), who pick at the evidence and do not succeed in producing an alternative historical context which fits all the elements of 9:22 so well.

(3) In particular, there is no clear evidence of an official policy of excluding Jews who believed in Jesus from the synagogue during the same period. Although church and synagogue pulled apart in the Gentile mission, there is no indication of such a disruption within the Jewish mission (cf. Acts 21:20-21). Thus, when Josephus writes of Syria in the period prior to the Jewish war, he seems to know of no faction within the Jewish communities excluded from the synagogue. And even in the Gentile mission it is significant that (prior to the Neronian persecution at least) the Roman authorities thought of Jewish-Christian controversy as an internal Jewish affair (Acts 18:15; Suetonius, *Claudius* 25.4).[28] (4) The degree to which the Pharisees emerge in the Fourth Gospel as the dominant force in Judaism, in contrast to the other Gospels (even "many of the rulers" fear "the Pharisees" — 12:42),[29] is surely best explained as a reflection of the growing dominance of the rabbinic authorities within Judaism during the Jabnean period.

Finally, (5) there is enough evidence to indicate that it was precisely during this period that rabbinic Judaism began to take deliberate steps to mark itself off from other claimants to the broader heritage of pre-70 Judaism. It should be noted that this last point does not depend on establishing a precise text and date for the twelfth Benediction, the *birkat-ha-minim,* or on postulating a specific reference to Christians in this malediction on heretics.[30] It is enough to note that rabbinic tradition traces the composition of the *birkat-ha-minim* back to the time of Gamaliel II (*b. Ber.* 28b)[31] and that it was probably aimed at those regarded by the rabbis as (Jewish) sectarians, including Jewish Christians.[32] The point then is that the independent evidence of Jewish tradition confirms what the internal evidence of the Fourth Gospel made probable anyway (cf. also Justin, *Dialogue* 16; 47; 96) — viz., that rabbinic Judaism began to take steps in the late first century and early second century to exclude

---

28. The recognition that Christians were an entity distinct from the Jews is first attested by Tacitus (*Annals* 15.44.2-5), though it is significant that Tacitus accuses them of "hatred of the human race," that is, the old charge regularly brought against the Jews — see M. Stern, *Greek and Latin Authors on Jews and Judaism* II (1980) 93.

29. See, e.g., Martyn (n. 25), 84-89; Lindars, *John* (n. 15), 37; H. F. Weiss, *TDNT* IX, 43-45.

30. Martyn (n. 25), 58, assumes too quickly that Christians (= Nazarenes) were explicitly mentioned in the Jabnean form; but see the fuller discussions listed in n. 32 below.

31. The period of Gamaliel II's ascendancy at Jabneh is usually reckoned from about 80 to 115. Most scholars accept a date for the *birkat-ha-minim* in the middle 80s, though note Martyn's (n. 25) increased caution and its reasons, discussed in his 1979 edition (nn. 69, 75).

32. See particularly W. Horbury, "The Benediction of the *Minim* and early Jewish-Christian Controversy," *JTS* 33 (1982) 19-61, which includes discussion of the too cautious treatment by R. Kimelman, "*Birkat-Ha-Minim* and the Lack of Evidence for an Anti-Christian Jewish Prayer in Late Antiquity," *Jewish and Christian Self-Definition* II: *Aspects of Judaism in the Graeco-Roman Period,* ed. E. P. Sanders (1981) 226-44, 391-403; see also A. F. Segal's note in the following essay (409f.; n. 57) cited below (n. 62); earlier bibliography in Wengst (n. 3), notes to pp. 53ff.

various expressions of heterodoxy, which from the point of view of (newly) normative Judaism had come to be regarded as heresy — including Jewish Christian belief in Jesus as Messiah.

It is possible therefore to reach the fairly strong conclusion that the Fourth Gospel itself reflects the situation confronting the Johannine author/school/community in the late first century of our era — a situation where the Jewish Christians concerned saw themselves threatened by the world as represented particularly by the Jewish authorities where they were.[33] The fact that christology seems to have been the focal point of the confrontation between the Fourth Evangelist and "the Jews" provides strong encouragement for us to investigate the issues involved more closely in the hope of shedding further light on the historical context of the Gospel and on the reasons for its distinctive christological emphases.

5

The second stage of our inquiry is to question more closely why it was that the Christian confession of Jesus as Messiah provoked such confrontation between the Johannine Jewish-Christian "sect" and "the Jews." We can hope to shed some light on these questions both from the Fourth Gospel itself and from what we know of Judaism between the revolts.

5.1. What were the particular issues at stake so far as "the Jews" were concerned in their confrontation with Jesus? It was not simply the assertion that Jesus was Messiah, which might well have remained largely unexceptionable or at least nonheretical in itself. What caused the trouble was the fact that the Messiah claim was itself a summary for a much fuller christology — all in fact that is expressed more adequately, so far as John is concerned at any rate, in the title *"Son of God."* To defend and win belief in Jesus as the Son of God is the Evangelist's stated aim in 20:31, where "Son of God" is the necessary supplement to and explanation of the less provocative "Messiah" claim (similarly 11:27). And it is precisely on the grounds that Jesus "made himself Son of God" that "the Jews" denounce Jesus to Pilate (19:7).

33. Wengst (n. 3) thinks it possible to locate the Johannine community with some precision within the southern part of Agrippa II's kingdom, in the territory of Gaulanitis and Batanea (77-93); but it is enough for our purposes to note that there is at least one setting in the general area of the eastern Mediterranean which matches the probable historical context of the Fourth Gospel so well. Cf. O. Cullmann, *The Johannine Circle* (1976) 59f. On the "sectarian" consciousness of the Johannine community, see particularly Meeks (n. 5) and D. M. Smith, "Johannine Christianity: Some Reflections on Its Character and Delineation," *NTS* 21 (1974-75) 222-48.

When we unpack this claim and the reasons for its offensiveness to Jewish ears, it becomes clear that one of the main contentious points revolves around the question of Jesus' *origin:* Where has he come from? — from Bethlehem, from Galilee, from where? The Gospel reader, of course, knowing full well the Evangelist's answer — "from his Father in heaven" (see particularly 6:41; 7:27-29, 42, 52; 8:23; 9:29; 19:9). Most disturbing of all to "the Jews" is the inference they draw that in claiming to be Son of God, Jesus has made himself "equal to God" (5:18), indeed has made himself *God* (10:33)[34] — a significance for "Son of God" which the Evangelist, of course, wants to press home on his own account (1:1, 18; 20:28).

That it is the question of Jesus' heavenly origin and status which is mainly at issue in all this is confirmed by the most distinctive feature of the Johannine Son of man sayings. The offense of Jesus' teaching is both heightened and (if it can be accepted) resolved by reference to the Son of man's descent from heaven and ascent to heaven (3:12-13; 6:61-62).[35] Bound up with this is one of the most consistent emphases of the Fourth Gospel, on Jesus as the bearer of divine revelation — the Son of God who makes known the heavenly mysteries with authority, precisely because he has been sent from heaven and speaks of what he has seen and heard with his Father (see particularly 1:17-18, 49-51; 3:10-13, 32; 7:16-18; 8:14, 28, 38; 12:49-50; 14:10; 15:15; 17:14).

It is clear then that what is at stake for the Johannine community is the full significance of the confession "Jesus is the Christ, the Son of God." And what is of particular importance for the Evangelist, and particularly contentious to the Jews of his time, is the claim that this confession includes belief that Jesus came from heaven and speaks with the authority of God.[36]

5.2. When we set this fuller picture of John's christology into the context of post-70 Judaism, it quickly becomes apparent that there are some striking overlaps with the Johannine concerns. As has been more clearly perceived in the past few years, Judaism between the two revolts was not yet the massively uniform structure embodied in the Mishnah and Talmuds.[37] The disappearance of other parties (Sadducees, Zealots, Essenes) did not mean a disappearance

---

34. $\mathfrak{P}^{66}$ reads θεόν.

35. "Wherever the [ascent/descent] motif occurs, it is in a context where the primary point of the story is the inability of the men of 'this world,' pre-eminently 'the Jews,' to understand and accept Jesus" — Meeks (n. 5), 58.

36. The subsequent ascent through death and resurrection is, of course, also of crucial significance for John's christology, as I have myself noted elsewhere ("John 6 — a Eucharistic Discourse?" *NTS* 17 [1970-71] 328-38; also *Unity and Diversity in the New Testament* [1977] 301-2), but to include that aspect within the present essay would enlarge the discussion too much (though see below, section 9.2).

37. See now the welcome English translation of G. Alon, *The Jews in Their Land in the Talmudic Age* (1980).

of other facets of pre-70 Judaism. In particular, recent scholarship has reminded us of two other important strands of that broader Judaism which survived the destruction of the temple — the apocalyptic and merkabah mystical traditions.[38] Several points of relevance for our inquiry emerge here.

First, we should note the extent to which these two strands themselves overlap. Both apocalyptic and merkabah mysticism are characterized precisely by their claim to a direct knowledge of heavenly mysteries, either by means of a vision, or, more frequently, by means of an ascent to heaven.[39] Such ascents to heaven are attributed not only to Enoch (*1 En.* 14:8ff.; 39:3ff.; 70–71; *2 En.* 3ff.) and to Abraham (*T. Abr.* 10ff.; *Apoc. Abr.* 15ff.; cf. also 4 Ezra 3:14; *2 Baruch* 4:4), but also to Adam (*Life of Adam and Eve* 25-29), to Levi (*T. Levi* 2:5ff.), to Baruch (*2 Baruch* 76; *3 Baruch*) and to Isaiah (*Ascension of Isaiah* 7ff.; cf. Sir. 48:24-25)[40] — most of these reports are either roughly contemporary with or predate the period in which we are interested.[41] So too the account of Moses' ascent of Mt. Sinai (Exod. 19:3; 24:18) evidently encouraged several circles within Judaism to view it as an ascent to heaven (Philo, *Mos.* 1.158; *Quaestiones et Solutiones in Exodum* 2.29, 40, 46; Josephus, *Ant.* 3.96, *2 Baruch* 4:2-7; pseudo-Philo, *Biblical Antiquities* 12:1; *Memar Marqah* 4:3, 7; 5:3; *2 Baruch* 59).[42] Likewise the practice of merkabah mysticism, in which one sought by meditation, particularly on the chariot vision of Ezekiel 1 (but also passages like Isaiah 6 and Dan. 7:9-10, as well as the story of creation in Genesis 1), to experience for oneself a mystical ascent to or revelation of the throne of God, seems to have been already well established in our period.[43] Such interest is evident already in *1 En.* 14, is hinted at in Sir. 49:8, and is clearly attested in the so-called "angelic liturgy" of Qumran (4QS1 [4QŠirŠabb] 40.24).[44] Not least relevant

38. See particularly I. Gruenwald, *Apocalyptic and Merkabah Mysticism* (1980); C. Rowland, *The Open Heaven: A Study of Apocalyptic in Judaism and Early Christianity* (1982).

39. This overlap has been obscured by identifying apocalyptic too closely with eschatology. See particularly the important corrective by Rowland on this point (n. 38). D. J. Halperin, *The Merkabah in Rabbinic Literature* (1980) does not take sufficient account of this overlap.

40. Note also the "final" ascents of Elijah (esp. 2 Kdms. 2:11; Sir. 48:9-10; *1 En.* 90:31), Ezra (4 Ezra 14:9), and Abel (*Testament of Abel* 11; *Ascension of Isaiah* 9:8).

41. For fuller detail see A. F. Segal, "Heavenly Ascent in Hellenistic Judaism, Early Christianity, and Their Environment," *ANRW* 2/23/2 (1980) 1352-68.

42. See particularly Meeks (n. 24), 110-11, 120-25, 147-49, 156-59, 206-9, 241-44; idem, "Moses as God and King," *Religions in Antiquity: Essays in Memory of E. R. Goodenough*, ed. J. Neusner (1968) 354-71.

43. Modern interest in merkabah mysticism as a feature of second temple Judaism derives chiefly from G. G. Scholem, *Major Trends in Jewish Mysticism* (1941, reprint 1961) esp. 42-44.

44. J. Strugnell, "The Angelic Liturgy at Qumran," *Vetus Testamentum* Supplements 7 (1959) 318-45. See further C. Rowland, "The Visions of God in Apocalyptic Literature," *JSJ* 10 (1979) 137-54. In a paper delivered at the SNTS Conference in Leuven, Belgium, 1982, H. C. Kee argued that Joseph and Asenath stands within the merkabah mystical tradition of Judaism ("The Socio-Cultural Setting of *Joseph and Asenath*," *NTS* 29 [1983] 394-413).

here are the appearance in some of these visions of a glorious being closely related in appearance to God (Ezek. 8:2 compared with 1:26-27; Dan. 7:13 LXX; 10:5-6; *Apoc. Abr.* 10; *Apocalypse of Zephaniah* 9:12–10:9)[45] and the motif of the transformation into angel-like form of the one who ascends himself, notably Moses and Isaiah (see above), and most strikingly Enoch (*1 En.* 71:11; *2 En.* 22:8; *Ascension of Isaiah* 9:9), who is identified as the Son of man in the Similitudes of Enoch (*1 En.* 71:14) and subsequently as Metatron in *3 Enoch* 3-16.[46]

Second, we should note also that *both* early Christianity *and* the Jabnean sages were not unaffected by such tendencies within Judaism. Paul's account of a visionary ascent to the third heaven (2 Cor. 12:2-4) may well support the view that Paul himself was familiar with the practice of merkabah mysticism,[47] and the vision of John the seer (Rev. 1:13-16) has some striking points of contact with the earlier visions of Ezekiel 1 and of Daniel (Daniel 7; 10:5-6).[48] As for the rabbis, there is strong evidence that Johanan ben Zakkai, who played the leading role in initially reestablishing rabbinic Judaism at Jabneh, was himself greatly interested in the chariot chapter of Ezekiel 1 and probably practiced meditation on it (*Tosephta Ḥag.* 2:1 and parallels).[49] More striking is the tradition about the four sages who "entered the garden *(pardes)*" (*Tosephta Ḥag.* 2:3-4 and parallels). As most agree, the tradition probably refers in a veiled way to a vision of the chariot throne of God. This is confirmed by such fuller information as we have about these rabbis.[50] One of them, Elisha ben Abuyah, is remembered as an archheretic, because in his vision of heaven he mistook the glorious figure sitting on a great throne (Metatron) as a second power in heaven — thus denying the unity of God (*b. Ḥag.* 15a; *3 Enoch* 16); one of the starting points for this "two powers" heresy seems to have been speculation on the plural thrones

45. Rowland (n. 38), 94-103, though unfortunately he fails to ask whether similarities in such visionary appearances may be due simply to the seer having to draw on a common but inevitably limited stock of imagery deemed appropriate to describe glorious heavenly beings. See also R. Bauckham, "The Worship of Jesus in Apocalyptic Christianity," *NTS* 27 (1981) 322-41, here 323-27.

46. See also J. A. Bühner, *Der Gesandte und sein Weg im 4. Evangelium* (1977) 353-62. In his otherwise valuable exploration of the historical context of the Fourth Gospel, Wengst (n. 3) unfortunately ignores this whole dimension almost entirely — taking note of Meeks only in passing and dismissing Bühner in a footnote (17, n. 24).

47. J. W. Bowker, " 'Merkabah' Visions and the Visions of Paul," *Journal of Semitic Studies* 16 (1971) 157-73: ". . . Paul practiced *merkabah* contemplation as an ordinary consequence of his highly extended Pharisaic training" (172).

48. C. Rowland, "The Vision of the Risen Christ in Rev. 1,13ff.: The Debt of an Early Christology to an Aspect of Jewish Angelology," *JTS* 31 (1980) 1-11.

49. See J. Neusner, *A Life of Yohanan ben Zakkai* (²1970) 134-40; Gruenwald (n. 38), 75-86; Rowland (n. 38), 282-305. Halperin (n. 39), 107-40, is more skeptical.

50. Gruenwald (n. 38), 86-92; Rowland (n. 38), 306-40. Halperin (n. 39), 98-92, disputes the link to merkabah mysticism.

in Dan. 7:9.[51] There is also a tradition regarding another of the four, the famous rabbi Akiba, in which he is rebuked for his speculation as to the occupant of the second throne in Dan. 7:9 (*b. Ḥag.* 14a; *b. Sanh.* 38b).

Third, we know that there were already strong reactions against some of these tendencies in apocalyptic and merkabah speculation. Sir. 3:18-25 can be readily understood as an exhortation to refrain from speculations involving visionary experiences.[52] And 4 Ezra 8:20f. seems to be directed against claims to be able to see and describe God's throne.[53] In specifically Christian circles we may recall the strong warnings against angel worship in Col. 2:18 and Hebrews 1–2,[54] and the early churches' hesitation over granting too much authority to the book of Revelation. Similarly, the rabbinic polemic against angelology probably goes back to our period,[55] there are explicit cautionary notes concerning the chariot chapter in the Mishnah (*m. Ḥag.* 2:1; *m. Megilloth* 4:10), and the apostasy of Elisha ben Abuyah is a notorious fact elsewhere in rabbinic tradition.[56] We may also note how frequently subsequent rabbinic polemic against the *minim* consists in a defense of monotheism, the unity of God.[57]

5.3. All this evidence points strongly to a threefold conclusion. (1) There was evidently considerable interest in the possibility of gaining heavenly knowledge through visions and heavenly ascents in the period between the two Jewish revolts. (2) This interest is reflected in the Fourth Gospel as well as in our other sources from this period. (3) There were various degrees of misgiving about and hostility to this interest as too speculative and dangerous among both Christians and the rabbis.

6

The main question which remains for us therefore is: Does an awareness of *this* context, of these crosscurrents in Jewish and Christian thinking during the period in which the Fourth Gospel was probably written, help us to make clearer sense of the Johannine distinctives? If we return again to the Gospel

51. See A. F. Segal, *The Powers in Heaven: Early Rabbinic Reports about Christianity and Gnosticism* (1977) particularly 33-67, 148-49.
52. Gruenwald (n. 38), 17-18.
53. Rowland (n. 38), 54-55.
54. See also Bauckham (n. 45).
55. P. S. Alexander, "The Targumim and Early Exegesis of 'Sons of God' in Gen 6," *JJS* 23 (1972) 60-71; see also J. Goldin, " 'Not by Means of an Angel and Not by Means of a Messenger,' " *Religions in Antiquity* (n. 42), 412-24.
56. See Rowland (n. 38), 331-39.
57. See the texts collected by R. T. Herford, *Christianity in Talmud and Midrash* (1966) 291-307.

itself, we should now be in a better position to appreciate some of John's finer points as he seeks to promote faith in Jesus as the Christ, the Son of God, to hear more of the nuances which a first-century reader would have been expected to observe. We will have time to note only a few key examples.

6.1. The prologue ends with the highest claim for the revelatory significance of Jesus: "No one has ever seen God; the only Son/God . . . has made him known" (1:18). True knowledge of God comes through only one — Jesus, the incarnate Logos. The reader is probably intended to bear this blunt assertion in mind when he comes to the next climax of christological confession — the exchange with Nathanael (1:47-51).[58] The train of thought is at first puzzling, but it gains invaluable illumination from the background sketched out above. In mystical thought "Israel" is taken to mean "he that sees" or "he that sees God" (as often in Philo).[59] Nathanael is presented as "a genuine Israelite," who has begun to believe in Jesus ("rabbi, Son of God, King of Israel" — 1:49). But Jesus replies that he will see more than that — a vision just like that of the first Israel (Jacob — Gen. 28:12), where the central feature will be the Son of Man mediating between heaven and earth (1:51).[60] For no one else has seen God — not Moses (1:17; cf. Exod. 33:20; Deut. 4:12), and not even Israel. The true Israelite is thus encouraged to "see" that all God's self-revelation now comes to focus in and through Jesus (1:18, 51); God can only be seen to the extent that one sees him in and through (the revelation of) Christ.

John 1 links with John 3 in that another sympathetic Jew (3:2) needs similar instruction. Though "a teacher of Israel" (3:9), Nicodemus has no idea how one can "see the kingdom of God," how it is possible to "enter the heavenly realm" (3:3, 5).[61] Such knowledge cannot be attained by an ascent to heaven — "*no one* has ascended into heaven" (3:13). This sweeping assertion can hardly be other than a polemic against current beliefs in the possibility of such heavenly ascents, through contemplation on the divine chariot or otherwise.[62] Such

---

58. Cf. M. de Jonge, *Jesus: Stranger from Heaven and Son of God* (1977) 83: "1,19-50 stands between 1,18 and 1,51, both dealing with the heavenly status of the One to whom all the designations in the intermediate section point in their own way."

59. See references in vol. X of the Loeb edition of *Philo*, p. 334, note; J. Z. Smith, "The Prayer of Joseph," *Religions in Antiquity* (n. 42), 265-68.

60. Cf. H. Odeberg, *The Fourth Gospel* (1929) 33-40; Dodd (n. 23), 245-46; N. A. Dahl, "The Johannine Church and History," in *Current Issues in New Testament Interpretation*, ed. W. Klassen and G. F. Snyder (O. A. Piper FS; 1962) 136, notes that "in the Haggadah, Genesis 28,12, like other visionary texts, is often combined with Daniel 7 and Ezekiel 1"; P. Borgen, "God's Agent in the Fourth Gospel," *Religions in Antiquity* (n. 42), 145-46.

61. In John the kingdom of God = "the heavenly realm on high to which the divine envoy leads (cf. 14:3; 12:26; 17:24)" — R. Schnackenburg, *The Gospel according to St. John* I (1968) 366f.

62. Odeberg (n. 60), 72-98; Meeks (n. 24), 295-301; F. J. Moloney, *The Johannine Son of Man* (1976, [2]1978) 54-57; A. F. Segal, "Ruler of This World: Attitudes about Mediator Figures and the Importance of Sociology for Self-Definition," *Jewish and Christian Self-Definition* (n. 32), 245-68, esp. 255f.

knowledge of heavenly things is possible *only* for him who *de*scended from heaven, the Son of Man (3:12-13). Mention of Moses in the following verse and the return to the same theme in 3:31-36 ("he who comes from above is above all") effectively distances this Son of Man from any competing claims about the heavenly commissions of Moses and John the Baptist (cf.1:6, 17). Not even Moses ascended to heaven, and the Baptist remains rootedly "of the earth."[63] True knowledge of heaven comes only from Christ, he who is from above and bears witness to what he (alone) has seen there.[64]

In John 6 the narrative moves with fine dramatic sense from the enthusiastic recognition of Jesus as "the prophet who is to come into the world" (6:14), the prophet like Moses who could be asked to repeat the miracle of manna (6:31), to the point where many of his own disciples take offense (6:60f., 66). What causes the offense is the way in which the category of prophet is transcended and left behind: to speak of Jesus as "him whom God sent" (6:29) is only adequate if by that phrase is meant "sent from heaven," without implication of any previous ascent; his subsequent ascent is to "where he was before," to his place of origin (6:62). Moses too is pushed to one side (6:32). The manna miracle does not exalt Moses, as the Jews assumed;[65] that model of divine mediation (cf. Deut. 18:18) is inadequate to express the significance of Jesus. The direct communication from God promised by Isa. 54:13 is now a reality in Jesus (not the Torah); he is the yardstick by which all claims to knowledge from God must be tested, for only he has seen the Father (John 6:45-46).[66] Thus the experience which mediates eternal life is believing recognition that Jesus is himself from God, the living bread which came down from heaven, the life from God incarnate in Jesus (6:35-58).

Finally, we might note in chs. 7 and 12 some indication that John's constituents were aware of wider speculations within Judaism about the Messiah's origin and end. Some thought simply in terms of Davidic descent and birth at Bethlehem (7:42); others, who claim that no one knows where the Christ comes from (7:27), may thereby allude to the sort of speculation we find in the Similitudes of Enoch, in 4 Ezra and *2 Baruch*, about the hiddenness of the Messiah in the divine purpose (in heaven? *1 En.* 48:6-7; 62:7; 4 Ezra 7:28; 12:32; 13:26, 32, 52; *2 Baruch* 29:3; 39:7).[67] So too the crowd's opinion "that the Christ remains forever" (John 12:34) may well reflect the sort of

63. Cf. Targum Neofiti on Deut. 30:12, cited below in section 7.2.

64. Cf. Meeks (n. 5), 52-57, though to insist that "the one born from above/from the spirit" can *only* be the Son of Man, Jesus (53), is overscrupulous. See also J. H. Neyrey, "John 3 — A Debate over Johannine Epistemology and Christology," *NovT* 23 (1981) 115-27.

65. Cf. particularly G. Vermes, " 'He is the Bread': Targum Neofiti Exodus 16,15," *Post-Biblical Jewish Studies* (1975) 139-46.

66. See particularly P. Borgen, *Bread from Heaven* (NovTSup 10; 1965) esp. 150-54.

67. De Jonge (n. 58), 90-91.

speculation that various heroes of the past had been translated or apotheosized to heaven, in some cases at least without tasting death (Enoch, Elijah, Abel? Moses? Ezra),[68] or (less likely) the targumic tradition which found in Isa. 9:5's phrase "everlasting Father" a reference to the eternal existence of the Messiah.[69] The Fourth Evangelist does not respond directly to such queries. He simply drives on singlemindedly toward the climax of each of these sections (8:48-59; 12:44-50), in which the emphasis on the continuity between the Father and the Son transcends all such speculations and leaves them behind.

These examples must suffice to show how central it is for John that *Jesus is from above,* and because he is from above, *he brings and embodies the truth,* the true knowledge of God and of heavenly things.

6.2. What is the Fourth Evangelist trying to do in all this? Clearly he is in touch with something at least of the range of theological reflection about God, about God's favored servants, about the means of gaining heavenly knowledge, particularly through ascending to heaven — the sort of speculation, in fact, which we know was current toward the end of the first century. Some of this reflection he merely acknowledges in passing: some he makes use of. He maintains the Christian claim to the messiahship of Jesus without debating all the questions being discussed. The language of heavenly ascent and descent is taken over for his own purposes. One of his chief categories, Jesus as the one sent from God, is an elaboration of a familiar prophetic category — the prophet as the agent of God.[70] But clearly he also sees Jesus as transcending such categories as "prophet" and "king" and even "Messiah."[71] Clearly he wants to say more — much more. What precisely is this "more"? And why does it bring the wrath of "the Jews" upon the Christian believers?

The answer most probably is bound up with these points that John has taken such care to emphasize so much, those claims which prove so contentious to "the Jews." One is John's claim of a *heavenly origin* for Jesus the Messiah, a heavenly origin which goes back to the beginning of time. Jesus is not one whose claims on our attention derive from an ascent to heaven; they derive rather from the fact that he descended from heaven. The other is John's claim for *a closeness of continuity* between Father and Son which is more than simply identity of will or function: the Son is so like, so close to the Father, that we can even speak of some kind of identity of being (he makes himself God; he and the Father are one).

The importance of these points receives striking confirmation when we compare the findings of the two studies which, more than any other in recent

68. See above, section 5.2 and n. 40; cf. Barrett (n. 13), 427.
69. See particularly B. McNeil, "The Quotation in John 12:34," *NovT* 29 (1977) 22-33.
70. See particularly Bühner (n. 46), part three.
71. See particularly the two essays on these three titles by de Jonge (n. 58), chs. 3 and 4.

Let John Be John: A Gospel for Its Time   365

years, have succeeded in setting the Fourth Gospel's christology within the
historical context of late first-century Judaism. In his ground-breaking investigation of the background to John's christology, W. A. Meeks recognized one
major point of distinctiveness: the Johannine "pattern of *descent/ascent* of a
heavenly messenger has no direct parallel in the Moses traditions (of Jewish
and Samaritan theology)."[72] Subsequently Meeks also conceded de Jonge's
criticism that "Jesus' kingship and his prophetic mission are both redefined
in terms of the *unique relationship* between Son and Father, as portrayed in
the Fourth Gospel."[73]

The other most thorough recent investigation of the background of the
Fourth Gospel's christology, by J. A. Bühner, highlights — by failing to explain — precisely the same two points. He attempts to root the idea of the
Son's preexistence in the *Berufungsvision* of the prophet, interpreted in the
light of the fact that the same commissioning formula (God sent) is used also
of angelic messengers.[74] But the idea of Jesus as a glorious angel, even an
angel like the figure of Ezek. 8:2 or Jaoel in the *Apocalypse of Abraham,* is
simply not present in John:[75] In 1:51 the Son of man seems to be of a different
order from "the angels of God"; and the polemic of 3:13 seems likewise
intended precisely to distance Jesus, the Son of man, from such visionary
ascents.[76] The commissioning formula is too narrow a base to sustain such a
thesis. John's language almost certainly grew out of this kind of talk of divine
commissioning of the prophet, but his christology is neither contained in nor
explained by it — particularly, once again, his emphasis on a *preexistence* that
is precosmic (as in 8:25 and 17:5), or his emphasis on a *unity* between Father
and Son (as in 1:18 and 10:30) which goes far beyond the identity of sender
and sent on the *šālîaḥ* model.

The very fact that John moves beyond such background parallels at just
these points strengthens the impression given by passages like those examined

72. Meeks (n. 24), 297.

73. De Jonge (n. 58), 52; Meeks (n. 10), 173.

74. Note also the important earlier study of the question from this aspect by Borgen
(n. 60).

75. Possible parallels like 11QMelch (?) and the Prayer of Joseph hardly provide encouragement for the thesis. Other examples of descending angels (collected by C. H. Talbert,
"The Myth of a Descending-Ascending Redeemer in Mediterranean Antiquity," *NTS* 22 [1975-
76] 422-26, and *What Is a Gospel? The Genre of the Canonical Gospels* [1977] 57-61) are only
"short-term visitors."

76. According to 1:51 ascent precedes descent even in the case of the angels of God.
Both Bühner (n. 46) and P. Borgen, "Some Exegetical Traditions as Background for the Son of
Man Sayings in John's Gospel (John 3,13-14 and Context)," *L'Évangile de Jean* (n. 2), 243-58,
argue that the Fourth Evangelist's language implies a *previous* ascent, to "become" the Son of
Man, prior to his descent as Son of man (in Borgen's case, an "ascent" in preexistence). But
this forces too much upon the language and throws the Johannine christology into confusion
(the Logos "ascends" to become the Son of man?!); cf. Barrett (n. 13), 213.

above (section 6.1), that it is precisely these two points which John wishes to emphasize. In presenting Jesus as the Messiah, the Son of God who is also the Son of man, the Fourth Evangelist wants to persuade his readers of *a heavenly origin* for Jesus the Messiah which goes back to the beginning of time, and of *a closeness of continuity* between Father and Son which is more than simply identity of will or function. From where then does he derive these emphases? Our task remains incomplete unless we can clarify the source of these key Johannine distinctives.

In fact, the Fourth Evangelist himself probably gives us the decisive clue, in the prologue. The prologue seems to be intended to provide a category or model, that of Wisdom or Logos,[77] in terms of which the reader can (and should) understand the christology of the whole.[78] In the final stage of our attempt to illuminate the Johannine distinctives in the light of John's historical context we shall focus therefore on John's Wisdom christology.

7

Does the Wisdom christology of the prologue explain these points of distinctiveness which our *religionsgeschichtliche* investigation has brought to the fore?

7.1. It is often assumed that the Wisdom/Logos motifs are more or less confined within the prologue, and so are without relevance to the rest of the Gospel. On the contrary, however, language and imagery from the Wisdom/Logos tradition occur repeatedly in the Fourth Gospel, as R. E. Brown in particular has shown.[79] These include, not least, the idea of being sent or descending from heaven, as in 3:13 (the nearest parallels are in Wis. 9:16-17; Bar. 3:29; *1 En.* 42 — both descent and ascent),[80] and the "I am" statements,

---

77. Wisdom and Logos are virtually synonymous so far as our present inquiry is concerned; see Dunn (n. 10), index under "Word and Wisdom."

78. I find it impossible to regard the prologue of John's Gospel as redactional (i.e., added after the Fourth Evangelist put the Gospel into its present form); the themes of the prologue are too closely integrated into the Gospel as a whole and are so clearly intended to introduce these themes that such a conclusion is rendered implausible.

79. Brown (n. 24), esp. cxxii-cxxv and index under "Wisdom."

80. To reject a Wisdom background at this point on the grounds that the language parallels are not close enough (the usual objection) is to refuse to allow the Fourth Evangelist any creativity of his own — an implausible evaluation, considering the distinctive character of the Gospel. Closer parallels, as in later Gnosticism, probably imply dependence — on John! Since the Gnostic Sophia myth is also dependent on the *Jewish* Wisdom tradition (G. W. Macrae, "The Jewish Background of the Gnostic Sophia Myth," *NovT* 12 [1970] 86-101), it is wiser to conclude that the descent/ascent motif in its Johannine form is a creation of the Johannine school itself, formed precisely by the conviction that the full significance of Jesus could be grasped only in terms of the identification of Christ as Wisdom.

which can be paralleled both in first person singular speech (Proverbs 8 and
Sirach 24) and in content (e.g., light — Wis. 7:26, 29; food and drink — Sir.
24:19-22; shepherd — Philo, *Agr.* 51; *Mut.* 116).[81] Most important of all, it is
only in the Wisdom/Logos tradition of the Jewish background that we have
anything really close to the synthesis of Johannine conceptuality — a Wis-
dom/Logos which is distinct from all other potential intermediaries, angelic or
human, precisely by virtue of *its precosmic existence with God* (e.g., Prov.
8:27-30; Sir. 24:9; Wis. 9:9), and precisely by virtue of *its close identity with
God* (e.g., Ps. 33:6; Wis. 7:25; Philo, *Opif.* 24; *Sacr.* 64). The point of distinctiveness being that Wisdom/Logos is *not* a heavenly being over against God, but
is *God himself, God in his self-manifestation,* God insofar as he may be known
by the human mind.[82] It is precisely for this reason, because the Son is the
incarnate *Logos,* God in his "knowability" and "visibility," that the *Son* can say,
"He that has seen *me* has seen the *Father"* (12:45; 14:9). In a similar way, the
working out of the "glory" motif of the prologue (1:14) includes the otherwise
puzzling 12:41 ("Isaiah saw his glory and spoke of him"), where Isaiah's vision
of the *Lord* sitting on his throne (Isaiah 6) is interpreted as a vision of *Christ's*
glory — presumably because for the Fourth Evangelist Christ is to be identified
not with one of the seraphim, as in some later Christian thought, but as *the
shekinah of God,* the visible presence of God himself.[83]

The key then to understanding the Johannine distinctives in his presentation of Jesus as Messiah, Son of God, and Son of man, is to see these titles
primarily as *an elaboration of the initial explicit identification of Jesus as the
incarnate Wisdom/Logos* — an identification taken over certainly from earlier
Christian tradition,[84] but expounded in John's own distinctive fashion. It is this
which alone satisfactorily explains John's repeated emphasis on the direct
continuity between this Jesus and God from the beginning of time. The revelation which Jesus brings seems to be so limited, precisely because what he reveals
is not information but, quite simply, God, that he is God in his self-revelation.[85]
This is what it means for the Fourth Evangelist to confess Jesus as the Messiah,
the Son of God. It is this faith which he wants to win or sustain in his readers.

81. Cf. particularly E. Schweizer, "Zum religionsgeschichtlichen Hintergrund der 'Sendungsformel' Gal 4,4f.; Rom 8,3f.; Joh 3,16f.; 1 Joh 4,9," *Beiträge zur Theologie des Neuen
Testaments* (1970) 83-95. On 8:58 see esp. Lindars, "Discourse and Tradition" (n. 15), 96.
82. See my *Christology* (n. 10), 168-76, 217-30.
83. Cf. Dahl (n. 60), 131-32. On the shekinah as the immediate presence of God, see
A. M. Goldberg, *Untersuchungen über die Vorstellung von der Schekhinah in der frühen rabbinischen Literatur* (1969); E. E. Urbach, *The Sages: Their Concepts and Beliefs* ([2]1979) ch. 3.
84. See below, section 9.2.
85. Cf. E. Haenchen, " 'Der Vater, der mich gesandt hat,' " *NTS* 9 (1962-63) 208-16,
reprinted in *Gott und Mensch* (1965), 68-77, esp. 71-73; Wengst (n. 3), 101-4. My formulation
alludes, of course, to Bultmann's famous comment: "Jesus as the revealer of God reveals nothing
but that he is the revealer" (*Theology of the New Testament* II [1955] 66).

7.2. The coherence of this exegesis (on internal grounds) is confirmed by the fact that this understanding of John's claims regarding Christ provides an excellent explanation for the fierceness of the rabbinic opposition to the Jesus of the Fourth Gospel. As we have already noted (section 5.2 above), the Jabnean rabbis were at least to some degree engaged in a similar interaction with these other (apocalyptic and mystical) strands of Judaism to that which we find in the Fourth Gospel. And in a similar way they were both drawing *on* that broader tradition, *and,* over the period between the two Jewish revolts, beginning to distance themselves from unacceptable elements within it.

The difference was that while the Christians were focusing what they wanted to say on *Jesus,* the rabbis were focusing on the *law.* Clear hints of this fact, so abundantly obvious from rabbinic sources, occur at several points in John (7:49; 9:28-29; 12:34; 19:7). Already within the Wisdom tradition a firm equation between Wisdom and Torah had been established (Sir. 24:23, 25; Bar. 3:36–4:4). And the rabbis probably took up and developed this equation just as the Christians were developing the identification of Wisdom with Christ. One indication may lie in the fact that Deut. 30:12-14, which the Baruch passage just cited referred to Wisdom, was interpreted by Targum Neofiti with reference to Moses and the law: "The law is not in the heavens, that one should say: Would that we had one like Moses the prophet who would go up to heaven and fetch it for us. . . ." And certainly we can have little doubt that the allusions to "the gift of God" and "living water" in John 4:10 have in mind the rabbinic readiness to use such phrases of the Torah.[86] In effect, what the Christians were claiming for Christ, the rabbis were claiming for the law. And quite soon (we do not know how soon) they began to speak of the law as preexistent[87] — just as Christians had begun to speak of Christ in the same way.

More important still, what we see reflected in the Fourth Gospel is the debate between Christian and rabbi at a crucial stage in these mutual developments. On the one hand, we see the Fourth Evangelist disputing the rabbinic exaltation of the law: the law is *not* the climax of God's revelation, *Christ* is the climax; the law bears witness to *him* (1:45; 5:39, 46). Beside the fullness of divine revelation in Christ, the law is defective (1:17). Compared with the climactic revelation of Christ, the revelation given through Moses, Sinai and the whole wilderness period is deficient (3:9-15; 5:37-47; 6:35-58; 7:14-24; 10:34-36).[88] The Wisdom of God is present in the Torah, but present in fullness

---

86. Barrett (n. 13), 233.

87. Texts are gathered in SB II, 353-55. See Dunn (n. 10), ch. 6, n. 43.

88. See particularly the richly seminal study of Dahl (n. 60), 133; Meeks (n. 24), 287-91, 299-301; idem, "The Divine Agent and His Counterfeit in Philo and the Fourth Gospel," *Aspects of Religious Propaganda in Judaism and Early Christianity,* ed. E. Schüssler Fiorenza (1976) 43-76, here 56-58; de Jonge (n. 58), 56-58; and exposition with notes, section 6.1 above.

only in Christ. Christ, *not* the Torah, is the embodiment of divine Wisdom, the incarnation of God's Word.

On the other hand, at one and the same time, we see reflected the *rabbinic* opposition to the *Christian* claim regarding Christ. As the Fourth Evangelist protests against the rabbinic exaltation of the law (and by implication, the rabbinic equation of Wisdom with the law), so the rabbis protest against the Christian identification of Wisdom as Christ. "The Jews" recognized that so to identify Christ with Wisdom/Logos, the self-expression of God, was to make Jesus equal with God (5:18), was to make him not simply an angel or heavenly figure (like Enoch), but *God* (10:33). The equation of Wisdom with the Torah was attractive as an alternative, presumably not least because it posed no such threat to Jewish monotheism. But "the Jews" could not understand John's christology except as a severe threat to the unity of God — just as John no doubt considered their overexaltation of Moses and the law a threat to the claims of the revelation given in and through Christ. Evidently then, in rabbinic eyes, the Fourth Evangelist and his community/school belonged with those others within Judaism who were speculating too unguardedly (not least about the vision of Daniel 7), on the basis of revelation they claimed to have received, and who, in consequence, were endangering the primary axiom of Judaism — the oneness of God.

In short, what we see reflected in the Fourth Gospel is a three- (or even four-) way dialogue — the Fourth Evangelist in dialogue with broader strands of apocalyptic and mystical Judaism, with the rabbis of Jabneh, and possibly with other Christians too.[89] The Fourth Evangelist draws on this larger heritage, both Christian and Jewish, as the others do in their own way. And, under the inspiration of the Spirit of Jesus (14:26; 16:13-15), and in debate with these alternative theologies of revelation and salvation, he presents his own faith centered on Jesus the Christ, the Son of God.

8

8.1. This essay has attempted to take the first step toward clarifying the Gospel of John in its relation to the gospel particularly as presented by the other three Evangelists. As a first step it seemed necessary to try to understand John in its own terms, to seek to clarify the distinctive features of the Fourth Gospel's presentation of Christ by situating it as far as possible within the context in which and in relation to which it was written. Over against those who have

---

89. Cf. Segal (n. 62), 256. On the intra-Christian dialogue see above, n. 17; also de Jonge (n. 58), 99.

left out that first step and have sought to understand John's christology *too quickly* as an expression of later orthodoxy (or later heresy) or in relation to the historical Jesus *per se,* it is important for exegesis to insist that John must first be allowed to be itself before its relation to other expressions of the gospel can be properly and fully explored. Insofar as we have been able to fulfill even that modest aim within the scope of this essay, we can now attempt to draw out the most obvious and potentially important conclusions, before finally reflecting briefly on the next step, for which we have only been able to prepare.

8.2. One immediate result is in effect quite *a major shift in perspective.* The apparent dominance of the Son of God category over the initial Logos category is misleading. Rather, the Fourth Evangelist evidently intended what is in fact the much vaguer title (Son of God)[90] to serve as a vehicle for his basically Wisdom christology. The Fourth Evangelist really did intend his Gospel to be read through the window of the prologue. The *Son of God* reveals nothing other than that he is the *Wisdom of God,* God in his encounter with humankind. The late first-century Jewish desire for knowledge of heavenly things is met in Jesus, because he is the Logos of God, God insofar as he may be known and seen by humankind: whoever has seen the Son has seen the Father (12:45; 14:9).

To put it another way, by reading the Father-Son language in the light of the Wisdom/Logos prologue, the range of options possible in the title Son of God is narrowed dramatically. Over against any who might be content with a prophet christology, or a merely Davidic Messiah christology, John insists unreservedly on a Wisdom christology. In modern terms, which echo John's to a significant degree, the Fourth Evangelist insists that a christology "from below" is inadequate (a christology of inspiration or mystical ascent or apotheosis). The meaning of Christ cannot be expressed except as a christology "from above." Over against any who might offer an alternative theology of revelation and redemption (through Torah or angel?) he insists that Christ alone is able to reveal God, to bring the true knowledge of God, to mediate the fullness of his grace (1:16-18). And that can only be because he is the Wisdom of God incarnate, the fullest possible embodiment in human flesh of God in his outreach to this world.

8.3. It follows that in a vitally important sense, for the Fourth Evangelist, *theo*logy (in the narrower sense) is more important than *christ*ology.[91] We only let John be John if we recognize that the primary debate the Fourth Evangelist engaged in with the rabbis was actually a debate about *monotheism.*

---

90. Dunn (n. 10), 14-16.
91. Cf. C. K. Barrett, "Christocentric or Theocentric? Observations on the Theological Method of the Fourth Gospel" (1976), in idem, *Essays on John* (1982) 1-18.

The Fourth Gospel belongs, in *religionsgeschichtliche* terms, to that diverse body of late first-century and early second-century Jewish piety and literature that explored the boundaries of earlier conceptualities of deity and revelation within a framework of monotheism. Set against that context, what we see is John in effect claiming that Christian revelation could not be expressed without understanding Jesus in full-blown Wisdom terms, without, in that sense, redefining the basic category of Jewish monotheism itself. The Fourth Evangelist had no intention of breaking or moving out from that category. Precisely because Wisdom/Logos rather than Son of God is his primary category, he remains a monotheist — for while "Son" is more fitted to express distinction and relation (as Athanasius realized), "Logos" by definition better expresses sameness and continuity.[92] But "the Jews" focused more on the talk of sonship and heard it as a blasphemy against the unity of God. At this point the Fourth Gospel becomes a valuable witness not only to the development of early Christian theology, but also to the tensions within late first-century Judaism, important background for understanding the subsequent rabbinic rejection of the two-powers heresy.

This insight enables us to sharpen our initial criticisms both of subsequent Christian interpretation of John in relation to Nicene orthodoxy, and of the earlier *religionsgeschichtliche* interpretation of John (section 2 above). On the one hand, the Fourth Gospel is not speaking to a trinitarian debate about the interior relationships within the Godhead. It is speaking to a discussion about monotheism, advocating the necessity of identifying Jesus with God insofar as God makes himself known to humankind. Thus, for example, to understand John's frequent talk of the Son's obedience to the Father as an assertion of the Son's *subordination* to the Father is anachronistic and not quite to the point.[93] It would be more accurate to say that the Fourth Evangelist's intention was to emphasize the *continuity* between Father and Son, the continuity of Wisdom/Logos: he is doing the same work as God (5:17); his hand and the Father's hand are one (10:28-29); he speaks with the authority of God (14:10).[94] The issue here is not so much one of *relation* between Father and Son, as of the validity of the Logos-Son's *revelation* of the Father.[95] If the Fourth Gospel is interpreted

---

92. Hence the ambiguity between *logos* = unuttered thought, and *logos* = uttered thought, for *logos* denotes precisely the continuity between the same thought in its unexpressed and expressed forms. Cf. the ambiguity of Philo, *Sacr.* 80-83; *Ebr.* 157; *Somn.* 1.102-14.

93. Cf., e.g., the "subordination" of the uttered *logos* to the expressed *logos* in Philo, *Abr.* 83.

94. Cf. Käsemann (n. 8), 25: "John's peculiarity is that he knows only one single dogma, the christological dogma of the unity of Jesus with the Father"; and Appold in n. 95 below.

95. Cf. particularly M. L. Appold, *The Oneness Motif in the Fourth Gospel* (WUNT 1; 1976) 18-34; "John's christology leaves no room for even incipient subordination" (22)! I would thus want to qualify Barrett's otherwise important counteremphasis, " 'The Father Is Greater than I' John 14,28: Subordinationist Christology in the New Testament" (1974), in *Essays* (n. 91), 19-36.

primarily as an exposition of the relationship between the Father and the Son, it becomes difficult to avoid slipping over into a form of bitheism or tritheism — as popular treatments purporting to expound the orthodox trinitarian faith often demonstrate. Rather, the Fourth Evangelist's contribution to that subsequent stage of Christian reflection is that *by his presentation of the Logos-Son he established monotheism as the primary framework for further thought.* That presumably is why the next main stage in the intra-Christian discussion was debate concerning the modalist option. And, more important, that is why when "Logos" finally gave way to "Son" as the primary category of christology, Christian belief in the oneness of God was not threatened — because the earlier Logos christology pioneered by John had already secured the base of Christian monotheism. From John onward, to understand the Son other than as the Logos-Son is to misunderstand Christianity.[96]

On the other hand, by thus letting John be John we can recognize more clearly that both "sides" of the earlier *religionsgeschichtliche* investigation are partly right and partly wrong. Meeks, Borgen, Bühner, et al. are right in seeing late first-century Jewish thought as John's primary historical context; but they have not given enough weight to the significance of Wisdom/Logos as John's dominant leitmotif.[97] Bultmann and his followers were right insofar as they recognized that the "Wisdom myth" is the decisive extra factor in John's christology; but in interpreting this Wisdom tradition in the light of or as a precursor to the Gnostic redeemer myth, they distorted the picture even more. The key is to recognize that what John draws on is the wisdom tradition *within* Judaism — where Wisdom/Logos is not understood as a divine being distinct from God, interpreted as an "intermediary being" between God in his lofty transcendence and his world,[98] but rather where Wisdom is understood precisely as the expression of God's *immanence.*[99] It is precisely because the incarnate Logos has made God visible in his immanence that the heavenly ascent or mystical vision is unnecessary,[100] just as it is precisely because the immanent God has made himself known in the man Jesus that the equation of Wisdom with Torah is inadequate.

In short, however we may think John's Logos-Son christology stretches monotheism, it is only when we understand John as an expression of Christian monotheism that we understand it aright.

96. See my debate with Maurice Wiles in chapter 16 above.

97. Bühner (n. 46) dismisses the possibility of Wisdom influence on John's christology in far too casual a manner (87-103, 411); but Borgen (n. 60), 146, and Meeks (n. 5), 59, 61, recognize its importance without giving it primary weight.

98. W. Bousset and H. Gressmann, *Die Religion des Judentums im späthellenistischen Zeitalter* (HNT 21; [4]1966) 319.

99. See Dunn (n. 82 above); chapter 20 above.

100. Contrast Scholem (n. 43), 55: in merkabah mysticism "the idea of the Shekinah and of God's immanence plays practically no part at all."

9

Finally, we must ask what light our findings throw on the larger questions of this symposium. Now that we have come to a clearer understanding of John in its own terms, what corollaries follow for our understanding of John's relation to the other Gospels? If we now understand better the emphases and motivations of the Johannine distinctives, what pointers do they provide for the next stage of an inquiry into the continuities and discontinuities between John and the earlier tradition on which John draws?

9.1. The most striking point to emerge from our study in this connection must be *the extent to which the Johannine distinctives have been formulated out of John's interaction with the other strands of late first-century Judaism.* In terms of the tradition history of the material incorporated into the Fourth Gospel, it would appear that some of John's key emphases belong (in their Johannine formulation at least) to the later stages of that tradition history — in particular, the question of Jesus' origin, John's insistence that Jesus descended from heaven, and the assertion of Jesus' precosmic existence with God and identity as Son of God with the Father.

Equally striking, however, is the degree to which these Johannine distinctives mark John off *both* from earlier forms of the Jesus-tradition *and* from its context within late first-century Judaism. It is *not* the case that John's differences from the earliest Jesus-tradition can be explained simply by John's drawing ideas from the contemporary melting pot of religious reflection; John's emphases are distinctive also when set against the broader context of the late first century and are better explained as John's development of the *earlier Christian tradition.* Nor is it the case, conversely, that John's differences from its historical context are to be explained simply as elements drawn from the earlier Jesus-tradition; the Johannine formulation presupposes too much of the issues and speculations which came to the fore in the late first century, so that if the Johannine distinctives *are* derived from the earlier Christian tradition, they have to be explained as a *development* of that tradition.

In short, if we are to do justice to the Johannine distinctives, we have to see them as a development of the Jesus-tradition designed to express the truth of Jesus as understood within the Johannine circle. It was a development which was actually part of the late first-century exploration of the conceptualities available and appropriate to talk of God's revelation and salvation, and which probably was in the vanguard of the exploration. It was a developing theology which was partly reacting against other strands of that exploration and partly stimulating reaction from others (the rabbis in particular), and which was in process of formulating a distinctive *Christian* theology which would be increasingly unacceptable for the rest of Judaism, being perceived as a denial of the unity of God.

9.2. Clearly, then, more study is required of what precisely is involved in this *development* of the earlier Christian traditions about Jesus. Does such clarification as we have achieved of the later stages of the tradition history of John's material throw any light on the earlier stages?

One thing can be said straightaway. Our findings do not require us to modify in any degree our earlier recognition of the many points of continuity between John and the earlier Synoptic tradition (section 3.2 above). On the contrary, the recognition that what we have in John is development of the earlier Christian tradition underscores the importance of these points of continuity. Moreover, we can trace something of the course of the development even of John's distinctives, particularly his Wisdom christology and his emphasis on Christ's preexistence, in the Wisdom christology of Paul and of Hebrews (1 Cor. 8:6; Col. 1:15-20; Heb. 1:3-4).[101] Even John's integration of a Wisdom christology (Jesus identified *as* Wisdom) into the Jesus-tradition is paralleled in some degree in the Matthean redaction of Q at three or four points (Matt. 11:19/Luke 7:35; Matt. 11:25-30/Luke 10:21f.; Matt. 23:34-36/Luke 11:49-51; Matt. 23:37-39/Luke 13:34f.).[102] It is not so much the *content* of the Fourth Evangelist's distinctive christology which marks him out, then, as the *way* in which he formulates it, as the *degree of development* of Jesus-tradition which distinguishes the Fourth Gospel from the Synoptics — the style of elaborate discourse and self-testimony, with only minimal parallel in the Synoptic form of the tradition.

Another striking fact is that the Fourth Evangelist obviously felt it necessary to retain the format of a *Gospel*. For all its differences from the Synoptics, John is far closer to them than to any other ancient writing. Although it is the discourses of Jesus which are the most elaborated feature of John's Gospel, the Evangelist did not elect to present a document consisting solely of the discourses or sayings of the redeemer (we may contrast Gnostic equivalents like the *Gospel of Thomas, Thomas the Contender,* and *Pistis Sophia*). Rather he chose, and chose deliberately, to retain the developed discourse material within the framework of a Gospel as laid down by Mark — traditions of Jesus' miracles and teaching building up all the while to the climax of the cross.[103]

All this highlights what in many ways is the most fascinating aspect of the Fourth Gospel — the fact that the author(s) felt *both* free toward the Jesus-tradition (the degree of development) *and* bound to it and its Gospel

101. See Dunn (n. 10), 176-96 and 206-9.
102. See Dunn (n. 10), 197-204. To my bibliography there add M. Hengel, "Jesus als messianischer lehrer der Weisheit und die Anfänge der Christologie," in *Sagesse et Religion* (1979) 148-88, here 149-60 (English translation in *Studies in Early Christology* [Edinburgh: Clark, 1995]).
103. Cf. Dunn (n. 36), 287, 301f., 307.

framework at one and the same time. It is this interplay of freedom and constraint — greater freedom than we find in the Synoptics, greater restraint than we find in the Gnostic equivalents — which requires more detailed study. How could John think that such a degree of development was still being true to the word "from the beginning"? Did he exercise sufficient restraint? — the implication that some of the Johannine community went off into a docetic christology (1 John 2:19) and 1 John's increased emphasis on continuity with the original word (1 John 1:1; 2:7, 24; 3:11) serve only to sharpen the question.[104] Does the Fourth Gospel provide an exemplary case study of how to reexpress the gospel in the different and constantly changing circumstances of a later era while remaining true to the earlier tradition of the gospel — or a cautionary tale? These are some of the issues at stake in a fuller investigation of the actual tradition-historical process, which began with the Synoptic-like sayings from the earliest Jesus-tradition scattered throughout the Fourth Gospel and which ended with the elaborate discourses of the Fourth Gospel, itself aimed at presenting the gospel to a later audience. Such an investigation would provide an agenda in itself for another symposium. Hopefully we have succeeded in letting John be John, but perhaps the greater challenge is to let John's gospel be John's Gospel — both *gospel* and *John's* Gospel!

---

104. See particularly Brown (n. 2), 109-23.

21

Christology as an Aspect of Theology

Introduction

In a recent essay Lee Keck picks up Nils Dahl's observation "that the understanding of God has been the neglected factor in the study of New Testament
theology as a whole" and adds, "This is particularly true of the study of NT
christology."[1] This is the theme I wish to seize upon, gladly acknowledging
the stimulus I have received from Keck's own contributions in this area, as
from his earlier work on the historical Jesus,[2] and offering this small token
of appreciation in return.

The essential problem of a christology which emphasizes the divine
identity and significance of Jesus[3] is that it runs the constant danger of pulling
christology apart from theology (in the specific sense of "doctrine of God").
In more visual terms, christology "from above" runs the risk of leaving God
in the background, an absentee landlord who has handed over the adminis-
tration of his affairs to his son (cf. Mark 12:1-9!). A theology centering in
Christ can actually result in the downgrading of God. The greater the significance attributed to Jesus or the Christ-event, the greater the thrust toward

1. L. E. Keck, "Toward the Renewal of New Testament Christology," *NTS* 32 (1986)
362-77, here 363, citing N. A. Dahl, "The Neglected Factor in New Testament Theology,"
Reflection 73 (1975) 5-8. Similarly, J. C. Beker, *Paul the Apostle: The Triumph of God in Life
and Thought* (Philadelphia: Fortress, 1980) 355-56.

2. Particularly his work as editor of the Lives of Jesus series and as author of *A Future
for the Historical Jesus* (Nashville: Abingdon, 1971; London: SCM, 1972).

3. In the same essay Keck defines "the true subject-matter" of christology as "the
construal of Jesus' identity and significance" ("New Testament Christology," 372).

Reprinted by permission from *The Future of Christology: Essays in Honor of L. E. Keck,* ed.
A. J. Malherbe and W. A. Meeks, 202-12. Copyright © 1993 by Augsburg Fortress.

either modalism or bitheism/tritheism, rather than Trinity.[4] We need not illustrate this here by reference to the Jesuism of so much Protestant piety.
Already in the Nicene Creed the danger was apparent. For it talks of Jesus
Christ who "came down from heaven," as though the Word become incarnate
was a person in the same sense that the Messiah, Jesus of Nazareth (or you
or I), was a person.[5] And in the Western addition of the *filioque,* the danger
is all too present of depicting the Son as a separate and even independent
source (or principle or cause) of divinity from the Father — as the Eastern
churches have always protested.[6] In such a case the ancient myth which many
scholars set at the back of the vision(s) of Dan. 7:9-14 may still retain and
exercise its power: the one like a son of man as the younger god who usurps
the throne and authority of the Ancient of Days.[7] Indeed some would argue
that it was precisely belief in *two* gods — the High God (El Elyon) and Yahweh
or a supreme angel — which explains how it was that belief in the deity of
Jesus could become so quickly established, even within a Jewish matrix.[8]

It is important, therefore, to realize once again that in the New Testament
christology functions within theology, the divine significance of Christ is
actually a subcategory of the doctrine of God, the divine identity of Jesus
Christ is held firmly within the framework of the Christian (as well as Jewish)
axiom that God is one.[9] In the space available here, the point can only be
illustrated in an all too summary way from four of the New Testament authors.

"God in Christ" — Pauline Christology

We naturally start with the earliest New Testament writer — Paul. And the
obvious place to start in Paul is with the emphases of such passages as Rom.

---

4. See, e.g., the warnings in K. Rahner, *The Trinity* (London: Burns and Oates, 1970)
42-45; also idem, *Foundations of Christian Faith* (London: Darton, 1978) 133-37.

5. G. W. H. Lampe (*God as Spirit: Bampton Lectures, 1976* [Oxford: Clarendon, 1977])
gave particular emphasis to this danger. According to Beker, "Nicaea and Chalcedon . . . actually
fostered a type of Christomonism" (*Paul,* 358).

6. See, e.g., L. Vischer, ed., *Spirit of God, Spirit of Christ: Ecumenical Reflections on
the* Filioque *Controversy* (London: SCM; Geneva: WCC, 1981) 11, 58.

7. See those cited by F. H. Borsch, *The Son of Man in Myth and History* (London: SCM,
1967) 141-42; C. Colpe, ὁ υἱὸς τοῦ ἀνθρώπου, *TDNT* VIII (1972) 416-19.

8. See particularly P. Hayman, "Monotheism — A Misused Word in Jewish Studies?"
JJS 42 (1991) 1-15; M. Barker, *The Great Angel: A Study of Israel's Second God* (London:
SPCK, 1992).

9. The most important attempt to provide a corrective of which I am aware is W. Thüsing,
*Per Christum in Deum. Studien zum Verhältnis von Christozentrik and Theozentrik in den
paulinischen Hauptbriefen* (3d ed.; Münster: Aschendorff, 1986), though, significantly, it seems
to have been largely ignored; so, e.g., by L. J. Kreitzer, *Jesus and God in Paul's Eschatology*
(JSNTSS 19; Sheffield: JSOT, 1987).

5:8 and 2 Cor. 5:19. According to Paul, Christ's death was the demonstration (συνίστησιν) of *God's* very own love (ὁ θεός in the place of emphasis) (Rom. 5:8). On the cross "God was in Christ [ἐν Χριστῷ] reconciling the world to himself" (2 Cor. 5:19). Other examples of this neglected use of the familiar ἐν Χριστῷ motif are Rom. 8:39 and 1 Cor. 1:4 (the love/grace of God in Christ Jesus).[10] Such usage should not be reduced simply to the recognition that the sacrificial victim was provided by God (Rom. 3:25), important as that recognition is for any appreciation of both Jewish and Christian theology of sacrifice. Nor is it simply a variant affirmation of Jesus' prophetic inspiration (the Jesus-prophet motif is hardly prominent in Paul). We need to take more seriously what Paul actually says. In some sense, which Paul does not elaborate in these passages, God was acting in and through Christ, so that Christ's death in particular was an enactment of God's love.

The same point comes to the fore in Paul's talk of God's faithfulness. Christ is the expression and proof of *God's* faithfulness (Rom. 15:8; 1 Corinthians 8–9; 2 Cor. 1:18-20). In contrast, the idea of *Christ* as "faithful" is markedly lacking;[11] and when it does appear clearly, in what are now usually taken as post-Pauline epistles (2 Thess. 3:3; 2 Tim. 2:13), it seems to be modeled on the earlier statements of God's faithfulness,[12] probably thus still reflecting the earlier insight that Christ's function within this theme is to express the faithfulness of God. The theme is certainly important within Romans, Paul's most theologically schematic letter, though it has not been given the prominence it deserves,[13] its significance presumably obscured by the fact that the common motif in Hebrew (אֱמוּנָה) has been dispersed across the sequence of Greek equivalents (πίστις, ἀλήθεια, and δικαιοσύνη). But when such key passages as Rom. 1:17, 25; 3:3-7, 21-26; and 15:8 are taken together with chs. 9–11 as a whole (with 9:6 as the thematic text), its importance is hard to ignore. Most striking of all is the way Paul can express his confidence in God's faithfulness (to Israel) in the climactic argument of Romans 11 without giving christology as such (that is, the distinctively Christian reformulation of the messianic hope) very great prominence. Even though

---

10. Neglected even by Thüsing *(Per Christum in Deum)*, despite his ch. 2, "Die Theozentrik des In-Christus-Seins."

11. It is one of the weaknesses of the renewedly popular view that πίστις χριστοῦ refers to the faith/faithfulness of Christ rather than to the more traditional "faith in Christ" (a view which Keck also espouses; see his " 'Jesus' in Romans," *JBL* 108 [1989] 443-60, esp. 452-57), that it detracts attention from the more important motif of *God's* faithfulness. See further my "Once More πίστις χριστοῦ," *SBLSP* 1991 (Atlanta: Scholars, 1991) 730-44.

12. BAGD, πιστός 1aβ.

13. Exceptions include W. S. Campbell, "The Freedom and Faithfulness of God in Relation to Israel," *JSNT* 13 (1981) 27-45; J. C. Beker, "The Faithfulness of God and the Priority of Israel in Paul's Letter to the Romans," *HTR* 79 (1986) 10-16. But these naturally relate the issue to "the problem of Israel" more than to christology.

for Paul the faithfulness of God has come to supreme expression and focus in Christ, it is the faithfulness of God which is the dominant theme rather than the christology (hence 15:8).

What then of those passages in Paul which seem to affirm the deity of Christ in less controlled ways? — that is, without setting the christological affirmation so clearly *within* theology as in the cases already instanced. One thinks at once of the astonishing application of LXX κύριος (= the Lord God) to Christ, particularly in Phil. 2:9-11 (clearly echoing the strongly monotheistic Isa. 45:23). But this should not be understood as attributing a distinct or different lordship to Christ: Isa. 45:23 can be echoed precisely because what is conceived is part of the worship due the one God; hence in the hymn itself the confession of Jesus Christ as Lord is εἰς δόξαν θεοῦ πατρός (Phil. 2:11).[14] Moreover, Paul seems to be at some pains to emphasize that this lordship of Christ is granted by the Lord God (Ps. 110:1) and is wholly consistent with the unity of God (1 Cor. 8:6). Christ is Lord only as an expression of the one God's lordship: God is still "the God and Father of our Lord Jesus Christ" (Rom. 15:6; 2 Cor. 1:3; 11:31; also Eph. 1:3, 17; Col. 1:3; 1 Pet. 1:3); the climax of Christ's lordship will be his own "subjection to the one who put all things under him, so that God may be all in all" (1 Cor. 15:28). Indeed, we could say that Christ's lordship is as much an expression of Adam christology as anything else: the subordination of enemies (to the Lord — Ps. 110:1) is evidently understood by Paul (and other New Testament writers) as equivalent to or part of all things being put in subjection (to Adam — Ps. 8:6).[15] As Adam's dominion over all things was intended as the exercise of God's own authority as Creator, so with the lordship of the exalted Christ (hence also the sequence of authority in 1 Cor. 3:23 and 11:3).

The conflation of Adam and Lord christology as subsets of theology is reflected also in Paul's use of the εἰκών and δόξα motifs. Christ is the image of God precisely in that he embodies the highest expression of God's creative power and purpose, and thus serves as the pattern and template for that re-creation of humanity which is God's continuing purpose of salvation: hence Rom. 8:29 (absorbing the motif of Christ as Son), 1 Cor. 15:49 (Adam Christology), and the ambiguity as to whether the "image" refers to God or Christ in 2 Cor. 3:18 and Col. 3:10. Christology is a subset of theology not least because if God is to be all in all, then *all*-ologies (cosmology, soteriology, etc.) are, properly speaking, subsets of *theo*-logy. Likewise with δόξα, linked with the εἰκών theme in 2 Cor. 3:18 and 4:4. As Beker points out, in Paul,

---

14. See further Thüsing, *Per Christum in Deum,* 55-60.

15. Note the way in which Ps. 8:6 is merged with Ps. 110:1 in Mark 12:36 par.; 1 Cor. 15:25-27; Eph. 1:20-22; Heb. 1:13–2:8; and 1 Pet. 3:22; see further my *Christology in the Making* (London: SCM, 1980; 2nd ed., 1989) 108-13; and ch. 13 above.

δόξα refers overwhelmingly to the glory of God (Rom. 1:23; 3:23; 5:2; 6:4; 9:23; 15:7, etc.). The relatively fewer references to the "glory of Christ" (1 Cor. 2:8; 2 Cor. 3:18; 4:4; cf. 2 Cor. 8:19, 23; 2 Thess. 2:14) are to be taken either as anticipations of the final glory of God[16] or in terms of Christ manifesting what of God is perceptible to human sight. As with the theme of lordship, so here, the glory of Christ is not understood by Paul as a different glory from that of the glory of God; it *is* the glory of God.

This points to what is probably the best way to understand the passage usually taken to be the clearest application of θεός to Christ within the Pauline corpus[17] (albeit in the deutero-Pauline) — Tit. 2:13: the appearance of Jesus Christ (1 Tim. 6:14; 2 Tim. 1:10; 4:8) is the "appearance of the glory of our great God and Savior,"[18] as he also was the appearance of "the goodness and loving kindness of God our Savior" (Tit. 3:4); in the Pastorals, God is more frequently described as Savior (1 Tim. 1:1; 2:3; 4:10; Tit. 1:3; 2:10; 3:4) than Christ (2 Tim. 1:10; Tit. 1:4; 3:6), that is, not two Saviors but the one saving action.

In the light of all this, the references to Christ as having a preexistent role in creation (particularly 1 Cor. 8:6 and Col. 1:15-17) fall into place. For, as is generally recognized, this motif in Pauline christology emerges from the application of wisdom terminology to Christ; that is, to be more precise, the language of these passages is language which was characteristically used of divine Wisdom in Jewish wisdom literature (e.g., Ps. 104:24; Prov. 3:19; 8:22, Sir. 24:3, 9; Wis. 7:26; 8:4-6) and which would no doubt have been recognized as such by those familiar with (particularly) diaspora Jewish apologetic.[19] This Wisdom is frequently taken as a "hypostasis" or "intermediary" between God and the cosmos. That, however, is to mishear the vivid metaphorical character of such speech and thus also to misread the strategy of Jewish apologists for the one God, as one who acts not through or in conjunction with other deities but precisely through his *own* wisdom, spirit, name, glory, etc. This creating, sustaining, saving outreach of the God of Israel (and of the world) they saw embodied definitively in the Torah (Sir. 24:23; Bar. 3:9–4:4). In a similar, but still bolder, way Paul and other early Christians saw the same divine Wisdom most clearly and definitively embodied in Christ — which for Paul meant most clearly and definitively in the cross (1 Cor. 1:22-25)! That

---

16. Beker, *Paul the Apostle,* 362-63.

17. Rom. 9:5, of course, is regularly taken as referring to Christ as God. For myself, however, I find it virtually impossible to argue that any Jew, or Gentile as familiar with Jewish theology as Paul assumes the readers of Romans to be, would think to read the benediction to "God over all things" as referring to the Jewish Messiah. For fuller discussion, see J. D. G. Dunn, *Romans* (WBC 38; Dallas: Word, 1988) 528-29.

18. See esp. V. Hasler, "Epiphanie and Christologie in den Pastoralbriefen," *TZ* 33 (1977) 193-209, here 201.

19. See more fully, and for what follows, Dunn, *Christology,* ch. 6.

this (similarly) apologetic strategy was recognized by Paul's Jewish opponents is indicated by the fact that christology does not seem to have been an issue for them: they evidently did not see Paul's Wisdom christology as a compromise of or threat to their more traditional Wisdom theology, but as an (alternative) expression of it.[20] They evidently saw no inconsistency when Paul expressed his Wisdom christology in the same breath that he affirmed the *Shema* (1 Cor. 8:6); the one who is the wisdom of God embodies "all the fullness of God," through whom he reconciles all things to himself (Col. 1:19-20; 2:9).

In short, Pauline christology again and again in its "highest" moments shows itself to be in essence an aspect of theology.[21]

"God with Us" — Matthean Christology

Here we can be briefer. Of the Synoptics, Matthew clearly contains the "highest" christology, not simply by his incorporation of a birth narrative (a feature he shares with Luke), but in the way he uses it to strike a thematic note for his Gospel and in the way, unlike Luke, he develops the wisdom motifs present in the Q material into a more explicit Wisdom christology.

I refer in the first place to his incorporation of Isa. 7:14 as the first of his sequence of Scripture fulfillments (1:23). The focus of discussion here has traditionally been on the thought of virginal conception. But the main emphasis for Matthew falls rather on the second half of the quotation: "and his name shall be called Emmanuel (which means, God with us)." Jesus is thus presented as the one who fulfills the prophetic promise of "God with us," that is, as the one who so fully embodies the divine presence that he can be called, in a more than metaphorical sense, "God with us."[22] That so to read Matt. 1:23 is in tune with Matthew's own intention is confirmed by 28:18-20. In the final words of the whole Gospel, the promise of divine presence is reaffirmed: the risen Christ has been given "all authority in heaven and on earth" (28:18); as the exalted one he continues to embody the divine ἐγώ εἰμι, continues (as in 1:23) to embody the divine presence μεθ' ὑμῶν (28:20). The two christo-theological words form an

20. Unlike the Jewish opponents in the background of John's Gospel; see below, pp. 369, 385.

21. Regrettably there is too little space to go into the complexities of the further relationship in Paul between God, Christ, and the Spirit of God. But see Thüsing, *Per Christum in Deum,* ch. 4, and Dunn, *Christology,* 141-49.

22. See, e.g., W. D. Davies and D. C. Allison, *Matthew 1–7* (ICC; Edinburgh: Clark, 1988) 217. A full treatment of the theme is provided by D. Kupp, *Matthew's Emmanuel* (Cambridge: Cambridge University, 1996).

inclusio, clearly intended to bracket the whole Gospel, and thus indicate the framework or fundamental structure of the Matthean christology within which the whole has to be read. Thus, in particular, we are not surprised to find, in the chapter which most clearly looks to the future of the Christian churches, a further expression of the same theme, in the promise that where two or three are gathered in his name, ἐκεῖ εἰμι ἐν μέσῳ αὐτῶν (18:20), a further expression, that is, of divine presence christology.[23]

As to Matthew's Wisdom christology, I need do no more than give a reminder of the generally accepted point that Matthew has redacted the Q material at several places to transform the picture of Jesus the teacher of Wisdom into that of Jesus as himself identical with Wisdom.[24] Given the understanding of divine Wisdom within contemporary Judaism, already noted, the same point emerges: in Matthew, Jesus is portrayed as the embodiment of the divine Wisdom which is God in his outreach to his creation. Jesus as divine Wisdom is synonymous with Jesus as "God with us."

Here too, then, we have christology entirely in the service of theology.

"Equal with God" — Johannine Christology

As Bultmann recognized, the main thrust of John's Christology is to present Jesus as the bearer of divine revelation: "Jesus as the revealer of God reveals nothing but that he is the revealer."[25] The observation is soundly based but misleadingly formulated, in effect making the same mistake of focusing too narrowly on the christology. What Bultmann ought to have said is: "Jesus as the revealer of God reveals nothing but that he is the revealer *of God.*"[26]

The point is that each of the distinctive motifs of Johannine christology

---

23. Frequently cited is the rabbinic parallel in *m. Aboth* 3:2 ("If two sit together and the words of the Law [are spoken] between them, the divine presence [the Shekinah] rests between them"), where the Shekinah likewise is a way of speaking of the divine presence, as characteristically in rabbinic thought; see, e.g., A. M. Goldberg, *Untersuchungen über die Vorstellung von der Schekhinah in der frühen rabbinischen Literatur* (Berlin, 1969); E. E. Urbach, *The Sages: Their Concepts and Beliefs* (2nd ed.; Jerusalem: Magnes, 1979), ch. 3: "The *Shekhina* — The Presence of God in the World."

24. Matt. 11:19/Luke 7:35; Matt. 11:25-27/Luke 10:21-22 with Matt. 11:28-30 (cf. Sir. 51:23-26); Matt. 23:34/Luke 11:49; Matt. 23:37-39/Luke 13:34-35. See esp. M. J. Suggs, *Wisdom, Christology and Law in Matthew's Gospel* (Cambridge: Harvard University, 1970), chs. 2-3; C. Deutsch, "Wisdom in Matthew: Transformation of a Symbol," *NovT* 32 (1990) 13-47.

25. R. Bultmann, *Theology of the New Testament* II (London: SCM, 1955) 66.

26. In what follows I have space only to outline briefly what I have attempted to argue in more detail in ch. 20 above and in *The Partings of the Ways* (London: SCM; Philadelphia: TPI, 1991) §§11.5-6.

have this same function — presenting Jesus as the one who reveals God, God's grace and truth (חֶסֶד וֶאֱמֶת),[27] most clearly and definitively. He is the Logos become flesh (1:14): like the earlier Wisdom christology, a bolder claim than the more traditional identification of divine Wisdom with the Torah (hence 1:17), but more bluntly posed, given the more negative overtones attaching to "flesh" in John (1:13; 3:6; 6:63; 8:15); and, like the earlier Wisdom christology, a claim that Christ has embodied the self-revelation of God toward his creation.[28] He is the μονογενὴς θεός who alone has "seen God," and who thus alone can "make him known" (1:18); hence to have seen him is to have seen the Father (6:46; 12:45; 14:9); the Israelite who sees his real significance is the true Israelite who "sees God" (1:47-51).[29] He is the Son of man descended from heaven, and hence alone able to reveal the mysteries of God in heaven (3:12-13, 31-33). He is the Son sent by the Father, who embodies the full authority of God (3:34-35), who does what the Father does (5:17, 19), who has life in himself as the Father has life in himself (5:26), and so on. He is the divine "I am," who not only utters the word of God but who also embodies in himself the self-revelation of God, those images, for example, of light, food and drink, and shepherd (John 6:51-58; 10:14; 12:8) by which God's self-revelation in Wisdom was characterized (as in Wis. 7:26, 29; Sir. 24:19-22; Philo, *Agr.* 51; *Mut.* 116). The glory of God (the manifestation of God in glory) which Isaiah saw in the Temple (Isa. 6:1) is now embodied in him (John 12:41), and most clearly in his fleshness (1:14) and in his death (12:33; 13:31).

At all these points it is Jesus as the revealer of God who is presented to us. This is probably the key to the oft-noted tension between assertions of oneness with the Father alongside assertions of the Father's superiority (as in 10:29-30).[30] For these two are not antithetical assertions, nor intended as precursors of the nicely balanced assertions of the Son's oneness with and subordination to the Father, as in the later trinitarian treatises. Rather they are

27. For the importance of the hendiadys in Hebrew theology, see A. Jepsen, *TDOT* I, 313-16; H. J. Zobel, *TDOT* V, 57. Despite, or perhaps because of, his dependence on and admiration for Bultmann's work, J. Ashton fails to advance beyond this insight (*Understanding the Fourth Gospel* [Oxford: Clarendon, 1991], part 3).

28. See, e.g., Dunn, *Christology,* ch. 8.

29. The Jacob who dreams of the ladder to heaven (Gen. 28:12-17; John 1:51) is, of course, the Jacob who sees God face-to-face and is renamed Israel (Gen. 32:28-30); in consequence "Israel" was often taken to mean "he that sees God" (as often in Philo).

30. See esp. C. K. Barrett, "Christocentric or Theocentric? Observations on the Theological Method of the Fourth Gospel," *La Notion Biblique de Dieu,* ed. J. Coppens (Paris: Duculot, 1976); reprinted in Barrett, *Essays on John* (London: SPCK, 1982) 1-18; idem, " 'The Father is Greater than I.' John 14:28: Subordinationist Christology in the New Testament," *Neues Testament und Kirche: Festschrift für Rudolf Schnackenburg* (Freiburg: Herder, 1974), reprinted in Barrett, *Essays,* 19-36. See also the review and discussion in D. A. Carson, *Divine Sovereignty and Human Responsibility: Biblical Perspectives in Tension* (Atlanta: John Knox, 1981) 146-60.

assertions that, even as the Logos becomes flesh, Jesus expresses the full authority of the Father; it is to enhance his own authority, that is, as the authority of God, that the Johannine Jesus emphasizes his commissioning by God. So the claim to oneness with the Father is but another way of saying the same thing.[31] That is why both the opposition reflected in John and John himself can take with such full seriousness the affirmation that Jesus has made himself "equal with God" (5:18), indeed, has "made himself God" (10:33), and can be hailed as "my God" (20:28).

It was no doubt John's willingness to express the Christian claim with such boldness which caused "the Jews" of John's time to recognize (at last) a threat to Jewish monotheism and to insist that Jews who made such a confession of Jesus should be expelled from the synagogue (9:22). But John seems to have understood what he was doing simply as a way of underlining that it was the unseen God, the one God himself, whom Jesus revealed, and revealed with an incomparable fullness and finality. In short, the Johannine Christ is the medium of God's self-revelation, and, as such, Johannine christology functions as an aspect of his theology.

"The Throne of God and of the Lamb" — Apocalyptic Christology

The only other New Testament writing with a sustained "high" christology is the Revelation of John. What is most striking here is the opening vision of the exalted Christ in 1:12-16. For it is clearly a composite picture drawn (consciously or unconsciously) principally from the visions recorded in Ezekiel and Daniel (Ezek. 1:24, 26; 8:2; Dan. 7:9, 13; 10:5-6). That is to say, it draws on descriptions both of God and of a glorious angelic being, such as we find elsewhere at this time (e.g., *Apocalypse of Zephaniah* 6:11-15; *Apoc. Abr.* 10-11; *Joseph and Aseneth* 14:9-10). What needs to be noted here is the way in some of these visions and in Rev. 1:12-16 itself the images used of God and of the glorious angel seem to merge. The angel is a development from the angel of the Lord, who, in the Pentateuch, is the physical manifestation of God himself (e.g., Gen. 16:7-13; 21:17-18; 31:11-13; Exod. 3:2-6, 14); or, in terms drawn from Exod. 23:20-21, the angel is characterized as the one in whom God has put his name (hence the name of the angel in *Apoc. Abr.* 10:3 — Yahoel). And in Rev. 1:13-14 the seer draws on the descriptions both of the Ancient of Days and of the son of man-like figure (Dan. 7:9, 13).

31. See further M. L. Appold, *The Oneness Motif in the Fourth Gospel* (WUNT 1; Tübingen: Mohr, 1977).

Consistent with this is the fact that both God and Christ say of themselves, "I am the Alpha and the Omega" (1:8; 22:13); and that the Lamb seems to be sitting on God's throne (7:17; 22:1, 3).[32]

What is happening here? Is it that the vision of God is fragmenting (in a way analogous to the supposed hypostatization of Wisdom)?[33] I would say not. These are all better understood as attempts to envision and to speak of the mystery of God. For the apocalyptic visionary, visions of a glorious being, dazzling in appearance, were the best he could hope for. The echoes of the fullest revelations hitherto afforded (Exod. 33:18-23; Isa. 6:1-5; Ezek. 1:26-28; Dan. 7:9-10) are intended (consciously or unconsciously) as precisely that — echoes which enhance the authority of the vision, echoes which invite the reader to recognize a true sight of God's glory and revelation of God's will. Again it is the closeness and continuity between the one God and what is seen that is the point of emphasis, a centripetal rather than a centrifugal force.

There is, however, one major difference between the Christian seer and the other apocalyptists. They were careful to retain a clear distinction between God and the glorious angel, by insisting that the angel should not be worshiped (*Apocalypse of Zephaniah* 16:15; *Apoc. Abr.* 16:3-4; 17:2). In Revelation, on the other hand, the Lamb is the subject of worship and adoration just like that given to God (Revelation 4–5). Yet this, too, is best seen as an expression of the same apocalyptic tendency. For it is not two separate acts of worship which are being directed to two separate beings, but one and the same worship (5:13; 7:10) to those who sit as God on the one throne (7:17; 22:1, 3). That which is seen through the shimmering and dazzling light of heavenly vision all serves to reinforce the Christian conviction that it is the Lamb (slain and alive again) who is the clearest manifestation of the one God.

Here too, therefore, like John the Evangelist, though pressing hard at the frontiers of human attempts to speak of God, John the seer evidently intended his christology as an expression of his theology.

Conclusions

In some ways our findings are unsurprising — a merely traditional restatement of classic christology, some might say. Yet the fact is that there is an ongoing and recently revitalized debate as to whether Judaism was after all monotheis-

---

32. For more details, see Dunn, *Partings*, 215-20.

33. So esp. C. Rowland, *The Open Heaven: A Study of Apocalyptic in Judaism and Early Christianity* (London: SPCK; New York: Crossroad, 1982) 96-97, 100. But see also L. W. Hurtado, *One God, One Lord: Early Christian Devotion and Ancient Jewish Monotheism* (Philadelphia: Fortress; London: SCM, 1988) 85-90.

tic, with the corollary drawn by one side that Christianity simply *took over the idea of a second god* already present in Judaism.[34] In marked contrast, M. P. Casey can argue that precisely by calling Jesus God, Christianity became Gentile and *abandoned* Jewish monotheism.[35] And at the level of popular Christianity almost certainly there is considerable *functional tritheism or bitheism.*

Our findings are therefore important. For they remind us that the Christian gospel has to do first and last and foremost with God. They remind us that Christian faith is primarily faith in the one God, Creator, Savior, Judge. We have looked at those Christian canonical texts which are normally understood to present a "high" christology. In each case we have seen that the writers had no thought to present Christ as an alternative to God, as an object sufficient in himself of Christian worship. Do not misunderstand me. The Christ of the New Testament writers is worthy of the highest praise, devotion, and worship, as the one in whom heaven and earth come together, as the one in whom God comes to fallen humanity, as the one who embodies the divine presence and grace in ultimate degree (in death and life, as well as resurrection and exaltation), as the one through whom believers see God and present their prayers. But it is in this role that he is most worthy of worship; and worship which stops at him and does not pass through him to God, the all in all, at the end of the day falls short of Christian worship.

34. See above, n. 8.
35. M. P. Casey, *From Jewish Prophet to Gentile God: The Origins and Development of New Testament Christology* (Cambridge: Clarke, 1991); see also ch. 22 below.

22

The Making of Christology
Evolution or Unfolding?

There is no question that we have to speak of the development of christology in the earliest decades of Christianity. At the beginning of that period and within the area where Christianity began there was no thought of a Messiah figure being crucified, raised from dead, and designated θεός. Less than one hundred years later such claims were being made regarding Jesus (particularly in John 20:28) and indeed already being taken for granted (at least in Ignatius, *Ephesians* inscr; 1:17; 7:2; 15:3; 18:2; 19:3, etc.).[1] Clearly something was being said at the end of the period which had never been said before. In that sense at least we must speak of development of ideas and usage.

But that conclusion simply opens up the more important question: What do we mean by "development"? Do we mean the outworking of what was always there in principle or *in nuce* — the organic development of the seed into the plant, of the acorn into the oak? The fuller christology of the late first century and early second century (and beyond) could then be said to be simply the recognition of what had always been true of Jesus and only awaited the eye of faith to see with increasing clarity. Just as the rabbinic (oral) tradition could be defined by the rabbis as the "Torah received by Moses at Sinai" and handed down through Joshua, elders, and prophets to the great assembly (*m. 'Abot* 1:1), so the developed christological formulations of later centuries could be traced back to Jesus and the apostles. This in effect has been the

---

1. Further details in W. R. Schoedel, *Ignatius of Antioch* (Hermeneia; Philadelphia: Fortress, 1985) 39.

Originally published in *Jesus of Nazareth, Lord and Christ: Essays on the Historical Jesus and New Testament Christology,* ed. J. B. Green and M. Turner (I. H. Marshall FS; Grand Rapids: Eerdmans, 1994) 437-52.

classic view of christological development, defended in more extensive principle by Newman[2] and in recent New Testament scholarship by Moule.[3] The
claim by Hengel that "more happened" in christology in the first two decades
of Christianity "than in the whole of the next seven centuries,"[4] amounts to
the same thing.[5] And Howard Marshall follows a similar line in *The Origins
of New Testament Christology:* "Behind the development there stands the
figure of Jesus and the claim, indirect or direct, which he made for himself";
"the divinity of Jesus . . . emerged as the inescapable corollary of Jesus'
position."[6] For want of a better label I put this perspective under one of
Newman's terms, "unfolding."

The alternative view is that earliest christology developed by accretion,
that is, in crude terms, by adding on new ideas and claims which were not
implicit in or native to the earliest response to Jesus. This can be characterized
more carefully as the model of "evolution" — that is, development by inner
change, from one species to another, where there is, of course, continuity
between what went before and what develops out of it, but where changing
environment makes it necessary for the organism to adapt and thus to evolve
into something different. This in effect was the classic rationalist response to
traditional christology. It naturally found a definitive precedent in the emergence of a clear model for "evolution" in the work of Darwin and was
variously espoused in the liberal Protestantism of Harnack and the *reli-
gionsgeschichtlich* approach of Bousset and Bultmann.[7] However, reaction to
the particular theses of the latter in the intervening decades of New Testament
scholarship has tended to cloud the hypothesis of evolutionary development
and to detract from its credibility. And it is only in the last few years that it
has gained a new champion and a fresh, sophisticated version.

I refer to the revised version of M. Casey's Cadbury Lectures delivered
at the University of Birmingham in 1985 and published under the title *From
Jewish Prophet to Gentile God: The Origins and Development of New Testa-*

---

2. J. H. Newman, *An Essay on the Development of Christian Doctrine* (first published
1845).

3. C. F. D. Moule, *The Origin of Christology* (Cambridge: Cambridge University, 1977).

4. M. Hengel, *The Son of God* (London: SCM, 1976).

5. See, e.g., Hengel, *Son of God*, 71: "There was an inner necessity about the introduction
of the idea of pre-existence into christology."

6. I. H. Marshall, *The Origins of New Testament Christology* (Leicester: Inter-Varsity,
1976) 128-29. Other recent monographs which focus largely on the initial impact of Jesus and
his resurrection include P. Pokorný, *The Genesis of Christology* (Edinburgh: Clark, 1987); and
M. de Jonge, *Christology in Context: The Earliest Christian Response to Jesus* (Philadelphia:
Westminster, 1988).

7. A. Harnack, *What Is Christianity?* (first published 1900); W. Bousset, *Kyrios Christos:
A History of the Belief in Christ from the Beginnings of Christianity to Irenaeus* (1913; [2]1921;
ET, Nashville: Abingdon, 1970); R. Bultmann, *Theology of the New Testament* I (London: SCM,
1952) §15.

ment Christology.[8] The issues it raises are so important that I propose to devote the rest of this essay to discussion of Casey's thesis.

1

Casey begins by proposing a new way of analyzing the evidence, which he then uses to elaborate a new theory to explain why New Testament christology developed as it did. The major concept is that of *identity.* The identity of a group is "everything which is perceived[9] to make it that group and not another group" (11). What that means in practice is the recognition of a sequence of *identity factors,* whose distinctiveness either characterizes or focuses or encapsulates or together builds up to embody the group's identity. For the purposes of his study he specifies eight identity factors of Second Temple Judaism — ethnicity, Scripture, monotheism, circumcision, Sabbath observance, dietary laws, purity laws, and major festivals. He notes that it is not a simple matter of all or nothing. Ethnicity is obviously a key factor, and indeed may be an overriding factor: "People may be perceived as Jewish if it is the only one of the eight identity factors that they have, and they may be perceived as Gentile if they have all the other seven identity factors, but not ethnicity" (14). The fact that five of the eight identity factors "may reasonably be perceived as social factors which have received religious legitimation" (16) leads to the further observation that "when a religion is coterminous with an ethnic group, its identity factors are both social and religious" (17). He also maintains that "a concept of orthodoxy is necessary," with "orthodox Jews" defined as those who, in opposition to threats of assimilation, sought to ensure the observation and application of the law to the whole of life — the law thus elaborated and enacted being seen in this way to embody Jewish identity (17-19).[10]

On this base Casey's thesis can be stated in straightforward terms. As long as the earliest Christian community was Jewish in self-identity, the crucial developments in christology of affirming the deity and incarnation of Jesus

8. P. M. Casey, *From Jewish Prophet to Gentile God: The Origins and Development of New Testament Christology* (Cambridge: Clarke; Louisville: Westminster, 1991). I am grateful to Dr. Casey, my former colleague at Nottingham, for his readiness to comment on the first draft of this essay and to help remove possible misrepresentations or misunderstandings of his argument.

9. The use of the passive voice at this foundational point in Casey's procedure is significant. It naturally raises the question: "perceived" by whom? As we shall see, this simple question has important ramifications.

10. Note also Casey, *Jewish Prophet,* 61-64: Jesus was in conflict with "the orthodox wing of Judaism."

could not happen. The crucial identity factor of Jewish monotheism inhibited and limited the development of christology. That limiting factor was only finally removed in the Johannine community. There the sharpness of the confrontation with "the Jews" indicates that the author had Gentile self-identification. This implies in turn that the identity factor of monotheism either was no longer such a constraining factor or was no longer operative at all. "The removal of the Jewish restraint after A.D. 70, leaving the Johannine community with Gentile self-identification, was the decisive step which ensured that Jesus was hailed as God . . ."; "this Gentile self-identification was a necessary cause of belief in the deity of Jesus, a belief which could not be held as long as the Christian community was primarily Jewish" (37-38). Here, clearly, the evolutionary hypothesis receives very strong statement. It is not simply the case of a changing environment permitting a development which would have been inhibited elsewhere, but of the changed environment actually *causing* the development — a development, that is, which would not have taken place without that change from Jewish to Gentile self-identity.

2

We can be grateful to Casey for bringing the category of identity into play so fully. As others have recognized, the question of how individuals and groups saw themselves and defined themselves over against others is bound to be critical in any attempt to sketch out the history of a movement, particularly in its beginnings.[11] Moreover, within the list of identity factors selected (somewhat arbitrarily) by Casey, ethnicity was undoubtedly a crucial factor. It could indeed be said that that alone was sufficient to ensure that Christianity became something different from Judaism. That is, as more and more Gentiles joined what started as Jewish sect, without becoming Jews (proselytes), it was inevitable that a Judaism for which ethnic Jewishness remained the fundamental identity factor would have to disown that sect. We should note nevertheless that a vital and continuing *Jewish* Christianity meant that the process was much more drawn out than is normally recognized.[12]

A more important point of critique, however, is Casey's failure to recognize the extent to which there was (and still is) a tension between ethnic and religious identity in Judaism. Ethnicity may be fundamental, but is it

11. See, e.g., E. P. Sanders et al., ed., *Jewish and Christian Self-Definition* (3 vols., London: SCM, 1980-82); J. Neusner and E. S. Frerichs, *"To See Ourselves as Others See Us": Christians, Jews, "Others" in Late Antiquity* (Chico: Scholars, 1985).

12. See my *The Partings of the Ways between Christianity and Judaism* (London: SCM, 1991) ch. 12.

decisive? Orthodox and the various branches of hasidic Judaism today in Israel would certainly want to raise questions here. "Who is a Jew?" is as lively an issue as it has ever been. Are nonreligious Jews (apostates), or Gentiles who have converted to liberal Judaism, or Jews who have become Christians, really "Jews"? And, more to the immediate point, the issue was just as lively in the first century also. It is relevant here to recall that Josephus uses the name "Jews" for the exiles returning from Babylon, rather than for those who had remained in Judea throughout (*Ant.* 11.173), that he shows clear disapproval of the Samaritans calling themselves "Jews" (*Ant.* 11.340-41), and that he refrains from calling the apostate Tiberius Alexander a "Jew" (cf. *Ant.* 20.100). It is still more relevant to recall that Paul is able to dispute the definition of "Jew" (Rom. 2:28-29) while both speaking of his life "within Judaism" as something belonging to the past (Gal. 1:13-14) and claiming still to be an "Israelite" (Rom. 11:1). In all these cases religious and ethnic identity are being held in uncomfortable tension.

The problem is exacerbated by introduction of the concept of "orthodoxy." For the reality of the matter is that different groups within late Second Temple Judaism regarded themselves as in effect the only truly "orthodox," the only truly loyal to the covenant and to the law. Their faithfulness to a Zadokite priesthood, their observation of (what they regarded as) the (only) correctly calculated feasts, their commitment to their own sectarian halakhah (interpretation of the law), all carried the corollary in different degrees that the other sects, and probably the larger mass of Jewish people, were "unorthodox," or in their own terms, "sinners," "impious," "ungodly." Such factionalism within Second Temple Judaism can be clearly seen not only in the writings of the Qumran Essenes, but also in such writings as *1 Enoch, Jubilees,* the *Psalms of Solomon,* and the *Testament of Moses.*[13] By using the term "orthodox" of the Pharisees (61-64) Casey is viewing the time of Jesus from a post-70 rabbinic perspective, with inevitably distorting effect.

The point is this: with such disagreement and dispute so obvious within the Jewish writings of the period, can we speak so straightforwardly of "Jewish identity"? In fact many historians of the period, not least Jewish scholars, find it necessary to speak of Second Temple Judaisms (plural) rather than simply of Judaism (singular), or indeed, if the word is appropriate for the time of Jesus, of competing orthodoxies. In other words, Casey is running the danger of postulating a too simplified and uniform concept of Jewish identity. Of course he recognizes the dangers and tries to meet them by speaking of "an identity scale" (12). But nonetheless he does not really grapple with the problem of an identity which was itself developing (or evolving), or of identity factors disputed in what they amounted to and in

13. I may refer again simply to my *Partings,* 102-7.

their degree of relevance. Hence the earlier question: "perceived" by whom?[14] For an outsider might perceive "Judaism" to be more coherent and internally consistent than an insider.[15] On the other hand, an insider could well be more concerned with internal boundaries, and regard them as in effect more important than the external boundaries which marked out all Jews.[16] Identity markers as perceived from outside might well have different values from the way they were perceived from inside.

Here it may be significant that Casey ignores what surely must be regarded as one of the chief identity factors of Second Temple Judaism — that is, the Second Temple itself.[17] Judea was a temple state — a political entity whose identity (political, social, economic, and religious) was wholly bound up with the temple. But, of course, the direct relevance of the temple as then constituted to the practice of Judaism was one of the more disputed features of Second Temple Judaism, as, once again, the Dead Sea Scrolls and such writings as the *Psalms of Solomon* attest, given also, not least, that the majority of Jews lived outside Israel and would probably have been unable to attend the temple more than once or twice in their lives. Yet the loss of the temple in 70 C.E. was not a fatal blow to Judaism; instead, it led into the greatest inner transformation of Judaism (should we say unfolding or evolution?) that Judaism recognizes — from a religious system dominated by priest and cult to one dominated by rabbi and rabbinic interpretation of the Torah. Fully to appreciate the transformation of a Jewish sect into Christianity, one has to be able to compare these two transformations (from Second Temple Judaism to Christianity and from Second Temple Judaism to rabbinic Judaism) with each other. Otherwise the concept of "Jewish identity" is being given artificial value and unhistorical coherence and consistency.

And if Jewish identity in the Second Temple period was that much less clearcut, it should further warn us against a too simple juxtaposition and antithesis of "Jewish identity" with "Gentile identity." This is particularly pertinent in the case of the Fourth Gospel. Casey's whole thesis, in fact, swings on his assertion that the Fourth Evangelist "wrote as a member of a group who had Gentile self-identification" (27), and whose christology therefore breached the constraints of *Jewish* monotheism. But given the complexities and tensions already noted, the issue needs much more careful handling. It is

14. See above, n. 9.
15. This is the implication of Mark 7:3-4, where the note added assumes that Pharisaic halakhah was followed by all Jews.
16. The most striking example of this within Second Temple Judaism are the Qumran Essenes, who regarded themselves as "the sons of light" and (apparently) all others, including all other Jews, as "the sons of darkness."
17. Contrast my *Partings,* ch. 2, where I designate the temple as one of the four pillars of Second Temple Judaism.

not settled, for example, by noting that John speaks of "the Passover of the Jews" (John 2:13); the presence of even a minority of Gentiles among the recipients of the Gospel would be sufficient to explain such notes of explanation. And talk of "your/their law" when Jesus is speaking to or about "the Jews" (8:17; 10:34; 15:25) need only imply a group of Jews whose identity as Jews was closely bound up with the law (as interpreted by them).

Even the frequent references to "the Jews" do not settle the matter. The many hostile references surely indicate a breach with those so designated; but most scholars identify "the Jews" in these passages with the Jewish authorities in the area where the Johannine congregations were meeting. And it still leaves a similar range of references where "the Jews" in question are the common people, the crowd. What is interesting about them is that they stand in the middle between Jesus on the one hand and "the (hostile) Jews" (= the authorities) on the other. They are presented as a shifting, ambivalent mass, for whose loyalty Jesus and the authorities are in competition, and where the clear hope is that many of them, like Nicodemus and the blind man of John 9 (even the many "authorities" of 12:42), will take their courage in both hands and declare for Jesus. In other words, the drama being played out in the Fourth Gospel, above all in existential terms for the Johannine communities themselves, is still an intra-Jewish drama, where Jews (and Gentiles) were contesting with other Jews the common Jewish heritage and the allegiance of still uncommitted Jews.[18]

It should be said that Casey is not oblivious to this problem — the problem of identifying identity in too clearcut terms, the problem of defining self-identity. Unfortunately, however, his allusions to the problem only help to compound it. For he speaks of "assimilating Jews" (32-34) and even of "former Jews" (33). At what point an "assimilating Jew" becomes a "former Jew" (= a Gentile?) is not clear. How can an ethnic Jew become a "former Jew"? Nor does he say anything of the blurring of boundaries from the other side, that is, in the cases of proselytes and God-fearers; or indeed of the other Jews (*minim* = heretics) rejected by the post-Yavnean sages. In other words, the concepts of "Jewish identity" and "Gentile identity" can simply not be drawn as sharply as he strives to do. And, in particular, the arguments that there was in effect a shift in identity between the earlier and other Christian (diaspora) communities and the Johannine community, and that the Johannine community had a "Gentile," that is, non-Jewish identity,[19] are altogether too

18. For fuller detail see my "The Question of Anti-Semitism in the New Testament Writings of the Period," in *Jews and Christians: The Parting of the Ways AD 70-135,* ed. J. D. G. Dunn (Tübingen: Mohr, 1992) 177-211; here 195-203; more briefly in *Partings,* 156-60. For the two levels on which John's Gospel must be read, see particularly J. L. Martyn, *History and Theology in the Fourth Gospel* (rev. ed., Nashville: Abingdon, 1979).

19. "Gentile," of course, is itself a *Jewish* term of identification.

casually drawn, not least when they are the hinge on which his overall argument turns. This alone would be sufficient to put a very large question mark against Casey's thesis of christological development.

3

Casey is also to be commended for his analysis of other messianic and intermediary figures in Second Temple Judaism (ch. 6) which provide parallels or analogies with earliest Christian evaluation of Jesus. The presence and significance of such parallels has been one of the major subjects of debate in regard to New Testament christology over the past twenty years. But Casey has added a potentially helpful distinction between "static parallels" and "dynamic parallels." The former indicate a category which may simply have been transferred to Jesus from another figure; the latter denote "an intermediary figure (which) was involved in a process which increased its status, or function, or both" (78). Instances of the former are "Lord," "Messiah," and "Son of God," and, more surprisingly, preexistence; more surprisingly, since it is at least arguable that preexistence was a more dynamic category as it itself developed from a concept of "ideal" preexistence to one of "real" preexistence.[20] Under the heading of "dynamic parallels" he lists no less than sixteen figures who were held by some Jews "to be of unusually elevated status," including the future Davidic king, Abel, Elijah, Enoch, Jacob, Melchizedek, Michael, Moses, Wisdom, and Word. A common feature is that "most of them were closely associated with the identity of the Jewish people, and they underwent striking developments of their status and functions during the Second Temple and early rabbinical periods" (85), especially Enoch and Wisdom.

There are two features of this inner-Jewish development on which Casey focuses as of particular significance for his thesis. The first is that "we can detect a social subgroup attached to each of them (Enoch and Wisdom), and each of them in some way indicates or embodies the identity of that group. This illuminates the nature of the cause of these developments. They were caused by the needs of the community." Such parallels lead us naturally to expect that the figure of Jesus would develop in status similarly in accordance with the needs of the early Christian community (92). This is all posited in a logical and winning way. But it involves a number of significant jumps, where

---

20. As the recent study of J. Habermann, *Präexistenzaussagen im Neuen Testament* (Frankfurt: Lang, 1990) 26, notes, this distinction goes back at least to W. Beyschlag's *Christologie des Neuen Testaments* (1866).

the claim is simply stated and neither worked through nor defended. From observing that a subgroup can be hypothesized behind each of the figures of Enoch and Wisdom, the deduction is made that the figures indicate or embody (two significantly different claims) the identity of these subgroups, and then the further jump is taken to the claim that the developments in these figures were *caused* by the *needs* of these subgroups. The argument is certainly plausible. But when it is so fundamental and vital to Casey's thesis one would have hoped that it might be argued with more documentation and detail, rather than being simply asserted. Of course Casey would readily admit that very little is known about these subgroups (86-89). But that simply reinforces the imprudence of drawing such firm and clear conclusions on the basis of so little hard evidence.

The second important feature about this inner-Jewish development of intermediary figures for Casey is that it was "inner-Jewish"; that is, it was held within the constraints of Jewish monotheism. "No other serious limitation may be observed. In particular, there was no general bar to prevent the transfer of status and functions from one intermediary figure to another" (93). At this point I am in substantial agreement with Casey. I too am persuaded that monotheism was one of the "four pillars" of Second Temple Judaism and that it was the Christian redefinition of this fundamental axiom of Judaism which resulted in the most decisive partings of the ways between Christianity and Judaism.[21]

At the same time, however, we should note that there are not a few scholars who would question whether Jewish monotheism was quite so firm and unyielding as both Casey and I claim. The most thoroughgoing examples are the recent contributions by Hayman and Barker, who argue that in fact Israel was never as monotheistic as is usually assumed.[22] Rather, they claim, the more ancient belief was of a High God (*'El 'Elyon*) who had several Sons of God, of whom Yahweh was one, to whom Israel was given as his heritage (as in Deut. 32:8-9 LXX), and this ancient belief lies behind subsequent talk in particular of a supreme angel. The significance of such a thesis for developments in christology is clear. "The fact that functionally Jews believed in the existence of two gods explains the speed with which Christianity developed so fast in the first century towards the divinization of Jesus."[23] "Yahweh, the Lord, could be manifested on earth in human form, as an angel or in the Davidic king. It was as a manifestation of Yahweh, the Son of God, that Jesus was acknowledged as Son of God, Messiah and Lord."[24]

---

21. *Partings,* chs. 2, 11.
22. P. Hayman, "Monotheism — A Misused Word in Jewish Studies?" *JJS* 42 (1991) 1-15; M. Barker, *The Great Angel: A Study of Israel's Second God* (London: SPCK, 1992).
23. Hayman, "Monotheism," 14.
24. Barker, *Great Angel,* 3.

This is not the place to engage in a thorough study of the arguments mounted by Hayman and Barker. It must suffice to note that the perception of a strong monotheism at the heart of Judaism from the exile onward remains hard to discount to the extent that Hayman and Barker argue for. It is not a matter simply of the evidence of the *Shema* (Deut. 6:4) and Second Isaiah (especially Isa. 45:20-25). The same common self-perception is evident also in such worldly-wise Jews as Philo and Josephus,[25] and witnessed in the Jesus tradition (cf. Mark 12:29-30 par.). Judaism was similarly perceived from without by those who found its monotheistic denial of other gods a mark of atheism — as in the case of Celsus: "The goatherds and shepherds who followed Moses as their leader were deluded by clumsy deceit into thinking that there was only one God . . . (and) abandoned the worship of many gods. . . . The goatherds and shepherds thought that there was one God called the Most High, or Adonai, or the Heavenly One, or Sabbaoth, or however they like to call this world; and they acknowledged nothing more" (*Contra Celsum* 1.23-24). Philo, we should note, was a prominent exponent of the sort of language and conceptuality which Barker cites as evidence for a strong strand of apocalyptic (non-Palestinian) Judaism.[26] And Celsus, too, was obviously well aware of the range of titles used for God within Judaism. But neither saw any contradiction between that wider conceptuality and usage and the assertion/recognition of Judaism's strong and consistent monotheism. Since those named were capable of highly sophisticated thought and nuanced expression, we should give such assertions/recognitions full weight.

Others have used much of the same evidence to draw less radical conclusions: that the LXX of Dan. 7:13 ("came *like* the Ancient of Days," instead of "came *to* the Ancient of Days") indicates a readiness within apocalyptic Judaism to recognize a heavenly being like God;[27] that the glorious angel of such passages as Ezek. 8:2 and Dan. 10:5-6 indicates a "bifurcation" within the Jewish conception of God;[28] or, more commonly, that the figure(s) of divine Wisdom (and Logos — Philo) mark already the hypostatization of a divine attribute.[29] Again, I beg to disagree; in such characterizations not

---

25. Philo, *Decal.* 65: "Let us, then, engrave deep in our hearts this as the first and most sacred of commandments, to acknowledge and honor one God who is above all, and let the idea that gods are many never even reach the ears of the man whose rule of life is to seek for truth in purity and goodness"; Josephus, *Ant.* 5.112 — "to recognize God as one is common to all the Hebrews."

26. Barker, *Great Angel*, ch. 7.

27. Cf. S. Kim, *"The 'Son of Man' " as the Son of God* (WUNT 30; Tübingen: Mohr, 1983) 22-24.

28. C. Rowland, *The Open Heaven: A Study of Apocalyptic in Judaism and Early Christianity* (London: SPCK; New York: Crossroad, 1982) 96-97, 100.

29. E.g., M. Hengel, *Judaism and Hellenism* (2 vols., London: SCM, 1974) I, 154-57, 312.

enough allowance is being made for the vigor and flexibility of Jewish apocalyptic writing or Wisdom speculation.[30] Certainly the language indicates a
willingness to explore different ways of speaking of the reality of God and
of God's interaction with his world. But evidently a Philo could engage in
such speculation and still say, and fully mean, the *Shema*.

The real point to emerge from all this is not that Judaism contained a
large and prominent segment which had abandoned monotheism, but that
(prior to the second century C.E. at least) Judaism's monotheism was able to
contain within itself a vigor of metaphorical language and apocalyptic vision
which indicates how rich and diversely textured that monotheistic axiom
actually was. I do not exclude the probability that many Second Temple Jews
were functionally polytheistic; that is, that the more speculative language or
visionary experience in unsophisticated hands effectively resulted in a breach
of Jewish monotheism. In the same way I suspect that many Christians today
who think they are trinitarians are actually tritheists (or christotheists), because
the highly technical distinctions within the doctrine of the trinity pass them
by. Nor do I ignore the fact that sometime early in the second century rabbinic
Judaism took fright at the possible deduction to be drawn from visions of
glorious heavenly figures and denounced the declaration that there are two
powers in heaven as heresy.[31] But it seems to me still to be a proper and
accurate summary of Second Temple Judaism, as expressed in the writings
which have come down to us from that period or which bear witness to that
period, that Second Temple Judaism was through and through monotheistic
in character.

It should be clear enough where all this bears upon Casey's thesis. At
the very least, it means that Jewish monotheism is a much less clearly defined
or, indeed, much less firm identity marker than Casey assumes. If the arguments of Hayman and Barker, or the other less radical views, have any
substance in them, then we must acknowledge a legitimate dispute as to
whether Judaism was wholly monotheistic at all. And if monotheism had never
wholly carried the day within Judaism, or if Jewish monotheism had been
decisively eroded or diluted well before Jesus appeared on the scene, then it
is quite possible to accommodate the developing christology of the first two
Christian generations wholly within Judaism. If, alternatively, as Casey and I
believe, Jewish monotheism remained as a strong identity factor throughout
Second Temple Judaism, the consequences differ only slightly for Casey's
thesis. For then we are confronted with a monotheism which contained within

30. See further my *Christology in the Making* (London: SCM, [2]1989); also *Partings,* chs.
10-11.
31. See particularly A. F. Segal, *Two Powers in Heaven: Early Rabbinic Reports about
Christianity and Gnosticism* (Leiden: Brill, 1977).

it richly diverse ways of speaking of divine immanence. In particular, it becomes quite possible to accommodate the developments marked by the Christian apocalypse of John (Revelation) wholly within the stream of *Jewish* apocalyptic visionary speculation. And even the rich developments of the Gospel of John's christology can be seen primarily as an extension of the Jewish fascination with divine revelation which was the driving force of apocalyptic and mystical trends *within Judaism* at that time. To be sure there were Jews ("the Jews" = the Jewish authorities of the region) who believed that John's Christ had threatened the unity of God (John 5:18; 10:33); but it was probably the same Jews (the early rabbis) who believed that the apocalyptic and mystical concerns of other Jews with glorious heavenly beings other than Yahweh was equally threatening to the unity of God. The point is that such developments could, and did, take place wholly within a Jewish context. It is simply not true that "the deity of Jesus is a belief which could have developed only in a predominantly Gentile church," and at least highly questionable whether "the deity of Jesus is . . . *inherently* unJewish."[32] Once again the transition from Jewish identity to Gentile identity has been too casually drawn. The development within the New Testament is not so much from Jewish prophet to *Gentile* God, as from Jewish prophet to *Jewish* God; it is precisely that development and the problems it caused within Judaism which is reflected in the Fourth Gospel.

4

A third element of his thesis on which Casey is vulnerable is in his postulation of what can only be characterized as a rather onesided and reductivist development schema. It revolves around what Casey sees as the interaction of identity, social cohesion, and christology, in what boils down to an explanation of the development of christology as the result of essentially social factors. The schema depends on two principal assertions.

The first is that "the whole of Jesus' ministry could be perceived" "to embody Judaism as a religion," "as the embodiment of Judaism as it should be" (72) — and not only "could be," but was so perceived. "Jesus offered people the spiritual centre of Judaism"; "from the disciples' perspective he was the embodiment of Judaism itself." Consequently the group around him could also be perceived to have embodied Judaism as it should be; as a result Jesus "was himself the visible embodiment of Jewish identity, and the source of the recreation of the Jewish identity of his disciples" (73-74). This claim

32. Casey, *Jewish Prophet,* 169, 176.

is central to Casey's thesis, for in his view it is Jesus' embodiment of the identity of Judaism which was the original driving force behind early Christian belief in the resurrection of Jesus (100, 105) and which thus set the whole development in train. Likewise it was his first disciples' perception that he embodied "all that was right, all that was religious and salvific, in Judaism, without ethnic customs such as circumcision and dietary laws (which) drove christology upwards, and drove it more vigorously than comparable figures because of the uniqueness of the community" (136). This aspect of the thesis is summarized in the final chapter: "the relationship between identity and christological development is to some extent one of cause and effect" (162).

The penultimate quotation, however, brings in the other key feature in the schema. The Gentile mission was the additional driving force behind christological growth. It was this mixed community of Jews and Gentiles which needed the figure of Christ to be powerful enough to hold it together (137). Again the development is one of cause and effect: the "decline in the observance of the Jewish Law in the Christian community drastically increased the requirement for a higher christology"; "the conflicts intensified by war between Israel and Rome drove christological development up to the deity of Jesus" (138); the secondary material expressing higher christology "has been produced most extensively at those points where the community needed it most" (153). In short, "the development of christology . . . was, and has remained, a means of holding together a large social group" (176).

This reconstruction is open to a number of criticisms. One is the degree of arbitrariness with which the first assertion is introduced and the lack of fit between the reconstruction and the data. With what justification can it be claimed that Jesus was perceived as "the embodiment of Judaism itself"? The claim is fundamental and far-reaching, but it is simply asserted, and the material reviewed by Casey (72-73) does hardly anything to justify the claim itself. It is certainly fair to argue that Jesus and the disciples' commitment to him is what marked them off from the rest of Judaism (74); but that is not the same as saying that they perceived Jesus to embody Judaism itself. We have already noted that the category of Judaism and Jewish identity was much more contested and much less clearly drawn at that time than most (including Casey) assume. And while it is highly probable that Jesus was seen by the Evangelists as replaying the role of Israel (as in Matt. 4:1-11), it is less clear that Jesus was so seen during his ministry.[33] Rather the implication of Jesus' having chosen twelve disciples is that *he saw them* as embodying Israel, and himself as somehow over against them. At the very least Casey has to argue his case, not simply assert it.

---

33. Casey himself attributes the reference to Jesus of the humanlike figure ("one like a son of man" = the saints of the Most High) of Dan 7:13-14 to post-Easter reflection.

There is also a degree of tension between the two postulated causes of christological development which requires more clarification than Casey provides. For the more it is claimed that Jesus was seen as the embodiment of Judaism the less easy is it to explain how and why the movement focused on this Jesus first opened the door to Gentiles. The second cause (mixed community, growing Gentile self-identity) is itself not explained, and cannot be explained from the first cause (Jesus as embodying Jewish identity). Jesus was not remembered as advocating outreach to the Gentiles; nor is he ever remembered as saying anything whatsoever on the most crucial issue of all (whether Gentile converts should be circumcised) — a surprising fact if indeed other passages in the Synoptic Gospels have been produced to meet the community's need. And while passages like Matt. 5:17-20 and 10:5-6 could be explained as occasioned by a (self-?)perception of Jesus embodying Jewish identity, their presence in the Jesus tradition simply serves to underline the difficulty of explaining the Gentile mission on Casey's thesis. In other words, Casey's postulated causes are insufficient to explain developments which he sees as fundamental to the growth of christology, and indeed, if anything, make these developments harder to explain.

This reflection leads into the second main point of criticism: that Casey's reductivist sociological explanation needs at least to be supplemented and corrected by the hypothesis of other causes. Has Casey actually uncovered the dynamic of the development of earliest christology? He has indicated social factors which must have played some role in contributing to and shaping that development. It may be that he has indicated a necessary cause of the development. But has he uncovered the necessary and sufficient cause, sufficient to explain all the relevant data which make up New Testament christology? Was there not also a more important inner dynamic within the christological development, which no doubt interacted with the social forces but which is not to be wholly explained by them?

For instance, Casey's discussion of the category of "Messiah" operates with a too static category (42-43) and allows too little for the impact of Jesus himself on the designation, giving it his own evolutionary twist to a fluid Jewish messianology.[34] We could also note that Casey's assertion that Jesus was perceived to embody Judaism itself introduces an element of internal dynamic which he ignores. The more that claim can be pushed, the more we have to ask whether Jesus' first disciples could reach such a conclusion without any stimulus or encouragement from Jesus himself ("Jesus offered people the spiritual centre of Judaism"), and the more we have to reckon with the

---

34. Casey's assertion that "the messiah was not a title in Second Temple Judaism" (42) is strictly correct, but the usage of *Pss. Sol.* 17:32 and 1QS 9.11 and 1QSa 2.20 is surely sufficient indication of belief in a royal Davidic Messiah; see further chapter 5 above.

possibility that Jesus saw himself as in some sense a focus for Israel and its people's hopes, with all that implies in terms of Jesus' own self-understanding as a representative figure. An *individual* who thus expresses the corporate identity of Israel/Judaism ("embody" is Casey's term) immediately suggests a royal or priestly figure, or indeed an image like the suffering servant of Isaiah 53 or the human-like figure of Dan. 7:13-14. In other words, Casey himself may open the door to the recognition that Jesus made or implied high claims for his own significance, claims which would themselves be sufficient cause to explain much of the subsequent development in christology. At the very least, Casey needs to explicate his own hypothesis with greater care.

The analysis of the crucial belief in Jesus' resurrection is similarly incomplete. Casey is surprisingly confident that only "resurrection was the culturally relevant form of vindication" which Jesus could have looked for (52, 102-3). What of the exaltation or translation long ago attributed to Enoch and Elijah or to the martyred righteous in Wisdom 5, or implied in the triumph of the saints of the Most High in Daniel 7, or attributed to such great saints as Moses, Baruch, and Ezra at around this time?[35] It is by no means clear that Jesus was bound to use the category of resurrection (Aramaic קום) in expressing a hope of vindication, or that the first disciples seeing visions of Jesus after he was dead should conclude therefrom that he had been resurrected rather than taken to heaven. On the contrary, given that Jesus' resurrection was self-evidently *not* part of the general resurrection at the end of time, the conclusion of the first Christians that that is what had happened to Jesus is all the more surprising — precisely because a less problematic category lay close to hand (post-mortem exaltation to heaven). Again we are forced toward the conclusion that external factors and availability of suitable categories were not the sufficient cause to explain the earliest belief in Jesus' resurrection. Rather we must assume an inner dynamic which shaped the categories as well as being shaped by them. Without more allowance for that inner dynamic than Casey allows, the development of christology cannot be adequately grasped.[36]

Other elements within the inner dynamic of developing christology could be mentioned. For example, Casey refers at one point to "the gift of the Holy Spirit" and to the "religious and emotional experience of new revelation" (108), without apparently considering what this might have meant for christological development. And he is so confident that the changing character of

35. See further, e.g., my *Partings,* 186-87.

36. Casey's discussion of the resurrection narratives leaves a good deal more to be desired. For example, he notes that the discrepancies between the different Gospel accounts "are too great to have resulted from accurate reporting of a perceptible event" (99); he does not seem to allow the possibility of *confused* reporting of a perceptible event! And he ignores such questions as why the report of an empty tomb should be attributed to women and why there was no early tomb veneration at an undisturbed tomb.

earliest mission (to Gentiles as well as Jews) was the cause of developments in christology that he fails to consider whether the influence was not as much or more the other way: that it was the christology which resulted in the opening to the Gentiles, as the New Testament writers certainly believed (e.g., Matt. 28:18-20; Gal. 1:15-16). Putting the same point in other terms, Casey seems to assume that Paul's own experience was simply a confirmatory factor, that is, presumably, of developments determined entirely by social pressures, without asking whether Paul's experience (as Paul himself understood it, of Christ) was not itself one of the major factors which achieved the revolution of the Gentile mission (e.g., again Gal. 1:15-16).[37]

Above all, Casey has ignored the whole dynamic of early Christian worship. This is most serious since it is precisely the thesis of the other recently published monograph which also seeks to explain the transition from Jewish monotheism to Christian belief in the deity of Christ that this transition can only be explained in terms of the cultic veneration of Christ and the generative power of religious experience.[38] And it is all the more serious since worship and religious experience are such common factors in the other apocalyptic and mystical explorations of divine transcendence and immanence, of which Casey is well aware, as they are, for example, in Revelation and the christological hymns in the New Testament. Casey may mean, of course, to include all this within his social description of such communities. But the factors are surely of too obvious importance to be so absorbed within or reduced to social forces. And without taking them into account it is highly dubious whether any explanation of christological development could be counted adequate.

5

In short, Casey's monograph is a stimulating and provocative attempt to trace the development of christology in evolutionary terms, as the effect of social causes — namely, the way in which Jesus embodied the identity of the new movement, and the way in which the expansion of that movement to include Gentiles caused the movement's primary identity factor (Christ) to gain increasing significance, until the predominance of Gentiles within the movement made it possible/inevitable that the constraint of Jewish monotheism be slackened and abandoned. The thesis is to be welcomed precisely because it

37. But I am not sure that I have understood Casey's logic here: "Paul's christological developments can be traced without much reference to experience because they were so closely related to experience that they were confirmed by experience" (131).

38. L. W. Hurtado, *One God, One Lord: Early Christian Devotion and Ancient Jewish Monotheism* (Philadelphia: Fortress, 1988).

highlights the social factors so clearly, and can therefore serve as a standing reminder not to ignore or unwisely discount such factors.

Unfortunately, however, Casey works with a too simplified concept of Judaism and of Jewish identity, and thus with a too simplified appreciation of the richness and diversity of reflection on divine immanence which was possible and is attested within Jewish monotheism. Moreover, his social analysis does not sufficiently explain all the relevant data and discounts to a serious degree what arguably were the principal factors in the development of christology — namely (using theological shorthand), the impact of Jesus, the impact of Jesus' ministry and teaching, the impact of the resurrection of Jesus, the impact of the Spirit of God, and the generative power of religious experience and of worship of God through Christ particularly in and through the preaching and teaching of religious geniuses like Paul and John.

That such a process is not simply to be described as "evolution" should be clear enough. Whether it can be described simply as an "unfolding" is less clear, since the process of conceptuality in transition within historical contexts themselves undergoing change is not easily categorized, as I have tried to explain elsewhere.[39] But that it involved an inner dynamic (the inner dynamic of religious experience and worship) and that it was understood by the participants as an unfolding of the truth of Christ is sufficiently clear, and with that we probably have to be content.

---

39. See chapter 18 above, pp. 291-93. But Newman's idea of development/unfolding (*Essay*) was also nuanced and reflected changing circumstances.

23

Why "Incarnation"?
A Review of Recent
New Testament Scholarship

1. Introduction

In casting around for an appropriate theme to contribute to Michael Goulder's Festschrift, I naturally fell to reflecting on the debate regarding the incarnation in which Michael played a prominent part.[1] The question which came to me afresh was the old one: What was the theological (or historical) logic which brought about the doctrine of the incarnation?

He will not need reminding that there have been many answers to this question. The view of traditional orthodoxy is that it emerged directly from Jesus' own self-consciousness of divinity and/or preexistence.[2] Alternatively, for some it was an inevitable corollary to the conviction that Jesus had been raised from the dead and exalted to God's right hand.[3] For others it was very much bound up with the impact of Paul's conversion experience on the Damascus road — Paul realizing that what he was seeing was the preexistent glory of God.[4] For others again it was a consequence of Christianity spreading into wider circles and being influenced by other systems of religious

1. J. Hick, ed., *The Myth of God Incarnate* (London: SCM, 1977); M. Goulder, ed., *Incarnation and Myth: The Debate Continued* (London: SCM, 1979).

2. E.g., H. P. Liddon, *The Divinity of Our Lord and Saviour Jesus Christ* (London: Rivingtons, 1878); A. E. J. Rawlinson, *The New Testament Doctrine of the Christ* (London: Longmans, 1926) 122.

3. Cf. A. Harnack, *History of Dogma* (London: Williams and Norgate, 1897) I, 325: "This post-existence of his gave to the ideas of his pre-existence a support and a concrete complexion which the earlier Jewish theories lacked."

4. Cf., e.g., J. W. Fraser, *Jesus and Paul* (Sutton Courtenay: Marcham, 1974) 67.

Originally published in *Crossing the Boundaries: Essays in Biblical Interpretation in Honour of M. D. Goulder,* ed. S. E. Porter et al., 235-56. Copyright © 1994 E. J. Brill and used by permission.

thought — whether the "Hellenizing" process of Harnack, the Gnostic re-deemer myth of Bultmann, or the Samaritan incarnational theology of Simon Magus as argued by Goulder himself.[5] And of course the classical theological logic is that of Gregory Nazianzen: "What has not been assumed cannot be restored"; that is, without incarnation, salvation could not have been achieved.[6]

In the fifteen to twenty years since *The Myth of God Incarnate* the debate on such questions has gone on apace. Indicative of the continuing interest in these and other aspects of New Testament christology and the wide range of scholars involved in the discussions has been the number of Festschriften and doctoral theses devoted to New Testament christological themes.[7] It cannot be said that the disputes have been resolved, though certainly the issues have been further clarified and a measure of consensus achieved on a number of important points. At any rate, since the doctrine of the incarnation is at the heart of Christian theology it may be worth reviewing the *status quaestionis* on the incarnation in the light of that debate.

5. Harnack, *History*, 318-31; R. Bultmann, *Theology of the New Testament* I (London: SCM, 1952) 164-83; M. Goulder, "The Two Roots of the Christian Myth," in Hick, *Myth*, 64-86; also "The Samaritan Hypothesis," in Goulder, *Incarnation*, 247-50.

6. *Epistle* 101.7, cited, e.g., in J. N. D. Kelly, *Early Christian Doctrines* (London: Black, [2]1960) 297.

7. Without attempting a complete listing we may mention *Christ the Lord*, ed. H. H. Rowdon (D. Guthrie FS; Leicester: Inter-Varsity, 1982); *The Glory of Christ in the New Testament*, ed. L. D. Hurst and N. T. Wright (G. B. Caird FS; Oxford: Clarendon, 1987); *From Jesus to John: Essays on Jesus and New Testament Christology*, ed. M. C. de Boer (M. de Jonge FS, JSNTSS 84; Sheffield: JSOT, 1993); *The Future of Christology*, ed. A. J. Malherbe & W. A. Meeks (L. E Keck FS; Minneapolis: Fortress, 1993); *Jesus of Nazareth: Lord and Christ*, ed. J. B. Green (I. H. Marshall FS; Grand Rapids: Eerdmans, 1994).

Note also, e.g., the various symposia on New Testament christology produced during the last ten years in North America: R. Jewett, ed., *Christology and Exegesis: New Approaches*, *Semeia* 30 (1984); H. Anderson et al., *Perspectives on Christology* (Nashville: Exodus, 1989); J. H. Charlesworth, ed., *The Messiah: Developments in Earliest Judaism and Christianity* (Minneapolis: Fortress, 1992); R. F. Berkey and S. A. Edwards, *Christology in Dialogue* (Cleveland: Pilgrim, 1993).

Theses include S. Kim, *The Origin of Paul's Gospel* (WUNT 2/4; Tübingen: Mohr, 1981); W. R. G. Loader, *Sohn und Hoherpriester. Eine traditionsgeschichtliche Untersuchung zur Christologie des Hebräerbriefes* (WMANT 53; Neukirchen: Neukirchener, 1981); M. Müller, *Der Ausdruck "Menschensohn" in den Evangelien. Voraussetzungen und Bedeutung* (Leiden: Brill, 1984); G. Schimanowski, *Weisheit und Messias. Die jüdischen Voraussetzungen der ur-christlichen Präexistenz-christologie* (WUNT 2/17; Tübingen: Mohr, 1985); L. J. Kreitzer, *Jesus and God in Paul's Eschatology* (JSNTSS 19; Sheffield: JSOT, 1987); S. E. Fowl, *The Story of Christ in the Ethics of Paul: An Analysis of the Function of the Hymnic Material in the Pauline Corpus* (JSNTSS 26; Sheffield: JSOT, 1990); J. Habermann, *Präexistenz-aussagen im Neuen Testament* (Frankfurt: Lang, 1990); D. B. Capes, *Old Testament Yahweh Texts in Paul's Chris-tology* (WUNT 2/47; Tübingen: Mohr, 1992).

2. Jesus' Own Self-Consciousness and the "Son of Man" Debate

Fundamentalists and near fundamentalists will continue to hold that John's Gospel provides a transcript of Jesus' own words, or at least an accurate reflection of Jesus' own self-consciousness. But for the great bulk of New Testament scholarship that view is no longer an option, given the characteristic, marked, and dramatic contrast between Jesus' self-presentation in John's Gospel and that in the other three.[8]

In the Synoptics the closest parallel is the famous "Johannine thunderbolt" in Matt. 11:27/Luke 10:22. But here too the unusualness of the formulation raises the suspicion in most minds that the saying has been at least elaborated in the course of transmission. In which case the underlying (original?) saying might well simply have been a claim to insight not so very different from that of the teacher of wisdom.[9] At this point the basic problem is the limitation of our methodology. The historical-critical method anyway finds it very difficult to recognize the "new," and virtually impossible to recognize the "unique." So it is very difficult methodologically to mount a successful argument that a saying, which stands so much on its own within the Synoptic tradition, and which certainly reflects (in at least some measure) the high christology of the early churches which cherished it, can be traced back to Jesus in its present form. This consideration, it is true, does not amount to a denial that Jesus did or could have spoken these words, but it does mean that they cannot be shown to go back to Jesus with any confidence. And that makes Matt. 11:27/Luke 10:22 a very insecure foundation on which to build a conclusion regarding Jesus' self-consciousness of preexistence.[10]

Similar cross-examination leaves the testimony of the other Synoptic references to Jesus as "the Son" (Mark 13:32 and 12:6) equally ambiguous.[11] There remains a somewhat surprisingly strong consensus that Jesus' own spirituality was distinctive for its use of "abba" in address to God.[12] And

8. The point is a commonplace in Johannine scholarship — see, e.g., the various contributions in *The Four Gospels 1992*, ed. F. van Segbroeck et al. (F. Neirynck FS; Leuven: Leuven University, 1992) III, chs. 83-86; for my own perspective see *The Evidence for Jesus* (London: SCM, 1985) ch. 2; also chapter 21 above.

9. Cf., e.g., the careful discussion of W. D. Davies and D. C. Allison, *Matthew* II (ICC; Edinburgh: Clark, 1991) 282-87.

10. Note however the confidence with which E. P. Sanders, *Jesus and Judaism* (London: SCM, 1985), has concluded that Jesus saw himself as a spokesman for God (280-81, 287-88).

11. See, e.g., R. Leivestad, *Jesus in His Own Perspective: An Examination of His Sayings, Actions, and Eschatological Titles* (Minneapolis: Augsburg, 1987) 110-13; M. D. Hooker, *Mark* (London: Black, 1991) 276, 323.

12. N. Perrin, *Rediscovering the Teaching of Jesus* (London: SCM, 1967) 40-41; W. Kasper, *Jesus the Christ* (London: Burns and Oates, 1976) 109-11; B. van Iersel, " 'Son of God' in the New Testament," in *Jesus, Son of God?* ed. E. Schillebeeckx and J. B. Metz

justifiably so: it is the only reasonable conclusion to be drawn from the fact that the early Greek-speaking churches preserved this Aramaic usage in their own prayer, and did so precisely as a distinctive mark that they shared in the Spirit of Jesus and in his sonship (Rom. 8:15-17; Gal. 4:6-7).[13] But even so, all that that tells us is that Jesus was remembered for the intimacy of his sense of sonship to God. Of itself it says nothing about consciousness of preexistence or incarnation.[14]

The main battleground at this point remains the significance of "the Son of man" formulation in the Synoptics. Here a remarkable gap has opened up particularly between British scholarship and the rest of Europe. The dispute is complex and involves several interrelated issues.

The dispute in the first place is over the status of the human-like figure in the vision in Dan. 7:13-14. Here it is impossible to speak of consensus. Those who maintain that the "one like a son of man" symbolizes "the saints of the Most High" base their conclusion primarily on the fact that what is given to the human-like figure in 7:14 is so similar to what is given to the saints in 7:18, 22, and 27 that the two must be one and the same.[15] But others argue with equal conviction that the "son of man" must have been intended as a heavenly individual — an angel or other divine being, albeit representative of Israel in at least some degree.[16] This is the basis for the argument of several recent contributions that Jesus himself in using the phrase "the Son of man" identified himself with the Danielic figure, that is, as a "divine figure," "a heavenly Being."[17]

What is surprising in the latter case, however, is the complete failure to take account of what has for long appeared to me as one of the major considerations, if not the major consideration in determining the original significance of the phrase as used in Daniel 7. I refer to the strong implication that the double vision constitutes a powerful adaptation of the creation myths

(Concilium 153; Edinburgh: Clark, 1982) 40-41; R. H. Fuller and P. Perkins, *Who Is This Christ? Gospel Christology and Contemporary Faith* (Philadelphia: Fortress, 1983) 21; J. Gnilka, *Jesus von Nazareth. Botschaft und Geschichte* (Freiburg: Herder, 1990) 264-66; G. Vermes, *The Religion of Jesus the Jew* (London: SCM, 1993) ch. 6.

13. See my *Christology in the Making* (London: SCM, 1980, ²1989) 26-28; also *Romans* (WBC 38; Dallas: Word, 1988) 453-54.

14. Despite J. Moltmann, *The Way of Christ: Christology in Messianic Dimensions* (London: SCM, 1990) 142-45, who also still uses earlier formulations of J. Jeremias without acknowledging the degree of refinement necessary.

15. See, e.g., L. F. Hartman and A. A. Di Lella, *Daniel* (AB 23; New York: Doubleday, 1978) 85-102; cf. J. Goldingay, *Daniel* (WBC 30; Dallas: Word, 1989) 167-72, 176-78.

16. J. J. Collins, *The Apocalyptic Vision of the Book of Daniel* (Missoula: Scholars, 1977) 141-46; A. Y. Collins, "The 'Son of Man' Tradition and the Book of Revelation," in Charlesworth, ed., *The Messiah*, 536-68, here 550.

17. S. Kim, *"The 'Son of Man' " as the Son of God* (WUNT 30; Tübingen: Mohr, 1983), citation from p. 36; C. C. Caragounis, *The Son of Man* (WUNT 38; Tübingen: Mohr, 1986) 80-81, 250; B. Witherington, *The Christology of Jesus* (Minneapolis: Fortress, 1990) 233-62.

of Genesis 1 and 2. As in Genesis 1 and 2 the act of creation consists in making "beasts" and "man," so in Daniel 7 there emerge from "the great sea" (primeval chaos) beast-like figures, and then there appears a human-like figure. And as in Genesis 1 and 2, the man is clearly the crown of creation and is explicitly given dominion over the beasts, so in Daniel 7 the human-like figure is the climax of the vision and is given dominion over the nations represented by the beasts. Now, since the beast-like creatures are so clearly identified with the nations which had afflicted Israel (the saints of the Most High), the inference is hard to escape that the human-like figure was similarly intended to represent Israel, the victim of the hostile nations. In other words, Daniel 7 is almost certainly an example of what we find elsewhere also, viz., the adaptation of the creation myths to express Israel's conviction that she herself was the climax of God's creative purpose.[18] In which case it is at least highly dubious that the human-like figure was intended to be understood, like the beast-like figures, as anything other than a symbol for a national body.

The second area of dispute focuses on the significance of the use of Daniel 7 in the Similitudes of Enoch (*1 En.* 37–71) and 4 Ezra 13. The dispute is whether there is any evidence that within Second Temple Judaism the Danielic son of man was understood as a heavenly figure (= the Messiah). A strong consensus, particularly in German scholarship, continues to give a surprisingly confident answer in the affirmative.[19] The dispute focuses particularly on the dating of the Similitudes. Those just referred to tend to assume that the Similitudes must be dated to the late first century B.C.E. (principally on the basis of an allusion to the Parthian invasion of 40-38 B.C.E. in *1 En.* 56:5-7), or at least to the early first century C.E., by which they mean prior to Jesus, or (the argument becoming steadily weaker) as representing a well-known view current at the time of Jesus. However, the absence of any copies of the Similitudes in the Qumran library, despite Qumran's evident interest in Daniel and in the other parts of the Enoch corpus, has been a major factor in persuading a good many others that while a first-century date for the Similitudes is very likely, that conclusion cannot be pressed to an early or pre-Jesus date.[20] In addition, more note should have been taken of the fact that both the Similitudes and 4 Ezra introduce what are evidently interpretations of the vision of Daniel 7 as though they were fresh interpretations — that is, implic-

18. This theme has been examined by my pupil David Goh in *Creation and the People of God* (Durham Ph.D. thesis, 1994).

19. See, e.g., W. G. Kümmel, *Jesus der Menschensohn?* (Stuttgart: Steiner, 1984); P. Stuhlmacher, *Jesus von Nazareth, Christus des Glaubens* (Stuttgart: Calwer, 1988) 29-30; Gnilka, *Jesus,* 260-64; J. J. Collins, "The Son of Man in First-Century Judaism," *NTS* 38 (1992) 448-66.

20. See particularly the sequence of articles by J. H. Charlesworth, M. A. Knibb, and C. L. Mearns in *NTS* 25 (1978-79) 315-23, 345-59, 360-69; J. H. Charlesworth, *The Old Testament Pseudepigrapha and the New Testament* (SNTSMS 54; Cambridge: Cambridge University, 1985) 89.

itly denying that it was an established interpretation; also that in 4 Ezra 13 the figure is identified not as the "Son of man," but simply as the "man," indicating a continuing awareness of the idiomatic (that is, nontitular) force of the phrase ("son of man" = "man").[21]

These latter considerations should be sufficient to indicate how flimsy or at least suspect is any argument based on the assumption that there was a pre-Christian Jewish belief in a heavenly figure identified with the Danielic son of man. And when it is further recalled that no record is extant of Jesus being hailed or confessed as this son of man or questioned as regards this son of man, then the argument becomes very suspect indeed. The old appeal to Luke 12:8, on the ground that it presupposes a distinction between Jesus and a heavenly Son of man,[22] has become more muted recently, since the presupposition itself is at best dubious. The more recent debate has served therefore to underline that the grounds for saying that Jesus identified himself with a (preexistent) heavenly figure (the Son of man) are too weak to provide any secure foundation for a stronger christological conclusion.

A third dispute which continues to rumble is whether the phrase "the son of man" is simply the Aramaic idiom = "man" or "one," or was titular from the first ("the Son of man"). The same division is to be found here, with English-speaking scholarship now quite strongly favoring the former,[23] and the above considerations also pointing in its direction. This is not to exclude the possibility that Jesus himself drew upon the Danielic vision to inform his own sense of mission and expectation as to its outcome,[24] but that would be a future expectation, and it would be a substantial leap beyond the evidence to conclude that Jesus thought of himself as a heavenly figure come to earth.[25]

In short, the recent debate has provided no stronger grounds for the argument that Jesus saw himself as the incarnation of a preexistent heavenly being, and if anything has strengthened the case against. Of course, the question of continuity between what Jesus believed about himself and what Christianity subsequently proclaimed about him remains an important one.

21. See further particularly M. Casey, *Son of Man: The Interpretation and Influence of Daniel 7* (London: SPCK, 1979) 99-112, 122-29.

22. E.g., G. Bornkamm, *Jesus of Nazareth* (London: Hodder, 1960) 176; F. Hahn, *The Titles of Jesus in Christology* (London: Lutterworth, 1969) 28-31.

23. See particularly Casey, *Son of Man;* B. Lindars, *Jesus Son of Man: A Fresh Examination of the Son of Man Sayings in the Gospels* (London: SPCK, 1983); D. R. A. Hare, *The Son of Man Tradition* (Minneapolis: Fortress, 1990).

24. Still maintained by E. Schweizer, *Jesus Christ: The Man from Nazareth and the Exalted Lord* (Macon: Mercer University, 1987) 45-48.

25. K. J. Kuschel, *Born Before Time? The Dispute over Christ's Origin* (London: SCM, 1992) 228-32, notes the strong consensus on this point.

But those who have argued for continuity seem to have been content for the most part to find that continuity rooted in Jesus' sense of intimate sonship and expectation of eschatological vindication. Beside this characteristic forward look in the Jesus tradition there is no comparable backward look prior to John's Gospel.

3. The Exalted Lord

There is no doubt that to the resurrection of Jesus must be attributed a decisive, if not the decisive impulse in the emergence of a "high" christology.[26] The question remains, however, whether that initial impulse was exclusively forward-looking, eschatological, and parousia-oriented, or whether it also contained an unavoidable inference that he who was (now) so exalted must have been divine from the first.

The debate here has in effect been between those content to recognize a developing christological pattern, with thought of preexistence and incarnation as part of a later stage (not necessarily a straightforward linear development), and those who have found it possible to maintain that all the basic elements of classical christology (including preexistence and deity) were in place within the first few years of Christianity's existence, that is, before Paul's own major written contribution.

The latter argument can be put forward on several grounds. One is the significance of the conviction that Jesus had been exalted to God's right hand. That conviction is abundantly clear in our earliest sources, in echoes of the very early proclamation and confession. So in particular in regard to the still largely unchallenged assumption that the use of Ps. 110:1 expresses one of the first attempts by the post-Easter believers to make sense of what had happened to Jesus (e.g., Acts 2:34-35; Rom. 8:34; 1 Cor. 15:25; Heb. 1:3, 13; 1 Pet. 3:22).[27] What is now being more fully appreciated, however, is that there was quite a widespread belief in second Temple Judaism that various

---

26. See particularly P. Pokorný, *The Genesis of Christology: Foundations for a Theology of the New Testament* (Edinburgh: Clark, 1987).

27. The influence of N. Perrin, "Mark 14.62; The End of a Christian Pesher?" *NTS* 12 (1965-66) 150-55, reprinted in his *A Modern Pilgrimage in New Testament Christology* (Philadelphia: Fortress, 1974) 10-18, has been substantial. Cf., e.g., W. H. Kelber, ed., *The Passion in Mark* (Philadelphia: Fortress, 1976) 71; C. R. Kazmierski, *Jesus, the Son of God: A Study of the Markan Tradition and Its Redaction by the Evangelist* (Würzburg: Echter, 1979) 167-85; D. Juel, *Messianic Exegesis: Christological Interpretation of the Old Testament in Early Christianity* (Philadelphia: Fortress, 1988) 144-46. But see now R. H. Gundry, *Mark* (Grand Rapids: Eerdmans, 1993) 912-14, and R. E. Brown, *The Death of the Messiah* (New York: Doubleday, 1994) 488-515.

heroes of the faith had been exalted to heaven (Adam, Abel, Enoch, Abraham, Elijah, etc.), without the corollary being drawn that they had previously come down from heaven and from a preexistent state there.[28]

The same considerations bear upon the corollaries which some have drawn from the fact that roles previously ascribed solely to God seem to have been attributed to the exalted Jesus more or less from the beginning.[29] For the same tendency is evident in the same accounts of the exaltation of Israel's heroes,[30] and Paul can even talk of the saints judging the world and angels (1 Cor. 6:2-3). Such language born of apocalyptic or mystical vision came to be seen as a threat to Jewish belief in God only later, as when rabbi Akiba (early second century C.E.) was rebuked for his speculation that the other throne implied in the plural "thrones" of Dan. 7:9 must be for the Messiah (b. Ḥag. 14a).[31]

A third area of debate here is whether the exalted Jesus was worshiped more or less from the first.[32] Certainly we should recognize the internal dynamic of Christian experience and worship as a major factor in christology breaking through the constraints of Jewish monotheism,[33] as against the view that social and cultural factors provide sufficient explanation by themselves.[34] The question, however, is when we can first properly speak of Christians "worshiping" Jesus, as distinct from invoking him or singing hymns in his praise. The degree of hesitation on this point in the case of Paul himself, who more typically prays *through* Jesus to God rather than *to* Jesus (Rom. 1:8; 7:25; 2 Cor. 1:20; Col. 3:17), should make us still more hesitant about at-

28. L. W. Hurtado, *One God, One Lord: Early Christian Devotion and Ancient Jewish Monotheism* (Philadelphia: Fortress, 1988); P. M. Casey, *From Jewish Prophet to Gentile God: The Origins and Development of New Testament Christology* (Cambridge: Clarke; Louisville: Westminster, 1991) ch. 6; J. D. G. Dunn, *The Partings of the Ways between Christianity and Judaism* (London: SCM; Philadelphia: TPI, 1991) ch. 10; cf. A. Chester, "Jewish Messianic Expectations and Mediatorial Figures and Pauline Christology," in M. Hengel, ed., *Paulus und das antike Judentum* (WUNT 58, Tübingen: Mohr, 1991) 17-89. It remains difficult to know how to relate the Melchizedek of 11QMelch to the Melchizedek of Genesis 14. And while *The Prayer of Joseph* presents Jacob as the "incarnation" of the angel Israel, the unusualness of the thought (an angel "tabernacling among humans") and the uncertainty of the dating (first century C.E.?) make it difficult to evaluate its relevance. On the rabbinic tradition which identified Phinehas with Elijah, see R. Hayward, "Phinehas — the Same Is Elijah: The Origins of a Rabbinic Tradition," *JJS* 29 (1978) 22-34.

29. See particularly M. M. B. Turner, "The Spirit of Christ and Christology," in *Christ the Lord,* ed. Rowdon, 168-90; Kreitzer, op. cit.

30. So, e.g., with regard to Moses in *Ezekiel the Tragedian* 68-82 and Josephus, *Ant.* 3.96-97; 4.326.

31. See further A. F. Segal, *Two Powers in Heaven: Early Rabbinic Reports about Christianity and Gnosticism* (Leiden: Brill, 1977).

32. So argued by R. T. France, "The Worship of Jesus: A Neglected Factor in Christological Debate?" in *Christ the Lord,* ed. Rowdon, 17-36.

33 So, rightly, Hurtado, *One God.*

34. *Pace* Casey, *Gentile Prophet;* see chapter 22 above.

tributing such worship to a still earlier stage.[35] And the confusion between different Christian traditions to this day as to whether Mary, mother of Jesus, is worshiped or only venerated is a warning of how far language can be stretched on this point.[36]

Correlated with this experientially based approach is the argument over how the exalted Jesus was experienced by the first Christians. In the absence of firsthand reports prior to Paul the argument naturally focuses on Paul's own testimony. One area is his own conversion experience, where 2 Cor. 4:4-6 in particular can be taken to imply that what Paul saw on the Damascus road was Christ as the "image of God," with all that that implied for the divinity of Christ and his protological relationship with God.[37] Alternatively, or in addition, it can be argued that the "in Christ" language of Paul implied an understanding of the exalted Christ not just on the analogy of a vindicated, apotheosized hero, but as a corporate person, as more than individual, that is, as one who not only is divine but always has been divine.[38] Certainly the language of these texts and their implicit christology are most striking, but they are also puzzling, and in the end of the day the full christological corollary of these texts is opaque.[39] Whether we should best speak of a kind of mystical perception of the exalted Christ,[40] and whether in consequence we should use such language to derive dogmatic corollaries, particularly about Christ's divinity or preexistence, are issues which can be posed, but without much hope of achieving a firm conclusion.[41]

A further issue correlated within the Pauline corpus has recently been revitalized: whether the title "Lord" as applied to Jesus implied that Paul identified Jesus with God; and whether Paul spoke of Jesus explicitly as "God." The former has recently been strongly reaffirmed on the familiar

35. Worship of Jesus as such is only clearly envisaged in Revelation; see R. Bauckham, "The Worship of Jesus in Apocalyptic Christianity," *NTS* 27 (1980-81) 322-41; and my *Partings,* 215-20. On the confusing issue of an angel christology in Revelation, as posed particularly by C. Rowland, *The Open Heaven* (London: SPCK, 1982), see now P. R. Carrell, *Jesus and the Angels* (Cambridge: Cambridge University, 1997).

36. See further L. Hurtado, "What Do We Mean by 'First-Century-Jewish Monotheism'?" in *SBL 1993 Seminar Papers,* ed. E. H. Lovering (Atlanta: Scholars, 1993) 348-68.

37. See particularly Kim, *Origin.*

38. C. F. D. Moule, *The Origin of Christology* (Cambridge: Cambridge University, 1977): "If this Jesus of history turns out, in subsequent Christian experience, to be eternal and more than individual but still personally identified with the One who was known as Jesus, how are we to deny him a personal pre-existence comparable to this?" (p. 139).

39. The debate on the significance of Paul's "in Christ" motif has not really moved forward in the period reviewed.

40. See also A. F. Segal, *Paul the Convert: The Apostolate and Apostasy of Saul the Pharisee* (New Haven: Yale University, 1990).

41. A major point which has been largely ignored in my own *Christology* is the importance of recognizing that in New Testament christology in particular we are confronted with "conceptuality in transition"; see pp. 275-78, 291 above.

ground that Paul used Old Testament Yahweh *(kyrios)* texts in reference to the exalted Christ, thus fully identifying Christ with Yahweh.[42] Certainly the association of the exalted Christ with God the Father in blessing and benediction is a remarkable feature of Paul's christology; but its significance in terms of preexistent divinity ascribed to the exalted Christ is by no means clear. And the fuller case has been markedly weakened by failure fully to integrate such passages as 1 Cor. 15:24-28 and talk of "the *God* and Father *of our Lord* Jesus Christ" (Rom. 15:6; 2 Cor. 1:3; 11:31) into the discussion. The consequence is that the tension between the functional and ontological christology implicit in the reference of *kyrios* to Christ remains obscure and unresolved.[43]

The latter dispute, on whether *theos* was used by Paul of Christ, is posed by Rom. 9:5 in particular, with scholars almost equally divided on how the passage should be punctuated.[44] Too neglected, however, has been the appreciation of the text's immediate context — that is, of an awareness of Paul's careful speaking to Jewish sensibilities and privileges, in which the Messiah is chiefmost of Israel's blessings (9:4-5), and in which the whole treatment climaxes in a paean of praise to God alone (Rom. 11:33-36). In such a context it is hardly likely that Paul would have expected the benediction to "God who is over all" to be attributed to other than the one God of Israel's faith.[45]

The most persuasive line of argument that belief in the preexistent divinity of Christ was formulated early has been based on the Philippian hymn (Phil. 2:6-11).[46] For some it has provided the primary evidence for the conclusion that the most significant developments in christology had already taken place within the first twenty years of Christianity.[47] Not, however, in terms

42. Capes, citing Rom. 10:13; 14:11; 1 Cor. 1:31; 2:16; 10:26; 2 Cor. 10:17; 2 Tim. 2:19. Cf. also Kreitzer.

43. Neither Capes nor Kreitzer pays any heed to the more subtle analysis of the relation between Jesus and God in W. Thüsing, *Per Christum in Deum. Studien zum Verhältnis von Christozentrik und Theozentrik in den paulinischen Hauptbriefen* (Münster: Aschendorff, 1965); see further Thüsing's contribution to K. Rahner and W. Thüsing, *A New Christology* (London: Burns and Oates, 1980).

44. For Jesus ascribed as "G/god" see, e.g., C. E. B. Cranfield, *Romans* (ICC; Edinburgh: Clark, 1975, 1979) 464-70; L. Morris, *Romans* (Grand Rapids: Eerdmans, 1988) 349-50; J. A. Fitzmyer, *Romans* (AB 33; New York: Doubleday, 1993) 547-49; M. J. Harris, *Jesus as God* (Grand Rapids: Baker, 1993).

45. See my *Romans,* pp. 528-29; also P. Stuhlmacher, *Römer* (NTD 6; Göttingen: Vandenhoeck und Ruprecht, 1989) 131-32; Kuschel 301-3.

46. Although the hymn can fairly be reckoned as "pre-Pauline," that should not be taken to mean pre-Paul's conversion, or even pre-Paul's earliest writings.

47. So particularly and repeatedly M. Hengel, e.g., *Son of God* (London: SCM, 1976) 1-2; also "Hymns and Christology," *Between Jesus and Paul* (London: SCM, 1983) 94-95; also "Christological Titles in Early Christianity," in J. H. Charlesworth, ed., *The Messiah,* 425-48, 440-44.

of Hellenization; the hymn is constructed and permeated throughout with Old Testament themes.[48] Nor in terms of the so-called Gnostic redeemer myth, whose character as a wild goose chase has become increasingly recognized in the past few decades.[49] Others have found it more persuasive to read the hymn as a poetic account of Christ's saving actions either as a following out of the course of Adam (to death) and divine purpose for Adam (God's regent over the rest of creation),[50] and/or by drawing in something of the wisdom paradigm of the righteous man vindicated (e.g., Wis. 4.7–5.8).[51] But if indeed the main focus of the hymn is on the saving action described therein and its main function is to present Christ as an ethical example,[52] it raises the question as to whether any precise definition was intended as to what the state was which Christ voluntarily abandoned. Adam, beginning in, as we would say, mythical prehistory, could certainly serve as a pattern for truly human conduct; as could the righteous man freely giving himself to an unjust lot and fate. Despite the majority view (the hymn assumes Christ acting in a preexistent state) there are important demurrers which call for caution in drawing any dogmatic corollaries on the subject of Christ's incarnation.[53]

In short, there is no doubt that the first Christians quickly began to associate Christ with God, at least as God's primary agent and regent in carrying through God's saving purpose to reclaim humanity and creation to his sole lordship. Whether or how quickly a corollary was drawn as to Christ's preexistent divinity and incarnation is a matter of continuing dispute. It is still less clear whether such a reading back of Christ's exalted status into a preexistent state carried any added significance for a soteriology

48. See particularly O. Hofius, *Der Christushymnus Philipper 2.6-11* (Tübingen: Mohr, 1976, [2]1991).

49. See, e.g., my *Christology,* ch. 4; E. Schweizer, "Paul's Christology and Gnosticism," in *Paul and Paulinism,* ed. M. D. Hooker and S. G. Wilson (C. K. Barrett FS; London: SPCK, 1982) 115-23; Kuschel, 248-50. Goulder's Samaritan hypothesis does not seem to have gained support.

50. See particularly J. Murphy-O'Connor, "Christological Anthropology in Phil. 2.6-11," *RB* 83 (1976) 25-50; Dunn, *Christology,* xviii-xix, 114-21; also *Partings,* 193-95; H. Wansbrough in *NJB;* J. Macquarrie, *Jesus Christ in Modern Thought* (London: SCM; Philadelphia: TPI, 1990) 56-59. Otherwise, C. A. Wanamaker, "Philippians 2.6-11: Son of God or Adamic Christology?" *NTS* 33 (1987) 179-93; N. T. Wright, *"Harpagmos* and the Meaning of Philippians 2.5-11," *JTS* 37 (1986) 321-52.

51. Kuschel, 255-66, following particularly D. Georgi, "Der vorpaulinische Hymnus Phil 2.6-11," in *Zeit und Geschichte,* ed. E. Dinkler (R. Bultmann FS; Tübingen: Mohr, 1964) 263-93.

52. See particularly Fowl, *Story,* chs. 3-4.

53. In view of Kuschel's support for a Wisdom christology here his comments on pp. 262-63 assume greater importance; note also Wright's comments in his *The Climax of the Covenant* (Edinburgh: Clark, 1991) 95-97. On 2 Cor. 8:9 my observations in *Christology,* 121-23, seem to have attracted little notice; see, e.g., V. P. Furnish, *2 Corinthians* (AB 32A; New York: Doubleday, 1984); M. de Jonge, *Christology in Context: The Earliest Christian Response to Jesus* (Philadelphia: Westminster, 1988) 197; but see also Kuschel, 295-97.

focused so exclusively on cross and resurrection. For myself it remains critically decisive that Paul's christology seems to have created no problems for his Jewish (-Christian) opponents, unlike his teaching on the Torah. That is to say, his christology seems to have posed no threat to the axiomatic Jewish monotheism of the time.[54] However, we have still to look at the principal evidence on this subject.

4. Jesus as Divine Wisdom

The strongest consensus to emerge from the past thirty-forty years has been that the main current of christological development flowing through the first century C.E. was wisdom christology.[55] This conviction has two principal elements. First, that through the course of Second Temple Judaism the heavenly (female) figure of divine wisdom became prominent in talk of creation, revelation, and redemption (Job 28; Proverbs 8; Sirach 24; Baruch 3–4; Wisdom *passim,* and also in Philo). And second, that Jesus was identified with this figure in a sequence of texts: in the Pauline corpus, particularly 1 Cor. 8:6 and Col. 1:15-17; elsewhere in Matthew, particularly 11:25-30 and 23:34, and Heb. 1:2-3; and particularly in John's Gospel, in the prologue (logos and wisdom christology being more or less one and the same) and underlying other christological images (light, drink, shepherd, etc).[56] However, there are still matters of considerable dispute of direct bearing on our question.

One is the status of the figure of divine Wisdom in Second Temple Jewish literature. The most prominent older view is that Wisdom was one of a number of intermediary figures which interposed themselves, as it were, between God, now thought of as distantly remote, and his creation.[57] This

54. See further Hurtado, *One God;* Casey, *Gentile Prophet,* ch. 8; chapter 11 above; Kuschel, 303-8; cf. Wright's concept of "christological monotheism" (*Climax,* chs. 5 and 6).

55. Particularly influential has been the article by E. Schweizer, "Zum religionsgeschichtlichen Hintergrund der 'Sendungsformel' Gal. 4.4f., Röm. 8.3f., John 3.16f., 1 John 4.9," *ZNW* 57 (1966) 199-210, reprinted in *Beiträge zur Theologie des Neuen Testaments* (Zurich: Zwingli, 1970) 83-95. In recent study see particularly my *Christology,* ch. 6, Schimanowski, Habermann, and Kuschel.

56. See, e.g., R. E. Brown, *John 1–12* (AB 29; New York: Doubleday, 1966) cxxii-cxxv; Dunn, *Partings,* 227; M. Scott, *Sophia and the Johannine Jesus* (JSNTSS 71; Sheffield: JSOT, 1992) ch. 3.

57. Influential here has been the formulation of W. Bousset and H. Gressmann, *Die religion des Judentums im späthellenistischen Zeitalter* (HNT 21; Tübingen: Mohr, 1925, [4]1966) 319; cited, e.g., by M. Hengel, *Judaism and Hellenism* (London: SCM; Philadelphia: Fortress, 1974) I, 155.

encouraged the idea of Wisdom as a heavenly being distinct from God[58] and has contributed to the near *reductio ad absurdum* thesis that Judaism, despite its fundamental confession of monotheism (the Shema — Deut. 6:4), after all did make room for belief in two gods, so that Jesus' divinity was simply the consequence of his identification with Wisdom.[59] However, in sharp contrast, the great preponderance of scholarship has continued to insist that Wisdom is a poetic personification of God's wisdom, the wisdom with which he created and which he ever seeks to communicate to his people in revelatory and saving power, the wisdom embodied for Israel in the Torah (Sir. 24:23; Bar. 4:1).[60]

A second issue of continuing controversy is when the identification of Jesus with Wisdom first becomes evident in the Christian corpus. There is still general agreement that within the Jesus tradition the identification first appears with Matthew's use of "Q" tradition; that is, the Q and earlier forms of the Jesus tradition (so, including Jesus himself) did not make this identification; in the tradition prior to Matthew Jesus is still teacher and ambassador of Wisdom.[61]

In Paul, however, there is continuing dispute over the tradition Paul used. Does the similar wording of Rom. 8:3 and Gal. 4:4 ("God sent his Son"), when taken with John 3:16-17 and 1 John 4:9-10, indicate an already established (pre-Pauline) formulation? And does it presuppose a sending from heaven (as in the later Johannine context), or the heavenly commission of a prophet? The parallel with Wis. 9:9-10 certainly weighs in favor of the former.[62] But nagging questions persist:[63] whether such an identification of Jesus with Wisdom could have been so casually assumed in its earliest form, where, all agree, the thrust of the sentence in both cases drives towards a cross-effected redemption; whether an echo of the parabolic language and prophetic imagery of Mark 12:6 is not a more likely explanation;[64] and

---

58. See, e.g., I. H. Marshall, "Incarnational Christology in the New Testament," in *Christ the Lord,* ed. Rowdon, 9, n. 22. Resort continues to be made to the intermediary category of "hypostasis" — so, e.g., H. Gese, *Essays on Biblical Theology* (Minneapolis: Augsburg, 1981) 192-93 — but only by ignoring the older warnings of the inappropriateness of this language, e.g., of G. L. Prestige, *God in Patristic Thought* (London: SPCK, [2]1952, 1964) xxviii, and J. Marböck, *Weisheit im Wandel: Untersuchungen zur Weisheitstheologie bei ben Sira* (Bonn, 1971) 129-30; see also now Kuschel 195-96.

59. P. Hayman, "Monotheism — A Misused Word in Jewish Studies?" *JJS* 42 (1991) 1-15; M. Barker, *The Great Angel: A Study of Israel's Second God* (London: SPCK, 1992).

60. See my *Christology,* 168-76, and others cited there; also Hurtado, *One God,* ch. 2; Casey, *Gentile Prophet,* 88-90; Kuschel, 185-87.

61. The view of M. J. Suggs, *Wisdom, Christology, and Law in Matthew's Gospel* (Cambridge: Harvard University, 1970), still holds sway; see, e.g., M. Sato, *Q und Prophetie. Studien zur Gattungs- und Traditionsgeschichte der Quelle Q* (WUNT 2/29; Tübingen: Mohr, 1988) 160-61; Kuschel, 240-43. Still peerless on the birth narratives of Matthew and Mark is R. E. Brown, *The Birth of the Messiah* (New York: Doubleday, [2]1993); see also Kuschel, 308-26.

62. Here the influence of Schweizer continues to be strong (see above n. 55).

63. See again Dunn, *Christology,* xvii-xviii and 38-45; Kuschel, 272-77, 300-301.

64. Fuller and Perkins, 46-47.

whether those who continue to hear the language of preexistence here[65] are not listening with ears attuned too much by the taken-for-granteds of the classic christology of later centuries.

On other early Pauline texts, and here the second issue of dispute begins to give way to the third, it is hard to get a firm handle on their significance for our question. The most explicit identification of Christ with wisdom comes in 1 Cor. 1:24 and 30: but it is equally explicitly the crucified Christ who is so identified, and is this wisdom or Wisdom that is in view?[66] In 1 Cor. 10:4 Christ is identified with the rock in Israel's wilderness wanderings, which elsewhere is identified with Wisdom; but is the identification more than typological (cf. 10:11 — *typikōs*)?[67] And in Rom. 10:6-10 Christ is read into Deut. 30:12-13 in the same way that Wisdom is read into the older Jewish interpretation of the same passage (Bar. 3:29-30); but again the parallel seems to be drawn with the death and ascension of Christ, rather than with preexistent Wisdom as such.[68]

Even in the case of 1 Cor. 8:6 it seems to have been difficult to draw clear conclusions. There is wide agreement that the "through him all things" is the language of creation, language used typically of divine Wisdom (e.g., Ps. 104:24; Prov. 3:19; Philo, *Det.* 54). But how was this confession of the one Lord intended to cohere with the continuing confession of the one God, "from whom all things"? Is this a confession only of the exalted Christ, who, according to other texts, only received the title "Lord" at his resurrection/exaltation (Acts 2:36; Rom. 10:9; Phil. 2:9-11)? In which case, should we understand the language of the second half as referring to the new creation ("through him all things and us through him"), itself the climax of the divine purpose for the first creation ("from him all things and us for him")?[69]

On the other hand, is there much point in disputing the implication that

65. E.g., C. E. B. Cranfield in *Glory of Christ,* ed. Hurst and Wright, 270-72; Hengel in Charlesworth, ed., *The Messiah,* 440, n. 49; Fitzmyer, *Romans,* 484-85; and the brief review in R. N. Longenecker, *Galatians* (WBC 41; Dallas: Word, 1990) 167-70.

66. The one point of agreed clarity has been that the language and argument of 1 Corinthians 1–2 do *not* require the presupposition of a Gnostic-Wisdom christology on the part of Paul's opponents — the older view of U. Wilckens, *Weisheit und Torheit* (Tübingen: Mohr, 1959) 68-76; also *TDNT* VII, 519-20; but see, e.g., J. A. Davis, *Wisdom and Spirit* (Lanham: University Press of America, 1984); G. D. Fee, *1 Corinthians* (Grand Rapids: Eerdmans, 1987) 65, n. 79.

67. See, e.g., my *Christology,* 183-84; E. Schweizer, "Jesus Christus," *TRE* XVI (Berlin: de Gruyter, 1987) 687; Kuschel, 280-85; otherwise, e.g., C. Wolff, *I Korinther 8-18* (THKNT 7/2; Berlin: Evangelische Verlagsanstalt, 1982) 42-43; Fee, 449; E. E. Ellis, "*Christos* in 1 Corinthians 10.4, 9," in *Jesus to John,* ed. de Boer, 168-73.

68. See my *Christology,* 184-87; also *Romans,* 605-6. But Morris (383) and Fitzmyer (590) continue to assume an allusion to incarnation in 10:6.

69. J. Murphy-O'Connor, "1 Cor. 8.6: Cosmology or Soteriology," *RB* 85 (1978) 253-67, followed by Kuschel, 285-91.

Christ is identified with preexistent Wisdom in 1 Cor. 8:6, since that identification seems so far beyond dispute in the case of Col. 1:15-17 and Heb. 1:2-3? Whatever issues of preexistence and incarnation might be avoided in these earlier texts, they can hardly be avoided in these later texts. Even so, however, that simply clears the deck for the third and most crucial issue in current debate: what did this use of Wisdom language for Christ, this implied identification with the wisdom by which God created all things, amount to? Here the first issue (who or what was divine Wisdom in Second Temple Judaism?) can actually be determinative: those who think Wisdom was already understood as a second divine being in pre-Christian Judaism making the obvious deduction;[70] and those who think of Wisdom as a poetic personification reading the Colossian hymn as an assertion of Christ's cosmic revelatory and redemptive significance (1:20-22), analogous to the identification of primal Wisdom with the Torah in Sir. 24:23 and Bar. 4:1.[71]

Puzzling for those who wish to maintain a more "orthodox" interpretation of the Colossian hymn is how to correlate it with the expressions of later orthodoxy: particularly when 1:15 would seem to lend itself to an Arian interpretation and 1:18-19 would seem to favor some form of Adoptionism or Nestorianism.[72] And should we be content to read the hymn as though it were a statement of dogmatic definition, with a role in creation attributed to the crucified Christ (as distinct, dogmatically, from the Wisdom/Logos become flesh of John's Gospel)?[73] Here again it seems to me of critical significance that such attribution to Christ was not seen as likely to be controversial for Jewish monotheism, either by the writer of Colossians or for the principally Jewish alternative at Colossae.[74]

In short, despite repeated expositions, the key exegetical-theological conundrum has hardly been grasped here. If Col. 1:15-20 and Heb. 1:2-3 (at least) represent anything like a breakthrough to a new theological conception (incarnation), then why is it not presented as such a breakthrough, with the correlative surprise or indignation of Christianity's opponents indicated? Whereas, if the christology of these passages was perceived by Christians

70. See above, nn. 57-59.

71. Dunn, *Christology,* ch. 6; Fuller and Perkins, ch. 5; Kuschel, 327-40. On Heb. 1:2-3 see also M. E. Isaacs, *Sacred Space: An Approach to the Theology of the Epistle to the Hebrews* (JSNTSS 73; Sheffield: JSOT, 1992) 186-204; L. D. Hurst, *The Epistle to the Hebrews: Its Background of Thought* (SNTSMS 65; Cambridge: Cambridge University, 1990) 113-19.

72. See further my *Christology,* 191-93, in critique of P. Benoit, "Body, Head and *Pleroma* in the Epistles of the Captivity," *Jesus and the Gospels* II (London: Darton, 1974) 51-92.

73. J. F. Balchin, "Paul, Wisdom and Christ," in *Christ the Lord,* ed. Rowdon, 215 — "the plain meaning here is that Christ pre-existed the creation of the world"; de Jonge, 121-22, but note also the more subtle analysis in 194-99 and Macquarrie, 388-92.

74. On the latter see now T. J. Sappington, *Revelation and Redemption at Colossae* (JSNTSS 53; Sheffield: JSOT, 1991).

and opposition as simply an extension or adaptation of older ways of conceptualizing divine revelation, then can we yet speak of such a breakthrough?[75]

In contrast, it is precisely such a sense of breaking new ground which comes to expression in John's Gospel, initially in the prologue (1:14-18) and the testimony of the Baptist (1:6-8, 15, 20, etc.), and subsequently in the reaction both of sympathizers and opponents (5:18; 6:52, 60-66; 10:33). Here there is no dispute as to the preexistence of the Logos-Son, and little dispute that the concept of incarnation really has emerged.[76] What does remain unclear, however, is whether a more literal imaging (Son) has here overtaken the earlier language of poetic personification (Logos/Wisdom). Having suggested an affirmative answer initially,[77] I am myself now more doubtful and find a greater consistency within the document when the Son christology is understood as a sustained elaboration of the prologue's Logos christology.[78] Either way, however, there is no question that what is in view is God's Word/self-expression (Son), preexistent with God from the beginning, and little doubt that a "real" incarnation was intended.

The continuing endeavor to set the Gospel more fully against the context of late first-century Judaism has also made it clearer that John portrayed Jesus as *the* revealer of God, over against other claims to definitive revelation, whether in Torah or through vision of or mystical ascent to heaven (1:17-18, 51; 3:13; etc.).[79] Which in turn has made it difficult to doubt that it was precisely the language of preexistence and conception of incarnation in reference to Jesus which was seen by Jewish opposition as a threat to the unity of God and so as the first real breach (perceived as such) with the Jewish monotheistic axiom.[80]

75. This conundrum continues to plague Hurtado's more recent work (n. 36).

76. Although it has been disputed by E. Käsemann, *The Testament of Jesus* (London: SCM, 1968), and K. Berger, "Zu 'das Wort ward Fleisch' John 1.14a," *NovT* 16 (1974) 161-66; but see my *Christology,* 347, n. 104; M. M. Thompson, *The Humanity of Jesus in the Fourth Gospel* (Philadelphia: Fortress, 1988) ch. 2 (but insufficiently nuanced on pp. 49-50); U. Schnelle, *Antidocetic Christology in the Gospel of John* (Minneapolis: Fortress, 1992) 221-22.

77. *Christology,* 239-50. In his critique of this earlier formulation (637, n. 63) Kuschel has missed the revision of my views put forward in the literature in n. 78.

78. See chapter 21 above; also my *Christology,* xxvi-xxx (= pp. 307-12 above). See also J. A. T. Robinson, "Dunn on John," *Theology* 85 (1982) 332-38, and my debate with M. Wiles, chapter 16 above; Kuschel, 383-89; and contributions by M. de Jonge, G. R. Beasley-Murray, and J. Painter in *Four Gospels* (Neirynck FS) III, chs. 88-90.

79. Particularly J. A. Bühner, *Der Gesandte und sein Weg im 4. Evangelium* (Tübingen: Mohr, 1977); but see also J. Ashton, *Understanding the Fourth Gospel* (Oxford: Clarendon, 1991); W. Loader, *The Christology of the Fourth Gospel* (Frankfurt: Lang, [2]1992).

80. Dunn, *Partings,* 220-29.

5. Conclusions

At this point I can hear a typical Goulder chuckle and the teasing retort, So what? All this is an interesting historical exercise, like so many of those carried through by Michael himself. But is it of any more significance than that? I think so.

First, it shows something of the character of a clear process of development through the first two generations of Christianity — not necessarily a straight or single linear development, but a developing process nonetheless. This is the case at whatever point(s) the ideas of personal preexistence and incarnation first emerged in Christian talk about Jesus. The development indicates that earliest Christian thought was not static, but involved the creative use of older language and conceptuality as these first Christians tried to make sense of what Jesus had done and what he continued to mean for them. The fascination of the historical study at this point is the sense it gives of standing within a process in which conceptuality was being transformed, remolded, and minted afresh to give it new capacity, to enable it to convey ideas which had quite literally never been thought before. That tells us something about the power of religious experience (not to say revelatory experience), and of language, to adapt with fresh insight to express new truth as newly perceived truth. Such a historical finding, more sensitive to the reality of conceptuality in transition, is much to be preferred to cruder versions of whole theologoumena simply taken over from other systems or created to appeal to new constituencies. Such a recognition of and respect for the character of earliest Christian theologizing is a considerable gain, and not least for anyone who thinks it important to correlate contemporary Christianity in at least some degree with the Christianity of its canonical documents.[81]

Second, there is a substantial consensus of current historical scholarship which finds a strong line of continuity running through the process. A developing continuity, in the first place, between the Jesus tradition and the christology of the later theologians Paul and John. It is hardly coincidental that designation of Jesus as God's Son can both be rooted so credibly in Jesus' own prayer life and provide the vehicle of the "sending" formula in Paul (Rom. 8:3; Gal. 4:4), which evidently served as a transition to the full-blown Logos-Son christology of John. The transition from Jesus as teacher and ambassador of Wisdom (Q) to Jesus identified with Wisdom (Matthew) takes place almost imperceptibly within the developing Jesus tradition itself. And it must be significant that what can still be called the highest christology in the New

---

81. These and the following observations provide a partial, but only partial, response to the strictures of L. E. Keck, "Toward the Renewal of New Testament Christology," *NTS* 32 (1986) 362-77; also in *Jesus to John,* ed. de Boer, 321-40.

Testament (John's Gospel) consists of reflections on the significance of things Jesus said and did (as well as of his revelatory significance as a whole) and precisely in the form of discourses in the mouth of Jesus himself and the controversies his words provoked. This fact, that such a clear continuity can be drawn between Jesus' own teaching and subsequent appreciation of Jesus in the light of his cross and resurrection, cannot but be of primary importance for Christianity's own self-understanding and relationship with what it has for so long regarded as the determinative event in history, the incarnation and ministry of Jesus of Nazareth.

A developing continuity, in the second place, with pre-Christian Jewish reflection on divine self-revelation in, through, and as Wisdom and Logos in particular. Here again the fact that there continues to be such a lively debate as to the point of transition in *Jewish* thought between poetic personification and hypostasis or distinct person is indicative. As is the fact that the earliest preexistence christological reflection in Christian circles took place in such characteristically Jewish terms. To speak of a kind of "binitarianism" within Second Temple Jewish understanding of God as one (that is, God as transcendent and God as immanent in his Wisdom, Logos, etc.) is no strain on the evidence. The most immediate parallel and precedent to the thought of Wisdom incarnated in Jesus may be said to be that of Wisdom identified with Torah. And it would appear that the recoil of rabbinic Judaism around the turn of the first-second century C.E. was as much a recoil from the dangers of apocalyptic and/or mystical vision of God as from the emerging incarnation theology of Johannine Christianity. This fact, that Christianity's most distinctive doctrine emerged wholly within and as part of Christianity's original Jewish matrix, cannot but be of continuing importance for Christianity's own self-understanding.

And a developing continuity, in the third place, between these early, first-century reflections on the significance of Christ, and the subsequent christological dogmas. Here it cannot but be important that it was precisely the Logos-Son christology of John's Gospel which continued to carry the main weight of christological reflection through the second century toward Nicea. Also that the first great christological controversy was the still essentially intra-Jewish one on the monotheistic implications of this christology, and that the Christians emerged maintaining the unity of God as still axiomatic (despite rabbinic rebuttal). In other words, these important developments in christology are to be understood not simply as the result of Christianity becoming more Gentile in composition and thought, and certainly not as a succumbing to Greek categories and philosophy or as merely incorporating syncretistic-fashion elements of alien systems (Samaritans or otherwise). There are paradigms of continuing value here for Christianity's continuing need to adapt to and speak with other religions and philosophies.

Finally, the why question. Why incarnation? The answer has been made only a little clearer by recent discussion. But at least we can say that we have to recognize as historians that there must have been several compulsions working within first-century christological development. One was evidently a sense that it was not enough to remain focused on Jesus' death and resurrection, as though salvation was primarily future-oriented and constituted some denial of the old creation. The necessity of a fuller correlation between old creation and new was somehow given within the dynamics of the process. Another was evidently that the first Christians found themselves compelled by their memory of Jesus and continuing spiritual experience to conclude that Jesus provided not just the pattern of humankind (Adam christology) but also the paradigm for God's self-revelation (Wisdom christology), the image of God in this twofold sense. In other words, the idea of incarnation seems to have been simply the articulation of a growing sense that Jesus shows what God is like more clearly than anyone or anything else, that it is Jesus who above all reveals God to humankind, a climactic though not necessarily exclusive claim.

24

He Will Come Again

Introduction

One thing we can be sure about: that over the next five years the subject of eschatology will gain increasing prominence. As we draw steadily nearer to the close of another millennium, enthusiastic speculation regarding the eschaton, the end events, is bound to rise. I am no prophet, nor even the son of a prophet; but still I make that prediction with confidence. Those who believe that they have been given a preview of the divine timetable for history's grand finale could hardly fail to see significance in such an auspicious date. And high on the eschatological agenda for anyone influenced by Christian tradition is bound to be the topic of the Second Coming. Anyone looking for the soon coming of our Lord could hardly fail to find the year 2000 a likely candidate.

Does such speculation increase our hope? Or does it increase our embarrassment? There is no way of avoiding either the one or the other, is there? For the coming again of Christ is quite central in the earliest Christian documents; as also in the creeds, doctrinal statements, and liturgies of the churches. From the earliest formulation that we have in Aramaic, "Maranatha, Our Lord, come" (1 Cor. 16:22), to the eucharistic acclamation, "Christ has died, Christ is risen, Christ will come again," the hope is constant and is repeatedly reaffirmed.

So what are we to say about this hope today? In a day when the currency of eschatological hope is subject to the inflation of rising expectation, which also means that the currency is losing its value, what are we to say? In the face of repeated disappointments of that hope and many earlier devaluations

---

A version of this lecture was published in *Interpretation* 51: 42-56. Copyright © 1997 and used by permission.

424

of that currency over the centuries, what are we to say? "He will come again," we boldly confess. But what are we actually saying? What do we Christians believe?

1. The Nature of Hope

It only takes a little study of the theme to remind us of two important features of biblical hope. On the one hand, biblical hope is a *confident* hope. This is one of the points at which biblical vocabulary differs from Hellenistic vocabulary. In classical Greek thought there is an inescapable sense of uncertainty about the future — rather like our own use of the term: "I hope I may see you next summer (but I am not confident that I will)." But in biblical thought hope is closely allied to trust, trustful hope, hope as confidence in God. Of this trustful hope, Abraham is the great example, as one who in trustful hope accepted God's promise of a son when he and his wife were long past child bearing (Romans 4).

At the same time, however, biblical hope is a constantly *redefined* hope. It is a hope in which the balance between the already and the not yet has never been finally resolved. Let me try to document this briefly.

Two of the great paradigms of the eschaton in the Bible are the entry into the promised land and the return from exile. You will remember how the letter to the Hebrews makes such effective use of the idea of the promised rest of the promised land. The Christian pilgrimage is like the people's wandering in the wilderness; and so, according to Hebrews 4, "there remains a rest for the people of God" into which they have still to enter. In other words, the great goal of the promised land is incomplete, in part at least only a shadow of what is still to come.

Similarly the exile became for many Jews an image of their being under the curse of God upon their disobedience, and the longed-for return from exile became a continuing metaphor for their restoration as God's favored nation. So the great prophets of the school of Isaiah depict the restoration of Israel and the longed-for return to Judea in classic images of eschatological renewal and of paradise restored — the child playing over the hole of the asp, and the wolf and lamb feeding together (Isa. 11:6-9; 65:25). And the seer of Revelation, the Christian apocalypse of John, is not the only one to use Babylon as the metaphor of the final opposition to God (Rev. 14:8, 17-18).

In other words, in both cases, both promised land and return from exile, the hope fulfilled fell short of the hope expressed, and the realization of hope was understood as only a partial fulfillment of that hope. Yet, the partial fulfillment did not undermine or falsify the hope but became the springboard for a fresh articulation of hope. The already did not completely express the fullness of hope, so that the unrealized not yet became the basis of hope reexpressed.

So also with the first coming of Christ. It was itself the fulfillment of eschatological hope. Yet the figure expected by John the Baptist was to be one who would bring final judgment — the unfruitful trees to be cut down and cast in the fire, the chaff likewise to be burned with unquenchable fire (Matt. 3:10, 12). The hope of the royal Messiah was for one who would restore the glory of his father David's reign (Ps. 2:7-9; Ezek. 34:20-31, etc.). What a surprise Jesus was! What a disappointment to so many. The predictions of kingly glory and of judgment on the nations were not fulfilled. Jesus did not fulfill all hopes for the age to come. In the light of Jesus' coming, Christians had to redefine the biblical hopes they inherited — above all to hope of a Messiah who must suffer and die.

At the same time, the images used by Jesus, the blind to see, the deaf to hear, the lame to walk, the poor to have good news proclaimed to them (Matt. 11:5), were the Isaianic images used for the age to come, for paradise restored (Isa. 29:18-19; 35:5-6; 61:1-2). There *was* fulfillment. In some sense the new age had come. And yet at one and the same time, it had not yet come. For still today we pray, as he himself taught us, "May your kingdom come" — the kingdom which he also said "had come upon them" in his ministry of exorcism (Matt. 12:28). The "not yet" remains; the "already" has not sucked out the fullness of the "not yet." The hope is reaffirmed even as it is redefined. Thus again is illustrated the nature of biblical hope — both realized and renewed, without the one causing the other to be denied.

Consequently we are not alarmed when we realize that Jesus' own expectation is unclear to us, and probably was unclear to him. What did he hope for? The scholars are confused on this, because the data is confusing. He proclaimed the coming of the kingdom; that is clear: "The kingdom of God is at hand; repent!" (Mark 1:15). But did he mean by that, the restoration of Israel or the coming of the end of the world? The former might seem a disappointingly narrow hope to attribute to Jesus. But why then does Luke represent the disciples as responding to the risen Jesus' exposition of the kingdom with the question, "Will you at this time restore the kingdom to Israel?" (Acts 1:6)? And the latter, the end of the world, an exposition of the coming kingdom from which Albert Schweitzer will not let us escape, poses still more difficult questions for us. Was Jesus' hope for his own generation not after all fulfilled? Jerusalem was destroyed indeed, but have the stars fallen from heaven and the angels come to gather the elect (Mark 13:25, 27)? So Jesus' own hope belongs to the same tradition of biblical hope realized but not completely, an already which still leaves a not yet outstanding as the substance of hope freshly reminted.

And what of Jesus' talk of the coming of the Son of man? The language is ambiguous. Did he mean a coming of the Son of man to God — a hope of vindication and exaltation? So the clear echo of Daniel's vision in all the relevant New Testament passages might suggest (Dan. 7:13-14). Or did he envisage the Son of man, or himself as the Son of man, coming again from heaven to earth? So some expressions of the hope seem to indicate (Mark 14:62). And yet, can we be sure? Is there here again a meshing and mixing of hope realized and hope redefined, of already and not yet?

Or consider the similar way in which the event of Pentecost is presented as the fulfillment of eschatological hope, hope of the age to come. Not only is the outpouring of the Spirit "on all flesh" a typical way of envisaging the new age (Joel 2:28-32). But the prophecy of Joel, fulfilled at Pentecost, according to Acts, includes talk of the sun turned to darkness and the moon to blood in anticipation of the coming of the day of the Lord (Acts 2:20). This, according to Luke's version of Joel's prophecy, would happen "in the last days" (2:17). But, despite the absence of such cataclysmic end-time happenings, Luke regards this hope as fulfilled at Pentecost. The hope is fulfilled, but not in the way that the prophet seems to have envisaged. The hope is reaffirmed even as it is redefined.

It is not surprising then, when we turn to focus on the hope of the coming again, that there should be something of a similar or equivalent ambiguity. Jesus spoke of the coming kingdom. But if it was not tied to the restoration of Israel, to what extent was it fulfilled in Pentecost? Was it there that the some who were with Jesus after the confession of Caesarea Philippi saw the kingdom of God come with power before they tasted death (Mark 9:1)? And if he spoke of the coming of the Son of man other than as referring to his own vindication after death, why is this language not picked up elsewhere in the New Testament, in the other earliest Christian expressions of parousia hope?

Or again, can we rule out the possibility, popular earlier in this century, that the Maranatha prayer, "Come Lord Jesus," was used as a eucharistic prayer — "Come to us Lord as we gather two and three in your name to partake of your body and blood"; "Make yourself known to us in the breaking of the bread, as you did to the two at Emmaus" (Luke 24)? Can we not speak of a "coming again" in the Lord's Supper? And John in his Gospel seems to suggest that Jesus' promises to his disciples in the farewell discourses, that he would not leave them desolate, but would come to them, were to be fulfilled in the coming of the Spirit of Truth, the place of the first Paraclete filled by the coming of the other Paraclete (John 14). Here again we find a tension built into the parousia hope, a tension between already and not yet, between reaffirmation and redefinition.

Not least we should note the confusion which we bring upon ourselves when we take the scattered references to and pictures of the hoped-for coming again and try to build from them a single coherent whole — the uncertainty on how to correlate Jesus' anticipation of the coming kingdom and his own resurrection and coming again, the lack of clarity between allusions to Christ's kingdom and the kingdom of God (1 Corinthians 15), and the confusion which seems to emerge when we try with insufficient thought or justification to correlate the 1 Thessalonians vision of Christ meeting the saints in the air and the Revelation's talk of a thousand-year reign, with the endless disputes which result between pre- and post- and a-millennialism, and between pre- and post-rapture tribulation scenarios.

The simple fact is that biblical hope has never been a matter of straightforward prediction. Confident, yes! Confident in God, above all! But confident as to what all would be involved in the fulfillment of that hope, No! Jesus himself warns us of the dangers of speculating on this point and of building anything on these speculations. Questions about who will be whose wife for the much married woman are inappropriate: the one thing we can be sure of, the life of the world to come will not be determined by the rules governing present-day society (Mark 12:18-27). Again, no one knows the day or the hour, not even the angels, not even the Son, but only the Father (Mark 13:32): there is an unknown quality, an unknowableness about God's future, which means that confidence in God can remain strong without being specific; the hope is in God, not in the particulars of what God will do. And again, God can repent and change his mind: the unfruitful tree can be given another year to show whether it is after all fruitful (Luke 13:6-9); Nineveh can repent and be spared, even if prophet Jonah is outraged at the seeming falsification of his prophecy of doom. We may be confident in God — yes, indeed! But in the matter of final judgment he is unpredictable in terms of human schematization, since his mercy runs far beyond what we would think proper or could predict, however inspired.

The nature of biblical hope, therefore, should be allowed to guide us in the formulation of our own hope, and not least on the subject of eschatology in its traditional sense, "the final things." Central to that eschatology, the coming again of Christ is part of that hope, and our articulation of that hope must be in tune with the nature of biblical hope as a whole. This means that the hope can be reaffirmed with confidence, but the elements which go into any description of what is hoped for are subject to the "principle of indeterminacy." The repeated redefinition involved in the restatement of biblical hope leaves us no choice. The tension between the already and the not yet means that the shape of the not yet is both clarified in some degree, since it will accord with the already, and obscured in some degree, since it remains unclear what all belongs to the not yet.

This brings us to our second main line of reflection.

2. The Language of Our Hope

It is a striking feature that so much if not most of the biblical language related
to the coming again of Christ is the language of *vision*. The most characteristic
imagery which at once jumps into our minds is that of the Christ coming on
clouds. "Behold, he is coming with the clouds," cries the seer of Revelation
at the beginning of his series of heavenly visions (Rev. 1:7) — an imagery
captured so well in Wesley's great hymn, "Lo, he comes with clouds descending."

Now we know that in apocalyptic vision clouds functioned as a means
of heavenly transport (in the New Testament Mark 13:26; 14:62; Acts 1:9;
1 Thess. 4:17; Rev. 11:12) and as a symbol of divine majesty and authority.
Thus in Ezekiel's archetypal vision of the chariot throne of God, the vision
is of "a great cloud" which came out of the north, in the midst of which was
the fire and the living creatures and the chariot itself (Ezekiel 1). So also in
the other archetypal vision of Daniel, the one like a son of man came with
the clouds of heaven (Dan. 7:13). It is important for us to grasp that the
symbolical force of this language would have been fully appreciated by the
prophets and seers. They would not have expected their readers simply to take
it at face value. Any more than Daniel would have expected his readers to
think the extraordinary beasts, which came up out of the sea earlier in his
vision (7:3-8), were intended to denote actual beasts. The apocalyptic visionary worked with symbolical language all the time.

This is clearest in the Christian canonical apocalypse, the Revelation of
John. Anyone who is familiar with it knows that it is stuffed full of symbolism
— bowls and trumpets, strange portents and bizarre beasts. It is the one book
in the New Testament where the normal rules of biblical exegesis do not apply:
in Revelation a *literal* interpretation is usually a *false* interpretation. It is in
the nature of apocalyptic vision that what is seen and described is more symbol
than anything else. So with reference to the coming again, the language of
hope is the language of vision is the language of symbol. If we forget this in
interpreting the Christian hope we simply store up for ourselves trouble and
confusion — as the history of interpretation of the Revelation of John illustrates all too well.

Another way to put this is to recognize that in talking of the coming
again we are talking about events which transcend history, which bring history
to an end as we have experienced it hitherto. In this we may see a parallel
between talk of the beginning and talk of the end: in this too, *Endzeit* is as
Urzeit. Despite a certain amount of discomfort, still continuing in some quar-
ters, we have grown accustomed to recognize that the biblical accounts of
creation depict events beyond time. We use the word "myth," not in the sense
of *un*historical, but in the sense of denoting that which is *beyond* history, that

for which scenes drawn on the template of human history can function only metaphorically or allusively. How else can we speak of what precedes history as we know it? Again, as we Christians have struggled to come to terms with, it is not a question of myth denoting falsehood, but of myth denoting a truth which can only be expressed by picture language and imagery. The myth of the beginnings of the world and of humankind is true in the way that a great poem or a great painting may be true.

Somewhat to our surprise, cosmologists and astrophysicists have been coming to equivalent conclusions for some time, with such concepts as curved space, antimatter and of time so speeded up that what proponents of the big bang claim to have happened within the first second simply outruns the scope of our rational imagination. Augustine was a lot smarter than most of his readers recognized for centuries when he said that God created with time — not that he created in time, nor that he created time, but that he created with time. The fact is that when we speak of events outside the realms of our normal space-time complex we simply cannot avoid using language in a metaphorical, analogical way, when the words used can no longer have a straightforward one-to-one correlation with that to which they refer.

The same is true for the other end of time, marked as we believe it to be by the second coming. Once we leave aside the more bizarre imagery of the apocalyptic visions we are actually left with a fairly small number of metaphors. The principal ones are the coming in clouds, the throne and judgment seat, and resurrection itself, a term which in itself simply denotes getting up or arising. The point which I am emphasizing is simply that they are metaphors. Their truth is not to be thought of as exhausted by or dependent upon reading them as literal descriptions — any more than the truth of the cosmos is exhausted by or dependent upon reading it in terms of Newtonian physics. We rightly recognize that it is no rebuttal of a confession that Christ will come in clouds to note the physical fact that clouds are too insubstantial to provide a platform for any solid body. The language we use at such times is an attempt to express what we cannot fully express by language, and can only begin to express when language functions as metaphor, metaphor functioning as another way of depicting reality.

Another aspect of the same feature comes to focus in one of the principal texts relating to the second coming, Acts 1:11 — the words of the angel to the disciples at Jesus' ascension: "Men of Galilee, why do you stand looking up toward heaven? This Jesus, who has been taken up from you into heaven, will come in the same way as you saw him go into heaven." Clearly the language used expresses the cosmology of the time — of heaven as a place above the earth. So for Jesus to go to heaven could only be expressed, could only be seen in terms of the conceptuality of the time, as a "being taken up into heaven." This is the issue which Bultmann saw so clearly, and tried to resolve so inadequately, in his essay on demythologizing. The language used by the ancients could only express what they saw and understood within the horizon of their own conceptuality. Again, it is not a question of truth or untruth. It is simply that language is the coming to birth of conceptions, and ideas and insights which have not yet been conceived cannot yet come to expression in language.

The fact then that we self-styled "moderns" are heirs of a different conceptuality, enriched by centuries of discovery and reflection, the fact that we see the cosmos differently and can no longer think of heaven as "up there," should neither disturb us nor cause us to see Bultmann's problem of myth as a threat. Of course, we can still smile tolerantly when Yuri Gagarin, the first Russian cosmonaut, says, "There is no God; I've been up there, and I didn't see him." Of course we use the word "heaven" both for the vault above and for the "place" where God is, and do so without confusion and without embarrassment. Of course, we can still speak of the "ascension" of Jesus, even though the metaphor is of a physical "going up." For the issue simply reminds us that all our metaphors are drawn from our experience and understanding of reality but go beyond that experience and understanding. It is not the case of ancient metaphor confronting modern fact, so much as of ancient metaphor compared with modern metaphor. For in all things which transcend human experience we have no choice but to use metaphor.

And if this is true of the ascension, and if indeed the ascension is the pattern for the coming again, as Acts 1:11 affirms, then presumably the same is true of the coming again. As with vision, as with myth, so with metaphor, all are a recognition that as Christians we have to speak of that of which our everyday experience and conceptuality and language give us only inklings, "rumors of angels," the already but not yet the not yet. Even those who attempt to describe "near-death" experiences find the same problem and inadequacy of language. To speak of the second coming as metaphor or myth, then, is not to deny it or to play it down but to recognize the character of the language of hope. And to deny the language of hope its metaphorical character is to particularize and specify the terms of that hope in a way that Jesus and the biblical writers repeatedly warn us against. We acknowledge this all the time, do we not, in our worship and liturgies. We are not put off our stroke or tempted to abandon our faith by the inadequacies of the metaphors we continually use in talk of heaven and the hereafter. We enthusiastically sing of being gathered by the crystal sea, of sitting on thrones and casting crowns before him, of endlessly acclaiming "Worthy is the Lamb," of the rapture when we lie prostrate before the throne and gaze on the Father, and so on. Do we mean this language literally? Surely not. To take it literally is *not* to take it seriously; on the contrary, it is to diminish it. If ever we think we have grasped the reality of heaven in the words we use to describe it, we are to be pitied not commended.

Francis Thompson has a poem entitled "Little Jesus."

Didst Thou sometimes think of *there*
And ask where all the angels were?
I should think that I would cry
For my house all made of sky;
I would look about the air,
And wonder where my angels were;
And at waking 'twould distress me —
Not an angel there to dress me!
. . . .
And didst Thou play in Heaven with all
The angels that were not too tall,
With stars for marbles? Did the things
Play *Can you see me?* through their wings?
And did Thy mother let Thee spoil
Thy robes, with playing on *our* soil?
How nice to have them always new
In Heaven, because 'twas quite clean blue!

Do we wriggle uncomfortably in our seats at such extravagance? We shouldn't, should we? For Thompson catches well the tone of childish wonder. And who of us would want to say that a child's vision of heaven was wrong or inappropriate? — especially with the words of Jesus himself ringing in our ears: "unless you convert and become like little children you will never enter the kingdom of heaven" (Matt. 18:3). Most of us, after all, have no doubt sung many times, "There's a friend for little children above the bright blue sky." And would we wish to deny its sentiments in the presence of our children? The vision of heaven which we express in our words has to be appropriate to our level of understanding, however inadequate. And that is as true of our adult language of heaven as it is of a child's. For in the mysteries of the faith we are all children, however mature we may be in the Spirit, and our language, however sophisticated, shares something of Thompson's naive innocence.

How could it be otherwise? When the author of Revelation in his description of heaven says, "and the sea was no more" (Rev. 21:1), was he expressing a hope framed in terms of his own, presumably unhappy experience of the sea, or was he affirming that heaven would be a place of disappointment for all who love the sea? Or when 2 Thessalonians envisages the climax of hostility to God as "the son of perdition," "the lawless one (masculine)" taking his seat in the temple of God (2 Thess. 2:3-10), are we intended to understand that that preview of the end events can only be realized by a male figure sitting down in a rebuilt Jerusalem Temple? No, No! This is the language of imagery, and we abuse the language, diminish its imagery and disdain its writers if we insist that it can have no other than a literal reference.

To take but one other example — from the other place. We are all accustomed to the biblical vision of hell, predominantly in terms of fire that burns without being quenched. The imagery was in part at least drawn from the fires of Gehenna, the constantly smoldering rubbish dump outside the walls of Jerusalem. And the imagery has been constantly repeated in art and literature all down the centuries. Are we to take that imagery literally? What then of Dante's portrayal in *The Divine Comedy* of the deepest circle of hell as a deep frozen lake in which the souls of the tormented are forever trapped? Or C. S. Lewis's portrayal in *The Great Divorce* of hell as a depressingly gloomy, smoggy city? Are these alternative images rendered false by the predominant canonical one? Surely not. Were Dante and Lewis wrong to depart from the biblical metaphor? Surely not. A metaphor by its very nature is not, cannot be a literal description. The more appropriate answer is to say that all three are attempts to portray an unimaginable human future in terms drawn from the more horrific experiences of human life. Here once again language falls far short of what we are trying to say.

To sum up our second line of reflection, then, the language of our hope, and particularly our hope of heaven and of Christ's coming again, shares a basic deficiency with all our language about the divine and the beyond. It simply cannot express a reality which goes beyond anything those who speak with human speech have experienced. Even their visions are still only visions, and when put into words are constrained by the concepts and words available to them from the store of human discourse. Or else they hear things in their vision "that are not to be told, that no mortal is permitted to repeat" (2 Cor. 12:4). For in both cases the reality thus envisaged far surpasses the power of human speech to express. As with our talk of the beginning of all things, so with our talk of the end. It is all metaphor, whether the metaphor of a garden paradise or the metaphor of a big bang, whether the metaphor of a descent from heaven on clouds, or the metaphor of a wedding feast. There is no single or multiple description of heaven or of Christ's return which is adequate to express a reality beyond words, a reality beyond our experience and understanding.

In short, in this, as in all our talk of God, our language is an icon, and only functions properly when it functions as an icon, that is, as a window through which we look to the spiritual reality beyond. And as with all icons, the danger is always present that we will turn the icon into an idol, that we will cease to look through the metaphor and instead focus our attention on the metaphor itself, and so give the language the devotion which belongs to our God and to his Christ alone. In terms of our present topic, the danger is that we will forget the symbolical character of our talk of Christ's coming again, will forget that the reality confessed is far greater than our human language can express, and will focus our attention upon that language in a pedantic way which turns our attention away from God and his Christ and leaves us expressing our devotion to idols made of human words and verbal images.

3. The Christ — Focus of Our Hope

This brings us to our third and final line of reflection — the key issue: What, then, is our hope? What are we confessing when we confess that Christ will come again? To which the short answer is: We are confessing Christ. We are confessing God in Christ. We are confessing God's purpose summed up in Christ. Let me try to elaborate in the space remaining.

First we need to recall that an eschatological hope is something distinctive within the monotheistic traditions which stem from the religion of Israel. The religions of the East more typically have a cyclical view of time; the religions of the West more typically a linear view of time. I still remember the impact this point made upon me when I first encountered it as a student in John Baillie's *The Idea of Progress*. We see some affirmation of this basic worldview in the irreversible forward steps which have characterized our own entry into the modern period — the development of printing, of human flight, of radio and TV, the current revolution in information technology, none of which are reversible.

We should not downplay the extent to which such progress has been inspired, made possible, and to a degree validated by Christian theology, by Christian eschatology. Just so long as we don't make the mistake of the Victorians and the nineteen-century liberal Protestants in assuming that scientific progress must lead to moral progress. The events of the twentieth century surely highlighted that fallacy once and for all! The more realistic appropriation of Christian eschatology should have reminded us long before World War One that the Christian visions of the future have included plenty scope for evil as well as for the final triumph of good.

My point here, however, is that in the attempt to speak of eschatology, in the attempt to envisage the future and the end, Christ is the distinctive Christian contribution. For Christians the coming again of Christ is a way of affirming that Christ is the goal and climax of human history. The forward-moving line of human progress reaches its end in Christ. In this we share the traditional hope of Jews past and present: that the world to come will be inaugurated by the coming of the Messiah. In the words of Isaiah, reworked by Paul, "Out of Zion will come the deliverer; he will turn away ungodliness from Jacob" (Rom. 11:26 = Isa. 59:20-21). The only difference is that we Christians believe we know who that deliverer, who that Messiah is — Jesus the Christ. But the hope is essentially the same, reaffirmed even as it is redefined. The hope is expressed in the language of metaphor, but it is a confident hope nonetheless.

Secondly, we should recall again the slogan in Jewish-Christian eschatology that the End time will be as the Beginning time, *Endzeit* as *Urzeit*. For it reminds us that the role of Christ at the end may be analogous to the role attributed to him at the beginning. The idea of Christ as agent in creation itself is as old as Paul: "for us there is one Lord, Jesus Christ, through whom all things and we through him" (1 Cor. 8:6); "who is the image of the invisible God, firstborn of all creation, for in him were created all things, . . . all things through him and for him have been created" (Col. 1:15-16).

What did Paul mean by such language? The growing consensus of scholars who have studied such language is that Paul did *not* intend to affirm that Jesus of Nazareth as such was there in the beginning; that would be a step on the road to bitheism. Rather he was using the language, developed by Jewish wisdom writers, to speak of divine Wisdom: Wisdom who, in the poem of Proverbs 8, was with God at the time of creation like a master worker or a little child, daily his delight rejoicing before him always (Prov. 8:30); or who, in the Wisdom of Jesus ben Sira, came forth from the mouth of the Most High, and covered the earth like a mist, who was given to Israel as its inheritance and is now embodied in the Torah (Sir. 24:3, 8, 23). This is the wisdom by which God has made all things, the wisdom by which he founded the earth (Ps. 104:24; Prov. 3:19).

And what is this wisdom? It is simply God's wisdom. The poems of Proverbs and ben Sira are simply vivid elaborations of the basic metaphor, ways of saying in imagination-stirring terms that creation was not irrational or purposeless but an act of God's wisdom. The cosmos is not nonsense. It is creation; it makes sense — God's sense! In other words, the figure of Wisdom is simply a way of speaking of God in his action and relationship toward the world he has made. That's why the Wisdom of Solomon can speak of the acts of God toward humanity and on behalf of the patriarchs and Israel as the acts of Wisdom. For Wisdom is the face of God turned to his world and his people.

So when Paul and other New Testament writers use such language of Christ they are speaking not of some other divine being other than the one God of Israel. Like their predecessors, the Jewish wisdom writers, they are speaking of the way in which God relates to his world and his people. And what they are saying is that Christ demonstrates the character of God's outgoing creative and redemptive power. As ben Sira and other wisdom writers saw this divine Wisdom embodied in the Torah, so Paul and the other Christian writers saw this divine Wisdom embodied in Christ. Christ reveals God to us, the God who creates in wisdom. Christ is the climax, the epitome, the incarnation of that divine Wisdom. He shows us what God is like; he reveals to us what creation is all about. Apart from anything else, Christ as Wisdom underlines the insight, rooted deep in our Scriptures, that spirituality is not something divorced from creation, that in no way should salvation be seen as rescue from creation. In Wisdom christology creation and redemption are two sides of the same coin.

And what does this say to our present concerns? If indeed the End is to be as the Beginning, then could it be that the language describing Christ's involvement in the End plays an analogous function to the language describing Christ's involvement in the Beginning? Is the same basic insight involved here? That the End will be as Christ-focused as the Beginning, that Christ embodies the character of the End in as definitive and final a way as he embodies the character of the Beginning? Christ, coming again in new creation, is, as Christ, agent of the old creation? But if so, the point is the same in both cases: to speak of Christ as a way of confessing our faith in God, as a God whose initial purpose was not only wise but will in the end, will as the end achieve the goal intended for it in the beginning.

Something at least of this is surely expressed in two biblical passages central to our concerns. First, Ps. 8:4-6, as taken up and interpreted in the New Testament, in Heb. 2:6-8 in particular: the purpose of God in making humankind — made a little lower than God, crowned with glory and honor, given dominion over the works of God's hands, with all things subservient — has not been fulfilled in humankind as we know it. But it has been fulfilled in Christ — made a little lower than the angels, but now crowned with glory and honor (Heb. 2:6-9), to whom all things will be made subservient (1 Cor. 15:25-27). Christ in his dominion over all fulfills the purpose of God in making humankind in the first place. Second, and correlated with the first, 1 Cor. 15:20-28: when this dominion over all is completed, including the last enemy, death, then Christ himself will be subservient to God, "so that God may be all in all." Final time indeed as Primeval time, when the process begun with God alone in creation *ex nihilo* climaxes in God alone as all in all.

Here again we can conclude that any christology, any eschatology, which sets creation and salvation in antithesis is at odds with the Christ-focus of both. But also that any spirituality or theology which separates Christ from God or focuses on Christ in forgetfulness of God is at odds with the consistent and fundamental God-centered monotheism of our Scriptures. Consequently, we may say again, confession of Christ's coming again is, like confession of Christ's role in creation, a confession primarily of God, of God's wisdom and purpose, but of that wisdom and purpose as focused in Christ, as the character of God in his wisdom and purpose finally and most fully illuminated by and embodied in Christ. The doctrine of the second coming is at its heart the Christian attempt to say that God's final purpose, like his original purpose, is Christ-focused, is Christ-shaped.

This line of reflection leads at once into our third and final point. That we already know the character of the end, because we know the character of Christ. Christ as the midpoint of time shows us what the unveiling of God's purpose for the end will be like, just as it shows us what the unveiling of God's purpose in the beginning was like. We already know the end, because we already know Christ.

This is surely the great lesson to be learned from the strong realized eschatological emphasis of our founding Scriptures. That in Christ the end has somehow already arrived. The kingdom of God has come in his exorcisms (Matt. 12:28). The resurrection of the dead has begun in his resurrection (Rom. 1:4); it is the *aparche,* the firstfruits, the beginning of the eschatological harvest of dead bodies (1 Cor. 15:20). So too the Spirit is the *arrabon,* the down payment and guarantee of that complete redemption (Rom. 8:23), which will include the transformation of the *soma psychikon* into the *soma pneumatikon,* of the body enlivened by the psyche into a body enlivened by the Spirit (1 Cor. 15:45-50). Or in alternative terms, the Spirit-Paraclete as the coming again of the first Paraclete (John 14; 1 John 2:1).

All this imagery was born of the sense pervasive among the first Christians that they were already experiencing the powers of the age to come (Heb. 6:4-5); they already knew the end because they were already recipients of its blessings. They were already part of the "new creation" (2 Cor. 5:17; Gal. 6:15). That was why delay of the parousia was never as serious a problem for early Christian theology as so many theologians of this century have thought. Simply because the imminence of the end was not constitutive of their view of the end. What was constitutive was their recognition of its character as defined by and come to focus in Christ — the kingdom to come already manifest in the ministry of Jesus of Nazareth; the Spirit of the end time now understood as the Spirit of Christ, the Spirit that inspired the ministry of that Jesus. As Oscar Cullmann pointed out in his *Christ and Time,* the delay of Christ's coming again was no great problem for the first Christians because the spring of their hope was in Christ's first coming. In similar terms we may add, the unclarity of their unrealized eschatology was no problem because its defining moment lay in the realized eschatology of Easter and Pentecost.

The struggle which the first Christians had to hold together the potentially divergent strands of their faith and hope points in the same direction. If Paul is any guide, the overlapping and sometimes conflicting images and metaphors which they used to express their worship all came to nothing if they did not find their resolution in Christ. What did it mean for them to speak of their being "in Christ," of being baptized "into Christ," of coming to the Father "through Christ," of their community as "the body of Christ," of the Spirit as "the Spirit of Christ"? Certainly not that they thought of Christ as dead and gone. Certainly not that they were merely celebrating Christ the great teacher: to collapse such language into an affirmation of the influence of Jesus' teaching is to cut out the living heart of earliest Christian worship.

But how did they conceive of him, the living present Christ? How did they picture this Christ in their minds? Christ as Jesus of Nazareth sitting on a throne in heaven beside God? Christ as a kind of universal atmosphere or fluid in which they lived? Christ as a huge cosmic body? Or what? Pursuit of such questions is likely to be as fruitless as the quest for the Primal Man myth of pre-Christian Gnosticism, a wild goose chase which dominated New Testament scholarship in the middle decades of this century.

The point surely is that the first Christians were ransacking their language and imagery to express the conviction that Christ, the risen Christ, Christ from the other side of death, Christ the embodiment of God's wisdom, Christ as the face of God turned to his world, was still with them, still determining their being as they focused their worship of God through him. They could not give further content to their faith except in and through this language and imagery. "In Christ" said it all. To say more was to say less.

And is it not the same with our talk of Christ's coming again? To tie that confession to a literal coming of Jesus in the clouds of heaven is to limit it. To reduce it to the level of a live television report of Jesus' descent on the Mount of Olives, which could be seen simultaneously all over the world, on all channels, is to lose sight of the deeper significance of the language, to linger on the letter and lose the Spirit. Not that the language should be abandoned. Not at all! The words of our confession are the means by which we express this great Christian conviction, this great truth of universal significance. Christ will come again! But the imagery itself is not the reality. The reality is far greater than the imagery. We must not fall into the trap of making the icon into an idol.

4. Conclusion

Perhaps it would be helpful to see a parallel between our confession of Christ's coming again and our confession of Jesus as the Son of God. By the imagery of "son" we do not mean that Jesus was literally God's Son by God having sexual intercourse with a woman. That would be to reduce our confession of Jesus' divine sonship to the level of the lewd legends of Zeus in his amorous dallyings with earthly women. But that does not mean we abandon the language of divine sonship for Jesus. Not at all! Christian worship and thought down through the centuries, from the beginning, has recognized that there is no better way of expressing the intimate relation between God and Jesus. That is to say, we recognize that the language is metaphorical, that it is, strictly speaking, inadequate to the task. But we recognize equally that there is no better, no more fitting imagery than that of Jesus as God's Son.

So too with our hope of Christ's coming again. There is an uncertainty about it which pervades all human prediction about God's future purpose. It is the language of vision and metaphor. It is therefore, strictly speaking, inadequate to the task, as is all human speech about God. But it is the best we have and we should neither be embarrassed about it nor should we abandon it. For it tells us and enables us to tell the world that the future is not random and pointless; God's purpose still prevails and drives forward to the climax of his-story. It tells us and enables us to tell the world that the future has a Christ-shape and a Christ-character. The future will not come to us as a total surprise. For the God we encounter at the end of time will be the God who encounters us at the midpoint of time, God in Christ. And the Christ we encounter at the end of time will be the Christ we encounter in the Gospels, the Christ we encounter in our worship, in the Spirit, in Christ and through Christ to God the Father. We believe that this Christ will come again. "Maranatha. Come, Lord Jesus."

INDEX OF MODERN AUTHORS

Allison, D. C., 177n.23, 180
Augustine, 430
Aulén, G., 49

Baillie, John, 434
Balchin, J. F., 273, 277, 299n.27
Barker, M., 396, 397, 398
Barrett, C. K., 199n.38, 208, 243,
    249n.33, 251n.48
Barth, Karl, 51, 53
Baur, F. C., 144
Beker, J. C., 380
Betz, Otto, 70
Black, Matthew, 75, 83n.11
Boismard, M. E., 141n.38
Boobyer, G. H., 63n.14
Borgen, P., 365n.76, 372
Borsch, F. H., 71, 318
Bousset, W., 164n.32, 191, 318,
    319n.16, 389
Bouttier, M., 125n.44
Bowersock, G. W., 302n.46
Brandenburger, E., 137, 138, 161
Brown, D., 299n.27
Brown, R. E., 51, 366
Bruce, F. F., 243
Bühner, J. A., 262, 365, 365n.76, 372
Bultmann, R., 40, 53, 66-67, 70, 71, 77,
    127n.5, 135n.23, 191, 315, 317, 318,
    319, 340, 348, 349, 353, 372, 383,
    389, 406, 431
Burkill, T. A., 60n.6, 64n.16

Burrows, M., 108n.43

Cadbury, H. J., 242
Casey, M. P., 387, 389-96, 398, 399-404
Collins, A. Yarbro, 83n.11
Conzelmann, H., 65n.19, 243, 244
Cross, F. M., 108n.43
Cullmann, O., 242

Dahl, Nils, 377
Dante, 433
Davies, W. D., 130
de Jonge, M., 216
Dinkler, E., 68
Dodd, C. H., 65, 206, 351

Fjärstedt, B., 180
Foerster, W., 242
Fossum, J. E., 305
Franklin, E., 244
Friedrich, G., 197
Fuller, R. H., 298n.26
Furnish, Victor, 173, 189n.73

Goldberg, A. M., 329-30
Goulder, M., 406, 421
Gressmann, H., 318, 319n.16
Gruenler, R. G., 271, 273-74, 300n.30
Gruenwald, I., 307
Grundmann, W., 66, 214
Gunkel, H., 158, 160n.21

Haenchen, Ernst, 68, 243, 250n.45
Hahn, Ferdinand, 67, 68, 127, 215, 243
Hanson, A. T., 271, 272-73, 276, 277
Harnack, A., 389, 406
Hayman, P., 396, 397, 398
Hays, Richard, 187
Headlam, A. C., 143
Heitmüller, W., 191
Hengel, Martin, 213, 223n.32, 229, 318, 389
Hermann, Ingo, 115, 120-21, 124
Higgins, J. B., 325
Hill, D., 209
Holladay, Carl, 279-86, 301, 303
Hooker, Morna D., 75, 190, 232
Hultgren, A. J., 298n.26
Hurst, L. D., 297n.21
Hurtado, L. W., 298n.26, 301, 303, 309, 310n.80

Janowski, B., 202
Jeremias, J., 96, 97, 105n.32
Johnson, L. T., 243
Jones, D. L., 244
Judge, E. A., 216n.15

Käsemann, E., 161, 197, 349
Keck, Lee E., 59n.3, 301n.39, 377
Kee, H. C., 359n.44
Kierkegaard, Søren, 75
Kim, S., 304, 305
Kreitzer, L. J., 296n.20
Kümmel, W. G., 123n.35

Lampe, G. W. H., 54
Lewis, C. S., 433
Lightfoot, R. H., 69
Lindars, B., 319
Linnemann, E., 128n.11, 135n.26
Lohmeyer, E., 70
Lonergan, B., 268
Longenecker, Richard, 75
Luz, Ulrich, 59

Marböck, J., 330
Marshall, I. H., 273, 276, 277, 389
Martin, R. P., 192n.10, 297n.23
Martyn, J. L., 355n.25
Marxsen, W., 65n.19
Meeks, W. A., 365, 372

Michel, O., 140n.36
Miller, E. L., 341n.83
Montefiore, C. G., 71
Morris, L., 207, 209
Moltmann, J., 53
Moule, C. F. D., 160n.18, 244, 342n.86, 389
Mowinckel, S., 325

Neirynck, Frans, 185, 186
Neusner, J., 99-100
Newman, J. H., 389
Nineham, D. E., 69

O'Neill, John C., 65, 244
Otto, R., 333n.63

Pannenberg, W., 53, 190
Payne, P. B., 300n.30
Pesch, R., 243

Reicke, B., 150n.70
Reitzenstein, R., 164n.32
Resch, Alfred, 173
Robinson, J. M., 62
Rowdon, H. H., 271
Rowland, Christopher, 286, 305, 306n.66, 307, 360n.45

Sanday, W., 143
Sanders, E. P., 93n.26, 100-103, 329, 407n.10
Sanders, J. T., 318
Schiffman, L. H., 80n.2
Schildenberger, J., 123n.35
Schillebeeckx, E., 53
Schmidt, K. L., 145n.53
Schmithals, W., 124
Schneider, G., 143n.44, 149n.68, 150n.73, 243, 244, 250, 250n.45
Schulz, S., 318, 329
Schweitzer, A., 51, 93, 426
Schweizer, Eduard, 62, 64, 127, 128, 129, 140, 147, 148, 149n.66
Segal, A., 279-86, 301n.40, 328n.45
Smith, J. Z., 286
Smith, Morton, 285

Taylor, Vincent, 69
Thompson, Francis, 432

Thompson, Michael, 173
Tiede, D. L., 280
Turner, Nigel, 123

van Unnik, W. C., 116n.2
Vermes, Geza, 75
Vielhauer, P., 60n.7

Walter, Nikolaus, 185, 186
Wanamaker, C. A., 297n.21
Wedderburn, A. J. M., 183, 186

Weeden, T. J., 67, 68
Weiser, A., 243
Weiss, J., 51
Wengst, K., 317, 357n.33, 360n.46
Whiteley, D. E. H., 132n.21, 209
Wiles, Maurice, 257-61, 262
Wrede, Wilhelm, 57-58, 61, 62, 63n.14,
    65, 66, 68, 69, 72, 76
Wright, N. T., 206n.68, 296n.18

Young, F., 318

INDEX OF SCRIPTURE
AND OTHER ANCIENT WRITINGS

OLD TESTAMENT

Genesis
1	359
1–2	409
1:26	325, 328
1:26-27	41
1:27	277, 296
2–3	285
2:7	155, 157
2:19	296, 325
2:22-24	296
3:5	41, 296
5:3	277
5:24	224, 272, 300, 319
6:1-4	35
6:2	322
6:4	35, 322
6:16	197
12:3	175
14	321
16:7-13	385
18	35, 97
21:17-18	385
27:29	175
28:12	362
31:11-13	385
32:24-30	35

Exodus
3:2-6	323, 385
3:14	24, 45, 385
4:22	8
14:19	323
14:24	323
19:3	359
23:20	323
23:20-21	385
23:21	324
24:18	359
33:2	323
33:3	323
33:18-23	386
33:20	362
34:29-35	117, 118-21
34:34	17, 122, 123, 124

Leviticus
4	202
4:3	81
4:5	81
4:16	81
5	38
5:6-7	198
5:11	198
6:22	81
16:3	198
16:5	198
16:9	198

16:21	202
17:10-12	203
19:18	178, 182
21:17-18	109
21:17–24:37	106
21:18	109
24:14	202

Numbers
6:16	198
7:16	198
8:10	202
16:22	146
24:9	175
25:10-13	81
27:16	146
27:18	202
27:23	202

Deuteronomy
1:11	250
4:12	362
6:4	285, 306, 397, 417
12:23	203
15:21	109
18:15	6, 333
18:18	6, 333, 363
21:23	220, 223
30:7	187

30:11-14	187, 188	Job		8:1-35		331
30:12-13	234, 418	1:6-12	8, 322	8:22	42, 48, 234, 258,	
30:12-14	368	2:1-6	322		381	
32:8	322	11:14	330	8:25	42, 234	
32:8-9	396	14:1	194	8:27-30	367	
32:35	187	15:14	194	8:30	83, 329, 435	
34:5	321	25:4	194	9:1-6	331	
34:9	202	28	416	25:21	187	
		29:15	109			
Joshua		38:7	322	Isaiah		
5:13-15	35			6	24, 359	
		Psalms		6:1	45, 384	
Judges		2:2	80	6:1-2	90	
2:1	323	2:7	12, 35, 37, 285	6:1-5	386	
6:34	32	2:7-9	426	6:5-8	42	
13:5	122	8:4	9, 94	7:14	50, 382	
14:19	35	8:4-6	14, 194, 195,	8:14-15	122	
			232, 285, 336,	8:17-18	122	
			436	11:1	122	
1 Samuel		8:5	296	11:1-2	80	
2:10	80	8:5-6	296	11:1-5	5	
7:13	249	8:6	15, 41, 337, 380	11:6-9	425	
12:15	249	24:11	207	17–19	7	
		29:1	322	27:1	331	
2 Samuel		31:6	250	29:18-19	426	
3:12	249	33:6	45, 367	31:3	146	
5:6	109	45:4	330	33:5-6	109	
5:8	109	45:6	16, 35	35:5-6	109, 426	
5:9	109	82:6	16, 35	35:5-7	7	
7:12-14	71, 80	84:9	81	42:1	37	
7:13-14	5, 87	85:10	330	43:10	24, 45	
7:14	8, 95	89:6	322	45:20-25	397	
		89:26-27	35	45:21-23	337	
1 Kings		89:51	80	45:23	225, 380	
18:46	35	104:24	381, 418, 435	49:1-7	42	
19:16	81	105:15	81	49:18	38	
		106:30-31	83	51:9	330	
2 Kings		107:42	330	51:17-23	10	
1:8	320	110	285	53	82, 92, 93-94,	
2:11	224, 300, 319	110:1	12, 41, 71, 232,		200	
2:15	81		252, 337, 380,	53:4	182	
2:16	249		411	53:4-6	42	
5:18	207	110:4	19, 321, 333	53:10	198	
		132:17	80	53:10-11	10	
				54:13	363	
2 Chronicles		Proverbs		59:20-21	435	
29:23-34	198	1:20-33	331	61:1	274	
		3:19	42, 234, 381,	61:1-2	6, 81, 90, 91, 94,	
Nehemiah			418, 435		426	
10:33	198	8	416	62:5	38	

65:25	425		335, 360, 385,	1:18	22
			397, 429	1:20	22, 323
Jeremiah		7:13-14	402, 408, 427	1:22-23	22
1:7	42	7:18	325, 408	1:23	22, 44, 382
20:9	35	7:22	325, 408	2:4	22
23:1-6	38	7:27	325, 408	2:13	323
23:5	80	8:16	322	2:15	22
32:6-9	122	9–10	359	2:17-18	22
33:15	80	9:21	322	2:19	323
51:34-37	331	9:25-26	80	2:23	22, 122
		10:5	324n.33, 336	3:7-12	93, 333
Ezekiel		10:5-6	22, 305, 360,	3:10	426
1	359, 429		385, 397	3:12	426
1:24	22, 336, 385	10:13	83, 322, 323	3:17	22
1:26	305, 324, 385	10:20	323	4:1-11	400
1:26-27	360	12:1-2	93	4:3-6	22
1:26-28	386			4:14-16	22
2:2	35	**Joel**		5–7	172
2:3	42	2:28-32	427	5:3	90, 110
8:2	22, 305, 324,	2:32	225, 251, 337	5:3-4	6
	360, 365, 385,	2:39	251	5:9	177
	397	3:1	81	5:11	9
29:3	331			5:11-12	93
34:10-16	38	**Haggai**		5:17-20	401
34:20-24	38	2:23	80	5:23-24	221
34:20-31	426			5:31-42	7
34:23	88	**Zechariah**		5:43	178
34:24	80	3:4	80	5:43-44	175
37:25	80	3:8	80	5:44	174
40–48	70	4	81	6:13	93
42:13	198	6:12	80	6:22-23	93
43:2	336	9:9	69	7:21	22
43:19	198	11:13	122	7:24-27	8
45:18-22	199			8:11-12	98
		Malachi		8:17	22, 182
Daniel		1:8	109	8:29	22
7	10, 82-83, 92,	3:1	82	8:31	94
	93-93, 226, 331,	3:1-3	335	9:27	22
	360, 369, 409	3:2	333	9:31	94
7:1-2	326	4:5	6, 81, 319, 333	10:5-6	11, 401
7:3	326			10:7	93
7:3-8	429			10:16	179
7:9	326, 327, 335,			10:23	93, 335
	336, 361, 385,	**NEW TESTAMENT**		10:32	8, 9
	412			10:32-33	22
7:9-10	386	**Matthew**		10:33-34	94
7:9-14	305, 378	1–2	44	10:37	8
7:13	9-10, 13, 22, 37,	1:1	22	10:39	93
	94, 285, 304,	1:8	39	10:40	91, 351
	325, 326, 328,	1:17	22	11:2	22

11:5	6, 90, 109, 110, 333, 426	21:13	122	1:25-28	64
		21:14	109	1:27	7, 62
11:5-6	7	21:15	22	1:28	62
11:7-11	320	21:46	90	1:34	58, 61, 77
11:9	90	22:1-10	38, 178	1:38	66
11:10	91, 333	22:1-14	98	1:43-45	58, 64
11:11	194	22:2	99	1:44	59
11:14	333	23:10	22	1:45	63
11:19	22, 44, 97, 98, 184, 374	23:29-36	93	2:1–3:6	74, 172
		23:29-37	10	2:5	38
11:25-26	8	23:34	416	2:5-10	300
11:25-30	22, 44, 374, 416	23:34-36	22, 44, 374	2:10	8, 9, 38, 64
11:27	9, 37, 351, 407	23:37	10, 93	2:12	63
12:17-21	22	23:37-39	22, 44, 374	2:15-16	97
12:23	22, 334	24:5	22	2:16	98, 99
12:28	7, 76, 178, 273, 426, 437	24:27	13	2:16-17	184
		24:37	13	2:17	7, 64, 98, 183
12:41	91	24:42	177, 180	2:18-19	97
12:50	22	24:43	176, 177	2:19	38, 98
14:33	22	24:44	13, 335	2:23–3:5	178
15:1-2	98	25:1	99	2:28	9, 64
15:11	175	25:1-13	38	3:3	63
15:20	98	25:10	98	3:11	19, 58, 61
15:21-28	98	25:13	177	3:20	63, 97
15:22	22	25:31	335	3:22	10, 33, 59
15:24	91	26:61	70	3:23	7
15:30-31	109, 109n.45	26:63	22	3:26	59
16:14	81, 321n.24	27:9-10	22, 122	3:27	7, 64
16:16	22	27:37	70	3:28-29	9
16:17	22	27:40	22, 70	3:28-33	7
16:17-19	67, 88	27:43	22	4:3-8	38
16:19	38	27:51-53	12	4:9	74
16:20	22	27:54	22	4:10	74
16:28	9, 335	28:18	44	4:10-13	58
17:5	22	28:18-20	11, 382, 403	4:11	59, 60, 74
17:20	176	28:19	22	4:13	19
18:3	351, 432	28:20	22, 44	4:21-22	74
18:10	22			4:23	74
18:12-13	351	Mark		4:26-29	38
18:18	38	1:1	19	4:33	74
18:19	22	1:2	333	4:34	58, 60, 64
18:20	22, 44, 383	1:3	66, 82	4:35–5:43	172
19:19	178	1:6	320	5:1-20	62
19:28	13, 39, 225, 272, 300, 335	1:7	82	5:6	58
		1:8	12	5:7	19
20:30-31	22	1:11	13, 19	5:19	63
21:4	22	1:15	93, 426	5:35	7
21:5	122	1:21-45	59	5:37	63, 64
21:9	22, 136	1:23-25	58	5:40	59
21:11	90	1:25	61	5:43	58

6:1-6	59	8:33	66	12:1-9	6, 93, 377
6:2	7	8:38	7, 64	12:2-6	42
6:2-3	63	9:1	93, 427	12:6	16, 407, 417
6:4	6, 37, 90, 93	9:2	64	12:8	19
6:6-13	173	9:2-8	321n.26	12:12	64
6:14	59, 63, 224	9:7	19, 91, 333	12:18-20	224
6:15	6, 81, 86, 90, 91,	9:8	81	12:18-27	428
	320	9:9	11, 58	12:29-30	397
6:30	87	9:11	82, 320	12:31	178
6:30-44	97	9:11-13	333	12:33	178
6:31	63, 97	9:12	19	12:35-37	13, 63, 136, 337
6:34	98	9:13	91	12:36	194
6:41	97	9:14-29	62	12:42-43	110
6:45	6, 66	9:15	74n.51	13:2	87
6:46	66	9:17	7	13:3	58, 64
6:50	23, 351	9:20	58	13:5-8	93
6:51-52	60, 77	9:25	59	13:17-20	93
7:1	99	9:28	58	13:22	19
7:1-5	98	9:30	58	13:25	426
7:1-23	101, 178	9:30-32	64	13:26	335, 429
7:3-4	393n.15	9:31	10, 11, 19, 58	13:27	426
7:15	176, 184	9:31-32	64	13:29-30	93
7:17	60	9:32	60	13:32	9, 37, 407, 428
7:17-23	58, 64	9:33-50	173	13:33-37	177
7:18-20	176	9:37	7, 37, 91	14:3	97
7:19	184	9:38-39	7	14:6-9	98
7:24	58, 63	9:50	177	14:8	10
7:24-30	62, 98	10:10	60	14:17-25	97
7:31-37	63	10:15	351	14:22-23	97
7:33	59	10:17	7	14:22-24	23
7:36	58, 64	10:19	178	14:22-25	64
8:1-10	97	10:20	7	14:24	10, 13, 94, 199
8:14-21	19	10:21	110	14:25	11
8:15-21	64	10:32	74n.51	14:33	92
8:17-21	73	10:32-34	58, 64	14:35	66
8:22-26	63	10:33-34	19	14:36	8, 10, 92, 140,
8:26	58	10:34	10, 11		260
8:27	66, 87	10:35	7	14:40	77
8:27-30	6, 68	10:38	10	14:55	70
8:27-33	64	10:38-39	19, 92	14:57-61	87
8:28	6, 59, 63, 81, 86,	10:45	10, 19, 21, 51,	14:58	70, 87
	91, 320		64, 93	14:61	70
8:28-29	91	10:46	59, 63	14:61-64	19, 215
8:29	67, 334	10:47	58, 65	14:62	6, 9, 13, 71, 73,
8:30	58, 72, 76, 88	10:47-48	87		89, 335, 351,
8:30-31	19	11:15-17	87		427, 429
8:30-33	6	11:23	176	15:1-4	87
8:31	9, 10, 11, 58, 68	11:28	7	15:2	6, 89, 215
8:31-33	64, 89	11:32	6, 90	15:5	74n.51
8:31–9:1	19	11:49	122	15:23	181

15:26	5, 70, 86, 215	6:22	9	13:34	10, 13, 93, 374
15:29	70	6:22-23	93	14:1	97, 103
15:32	215	6:27-38	173	14:1-24	98
15:34	8, 42	6:48-49	180	14:7-24	184
15:35	320n.18	7:22	6, 90, 109, 110,	14:12-21	107-10
15:36	181		333	14:12-24	178
15:39	19, 65	7:22-23	7	14:13	98, 99, 110, 111,
		7:24-28	320		179
Luke		7:26	90	14:16-24	98
1:2	27, 45	7:27	91, 333	14:21	98, 99, 110, 111
1:8-23	20	7:31-35	7, 37	15:2	97, 98
1:11	323	7:34	97, 98, 184	15:4-6	23
1:15	20, 33	7:34-39	179	15:4-7	38
1:16	333	7:35	13, 374	15:11-32	38
1:17	81	7:36	97, 103	15:23-24	98
1:19	323	7:36-50	98	15:32	98
1:26	323	9:8	224	16:15	251
1:26-38	334	9:18	172	16:16	91
1:35	20, 150	9:28-29	172	16:19-31	110
1:41	20	9:31	20, 321n.26	16:34	251
1:67	20	10:1-22	8	18:7-8	21
1:67-69	20	10:7-8	98	18:8	335
1:69	21	10:9	21, 93	19:5-7	97
1:76	333	10:11	21, 93	19:7	98
2:9	323	10:16	91	19:8	110
2:11	21	10:18	7	19:9	21
2:22-51	20	10:20	180	19:11	21
2:25	20	10:21	20, 374	19:12-27	38
2:30	21	10:21-22	7, 13	20:9	21
3:4-6	20	10:22	407	20:47-51	93
3:6	21	10:39	97, 98	21:8	21
3:7-9	93, 333	11:2	8	21:32	21
3:16	300, 333	11:4	93	21:34-36	177
3:16-17	93	11:20	7, 20, 178	22:19-20	21, 23
3:21	172	11:31	13	22:27	21
3:21-22	20	11:32	91	22:30	98, 225, 272,
3:22	20, 21, 150	11:37	97, 103		300, 335
4:1	20	11:39-41	98	22:37	13
4:14	20	11:49	13	23:37	93
4:16-22	20	11:49-51	7, 374	23:38	70
4:16-30	90	12:8	9, 335, 410	23:46	243
4:18	20, 21, 110, 150,	12:35-37	98	24	427
	333	12:35-48	180	24:19	20, 90
4:18-19	6, 37, 90	12:39	177	24:26	12
4:43	91	12:40	335	24:26-27	20
5:15	172	12:49-50	10	24:30	98
5:20	90	13:6-9	428	24:30-31	97
6:12	172	13:26-27	98	24:39-43	21
6:20	99, 110	13:28-29	98	24:44-48	20
6:20-21	6	13:33	6, 90, 93	24:45	251

24:46	12	2:17	181	6:15	5, 6, 65, 88
24:52-53	20	2:19	70, 87	6:20	23
		2:22	11	6:27	151
John		3:2	362	6:29	363
1:1	358	3:3	159, 351, 362	6:31	363
1:1-2	24	3:5	159, 351, 362	6:32	363
1:1-3	45	3:6	25, 45, 384	6:35	24
1:1-11	338	3:9	362	6:35-40	25
1:3-5	24	3:9-15	368	6:35-58	363, 368
1:5	25	3:10-13	308, 358	6:38	340
1:6	363	3:11-13	24	6:41	358
1:6-8	420	3:12-13	45, 308, 358,	6:41-42	308
1:6-9	354		363, 384	6:45-46	308, 363
1:9-10	24	3:13	26, 308, 335,	6:46	24, 45, 384
1:11	25		362, 365, 366,	6:51	25, 46
1:12-16	385		420	6:51-58	23, 384
1:13	25, 45, 384	3:14	26, 46	6:52	420
1:14	24, 25, 45, 48,	3:16	24	6:53	351
	54, 144, 165,	3:16-17	417	6:53-56	25
	235, 258, 289,	3:18	24	6:53-58	46
	290, 307, 308,	3:19-21	25	6:57	25
	338, 340, 349,	3:28-31	354	6:60	46, 363
	367, 384	3:31-32	308	6:60-62	45
1:14-18	420	3:31-33	24, 384	6:60-66	420
1:15	354	3:31-36	363	6:61-62	308, 358
1:16-18	370	3:32	308, 358	6:62	26, 335, 363
1:17	24, 338, 362,	3:34	151	6:63	45, 159, 384
	363, 368, 384	3:34-35	384	6:66	363
1:17-18	308, 358	4:10	26, 159, 368	6:68-69	354
1:18	24, 27, 45, 308,	4:14	26, 159	7:1	355
	309, 338, 358,	4:19	91, 136	7:12-15	354
	362, 365, 384	4:25	24	7:13	355
1:19	355	4:26	88	7:14-24	368
1:19-22	86	4:34	26	7:16-18	308, 358
1:20	5, 354, 420	4:42	21	7:25-27	354
1:21	6, 320, 335	5:3	109	7:27	363
1:23	82	5:16	355	7:27-29	308, 358
1:24	355	5:17	308, 371, 384	7:28	136
1:29	25, 199	5:18	24, 45, 224, 277,	7:30	25
1:32	26		310, 369, 385,	7:31	354
1:33	26, 151		399, 420	7:32	355
1:41	24, 354	5:19	351, 384	7:38	122, 159
1:45	354, 368	5:19-23	25	7:39	26, 159
1:47-51	24, 45, 308,	5:26	384	7:40	6, 81, 91, 136
	362, 384	5:26-27	25	7:40-44	354
1:49	354	5:37-47	368	7:42	136, 308, 358,
1:49-51	308, 358	5:39	368		363
1:51	335, 365, 420	5:46	368	7:49	368
2:4	25	6:14	6, 81, 91, 136,	7:52	6, 81, 308, 333,
2:13	394		363		354, 358

8:12	24, 354	12:23	25, 26	18:12	355
8:13	355	12:23-24	46	18:33-37	73
8:14	136, 358	12:27	25	19:7	357, 368
8:15	136, 384	12:32	12, 25, 26	19:9	308, 358
8:17	394	12:32-33	46	19:19	70
8:20	25	12:33	384	19:28-29	181
8:21-47	355	12:34	354, 363, 368	19:30	26, 152
8:22	355	12:41	24, 45, 308, 367,	19:31	355
8:23	308, 340, 358		384	19:34	25, 26
8:24	24	12:42	354, 356, 394	19:34-35	25
8:25	354, 365	12:44-50	364	19:35	351
8:28	24, 26, 308, 358	12:45	308, 341, 367,	19:38	355
8:38	340, 358		370, 384	20:2-9	351
8:48	354	12:47	333	20:17	26
8:48-59	364	12:47-48	91	20:19	355
8:52-53	91	12:49-50	358	20:21-23	26
8:53	354	13:1	25	20:22	38, 159
8:58	24, 45, 308, 341	13:10	25	20:23	300
9:13	355	13:19	308	20:26-29	26
9:16-17	354	13:20	351	20:28	24, 45, 354,
9:17	91	13:30	25		358, 385, 388
9:18	355	13:31	26, 46, 384	20:31	23, 24, 159, 353,
9:22	215, 354, 355,	14	427, 437		357
	385	14:3	26	21:19	46
9:28-29	368	14:5-11	354	21:24	351
9:29	308, 358	14:6	24		
9:29-33	354	14:9	25, 45, 308, 341,	Acts	
10	23		367, 370, 384	1:2	20
10:1-5	351	14:10	308, 358, 371	1:3	21
10:14	384	14:15-26	26	1:4	98
10:15	351	14:25-31	25	1:5	20, 300
10:19-21	354	14:26	26, 369	1:6	250, 426
10:24	354	15:15	358	1:6-8	21
10:25	25	15:18-25	355	1:8	20
10:28-29	308, 371	15:25	181, 394	1:9	429
10:29-30	384	15:26	25, 26	1:11	430-31
10:30	25, 308, 341,	15:27	352	1:16-20	20
	365	16:2	354	1:20	122, 181
10:33	24, 45, 47, 224,	16:7	26	1:21	250
	277, 310, 354,	16:10	26	1:24	242, 243, 248,
	358, 369, 385,	16:12-15	26		250
	399, 420	16:13	352	2:1-4	20
10:34	394	16:13-15	369	2:4	20, 158
10:34-36	368	16:28	340	2:16-21	20
10:36	340	17	350	2:17	427
10:37-38	25	17:1	25, 26	2:17-18	20
11:27	24, 354, 357	17:5	260, 340, 365	2:20	249, 427
11:41-42	260	17:14	358	2:20-36	251
12:8	384	17:24	340	2:21	21, 243, 249,
12:16	26	18:3	355		252, 253

2:22	20	6:3	33	11:2-3	175
2:23	150	6:5	33	11:8	248
2:24-32	11	6:14	70, 87	11:16-17	249
2:25	249	7:31	249	11:17	250
2:25-36	20	7:33	249	11:20	13
2:29	136	7:35	249	11:21	249, 250
2:30	136	7:37	20, 91, 333	11:23	250, 251
2:32-33	12	7:41	20	11:24	250
2:33	12, 20, 21, 39,	7:48	20	12:7	249
	158, 300	7:49	249	12:9	21
2:34	12, 249, 252	7:56	9, 335	12:11	249
2:34-35	411	7:59	242, 243, 248	12:22	272, 300
2:36	13, 242, 243,	7:60	242, 248	12:23	249
	249, 252, 253,	8:14	250	12:24	249
	418	8:16	250	13:1	84, 171
2:38	251	8:17-20	225	13:2	250
2:39	253	8:18	158	13:5	250
2:42	13	8:18-19	21	13:7	250
2:46	20	8:22	250	13:10	249
2:47	250	8:24	250	13:10-12	252
3:1	221	8:25	249, 250	13:11	249
3:1-10	20	8:26	249	13:12	250
3:6	21	8:32-33	82	13:23	21, 136
3:13	21	8:39	249	13:26	21
3:16	21	9:1	250	13:29-30	21
3:18	12	9:2	216	13:30-37	11
3:19-21	13	9:10	21	13:33	12, 13
3:20	249, 335	9:14	242, 251	13:43	250, 251
3:22	20, 91, 249, 333	9:15	20	13:44	250
3:26	21	9:17	242	13:45-50	20
4:1-2	11	9:20	13	13:46	250
4:10-12	21	9:21	242, 251	13:48	250
4:11	122	9:31	249	13:49	250
4:12	21	9:35	250	14:3	251
4:26	249	9:42	250	14:15	250
4:27	21	10:3	249	14:23	242, 250
4:29	248	10:4	248	14:26	251
4:30	21	10:14	175, 248	15:8	250
4:31	21	10:33	252	15:11	21, 251
4:33	11	10:36	27, 242, 243,	15:17	249
5:9	249		249, 252	15:19	250
5:14	250	10:36-38	45	15:35	250
5:19	244, 249	10:36-39	20	15:36	250
5:20-21	20	10:38	20, 21, 150, 333	15:40	251
5:30	21, 220, 223	10:39	220, 223	16:7	12, 21, 152, 249
5:31	21	10:39-40	21	16:14	251, 252
5:34-39	213	10:40-41	11	16:15	250, 252
5:42	20	10:42	21	16:31	21, 250, 252
5:9	244	10:43	21	16:32	250, 252
6–7	213	10:46	158	16:34	250

17:11	216	1:3-4	126-53, 188, 230	5:12-21	14, 161, 192, 231, 233, 296
17:13	250	1:4	13, 17, 437		
17:18	11	1:7	127, 226, 235	5:14	193
17:24	249	1:8	16, 226, 412	5:15	166
17:28	31	1:17	122, 235, 379	5:15-19	41, 194, 231
17:30-31	11	1:18	207	5:19	14
17:31	21	1:18-32	208	5:21	127
18:8	250	1:18–3:20	230	6:1-11	233
18:9	21	1:19-25	231	6:3	196
18:11	250	1:19-32	187, 188	6:3-4	196, 205
18:15	81, 356	1:23	192, 381	6:3-6	15
18:18	81	1:25	235, 379	6:4	152, 381
19:6	158	2:1-5	219	6:5	162, 193, 205
19:9	216	2:17	219	6:5-8	14, 205
19:10	250	2:17-29	219	6:6	193
19:13-19	7	2:28	132, 149	6:7	208
19:20	250	2:28-29	392	6:7-10	210
20:19-35	249	3:3-7	235, 379	6:8	196
20:21	250	3:9-20	219	6:9	208
20:24	251	3:20	131	6:9-10	195
20:28	21	3:21-26	219, 230, 379	6:10	193
20:32	250, 251	3:23	232, 381	6:11	196
21:7-36	20	3:24-25	209	6:17	181
21:13	252	3:24-26	230	6:19	132
21:14	249, 252	3:25	14, 51, 197, 198, 200-201, 206, 207, 221, 223, 235, 379	6:27-28	174
21:20-21	356			7:1-6	199
21:26	222			7:3	148
21:27	222			7:5	131, 135, 149, 193
21:28	222				
22:4	216	3:25-26	188		
22:14	242	3:27	220	7:7-11	296
22:16	242, 251	3:27–5:1	219	7:7-12	232
22:17-21	21	3:30	236	7:14	193
22:21-22	20	4:1	132, 133	7:18	131, 193
22:22	216	4:4	133	7:24	162, 193
23:6	224	4:6-8	133	7:24-25	210
23:6-9	213	4:16	133	7:25	16, 127, 131, 138, 139, 193, 226, 412
24:5	216	4:24-25	188		
24:25	21	4:25	12, 82, 200, 221, 230		
26:13-19	21			8:1	211
26:18	250	5:1	127, 233	8:2	159
26:20	250	5:2	381	8:3	14, 15, 16, 42, 43, 131, 139, 140, 166, 192-94, 197, 198, 200, 201, 203, 204, 221, 232, 294, 295, 296, 417, 421
26:21	20	5:5	124, 158		
26:23	141	5:6	195		
27:23	249	5:6-8	200, 223		
28:25-28	20	5:6-9	221		
28:28	21	5:6-11	51		
		5:8	195, 379	8:4	127, 133, 138
Romans		5:9	200	8:4-5	183
1:3	169, 195, 215	5:11	127		

8:5	131, 135	10:6-8	234	15:6	16, 127, 225,
8:6	132	10:6-10	418		337, 380, 414
8:7	131	10:9	11, 13, 16, 188,	15:7	214, 381
8:8	131, 135, 149		418	15:7-13	235
8:9	17, 124, 125,	10:9-10	230	15:8	379, 380
	132, 144, 152,	10:9-13	252	15:8-9	184
	160	10:12	243	15:19	124
8:9-11	17, 125	10:13	16, 225, 251, 337	15:30	127
8:10	138, 139, 162	10:18	122	16:19	179-80
8:10-11	205	11:1	392		
8:10-13	210	11:8	122	1 Corinthians	
8:11	11, 17, 152, 163,	11:14	130	1:2	127
	188, 276	11:17-24	219	1:4	379
8:12	131, 138, 139	11:26	217, 435	1:5	158
8:13	124, 162	11:33-36	414	1:7	158
8:14	17, 141	11:35	122	1:11	17
8:15	17, 140, 141,	12:2	163	1:13	188, 214
	158, 160	12:5	196	1:14	17
8:15-16	8, 124, 181	12:9-21	188	1:20	134
8:15-17	15, 194, 277,	12:14	173, 174, 180	1:22-24	235, 338
	408	12:15-21	187	1:22-25	43, 381
8:17	14, 138, 140,	12:17	173, 180	1:23	12, 195, 212,
	160, 162, 196,	12:18	177		217, 218, 230
	210, 232	12:19	122	1:24	16, 144, 234, 418
8:17-23	205	12:21	180	1:25	133
8:19-23	232	13:7	173, 180	1:26	133
8:22	133	13:8-10	13, 182, 183	1:29	131
8:23	141, 163, 437	13:9	177-78, 180	1:30	15, 144, 234,
8:24	164	13:14	127, 131, 140,		338, 418
8:29	14, 15, 163, 166,		163, 183, 232	2:2	12, 195, 230
	233, 237, 304,	14:1–15:6	182	2:4-5	124
	336, 380	14:9	12, 188	2:8	381
8:29-30	232	14:12-14	179	2:9	122
8:32	200, 221	14:13	180	2:10	125
8:34	12, 13, 188, 230,	14:13-14	173, 183	2:12	17, 124, 125
	411	14:14	175, 180, 184,	2:16	16
8:39	196, 379		186	3:1	155
9:3	133, 215	14:15	188	3:10-14	180
9:5	133, 214, 217,	14:17	178-79, 180, 184	3:16-18	123
	338, 381n.17,	14:17-18	183	3:18	124
	414	14:18	180, 215	3:23	16, 236, 380
9:6	235, 379	14:21	217	4:8	155
9:7-8	121	14:23	218	4:12	175
9:8	133	15:1	180	4:17	140
9:19-21	219	15:1-2	183	4:20	178
9:23	381	15:1-3	232	5:5	131
9:32-33	217	15:1-5	181	5:7	14, 199, 221
9:33	122	15:2	140, 180, 182	6:2	272, 300, 335
10	187	15:3	214	6:2-3	39, 225, 412
10:5-9	121			6:9-10	178

6:9-11	124, 179	13:2	176	2 Corinthians			
6:14	152, 188	15	428	1:3	16, 225, 337,		
6:16	130	15:1-8	170		380, 414		
6:16-18	122	15:3	12, 171, 200, 221	1:5	162, 232		
6:17	17, 125, 160	15:3-4	188	1:17	133		
7:10-11	169, 174, 185,	15:3-8	52, 230	1:18-20	379		
	187	15:5-12	227	1:20	16, 226, 235, 412		
7:28	130-31	15:12	155, 188	1:21	140, 163, 196		
7:29-31	13	15:12-19	230	1:21-22	17		
8–9	379	15:12-20	11	1:27	134		
8:5	39	15:13-32	155	2:18	380		
8:5-6	16	15:20	12, 139, 152,	3:6	159		
8:6	16, 39, 42, 144,		161, 192, 437	3:7-9	159		
	225, 226, 227,	15:20-22	14, 41, 166, 231	3:7-18	117-20, 157		
	234, 235, 236,	15:20-23	295	3:16	116, 122, 159		
	237, 252, 299,	15:20-28	436	3:17	17, 115-25, 159		
	310, 337, 338,	15:21	336	3:18	17, 125, 138,		
	339, 374, 380,	15:21-22	14, 195, 296		141, 144, 163,		
	381, 382, 416,	15:22	166, 196, 231		165, 183, 304,		
	418, 419, 435	15:24	16, 236		381		
8:8	16	15:24-28	337, 414	3:18–4:4	238		
8:10	218	15:25	12, 16, 337, 411	3:18–4:6	232, 336		
8:11	188	15:25-27	15, 232, 237	4	180		
8:13	217	15:25-28	225	4:4	163, 183, 304,		
8:18-21	194	15:27	14, 194-95, 296		380, 381		
9:8-10	157	15:28	16, 236, 237, 380	4:4-6	413		
9:14	169, 174, 185,	15:35-50	155	4:6	14, 183		
	187	15:39	130	4:7–5:5	17, 164, 205		
9:19-21	222	15:40	156	4:10	205		
9:20	194	15:42-44	156	4:10-12	139, 210, 232		
10:1-5	119n.16	15:44	139, 152, 157	4:11	132, 162		
10:1-12	155	15:44-45	197	4:14	233		
10:4	119, 215, 273,	15:44-49	231, 276, 295	4:14-15	197		
	418	15:45	17, 54, 126,	4:16	139, 162		
10:9	215		140n.34, 144,	4:16-18	232		
10:18	132		152, 154-66,	4:16–5:5	138		
11:1	140, 191		211, 296	5:5	17, 163		
11:2	13, 84, 171	15:45-49	14, 15, 156,	5:14	14, 166, 196,		
11:3	16, 215, 236		192, 304		203, 209, 210		
11:23-25	169	15:45-50	41, 437	5:14-15	200, 221		
11:23-26	169	15:46-49	164	5:14-21	218		
11:25	94	15:47-49	336	5:15	196, 197		
12:2	159	15:49	141, 163, 238,	5:16	133		
12:3	16, 17, 125, 144,		380	5:17	196, 197, 437		
	160	15:50	130, 156, 178	5:18-20	223		
12:4-6	17, 125	15:51	155	5:19	16, 196, 209,		
12:12	196, 215	15:54-55	122		235, 379		
12:13	196	16:22	13, 13, 424	5:21	14, 42, 195, 199,		
12:27	196, 233				200, 201, 203,		
12:28	84, 171						

	204, 209, 221, 230, 232
6:2	121
7:1	130, 131, 193
7:5	130
7:33	134
8:8	140
8:9	14, 41, 181, 232, 276
8:19	381
8:23	381
10–13	227
10:1	13, 169, 181
10:2	133
10:3	131, 135
11:2	215
11:4	212, 227
11:7	183
11:18	133
11:31	16, 225, 337, 380, 414
12:2-4	360
12:4	433
12:7	131
13:4	17, 152
13:11	177

Galatians

1:1	11
1:4	200, 220, 221, 230
1:10	140
1:13-14	214, 392
1:15-16	184, 403
1:16	14, 131, 160n.21
1:18	171, 181
2:4	196
2:11-15	184
2:12	175
2:16	131
2:19	162
2:19-20	196, 205
2:19–3:1	218
2:20	125, 131, 138, 200, 210, 221, 230
3:1	12, 195, 230
3:3	132
3:5	124, 158
3:8	157, 122

3:13	14, 200, 204, 212-13, 217, 218, 220, 221, 232
3:14	220
3:16	196
3:20	15
3:26-28	233
3:26-29	196
3:27	15, 196
4:1-6	199
4:3	194
4:4	14, 16, 42, 43, 169, 232, 276, 294, 296, 417, 421
4:4-5	14, 194, 204, 285
4:4-7	15, 184
4:5-7	194
4:6	8, 17, 124, 125, 140, 144, 152, 159, 160
4:6-7	179, 277, 408
4:9	194
4:13	130, 133
4:19	120, 125, 138, 163, 199
4:21	194
4:21-31	157
4:25	119
4:29	133, 135
5:11	217
5:13	131
5:14	178, 182, 183
5:16	132
5:17	132, 138
5:18	159
5:19	132
5:21	178
5:22	124
5:24	131, 215
6:2	182, 183
6:6	84, 171
6:8	131
6:12	131
6:14	162, 205
6:15	437

Ephesians

1:3	16, 380

1:3-14	17
1:7	200
1:13-14	179
1:14	163
1:17	16, 159, 337, 380
1:18	125
1:20	11
1:20-22	41, 232
1:22	14, 194, 337
1:33	337
2:3	131
2:5	196
2:11	132
2:11–3:13	17
2:13	200
2:14	131
2:15	15
3:10	18
4:4-6	18
4:8	122
4:8-11	121
4:13	15
4:15-16	18
4:20	140, 191
4:22-24	15, 232
4:24	140, 183
4:32–5:2	140
5:2	200
5:14	122
5:18	33
5:23-27	18
5:25	200
5:29	130
5:31	130
6:5	133
6:6-9	133
6:12	131
7:2	3

Philippians

1:15	215
1:17	125, 215
1:19	17, 144, 152, 160
1:22	132
1:23	196
1:24	132
2:1	196
2:5-8	140, 181
2:6	144
2:6-7	277

2:6-8	232	1:20	200, 225	5:6	180
2:6-11	40, 41-42, 48,	1:22	131	5:9-10	200, 221
	54, 194, 226,	1:24	132, 139, 140,	5:10	196
	233, 236, 257,		163, 210	5:13	173, 176, 177,
	277, 284, 295,	1:26-27	17		180
	296, 317, 414	1:28	196	5:15	173, 180
2:7	14, 49, 53, 145,	2:1	130	5:16	180
	161, 166	2:2	17		
2:7-8	194	2:3	18	2 Thessalonians	
2:8	14, 139	2:5	131	1:5	178
2:9	12	2:6	13, 84, 140, 171,	2:3-10	432
2:9-11	11, 13, 16, 39,		183, 191	2:12	124
	230, 235, 252,	2:8	183	2:14	381
	380, 418	2:8-10	334	2:15	13
2:10	225, 337	2:9	15, 43, 340, 382	3:3	379
2:11	225, 310, 337	2:11	131	3:6	171
2:15	179	2:12	11		
3:3	132, 149	2:13	131	1 Timothy	
3:4	132	2:15	15, 49	1:1	381
3:6	214	2:18	131, 334, 361	1:15	18
3:10	139, 140, 163	2:20	196	2:3	381
3:10-11	14, 17, 205,	2:23	131	2:5-6	18
	210, 232	3:1	196	3:16	18, 129, 147,
3:20	276	3:2–4:1	133		149-50, 152
3:21	14, 41, 120, 138,	3:3	196	4:10	381
	139, 163, 194,	3:9-11	15, 232	6:3	18
	232, 336, 337	3:10	163, 183, 238,	6:13	18
			336, 380	6:14	18, 381
Colossians		3:17	16, 226, 412		
1:3	16, 337, 380	3:22	133	2 Timothy	
1:13	15			1:9-10	18, 44
1:15	48, 144, 225,	1 Thessalonians		1:10	381
	235, 238, 314	1:5	124	2:8	18
1:15-16	435	1:6	124, 140, 158,	2:13	379
1:15-17	16, 234, 381,		191	4:1	18
	416	1:9-10	13	4:8	18, 381
1:15-20	40, 42-43, 44,	1:10	11		
	54, 226, 236,	2:12	178	Titus	
	258, 273, 277,	2:14	196	1:3	381
	284, 294, 295,	2:15	84	1:3-4	18
	297, 298, 303,	3:6	84	1:4	381
	310, 334, 339,	3:11-13	226	2:10	18, 381
	374	4:1	171	2:13	16, 18, 236, 343,
1:15-22	419	4:13-18	13		381
1:16	338	4:14	12	3:4	18, 381
1:18	14, 163, 166,	4:15-17	174n.17	3:5-7	18
	233, 235	4:17	429	3:6	18, 381
1:18-19	299	5:2	13, 173, 176,		
1:19	15, 143		177, 180	Hebrews	
1:19-20	382	5:4	176, 180	1–2	361

1:1-2	19	James		5:6-8	27
1:1-3	44, 236	1:5	22	5:7	12
1:2	340	1:22-23	22	5:20	27
1:2-3	18, 416, 419	2:8	178		
1:3	12, 48, 49, 338,	4:5	122	2 John	
	411	4:12	22	7	26, 148
1:3-4	374	5:6	22		
1:4-16	19	5:7-8	13, 22	Revelation	
1:5	334	5:12	13, 22	1:7	429
1:13	12, 411			1:8	23, 305n.61, 386
1:13–2:8	41, 232	1 Peter		1:12-16	385
2:4	158	1:3	18, 380	1:13-14	306, 385
2:5-18	161, 233	1:11	18, 152	1:13-16	35, 305, 335,
2:6-9	14, 44, 121, 194,	1:12	12		360
	436	1:18-19	199	3:3	177
2:6-17	18	1:19	18	3:21	23
2:6-18	336	1:20	18, 44	4:9-10	23
2:7	296	2:8	122	5:1	23
2:7-9	296	2:21-25	18	5:5	12, 23
2:9	195, 296, 337	2:22-25	82	5:6	12, 23
2:9-18	340	2:24-25	12	5:7	23
2:13	122	3:9	175	5:8	23
3:1-6	19	3:17-18	18	5:12-13	23
3:7-19	121	3:18	129, 149, 150,	5:13	23, 386
4:14	13		152	6:1	23
5:1-10	19	3:18-21	18	6:16	23
5:5	12	3:21-22	12	7:10	23, 386
5:5-10	340	3:22	12, 41, 194, 232,	7:14	23
5:6	333		337, 411	7:15	23
5:7	86	4:6	18, 150	7:17	23, 305n.61, 386
5:7-10	44	4:13-14	18	11:3	81, 320
5:10	333			11:3-12	321n.26
6:4	159	2 Peter		11:12	429
6:4-5	437	3:10	177	12:7-9	323
6:20	333			12:11	23
7:3	44, 333	1 John		14:8	425
7:16	19	1:1	27, 375	14:17-18	425
7:17	333	1:1-3	27	16:15	177
7:21	333	2:1	437	19:4	23
8:1–10:18	221	2:7	375	19:7-8	23
9:11-12	12	2:18	26	19:11	12
9:14	152	2:19	26, 375	21:1	432
9:26	44	2:22	26	21:2	23
10:5	44, 121	2:24	375	21:5	23
10:5-10	121	3:11	375	21:6	23
10:37-38	122	4:1-2	27	21:9-14	23
13:2	97	4:2	148	22:1	23, 305n.61, 386
13:8-16	19	4:2-3	26	22:3	386
		4:3	26	22:13	23, 305n.61, 386
		4:9-10	417	22:20	13

APOCRYPHA

Tobit
12:15   13, 83, 322
14:2   109

Judith
10:13   146

Wisdom of Solomon
2:13-18   8, 35
2:16-18   37
2:23   296, 328
2:23-24   231
2:24   296
4:7–5:8   415
5   402
5:1-5   10
5:5   224
5:15-16   224
6:18   331
7:25   367
7:26   42, 44, 234, 367,
              381, 384
7:29   367, 384
8:4-6   381
9:1-2   45
9:4   83
9:9   367
9:9-10   417
9:10   44
9:16-17   366
9:17   16, 45
9:40   329
10–11   235
10–19   235
13–15   187
16:7   331
18:15   329
18:15-16   35

Sirach
3:18-25   361
5:5-6   207
6:6   177
17:3   328
24   416
24:3   381, 435
24:5   83, 329
24:8   435

24:9   42, 234, 367, 381
24:19-22   367, 384
24:23   15, 36, 225, 234,
              298, 331, 368,
              381, 417, 419,
                       435
24:25   331, 368
45:2   224
45:23-24   81, 83
47:11   80
47:22   80
48:9-10   6, 81
48:10   320
48:24-25   359
49:8   359
49:16   328
51:1   331

4 Ezra
3:14   359
5:20   322
6:26   320
7:28   363
8:20   361
8:20-21   310
9:38–10:27   70
12:32   363
13   311n.81, 326,
              409, 410
13:1-3   326
13:26   363
13:32   226, 363
13:52   363
14:9   83, 272, 300

Baruch
3–4   416
3:9–4:4   234, 381
3:29   366
3:29-30   234, 418
3:36–4:4   331, 368
4:1   15, 36, 225, 298,
                  417, 419

1 Maccabees
2:54   81
2:57   80
4:46   81
14:41   81
18:12   83

2 Maccabees
1:4   251
1:10   81
7   223
7:14   92
7:23   10
7:33   223
7:37-38   223
7:38   93
8:24   109
8:29   223
15:12-16   321n.24
15:13   301

PSEUDEPIGRAPHA

2 Baruch
4:2-7   359
4:4   359
13:3   83, 272, 300
25:1   83, 272
29:3   363
39:7   363
59   359
76   359

3 Baruch   359

1 Enoch
1:1   102
1:7-9   102
5:6-7   102
6:10   35
9:1   322
9:1-3   83
9:3   322
12–16   224, 272, 300
12:4   83, 320
13:8   322
14   359
14:8   359
14:18-23   324n.33
15:8   146
20:1-8   322
37–71   226, 326, 409
37–72   311n.81
39:3   359
42   366
46:1-2   326

48:6-7	363
62:5	71
69:11	328
70–71	359
71:11	360
71:14	83, 320,
	326n.38, 328,
	360
75:3	322
80:6	322
82:4-7	102
82:10-20	322
85–90	328
89:59-65	322
90:20-25	322
90:29	70
90:31	81, 83, 225, 320
99:3	322
104:1	322
106:5	322

2 Enoch

3	359
22:8	224, 272, 300,
	320, 360
30:11	328

3 Enoch

3–16	320, 360
4	327
12:5	324
16	360
16:3	327

4 Maccabees

6–18	223
6:29	209
17:21	209, 223
17:21-22	198
17:22	93, 197

Apocalypse of Abraham

10	23, 324, 360
10–11	385
10:3	385
15	359
16:3-4	386
17:2	386

Apocalypse of Elijah

24:11-15	225, 320

Apocalypse of Zephaniah

6:11-15	385
9:12–10:9	360
16:15	386

Ascension of Isaiah

7	359
9:8	320
9:9	360
9:30	301

Assumption of Moses

10:1	322
10:2	323

Joseph and Aseneth

14:9-10	385

Jubilees

1:17	70
1:27	70, 322
1:29	322
2:2	322
4:22-23	39, 224, 272,
	300
4:23	83, 320
5:1-10	35
6:32-35	102
6:35	102n.24
13:25	321
15:31	322
22:16	102n.24
48:9-19	323

Life of Adam and Eve

25-29	359

Psalms of Solomon

3	102
13	102
15	102
16:14	146
17:23	5
17:32	80, 401n.34
18:57	80

Sibylline Oracles

2.187-89	320

Testament of Abraham

10	359
11	83, 225, 272,
	301, 320
13	225
13:1-6	39

Testament of Dan

6:1	322
6:2	322

Testament of Judah

21:2-5	81
25:2	322

Testament of Levi

2:5	359
3:5	13, 83, 322
5:6	322

Testament of Moses

7	102n.23
9:1	81
14	44

Testament of Reuben

5	35
6:8	80

JOSEPHUS

Antiquities

1.196	97
3.96	271, 301, 321,
	359
4.326	271, 301, 321
5.112	397n.25
6.166-68	87n.20
8.45-49	7
11.173	392
11.340-41	392
16.182	197
18.85-87	6, 90
20.97	6, 81
20.97-98	90
20.100	392

20.167	6	8-9	44	*Quod Deterius Potiori*
20.167-72	90			*Insidiari Soleat*
20.169-70	81	*De Posteritate Caini*		124	34
20.169-72	6	16-20	331	54	418
20.188	6, 90			

Jewish War

De Sacrificiis Abelis et Caini

QUMRAN DOCUMENTS

2.119-61	104
2.129-33	104
2.132	105
2.138-39	104
2.143	104
2.150	105
2.152	104
6:285	81

De Sacrificiis Abelis et Caini

8-10	321
9	16, 34, 44
64	367

1QapGen
| 22.14-7 | 321 |

De Somnis
| 1.65 | 331 |
| 1.65-69 | 45 |

1QH
1.10	322
2.8-19	102
2.32	110
3.25	110
5.16	110
5.18	110
5.22	110
6.13	83, 322
13.14	194
18.12-13	194
18.14-15	81
18.16	194

PHILO

De Virtutibus
| 62-65 | 331 |

De Abrahamo
| 107-14 | 97 |

De Vita Mosis
| 1.158 | 359 |
| 2.288 | 321 |

De Agricultura
| 51 | 367, 384 |

Every Good Man Is Free
| 81 | 104 |
| 86 | 104 |

1QM
11.9	110
11.13	110
13.10	323
13.14	110
17.6	323

De Cherubim
10	34
18	34
31	34
41	34
47	44
49	34
50	44
9-10	34

Legum Allegoriae
1.31	328
1.53	328
2.82	34
2.87	34
3.140-47	34
3.217	34
3.244	34
3.45	34

1QpHab
| 12.2-10 | 110 |

1QpNah
| 1.6-8 | 222 |

De Decalogo
| 65 | 397n.25 |

De Mutatione Nominum
56	331
116	367, 384
208	321

Quaestiones et Solutiones in Genesin
1.4	328
2.62	16
3.11	321

1QS
2.1-10	175
3.20	323
3.24	323
5.10-11	105
6.2	104
6.4-5	104, 108
6.8-9	104
6.10-11	105
6.16-17	105
6.20-21	105

De Opificio Mundi
16-24	330
24	367
134	328

Quaestiones et Solutiones in Exodum
2.29	359
2.40	359
2.46	359

De Plantatione
| 18 | 44 |

8.13-14	82	11QTemple		*Tosephta Ḥagigah*	
9.11	6, 80, 81, 82,	45.12-14	107	2:1	360
	401n			2:3-4	360
9.19-20	82	CD			
10.17-21	175	1.13-21	102	**OTHER ANCIENT**	
11.20-21	194	2.12	81	**WRITINGS**	
		5.18	323		
1QSa		6.1	81		
1.1	105	6.21	110	*1 Clement*	
2.3-9	179	7.20	80	10:7	97
2.3-10	106, 107	12.23	80		
2.5	109	14.14	110	Origen, *Contra Celsum*	
2.11-22	6, 81	14.19	80	1.23-24	397
2.12	80	19.10	80		
2.14	80	20.1	80	Cyprian, *Quod Idola Dii*	
2.17-21	105, 108			*Non Sint*	
2.20	80, 401n.34			11	33
		RABBINIC WRITINGS			
1QSb				*Didache*	
5.20	80	*b. Berakoth*		1:3	175
		28b	356		
4Q161	80			Epictetus	
		b. Ḥagigah		4.5.24	177
4QCDᵇ	107, 109	14a	361, 412		
5.1	80	15a	327, 360	*Epistle of Barnabas*	
7.4	109			12:10	136
7.4-6	107	*b. Sanhedrin*			
9.15	322	38b	324, 327, 361	*Gospel of Thomas*	
				14	175
4QFlor		*b. Shabbath*			
1.10-13	5, 80, 87	31a	177	Hermas, *Similitudes*	
1.11	80			5.6.5	33
		m. Aboth			
4QPat		1:1	388	Horace, *Odes*	
3-4	80	3:2	383n.23	1.2.41-52	34
4QpPs 37		*m. Ḥagigah*		Ignatius, *Ephesians*	
1.9	110	2:1	361	1:17	388
2.10	110			7:2	388
		m. Megilloth		15:3	388
4QS1		4:10	361	18:2	388
40.24	324, 359			19:3	388
		m. Ta'anith			
4QTestim		3:8	8, 35	Justin, *Apologia I*	
5-8	81			20-22	303
		m. Shebuoth			
11QMelch	6, 81, 83	1:7	202	Justin, *Dialogue*	
10	39, 272, 321, 324			8.4	320
13-14	225	Shemoneh 'Esreh 14	80	16	356
				47	356

49.1   320

96   356

Memar Marqah

4:3   359

4:7   359

5:3   359

Ovid, *Metamorphoses*

8.613-70   97

Pliny, *Epistles*

10.96.7   226

pseudo-Philo, *Biblical Antiquities*

12:1   359

48:1   81

Suetonius, *Claudius*

25.4   356

Tacitus, *Annales*

15.44.2-5   356n.28

15.44.3   87

Tertullian, *Adversus Praxean*

26   33

Virgil, *Eclogues*

4.6-10   34